1) Kökes Hartebeast — not seen
2) Klipspringer
   Vervet monkey
   Baboon
   Impala
   Grants Gazelle
   Garanuk
   Mongoose

   Abyssinian Hare
   Silver Back Jackle

A FIELD GUIDE TO THE

Mammals of Africa

including Madagascar

A FIELD GUIDE TO THE

Mammals of Africa

including Madagascar

Theodor Haltenorth
Helmut Diller

Translated by
Robert W. Hayman

COLLINS
Grafton Street, London

William Collins Sons & Co Ltd

London · Glasgow · Sydney · Auckland
Toronto · Johannesburg

ISBN 0 00 219778 2

Originally published as
Säugetiere Afrikas und Madagaskars
© BLV Verlagsgesellschaft mbH, München, 1977

© in the English translation William Collins Sons & Co Ltd, 1980

Reprinted 1984
Reprinted 1986 (twice)
Reprinted 1988
Filmset by Jolly & Barber Ltd, Rugby

Printed and bound by
South China Printing Co. Hong Kong.

Contents

6 CONTENTS

Preface

Africa, with its 30 million sq km of land, is a large and ancient part of the earth, which, after the appearance of mammals about 180 million years ago, became a nursery for mammalian evolution. Approximately 1500 species of mammals are known on the continent but up to the present they have been comprehensively listed in two systematic catalogues only, and have still not been fully described. In the nature of things the greatest number of species belong to small and inconspicuous forms, often nocturnal or burrowing, in particular insectivores, bats and rodents. These are largely unseen by most naturalists, animal lovers and tourists, and therefore are of less interest to them. To keep the present volume to a manageable size they have been omitted from it and the species covered consist of the large and medium-sized representatives of the mammals of Africa and Madagascar, as well as those species, widely known in or specially representative of Africa, viz., the ungulates, carnivores, monkeys and lemurs, hares, pangolins, seals, sea-cows, aardvarks, and the larger rodents (porcupines, cricetines, cane rats, maned rat, spring hare, gundis, scaly-tailed flying squirrels, and squirrels; the latter, owing to the great number of species, dealt with only briefly). Of the army of insectivores only the largest, the hedgehogs, elephant shrews and otter shrews are covered, the latter two families, being purely African, are described in detail. Of the Madagascan mammals the largest and best known are the lemurs and civets; for reasons of space the 10 rodent and 30 insectivore species are omitted. For the same reason the more than 200 bat species are not dealt with; of ssp. only the number is mentioned, except in some species where a common name is in use. Also, in the case of species whose main distribution lies outside Africa, the African ssp. are described. Further, the ssp. of Madagascan mammals and of the monkeys are described, since for these often no English descriptions have been available.

Regionally this book covers all Africa from the Mediterranean coast to the Cape of Good Hope, and the offshore islands from Fernando Póo to Zanzibar and Socotra, as well as Madagascar. It presents (so far as material allows) in summarised form, details of appearance, structure, measurements, weights, distribution, habitat, activity and locomotion, toilet, voice, sense organs, enemies, food, social life, breeding, growth and longevity of the species. But even the wealth of information here presented cannot be complete for, despite the intensive field work undertaken in Africa during the past 30 years, many species are still inadequately known.

Our heartfelt thanks go to Max Buhler in Pforzheim who played an important role in getting this work under way, Lothar Schlawe in Berlin for valuable information, Dr Ingrid Weigel and Liselotte Schon of the Library of Munich State Zoological Collection for friendly help in supplying references and to the staff of the BLV publishers for their understanding and help in the production of the book. The senior author also thanks his dear wife Charlotte for her unwearying patience during the making of the fair copy of the manuscript.

THEODOR HALTENORTH   HELMUT DILLER

Translator's Note

While attempting to produce a readable English version, rather than a strictly literal translation, of Dr Haltenorth's concise and highly informative text, I have followed his descriptions as closely as possible. Such modifications as may have been found necessary have been mainly confined to simplifying the complicated accounts in such subjects as habitats, territorial behaviour, daily activities, sociability, etc. For instance, under vocalisation, the original text uses as much as possible onomatopoeic renderings of mammalian language which may not lend themselves to English translation.

In the field of systematic arrangement and classification the original has generally been closely followed. There are however a small number of cases where the author's views on systematics are at variance with those widely held by most other workers on African mammalogy. Such divergencies have been noted in the translation without interfering with the original text. In this connection Mammals of Africa – an Identification Manual, by Meester and Setzer, 1974, has been an invaluable source of data and work of reference; it lists all African mammals down to ssp., with key characters, synonymies and distribution. As an agreed compilation by specialists in all groups it is likely to become a standard work of reference, and I have made full use of its findings in cases of disagreement over classification.

For the English reader the Bibliography has been revised with the emphasis on suitable English titles for reference or general reading.

Finally I wish to express my indebtedness to my wife for a great deal of patience and tolerance during the lengthy preparation of the translation, as well as practical help with the typescript.

Robert W. Hayman.
Ottery St Mary,
Devon. 1980.

Introduction

The Geological and Climatological History of Africa and Madagascar

In order to understand the unique and diverse composition of the mammalian world of Africa, it is necessary to review its geological and climatological history.

The mainland of Africa covers an area of 29,921,000 sq km. Taking into account the adjoining and outlying islands, Socotra, Seychelles, Amirantes, Madagascar, Comoros, Zanzibar, Pemba, Fernando Póo, Cape Verde Is., and Canary Is. as well as Madeira, and omitting the smaller coastal islands, we can add another 622,189 sq km.

In this area live about 1570 species, divided among 14 orders and 67 families. Of these, 13 orders, 38 families and 324 species, containing the largest and middle-sized species (see Preface) are presented in these pages.

Among the islands of Africa only Madagascar, Zanzibar, Pemba, Fernando Póo and some smaller offshore islands have any of the larger mammals. Madagascar, which separated from the African mainland in early times, has developed a specific fauna of its own, so that, whilst the others do not warrant separate treatment from the mainland, this island of 590,000 sq km does require a description of its larger mammals.

Through the whole span of geological time Africa has changed less than the other continents. It has been an age-old mainland on which animal life has developed over several hundred million years with few changes, apart from those of a purely regional nature.

During primeval times Africa was part of the vast southern continent or Gondwanaland, which included Australia, India, Madagascar, South Africa and South America. Towards the end of this period a large part of Southern Africa was covered by sea; afterwards the land reappeared, and underwent, with large parts of Gondwanaland, a first (Precambrian) glaciation.

During later ages, Africa – as part of the changing Gondwanaland, underwent – particularly in the North – several risings and lowerings of sea level (Transgression and Regression), and, with large stretches of Gondwanaland, was subjected to a second, severe glaciation (the Carbopermian), which in its extent and in its intermediate Ice Ages, is only comparable to the Quaternary Ice Ages of the northern hemisphere.

During the Mesozoic, or Middle period, of the earth's history (i.e. in the Triassic and Jurassic), Gondwanaland began to break up; the Indian Ocean and the Mozambique Channel came into existence, cutting off Madagascar from the mainland. In the north, the Tethys Sea still separated the northern continents from the southern, furthermore, as in the Devonian and Carboniferous epochs, it covered large parts of North Africa, linking the Mediterranean area with the West African Gulf of Guinea. From the Upper Cretaceous to the Miocene, i.e. for about 50 million years, Africa (at first still linked with India and Arabia, but later only with the latter) was an enormous island completely surrounded by sea.

With the Cenozoic Africa had largely assumed its present shape, and from the Eocene onwards, and between 20°N and the Cape, was already much as it is today, a good 60 million years ago. Then the Tethys Sea also left N. Africa, the Atlas mountains

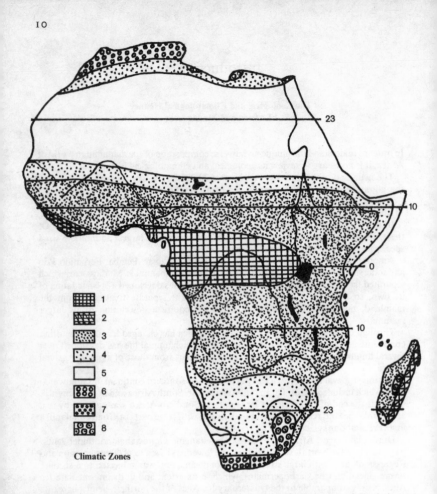

Climatic Zones 1 Tropical evergreen rain forest climate with double rainy season. 2 Tropical rain forest climate with one rainy season. 3 Tropical savannah climate with distinct dry season. 4 Steppe climate. 5 Desert climate. 6 Temperate dry summer climate. 7 Temperate moist climate. 8 Temperate dry winter climate.

were uncovered and were rejoined with the African continent. During the Oligocene Madagascar was joined to Africa, was separated again in the Miocene, and was nearly linked again in the Pliocene and Pleistocene by the narrowing and lowering of the Mozambique Channel. Arabia was still linked with Africa in the Eocene and Oligocene after India had been separated from Arabia in the course of the Paleocene. During the Miocene the Eastern Rift system, including the Red Sea, the Ethiopian and African

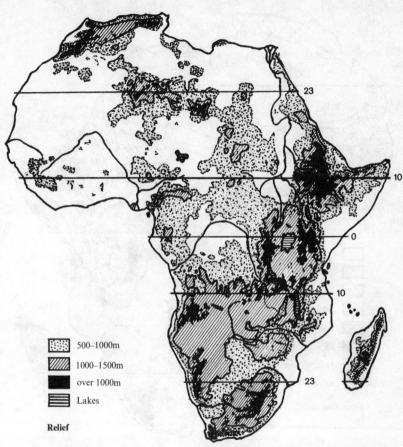

Relief

Legend:
- 500–1000m
- 1000–1500m
- over 1000m
- Lakes

Rift Valleys began to sink as the great south-eastern border ridge was lifted up. In the late Miocene first the northern part of the Red Sea, then by the late Pliocene the southern part also was formed. At that time the Isthmus of Suez rose and again blocked off the north of the Red Sea.

Thus the eastern Mediterranean, like the western, became an enclosed basin, with the Tunisian–Sicilian–Italian land bridge between the two. In the west the Gibraltar land bridge formed the barrier.

Geologically, up to the Middle Tertiary, Africa generally was raised no higher than the present average height of about 600m above sea level, with regional higher points reaching a maximum of 1500m above sea level. Continuous erosion had formed great plains. Only the remnants of the hard rock masses of the Palaeozoic, which had been raised in the Jurassic, were left by erosion on all sides as high island masses standing

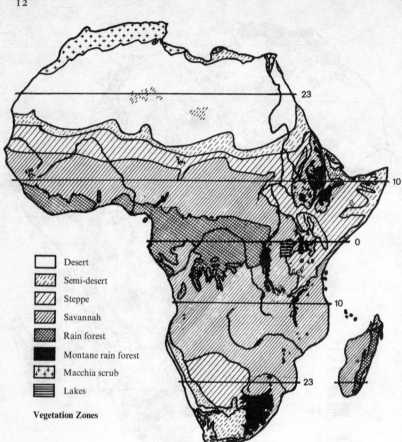

Desert

Semi-desert

Steppe

Savannah

Rain forest

Montane rain forest

Macchia scrub

Lakes

Vegetation Zones

over the plains, and from the Miocene onwards have never been significantly different from today. From the Miocene there remains one old formation, now low lying, which was an effective biogeographical land barrier, stretching along the northern rim of the Congo or Zaire basin from Ethiopia to the Gulf of Guinea. After the Miocene a depression was formed in the eastern section, through which the Lake Rudolf basin drained to the Nile, which had already formed its present great valley.

Towards the end of the Miocene a geological upheaval began which raised the great plains and the old plateaux of the Ethiopian highlands from heights of up to 1000m, to around 2500m. The latter, together with the highlands of Mid-Kenya (two of the biggest ancient mountain masses), became covered with great quantities of volcanic discharge during the Pliocene and Pleistocene. Independently of these vast continuous upheavals, local structural movements created the volcanic cones of Kilimanjaro, Meru, Kenya, Elgon and Mt Cameroon, whereas the Ruwenzori range, being nonvolcanic, was thrown up by a vast upheaval. In addition the Congo basin sank to form a great inland lake, and on its eastern rim a great highland area was thrown up.

These movements lasted until the middle of the Pleistocene, and in some parts still later, forming the Rift system, in which today lie the chain of lakes – Nyasa (Malawi), Tanganyika (Tanzania), Kivu, Edward (Idi-Amin), Albert (Mobuto), Rudolf, and the other smaller lakes. Lake Victoria, which had already been formed in the Miocene but disappeared in the Pliocene, was now re-formed, whereas the great central lake of the Congo became drained by the sinking of its western rim. Throughout the Pleistocene the great volcanoes mentioned above remained largely unaltered, whereas Rungwe, Marsabit, Kulal, Emi Koussi and others of the Sahara had only just been formed. Thus the main features of the African landscape which so fascinate us today, particularly in East Africa, were formed from the Miocene on.

During the Tertiary, when the climatic zones gradually emerged in Africa, the western parts offered more favourable conditions for rain forests than the eastern parts where the primitive forests were associated with the steppes. The northern monsoon zone was at first drier (in part close to semi-desert) and narrower, reaching to no more than 10°N. The southern monsoon zone, however, stretched all along the east side of the continent nearly to the Cape. The Sahara, Somalia and S. W. Africa are not only dry areas, but in part have been desert for a long time. Only during the Oligocene was there a moister climate in N. Africa. Naturally these climatic zones altered in width over such long periods, but it was only towards the end of the Miocene that the warm belts were reduced to the extent that the Mediterranean type of climate prevailed both in the north and in Cape Province. But these zones are unlikely to have been broader than they are now, at any time.

In the Pliocene the climate of S. Africa changed markedly between moist and dry. To what extent such changes affected N. Africa is still not known. In the Pleistocene, however, such changes were apparent in the whole of Africa. The periods of greater and lesser rainfall, the pluvial and interpluvial, coincided broadly with the cold and warm periods of the northern hemisphere. Distinction must be made between the isopluvial (times of increased rain throughout the year) and displuvial (times of increased summer rains but drier winters). These climatic oscillations changed the level of rivers and lakes by many metres, and the extent of the Sahara by several degrees of latitude. At times of minimal extension the residual desert was interlaced by rivers. Similarly the size of the snow and ice caps of the highest equatorial mountains varied considerably, giving height variations of between 500 and 1500m, as indicated by the traces of their lower edges.

Because of these ice cap variations it is estimated that in the equatorial warm belt the average temperature in the pluvial may have sunk between 3° and 5°. Only at such times could the northern temperate zone have advanced to the extreme limit of N. Africa.

History of the Mammalian World of Africa and Madagascar

The ancient continent of Africa played an important role in mammalian history. It is known that the first mammals lived about 170 to 180 million years ago in the Triassic period of the Mesozoic era. They originated from mammal-like reptiles, the so-called 'near mammals' or Therapsids, which by short evolutionary steps gradually acquired those characteristics which enabled them to be active at night, to survive in cooler climates and to penetrate into them and so conquer new habitats.

The main area of mammalian development was the huge southern continent, or Gondwanaland (see p. 9), and especially within the area that is now S. Africa, which provides us with the best evidence of that process. During the younger ages of the Palaeozoic, the Carboniferous and Permian, this ancient mainland block underwent several great glaciations which produced a long-lasting effect on the flora and fauna. Though living organisms had enough space to avoid the encroaching ice, they were nevertheless forced to adapt to new living conditions which were becoming continually harder because of the cooling climate. The flora had already developed from the spore-bearing fern-like plants, or Glossopterids, to a higher stage for growth on dry land, developing resistant seeds or fleshy fruits. As Gymnosperms (naked seeds, conifers) they led to the later, more highly developed Angiosperms (covered seeds, deciduous), whose shedding of foliage and protection of seeds enabled them to survive colder seasons. Their leaves, seeds and fruit provided a broad basis for nourishment for the reptiles, which were then the most highly developed form of terrestrial life. Adaptations of mouth and teeth enabled them to make full use of this form of nourishment. Up to that time the reptiles had lived mainly by predation, with uniform, pointed-tipped carnivorous-type teeth, but now the teeth began to differentiate into gripping front teeth (incisors and canines) and crushing back teeth or molars. With this development of the teeth came a general improvement of the body structure which gradually transformed some groups of reptiles into mammals, better capable of surviving the effects of glaciation than other groups which did not develop in this way. Thus the Carboniferous and Permian glaciations of Gondwanaland, and particularly of southern Africa, may well have been the main influence in the development of the mammals.

Among the more significant developments which produced the earliest mammals (apart from the differentiation of teeth for varied uses) came a general improvement of the body structure, such as a more efficient blood circulatory system, advanced reproductive systems through a placenta and mammary glands for feeding the young in parental care and, above all, the body covering of hair or fur to provide valuable insulation against severe climatic conditions. The physiological maintenance of a relatively controlled body temperature, independent of the environmental conditions, allowed a high level of activity in many and varied ways.

By the end of the Triassic, in the Rhaetian, 5 large groups of primitive mammals were already existing. During the next period, the Jurassic, mammals, either herbivorous, omnivorous or carnivorous, inhabited all the mainlands. It has been shown that already at that time 5 orders, 11 families, and about 70 genera were in existence. However, 4 of these orders died out between the Upper Jurassic and the Middle Cretaceous, also the 5th during the Eocene, but in the meantime, by the Late Cretaceous, the pouched mammals (Marsupialia) and the insectivores (Insectivora), the latter being the first of the placental mammals (Placentalia), had developed, leading to the higher mammals. At the beginning of the Tertiary, in the Palaeocene, the placentals were overtaking the marsupials with a series of further orders, namely bats (Chiroptera), early carnivores (Creodonta), early ungulates (Condylarthra), rabbits and hares (Lagomorpha) and rodents (Rodentia). During the Eocene these were quickly followed by new orders of placentalia, so that the total number of placental orders increased to 28, of which 17 still exist. From these Rhaetian beginnings with the primitive mammals they increased to 40 orders, 258 families, around 3000 genera, and a roughly-estimated perhaps 13,000 species, of which about a third, 4250, still exist.

In this brief outline of the evolutionary history of mammals Africa is important because of its own groups of forms and their later emigration in part to Europe and

Asia, and through the latter also to America, and also as a receiving country for Eurasian immigrants which later were transformed into purely African species. Moreover, Africa became a refuge for certain Tertiary species which, as faunal relics, survived there much longer than on the other mainlands.

In the **Late Eocene** and the **Early Oligocene** Africa was inhabited by a world of mammals which resembled that of Europe and Eurasia at that time, but which already included forms which can be considered as of entirely African origin. The trend towards a particularly African mammalian fauna was accented in the Oligocene. Such original African forms are the hyraxes (Hyracoidea), sea-cows (Sirenia), elephants (Proboscidea), aardvarks (Tubulidentata), Spring hares (Pedetidae), golden moles (Chrysochloridae), and the higher monkeys (Cercopithecoidea), as also the extinct Arsinotheriidae, which formed a heavy-footed family of the hoofed animals.

The hyraxes are probably descended from the Palaeocene African primitive ungulates of the order Condylarthra, and developed up to the end of the Miocene only in Africa. It was only at the beginning of the Pliocene that they spread to Europe and Asia. As well as the number of species, their bodily sizes up to tapir and rhinoceros dimensions, were well beyond today's forms.

The elephants, on the other hand, had their origins in a small, pig-like Eocene ancestor (*Moeritherium*) and developed a great variety of very large forms which leave the existing species in the shade. Until the Miocene the elephants were entirely African, and from there settled also in Europe, Asia and America; by the Early Miocene they were already found in S. America.

The sea-cows, herbivorous inhabitants of fresh, brackish and marine coastal waters, originated from the primitive ungulates which were closely related to the hyraxes and elephants. They appeared for the first time in the N. African Eocene (*Protosiren, Eotheroides*) and soon spread over suitable waters of other continents, being formerly much richer in species than today.

The aardvarks also seem to be descendants of Condylarthra, as indicated by many features of their structure. An ancestor (*Myorycteropus*) has been found in the African Miocene, and was much like today's descendant. In the Pliocene they also appeared in Europe and Asia, and in the Ice Age in Madagascar, but today they are only in Africa.

The spring-hares (like the aardvarks) first appeared in the African Miocene, closely resembling their descendants in Africa today.

The same can be said of the golden moles, which also originated in the African Miocene in a form closely resembling those of today, and which have never left the country.

The rhinoceros-sized Arsinotheriens were primitive ungulates (Paenungulata) carrying large, pointed, bony double nose horns, with a third smaller one on the forehead, and with 2 species in one genus and family formed a distinct order of heavy-footed ungulates (Embrithopoda), known only from the Lower Oligocene of Egypt. Thick-legged animals, they lived in the savannahs, feeding on the tough vegetation.

From the insectivores (Insectivora) the ancestors of the lemurs (Prosimii) had already originated in the Late Cretaceous, with squirrel-like forms, which until the Palaeocene produced a multitude of forms all over the world, in America leading to the broad-nosed monkeys (Platyrrhina or Ceboidea) and in the Old World to the narrow-nosed monkeys (Catarrhina or Cercopithecoidea). The latter, the so-called higher monkeys, seem to have been cradled in Africa, since by the Late Oligocene squirrel- to cat-sized ancestors (*Aegypto-, Para-, Propliopithecus*) had already appeared which split up into the modern monkeys (guenons, mangabeys, macaques, baboons, colobi) and to gibbons, anthropoid apes and perhaps primitive man. *Propliopithecus*, for example, already possessed the first characters of the later gibbons, and *Parapithecus* the later anthropoid apes.

During the **Eocene** primitive whales were also found in Africa (Archaeoceti), with *Protocetus, Basilosaurus, Eocetus, Prozeuglodon, Durodon*. Like the sea-cows, in the first place they were inhabitants of shallow waters, either sea coasts, or brackish, or fresh water. Since whales may be found today in all three types of water, the conclusion may be drawn that the terrestrial ancestors of the whales (which, according to recent research may have been primitive ungulates and not, as believed so far, among the primitive carnivores or insectivores) took to fresh waters first, then on to brackish coastal waters, eventually to become highly adapted to ocean life. The occurrence of primitive whales in Africa (especially N. Africa) does not itself prove that whales had African origins, since primitive whales are also found in the Eocene of Europe and N. America. Judging by the high degree of adaptation this order of mammals had reached by the Eocene, they must have been already in existence during the Late Cretaceous.

For the **Oligocene** of Africa, there is evidence that the following orders and genera were represented: insectivores or Insectivora (*Metolbodotes*), bats or Chiroptera (*Vampyravus*), rodents or Rodentia (*Phiomys, Metaphiomys*), flesheaters or Creodonta as primitive carnivores (*Sinopa, Metasinopa, Hyaenodon, Pterodon, Apterodon*), monkeys or primates (see above), elephants or Proboscidea (*Moeritherium, Palaeomastodon, Barytherium*), heavy-footed ungulates or Embrithopoda (*Arsinoitherium*), hyraxes or Hyracoidea (*Saghatherium, Geniohyus, Bunohyrax, Megalohyrax, Titanohyrax*), and ungulates or Artiodactyla (Anthracotheriidae with *Ragatherium, Brachyodus, Bothriogenys,* and *Bothriodon*).

The insectivores were the last representatives of a dying-out family, the 'mixed teeth' (Mixodectidae) which in N. America had already developed numerous species in the Palaeocene and Eocene, and whose teeth showed features of later families such as the first elephant shrews or Macroscelididae (*Metolbodotes*). The rodents already showed a certain resemblance to the purely African flying squirrels (Anomaluridae), among whose ancestors the Oligocene Theridomyidae genera *Phiomys* and *Metaphiomys* may belong. The primitive carnivores belonged to the Hyaenodontidae, which are of N. American descent, their more primitive genera of early genet-like or civet-like animals (*Sinopa, Metasinopa*) representing the first steps to the more hyaena-like Hyaenodontinae (*Hyaenodon, Pterodon, Apterodon*). The monkeys have already been mentioned. The elephants were still represented by the small Moeritherien (see above), but they had already developed in *Palaeomastodon* (or *Phiomia*) the larger Mastodontidae, whose name derives from the teat-like cusps of their molar teeth. With *Brachytherium* came a further family, the heavily-built Barytheriidae, always restricted to Africa. The hyraxes resembled tapirs and horses in size, and in part in other features. The ungulates first appeared in Africa with the 'heavy-footed animals' or Embrithopoda, and a primitive pig-like group (*Brachyodus, Mixtotherium*) belonging to the Anthracotheriidae, which may be considered as distant relations of pigs and ancestors of the hippopotamus. They came over from Europe with *Brachyodus* and *Bothriodon*, and together with *Rhagatherium* and *Bothriogenys* became purely African. They were heavy, stout-legged inhabitants of moist woodlands and lowlands.

During the **Early Miocene** the number of species in Africa continued to increase. On the one hand the elephants died out in the Miocene in their original forms of the Moeritheriidae and also the Barytheriidae (as did their relations the Arsinoitheriidae): on the other hand they reappeared in the form of new Mastodonts (*Buno-* or *Trilophodon*; *Zyglolophodon* or *Turiceus*; *Rhynchotherium*) which were joined in the Late

Miocene by *Tetralophodon*. *Rhynchotherium*, with its elongated trunk and stretched muzzle, carried a pair of medium-sized tusks in both upper and lower jaws.

Still to come in Africa was the new distinct family of flat-skulled 'frightful animals' (Deino- or Dinotheriidae), which also settled in Eurasia. Their tusks arose only from the sharply downward-angled front of the lower jaw. Presumably they were used for pulling down twigs, branches and creepers on which they fed. In the course of the Miocene they increased in size, became extinct in Eurasia during the Pliocene, and lived on in Africa until the beginning of the Ice Age.

During the Early Miocene the hyraxes were represented by several large-bodied genera (the early, rodent-like and upper hyraxes, *Pro-*, *Myo-*, and *Pliohyrax*), as well as the print-toothed *Protypotheroides* (so-named because of the pattern of their teeth). The Anthracotheriidae continued in part until the Pliocene with *Hyoboops* (*Merycops*) and *Brachyodus*. The primitive pig-like animals were followed by the true pigs (Suidae), which had as a branch form *Propalaeochoerus* (literally = primitive old pig), which already existed in Europe in the Oligocene, *Bunolistriodon* (with grooves between their molar cusps, hence the name) which was also found in Eurasia, and by the first bushpigs of Asian origin (*Palaeochoerus*), and also by still typical early forms such as the Diamond desert pig (*Diamantohyus*) which exhibited some peccary features. This animal, found in the S. African diamond desert, indicates the Old World origin of the New World peccaries of today.

Apart from the pigs other even-toed ungulates began to appear in the African Early Miocene; thus the first short-necked ancestors of the giraffes (still only roe or fallow deer sized) the so-called deer giraffes (*Climacoceras*). The giant *Libytherium* with its wing-like cranial processes is an indicator of the long development of the giraffes in Africa. Their branched, bony, skin-covered cranial processes were not shed like the antlers of deer later. Small ancestors of deer, the dwarf antelopes (Tragulidae) came in from Eurasia as the pig-like deer *Dorcatherium*, and in the aquatic musk deer or Chevrotain (*Hyemoschus*) their only slightly changed descendant has come down to the present time in the W. African primeval forests.

From the dwarf-antelope-like Eocene ancestors (*Archaeomeryx*) came the Early Miocene horned antelopes (Bovidae) which came from Eurasia. No larger than, and very similar to the duikers of today, with small backward sloping horns, was *Eotragus*, the herald of a great period for the horned Bovids of Africa.

With *Chalicotherium* (literally chalk animal) came many forms of the odd-toed ungulate family, the claw-hoofed-animals (Chalicotheriidae) from Eurasia into Africa. They had originated from the primitive hoofed animals (Condylarthra) in the Eocene of E. Asia and N. America. They were very large animals with horse-like heads, and looked half-way between horses and rhinoceroses. On their toes were powerful curved claw-like hoofs, possibly used like grapnels to pull up roots. By the beginning of the Villafranchian (Lower Pleistocene) the whole family had died out, and it was only with *Ancylotherium* in Africa that they persisted until the middle Ice Age.

Further odd-toed ungulates, *Brachypotherium* and *Aceratherium*, were the first of the rhinoceroses (Rhinocerotidae) in Africa. The family originated in dog-sized, hornless, ungulates in the Middle Eocene of Europe, and by the Late Eocene had already spread over Asia as well as N. America. The primitive odd-toed ungulates of the Early Eocene quickly proliferated, though at first they maintained a close resemblance to each other, so that at that time rhinoceroses, tapirs and horses differed little from one another. Out of a dozen families, the latter three families are the only survivors today. The majority of the numerous Tertiary species of rhinoceros were hornless. Oddly enough, the five surviving species today (Sumatran, Javan, Indian in Asia, and the black and white in Africa) are all horned.

Among the numerous early carnivores (Creodonta) which flourished during the Palaeocene and Eocene, only the hyaena-toothed animals of the genera *Hyaenodon*, *Metapterodon*, *Pterodon* etc. were still to be found in the Early Miocene in Africa. They died out in the Late Miocene like all the others before them. Only the Asiatic *Dissopsalis* genus of the Hyaenodontids was still existing at the beginning of the Pliocene. In the Eocene the terrestrial true carnivores (*Fissipeda*) had appeared and began to replace the early carnivores. In Africa the first Fissipeda, *Aelurogale* and *Pseudaelurus*, appeared in the Early Miocene. They came from the Late Eocene of Europe, and probably included in the Early Eocene the false sabre-toothed cats (Nimravidae). These took their name from the greatly lengthened upper canine teeth; other representatives of the family (*Eusmilus* in the Oligo-Miocene, *Sansanosmilus* in the Mio-Pliocene of Eurasia) led to the true sabre-toothed cats (Machairodontidae) of the Miocene. *Pseudaelurus*, for example, occupied a middle position between the Eo-Oligocene primitive cats (Proailuridae) and the true cats (Felidae) which rose during the Pliocene.

Among the smaller mammals of the African Early Miocene, purely African forms can be found, such as the early golden mole (*Prochrysochloris*) and the early spring-hares (*Para-* and *Megapedetes*). Both strongly resembled their existing descendants of today; a sign that both the golden moles (Chrysochloridae) as insectivores, and the spring-hares (Pedetidae) as rodents, had already passed the processes of high physical adaptation, on the one hand to a burrowing life, on the other to a rapid hopping, in the Palaeocene.

As already mentioned above, for the African Oligocene, the flying squirrel-like Theridomyidae produced further genera (*Paraphiomys*, *Diamantomys*, *Apodectes*, *Phthinilla*) during the Early Miocene. In addition to these climbing rodents, terrestrial rodents were already present, *Phiomyoides* and *Neosciuromys* represented the fore-runners of the cane rat (*Thryonomys*), a large stout rodent, weighing up to 9kg, living in reed beds and long grass, and *Pseudospalax* the burrowing rodents. Also, among the true hares (Lagomorpha) – an order which had been independent since the Palaeocene (having nothing in common with the rodents (Rodentia) apart from a superficial tooth similarity), piping hares (*Austro-* and *Kenyalagomys*), the first African representatives occurred in the Early Miocene, in S. Africa and Kenya. These immigrants, coming from Asia, constitute a family (Ochotonidae) of small animals, resembling guinea-pigs in size and appearance, within the hares (Lagomorpha). They inhabited mountains and steppes. They only appeared in Africa for a comparatively short period, and were already gone by the end of the Miocene. Today a number of species live in Asia and N. America.

In the **Middle Miocene** further mammals were added to those of the African Early Miocene already mentioned. Among the Insectivora appeared the long-legged, long-snouted rat-like giant elephant shrews (*Rhynchocyon*). They live unaltered in present-day Africa as representatives of the elephant shrew family (Macroscelididae). Further, tenrecs (*Protenrec*, *Erythrozootes*, *Geogale*) appeared as the first Madagascar hedge-hogs (Tenrecidae), a family still found only in Madagascar (*Geogale* remains un-altered to today). There were also the hairy hedgehogs (*Galerix*) which belong to a subfamily of the hedgehogs (Echinosoricinae or Gymnurinae), which had already lived in Europe in the Early Eocene, and at present can only be found in E. and S. Asia. In Africa and Europe they disappeared in the Late Miocene. Finally there also appeared the spiny hedgehogs (Erinaceinae) in the genera *Amphechinus* and *Gymnurechinus*.

Amphechinus as an early form still showed characters of the Echinosoricinae, but it had only a few spines or none at all, and came from the European Oligocene. *Gymnurechinus* is important as one of the close predecessors of the true hedgehogs (*Erinaceus*).

Among the monkeys (Primates) were the first galagos (*Progalago*), representing the lemurs (Lemuridae) and predecessors of the later, purely African galagos; also present were the first representatives of the true monkeys (Cercopithecidae) with *Mesopithecus*, distinct from the later colobus monkeys (Colobinae), the gibbon-like *Limnopithecus*, and the anthropoid-like *Proconsul* and *Sivapithecus*. *Limnopithecus* did not have the extremely long brachiating arms of the later gibbons. *Proconsul* was found as a dwarf chimpanzee-sized animal and a gorilla-sized species. Its foot structure indicated a functional resemblance to the human foot; in this respect it differed from the later man-like apes. *Sivapithecus*, which also lived in S.E. Asia in the Pliocene, appears to have been a fore-runner of the orang-utan. The co-existence of early forms of gibbon and various early man-like apes during the Middle Miocene makes it clear that the basic division of the higher primates into true monkeys, gibbons and man-like apes, and the branching out within the latter, had already begun during the Oligocene.

To all these Middle Miocene African mammals were added further hyraxes (*Meroehyrax*), rhinoceroses (*Turkanatherium*), the last hyaena-toothed carnivores (*Hyaenodon*), and the first of the bear-sized ancestors of the dogs (*Amphicyon*). The latter came from the European Oligocene and from the Middle Miocene of N. America and persisted up to the Pliocene in Eurasia and N. America.

In the **Late Miocene** of Africa, among the carnivores, appeared the first hyaenas (*Hyaena*), and the more primitive forest hyaena (*Ictitherium*), which although civet-like in form, already had hyaena-like teeth. Among rodents appeared hamster-like forms (*Cricetodon*, *Myocricetodon*) and ground squirrels (*Heteroxerus*). The aardvark was already the same genus (*Orycteropus*) as the animal of today. Elephants were still represented by mastodons (*Mastodon*) and dinotherians (*Dinotherium*), the sea-cows by an ancestral dugong (*Felsinotherium*) which was preceded by *Halitherium* in the Middle and Early Miocene. The anthracotherians still persisted up to the Pliocene. Towards the end of the Miocene there emerged from the odd-toed ungulates a rhinoceros (*Diceros* or *Atelodus*), and a still 3-toed horse (*Hipparion*), whereas the even-toed ungulates were already increasing the number of species with gazelles (*Gazella*) already similar to the present forms, and various antelopes (ancestral oryxes *Palaeoryx* and ancestral nylghai *Tragocerus*), okapi-like *Palaeotragus*, and cattle-like short-necked giraffes (*Helladotherium*).

There are few finds from the **Early Pliocene**, but many from the **Late Pliocene**, especially from the Villafranchian period. This covers the transition in time from the Pliocene (i.e. the end of the Tertiary), to the beginning of the Pleistocene or Quaternary or Diluvial (i.e. the beginning of the Ice Age).

The elephants began a process of change. The first true elephants (Elephantidae), represented by the southern elephants (*Archidiskodon*) replaced the last dinotheres (*Dinotherium*) as well as the mastodonts (*Bunolophodon*, *Mastodon*, *Pentalophodon*, *Stegolophodon*). The mastodonts, in the course of the Tertiary, had grown from rather small, long-muzzled and still short-trunked animals (*Palaeomastodon*) to ever larger animals with trunks always growing longer (*Stegomastodon* or *Stegodon*). In this process the muzzle became shorter, the lower tusks receded, and those of the upper jaw became longer. The molar teeth became reduced in number. The residual molars acquired extra pairs of cusps, as the names of the genera indicate (*Tri-*, *Tetra-*, *Pentalophodon*). Finally the pairs of cusps joined together to form transverse ridges (*Zygolophodon*, *Stegolophodon*, *Stegodon*) providing a unified chewing surface. The crowns remained low, however. At this stage the mastodonts, which were already elephant-like, died out in the Ice Age. During the Pliocene, however, from the pental-ophodonts there arose animals whose molars grew in height and in which the spaces between the transverse ridges became filled with cement. Thus, in the Villafranchian, with *Archidiskodon*, the first elephants appeared, their more efficient molar grinding surfaces enabling them to make use of wider food sources and new habitats, so that the mastodonts were displaced. From these first elephants came the true mammoth (*Mammuthus* or *Mammonteus*), and also, from a whole series of species of wide distribution, the 3 existing species (*Elephas maximus* in S. Asia, and *Loxodonta africana* and *pumilio* (but see note in text) from Africa.

The last of the 'claw-hoofed' animals, the Chalicotheriidae (see above) disappeared with the Dinotheres and Mastodonts. On the other hand, the even-toed ungulates increased in numbers of species. Primitive forest pigs (*Sivachoerus*), different developments of bush or river pigs (*Pro-, Post-, Potamochoerus*) and warthogs (*Omochoerus, Mitridiochoerus, Notochoerus, Phacochoerus*) were all represented. Among these, *Pro-* and *Postpotamochoerus* as well as at first *Microstonyx*, and later the warthogs, became steppe-living animals. A fore-runner of the warthogs was the rhinoceros-sized *Afrochoerus* with 4 long tusks. Hippopotamuses (*Hexaprotodon, Hippopotamus*) also appeared, and giraffes: (*Liby-, Griqua-, Sivatherium*) as short-necked giraffes with palmate horns, *Giraffa* with long neck and forehead cones). There were also camels (*Camelus*); cattle (true cattle, *Bos*; water and Cape buffaloes, *Bubalus* and *Syncerus*), giant-horned buffalo (*Pelorovis*) and the tahr-like *Numidocapra*, together with numerous gazelles and springbucks (*Gazella, Antidorcas*) and antelopes, populated the African plains. To a large extent the antelopes were already similar to today's: *Taurotragus* as elands, *Strepsiceros* as kudus, *Tragelaphus* as bushbucks, *Oryx* as gemsbucks, *Damaliscus* as topi, *Alcelaphus* as hartebeestes, *Redunca* as reedbucks, *Kobus* as waterbucks, and *Aepyceros* as impalas. *Menelikia*, on the contrary, was a less clearly defined primitive large antelope. The odd-toed animals showed more primitive forms (*Hipparion, Stylohipparion* as 3-toed horses) beside the modern forms (*Equus* with zebras and asses). However, it is not known whether the 'zebras' were striped. From the Middle Miocene onward a seal (*Pristiphoca*) frequented the coasts of the Tethys Sea, where today the Monk seal (*Monachus*) inhabits the Mediterranean and Black Sea. Among the rhinoceroses the white and black (*Ceratotherium* and *Diceros*) were already distinct. Otters (*Enhydridon, Lutra*) played in the waters. Wolf-like wild dogs (*Canis*), wolf-hyaenas (*Lycyaena*), sabre-toothed cats (*Homotherium, Machairodus*), and mongooses (*Herpestes*) hunted their prey, while macaques (*Libypithecus*) and round-snouted and gelada baboons (*Simopithecus, Theropithecus*) searched for their varied food. The gorilla-sized giant baboon (*Dinopithecus*) might also have been a predator in some circumstances to satisfy a need, as is the case sometimes with today's baboons.

Approximately 3 million years ago, and later, with the Australopithecines (*Australopithecus, Meganthropus, Paranthropus, Plesianthropus, Zinjanthropus*), the first prehistoric men appeared beside the man-like apes. Naturally aardvarks, hyraxes, golden moles, spring hares, more rodents and insectivores too, which were already known from earlier times, also still existed, although their existence can only be proved for later periods. Equally bats (Chiroptera) were certainly present, since this order had already produced well-developed representatives in the Eocene. Again, their existence was only proved for Africa in the Early Oligocene, and then again in the Diluvium. The long-lasting Tertiary Afro-Asiatic land connection facilitated the exchange of mammals, so that the structural differences between the mammals of the northern hemisphere and Africa have rarely exceeded specific and generic rank. Elephants, hyraxes, aardvarks, higher monkeys, and many artiodactyle ungulates migrated from Africa to Eurasia, and, in part, further to America, and horse-like animals, rhinoceroses and many artiodactyles moved from Eurasia to Africa. While at first it was particularly forest and bush species that were exchanged, later, from the end of the Miocene to the beginning of the Pliocene drying out, it was mainly steppe forms. In Africa itself, the Pliocene and Early Pleistocene mammalian fauna was largely uniform from north to south. With the Villafranchian the exchanges with Asia and Europe were almost completely stopped by the formation of the unbroken Red Sea rift and the Mediterranean barrier.

From then on the African mammals were isolated and underwent their separate development. This was especially so with the S. African forms, whereas N. Africa in the Middle Pliocene still received immigrants through the northern link. This isolation strengthened the early African forms in their independence (golden moles, elephant shrews, otter shrews, higher monkeys, elephants etc.) so that, for example, the African, and particularly the S. African elephants, became clearly distinct from all others. But from then on the bush pigs, forest hogs, warthogs, duikers, many antelopes, hartebeestes, topis, roan and kobs, bushbuck, reed buck, waterbuck, aardwolf, striped hyaena, bat-eared fox and hunting dog, are all to be considered as genuinely endemic Africans (i.e. found there and nowhere else).

In the Middle Pleistocene (c.400,000–150,000 BC) or shortly after (in S. Africa partly at first in the late Ice Age) the last representatives of the Tertiary animal world, which had found partial refuge in African isolation, disappeared. But in the middle Ice Age there appeared among the animal population of Africa dinotheres (*Dinotherium*), mastodonts (*Bunolophodon*), claw-hoofed animals (*Metaschizotherium*), 3-toed horses (*Stylohipparion*), short-necked giraffes (*Sivatherium*), sabre-toothed cats (*Machairodus*), giant-horned buffalos (*Pelorovis*), and wolf-hyaenas (*Lycyaena*), as well as elephants (*Palaeoloxodon, Loxodonta*), rhinoceroses (*Diceros, Ceratotherium*), zebras (*Hippotigris*) and asses (*Asinus*), hippopotamuses (*Hippopotamus*), warthogs (*Phacochoerus*), camels (*Camelus*), long-necked giraffes (*Giraffa*), gazelles (*Gazella*), hartebeestes (*Alcelaphus*), wildebeestes (*Connochaetes*), oryxes (*Oryx*), horse-antelopes (*Hippotragus*), elands (*Taurotragus*), reedbucks (*Redunca*), wild cattle (*Bularchus, Bos, Bubalus, Syncerus*), lions and leopards (*Panthera*), cheetahs (*Acinonyx*), hunting dogs (*Lycaon*), jackals (*Canis*) and foxes (*Vulpes*). From the beginning of the Villafranchian (about 1½ million years ago) to about the extreme end of the Middle Pleistocene (about 300,000 years ago), the early men gradually replaced the prehominids with forms of the Pithecanthropines (*Homo erectus, Telanthropus, Atlanthropus*). They themselves were further replaced by true man (Hominines) in the shape of Neanderthal man (*Homo neanderthalensis*), who was followed about 60,000 BC by modern true man (*Homo sapiens*).

The majority of forms were then already specifically identical with those existing today, such as white and black rhinoceroses, hippopotamuses, warthogs, long-necked giraffes, dorcas, Edmi and dama gazelles, hartebeestes, white-bearded gnus, oryx, eland, roan and sable, reedbuck, Cape buffalo, lion, leopard, spotted and striped hyaenas, jackal, hunting dog etc. Forms known at the beginning of the Ice Age but not yet recorded from the middle were naturally still there, since they persisted through the late and post-Ice Age times up to the present, like water buffalo, springbuck, bushbuck, kudu, waterbuck, impala, otter and mongooses. This also applies to all the related species still today typical of the African fauna, and that naturally like their relatives were also fully developed, so that besides the macaques, baboons and mangabeys, the guenons and colobus monkeys must have been already present, the more so if they could already have been found elsewhere, as, for example, the guenons in the Pliocene of India, where they no longer exist today, in contrast to the great number of African forms. Consequently the water chevrotains, duikers, dwarf antelopes, oribis, stein-bucks, klippspringers, gerenuks, situtunga, lechwe, bongos, nyalas, some viverrids (mongooses, genets, suricates, civets etc), small cats (Kaffir cat, jungle cat, black-footed cat, serval, caracal) foxes, pangolins, porcupines and numerous small mammals (shrews, otter shrews, bats, hares, mice, rats, mole-rats etc) have to be taken into account, as of generic or specific identity, if one wishes to obtain a clear picture of the profusion of African mammal species at that time.

About the middle of the Ice Age Africa was again linked with Europe by the land bridges of Gibraltar and Sicily, and with the Near East by the Suez bottleneck. This enabled animals from Europe and Asia, including the following species to enter N. Africa: Dwarf elephant (*Loxodonta jolensis = iolensis*), Mammoth (*Mammuthus primigenius*), Forest or Merck's and Woolly rhinoceros (*Dicerorhinus kirchbergensis = mercki, Coelodonta antiquitatis*), wild horses, wild boar (*Sus scrofa*), Red deer (*Cervus elaphus*), giant deer (*Megalocerus* or *Megaceroides algericus*), Mesopotamian fallow deer (*Cervus mesopotamicus*), Aurochs (*Bos primigenius*), Mouflon (*Ovis ammon musimon*), Barbary sheep (*Ammotragus lervia*), Alpine and Iberian ibexes (*Capra ibex* and *pyrenaica*), Brown and Cave bears (*Ursus arctos* and *spelaeus*), Red fox (*Vulpes vulpes*), Common otter (*Lutra lutra*), Lynx (*Lynx lynx*). However, these species did not advance beyond the southern edge of the Atlas Mts and the northern edge of today's desert. The changes in climate due to the Ice Age resulted in the pluvial and interpluvial periods which corresponded to the Ice and inter-Ice Ages of the northern hemisphere. The cooler pluvials favoured the development of forests, so that the animals of the Mediterranean region advanced further south, and species less sensitive to cold migrated from the north to Asia Minor, Syria, Palestine, Sinai and Ethiopia (e.g. snow mouse and ibex). The warmer interpluvials favoured the spread of savannahs and steppes, resulting in a migration of warmth-loving species to Egypt and Syria (e.g. giraffe, dorcas gazelle, oryx). In the second half of the Ice Age Thomas's camel (*Camelus thomasi*) lived in N. Africa. It was a two-humped camel and not a dromedary, 1.2 to 1.3 times larger than today's domestic camels. Up to now it has been recorded in an area from Morocco and Chad to Nubia, from the Middle Pleistocene to the early post-Ice Age. Presumably it came with the first-mentioned migrants from the north or north-east in the Middle Pleistocene and was probably a fore-runner of today's wild and domestic Bactrian camel.

While the Villafranchian mammal world in the whole of Africa was widely uniform, during the Middle Pleistocene the Tertiary members disappeared and the above-mentioned Eurasian immigrants came in from the north and northeast; they were however restricted to N. Africa. The late Ice Age pluvial, corresponding with the Wurm Ice Age, gave another rise to the spread of forests in the Atlas region and the Mediterranean borders, before historic man began the destruction of the soil structure, so that in the 7th century BC anthropoid apes still lived there. In addition the pluvial extended and widened the mid-African forest belt so that it reached the east coast, whereas in the interpluvial it receded, allowing contact between the dry regions of the southwest and northeast. This process, and the existence of the north-eastern immigrants, explains the formation of the zoo-geographical subregions of Africa (east, west, South African and Madagascan: the north belongs to the Palaearctic), as well as some of the present distribution gaps such as that between the northern and southern white rhinoceroses, or the southwestern and northeastern dikdiks, and finally these circumstances account for the presence of West African rain forest forms in the rain forests of the East African volcanic regions, such as the bongo on Mts Kenya and Meru.

Madagascar became separated from Africa in the course of the Mesozoic era, became reunited during the Oligocene, was separated again in the course of the Miocene, and then became very close to it during the Plio-Pleistocene through the narrowing and lowering of the Mozambique Channel. It was only during the Oligo-Miocene that the East African mammals had opportunities to occupy Madagascar. Since at that time a humid warm forest belt prevailed in the area of the southern monsoon belt, it was mainly some forest animals that came over, principally insectivores, carnivores, lemurs and rodents. The early Tertiary (Palaeocene) mammal world of Madagascar is still not known. Consequently the reason why these groups in particular should have settled, and not also others such as, for example, the African elephants, the anthracotheres, the dinotheres, primitive pigs, dwarf antelopes and early duikers (to name only a few of the distinctive forest forms of the Early Tertiary of Africa), remains unknown. The insectivores, carnivores, lemurs and rodents were enabled to spread all over the island without competition and develop suitable species for all habitats. This explains their great diversity of forms. The Middle Tertiary separation of Madagascar from Africa prevented later more highly developed and therefore more competitive animals arriving in the island, and so provided the circumstances in which the first immigrants could have become endemic settlers to the present day. Naturally these changed in the course of the following lengthy periods, mainly with regard to specific adaptations. Some species died out, others arose, but on the whole their ancient characteristics remained. Thus the investigator today, as in Australia and South America, those other two reservoirs of ancient forms, is confronted with animal forms much as they were 35–50 million years ago.

The Recent Insectivora of Madagascar have still maintained either their mouse-opossum like character (Bristly hedgehog, *Tenrec ecaudatus*) or elephant-shrew-like form (semi-bristly hedgehogs, *Hemicentetes*, 2 species), or may be hedgehog like, Hedgehog tenrec, *Setifer setosus*, Long-spined tenrec, *Echinops telfairi*, Short-spined tenrec, *Dasogale fontoynauti*, or mole-like (rice rat, *Oryzoryctes*, 3 species) or shrew-like (*Microgale*, 18 species) or otter-shrew-like (*Limnogale*, 2 species), or mouse-like (*Geogale aurita*), unchanged since the Miocene. Thus the 30 species of Madagascan insectivores occupy a wide range of habitats, with the roamers (bristly and semi-bristly hedgehogs and tenrecs), ground burrowers, climbers in thickets, and swimmers.

In the Oligocene, the period in which the ancestors of the Madagascan Carnivora came to the region, only the primitive carnivores (Creodonta) were well established in Africa. Besides, civets (Viverridae), which were also widely known in Europe and Asia, are the sole family of carnivores to which all recent Madgascan species belong. Finally, the Viverridae represent an ancient family, and among the living terrestrial carnivores (the cats, hyaenas, weasels, dogs, pandas and bears) are the earliest and yet, with 71 species today, the richest in number of forms. In Madagascar, too, the civets diversified. The 7 species belong to 7 distinct genera, and these to 3 separate subfamilies. The long isolation of the island accounts for 2 endemic subfamilies, (Cryptoproctinae and Galidiinae) which are found only in Madagascar. The third subfamily, Hemigalinae, with its 2 species Falanuk and Falanoka (*Eupleres goudotii* and *Fossa fossa*) has its other members curiously enough not in Africa but in S. Asia, where the Banded palm civet (*Hemigalus derbianus*), Owston's banded civet (*Chrotogale owstoni*), Hose's civet (*Diplogale hosei*) and Otter civet (*Cynogale bennetti*) are residual species further east in India, Sumatra and Borneo.

The largest Madagascan carnivore is the fox-sized Ferret-cat or Fossa, (*Cryptop-*

rocta ferox) which suggests the cats (Felidae) in structure, appearance and movements, and which therefore has the rank of subfamily in the civets, viz. Cryptoproctinae; it is considered to be the last survivor of the Early Tertiary pre-cats, (Proailurinae). The 4 Madagascan mongooses form a distinct subfamily (Galidiinae). Called mongooses, since they show a resemblance to those animals, they consist of Broad-striped (*Galidictis fasciata*), Narrow-striped (*Mungotictis decemlineata*), Ring-tailed (*Galidia elegans*), and Brown mongooses (*Salonoia concolor*).

The Primates reached Madagascar only in the form of lemurs (Prosimii) and have never reached a higher stage. On the other hand they developed a great variety of species, small (only mouse-sized) to anthropoid size. The latter must have been existing in the Pleistocene at least (*Megaladapis, Hadropithecus, Palaeopropithecus*) as peat bogs and caves indicate, and these must have died out after the arrival of man in early or historic times. Among these the giant lemur *Megalapadis* was about the size of a donkey.

The Madagascan lemurs developed within the suborder Prosimii their own infraorder (Lemuriformes), indicating their early palaeontologic isolation. Represented by 3 families with 10 genera and 19 species, they still show the wide range of forms produced in the course of their long development in the island. From the mouse-sized Mouse lemur (*Microcebus murinus*), with a HB length of about 10 cm, the smallest living primate, to the gibbon-sized indri (*Indri*), all intermediate sizes are represented. The mouse-lemurs may be said to replace the African pygmy flying squirrels, the lemurs (*Lemur*) replace the guenons, the Aye-aye (*Daubentonia*) with its powerful gnawing teeth and bushy tail suggests a large squirrel, the tail-less Indri (*Indri indri*, which also walks upright on the ground) suggests the gibbons, while the rock-loving Ring-tailed lemur (*Lemur catta*) suggests the macaques. The nocturnal habit so characteristic of the lemurs, together with their terrifying screams, earned the Madagascan lemurs their name in ancient Rome in reference to the alleged spirits of the dead. But there is some confusion owing to the Ring-tailed lemur and some other species of the genus *Lemur* being diurnal, as also the sifakas (*Propithecus*) and the indri.

The Rodents all remained small, mouse- or rat-sized, their structure so ancient that it is only in the Early Tertiary of Europe that their nearest relatives are found. They are represented in Madagascar by their recent 7 genera and 10 species, in one subfamily, the island mice (Nesomyinae) within the family of voles (Cricetidae). The large-footed mice (*Macrotarsomys*, 2 species) are like wood mice in appearance and habits. The Island mouse (*Nesomys*, 1 species) and the Naked-tailed mouse (*Gymnuromys*, 1 species) are rat-like, their habits little known. The Short-footed mouse (*Brachytarsomys*, 1 species) is rather vole-like but much larger, and its habits are similar. The dormouse-tailed *Eliurus* (2 species) is like a dormouse in form and also climbs. The Rabbit-mouse (*Hypogeomys*, 1 species), has habits like a rat, but lives like a rabbit, whose size it approaches, whereas the short-tailed mouse (*Brachyuromys*, 2 species) looks like voles and like them scuttles in grassy tunnels.

The Sucker-footed bat (*Myzopoda aurita*) appears to be a very old resident in Madagascar, distinguished by its sucking pads on base of thumb and sole of foot, and is found nowhere else. It constitutes a special family (Myzopodidae), as do the members of another similarly equipped family, Thyropteridae, of Central and S. America (1 genus, 2 species). The other 21 species of bats in Madagascar (3 fruit bats, 18 small bats) must have flown to the island much later, partly from the African mainland, partly from the east, not having developed any Madagascan families, not even a genus, rather at the most a few endemic species. In the Plio-Pleistocene, when Madagascar again came within closer range of the African mainland, bushpigs (*Pota-*

mochoerus) and hippopotamuses reached the island. The bushpigs have persisted, and up to the present are only subspecifically distinguishable from those of the mainland. The hippopotamuses apparently died out in prehistoric times, but it is also possible that man may have exterminated them. They belonged to a dwarf species (*Hippopotamus lemerlei*), which had a similar ancestor in the Early Pleistocene in E. Africa (*Hippopotamus imaginuncula*) and which, like this, also developed first in the Mediterranean islands. They are not closely related to the ancient Pygmy hippopotamus of W. Africa (*Choeropsis liberiensis*).

Aardvarks also once lived in Madagascar, as some Ice Age remains show. It also was probably exterminated by man. Equally, since the Early Tertiary, sea cows and whales lived in Madagascar's coastal waters. For the sea cow there is a Miocene dugong, (probably a *Halitherium*).

At the end of the Pleistocene, about 15,000 years ago, Africa was a unique giant zoo. At that time, on the African mainland, the following occurred (listed only by their families): golden moles (Chrysochloridae), hedgehogs (Erinaceidae), elephant shrews (Macroscelididae), shrews (Soricidae), otter shrews (Potamogalidae), bats (Chiroptera) including flying foxes and small bats, lemurs of the family loris (Lorisidae), monkeys (Cercopithecidae), anthropoid apes (Pongidae), hares (Leporidae), squirrels (Sciuridae), flying squirrels (Anomaluridae), spring hares (Pedetidae), voles (in the widest sense, Cricetidae), mole-rats (Rhizomyidae), rats and mice (Muridae), cane rats (Thryonomyidae), rock rats (Petromyidae), mole rats (Bathyergidae, Spalacidae), dormice (Muscardinidae), gundis (Ctenodactylidae), jerboas (Jaculidae), porcupines (Hystricidae), pangolins (Manidae), dogs (Canidae), bears (Ursidae), weasels (Mustelidae), civets (Viverridae), hyaenas (Hyaenidae), cats (Felidae), sabre-toothed cats (Machairodontidae), aardvarks (Orycteropidae), elephants (Elephantidae), hyraxes (Procaviidae), horses (Equidae), rhinoceroses (Rhinocerotidae), pigs (Suidae), hippopotamuses (Hippopotamidae), camels (Camelidae), chevrotains (Tragulidae), deer (Cervidae), giraffes (Giraffidae), and hollow-horned ruminants (Bovidae), including, in addition to cattle, wild sheep, wild goats, duikers, gazelles and antelopes.

In N. Africa alone man could encounter (to name only hoofed animals, predators and monkeys) – elephants, white and black rhinoceroses, wild horses, wild asses, zebras, warthogs and wild boars, hippopotamuses, camels, giant, red and fallow deer, long and short-necked giraffes, roan and sable antelopes, addax, hartebeestes, white-tailed and white-bearded gnus, elands, kudus, waterbucks, kobs, reedbuck, Grants – dama- and Soemmering's gazelles, dorcas – true-, red-fronted-, Heuglin's-, dune-, gazelles, gerenuks, Barbary sheep, ibexes, old-, water- and Cape-buffalos, aurochs, jackals, red-, sand-, pallid-, desert-foxes, hunting dogs, bears, polecats, weasels, striped weasels, ratels, otters, mongooses, genets, spotted and striped hyaenas, lions, leopards, cheetahs, servals, caracals, Kaffir and sand cats, Barbary apes, hussar or patas monkeys, baboons and probably also anthropoids. That is altogether 68 species. In addition, among the other larger forms the following are worth mention – hares, porcupines, aardvarks, ostriches and crocodiles.

Of this African paradise, once inhabited by over 100 million mammals, there now remains only a weak reflection. Since the end of the Ice Age the continuous drying-out of the country (partly brought about by man) has turned more than a quarter of the land area to desert. Hunting, settlement, exploitation of the soil, and destruction of habitat, have brought about extermination of big game populations in many regions. The relationship between man and game in Africa is a history extending over 100,000 years. Its description would require a separate book. In its course dozens of large mammal species vanished for ever. Already 50,000 years ago, at the end of the

Acheulian (Early Stone Age) more than 2 dozen genera of large mammals became extinct; to come nearer our own times the most recent were the Bluebuck, the Quagga, the Cape and Barbary lions.

In Madagascar also the animal paradise came to an end with the arrival of man in the Indo-Malayan invasion about AD 500–900, with the rapid extermination of 14 large lemurs and 4 giant ostrich species, and the deforestation going on to the present day.

Therefore may we hope that the following descriptions of the African and Madagascan mammals will help us to realise, in spite of the blood-letting already done, what a still precious inheritance we have to preserve for the future.

Abbreviations and Notes

The following abbreviations are used in the species descriptions:

A	Afrikaans	H	Horn length
F	French	Wt	Weight
G	German	N	North
MA	Malagasy	E	East
S	Swahili	S	South
HB	Head & body length	W	West
TL	Tail length	♂ =	Male
TTL	Total length (HB+TL)	♀ =	Female
Ht	Height at shoulder	Dent.	Dentition

All measurements in cm, all weights in grammes or kilogrammes according to size of each species.

In the dentition:

I = Incisors (gnawing teeth)
C = Canines (eye teeth)
P = Premolars (anterior cheek teeth)
M = Molars (posterior cheek teeth).

The dental formula consists of 1, number of incisors, 2, number of canines, 3, number of premolars, 4, number of molars. Usually only the number in one half of the jaw is shown. Therefore the total number of teeth is normally 4 times this figure. Where the number of teeth in upper and lower jaws differs, then the number in the upper jaw is placed before a stroke, and the number in the lower jaw is placed after the stroke (e.g. 2/3). Where the number varies within a species, 2 numbers are shown before or after the stroke (e.g. 1–2/1 or 1–2/2–3).

Distribution maps are placed as close to their species text as space allows. Where this is not on the same or facing page a cross-reference to the page on which they appear is given at the end of the paragraph on distribution.

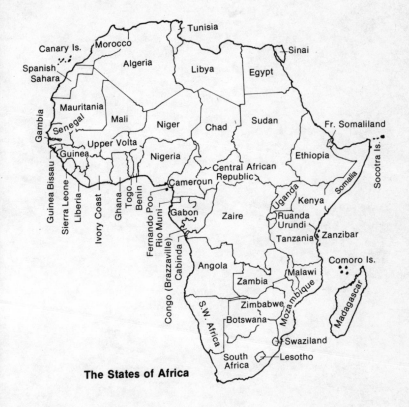

The States of Africa

Even-toed Ungulates, Artiodactyla

PIGS, SUIDAE

Medium-sized, thickset animals, rather short-legged, with elongated muzzle ending in a naked sensitive disc-like snout. Canines (tusks) often large. Face in part with knobs, warts, pads or hair tufts, or cheek beard. Toes number 4/4, secondary toes (2 & 5) shorter than front toes (3 & 4), normally not reaching ground. Skin thick, naked or thickly bristly, or woolly, with neck or dorsal mane. Young uniformly coloured or longitudinally striped. Sociable omnivorous feeders, do not chew cud. Originally only in the Old World, however introduced wild or as domestic animals and later becoming feral in New Guinea, Australia, Melanesia, New Zealand, Madagascar, N. & S. America and various other places and islands. Five genera with altogether 8 species, of which 4 genera each with 1 species in Africa including Madagascar.

BUSH PIG, RED RIVER HOG, *Potamochoerus porcus* (Linnaeus, 1758) **Pl. 1**
G. Buschschwein   F. Le Potamochère d'Afrique   A. Bosvark   S. Nguruwe
Identification. Body colour light reddish-brown (rain forest animals) to grey-brown, dark grey and brown with blackish-brown underside and black limbs (bush animals), whitish dorsal mane, long ear tufts. Young with light longitudinal stripes or rows of spots. Bush young in part with light feet, tail, and ear edge. Dent.: $3/3 \cdot 1/1 \cdot 4/3 \cdot 3/3 =$ 42, upper canine up to 10cm, lower up to 16cm. 6 (4) teats. Preorbital and foot glands present. MEASUREMENTS: HB 100–150, TL 30–45 Ht 55–80 (Senegal 100) Wt 45–120 (Senegal 150).
Distribution. Africa S. of Sahara, S. Ethiopia and S. Somalia southwards to S.W. Cape, also in Madagascar, Mayotte (Comoro Is.) Zanzibar and Mafia. 13 ssp. HABITAT: plains and mountains up to 4000m. Primary, secondary and gallery forests, bush, swamps, reed beds, high grass, forest patches, bush thickets in savannah, seldom in open savannah or steppe; also in cultivation where accessible. TERRITORY: large, extent of wandering not yet known. Said to be attached to particular habitats, wandering in search of ripe fruit over longer distances. Probably no defended area in the sense of territory. *Map p. 31.*
Habits. DAILY RHYTHM: undisturbed, may be active by day, but where hunted only at night or dusk. Resting places in thickets, brushwood, high grass, reed beds etc; access to water preferred. TOILET: scratching, cleaning, sliding, rolling, wallowing, on the other hand seldom licks or grooms. Good swimmer, ♀ does not lick or groom young. VOICE: grunting soft and regular as a contact sound, harsh and threatening in anger. Squeals in mating play or in danger, in young as contact call or fear signal. Blowing, puffing, sneezing when alarmed and as warning or threat signal. SENSES: scent very good, hearing good, vision fair. ENEMIES: principal predators leopard and lion; their extermination allows Bush Pigs to multiply. Parents defend young, using their tusks against leopards, dogs and sometimes man. FOOD: omnivorous: grass, plants, roots, bulbs, fruit, crops, seeds, fungi, small animals, young birds, carrion, trapped animals, earth at salt-licks. Its rooting in the soil very destructive to agriculture. SOCIABILITY: in family bands usually 6–12, sometimes up to 24 animals, led by an old ♂, sometimes in large bands up to 100 animals. Old ♂♂ may also be solitary. ♂ and ♀ association apart from pairing and rearing young probable.

Reproduction. Pairing probably occurs through the year but most litters are dropped at the most favourable food seasons, in E. & S. Africa mainly Oct–Mar, concentrating in Nov–Jan. Gestation 120–130 days, litter size generally 3–6, often up to 8, rarely 10. Probably 2 litters annually. ♀ makes nest lined with grass. Young live for some days in this. ♀ does not eat the afterbirth. Family lives in neighbourhood of birth place. Weight at birth 0.65–0.9; HB 45–65; weekly weight increment 0.8–1 up to 10 months. Fully grown at 2 years. Immature coat changes at $\frac{1}{4}$ year. Sex ratio about 1–1. SEXUALLY MATURE at $1\frac{1}{2}$–$1\frac{3}{4}$ years. LONGEVITY: 12–15 years.

GIANT FOREST HOG, *Hylochoerus meinertzhageni* Thomas, 1904   **Pl. 1**
G. Waldschwein, Riesenwaldschwein   F. L'Hylochère géant   S. Nguruwe
Identification. Muzzle very broad (up to 16cm). Below eyes and across cheeks broad fungus-like glandular skin swellings. Scent glands before eyes, and on foreskin. 4 teats. Dent.: $1/2 - 3 \cdot 1/1 \cdot 3/2 \cdot 3/3 = 32$–34. Upper C strongly curved backwards, underside smoothly polished (length up to 30cm), lower long, pointed, sharp edged, strongly pointing outwards; only these used as weapons. Skin ash-grey, hairs flattened, dark brown to black. West African animals somewhat less black, breast and flanks mixed with a little white. Corners of mouth and behind ears with light hair tufts. Young up to 3 months uniformly brown (in W. Africa paler, with dark lateral stripes and somewhat lighter ground), dorsal hairs elongated, mane-like. MEASUREMENTS: HB 155–180, TL 25–35, Ht 80–100. Wt 100–250. ♂ larger and heavier than ♀.
Distribution. Central African forest belt from Liberia to Cameroun, N. Zaire, Bahr-el-Ghazal, S. Ethiopia (Wollega and Jimma), Kenya and N. Tanzania. Often only isolated occurrences, or up to present not yet generally recorded. HABITAT: large forests with dense thickets, open stands of tall trees with clearings, in plains and mountains. In Kivu National Park also on bush-studded grassy plains. TERRITORY: living area large, visited in the course of repeated wanderings, but not marked or defended. Droppings often in same places, especially where grubbing for roots around fallen trees, resulting in large dungheaps.
Habits. DAILY RHYTHM: active mostly at night. Rest mid-day in dense thickets, pierced by tunnel-like runs, leading to nest-like resting places. Search for food in morning and evening. TOILET: as in Bushpig. VOICE: grunting and growling. Contact call a high barking 'wah-wah', sometimes also heard in playful defence. Fighting ♂♂ have very loud call, beginning softly, swelling to elephant-like trumpeting and ending in lion-like grunt. SENSES: hearing very sharp, scent good, sight moderate. ENEMIES: leopard and Golden Cat, but only for unprotected young. Defence, see Bushpig. Excited fighting ♂♂ foam at corner of eyes. FOOD: grass, plants, leaves, buds, roots, berries, fallen fruit, sometimes crops near native settlements in forests. No earth eating. SOCIABILITY: in families of 4–12 as in Bushpig and Wild Boar. Probably mate for life, or at least for the breeding season. Old animals protect the young together. Sometimes young gather in parties (possibly due to numerous ♂♂). Old animals sometimes solitary.
Reproduction. Barely restricted to particular season, young seen all the year; however locally Oct–Nov seems the preferred pairing season. Gestation 4–4$\frac{1}{2}$ months. Litter size 1–4 (sometimes up to 8). Often only 1–2 survive, due to clumsy mother's overlaying in nest. No details of life span known, probably like Bush-Pig and Wild Boar.

WILD BOAR, *Sus scrofa* Linnaeus, 1758   **Pl. 60**
G. Wildschwein   F. Le Sanglier
Identification. Form like European Wild Boar. Coat yellowish intermixed with dark

greyish-brown. Limbs, muzzle, around eyes, backs of ears, tail tuft, dark olive to blackish-brown. Young brown with 3–4 longitudinal yellowish stripes on each side. Dent.: 3 · 1 · 4 · 3. C sharp, upper 5–8, lower 6–9cm. Scent glands before eyes, on chin, foot joints and foreskin. 10–12 teats. MEASUREMENTS: HB 110–130, TL 15–21, Ht 70–90. Wt 60–130. ♂ larger than ♀.

Distribution. North Africa. In Morocco and Algeria as far as the Sahara Atlas south border; extinct in thickly settled districts. N. Tunisia (Khroumerie mountain forests and neighbourhood). In Libya only still in Leptis Magna and Cyrenaica. Exterminated in Egypt about 1900. In the Sudan, in Kordofan and Senaar, only feral domestic pigs, as also in the E. African islands of Mafia and Pemba. 1 ssp. Barbary Wild Boar, *barbatus* Sclater, 1860 (= *algirus* Loche, 1867; *sahariensis* Heim de Balsac, 1937). HABITAT: woodlands, copses, groves of trees, bushy thickets, macchia scrub, swamps, reed beds, esparto grass etc. in plains and mountains. Water for drinking and wallowing is a necessity. Locations vary according to food supply and cover. Where hunted leads an unsettled life. TERRITORY: see Bushpig.

Habits. DAILY RHYTHM: when undisturbed, mainly active in morning, late afternoon and evening, resting mid-day and at night. Where hunted is mostly nocturnal. TOILET: SENSES: FOOD: see Bushpig. VOICE: like Bush Pig. Rhythmic grunting of leading ♀♀ keeps the following young together. ♀ call to young to suckle 'oink-oink-oink'. At the danger alarm 'Wuff' of ♀ the young instinctively hide motionless in cover. Lost young squeal, ♀ replies with rattling grunts. Cries of young in distress alert all ♀♀ in the neighbourhood as well as the mother. Other calls have various meanings. Mother recognises her young by scent as much as by sound. ENEMIES: formerly lion and leopard, both today wholly or almost extinct. Defence, see Bush Pig. SOCIABILITY: family bands usually mothers with young, ♂♂ nearby. Often several bands near, with breeding ♀♀ apart and ♂♂ on guard. Old ♂♂ often solitary.

Reproduction. Farrowing season late winter and early spring according to regional climate. Gestation 112–120 days, litter 5–8 (4–12), 2 litters a year possible. Young suckle for 2–3 months, first solid food at 1–2 weeks. ♀ makes grass- or leaf-lined breeding nest, which may be left after 12–24 hours, depending on weather. At 1½–2 weeks body temperature reaches constant 40°. Weight at birth and development much as in Bush Pig. SEXUAL MATURITY: ¾–1½ years (the shorter time for ♀♀ in good beech mast year). LONGEVITY: 15–20 years.

WART HOG, *Phacochoerus aethiopicus* (Pallas, 1767) **Pl. 1**
G. Warzenschwein   F. Le Phacochère   A. Vlakvark   S. Nigri
Identification. Pelage only separate bristles, those from forehead to middle of back

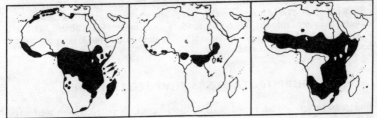

Wild Boar (N. of Sahara)   Giant Forest Hog   Warthog
Bush Pig (S. of Sahara)

long, forming yellowish to dark brown mane. Under edge of lower jaw with whitish whiskers (bristle fringe). Front of muzzle across canine roots very broad. Each side of head with 3 skin warts (infraocular, praeocular, and mandibular, the first in ♂ being up to 15cm long, the second in ♀ appearing late and weak). Young at first pinkish-grey haired, after a week grey. Skin of old animal grey and more or less wrinkled. Dent.: begining $1/3 \cdot 1/1 \cdot 3/2 \cdot 3/3 = 34$, then falling to $0/2 \cdot 1/1 \cdot 2/2 = 16$, or $0/2 \cdot 1/1 \cdot 1/1 = 12$. All I, often also all P and M fall out, except last M which becomes very elongated. Upper C semicircular in form, up to 60cm long. Scent gland below eye. 4 teats. MEASUREMENTS: HB ♂ 125–150, ♀ 105–140; TL ♂ 40–50, ♀ 35–40; Ht ♂ 65–85, ♀ 55–75: Wt ♂ 60–150, ♀ 50–75.

Distribution. Africa south of Sahara from Ghana to Somalia, thence southwards to Natal, S.W. Africa and Angola. 7 ssp. HABITAT: prefers treeless open plains and light savannahs, avoiding dense cover or steep slopes. Up to 2500m in mountains. Likes water for drinking and bathing, but can do without if necessary. TERRITORY: keeps to favoured locality even in drought and food shortage. Often shares territory with other bands. Droppings strewn about without any territorial marking. Ideal territory includes living and sleeping holes, watering places, wallows and rolling places, pasturage and shade. In favourable conditions one pair or band every 2sq km, even 3–4 or possibly more. *Map* p. 31.

Habits. DAILY RHYTHM: rest by night or at mid-day in an abandoned aardvark hole or self excavated termite hill, holes among rocks, cavities in the ground, or in emergency in bushy thickets. In morning and afternoon feeding, drinking, wallowing, and sand bathing, rubbing against trees or termite hills. TOILET: mutual grooming of neck, back and underside. Scratching, dust bathing, wallowing. Tolerate tick birds as destroyers of ticks, mites and fly grubs. VOICE: not very vocal; snorting and wooffiing in alarm and unease, tooth grinding in fury, high grunting in agitation. Young chirp. SENSES: scent and hearing best, sight better than in other African pig species. ENEMIES: lion and leopard principal enemies, cheetah sometimes takes young or isolated animals. ♂ protects family with lower tusks, as does ♀ with young. FOOD: principally short grass, also fallen fruit, green bark; during drought will dig with snout and canines for bulbs, tubers and roots. Sometimes also small mammals and carrion are taken. Avoids cultivation, therefore rarely harmful to crops. SOCIABILITY: family groups of parents and 2–4 young. Sometimes adopts orphans, sometimes previous year's young stay in family, sometimes two bands join together. Pair for the breeding season, but pairing for life not ruled out. Old ♂♂ may be solitary.

Reproduction. Pairing takes place as soon as previous young independent or sexually mature (♂ about 18–19 months, ♀ about 17–18). Regionally the pairing or littering season associated with the rains. Gestation 170–175 days. Litter size 2–4 (rarely more, up to 8 possible). Young leave hole after 1 week and start to eat grass. Suckle up to 3–4 months, but after 2 months milk only secondary nourishment. Wt at birth 0.8–1.2 (HB *c*. 35), Wt of yearling *c*. 27–30. Sex ratio in young and adults about 1:1. LONGEVITY: up to 18 years recorded in wild.

HIPPOPOTAMUSES, HIPPOPOTAMIDAE

Plump and thick-bodied, round-headed, short-legged, short-tailed even-toed ungulates with naked skin, very large tusk-like canines, small eyes and ears. Nostrils can be closed. Toes 4/4, lateral toes (2 and 5) rather shorter than anterior toes (3 and 4), joined by swimming webs. Aquatic, swimming and diving vegetarian feeders. No cud-chewing. 2 genera, each with 1 species, only in Africa.

HIPPOPOTAMUS, *Hippopotamus amphibius* (Linnaeus, 1758) **Pl. 2**
G. Grossflusspferd F. L'Hippopotame amphibié A. Seekoie S. Kiboko
Identification. Ears and nostrils capable of closure, jaws very deeply cleft, lower jaw rectangularly hinged. 4-toed feet webbed. Skin naked except for bristle hairs on muzzle and tail tip, with abundant mucous glands. Skin at birth pink, later greyish-brown, albinism rare. 2 teats. Dent.: $2 \cdot 1 \cdot 4 \cdot 3 = 40$. Both upper and lower C very large, curved, the lower up to 100cm on curve, weight up to 4kg. MEASUREMENTS: HB ϑ 320–420, $\mathcal{Q}$ 280–370; TL 35–50, Ht ϑ 140–165, $\mathcal{Q}$ 130–145. Wt ϑ 1500–3200, $\mathcal{Q}$ 1350–2500. ϑ on average larger and heavier than $\mathcal{Q}$.
Distribution. Now only S. of Sahara, in E. from N. Ethiopia southward to S.W. Mozambique, Transvaal, and northern S.W. Africa. Also on Mafia Is. (E. Africa) and Bijagos Is. (W. Africa). 4 ssp. HABITAT: small to large waters with flat banks, sand banks etc., bordering rich grass plains. Dense high reed beds and forested banks are avoided, and $\mathcal{Q}\mathcal{Q}$ with young also avoid strong currents and rocky shores. Water temperatures of $18°$–$35°$C are needed. Up to 2000m in mountains. Also on sea coasts. Home is always in water, sought in case of danger. Dive duration 1–5, rarely up to 15 minutes. TERRITORY: lying-up places on the banks are divided among individuals, the best held by the strongest $\vartheta\vartheta$. Areas of good pasturage are used in common. At various defecation sites all sexually mature $\vartheta\vartheta$ make their contribution in passing (scent-marking places). Highest population density along strongly winding, smooth-flowing rivers with numerous deep pools, where (as also on lake shores) there may be up to 100 animals or more per km. In rainy season $\vartheta\vartheta$ wander in search of fresh green often a km to new seasonal waters. *Map* p. 34.
Habits. DAILY RHYTHM: in daytime rest in or by the water, in evening go ashore to graze, the old $\vartheta\vartheta$ last. TOILET: nothing specific. Water keeps skin clean; the pink mucous secretion of skin glands protects the skin from effects of water, and also from drying too much on land. At times of excitement mucous secretions flow freely. VOICE: cattle-like bellowing with mouth open as ϑ threat or fighting challenge. Horse-like neighing when excited or alarmed. Mating call of ϑ a series of 3 notes (muh-muh-muh). Snorts through submerged nostrils (blowing), purpose unknown. SENSES: scent and hearing good, underwater sight only adequate, but above water not bad. ENEMIES: apart from man, few natural enemies; on land only groups of lions for solitary animals, and in water crocodiles are dangerous for young. $\mathcal{Q}\mathcal{Q}$ protect young bravely, if necessary also against ϑ. FOOD: soft short grass and other plants (40–60kg at each meal), fallen fruits, water vegetation only occasionally. In drought can fast for some weeks. SOCIABILITY: groups mainly of $\mathcal{Q}\mathcal{Q}$ (mothers with young and non-breeding young $\mathcal{Q}\mathcal{Q}$) watched over by old ϑ. Sexually mature $\vartheta\vartheta$ are kept on the edge of the group, at 8–10 years strong enough to fight older $\vartheta\vartheta$ for position. With increasing population there is more territorial fighting.
Reproduction. According to locality pairing takes place over the whole year. Gestation 225–257, in general 233–234 days. Generally 1 young, twins uncommon. Birth takes place according to circumstance, either in shallow water or on land (in that case $\mathcal{Q}$ makes grass or reed bed in hollow of bank, away from the herd). Birth weight 35–55, daily increment up to 6 months $c.$ 0.5. Suckle for one year, first solid food at 3 weeks. SEXUAL MATURITY ϑ 4–5, $\mathcal{Q}$ 3–4 (in captivity ϑ and $\mathcal{Q}$ about 3–4 years). 1st rut about 50 days after birth of young; if not impregnated, then repeated each 4

months. Normally 1 young each 1½–2 years. Sex ratio at birth 1:1 as in adults. LONGEVITY: 40–45 years (in zoo to 50 years).

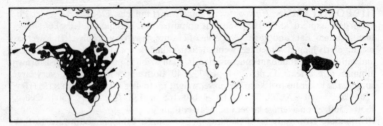

Hippopotamus   Pygmy Hippopotamus   Barbary Stag (Tunis)
                                                 Water Chevrotain
                                                 (Central Africa)

PYGMY HIPPOPOTAMUS, *Choeropsis liberiensis* (Morton, 1844)   Pl. 2
G. Zwergflusspferd   F. L'Hippopotame nain ou H. pygmé

Identification. Pig-sized. Tail flattened and on edge with bristles up to 1cm long. Front toes with short webs. Lateral toes rather long almost reaching ground. Skin smooth, naked, abundant pores, mucous secretion colourless. Colour greyish-brown, cheeks, throat and underside sometimes pink. As in Hippopotamus, penis curved backwards when urinating; 2 teats. Dent.: $2/1 \cdot 1/1 \cdot 4/4 \cdot 3/3 = 38$, lower incisors often lost. MEASUREMENTS: HB 170–195, TL 15–21, Ht 70–92, Wt 200–275, ♂ hardly larger than ♀.

Distribution. Coastal regions of W. Africa from R. Bufon in Guinea through Sierra Leone and Liberia to Bandama R. in Ivory Coast. Also 1300km further east in Niger delta (Owerri and Warre Provinces of Nigeria), where threatened or already extinct. 2 ssp.   HABITAT: swamp edges and bordering dense thickets by water in rain forest region.   TERRITORY: defended against other members of the species. Entrance in holes in bank or hole-like bush thickets, from which they wander for food. Also goes into high forest. Population low. On land, flees to water: in water, flees to land.

Habits. DAILY RHYTHM: roams by night, otherwise nothing known.   TOILET: see Hippopotamus, p. 33.   VOICE: pig-like grunting suggests sound of a rusty hinge (function not known). In anger a nasal snort, hissing with open mouth, tooth-grinding, in fear short snores, in mating play, lowing.   SENSES: hearing and scent better than sight.   ENEMIES: leopard, golden cat, others unknown. Defence with sideways blows of canines with open mouth. Flees (see TERRITORY).   FOOD: leaves, swamp vegetation, their roots and tubers (these dug out), fallen fruit.   SOCIABILITY: solitary; only meeting others at mating time. ♀ lives with young by herself.

Reproduction. Breeding season said to be at beginning of dry season (Nov–Dec). Gestation 180–210 days, 1 young at a birth laying up on land. Suckles lying on land or in shallow water 2 or 3 times a day. Daily weight increment 0.5. Solid food taken at 3 months. Suckles for many months. Young live with mother up to 3 years; latter has 1 young every 2 years. Wt at birth 5–7, Ht 27–30. Swimming in deep water is learnt.   SEXUALLY MATURE: at 3–5 years.   LONGEVITY: in captivity up to 30 years recorded.

CHEVROTAIN, TRAGULIDAE

Size of rabbit or hare, thickset, round-backed, small-headed, hornless, cloven-hoofed with slit-like nostrils, large eyes and small pointed or middle size rounded ears, with secondary toes (2 and 5) shorter than the anterior (3 and 4) and normally not reaching the ground. Dent.: $0/3 \cdot 1/1 \cdot 3/3 \cdot 3/3 = 34$. Upper C of ♂♂ elongated, dagger-like. Skin short-haired and smooth. Tail short, sometimes bushy. Goes on tip-toe, skulking in dense cover, solitary omnivorous feeder and chews the cud with plant food. 2 genera with altogether 4 species, in the Old World, of which 1 genus and 1 species in Africa.

WATER CHEVROTAIN, *Hyemoschus aquaticus* (Ogilby, 1841)   **Pl. 2**
G. Hirschferkel, Wassermoschustier   F. Le chevrotain aquatique
Identification. Hare-sized, hunch-backed, small-headed, nostrils narrow slits, naked muzzle with mobile snout, ears short. Legs slender and short, lateral toes 2 and 5 reduced. Tail bushy, reaching the heels. Pelage close and fine, longer on back of thighs than on posterior belly, lacking on back of feet between upper and lower toes. Upperside dark olive-brown, sometimes a blackish stripe from nose to forehead, belly and back of thighs brownish-yellow, conspicuous white pattern in form of spots on the back. 1–3 long stripes on flanks, chin, throat, breast band. Legs spotted; dorsal spots variable in form and number. Young colour like adults. Chin, anal and prepuce glands present, gall bladder present, 4 teats, larynx expanded, bladder-like (resonant). MEASUREMENTS: HB 75–85, TL 10–15, Ht 35–40, Wt 10–15.
Distribution. Guinea and Congo forest regions, from Guinea to Cameroun, Central African Republic, N. & E. Zaire, Gabon. HABITAT: primeval forests and moist gallery forests, thick undergrowth and nearby water essential. TERRITORY: local, small territory without fixed resting places and scent making spots (urine, droppings and chin-gland secretion scattered), each animal for itself, contact calls serve to space occupied areas. ♂♂ especially do not tolerate neighbours, using threatening gnashing to drive off intruders; no individual preserves and no rank order.
Habits. DAILY RHYTHM: active all night, ♂ 2, ♀ 1 rest periods at intervals by day resting in cover (thickets or holes in banks). TOILET: scratching with fore and hind feet and teeth and skin licking; the latter mutual only shortly during courtship and nursing small young by ♀, usually only sniffing. VOICE: short barks as contact calls (see Territory). ♀ confronting another ♀ a high rhythmic chatter (up to 8 a second). Bark as alarm note, loud grating bark when frightened, alerting associates, high screams as cry of distress when caught. ♂ in rut following ♀ utters short squeals, at which the sexually ready ♀ waits to be covered. SENSES: scent and hearing better than sight. ENEMIES: leopard, golden cat, civet, and for young also owls and other small predators. Bark in alarm, stands still or steals silently away; if danger near takes refuge in water, diving deeply and hiding under water. FOOD: omnivorous; grass, plants, leaves, fruit, insects, crabs, fish, small mammals, carrion, worms, roots unearthed with snout. With plant food chews the cud. SOCIABILITY: solitary, except at pairing time (see Territory).
Reproduction. ♂ find ♀ by scent, simple pairing without aggression; mating as in pigs. Gestation about 4 months, 1 active young. Young lies up for a week, ♀ comes to young only to suckle it. Suckling period 8 months, but solid food taken at 2 weeks. SEXUAL MATURITY: 8 months. LONGEVITY: not known.

DEER, CERVIDAE

In size from hare to horse, pointed paired hoofs, the front foot secondary toes (2 and 5) small to large (always however smaller than 3 and 4) and with lower or upper metacarpal ends visible but not in hind feet secondary toes. Tail absent or of medium length. Dent.: $0/3 \cdot 0-1/1 \cdot 3/3 \cdot 3/3 = 32-34$. Upper C long, short, vestigial or absent. Forehead with 2 short to long bony processes (antlers) on which all or most – yearly new skin (velvet) grows as far as the numerous ends (tines) round or partly flattened and broad shovel-like. At completion of growth the velvet falls off, and the antlers are carried for $\frac{1}{2}$ or more of the year. Solitary to sociable, cud-chewing vegetarian feeders. In all regions of Old and New Worlds. Introduced in Australia, Tasmania, New Zealand, New Caledonia. Mariannas, Mauritius, Comoro Is., Madagascar as well as numerous species spread over both the Old and New Worlds. 14 genera, with altogether 32 species, of which originally only one native species (Barbary Stag, a ssp. of Red Deer) exists in North Africa, though recently Fallow Deer (*Cervus dama*) in South Africa, Java Rusa (*Cervus timorensis russa*) in Mauritius, Anjouan and Madagascar, and Spanish Red Deer (*Cervus elaphus hispanicus*) introduced into Morocco and Fernando Poo.

BARBARY STAG, *Cervus elaphus barbarus* (Bennett, 1833) **Pl. 2**
G. Berberhirsch   F. Le Cerf de Barbarie
Identification. Somewhat smaller than Central European Red Deer. Summer coat light reddish-brown with long rows of whitish spots on the body, usually persisting throughout life. Rump pale yellowish. Winter coat longer, dark brown, spots barely or no longer visible, ♂ without rutting season mane on throat. Calf reddish-brown, rump whitish, usually on each side 6 rows of whitish spots between shoulders and thighs and 1–2 along throat. Dent.: $0/3 \cdot 1/1 \cdot 3/3 \cdot 3/3 = 34$. Scent glands present in front of eyes, mid-foot, between toes (latter only on hind foot) under tail and pygal area. ♂ also has glands behind chin, and ♀ above eyes, 4 teats. No gall bladder. Fully grown antlers *c.* 80cm long, spread around 65cm (record 98.7cm), circumference at base 15cm. Main beam moderate, colour dark to chestnut-brown. Tips lighter. Each antler 4–6 tines. Eight points normal, sometimes a weak extra tine or three-ended making cup-shape possible. MEASUREMENTS: Ht ♂ 130–140, ♀ 90–100; TL *c.* 15: Wt ♂ 150–225, ♀ 100–150.
Distribution. N.W. Africa, formerly Morocco to Tunisia, today a remnant in W. Tunisia, perhaps also E. Algeria. HABITAT: woods with dense undergrowth in plains, hills and mountains up to 600m (rarely up to 1200m). TERRITORY: no definite territory; outside breeding season ♂♂ and ♀♀ in separate areas. *Map* p. 34.
Habits. Wandering in early summer in the pastures of the Atlas Mts, in autumn down to valleys and river meadows. DAILY RHYTHM: during day rest in woodland thickets from spring to autumn, at night-time in fields and meadows to graze. TOILET: occasional scratching of fore-part of body with hind foot, leg licking, skin shivering, rubbing against trees, dusting in dry ground, in warm season wallowing (especially ♂♂) in pools and swampy lakes. Rub off dying velvet of antlers on trees and bushes. VOICE: calf bleats (contact call) variety of calls (recognition of mother, fear) a creaking like rusty lock (lost call). ♀ has special calls for young in breeding season. In rut ♂ 'bells', a succession of roaring sounds (young ♂♂ high, old ♂♂ deep) as challenge. A short 'wo-wo' is fear or alarm call. 'Aeugh' general contact call of both sexes. SENSES: scent very good, hearing good, sight moderate (movement and colour

recognised). ENEMIES: previously lion and leopard, both today nearly or quite exterminated. Otherwise man and feral dogs are main enemies. FOOD: grass, herbage, fungi, berries, shoots of bushes, trees, fresh leaves, meadow grass and farm crops. SOCIABILITY: in the rut both sexes together, otherwise adult ♂♂ separate; on the other hand ♀♀ with calves and immature fawn, family groups in separate areas.

Reproduction. Rutting season from beginning of Sep to end of Oct. ♂♂ and ♀♀ meet in clearings (rutting grounds). Roaring old ♂♂ fight each other to collect harem and keep rivals away. The severe persecution of the Barbary Stag in the last 100 years has resulted in the rut being less obvious. Calves are dropped from late April to early June. Gestation about 235 days 1 calf (able to run) at birth, twins rarely. For 2–3 weeks lies hidden, later follows the mother constantly. Suckling ends at next breeding of mother. SEXUAL MATURITY: $1\frac{1}{2}$ years. LONGEVITY: 12–15, sometimes up to 20 years. Fallow Deer have been introduced to Madagascar and S. Africa (see family introduction).

GIRAFFES, GIRAFFIDAE

Long-legged, long-necked, 180–580cm tall, even-toed ungulates with large eyes, small to large ears and medium length tail with terminal tuft. Forehead and crown with 2–5 skin covered horns. Okapi ♀ hornless. Secondary toes (2 and 5) absent except for rudiments. Ambling, cud-chewing, browsing inhabitants of high forest or savannah. 2 genera each with 1 species, in Africa only.

GIRAFFE, *Giraffa camelopardalis* (Linnaeus, 1758)   **Pl. 3**
G. Giraffe   F. La Giraffe   A. Giraf, Kameelperd   S. Twiga
Identification. Skin-covered horns in ♂♂ and ♀♀. Length up to 22cm. 1 pair on forehead, 2 smaller on crown, sometimes a stud or small horn between both pairs. (2, 4 or 5-horned). Horn diameter and skull weight in ♂ (skull as weapon in fighting rivals) considerably more than in ♀, namely 8–14: 2.5–5kg. Slit-like nostrils can be closed. Tongue as in Okapi, p. 38, but flesh-coloured. Secondary toes 2 and 5 absent. Middle line of back of neck with 5–13cm long mane of longer, stiffer hair, yellowish-red to dark brown. Body hair short, dense. Ground colour whitish-yellow to brown with fawn colour to blackish-brown spots. Spots shaped as in Pl. 3, transition between the 3 types shown. Individual and geographic pattern variations wide. Sometimes almost white or black or unspotted animals are found. Pattern of young as in adults. Dent.: $0/3 \cdot 0/1 \cdot 3/3 \cdot 3/3 = 32$. Gall bladder absent from birth. No skin glands, 4 teats. MEASUREMENTS: HB 300–400, TL 90–110, Ht at shoulder 270–330, Ht to crown with horns 450–580, Wt 500–800.

Distribution. Africa, S. of Sahara to E. Transvaal, Natal and N. Botswana. Reintroduced to S. Africa game reserves. 8 ssp. HABITAT: bush and tree savannahs (especially thorn acacias), up to 2000m from sparsely wooded grasslands to thickly overgrown savannah (Nyika, Bushveld, Miombo). TERRITORY: remains attached to large territories (some sq km), individual territories are not held. Territory used by whole family troop. Dominant ♂♂ with their wider view may add to their troop.

Habits. DAILY RHYTHM. Mainly feeding in morning 6–9am and afternoon (3–6pm); midday standing in shade, at night stand or lie (up to 1–2 hours) resting. TOILET: only rubbing (this is commonest), cleaning, licking and shivering: no water, mud or sand bathing, no scratching with feet. VOICE: harsh coughs, rumbles and grunts of ♂, a mixture of excitement and rival fighting. Calves and adults bleat in strong excitement, rising to a screaming bellow. A lost calf lows with closed mouth. Snorting through the nostrils seems to be a warning signal, a softer snorting or snoring seems an expression of difficulty, not well understood. SENSES: sight good (over 1km), colours distinguished; hearing and scent good. ENEMIES: lions a threat to young, protected by powerful kicks. FOOD: mainly (95 %) foliage of trees and bushes, buds, shoots, fruit; acacias preferred. Occasionally grass, plants, water melons. Maize and other crops are sought out. Salt and other mineralised earth gladly taken. When food is lush and soft, drinks once a week; when food is dry needs water at least every 2 days (30–50 l). SOCIABILITY: in small or large troops (mostly 2–6, less often 6–12, rarely 1–6 dozen). Centre of group is mother and family, several families making a troop. Old ♂♂ may wander and eventually form new associations. Thus new ♂ troops may be formed.

Reproduction. Gestation 400–468 days, average 440. No marked breeding season, however in E. Transvaal about 60 % of all births in summer (Dec–Mar). 1 active young at a birth, rarely twins. Wt at birth 45–70, Ht at shoulder 165–190. Suckle for 6–12 months. Births at intervals of 1½ years. Growth continues to 10 years. Sex ratio of adult ♂♂ to ♀♀ about 30–60:100. SEXUAL MATURITY: of ♀2½–3, ♂3–3½ years. LONGEVITY: up to 28 years in captivity.

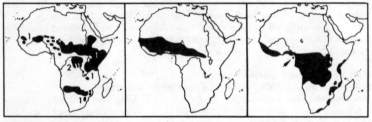

1 Giraffe   2 Okapi   Red-flanked Duiker   Blue Duiker

OKAPI, *Okapia johnstoni* (Sclater, 1901)   **Pl. 3**
G. Okapi   F. L'Okapi
Identification. Coat short, smooth, skin blackish, greasy, strongly scented. Short mane (1.5cm) along middle of neck to shoulders. Calf skin pattern much as adults, but brown part of coat is black at first, and forehead reddish-brown. From neck to root of tail in calf a 4cm long upright mane, but at 1½ years it disappears on the back, and on the neck is reduced to 1.5cm. Adult ♂ becomes somewhat paler than ♀. The number of blackish-brown transverse stripes on fore legs 5–8, on thighs up to 20. ♂ only has small skin-covered horns, the tips often worn bare. No gall bladder. Glands between toes on front and hind feet. 4 teats. Metacarpal and metatarsal remnants present on digits 2 and 5. Dentition as Giraffe. Nostrils slit-like, can be closed. Tongue long, rounded, front bluish-grey, extensile as far as eyes. MEASUREMENTS: HB. *c*.120, TL 30–40, Ht at crown, without horns, 170–180, Ht at shoulder 150–165, Ht at rump 130–155, H 15–26. Wt 250.

Distribution. Only in Zaire, and only in the mixed forest belt (Guinea and Equatorial type) of northern, eastern and southern central Congo basin, bounded in west by flood forest. Distribution includes long tongues of forest between the rivers Lomami and Zaire, Lomami and La Tshuapa, and La Tshuapa and Lomela. Okapi localities therefore in the Ubangui, Uelle, Aruwimi and Ituri rain forests from Libangi on the

Ubangui in the west, to near Lakes Kivu and Edward in the east, north to Faradje, south to Sankuru and Maniema districts, about 5°S. No ssp. HABITAT: depths of the lowland rain forests. Nearness to streams, rivers and occasional clearings, as well as firm ground, preferred. Swamps are avoided, but shallow water may be traversed if soil firm. TERRITORY: each animal has a home range of some hectares with clear borders. Population density not insignificant, perhaps half a dozen animals to each $2\frac{1}{2}$sq km.

Habits. DAILY RHYTHM: in wild unknown. TOILET: Skin cleaned by licking. Tongue can reach most parts of body including eyes and feet. Takes shower bath by trotting through water, afterwards licking skin dry. VOICE: not important; a cough (sometimes mixed with a high piping) as contact call. Snorts in excitement (anger or attack). Moaning sound when wounded. Calf has coughing contact call and other calls of alarm, when mother comes to help. SENSES: sight and hearing very good, sight good (important for food selection). ENEMIES: only leopard is threat to adults, for young calves also golden cat and perhaps serval. Main enemy the pygmy hunters – Okapis panic when they are near. FOOD: selective: leaves, buds, tender shoots, forest clearing grasses, ferns, fruit, fungi. Euphorbia plants (poisonous to humans) eagerly sought, as also manioc and sweet potato plants. Charcoal and mineral earths favoured. SOCIABILITY: normally solitary. Sexes meet only at pairing time. Previous year's calf presumably lives with or near mother.

Reproduction. Two main breeding seasons, May–Jun and Nov–Dec, though may pair in any month. Gestation 421–457 days, birth intervals 15–17 months. 1 young. Wt at birth 20–24, Ht at shoulder 72–83. Calf lies up for first 14 days, then follows mother. Suckles for 8–10 months. Strange calf may be adopted. Fully developed at 4–5 years. SEXUALLY MATURE: ♀ at 3 years, ♂ at 4. Horn growth begins at 12 months. LONGEVITY: 15–20 years in captivity.

HOLLOW-HORNED RUMINANTS, BOVIDAE

Size range from hare to cattle, small and elegant or large and heavy, even-toed ungulates. Forehead with 2 bony horn cores, covered with horny sheaths, continually growing as a pair (only the Indian 4-horned antelope has 4 horns). Pelage either scanty or long and thick, often with distinctive growth areas (beards, crests, ruffs, manes on neck, shoulders, back or belly etc.). Plesio-metacarpal (see Deer p. 36) completely lacking end joints of secondary toes (2 & 5). Dent. $0/3 \cdot 0/1 \cdot 3/3 \cdot 3/3 = 32$. Often gregarious, cud-chewing plant eaters in all types of habitat of Old and New Worlds. Introduced into S. America, New Zealand and Hawaii; not indigenous species also in N. America, S. Africa, such as domestic cattle, water buffalo, sheep and goats (in part feral), in part world-wide in distribution and also on oceanic islands. 42 genera with altogether 99 species, of which 72 species are indigenous in Africa.

DUIKERS or CROWNED ANTELOPES, CEPHALOPHINAE

Size of hare to Roe Deer, generally hunch-backed, slender-legged, short-tailed and smooth-skinned animals, with small simple horns, not reaching beyond the ears, generally in both sexes. Crown tuft generally present. Main hoofs narrow and pointed, lateral hoofs small. Scent glands in front of eyes, and often between toes as well as in inguinal region. Carpal and tarsal glands (leg tufts) uncommon. 4 teats. Gall bladder absent. Live solitary or in pairs, concealed in woodland thickets, only one species lives in bush or grasslands, 1 genus with 13 or 11 species, only in Africa.

DUIKERS, *Cephalophus*
G. Ducker   F. Céphalophes   A. Duiker
13 or 11 species, only in Africa. Form and habits very similar (except the Grey Duiker, subgenus *Sylvicapra*, see p. 46), so all generally grouped as Forest Duiker (subgenus *Cephalophus*).
Identification. Hare to Roe Deer size, round-backed, slender legs and heads. Eyes rather large. Ears short and round, or medium length and elliptical. Horns generally in ♂ and ♀ sloping backwards, short (not longer than ears) often concealed in crown tuft (especially ♀), with thick rings at base. Lateral hoofs small to medium. Tail short, round, generally with small terminal tuft. Pelage short and smooth, often thin on neck and shoulders, not grizzled, often with head crest. Scent glands: preocular (opening into a naked strip), generally also foot and inguinal glands. Leg tufts (tarsal or carpal glands) uncommon, latter the most obvious. 4 teats. No gall bladder.

RED-FLANKED DUIKER,   **Pl. 4**
Cephalophus (Cephalophus) rufilatus Gray, 1846
G. Rotflanken ducker   F. Le Céphalophe a flancs roux
Identification. Both sexes with horns, those of ♀ however only small tubercles. Lateral hoofs large, crown tuft well-developed, horns projecting beyond. Shoulder hair as long as body hair. Horns of ♂ slender and nearly straight, base somewhat ribbed, round in section, tips slightly curved upwards. Inguinal glands present, tail rather bushy. Body reddish-yellow or yellowish-red, or reddish-brown. A stripe from nose to forehead, or long stripe along dorsal line, and legs from rump downwards, blue- or brownish-grey or grey. Dorsal stripe widening from shoulder to middle of rump or root of tail. Sometimes whitish fetlock band. Crest and end of tail blackish. Tail blackish at start. Chin, throat, axillary and inguinal areas white. Young like adults. MEASUREMENTS: HB 60–70, TL 7–10, Ht 30–38, Wt 9–12, H ♂ 6–9.5, ♀ 3–4.
Distribution. Gambia to Cameroun, Ubangi-Shari, N. Zaire and W. Uganda. 2 ssp. HABITAT: Woodland edges and clearings, gallery forest strips, thickets in open country. Not in the closed inner regions of large forests. *Map* p. 38.

BLUE or MAXWELL'S DUIKER,   **Pl. 4**
Cephalophus (Cephalophus) monticola (Thunberg, 1789)
G. Blauducker   F. Le Céphalophe noir, Le Céphalophe de Maxwell   A. Bloubokkie   S. Paa
Identification. Horns in both sexes but sometimes absent in ♀. ♂ horns short, conical, bases strongly ridged, round in section, tips slightly turned up, ♀ horns shorter or absent. Muzzle somewhat trunk-like, mobile. Lateral hoofs small. Shoulder hair as long as body hair. Forehead crest short or absent. Tail rather bushy, beginning of underside naked. Body colour greyish-brown to dark greyish-brown, brownish-black or black with bluish sheen. Dark animals sometimes with rust-red tinge on shoulders and flanks. On blackish rump sharp edge to light rear border of thighs. Chin, underside of throat, breast and belly grey, light or whitish-grey. Back of nose, forehead and backs of ears darker than cheeks, sometimes light stripe over eye. Tail above, reddish to dark brown, underside grey to white. Young reddish-brown, underside lighter, at 2½ months the colour of neck and shoulder becomes darker and horn growth begins. MEASURE-MENTS: HB 55–90, TL 7–13, Ht 32–40, Wt 4–10, H ♂ 2.2–9.8, ♀ 0–4.
Distribution. From W. Africa (with Fernando Poo) to E. and S. Africa. 19 ssp. of which *maxwelli* (Gambia to Ghana) has formerly been considered a distinct

species. HABITAT: large and small forests, bush and gallery forest, thickets in open country. *Map* p. 38.

BANDED DUIKER or ZEBRA ANTELOPE, Pl. 4
Cephalophus (Cephalophus) zebra (Gray, 1838)
G. Zebraducker   F. Le Céphalophe zébré ou rayé

Identification. Both sexes with horns, ♂ horns short, conical, sharp-tipped, round in section at base. ♀ horns shorter. Forehead crest short or absent. Shoulder hair distinctly shorter than body hair. Lateral hoofs small. Inguinal and tarsal glands present. Tail tufted. Upperside of body light reddish-brown, with forehead, back of ears, nape, shoulders, end of rump and outside of limbs darker. Middle of rump and back of thighs lighter, inside of ears and thighs creamy. Back of nose brownish-black, also fetlocks and on leg joints. Tarsal gland (tufted) reddish-brown. Upperside of tail mixed red and black, underside white, end tuft black. 12–15 black transverse body bands between shoulders and croup, sometimes with shadowy stripes between. MEASUREMENTS: HB 85–90, TL *c.*15, Ht 40–50, Wt 15–20, H ♂ 4–48, ♀ 2–25.

Distribution. Sierra Leone to mid-Liberia and South West Ivory Coast. No ssp. HABITAT: Thickly wooded hill and mountain forests.

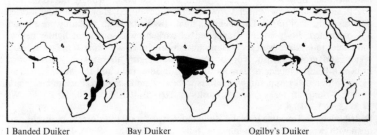

1 Banded Duiker   Bay Duiker   Ogilby's Duiker
2 Red Duiker

BAY DUIKER, *Cephalophus (Cephalophus) dorsalis* (Gray, 1846) Pl. 4
G. Schwarzrücken ducker   F. Le Céphalophe bai.

Identification. Both sexes with slender horns, weakly ridged at base, round in section, ♂ horns larger than ♀. Shoulder hair distinctly shorter than body hair, forehead crest well-developed, tail tufted. Lateral hoofs small. Inguinal glands present. Body colour brownish-yellow to dark brownish-red (flanks sometimes with individual white hairs) only armpits and groin at times lighter. Forehead crest reddish-black. Black stripe from behind nose to tail root, sometimes indistinct or lacking on nape and shoulder, as a rule sharply defined and sometimes broadening on the rump (sometimes with a few small yellow spots). Breast with blackish central line. Legs brown, darker below. Back of ears brownish-black; inside white. Tail black. Ssp. *castaneus* lips, chin and supra-orbital line white. Young entirely dark, blackish dorsal stripe only distinct on the rump, after ¼ year coloured reddish-brown with black dorsal stripe appearing. MEASUREMENTS: HB 70–100, TL 8–15, Ht 40–45, Wt 15–20, H 5.5–10.5.

Distribution. Sierra Leone to E. Zaire and N. Angola. 2–4 ssp. (see next species). HABITAT: thick forests, also dense secondary forest and thick jungle.

OGILBY'S DUIKER,   **Pl. 6**
Cephalophus (Cephalophus) ogilbyi (Waterhouse, 1838)
G. Ogilby Ducker   F. Le Céphalophe d'Ogilby.
Possibly only a form of the Bay Duiker.
Identification. Both sexes with horns, those of ♂ short and thick, slightly concave-curved, base strongly ridged, oval section, those of ♀ smaller and conical. Neck and shoulder hair shorter than body hair, forehead crest weak or absent, tail with small bushy tuft. Lateral hoofs small. Inguinal glands present. Body colour orange, redder on rump. From neck or shoulder black dorsal stripe to root of tail (widely varying, in ssp. *brookei* often ends 10cm before root of tail). Tail tuft mixed black and white. Legs light brown, towards the hoofs darker to brownish-black, fetlocks with whitish ring which may extend upwards as a stripe to the joint.   MEASUREMENTS: HB 85–115, TL 12–15, Ht *c.*55, Wt 14–18, H ♂ 8–12, ♀ *c.* 4.
Distribution. Upper and Lower Guinea forests from Sierra Leone to Cameroun and Fernando Poo. 2 ssp.   HABITAT: as previous species. *Map* p. 41.

RED DUIKER, *Cephalophus (Cephalophus) natalensis* (A. Smith, 1843)   **Pl. 5**
G. Rotducker   F. Le Céphalophe de Natal, Le Céphalophe rouge
A. Rooeduiker   S. Funo
Identification. Both sexes horned, ♂ horns short and thick, strongly ridged basally, oval in section. ♀ horns weaker. Crown crest well-developed. Hair on shoulder shorter than on body. Tail tufted. Lateral hoofs small. Inguinal glands probably present but not confirmed. Body colour orange-red to dark brown, somewhat lighter below, sometimes intermixed with grey. Nape greyish-brown. In ssp. *robertsi* breast, axillary region and groin whitish. Top of muzzle mouse-grey to blackish. Crown crest brownish-black. Outside of ears mouse-grey, insides, chin and throat whitish. Tail partly coloured as rump, tuft white. In ssp. *amoenus* and *natalensis* back of heels dark brown. Young all black.   MEASUREMENTS: HB 70–100, TL 9–14, Ht 35–45, Wt 11.5–13, H 3.3–10.6.
Distribution. S. Tanzania to Natal-Zululand. 5 ssp.   HABITAT: forests, bushveld, and bush with dense undergrowth in plains, hills and mountains. *Map* p. 41.

PETERS DUIKER, HARVEYS DUIKER,   **Pl. 5**
Cephalophus (Cephalophus) callipygus (Peters, 1876)
G. Petersducker   F. Le Céphalophe de Peters
Possibly only a form of Red Duiker.
Identification. Horns in both sexes similar, short, thick, heavily ridged at base, oval in section, tips slightly curved upward. Crown crest well-developed. Shoulder hair shorter than body hair. Tail tufted, lateral hoofs small. Inguinal glands present. Body colour light to dark reddish-brown (in ssp. *adersi* underside whitish). Posterior of body darker than anterior. Forehead dull brownish-red to black, crest reddish-brown, cheeks red to greyish-red. Outside of ears red to dark brown, inside, chin and lips white. Underside of tail, tail tuft, axillary region and groin and sometimes fetlocks of front legs whitish. Throat and breast red, latter with darker central stripe. Legs coloured as body, towards hoofs becoming darker (sometimes to black). Ssp. *callipygus* with narrow, reddish-brown to blackish dorsal stripe reaching the root of the tail, *adersi* with whitish transverse lines on lower edge of thigh (hip-stripes) and sometimes front and hind feet sprinkled with white. Young darker than adults (with dark ventral stripe) and becoming paler towards the front.   MEASUREMENTS: HB 80–115, TL 10–16.5, Ht 45–60, Wt 12–23, H 5.5–13.8.

Distribution. Gabon to S.W. Somalia, south to about a line between S. Cameroun and Dar-es-Salaam. 9 ssp. HABITAT: all types of forest, also in bush thickets and grassy jungles of the savannah; on Elgon, Kenya, Meru and Kilimanjaro up to 3000m. Vicinity of water preferred.

GABOON DUIKER or WHITE-BELLIED DUIKER, Pl. 5
Cephalophus (Cephalophus) leucogaster (Gray, 1873)
G. Weissbauchducker   F. Le Céphalophe à ventre blanc

Identification. Horns in both sexes, in ♂ short and thick, strongly ridged at base, oval in section, ♀ horns smaller. Shoulder hair shorter than on body, crown crest well-developed, tail tufted. Lateral hoofs small. Inguinal glands present. Upperside of body light to dark reddish-brown, a touch of grey on shoulder, the reddish-brown stronger towards the thighs. Muzzle, crown stripe and back of ears as well as dorsal stripe dark brown, crest light brown. Dorsal stripe between nape and shoulder strong or weak, between shoulders and tail black, sharply or irregularly edged, links up with red upperside of tail. Tail with underside naked at base, tuft black and white mixed. Chin, throat, breast, belly, inside of legs and back of thighs white, also the narrow streak on instep. Fetlocks greyish-brown. Young brownish-red mixed with grey, dorsal line wide and not well-defined. MEASUREMENTS: HB 90–100, TL 12–15, Ht 42–45, Wt 15–20, H 5–12.7.

Distribution. Cameroun, N. Zaire, besides bordering regions (E. Nigeria from Cross River eastward to L. Kivu) in Zaire south to 3°S, from Cameroun S. to mouth of Congo. No ssps. HABITAT: more in secondary than primary forest, also on forest edges, in gallery forest and in bushy thickets on edge of savannah.

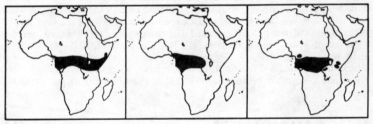

Peter's Duiker   Gaboon Duiker   Black-fronted Duiker

BLACK-FRONTED DUIKER, Pl. 5
Cephalophus (Cephalophus) nigrifrons (Gray, 1871)
G. Schwarzstirn ducker   F. Le Céphalophe à front noir

Identification. Both sexes horned. ♂ horns short and thick, strongly ridged, oval in section, tips very thin and straight, ♀ horns smaller and weaker. Shoulder hair nearly as long as body hair, in mountain animals the otherwise sleek hair rather woolly. Crest well-developed, tail without tuft. Inner hoofs very long and narrow (c. 3.5cm) lateral hoofs large. Inguinal glands present or absent. Upperside of body reddish to dark brown (shoulders sometimes blackish), underside rather lighter, lower breast with dark central line, belly with reddish-black spots. Legs as body, blackish at hoofs or fetlocks at least with black spots. Nose stripe and crest reddish-brown to black. Outside of ears black, inside with whitish spots. Chin, axillary region and groin whitish. Upperside of tail blackish, sometimes with red or whitish hairs, underside greyish-white. MEASUREMENTS: HB 85–107, TL 10–15, Ht 45–55, Wt *c.* 15, H ♂ 8–12, ♀ 4–8. **Distribution.** Zaire, from there to S. Cameroun, Gabon, Ruanda-Urundi, Uganda and mountain forests of Elgon, Kenya and Meru (up to 4300m) 5 ssp. HABITAT: swampy forest lands with dense undergrowth.

BLACK DUIKER, *Cephalophus (Cephalophus) niger* (Gray, 1846)   **Pl. 5**
G. Schwarzducker   F. Le Céphalophe noir
Identification. Both sexes horned, ♂ horn slender base weakly ridged, round in section, ♀ horn smaller. Shoulder hair shorter than on body, forehead crest well-developed. Tail tufted, lateral hoofs small. No inguinal glands. Body colour brownish-black to black, back and rump darkest, head, underside of neck and breast rather lighter, insides of thighs yellowish brown. Back of nose and forehead crest reddish-brown, middle of forehead sometimes black. Outsides of ears blackish-brown, inner side reddish. Tail black with some light hairs, tuft mixed black and white. MEASURE-MENTS: HB 80–90, TL 12–14, Ht 45–50, Wt 15–20, H ♂ 7.5–17.5, ♀ 2.5–3. **Distribution.** Sierra Leone to S.W. Nigeria. No ssp. HABITAT: forest edges, bushy thickets.

ABBOTT'S DUIKER, *Cephalophus (Cephalophus) spadix* (True, 1890)   **Pl. 6**
G. Abbott ducker   F. Le Céphalophe d'Abbott   S. Minde
Identification. Horns in both sexes similar, slender, base weakly ridged, round in section. Hair of shoulder shorter than on body, crest well-developed. Tail not tufted. Lateral hoofs small. Whether inguinal glands present is not yet proved. Body colour dark chestnut brown to black. Body and legs with individual white hairs. Forehead and crest reddish-brown, crest with some black and white intermixed. Face, chin, throat, backs of ears and underside of tail, naked. Upperside of tail dark brown, on the rump some greyish spots. MEASUREMENTS: HB 100–120, TL 8–12, Ht 50–65, Wt *c.* 50, H 10–12. **Distribution.** N. and S. Tanzania (Uluguru-Uzungwe, Rungwe Mts, Usambara Mts, Kilimanjaro, mountains between Babati and Mbulu up to 4000m). HABITAT: Dense forests.

YELLOW-BACKED DUIKER,   **Pl. 6**
Cephalophus (Cephalophus) sylvicultor (Afzelius, 1815)
G. Riesen or Gelbrücken ducker   F. Le Céphalophe à dos jaune ou de forêt
Identification. Similar horns in both sexes, thin, sharp-pointed, base weakly ringed, tips slightly curved downwards. Hair of shoulders shorter than on body, crest well-developed. Tail generally with small tuft, sometimes bushy, lateral hoofs short. In-guinal glands mostly absent. Upperside of body light to blackish-brown, back blackish-blue overwashed with whitish-yellow to orange wedge-shaped area whose tip reaches towards the shoulder and with hair long and erectile. Rump, behind the spot, with individual yellow hairs, tail blackish-brown. Crest reddish-brown mixed with black, back of ears also blackish-brown, inside greyish-yellow. Axillary region, under-belly and groin greyish-yellow. Lips, chin, throat, lower cheeks whitish-yellow to grey, yellow eyestripe not uncommon. Young wholly brownish-black, face somewhat lighter, lips, throat, and underside of tail whitish then becoming brown with greyish face, dark brown crest, similar legs and thighs, at 5 months gets a white dorsal patch

with some black tips and some white dorsal hairs; the dorsal patch becomes yellow and at 8 months full adult colour is attained. MEASUREMENTS: HB 115–145, TL 11–20.5, Ht 65–85, Wt 45–80, H 8.3–21.2

Distribution. From Senegal, Sierra Leone, Liberia etc. to Kenya, Zambia, N. Angola. 2 ssp. HABITAT: moist forests rich with dense undergrowth, including gallery forests and sometimes small savannah woodlands.

JENTINK'S DUIKER, Pl. 6
Cephalophus (Cephalophus) jentinki (Thomas, 1892)
G. Jentink ducker   F. Le Céphalophe de Jentink

Identification. Similar horns in both sexes, slender, nearly straight. Basally weakly ringed, round in section, ends pointed, only slightly curved down. Shoulder hair distinctly shorter than body hair, crest poor, tail nearly without tuft. Lateral hoofs small, inguinal glands present. Head, back of ears, neck and middle of breast as well as hoofs, blackish-brown to black. Lips, chin, inside of ears, shoulder band, legs, axillary region, groin and underside of tail whitish. Body, belly, thighs (sometimes also upper front legs) and upperside of tail slate-grey (sometimes with brownish wash), bristles of these regions in section semicircular, uppersides dark, underside light brown, tips white, giving the slate-grey overall colour. Young soft hair dark brown, somewhat mixed with whitish to cream, underneath somewhat lighter and greyish. Year old animal acquires adult coat. Up till now only 6 specimens in scientific collections. MEASUREMENTS: HB *c.* 135, TL *c.* 15, Ht 75–85, Wt up to 70, H 15.5–17.5.

Distribution. Liberia (Sharp Hill, Fali, Klosoke, Duotown, Geeke, Grand Gedah district, Nimba district, probable also in the adjoining W. Ivory Coast between Nimba and Sassandra rivers. No ssp. HABITAT: dense forests, large thickets.

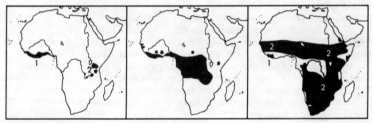

1 Black Duiker   Yellow-backed Duiker   1 Jentink's Duiker
2 Abbott's Duiker   2 Common Duiker

Habits of forest Duikers

TERRITORY: for Black-fronted Duiker and Common Duiker certainly, for other species probably where ♂♂ in captivity are unsociable (Maxwell's Duiker ♂♂ fight, by ramming and butting each other). Pair territory is marked by both sexes by the secretion of the preorbital glands on ends of branches in the runways and other objects. Pairs, or ♀ and young rub faces and horns together, or scent glands. Make tunnel-like runs in thick cover. Defecation and resting places are in thick bush or grassy thickets.

Yellow-backed Duiker also in breeding hollows. Territory size at most ½–1 dozen are (are = 0.025 acre). Very attached to particular site. Probably wandering short distances for ripe fruits. Territory marking with preorbital glands and/or dunghills.

Habits. DAILY RHYTHM: Black-fronted Duiker diurnal, other species active at dusk or night, resting by day. TOILET: mutual licking and grooming. VOICE: short snorts as excitement or anxiety calls, whistling, scream in terror, complaining or nasal contact call. SENSES: hearing and scent good, sight rather poor, but details not known. ENEMIES; leopard, golden and kaffir cats, serval, civets, jackals, diurnal birds of prey (especially crowned eagle), large owls, crocodiles, monitor lizards, pythons. Young are particularly at risk. Mother protects them with blows of front hoofs against small predators; usually seeks safety in flight, clearing obstacles up to 1.8m high. Maxwell's Duiker has lightning-like reactions when disturbed, confusing enemies and making escape likely. FOOD: leaves, buds, shoots, grass, herbs, berries, fruit, termites, ants, snakes, eggs, carrion, flesh. Protein needs met by eating eggs and young of ground-nesting birds, found by scent. Need little water. SOCIABILITY: solitary or in pairs, latter perhaps year-round. In Maxwell's Duiker life pairing known. Sometimes small parties of 1 ♂, 2 ♀ and their young. ♂ helps rear young.

Reproduction. Not restricted to any time of year, births known in all months. Gestation 7–8 months. 1 active young, twins rare. 2 litters in a year possible. ♀ on heat for ½–1 day, in rut again 4–6 weeks after birth of young. Licks young dry and eats afterbirth. Young lies with mother 2–3 days, is independent after 2–3 months. At 3 months is half-grown, at 9 months nearly full weight. Suckles 4–6 times a day for 1–3 minutes. First solid food about 2–3 weeks, weaned at about 5 months. SEXUAL MATURITY: ♀ ¾–1 year, ♂ ¾–1½ years. LONGEVITY: 10–12 years, in a zoo has reached 17¾ years.

COMMON or GREY DUIKER, Pl. 6
Cephalophus (Sylvicapra) grimmia (Linnaeus, 1758)
G. Kronenducker   F. Le Céphalophe du Cap   A. Duikerbok   S. Nsya

Identification. ♂ with horns, ♀ sometimes with, sometimes without, smaller than those of ♂. Horns straight, long, slender, upperside weakly keeled, base ringed, tips slightly upturned, rising from back of skull at angle of 40–50 degrees. Shoulder hair as long as body hair. Crown crest short or long. Tail tufted wholly or in part. Lateral hoofs small. Preorbital and inguinal glands present. Carpal and tarsal glands (brushes) sometimes conspicuous. Upperside of body sandy-coloured, often also below neck, breast and belly. Rear part of body usually darker than front. Breast and belly sometimes, inside of thighs, axillary region, throat and chin always, white. Forehead and crest yellowish to reddish-brown, sometimes washed with black. Nasal stripe narrow or broad, brown to black. Ear tips sometimes blackish. Fetlocks brown to black, this sometimes extending in front to first joint. Upperside of tail brown to black, underside and tip white. Young like adults but greyer. MEASUREMENTS: HB 80–115, TL 10–22, Ht 45–55, Wt 10–20. H 8–8.1. ♀ rather larger and heavier than ♂.

Distribution. Africa south of Sahara, and from Ethiopia southwards. Absent from coastal region of S.E. Tanzania. 19 ssp. HABITAT: all regions up to 4600m, except deserts and rain forests. TERRITORY: ♂♂ very pugnacious. Mark territory with preorbital gland secretions on ends of twigs. Regular runs, resting places and latrines are used. Resting places, especially on sandy soil, are made by scraping out hollows with hind feet. Population density in suitable locations 2–3 animals or more per square mile. Strongly attached to home area even when hunted, then becomes a furtive nocturnal animal. Also in neighbourhood of villages. *Map* p. 45.

Habits. DAILY RHYTHM: main periods of activity morning and evening or clear moonlit nights, resting in cover by day. Residence and activities always in thick cover. When disturbed steals away with lowered head and erect tail, after some distance stands still to look back. TOILET: details not known. VOICE: see p. 46. In great distress a hare-like scream of fear in adults, and loud bleating in young. SENSES: see p. 46. ENEMIES: numerous. Lion, leopard, serval, cheetah, caracal, kaffir cat, civets, hunting dogs, jackals, hyaena, ratels, baboons, python, crocodile, eagles and for young also large owls, monitor lizards and larger genets. For others see p. 46. FOOD: see p. 46. Often successful in capturing guinea fowl and francolins. Principal food leaves of trees and bushes, often standing up on hind legs. (Not done by Forest Duiker.) Fruit and grain important in dry season. (Soft fruit provides for liquid needs.) Does not drink in rainy season and only at long intervals in dry season. SOCIABILITY: primarily solitary, pair formation only at mating time.

Reproduction. In central Africa young at all seasons, further south births are mainly in the middle of dry and rainy seasons (Rhodesia), or middle of rainy season (Transvaal) or further south in the southern summer (Nov–Mar). Gestation $7-7\frac{1}{2}$ months. 1 active young, twins not recorded. Birth Wt 1.35–2.1, Ht 28–32. Sex ratio $\male\male-\female\female$ 1:1. Mother licks young to dry and mark it. Young lies up in cover. First green food after a few days. Horn growth begins after 1 month, reaching half length at 4 months. Adult in 6 months. SEXUAL MATURITY: $\female$ in 8–10, $\male$ in 12 months. As a rule 2 young born a year. LONGEVITY: in captivity 12 years recorded.

DWARF ANTELOPES, NEOTRAGINAE

Hare-sized without forehead crests, dainty and compact, round-backed antelopes. $\male$ only with small sharply pointed horns. Ears rather short, muzzle naked. Inner hoofs narrow and pointed. Lateral hoofs generally absent. Preorbital and foot glands present, no inguinal glands. 4 teats. Tail reaching half-way to heels. In regions densely overgrown. 1 genus with 3 species, in W.M.E. and S.E. Africa.

ROYAL ANTELOPE, *Neotragus (Neotragus) pygmaeus* (Linnaeus, 1758) **Pl. 7**
G. Kleinstböckchen   F. L'Antilope royale
Identification. Hare-sized, called by natives 'King of the hares' and so by Europeans 'Royal Antelope'. Horns only in $\male$, standing widely apart, directed backwards, to 3.5cm long. No lateral hoofs. Foot and preorbital glands present, latter not sunken, 4 teats. Pelage short and smooth, flanks and back of thighs longer, no forehead crest. Back of nose and forehead brownish-black, otherwise upperside dark reddish-brown to gold-brown. Underside white, back of front legs and front of back legs with narrow long white stripe. Tail short, tip rather bushy. Young rather darker than adults. Rudimentary upper canines sometimes present. Skull without rostral orifices (see following species). MEASUREMENTS: HB 40–50, TL 5–8, Ht *c*. 25, Wt 1.8–2.5.
Distribution. Sierra Leone, Liberia, Ivory Coast, Gold Coast (Ghana). No ssp. *Map* p. 48.
Habits. The 3 species of this genus are so alike in their habits that they are described together on p. 48.

BATES' DWARF ANTELOPE,   **Pl. 60**
Neotragus (Neotragus = Hylarnus) batesi (de Winton, 1903)
G. Batesböckchen   F. L'Antilope de Bates
Identification. As Royal Antelope, but rather larger. Horns only in $\male$ as in that species, 3–5cm. Very small lateral hoofs sometimes present, or replaced by naked

patch of skin. Upperside cinnamon-brown to brownish-black, cheeks, sides of neck, throat band and flanks yellowish-red to reddish-brown. Underside white or cream coloured. Ssp. *harrisoni* with white fetlocks and small white spot above the front foot. Skull like Royal Antelope, but with rostral vacuities (oval opening between the nasal process of the premaxilla and the maxilla). MEASUREMENTS: HB 50–55, TL 5–8, Ht *c.* 30, Wt 4–5.

Distribution. S. Nigeria east of the Niger, S. Cameroun, N. Gabon and N. Congo (Brazzaville), as well as further eastward from 24°E in Congo rain forest between *c.* 4°N and *c.* 4°S, with W. Uganda. 2 ssp.

Habits. See below.

SUNI, *Neotragus (Neotragus = Hylarnus) moschatus* (Van Duben, 1847) **Pl. 60**
G. Moschusböckchen   F. L'Antilope musquée   A. Soenie   S. Paa

Identification. Like Royal Antelope but rather larger. Horns only in ♂, length 6.5–13.3cm ringed for ¾ of height, slightly curved outward, position as in Royal Antelope. Upperside of body chestnut red to dark greyish-brown, washed with light brown; in ssp. *livingstonianus* flanks and legs reddish-brown, in *zuluensis* light reddish-brown, fetlocks dark brown. Chin and throat rusty-red to white; breast, belly, inside of thighs and underside of tail whitish-grey to white, upperside of tail dark greyish-brown to dark brown. The preorbital glands emit a strong musky scent, hence the name. Canines, skull, as Royal Antelopes' skull with rostral vacuities as Bates' Dwarf Antelope. MEASUREMENTS: HB 57–62, TL 8–13, Ht 33–38, Wt 4–6.

Distribution. From Tana River in E. Kenya (from there westward to Mt Kenya and Aberdares) through E. Africa southwards to N. Natal. West limits about 35°–38°E. Also on the islands of Zanzibar, Chapani, Bawane and Mafia. 5 ssp.

Habits. See below.

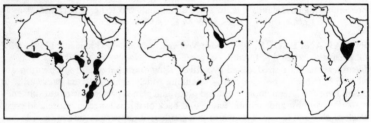

1 Royal Antelope   Salt's Dik-dik   Phillip's Dik-dik
2 Bates' Dwarf Antelope
3 Suni

Habits of Dwarf Antelopes

HABITAT: forest, gallery forest, woodland with dense undergrowth, bushy thickets and all kinds of grassy and bushy jungles, from moist to dry ground in plains and mountains up to *c.*2000m but Royal Antelope and Bates' Antelope are from moist forest regions, Sunis in dry bush. Also near human settlements, making nocturnal visits to plantations and market gardens if enough cover is nearby. TERRITORY: small, hardly more than 1/40 of an acre. Marking not, or barely done by preorbital scent glands, rather by dung heaps. DAILY RHYTHM: Royal and Bates' Dwarf Antelopes mainly at dusk or by night. Sunis mainly by day (morning and afternoon). TOILET: licking, nibbling, scratching. Tongue can clean cheeks and around eyes. Teeth nibble body, legs and tail, hind hoofs scratch head and fore part of body. Mutual nibbling and licking by partners. VOICE: a soft lowing sound as contact call in Royal and Bates' Antelopes. Sharp whistling snore 'tschi-tschi' alarm cry, and bush-buck-like, but weaker, belling warning and alarm cries of Suni. ♂ of latter bleats like goat when pursuing ♀. SENSES: hearing and scent good, better than sight. ENEMIES: all larger four-footed and feathered predators as well as big snakes. Suni jumps from hidden resting place usually at last moment; if man comes, sneaks off with weasel-like agility, dodging through the undergrowth, with a backward glance when about 100 yards away. Royal and Bates' Antelopes jump high, springbok-like, vertically, with rounded back and hanging legs, jumping over, if necessary 2.5m high obstacles, making off eventually by quick slipping and sneaking away with belly to ground. A standing Suni wags its tail, Royal and Bates' Antelopes generally carry it held tight. FOOD: leaves, buds, shoots, fungi, fallen fruit, some grass and weeds, sometimes field crops and vegetables. Drinking not necessary. SOCIABILITY: lifelong pairing very likely. Loose association of many animals in small clearings for grazing.

Reproduction. Gestation not known. 1 active young. Wt at birth 0.8–1. In Royal Antelope litter season Nov–Dec, weaning at about 2 months, maturity at about 1½ years. Further details unknown. LONGEVITY: in captivity, Royal Antelope 6 years, Suni 9 years recorded.

DIK-DIKS, MADOQUINAE

Somewhat bigger than hares, crown with crest, graceful slender-horned antelopes. Only ♂ with horns, small and pointed. Muzzle rather trunk-like, front part hairy. Ears medium. Inner hoofs narrow, pointed. Lateral hoofs very small. Tail only a stump. Preorbital and foot glands present. No inguinal glands. 4 teats. In dry bush country. 1 genus with 5 species in E. & S.W. Africa. 2 species have elongated snouts and the colour of the upperside differently arranged, on this account they have been placed in a separate subgenus, *Rhynchotragus*. Form and habits are much alike in all 5 species and are here described together.

Identification. Over hare-size, slender, ♀ averages 1/5th larger and heavier than ♂. Nose mobile, upper part of end slightly forked. ♂ with short (5–6, maximum 11.5cm long) horns, widely separated, inclined backwards. Lateral hoofs very small and blunt. Preorbital glands with roundish opening on a small naked circular area, foot glands present. 4 teats. Pelage uniform in type, thin, smooth, glossy, no undercoat, erect crest longer in ♂ than in ♀, horns almost hidden. Hair colour of pepper-and-salt type, body colour greyish-white to greyish-red or rust-red, back and neck greyish-white to greyish-yellow, underside white to yellowish-white. Young coloured like adults. Nasal bones moderate to very short, premaxillary bones narrowly elongated.

The first 3 species form the subgenus *Madoqua*. Nose on the whole only slightly elongated, nasal bones only moderately short, premaxillary front parts (rostrum) only moderately sloping, M_3 short and bilobed. Head and back colour separated by different colour of sides of neck. Only in E. & N.E. Africa.

SALT'S DIK-DIK, *Madoqua (Madoqua) saltiana* (Desmarest, 1816) **Pl. 7**
G. Eritrea-Dikdik   F. Le Dik-Dik de Salt
Identification. Back of nose, crest and backs of ears rusty-red in Ethiopian ssp.

cordeauxi intermixed with yellow and black. Cheeks, neck and throat pepper-and-salt like iron-grey. Back reddish-brown, somewhat overwashed with grey, flanks lighter (in *cordeauxi* nape grey to shoulders and also rump grey). Front of neck and breast reddish-grey. Legs rust-red. Chin, central line of belly and inside of thighs white to whitish-yellow. MEASUREMENTS: HB 55–60, TL 3–5, Ht 33–40, Wt 2.5–4, H up to 8.9.

Distribution. Kassala, Eritrea, Dire Dawa and Jebel Ahmer, and in mid-Ethiopia about Harar and westward to R. Hawash. 2 ssp.

PHILLIP'S DIK-DIK, *Madoqua (Madoqua) phillipsi* (Thomas, 1894)   **Pl. 7**
G. Rotbauchdikdik   F. Le Dik-Dik de Phillips
Identification. Back of nose, crown and backs of ears rust-red, in Guban (ssp. *gubanensis*) mixed with black and yellow. Chin, centre line of belly and inside of thighs white. Cheeks and neck (in *gubanensis* also shoulders, back, flanks and thighs) pepper-and-salt-like iron-grey, in *gubanensis* with narrow rust-red border on flanks. Front of breast and legs light rust-red. *Lawrencei* in Midjertain, Nogal and Obbia with broadly red flanks, as also on shoulders and lower thighs, sharply set off by grey of back. In *phillipsi* (N.E. Somalia) the dorsal grey overwashed with reddish, flank border line indistinct. In *hararensis* (Dire Dawa, Jebel Ahmer, Haud, Ogaden) back and thighs reddish-grey, flank – dorsal border strongly overwashed. MEASUREMENTS: HB 55–60, TL 3–5, Ht 33–38, Wt 2.5–3.6, H up to 8.3.
Distribution. Eastern mid-Ethiopia and northern Somalia, viz. Dire Dawa, Jebel Ahmer, Haud, Guban, Midjertain, Ogaden, Nogal and Obbia. 4 ssp. *Map* p. 48.

SWAYNE'S DIK-DIK, *Madoqua (Madoqua) swaynei* (Thomas, 1894)   **Pl. 7**
G. Kleindikdik   F. Le Dik-Dik de Swayne
Identification. Smallest of Dik-dik species. Back of nose, forehead, crest, back of ears and legs clear rust-red. Crest in part with yellow and black intermixed. Belly middle line and inside of thighs white. Cheeks and neck pepper-and-salt-like iron-grey, in ssp. *piacentinii* (N.E. Somalia, Midjertain and Nogal), also the rest of upper side of body. *Citernii* (Boran, Juba, Upper and Lower Webi Shebeli) with the red of legs tending to spread over the flanks and back, *erlangeri* (E. Arussi and W. Ogaden) with red also on shoulders and thighs, neck and cheeks still grey. MEASUREMENTS: HB 45–50, TL 3–5, Ht 30–33, Wt 2–2.5, H up to 7.3.
Distribution. Somalia and Ogaden between 9° and 5°N. 4 ssp. *Map* p. 48.

The following 2 species form the subgenus *Rhynchotragus* (Long-nosed Dik-Diks). Nose lengthened in trunk-like form, and with light groove on upper side, nostrils on the flat end. Neck and dorsal colour nearly or wholly uniform. Nasal bones very short, rostrum at first sloping steeply downward, then horizontal. M_3 three lobed. E. & N.E. Africa as well as Mid-Angola to S.W. Africa (Namaqualand).

GUNTHER'S DIK-DIK,   **Pl. 7**
Madoqua (Rhynchotragus) guentheri (Thomas, 1894)
G. Güntherdikdik   F. Le Dik-Dik de Guenther
Identification. Back of nose, head and back of ears light rust-red to greyish-red. Crest mixed black and white. Cheeks, neck, body and upper legs pepper-and-salt-like iron-grey, lower lips light rust-red. Chin, throat, breast, belly and inside of thighs white to yellowish-white. In ssp. *hodsoni* (Boran), flanks lighter than back with weak reddish-brown border line. In *smithi* (S.W. Ethiopia to N.E. Uganda and N. to mid Kenya)

whole middle of body washed with reddish-brown.   MEASUREMENTS: HB 55–65, TL 3–5, Ht 35–40, Wt 3.7–5.5, H up to 9.8.

Distribution. N. Somalia to S. Ethiopia and M. Kenya, as well as S.E. Sudan and N.E. Uganda. 4 ssp.

KIRK'S DIK-DIK, *Madoqua (Rhynchotragus) kirki* (Gunther, 1880)   **Pl. 7**
G. Kirkdikdik   F. Le Dik-Dik de Kirk   A. Damaralandse Bloubokkie
S. Dikidiki, Suguya

Identification. Back of nose, crown and back of ears light rust-red to greyish-red, crest mixed black and white. Neck, body and upper limbs pepper-and-salt-like iron-grey, but also varies to brownish-grey or reddish-grey. Chin, throat, breast and inside of thighs white to whitish-yellow. Lower legs light rust-red.   MEASUREMENTS: HB 55–57, TL 4–6, Ht 35–45, Wt 2.7–6.5, H up to 11.4.

Distribution. S. Somalia to S. Tanzania, otherwise M. Angola and as far as Namaqualand in S.W. Africa. 7 ssp of which only *damarensis* (Damara Dik-Dik) in S. W. Africa.

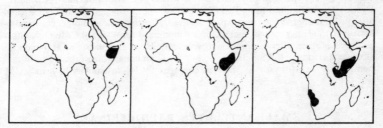

Swaynes Dik-dik   Gunther's Dik-dik   Kirk's Dik-dik

Habits of Dik-Diks

HABITATS: dry regions, stony rocky slopes, or sandy. The species of *Madoqua* more often in regions of low shrubby bush (bush steppe and scrubby semi-desert), while *Rhynchotragus* species prefer unbroken cover with rather higher, thicker, more bush cover (also with higher trees standing out). Where bush and bush-steppe are mixed, localities with representatives of both sub-genera may occur. Bushy thickets where isolated rocks occur provide a base and refuge, a vital necessity for the small weak animals. Also in the vicinity of villages if there is undisturbed scrubby cover, or *Opuntia* plains. In mountains up to 3000m.   TERRITORY: each pair of Dik-Diks remain attached to a favourable habitat with several clumps of bushes and a pile of rocks (kopje), with runs winding here and there. Distance between territories according to season or character of the vegetational growth 50–500m or more, corresponding to an average of one pair per $5\frac{1}{4}$ hectares. A territory has runs, places for resting, droppings, marked boundaries, the latter along runways and by dung-heaps, where tips of shoots and stems are marked by secretion of the preorbital glands. ♂ generally marks the most, defending his beat against rivals especially when ♀ is on heat. Dung heaps serve as boundary marks when 2 or 3 territories meet of use to all. Used mostly at different times, if not, and animals meet, then fighting takes place.   DAILY RHYTHM: mainly a short time before or after sunset. From 9 am dozing, cud-chewing or having short sleep. At noon wandering around, from late afternoon browsing again, with approaching darkness wanders freely. Around midnight a pause for rest, 1–2 hours before sunrise and up to about 9 am dozing again.   VOICE: calls in excitement, warning and fear a ringing 'Zick-zick' (hence the native name Dikdik). Cry of frightened young similar. Kirk's Dik-Dik ♀ has a neighing call to attract the distant ♂. A weaker 'zick-zick' whistle is a contact call, a warning from the parents for the young and a stimulating call of the breeding pair.   SENSES: sight, scent and hearing well developed.   ENEMIES: all larger predators of the environment (leopard, caracal, serval, kaffir cat, crowned eagle), further for the young monitor lizards and large snakes. Natives catch many with dogs and snares for the meat and skins.   FOOD: principal food – leaves of scrub, bushes, buds, plants, flowers, fruits beside grass, herbs, fallen fruit, especially acacia. Salt is an important item (in captivity may die after a week without it). Drinking not necessary; the liquid needed is found in the food. SOCIABILITY: life partners. Each pair lives together with latest and previous young. After sexual maturity seeks partner and territory.

Reproduction. Gestation about 6 months (Kirk's Dik-Dik 169–174, Phillip's Dik-Dik 152–177 days) 1 young twice yearly. Pairing season in E. Africa May and Nov, in E. Ogaden Apr to Jun, in Etosha Pan (S.W. Africa) Jul to Aug and Jan to Feb. ♀ eats afterbirth. Newborn young lies up for 2–3 weeks, after that follows mother constantly. First solid food after 1 week. Suckles for 3–4 months. Birth Wt 0.5–0.8, after 8 months as big as mother, after 12 months growth ends. Horn growth begins at 1 month. SEXUAL MATURITY: 6–8 months in ♀, 8–9 in ♂; young are then expelled from the home range.   LONGEVITY: in wild state average only 3–4, in captivity 10 years.

SMALL ANTELOPES, RAPHICERINAE

Size of Roe Deer or ⅓ less. Only ♂ with horns. No crown crest, sometimes vestigial. Nasal surface bare, ears medium to long. Inner hoofs narrow, pointed, lateral hoofs small, very small or absent. Tail short, only reaching ⅓ of distance to heel. Preorbital and foot glands present, inguinal and carpal glands present or absent. 4 teats. In grass and bush regions. Africa S. of Sahara. 2 genera with together 3 species.

STEINBOK, *Raphicerus (Raphicerus) campestris* (Thunberg, 1811)   **Pl. 7**
G. Steinböckchen   F. Le Steenbok   A. Steenbok   S. Dondoro
Identification. Resembling Common Duiker, somewhat smaller, rather round-backed. Only ♂ with horns, widely separated, smooth and upright. Ears large, preorbital glands with sunken opening in naked patch of skin. Toe and preputial glands present. Inguinal glands absent. 4 teats. Legs slender, lateral hoofs absent. Tail very short, naked below, long-haired above. Pelage short and smooth, upperside light reddish-brown to venetian, or orange-red or dark brown. Black wedge-shaped spot on upper edge of nose, light eye-ring, inside of ears with white-haired radial lines. Underside from chin to belly white to whitish-yellow, old ♂ usually darkest. Young like adults. Occasional albinos.   MEASUREMENTS: HB 70–90, TL 5–10, Ht 45–60, Wt 10–16, H 7–19, in ♀ rather larger and thicker than in ♂.
Distribution. From mid-Kenya and Angola S. to Cape. Absent in Zambia (except S.W.), Malawi, Mozambique, N. of Zambia and eastern Cape Province. 8 ssp.   HABITAT: open plains with scattered bush (grass, bushland and wooded savannahs) also in the Kalahari dunes and Karroo stoney plains, not on mountain tops, steep hills

or mountain slopes or boulder-strewn areas. Also near villages, airfields and culti-vated land. TERRITORY: sedentary, mark territory with facial scent glands and dung heaps. Solitary, only in pairs in breeding season. Population density 1–10 animals per square mile. *Map* p. 54.

Habits. DAILY RHYTHM: mainly diurnal, early morning and late afternoon, also active in light moonlit nights. Resting places under bushes or in grassy thickets or aardvark holes etc. In danger lies flat in high grass with head down. When large predators are near springs up suddenly with a snort of alarm, and with quick zigzagging gallop, head outstretched and occasional direction-finding leaps. Looks after *c*.100m. Does not leap over hedges or fences. When hunted with dogs may seek refuge in aardvark's or similar hole. TOILET: details not known. VOICE: snorts of fear (see Territory), scream-ing bleats in great distress, otherwise mute. SENSES: hearing sharp, further details unknown. ENEMIES: many predators from leopard to caracal, crowned eagle and python, and for the young also kaffir cat, jackal, ratel, baboon, monitor lizard. Mother defends young bravely against enemies as large as jackal. FOOD: mainly foliage of bush and trees besides grass and plants. Drinking not necessary (so also found in very dry areas) but watering places may be used. SOCIABILITY: see Territory.

Reproduction. Gestation $5\frac{1}{2}$–$5\frac{3}{4}$ months, exact details not known. 1 active young. Solid food taken after 2 weeks, weaned after 3 months. SEXUAL MATURITY: after 6–7 months for ♀, 9 months for ♂. At 12 months first birth possible, 2 births within a year as a rule. Littering season not limited though births are frequent from Sep–Feb, with peak in Nov and Dec. Sex ratio at birth locally sometimes double as many ♂♂ as ♀♀, in adults up to 80% more ♂♂ excess likely. However most common ratio for adults is 1:1. LONGEVITY: probably 10–12 years.

GRYSBOK, *Raphicerus (Nototragus) melanotis* (Thunberg, 1811)   Pl. 7

G. Greisbock   F. Le Grysbok   A. Grysbok   S. Dondoro

Identification. Closely resembles Steinbok (p. 52) but rather smaller and more stocky. Preorbital glands well-developed, foot glands present, no inguinal glands, ssp. *sharpei* ♂ with preputial gland. Horns only in ♂ as in Steinbok, in *sharpei* however notably short and sturdy. Lateral hoofs very small (*melanotis*) or absent (*sharpei*). Pelage rather stiff and wiry, from nape over neck and body to top of legs speckled with numerous individual white hairs (hence the name). *Sharpei* sometimes has small white complete spots on body. Pelage otherwise light to dark reddish-brown, throat reddish-yellow, breast and belly reddish and lighter than upperside, forehead sometimes with dark brown Y mark, from which a dorsal stripe can reach over the neck to shoulders. Inside of ears with white-haired radial stripes. Old and young ♂♂ darker than old and young ♀♀, otherwise pelage of young like adults. MEASUREMENTS: HB 65–75, TL 5–8, Ht 45–55, Wt 8–23, H 6.5–13 (*melanotis*), 4–10.5 (*sharpei*).

Distribution. From Tanzania southwards in E., S., S.W. Africa and S. Angola. 2 ssp. (treated as species by many authors): Northern or Sharp's Grysbok (*sharpei*), distri-bution separate from that of *melanotis*. Southern or Cape Grysbok (*melanotis*), Zululand to Cape Province. HABITAT: grassy plains with areas of thick bush, also in bush savannah and woodland savannah and at foot of low hills as well as in vineyards (*melanotis*) or preferably in stony or rock studded hills with bush, heath and grassy areas or plateaux including belts of reeds in waterside areas, but also bushy thickets on plains well away from hills (*sharpei*). TERRITORY: attached to particular locality, home range not large, with permanent sites for droppings, which with the scent from preorbital glands, serve to mark limits. Population density low, only about 1 animal to the sq km. *Map* p. 54.

Habits. DAILY RHYTHM: chiefly active in morning and late afternoon up to beginning of night. Under cover of darkness seeks out open areas. Resting places in bushy or grass thickets or in shade of rocks. In danger lies flat (see Steinbok, p. 52). If enemies approach springs out at 30–40m distance and runs like Steinbok (however without leaping up for better visibility or scenting), with sudden dives into cover as if swallowed up by the ground; hunted by dogs seeks refuge in holes like Grysbok. TOILET: details not known. VOICE: bleating screams when caught, otherwise mute. SENSES: large ears account for sharp hearing, other details not known. ENEMIES: see Steinbok. Not known whether mother defends young. FOOD: as in Steinbok. *Melanotis* eagerly eats grape-vine shoots. SOCIABILITY: solitary except at pairing time, even then partners lie up in separate hiding places.

Reproduction. Times of pairing and birth apparently not limited, young seen in all months. Further details not known, probably as Steinbok (see p. 52).

ORIBI, *Ourebia ourebi* (Zimmerman, 1783)   **Pl. 7**
G. Bleichböckchen   F. L'Ourébie   A. Oorbietjie   S. Taya
Identification. Long-legged, slender, somewhat higher towards the rear. ♂ with horns of medium length rising steeply and curving slightly forward, ringed on the lower third. Preorbital gland opening as a vertical fold before the front corner of the eye. Below the ear, a scent gland about the size of an old penny, naked, smooth black skin through which the secretion evaporates, to be dispersed by the fanning ears. Inguinal, foot and carpal glands present, knee tufts with long hairs. 4 teats. Underside of tail naked. Lateral hoofs small. Pelage short, smooth, sometimes rather longer and rougher. Upperside isabelline yellow, or reddish-brown. Lips, chin, throat, breast, belly, insides of thighs, back of hind legs as well as radial stripes on inside of ear, and spot or stripe over the eye, white. Outside of ears, edge of muzzle, preorbital gland area, under-ear and rounded forehead spot as well as upperside of tail or only tip of tail, brown to black. Fetlocks and knee tufts light or white. Young dark grey, in adult coloration at 5 weeks. Vestigial upper C. sometimes present. MEASUREMENTS: HB 92–110, TL 6–10.5, Ht 50–67, Wt 12–22, H 8–19; ♀ about ⅓ larger than ♂.
Distribution. Africa south of Sahara and Ethiopia outside closed forests. Now extinct in many localities. 13 ssp. HABITAT: large grassy plains preferred, with low growing herbage, open or only sparsely covered with scrub and trees. Ground bare or stony or rocky, in plains or slopes in hills and mountains up to 3000m. Water is welcome but can also be dispensed with. In suitable areas, also near villages. TERRITORY: pairs attached to permanent quarters, well marked runways, dropping and marking places (♂ marks area with preorbital gland secretions on stalks and ends of boughs).

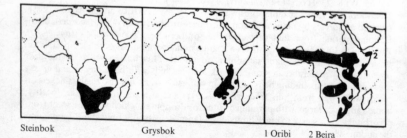

Steinbok   Grysbok   1 Oribi   2 Beira

Habits. DAILY RHYTHM: most activity morning, late afternoon and evening, if sky overcast then active longer by day, on moonlit nights also active. Resting places in depressions, grass tufts, besides bush or boulders. In proximity of enemies will lie quiet but if attacked will jump up and away with whistling fear call; quick escape with neck and tail horizontal (in places of poor visibility makes stiff legged bouncing leaps for locating position); beyond 100m stops to use nose and eyes. TOILET: no information. VOICE: apart from cry in fear nothing known. SENSES: no information. ENEMIES: enemy species much as for Steinbok (p. 52) other information not known. FOOD: mainly grasses and plants along with bush foliage. SOCIABILITY: see TERRITORY; no further information.

Reproduction. Gestation $6\frac{1}{2}$–7 months. Young born in tropical zone mostly shortly before or during rainy season. In sub-tropical zone, late spring to early summer. 2 births in a year as a rule. 1 active young. Wt at birth ♀ 1.6–1.8, ♂ 2–2.5, Ht *c.* 33. ♀ eats foetal sac and afterbirth, ♂ guards young strictly. In absence of parents young lies closely hidden. Young suckles 3 times a day, for 1–5 minutes. First green food after a week, after a month first cud-chewing, after 2 months is weaned, having reached $\frac{4}{5}$ths of the adult size. ♀♀ can breed again 1–10 days after giving birth. SEXUAL MATURITY: ♂ about 14 months (horns then 6–7cm long), ♀ about 12 months. LONGEVITY: 8–12, in zoo up to 14 years.

BEIRAS, DORCATRAGINAE

Size of Klippspringer. Only ♂ with horns. No crown crest. Ears very long and broad. Muzzle hairy, only naked around nostril edges. Main hoofs short and high. Front hoofs pointed, hind hoofs very broad and rounded. Lateral hoofs small. Tail reaching nearly halfway to heel. Foot glands present, no preorbital or inguinal glands. 2 teats. In semi-desert-like, bush regions, in stony or rocky hills or mountain regions of N.E. Africa. 1 genus with 1 species.

BEIRA, *Dorcatragus melanotis* (Menges, 1894)   **Pl. 7**
G. Beira   F. Le Beira

Identification. Klippspringer-size, though legs longer and slimmer. Head and tail longer, ears larger and prominent. Horns only in ♂, upright and wide apart, ringed at base. Preorbital and inguinal glands absent, foot glands present. 2 teats. Tail long-haired, reaching heel. Soles of inner hoofs with thick pads, lateral hoofs small with naked skin below. Pelage thick, erect, rather long, on belly and posterior edge of thigh somewhat longer. Upperside reddish to blue-grey, underside cream to white separated by dark brown flank stripe. White inside of ear interrupted by dark bare radial stripes. Coat of young like adult. MEASUREMENTS: HB 80–86, TL 6–7.5, Ht 50–60, Wt 9–11.5, H 9–13. ♀ rather larger and heavier than ♂.

Distribution. N. Somalia from Gulf coast to about 8°N. A threatened species. No ssp. HABITAT: Dry to desert-like bushy clad mountains and rocky stony hills with adjoining plateaux or mountain river plains. TERRITORY: attached to particular locality; population density low, no further information.

Habits. DAILY RHYTHM: morning and afternoon browsing, wandering, resting mid-day. TOILET: no particulars VOICE: not known. SENSES: sight and hearing very good. ENEMIES: caracal is main predator (for young, kaffir cat, jackal, hyena still a danger). Leopard (earlier or principal enemy) and lion, already nearly extinct and unimportant. FOOD: principally leaves of bushes as well as grasses and herbs. Independent of drinking water.   SOCIABILITY: pairs or families in small bands (perhaps 2–3 families), highest number a dozen.

Reproduction. No details known. Calving time said to be April. 1 active young. SEXUAL MATURITY and LONGEVITY: unknown.

KLIPPSPRINGER, OREOTRAGINAE

Twice size of hare. Generally only ♂ with horns. No crown crest, nose short, muzzle naked. Ears of medium length. Inner hoofs narrow, stands on tip toes. Lateral hoofs large. Tail a stump. Preorbital glands present. No foot or inguinal glands. 4 teats. Rocky outcrops in bush steppes south of Sahara. 1 genus with 1 species.

KLIPPSPRINGER, *Oreotragus oreotragus* (Zimmerman, 1783)   **Pl. 7**
G. Klippspringer   F. L'Oréotrague   A. Klipspringer
S. Ngurunguru, Mbuzi mawe

Identification. Stocky, round-backed, snout short, eyes, preorbital glands and ears large. Horns only in ♂ (except in ssp. *schillingsi* in S. Kenya, Tanzania, Ruanda-Urundi, where ♀ has weak horns) straight or slightly curved forward, ringed at base, wide apart and erect. Tail stumpy. Legs sturdy, metacarpals short, toe bones long. Main hoofs wide-spreading and long, only tips in contact with ground. Lateral hoofs medium sized, broad and long, flat, high placed. Foot and inguinal glands absent, preorbital glands present. 4 teats. Pelage uniform without underhair, individual hairs hollow and crinkled, stiff, brittle, easily shed, white basally, middle-olive to gold-brown, tips yellowish, the whole pelage colour pepper-and-salt effect. Hairs rustle when stroked. Upperside of body yellowish-gold or yellowish brown-tinged, or sandy or olivaceous. Back of nose, forehead, backs of ears as well as fetlocks brownish-black. Lips, chin, throat, around eyes, breast, belly, inside of legs, back of thighs, white to yellowish-white. Inside of ears white with black radial lines. Young coloured as adults.   MEASUREMENTS: HB 75–115, TL 7–23, Ht 47–60, Wt 10–18, ♀ somewhat larger and heavier than ♂, horns up to 16.

Distribution. From N. Nigeria to Somalia, thence S.W. to Cape, then northward to S. Angola. Absent between N. Nigeria and Bongo Mountains (Central African Republic) as well as further east to E. Equatoria (Sudan). In Sudan (geographic), Cape Province, Natal, Orange Free State and Transvaal largely extinct (still occurs in Kruger Park). 11 ssp.   HABITAT: on rocks of all kinds (granite, slate, limestone, sandstone etc.) from single boulders or kopjes and ridges (50–250m high rock summits) to boulder heaps, rocky hillsides, mountain massifs and slopes (up to 4000m). Thick bush as place of refuge is important. Rocks associated with bush are suitable whether in semi-desert, steppe, savannah, dry bush, dry wooded areas (in the latter also in invading grassy areas, so-called Dambos) in plains, hills and mountains.   TERRITORY: living space ranges from rock ridges or kopjes, mountain slopes with bush and nearby grassy spaces (only a small 7.5–9.5 hectares in size). Territory marked by scent gland secretions on twig ends and rock edges. Rest – sunning and dropping places, latter near territory border. Territory defended by ♂ against neighbours. Resident. Territory holders usually a pair or 1 ♂ and 2 ♀ ♀ with latest young (sometimes also still the last but one). In favourable localities about 50–100m for 1 pair. *Map* p. 59.

Habits. DAILY RHYTHM: most activity before and after noon also on moonlit nights up to midnight. During the day one (♂) or pair keep a motionless watch for hours from a high rocky lookout. In danger, a whistle-like nasal cry, repeated every 5 seconds (sometimes with quick jump off the spot) in breakneck dash from rocks into cover, after short flight scent for danger and look around. TOILET: no details known. VOICE: piping or whistling (see DAILY RHYTHM). In bad temper soft rattling like creaking door. Piercing cry in extreme danger. Short soft rustling of ♂ during pairing. SENSES: sight and hearing good, more important than scent. Details not known. ENEMIES: chief predators leopard, caracal and crowned eagle, of secondary importance kaffir cat, hyena, jackal, baboon, python; for young also the large birds of prey and monitor lizard. Humans capture Klippspringer easily in snares, so that whole regions (especially in S. Africa) are cleared of game. FOOD: *c.* 45% bush, plant and tree foliage, flowers and fruit, beard mosses, 55% grass and herbage. Stands on hind legs to reach foliage. In dry season drinking not necessary, the food supplies sufficient liquid. SOCIABILITY: probably mate for life, so normally occur in pairs.

Reproduction. Gestation about 7 months. Births sometimes limited (S.W. Africa Jul–Dec, Kruger Park Nov–Dec) partly unlimited (Zambia all the year). Two births a year, 1 active young. Ht at birth *c.* 25, Wt *c.* 1. Sex ratio 1:1. SEXUAL MATURITY: 1 year, ♂ looks for a territory, ♀ generally stays longer, may pair with parent. LONGEVITY: up to 15 years recorded in captivity.

BUSHBUCKS, TRAGELAPHINAE

Gazelle or cattle-like in size, ♂♂ (sometimes also ♀♀) generally carry spirally twisted and lyre-shaped horns. Sometimes horns simple (Asiatic representatives), sometimes 4 in number (Indian Four-horned Antelope). Pelage mostly smooth and short, but in part also longer, especially on nape, often on front of neck, sometimes with belly mane or forehead crest. Light (mostly whitish) body pattern on forehead, cheeks, throat, shoulder, body and thigh stripes or spots, or stripes and spots, leg and fetlock spots wholly or in part present. Preorbital and foot glands absent, generally lateral hoof- and 2–4 inguinal glands present. 4 teats. Forest, dense bush or bushy savannah, seldom live on open savannah. 3 genera with altogether 10 species, of which 2 genera each with 1 species in India. (Four-horned Antelope, *Tetracerus quadricornis*, and Nylghai, *Boselaphus tragocamelus*), the others, the true bushbucks or spiral-horned antelopes (*Tragelaphus*) in Africa south of the Sahara, including Ethiopia.

BUSHBUCK, *Tragelaphus (Tragelaphus) scriptus* (Pallas, 1776)   **Pl. 8**
G. Schirrantilope   F. L'Antilope harnaché, Le Guib   A. Bosbok
S. Pongo, Mbawala

Identification. Roebuck-like in size and form. Only ♂ with horns, front edge keeled, black with light tips, with 1–1¼ spirally twisted horns (sometimes also in ♀). Eyes and ears large. Tail bushy, reaching halfway to heel. Lateral hoofs small and flattish to medium sized and irregular. Preorbital and foot glands absent. 2–4 inguinal glands. 4 teats. Lateral hoof glands present. Pelage thin, smooth, sometimes longer on neck, breast and back of thighs, also often (particularly in ♂) a short dorsal line mane from shoulders to tail root. Old ♂♂ have head and upperside of neck very fine and short-haired, apparently almost naked. Colour and pattern varies greatly individually and geographically (for latter see Pl. 8). Often old ♂♂ and ♀♀ darker than young. Ground colour from dull yellowish-brown varying through yellowish-red, red, reddish-brown to dark reddish-brown or greyish-olive. White markings fully developed or partly reduced or slight. Forest forms mostly light reddish-brown with fully developed pattern (the ♂♂ dark), bush forms yellowish-brown to brownish-olive, pattern weak and incomplete, ♂♂ and ♀♀ alike. Young reddish-brown with complete white pattern, only weaker patterned than adults in the C. African ssp. *ornatus*. Sporadic albinos and dwarfed insular examples are known. MEASUREMENTS: HB ♂ 115–150, ♀ 105–130, TL 30–35, Ht ♂ 70–100, ♀ 65–85, Wt ♂ 40–80, ♀ 25–60, H ♂ up to 57, ♀ (rare) up to 30. Adult ♂ about half as heavy again as ♀ and so obviously larger.

Distribution. Africa south of Sahara, and from Ethiopia south to Cape Province (absent from western highlands of Transvaal, Orange Free State and Lesotho), from S.W. Africa (apart from N. Caprivi Strip), S.E. Angola and bordering W. Zambia. 8 ssp. HABITAT: undergrowth and thicket-rich country in level, hilly and mountain regions up to 4000m with swampy, moist or dry ground, usually near water (clearings or edges of primary and secondary forests, gallery forests, woodland, bush, high and reed-grass jungles in wooded savannah, bush savannah, also plantations and gardens). TERRITORY: separate in both sexes, each animal with territory of 15–35 hectares (♂ territory larger than that of ♀), each locality with runways, rest places, latrines; ground scrapings as marking spots though borders of neighbouring territories may overlap. ♂ with newborn and young animals form a small family. Very constant to locality. Population density in favourable areas averaging 0.1–2.5 animals per sq km with sex ratio 1:1. Often associate with baboons and green monkeys.

Habits. DAILY RHYTHM: most active early morning and later afternoon to evening, rest of day and in second half of night, resting; can also be active at those times if sky is overcast or moon shining, for 2–5 hours day and night. Where persecuted, a stealthy nocturnal animal. Good swimmer; jumps over fences to 2m high. TOILET: nostrils and lips cleaned by tongue. Teeth nibble from shoulder and breast backward to parts of body. Horns rub back and rump. Neck and cheek rubbed on prominent objects, chin and throat on soil. In pairing time, mutual licking and grooming of partner. VOICE: ♂ and ♀ a rough bark as alarm call (like Roe Deer fear cry) also grunting sounds. ♂ in pursuit of breeding ♀ a clicking-chirping 'teck-teck'. SENSES: scent and hearing (ears large) good, sight ability less. ENEMIES: principal enemy leopard, besides golden cat; for the young also, serval, caracal, kaffir cat, civet, python. Sometimes also lion, and by water, crocodile. A cornered ♂ fights bravely. FOOD: like Roe Deer, nibbles leaves of bushes, plants and trees, shoots, buds, fruits along with grass and herbs, vegetables and garden flowers, bark of trees (especially of citrus trees). Salt and mineral impregnated earth eagerly licked. SOCIABILITY: see TERRITORY.

Reproduction. Not seasonally separated; in part (C. Africa) possible in all months, otherwise birth mainly in dry season. Gestation 178–182 days. 1 active young. Wt at birth ♂ 3.5–4.2, ♀ 3.2–3.7, 2 births a year possible. Young lies up at first for a time, suckles for ½ year. Sex ratio at birth *c*. 1:1 in adults ♀♀ predominant. SEXUAL MATURITY: ♂ and ♀ 11–12 months. LONGEVITY: 12 years or more.

NYALA, *Tragelaphus (Tragelaphus) angasi* (Gray, 1849)   **Pl. 9**
G. Tieflandnyala   F. Le Nyala   A. Inyala

Identification. Resembling Bushbuck (p. 57). Horns only in ♂, blackish-brown to black, in spirals and stoutness as in Sitatunga, 1½–2 full spirals, 2 keels running nearly to the light tips. Tail bushy, in ♂ longer than in ♀ reaching ⅔ or ½ way to heel. Outer hoofs robust, those of hind feet with a glandular pad surrounded by tuft of hair. Preorbital and inguinal glands absent. 4 teats. Pelage short and smooth. ♂ with medial mane below from throat to groin and hind edge of thigh (sometimes also in axillary region) and on upperside from nape to root of tail. ♂ upperside slate-blue, weakly washed with ochreous, ♀ and young reddish-brown; young ♂ coloured at sexual maturity with slate-blue, which becomes the clear bicolour pattern of old ♂♂. White pattern, see Pl. 9, number of transverse body stripes always 8–13, the thigh spots 3–4. In old ♂♂ these may be reduced to few or none. MEASUREMENTS: HB ♂ 150–195, ♀ 135–145; TL ♂ 45–55, ♀ 40–50, Ht ♂ 100–121, ♀ 80–105; Wt ♂ 100–140, ♀ 85–90, H to 83.

Distribution. Eastern S. Africa between 30° and 35°E and 15°–28°S. Principal localities: (1) Northern: S. Malawi, south of Lake Nyasa and bordering regions of Mozambique, (2) Middle: northern part: along and between Rivers Buzi and Save in mid Mozambique; southern part: the triangular area Rhodesia – Mozambique – Transvaal (with Kruger Park) from which flow the rivers Nuanetsi, Bubye, Limpopo, Pafuri, Shingwedzi, Little and Great Letaba, Nantsi. (3) Southern: 2 larger regions west of Delagoa Bay in S. Mozambique, 1 smaller, N.W. and W. of St Lucia Bay in Natal. A nearby locality in Chewore Game Reserve on S. Bank of Zambesi on northern border of Rhodesia is doubtful. Introduced in Loskop Dam Nature Reserve in Transvaal and on farms in Natal and in Adelaide regions of Cape Province (Mozambique localities before civil war). No ssp. HABITAT: restricted to dense thicket areas in savannah, gallery forest or wooded patches, near water and in plains and hills, not on mountains. Localities isolated within the species overall distribution. HOME RANGE: c. 3–5 sq miles, sedentary, not territorial, ranges of troops overlap. Mkuzi reserve in Natal (15,500 hectares) holds 5,000 Nyalas, thus, on average, one to each three hectares.

Klippspringer Bushbuck 1 Mountain Nyala 2 Nyala

Habits. DAILY RHYTHM: mainly morning and evening, in dry season more by day, in rainy season more activity at night. Where hunted, very secretive nocturnal animals. TOILET: no details available. VOICE: hoarse grunting, deep piping. SENSES: scent and hearing good, sight not so good. ENEMIES: chief predator leopard, less so lion. For young also smaller carnivores, larger birds of prey and baboons are dangerous. When cornered a driven ♂ defends itself bravely, also against man. FOOD: foliage of trees and bushes, shoots, buds, bark, fruit and also some grasses and plants. To reach high foliage will stand on hind legs. SOCIABILITY: mostly in small troops of several ♀♀ with young, escorted by 1 old ♂ that is master of the troop and drives off young ♂♂, latter then forming separate troops. Old ♂ also solitary. Towards end of dry season gatherings of several troops (up to 50 animals together) are possible.

Reproduction. Mating and litter time partly seasonal to some extent, partly not (latter in Mozambique and Zululand, the first in Kruger Park where births are mainly in Jul–Nov, with peak Aug–Oct). Gestation 8½ months. 1 active young lies hidden

2–3 weeks. At birth HB 55–60, Ht 48–53, Wt 4.5–5.5. ♀ eats afterbirth and a week later mates again. SEXUAL MATURITY: ♀ at 11–12 months, ♂ about 1½ years. LONGEVITY: up to 16 years recorded.

SITATUNGA, *Tragelaphus (Tragelaphus) spekii* (Sclater, 1864)   Pl. 9
G. Sumpfantilope   F. Le Sitatunga   A. Water Koedoe   K. Nzohe

Identification. Like a long-legged Bushbuck (p. 57). Tail ⅔ distance to heel. Horns only in ♂ resembling Bushbuck, but stouter and longer, up to 1½ spiral twists, 2 keels, olive-greyish, brownish to brownish-black, tips light. Inner hoofs very long (up to 10cm), lateral hoofs 2–3cm without glandular pad tufts, backs of fetlocks naked. Preorbital glands absent. 2 (sometimes 4) inguinal glands. 4 teats. Coat thin, wispy, light oil and water-repellent, rather long, on ♂ neck sometimes lengthened, mane-like, on legs short and smooth. Uniformly coloured above and below, also ♂ and ♀ thus, or ♂ dark and ♀ light with clear white pattern. Newborn young mostly light like ♀. Young ♂♂ dark brown. Varying with ssp. and sex, colour from dark chocolate- to reddish-brown, to yellowish-brown or grizzled-grey. Body stripes 6–8, thigh spots 6–13. MEASUREMENTS: HB ♂ 125–170, ♀ 115–150, TL 18–30, Ht ♂ 85–125, ♀ 75–105; Wt ♂ 70–120, ♀ 40–105; H to 92.4.

Distribution. Africa between about 10°N (around Lake Chad to about 13°N) and 18°S, *viz.* from geographic S. Sudan and S. Ethiopia southwards to S.E. Angola, N. Botswana and S. Zambia, eastward to barely 34°E. On Rubondo Is. on Lake Victoria. Northward the west border is Togo (in Gambia almost, in Guinea – Bissau, Sierra Leone, Guinea and Ivory Coast extinct). In Liberia not present, in Nigeria threatened, in Malawi and Rhodesia practically also extinct, as in the Nzoia river swamps and Saiwa Swamp in Kenya. Threatened by hunting, and draining of swamps in many places. 5 ssp. HABITAT: swampy forests, gallery forests with swamps, reed or papyrus swamps, islands in lakes and rivers. Home swamps with tall grass, reeds and papyrus, rushes (up to 6m high) which completely conceal the Sitatunga, boggy soil with yielding grasses or water plant pads. TERRITORY: very localised. ♂ outside breeding season solitary in territory which may include several ♀♀. Home swamp depends on size, divided between several ♂♂ (border quarrels frequent). Seasonal flooding may make enforced herding together on flood-free places likely. *Map p. 62.*

Habits. DAILY RHYTHM: by day in swamp (often half submerged) resting in the reedy shade; morning and evening and sometimes also night-time feeding, also leaving the swamp after dark and browsing in neighbourhood. Feet adapted for running over yielding vegetation and pads of plants through the reedy jungles. Good swimmer. In flight from danger always makes for swamp or water, in danger dives strongly and submerged, remains hidden except for tip of nose. TOILET: as Bushbuck (see p. 57). VOICE: alarm cry as in Bushbuck; ♀ has a nocturnal sneezing call; ♂ pursuing ♀ has high-pitched mewing with mouth closed. Old and young bleat sometimes. Alarm signal a lowing. SENSES: hearing and scent the most valuable. ENEMIES: crocodile, leopard, python, and lion when the flooded ground dries out. Excessive flooding may drown young. Man is the chief enemy through poaching and destruction of habitat. A cornered ♂ defends itself courageously against dogs and man. FOOD: swamp- and water-vegetation, young grass on neighbouring meadows and field crops on farms near swamps. SOCIABILITY: see TERRITORY.

Reproduction. Gestation 225 days, mating and parturition times not restricted but may be affected by local conditions. 1 active young (rarely twins) instinctively seeks out higher and drier ground as rest place; in case of emergency the ♀ builds a raised platform of vegetation trodden underfoot. Young lies there about a month. Suckling period 4–6 months. SEXUAL MATURITY: ♀ about 1–1¾, ♂ about 1½–2 years. LONGEVITY: up to 19 years recorded.

MOUNTAIN NYALA,   Pl. 9
Tragelaphus (Tragelaphus) buxtoni (Lydekker, 1919)
G. Bergnyala   F. Le Nyale des Montagnes

Identification. Kudu-like, horns only in ♂, resembling closely those of Nyala, but spreading wider apart and therefore like Greater Kudu, with 1½–2 spirals, 2 keels to the light tips. Ears large, tail bushy, reaching heel. Lateral hoofs large and robust, close together. No preorbital glands, 2 inguinal glands, 4 teats. Coat of ♀ close, smooth and glossy, that of ♂ on neck, shoulder and back of thighs rather longer and stiffer with a 10cm long mane from nape to root of tail. Colour dark sandy greyish-brown to dark brown with whitish pattern (see Pl. 9). Number of transverse body stripes 2–5, body spots 6–10. Old ♂ darker than ♀, young ♂ browner than reddish-brown young ♀, latter with age becomes brownish-grey with faint white body stripes and spots. Calf bright yellowish-brown, white pattern as in adults but still lacking body stripes. MEASUREMENTS: HB ♂ 240–260, ♀ 190–200; TL 20–25, Ht ♂ 120–135, ♀ 90–100; Wt ♂ 180–250, sometimes 300, ♀ 150–200. H up to 118.

Distribution. Only Ethiopia, S. of 10°N, only in high mountains along the ranges from Chercher with Asba Tafari in E. over Gugu and Arussi Mts (Caca – Boset – Galana – Erosa – Chilalo Mts) in centre to Bali Mts southward to Limmu Mts near Yaballo in Sidamo. In addition in Wallega Mts in west middle Ethiopia. No ssp. described as yet, but on horn shape at least 3 exist. HABITAT: tree-heath zone between about 3500–3700m with thickets, clearings and morasses. Towards the rainy season (after the departure of the cattle herders and their herds) also in the deep thickets of *Hypericum*, *Hagenia* and *Juniperus* zones (3500–3350, 3350–3200, 3200 – 3000 – 2700m). In dry season also on moorland and alpine peak zone above the tree heaths (3700–4200m). TERRITORY: the female-led troops, which are joined by old ♂♂, stay closely within their home range, not leaving it throughout the year, but are not territorial. Population density in Arussi Mts averages about 2.4 (1.5–3.5) animals per sq km, in Bali Mts about 4.5 (2.5–6.9). Estimated population in the first about 4000–11,500, in the latter about 420–980. Menaced by habitat destruction and disturbance from humans (fire, wood-cutting, cattle grazing, cultivation, roads, hunting). *Map* p. 59.

Habits. DAILY RHYTHM: mostly active between 4pm to 8am. Old ♂♂ generally shorter active periods (5pm–7am). When undisturbed the more active by day, sunning and resting in open places, where disturbed, more nocturnal and thicket haunting. TOILET: no details known. VOICE: little known. When alarmed the ♀ troop leader utters a panting rather than a barking call. ♂ also calls in the same way but deeper and less often; a frightened bleat sometimes when danger is near. Sometimes a ♂ scares away a rival with loud raucous barks. SENSES: scent and hearing very good, sight less so, the distance from near objects poorly estimated and motionless observers down wind are not recognised. ENEMIES: chief enemy man (see TERRITORY). Natural enemies leopard which takes calves and young animals, but is poorly represented owing to persecution by man. FOOD: according to each season and locality, as well as leaves, buds and shoots of bushes and trees. also herbs and grasses, the latter eagerly sought as young growth on burnt areas or abandoned cattle kraals. SOCIABILITY: troops of ♀♀ with calves and young animals and the occasional associated old ♂. Strength of troop at highest a dozen, more often 4–6 animals. Young animals stay with mother until sexual maturity, then dispersed by old

♂, make up troops of young companions, later becoming solitary. Old ♂ sociable in breeding season. Apparently a marked excess of ♀♀.

Reproduction. Gestation not known, probably about 6 months. Breeding season in Bali Mts probably Nov–Dec, parturition Apr–Jun (rainy season), in Arussi Mts Oct–Dec, in Goba Mts Dec–Jan (dry season). 1 active young. SEXUAL MATURITY: ♀♀ about 2 years, ♂♂ somewhat later. LONGEVITY: further details of courtship, pairing, birth, rearing of young and growing up, ageing etc. not known.

LESSER KUDU, *Tragelaphus (Tragelaphus) imberbis* (Blyth, 1869)   Pl. 10
G. Kleinkudu   F. Le Petit Koudou   S. Tandala ndogo

Identification. Horns only in ♂, greyish-brown with horn-coloured tips, 2 long keels and 2½ spiral twists. Ears large and funnel-shaped. Tail bushy reaching ⅔ of way to heel. Front lateral hoofs small, hind short and robust, on the inside a hair tuft surrounding glandular pad. Preorbital glands absent, 2 inguinal glands, 4 teats. Hair short and close, short mane from nape (♂), or shoulders (♀) along dorsal line to tail root. Colour of ♂ bluish to slate-grey, ♀ reddish-brown, white pattern (see Pl. 10). Number of transverse body stripes always 11–13. Calf colour like ♀, young ♂ bluish-grey. MEASUREMENTS: HB ♂ 120–140 ♀ 110–130; TL ♂ 30–40, ♀ 25–30; Ht ♂ 95–105, ♀ 90–100; Wt 95–105, ♀ 80–95. H up to 91.

Distribution. Arid areas of east Africa between about 14°N and 8°S. Danakil, Harar, Arussi, Ogaden and Boran in Ethiopia, S. Guban in Somalia and from 8°N southwards further S.E. of Equatoria Province in Sudan and N.E. Uganda, as well as through Kenya and Tanzania southwards to about 8°S and 35°E with a gap in the grass savannah region north-east and east of Lake Victoria. Only at Speke Gulf is the S.E. shore of Lake Victoria reached. 2 ssp. HABITAT: dry thorn-bush country with dense thickets in plains and hills up to 1300m (the so-called Nyika). Sometimes also in savannah river gallery forests. TERRITORY: sedentary in habits. Home range about 2 sq km. Old ♂♂ not territorial. Young ♂♂ move further around. In favourable areas an average density over a year of 1–2 animals per sq km.

Habits. DAILY RHYTHM: mainly late afternoon, evening and early morning. TOILET: as in Bushbuck (see p. 57). VOICE: barking cry of fear, ♂ and ♀, as in Bushbuck; ♂ pursuing ♀ makes 'ummh' sound. SENSES: hearing and scent good, sight not so good. ENEMIES: chiefly leopard and hunting dog along with lion. Small calves are in danger also from serval, caracal, baboon and python. FOOD: principally foliage of trees and bushes, also in smaller quantities, grass, roots, fruit and herbs. Water is drunk where available, but a month without water is possible. SOCIABILITY: single, in pairs or in small parties (up to 6 animals) mostly several ♀♀ with young in neighbourhood of an old ♂. Young ♂♂ from 14 weeks form separate troops.

Sitatunga   Lesser Kudu   Greater Kudu

Reproduction. Gestation 222 days. Whether pairing or parturition is linked with any season is not known. In Ogaden, births Sep–Nov. 1 active young. Wt at birth 7–7.5. ♀ about to litter goes off apart. Young lie up a long time. SEXUAL MATURITY: about 1½–2 years. LONGEVITY: probably 12–15 years, not known certainly.

GREATER KUDU, *Tragelaphus (Tragelaphus) strepsiceros* (Pallas, 1766) Pl. 10

G. Grosskudu   F. Le Grand Koudou   A. Koedoe   S. Tandala mKubwa

Identification. Horns normally only in ♂, screw-like spirally twisted with 2 long keels and 2½ twists on the long axis, greyish-brown to dark brown, tips horn-coloured. Sometimes small horns in ♀♀. Ears and tail as in Lesser Kudu (see p. 66). Outer hoofs robust, innerside with hair tuft around glandular pad. Preorbital and inguinal glands absent. 4 teats. Coat short and smooth, about 10cm long hair crest from nape to root of tail (shorter hair in ♀). ♂ in addition has lower neck mane (hair up to 25cm long) from throat to base of neck. Coat colour brownish-grey, dull brown, reddish-brown or bluish grey, on anterior body old ♂♂ nearly blue grey. ♀ instead of neck mane has white stripes. White pattern (see Pl. 10). Always 2–3 cheek spots, and 4–12 transverse stripes on body. Number of body stripes varies also within the ssp. Calves and young animals more reddish-grey to light brown. MEASUREMENTS: HB ♂ 215–245, ♀ 185–235; TL 35–55, ♀ 30–50; Ht ♂ 130–150, ♀ 120–140; Wt ♂ 225–315, ♀ 180–215; H up to 181.

Distribution. From Lake Chad district, to eastward as far as Eritrea, Ethiopia and Somalia, from there southward through E. and S. Africa to the Cape and from there northward to mid-Angola. Distribution now discontinuous since in many regions, above all in S. Africa, exterminated. Re-introduced in Loskop Dam Reserve in Transvaal and introduced to New Mexico 1962. 4 ssp. HABITAT: stony ground preferred, lightly to thickly covered bushveld in hills and mountains, also in plains with similar cover, above all thick acacia-bush clad banks of seasonally dried out river beds. Watering places though important are not however vital. Vital on the other hand, thickets for resting by day. TERRITORY: Only old ♂♂ in the breeding season, maintain territory, defending it against rivals. Fighting sometimes fatal. Stay in territory so long as environment favourable otherwise seasonal change of quarters if necessary by further wanderings. Population density in suitable habitat averages ⅓–1 Kudu per sq km.

Habits. DAILY RHYTHM: by day resting in thick bush, late afternoon emerging to browse. Where undisturbed also before and after midday except in midday heat, but where hunted is a secretive nocturnal animal. TOILET: as Bushbuck (see p.57). VOICE: alarm cry like Bushbuck: old ♂ calls in pairing season sometimes like Bushbuck though more piping. ♂ follows ♀ on heat with 'ummh' sound (weak with closed mouth). ♀ and young ♂ moo with closed mouth (significance unknown). Calf has 'maaa' as contact call to mother and long 'oooo' as alarm, bringing the mother immediately to help. SENSES: scent and hearing very good, sight less so. ENEMIES: principal predator leopard, hunting dog, cheetah, lion but more for young and ♀♀ than old ♂♂. Young calves also threatened by serval, caracal, eagle and python. Escape from enemies generally only by flight, old ♂ seldom defends itself even if cornered, neither against dogs or humans. Obstacles are leaped over up to 2.5m high. FOOD: largely foliage of trees and bushes, additionally grass and plants. Chief fodder plants pod-bearing leguminosae, above all acacias. Sometimes makes nocturnal visits to plantations and vegetable plots. SOCIABILITY: mostly in small troops of several ♀♀ with their young, to which at times one or two old ♂♂ attach themselves. Number in troop 6–12, rarely 20–30. Larger troops (up to 100 or more) mostly towards the end of the dry season, assemblies in favourable feeding places. ♂♂ also in separate bands. Sex ratio at birth 1:1, but high mortality rate in young ♂♂ may alter this in adults to 2:1, or 5:1 for ♀♀.

Reproduction. Succession of breeding seasons from N. to S. (from October in N. to Feb–Mar in S.). Gestation about 7 months. 1 active young, lies closely for 2 weeks. Wt at birth about 15. Suckling period ½ year, first solid food about 1 month. SEXUAL MATURITY: ♀♀ 1¼–1½ years sometimes 1¾, ♂♂ 1¾–2 years; in ♂♂ formation of first horn spiral at about 2 years, full development of horns (2½ spirals) about 6–6½ years. Sex ratio at birth 1:1, however varies (see Sociability). LONGEVITY: in the wild average 7–8 years, but up to 23 years recorded in captivity.

BONGO, *Tragelaphus (Taurotragus) euryceros* (Ogilby, 1857)   **Pl. 10**
G. Bongo   F. Le Bongo

Identification. Resembling Nyala, but larger. Horns in both sexes, resembling Sitatunga, narrow lyre-shaped, with 2 longitudinal keels and 1½ spirals, brownish-grey to dark brown, tips light yellow, ♂ horns stouter than ♀. Latter just as long or a little longer. Ears long and broad. Broad muzzle surrounded by long tactile hairs. Tail hairs lengthened, with tuft at end reaching heel. Front lateral hoofs long and pointed, at base in contact, those of hind foot short and well separated. No preorbital, inguinal or foot glands. 4 teats. Pelage smooth, dense, in ♀ more glossy than ♂. Short hair crest along spine from nape to tail root. Coat colour in calf yellowish to light red (pattern clearly as in adults) sexually mature ♀ also stays like this, whereas ♂ darkens through mahogany and chestnut to blackish-brown. White pattern (see Pl. 10) as in Bushbuck, though reduction of the 2–3 cheek spots possible. Cheeks may be whitish below eyes. Throat spot absent. Leg spots and lower throat spots grey in old ♂, transverse body stripes always 9–14. MEASUREMENTS: HB 170–250, TL 45–65, Ht 110–130, Wt ♂ c.270, ♀ c.240, H up to 100.

Distribution. Forest regions of Africa between 10°N and 7°S from Sierra Leone to S. Sudan, Kenya and Tanzania, not in Dahomey and Nigeria. In S. Ethiopia several have been sighted and shot, but still no specimen in any scientific collection. In Kenya and Tanzania in mountain and volcanic forests (Kenya, Cherangasi, -Mau, -Kikuyu, -Eldoma, -Aberdare, -Kinango range. Mt Kenya, Ndasegara, Chepalunga forest; Tanzania: seen on Meru but still not collected; probably also on Kilimanjaro: on Elgon still not proved.). No ssp. HABITAT: the densest primary and secondary forests, bushy and bamboo jungles in plains and mountains up to 4000m. Also in large isolated forests. At night for short periods may leave dense cover to browse in clearings and plantations. Water must always be available. TERRITORY: apparently sedentary. Has special trails or water courses through territory. Whether territory is maintained is not known. Seasonally wandering around to particular feeding places is possible; also from forest to forest or mountain to mountain. *Map* p. 66.

Habits. DAILY RHYTHM: late afternoon, evening and early morning browsing, rest of day lying up in dense cover. When sky overcast sometimes seen at the edge of forest or thickets, also in the early morning or late afternoon, otherwise only leaves its forest hiding place under cover of darkness. TOILET: wallows in mud holes and rubs off the mud on tree trunks, like Red Deer. VOICE: alarm call like Bushbuck's (see p. 57), calf bleats; both uncommon. SENSES: hearing very good, like scent, but sight less so. ENEMIES: chief enemy leopard. Danger to calves from golden cat, and python. When cornered (by hunters and dogs) defends itself bravely; very dangerous. In full flight goes through densest thickets with horns laid along the back. FOOD: chiefly foliage of trees and bushes, a little grass and herbage. Stands erect on hind legs to reach leaves. Digs for roots with horns. Pith of fallen trees, charcoal, rotten fruit, and dead wood of the Croton tree (*Croton macrostachys*) are also eaten. A browsing nibbler like Roe, seeks titbits over a wide area. Saltlicks in demand. SOCIABILITY: solitary, in pairs, or in small parties of ♀♀ with young and 1 young ♂. Latter leaves the troop at times to go alone and join a solitary ♂, which only seeks ♀ at pairing time. Saltlicks possible rendezvous for several bands.

Reproduction. Gestation 9½ months. 1 active young Wt at birth *c.*22, Ht *c.*70, HB *c.*90, TL *c.* 23. Whether pairing and calving times are seasonally limited is not certain; births in Dec–Jan are known. Young lie up. A week-old ♀ has height of 70, at 12 months 120, Wt 112, H 10. SEXUALLY MATURE: at 20 months. LONGEVITY: up to 19½ years in captivity.

ELAND, *Tragelaphus (Taurotragus) oryx* (Pallas, 1766) **Pl. 10**
G. Elenantilope F. L'Elan(d) A. Eland S. Mbunju, Pofu

Identification. Ox-sized, but slender small hump on withers; small dewlap between throat and front of breast, large in old ♂♂. Horns in both sexes, in ♂ stouter than in ♀ (latter sometimes more or less strongly curved), 2 longitudinal keels, 1–1½ spiral turns, light grey to blackish-grey. Lateral hoofs large, hinder pair having glandular hair pad on inside. Preorbital and inguinal glands absent, 4 teats. Coat short and smooth, forehead crest (well developed in ♂), middle of dewlap with hair tuft (in ♀ longer than in ♂, though the latter dewlap larger), hair crest from nape to withers. Coat colour greyish-brown to dark reddish-brown, white pattern (see Pl. 10) strong to weak or faded according to ssp., with 2–15 transverse body stripes, more distinct at front than in rear; in young and ♀♀ clearer than in ♂♂, and in northern representatives more numerous and obvious than in the southern forms. MEASUREMENTS: HB ♂ 240–345, ♀ 210–270, TL ♂ 60–90, ♀ 50–80, Ht ♂ 140–180, ♀ 130–160, Wt ♂ 400–1000, ♀ 300–600, H ♂ up to 123, ♀ up to 66.

Distribution. Africa south of Sahara and Ethiopia excepting deserts and dense forests. Rinderpest, hunting and agriculture have led to disappearance, so is gone from west and middle geographic Sudan (apart from Senegal) in S. Tanzania, the whole Union of South Africa (except National Parks, game farms and nature reserves) and the greater part of Mozambique, S.W. Africa and Angola. 5 ssp, including *derbianus and gigas*, the so-called Giant Elands, in the north of the distribution, the first formerly from Senegal to N. Nigeria, today only remnants, the latter in N.Cameroun, S. Chad, N. Central African Republic, Bahr-el-Ghazal (S.W. Sudan) and N.E. Zaire (Garamba National Park). HABITAT: Giant Eland in somewhat thicker savannah, woodlands or bush-veld, with rather low cover, and interrupted by smaller or larger open plains, the others in more open country to semi-desert and in mountains up to 4500m. Forest edge specially is a haunt, but thick forest is always avoided. TERRITORY: in strict form not known, since in the chosen area of country the search for food and water goes on according to season, and they may stay in one location only a few days. Trees and bushes are marked with mud of moist earth or urine soaked forehead crest, a district so marked may be recognised on return. Wide ranging wanderings only in special circumstances (drought, etc.) when separate troops may join up to form a herd. In the Drakensberg in summer on the High Veld, winters in the Low Veld. Population density in favourable situation 1 animal each 9–10 hectares. *Map* p. 66.

Habits. DAILY RHYTHM: browses in mornings and afternoons, rests in shade at noon, at night only active in moonlight, otherwise resting. TOILET: no details known. VOICE: adults puff and grunt like cattle while grazing. Wounded, and in great danger, bellow like cattle. Mother calls calf with soft mew. Excited calf bleats. SENSES:

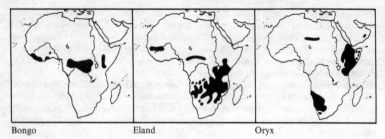

Bongo Eland Oryx

Common Eland sees well over long distances, scent also good, therefore moves mostly up wind. Giant Eland has especially good hearing and scent and has larger ears. ENEMIES: principal predators lion and hunting dog. Small calves are also preyed on by leopard, spotted hyaena, cheetah. Mother defends young bravely. Some mothers drive off if necessary hyaenas, leopards, cheetahs. At other times the Eland is timid and does not defend itself against man if wounded. If hunted, flees to a great distance. Can leap over obstacles up to 2m high. FOOD: in addition to grass and plants, also foliage of trees and bushes. Giant Eland takes more tree and bush foliage, Common Eland more ground vegetation. The first supplements its leaf browsing with grazing, if fresh and green; the latter its grazing in the dry season with trees and shrub foliage and shoots. Drinks morning and evening, or only once in 24 hours, can also go for a week or month completely without, if juicy melons, bulbs, tubers, onions and thick-leaved plants are available. Salt licks are used and also substitute salty and brackish water in salt pan regions. SOCIABILITY: in troops of $\frac{1}{2}$ to 1 or 2, rarely 3–4 dozen animals, sometimes association of several troops to form a herd or very large herd. A troop has normally several ♀♀ with young and 1♂, in larger troops also 2–3 old ♂♂, in herds even up to 12 ♂♂ and more (in rank order). Young ♂♂ form separate troops. Apart from the mating season old ♂ may also live alone.

Reproduction. ♀ sexually mature at $1\frac{1}{4}$–2 years (♂ also), has a 3-week cycle, gestation of $8\frac{1}{2}$–9 months (254–285 days), 1 active young, rarely 2. ♀ mates again soon after giving birth, so 2 births within a year possible. Sex ratio c.1:1, in adults often a considerable excess of ♀♀. One ♀ can give birth to 10–12 calves, if the normal length of life is reached. Main calving time in Kenya Oct–Nov, in Zambia, Malawi, Rhodesia Jul–Nov (peak period Aug–Sep), in W. Transvaal Mar–May, in E. Transvaal (Kruger Park) and S.W. Africa Aug–Sep. ♀ eats foetal sac and licks calf dry. Calf lies for 1 week, then follows ♀. Suckles at least $\frac{1}{2}$ year, first solid food at about 1 week. Wt at birth, ♂ 28–35, ♀ 23–31, maturity at about 7 years. Horn growth begins at about 1 month. LONGEVITY: 15–20 sometimes 25 years. Domestication. From 1892 in S. Russia, after 1945 also in Rhodesia and S. Africa to a moderate extent.

ROAN, SABLE and ORYX ANTELOPES, HIPPOTRAGINAE

Reindeer to horse-sized antelopes. Horns in both sexes, long spear-like or bow shaped or curling spirally on a twisted axis, in part with prominent rings. Hair mostly short and smooth, at times with mane on nape and anterior part of neck, or dewlap beard, or forehead crest. Preorbital and foot glands usually present, 4 teats. Inner hoofs high or flat, lateral hoofs large. Sociable in troops or herds. In open country to desert or savannah woodland or dry bushveld. 3 genera with total of 5 species in Africa and Arabia.

ORYX, *Oryx gazella* (Linnaeus, 1758) **Pl. 11**
G. Spiessbock   F. L'Oryx   A. Gemsbok   S. Choroa

Identification. Horns in both sexes, in ♀ rather thinner and with weaker rings, but somewhat longer than ♂; straight and lance-like or lightly to strongly curved like sabre: 15–30 prominent rings, ♂ with sturdier neck than ♀. Lateral hoofs large. Foot glands in fore and hind feet, 4 teats. Neck with short erect mane. Ssp. *leucoryx* and *gazella*, mostly with smaller throat mane, *callotis* ear tufts. Upperside whitish (*dammah* in part) or white (*leucoryx*) to light brown-reddish (*dammah* in part) or reddish-brown (*gallarum, callotis*) or brownish-grey to grey and whitish-grey (*annectens, beisa, blainei, gazella*). Black pattern on head, body and legs in *gazella* (the most conspicuous) to *dammah* and *leucoryx*, always slighter and paler. Calves of *dammah* and *leucoryx* light yellowish-brown without pattern, in forms from E. and S.E. Africa light brownish-red with faded dark pattern. General colouring of adult reached in 1 year. MEASURE-MENTS: HB 160–235, TL 45–90, Ht 85–140, Wt 55–255, ♂ ⅕ larger and heavier than ♀, H ♂ and ♀ 50–127 (*leucoryx* Ht 85–90, Wt 35–70; *dammah* Ht 110–125, Wt 180–200; others Ht 115–140, Wt 180–225).

Distribution. Originally all Africa apart from high mountains, large swamps and closed forests, also Arabia, Sinai Peninsula, Israel, Jordan, Iraq, and Syria. The species exterminated by man in recent times in ⅔ of these localities. In ancient Egypt *dammah*, and in the old civilisation of the Near East *leucoryx*, were kept in large numbers, half domesticated for sacrificial purposes. 7 ssp.: (1). North African Oryx or Scimitar Oryx (G. Sabelantilope; F. L'Oryx. algazelle ou l'Oryx blanc), *dammah*; 100 years ago North Africa from Rio de Oro and Senegal to Nile with northern border south edge of Atlas Mts., southern border between 14° and 12°N. Today extinct but for a small remnant on the south border of the Sahara between Air and Ennedi. (2) Arabian or White Oryx (G. Arabischer Spiessbock or Weisse Oryx; F. L'Oryx leucoryx) *leucoryx*; once in Arabia, Sinai Peninsula, Jordan, Israel, Iraq and Syria. Extinct in the wild state. About 100 animals at present in reserves. (3). Beisa (G. Eritrea Spiessbock; F. L'Oryx beisa; S. Choroa) *beisa*; Red Sea coastal region of Ethiopia, beside Eritrea and Somaliland, S. to about 6°N; extinct in Eritrea and Sudan, also elsewhere seldom met with. (4). Galla Oryx; *gallarum*; S. Ethiopia and S. Somalia with N. Kenya and S.E. Sudan. (5). Laikipia Oryx; *annectens*; Mt Kenya north of Tana R., westward to Karamoja and E. Uganda (in latter largely exterminated). (6). Fringe-eared Oryx or Kilimanjaro Oryx; *callotis*; Kenya S. of Tana R. and Aberdares to Masailand, S. of Kilimanjaro and Meru, west to the Great Rift and Sanjan plains. (7). Gemsbok (G. S. African Spiess-bock; F. Le Gemsbok; A. Gemsbok), *gazella*; Rhodesia (Matabeleland), S. Mozam-bique, Botswana, S.W. Angola, S.W. Africa and Cape Province. In south of distri-bution now only in reserves in north-central Cape Province and N. Transvaal. Intro-duced to New Mexico (U.S.A.) in 1962. HABITAT: open country in plains and hills apart from closed forest and large swamps: in each ssp. grassland to desert; *dammah* and *leucoryx* in impoverished steppes, semi-desert or deserts; *beisa* in dry steppes and semi-desert, in dry season in bush and tree savannahs; *gallarum, annectens* and *callotis* in grassland, bush steppe and dry savannah; *gazella* as in the foregoing, but also in semi-desert or desert. TERRITORY: none: steppe and savannah animals rather con-stant to locality; semi-desert or desert animals nomadic, their wanderings following the rainfall.

Habits. DAILY RHYTHM: main activity and browsing time early morning and late afternoon, also active in moonlight. TOILET: details not known. VOICE: weak. ♀ calls calf with soft low; ♂ grunts sometimes in pursuit of ♀, ♀ sometimes when cleaning calf after birth; calf bleats in fear, adults bleat when agitated. SENSES: sight, scent and hearing good. Desert and semi-desert animals can detect moving men (riders) and hear car and helicopter engines at a distance of 1km (usually take flight immediately because of past experience). ENEMIES: lion, leopard, hunting dog, and for small calves also hyaena, cheetah, caracal, serval, jackal; mother defends calf bravely. Man is principal enemy today. Adults when attacked put up a strong resistance against large predators, dogs and man, even spearing them to death. Do not leap obstacles, rather creep under or through them. FOOD: grass and plants, along with leaves and shoots of trees and bushes; in deserts thick-leaved plants, wild melons and other ground fruits as well as succulent roots, tubers and onions, which are dug out. Drinks daily if water available, in emergency will dig for it. In absence of water makes do with succulent fruits and tubers etc., and dew. SOCIABILITY: in pairs or small troops of ½ to 2–3 dozen, generally an old ♂ (leader and protector) with several ♀♀ and young; old ♂♂ also solitary. In semi-deserts and deserts sometimes herds of 30–200 (at an earlier period *dammah* on migration in several thousands).

Reproduction. Gestation 8½–10 months (*leucoryx* 255–260, *dammah* 242–256, others 260–300 days). Calving season varies regionally (Jul–Aug or Sep–Oct, or Sep–Dec, or Dec–Jan). 1 active young, twins rarely. ♀ nearing parturition goes aside, in *leucoryx* and *dammah* for 2–3 hours, otherwise 2–3 weeks, after which she rejoins the troop with the now active calf. Suckle for 3–4 months. Wt at birth 9–15, horns at birth already 1.5 in 6 months 45; suckling time 3½ months, in 4 months calf is ½ size of mother. Colour development begins at 3½, ends at 5 months. Sex ratio in adults of *gazella* about 2♀♀:1 ♂. SEXUAL MATURITY: 1½–2 years. LONGEVITY: 18–22 years recorded in captivity.

ADDAX, *Addax nasomaculatus* (de Blainville, 1816)   **Pl. 11**
G. Mendesantilope   F. L'Addax au nez tacheté
Identification. Reindeer size and build. Muzzle only a narrow strip between nostrils. Horns in both sexes, with 1½–3 (♂ 2½–3, ♀ 1½–2) large flattish spirals directed upwards and outwards, with 30–35 prominent rings in lower ⅔–¾. Hoofs low, in outline half-moon shaped, sole face flat, lateral hoofs large. Foot glands on fore and hind feet. 4 teats. Calf uniform pale reddish with dark crown and small forehead crest pad. Adult colour lightens with increasing age, often with individual variations. Winter colour dirty grey to greyish-brown; summer colour whitish grey-brown. MEASUREMENTS: HB 120–130, TL 25–35, Ht ♂ 105–115, ♀ 95–110, Wt ♂ 100–125, ♀ 60–90, H ♂ 60–109, ♀ 55–80; ♂ about ⅓ larger and heavier than ♀.
Distribution. 150 years ago still the whole of the Sahara and Libyan deserts from Rio de Oro and Senegambia to Egypt and Sudan, from the northern edge of the sand desert in Algeria, Tunisia and Libya to about 14°N in the south. In ancient Egypt probably also E. of the Nile, at that time commonly kept as a half domesticated sacrificial animal. Now exterminated except for a few last survivors in about ½ million sq km in the great desert of El Dschuf (Ed Djuf, El Djouf), between the Adrar mountains in Mauretania and Adrar mountains in Mali and in Tenere in Air to Ennedi (Niger and Chad Republics), in Kordofan, Darfur in M. Sudan already exterminated. The extinction of the last thousand animals may be expected soon. According to 1964 International Breeding Book *c.* 80 are in zoos. No ssp. HABITAT: ergs (dune deserts) and regs (gravel deserts). Today the remainder live in S. Sahara, north of the range of Scimitar Oryx. TERRITORY: none. Nomadic, following the rains (unusually good

weather brings rising humidity). Main migrations in the direction N.–S.–N. (Scimitar Oryx W.–E.–W.). In earlier times migrating herds of over 1000 common, today only a few hundred. *Map* p. 70.

Habits. DAILY RHYTHM: most active in early morning, evening and first half of night, during the day resting as much as possible in shade. TOILET: details not known. VOICE: little; a grunting and a bawling, however without explanation of significance. SENSES: sight, scent and hearing very good (see also Oryx p. 67). ENEMIES: previously on desert fringes lion, leopard, cheetah, hunting dog, and for calves also caracal, serval and hyaena, now only man. Like Scimitar Oryx subject to rinderpest. If cornered defends itself against man. FOOD: grass, plants, leaves of small bushes. Liquid needs obtained through sap of plants and dew, in case of emergency lives on its body fat, so a month or year-long existence possible without open water. In captivity drinks regularly. SOCIABILITY: in troops of 2–20 animals, on distant migrations large bands, in which ♂♂ and ♀♀ are under a leader.

Reproduction. Gestation 257–264 days. 1 active young; Wt at birth 4.8–7, 2–3 days after parturition ♀ is served again. Main calving seasons, earlier in N. Sahara end of winter beginning of spring, now in S. Sahara Sep–Oct and Jan–mid-Apr. SEXUAL MATURITY: ♀ 1½, ♂ 2¾ years. LONGEVITY: up to 19 years in captivity. Further details on courtship, pairing, birth, suckling time and growing up not known.

BLUEBUCK, *Hippotragus leucophaeus* (Pallas, 1766)   **Pl. 14**
G. Blaubock   F. L'Antilope leucophéage   A. Blaauwbok
Identification. Horns and form as Roan Antelope (below) but somewhat smaller. Horns in both sexes. Rings 28–35 in ♂, 20–26 in ♀. Tip of ear without hair pencil. Nape and dorsal mane only 2–3cm long, hairs on back of neck erect, underside of neck without mane. Upperside of body bluish-grey, underside whitish-grey. Mane, nose spot, forehead and front of legs brown, crown and back of ears light grey, muzzle, lips, chin, stripe above eye and hair tuft on skin over the preorbital gland yellowish-grey. Tail as Roan Antelope; preorbital and foot gland as Roan Antelope. Colour of young not known. MEASUREMENTS: HB ♂ 200–206, ♀ 188, TL ♂ 50–55, ♀ 49, Ht ♂ 105–106, ♀ 102, Wt probably ♂ 160–170, ♀ c. 150. H ♂ 55–61, ♀ 51–56.
Distribution. Swellendam region, south Cape Province. Exterminated 1800. HABITAT: partly open plains, partly hilly to mountainous country. Preponderantly lived in open plains. FOOD: mainly grass and plants. SOCIABILITY: in small troops of 5–6 animals, or in pairs. Old ♂ also solitary. Animal timid, taking to flight. Further details of habits unknown. *Map* p. 70.

ROAN ANTELOPE, *Hippotragus equinus* (Desmarest, 1804)   **Pl. 14**
G. Pferdeantilope   F. L'Hippotrague, Le Rouanne   A. Bastergemsbok
S. Korongo
Identification. Horse-sized. Horns in both sexes rising more or less steeply and curved backwards, the tips generally diverging, lower parts with 20–40 rings. Coat short and smooth. Short stiff mane from neck to withers and on front of neck. Ears long and narrow, tips with 3–5cm long tufts. Crown and back of ears light brown. Tail reaching heels, lower half tasselled. Upperside of body grey (ssp. *equinus*, S. Africa), fallow-brown to umber (*bakeri*, W. Ethiopia, S. Sudan, Uganda), pale brownish-red (*lang-heldi*, E. Africa), yellowish-brown (*koba*, Gambia to Cameroun), or ochreous-red (*scharicus*, Lake Chad and Shari region). Underside of body grey to yellowish-white. Neck mane greyish-brown with brownish-black edge. Tail hairs brownish-black. ♀ like ♂, horns rather weaker. Facial pattern of ♂ brownish-black to black, that of ♀

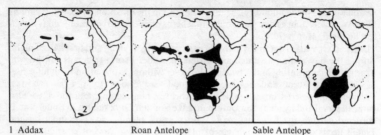

1 Addax   Roan Antelope   Sable Antelope
2 Bluebuck

and light brown calf (latter already with neck mane but still without tail tassel) brownish-red to dark brown. Preorbital gland under the skin distinguished by close-lying hair tuft. Foot glands present. 4 teats. MEASUREMENTS: HB ♂ 240–265, ♀ 220–245, TL ♂ and ♀ 60–70, Ht ♂ 150–160, ♀ 140–150; Wt ♂ 260–300, ♀ 225–275; H ♂ 70–100, ♀ 60–80.

Distribution. Africa south of Sahara. In geographical Sudan roughly between 15°–19°N from Gambia to W. Ethiopia, south through Central and E. Africa to S. Mozambique, E. Transvaal, Swaziland, N. Botswana, Ovamboland, Angola, S. and M. Zaire. In many regions extinct or threatened. Introduced to Rubondo Island in S. of Lake Victoria, Etosha Pan, S.W. Africa, in N. Transvaal, Natal. 6 ssp. HABITAT: open woodland or dry bush savannahs, gallery forest, light woodland in plains and hills up to 2000m. Nearby water necessary. TERRITORY: home range 50–100 sq km in size, within which wanderings only in dry season, otherwise very local, with troops of ♀ ♀ in ranges of 250–300 hectares including territories of 25–50 hectares marked (on ends of branches) and defended by ♂ ♂.

Habits. DAILY RHYTHM: morning and afternoon to nightfall feeding, over midday remain in cover. TOILET: details not known. VOICE: mostly silent, only a horse-like snort when alarmed. SENSES: sight, hearing and scent good. ENEMIES: lion, leopard, spotted hyaena, hunting dog, Nile crocodile; flees in files with sideways waving tails, old ♀ in lead, old ♂ ♂ following last of all. If attacked defends itself bravely. FOOD: predominantly medium height fresh grass (c. 90%) and foliage of bushes and trees. Drinks daily in morning and evening, also at midday in dry season. Can go without water for 2–3 days at the outside. SOCIABILITY: in small troops of 3–15, at most 25, only near end of dry season in herds of up to 60 or more. Mostly 1 old ♂, which keeps a strict watch on the troop, with several ♀ ♀ and young. Young ♂ ♂ in separate troops for 3–4 years, having been driven away from the ♀ troops at 2½–3 years by the old ♂. In rut ♂ and ♀ pair off. Sometimes solitary. Associate loosely with Oryx, Impalas, Wildebeestes, Buffaloes, Zebras or Ostriches.

Reproduction. Rival ♂ ♂ fight on their knees with violent backward sweeps of the horns. Gestation 268–286 days. Calving time in northern Africa November, in mid-East Africa Apr–Nov, sometimes Oct–Dec; in S.E. Africa Jan–Feb; in S.W. Africa Aug–Nov, in Zaire all year round, principally Feb–May. 1 active young. Wt at birth c. 16–18, after 1 month 32–34, horn growth begins at 1½ months. ♀ remains with young calf for some days or weeks, according to the district, apart, will also suckle an orphaned strange calf, suckling twice daily (morning and after the midday rest). SEXUAL MATURITY: 2½–3 years. LONGEVITY: in captivity up to 17 years.

SABLE ANTELOPE, *Hippotragus niger* (Harris, 1838)   **Pl. 14**
G. Rappenantilope   F. L'Hippotrague noir   A. Swartwitpens
S. Mbarapi, Pala-hala
Identification. Resembling Roan Antelope; somewhat smaller. Horns (in ♂ and ♀),
however, longer with 35–60 rings. Ears without terminal tuft. Underside of neck
without or with only poor mane. Upperside of body chestnut brown to black, ♀
markedly lighter than ♂ (spp. *roosevelti* ♀, S.E. Kenya and Tanzania chestnut-brown,
otherwise ♀ dark brown to brownish-black), old ♂ black. Facial mask pattern like
body colour. Back of ears and crown cinnamon brown. Mane from neck to shoulders
brown with black edge, in old ♂ black. Upperside of tail and tuft black. Underside of
body and narrow thigh band white. Calf light brown, mane and tail tuft black, white
areas (face, belly, back of thighs) as in adults, however at first still very fawn-coloured.
Preorbital and foot glands as Roan Antelope, 4 teats. MEASUREMENTS: HB ♂
210–255, ♀ 190–230, TL ♂ 45–75, ♀ 40–50, Ht ♂ 127–143, ♀ 117–135, Wt ♂
200–270, ♀ 190–230, H ♂ 80–165, ♀ 60–100.
Distribution. East and mid-Africa from S.E. Kenya to E. Transvaal, N. Botswana,
N.E. Kaokoveld, S. and mid-Angola, S.E. Zaire. Reintroduced to Swaziland. Previously in Orange Free State. In Orange Free State and Transvaal (apart from Kruger
Park) extinct; however has now been reintroduced. 3 ssp., of which the Giant Sable
(*variani*) with longest horns, in mid-Angola between upper Cuanza and Luando Rivers
(probably extinct as result of civil war) and small population in S. Zambia. HABITAT:
as in Roan Antelope but also in thick bushveld, not in open grass savannah.
ENEMIES: as in Roan Antelope, but flees in close troop. TERRITORY: troop inhabited area 240–280 hectares, ♂♂ territory therein 25–40 hectares, marked by
breaking off boughs of bushes with horns up to a metre high, and defended against
other old ♂♂, held for several months to 1 year. ♀♀ troops with young stay several
weeks to months, in S. Africa all year round, in old ♂ territory. Old ♂ pursuing ♀♀
during the rut keep them in territory by horn swinging and snorting.
Habits. DAILY RHYTHM: activity mainly in morning (7–10am) and afternoon
(2–5pm). TOILET, VOICE, SENSES, FOOD and SOCIABILITY: as in Roan. Troops
however on average larger.
Reproduction. Gestation 261–281 days. Main calving time in Kenya Jan–Feb and
Jul–Sep, in Angola May–Jul, Zaire Oct–May, N. Zambia Jun–Sep and Oct–Nov, S.
Zambia Jan–Mar and Jun–Oct, Rhodesia Dec–Jun, N.E. Botswana Jan–Feb, Caprivi Strip Dec–Feb, E. Transvaal Jan–Mar. ♀ goes apart in cover, calf stays with her
10, in *variani* 20 days, after that goes with mother to rejoin troop; ♀ eats afterbirth; Wt
at birth 12–14, rarely 16.5, horn growth begins at 1–1½ months, suckling period 8
months, first grass eaten at 1 month. SEXUAL MATURITY: 2½–3 years, first calf at 3
years, ♀ breeds up to 10–12 years, sex ratio at birth 1:1, in adults ♀♀ exceed
♂♂. LONGEVITY: up to 17 years in captivity.

REED AND WATER BUCKS, REDUNCINAE

Size of sheep to deer, horns only in ♂, short or long, simple, hooked or sickle or lyre-
shaped. Coat rather smooth and short, or somewhat longer, wispy and stiff, in part
with neck mane, throat and cheek beard. Tail reaching from ½ or ¾ or wholly to the heel,
bushy or with end tuft. 2 inguinal glands, 4 teats, foot glands sometimes present. Inner
hoofs short to long, lateral hoofs large, P^2 in *Redunca* very small or missing. Solitary, in
pairs, or in troops or herds, in flooded marsh, swampy regions or grasslands near water

or in dry high grass plains. 2 genera (*Kobus and Redunca*) with together 7 species in Africa. The genus *Pelea* (with 1 species) is in fact structurally partly related to the Reduncinae, but it is not certain that it belongs with this family. Its brain convolutions show resemblances to that of the gazelles.

DEFASSA or COMMON WATERBUCK, Pl. 12
Kobus (Kobus) ellipsiprymnus (Ogilby, 1833)
G. Wasserbock   F. Le Cobe defassa   A. Waterbok   S. Kuru

Identification. Size of Red Deer, though stouter-bodied. Only ♂ horned, 18–38 prominent rings, narrowly or widely spaced strongly curved backwards and upwards with weaker forward open curve. Inner hoofs narrow, pointed, outer hoofs sturdy, back of fetlocks hairy. Upperside of body varying from yellowish-brown (ssp. *unctuosus*, Gambia to Cameroun), reddish-brown (*defassa*, Ethiopia), sepia brown (*harnieri*, S. Sudan, N. Kenya, N. Uganda to Ruanda-Urundi) to greyish-red (*pallidus*, S. Somalia), grey (*crawshayi*, M. Zaire to Zambia and W. Tanzania) and greyish-black (*ellipsiprymnus*, Zambia to Zululand); flanks somewhat lighter, legs darker below. In S.E. Africa dark rump enclosed by white ring (ellipse) elsewhere whole rump whitish, in middle of E. Africa mixed forms between white-rumped and dark-rumped with white ring. No skin glands, except, in both sexes, sweat glands on whole body, most abundant on flanks, which provide a dark waterproofing secretion for the pelage, with a musky scent. 4 teats. Calf lighter than ♀. MEASUREMENTS: HB ♂ 190–220, ♀ 80–210, TL ♂ 35–45, ♀ 22–36, Ht ♂ 110–130, ♀ 100–125, Wt ♂ 170–250, ♀ 150–200, H 50–99.7. ♂ generally ½ to ¼ heavier and larger than ♀.

Distribution. Africa south of Sahara and from mid-Sudan, N. Ethiopia and S. Somalia southward to Transvaal, S. Botswana, N.E. S.W. Africa and S. Angola. 13 ssp. HABITAT: grass savannahs with bushveld or gallery forests or woodland patches as night refuge, with nearby standing water for daily drinking. TERRITORY: adults very local, ♂♂ in full vigour hold and defend marked territories to the water's edge usually for the whole year. ♀♀ troops wander through various ♂♂ territories; young ♀♀ and ♂♂ rove for a time here and there.

Habits. DAILY RHYTHM: seldom move far, and daily movements generally up to only ½ or 1km. Most active morning and afternoon to evening, otherwise resting. TOILET: no details known. VOICE: not often heard, mostly in alarm or in rut. Snores in sexual excitement, sometimes also in alarm. ♀ calls calf with soft 'Muh' calf answers a high bleating. SENSES: no details available. ENEMIES: lion, leopard, hunting dog, the latter seizing both breeding ♀♀ and calves. Where enough game available Waterbuck are avoided, after the first ½ year the flesh is tough and stringy, rank and musty scented. A solitary animal if disturbed often lies flat in concealment (see Reedbuck p. 78). When hunted may take to water; where shallow defending itself with horns and hoofs, or hiding in reeds submerged up to the nose, or swimming through floods. Wounded ♂ will even attack man. FOOD: 70–90% grass, rest foliage of trees and bushes. The grasses are species little used by other grazing animals. SOCIABILITY: troops of 1 ♂ and several ♀♀ with calves. Where old ♂♂ are territorial the whole year, ♀♀ troops wander through several territories. Young ♂♂ form troops near occupied territories.

Reproduction. Breeding season partly seasonal, partly all the year, according to location. Gestation 272–287 days. 1 active young, twins rare. Wt at birth *c.* 13. Suckling up to 6–7 months, horns begin growth at 5–6 months. SEXUAL MATURITY: ♀ 13, ♂ 14 months, ♀ will mate again 2–5 weeks after parturition though ♂ only establishes himself as the master buck in 4 years at the earliest, 6–7 normally. LONGEVITY: up to 18 years in captivity.

KOB, PUKU, *Kobus (Adenota) kob* (Erxleben, 1777)   **Pl. 12**
G. Grasantilope   F. Le Cobe de Buffon, Le Puku   A. Poekoe
Identification. Size of Roe Deer though body more thickset. Horns only in ♂, lyre-like and S-shaped in outline from base upwards, 10–15 rings. Small preorbital glands usually present, 2 (sometimes additional 2, vestigial) inguinal glands, foot glands sometimes vestigial, present on all four feet, or only on hind feet. 4 teats. Pasterns hairy. Upper side of body varying from light cinnamon colour (ssp. *kob*), yellowish-brown (*loderi*), dark-ochreous (*bahr-keetae*), and reddish-ochre (*ubangiensis*), to hazel-brown (*nigricans*), and blackish-brown (*leucotis*). *Leucotis* ♂ at sexual maturity changing from fox-brown to blackish-brown, with white around eyes, lips and throat and white ears.   MEASUREMENTS: HB ♂ 140–180, ♀ 125–150, TL ♂ 25–40, ♀ 18–30, Ht ♂ 80–105, ♀ 70–85, Wt ♂ 65–120, ♀ 50–70, H 30–69. ♂ about $\frac{1}{5}-\frac{1}{4}$ larger and heavier than ♀.

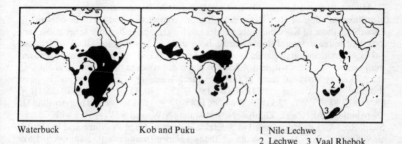

Waterbuck   Kob and Puku   1 Nile Lechwe
                                         2 Lechwe 3 Vaal Rhebok

Distribution. Sudan (geographic) from Senegal and Gambia to S.W. Ethiopia and W. Kenya besides N.E. Zaire, Uganda and Ruanda-Urundi on the one hand, and Central Africa (Malawi, S.W. Tanzania, Zambia) between 4° and 17°S. on the other hand. 12 ssp. of which best known: Senegal Kob (*kob*), W. Sudan (geographic) to N.W. Nigeria; White-eared Kob (*leucotis*), upper Shari to Bahr-el-Ghazal, Sennaar and S.W. Ethiopia, in eastern part between 11° and 14°N., already extinct; Uganda Kob (*thomasi*), region around northern half of Lake Victoria, eastwards to about 36°E.; Puku (*vardoni*), S. Zambia, M. and S. Zaire, N.E. Angola and Botswana, E. Caprivi. HABITAT: Open grassy plains, sometimes studded with bush and low woodland, also light woodland edges on savannah. Permanent water in neighbourhood necessary. TERRITORY: local, moving in home district usually less than 1km on average. Mature ♂♂ have an area within the territory (rutting place), ♀♀ and young move freely in or around, young ♂♂ in troops nearby. Where population is high perhaps a dozen small rutting grounds to one large one with arena as nucleus. Rutting ♀♀ each spend about 1 day on the rutting ground and are each served in turn by several ♂♂. Afterwards they return to the ♀♀ troop.
Habits. DAILY RHYTHM: active mainly early morning and late afternoon to dusk. Unattached single animals and small troops also during the day.   TOILET: no details known.   VOICE: unimportant. In excitement a whistling sound through the nostrils, 1–5 times. ♂ blows softly during pairing play; whistles 1–5 times after mating. ♀ and young have call sound for one another. Fear cry of young high bleating.   SENSES: no details known.   ENEMIES: lion, leopard, spotted hyaena, hunting dog and for young also serval. A solitary animal may lie flat when disturbed (see Reedbuck p. 78).

FOOD: principally grass and herbage, occasionally foliage of trees and bushes. Drinks daily. SOCIABILITY: troops of 2–40 animals, rarely up to 100, of ♀♀ with young and 1 or several old ♂♂. Young ♂♂ in separate troops. During breeding season territorial occupation by old ♂♂.

Reproduction. Mating time not seasonally restricted. Pairing possible over whole year. Gestation 261–271 days. 2 births a year possible. ♀ mates again 10–40 days after parturition. 1 active young, Wt at birth 4–5, after 7 months ♂ ⅓ ♀ ½ of adult weight, and ♂ and ♀ half adult size. Young mortality rate in first 7 months about 50%. Horn growth begins at 5 months, after 1 year as long as ears. Suckles 6–7 months, mature in 2 years. SEXUAL MATURITY: ♀ from 13, ♂ from 14 months, though only after 3–4 years can ♂ be active in rutting ground.

LECHWE, *Kobus (Hydrotragus) leche* (Gray, 1850) **Pl. 12**
G. Moorantilope or Litschi   F. Le Cobe lechwe   A. Basterwaterbok
Identification. Size of Roe Deer, though more compact in body. Horns only in ♂, resembling those of Kob, but more slender and longer, about 20 rings. Inner hoofs very long and narrow, lateral hoofs sturdy, both pairs wide-spreading. Back of fetlocks naked. 2 small inguinal glandular sacs. 4 teats. Upperside of body yellowish-brown; *smithemani* ♂ colours within 3–4 years to blackish-brown to near black, also old ♀♀ are darker; in *kafuensis* front of fore legs black reaching to upper legs and front of shoulder. MEASUREMENTS: HB ♂ 160–180, ♀ 130–170, TL ♂ 33–45, ♀ 30–35, Ht ♂ 85–110, ♀ 85–95, Wt ♂ 85–130, ♀ 60–95, H 45–92. ♂ ⅕ to ¼ larger and heavier than ♀.
Distribution. S.E. Zaire, Zambia, N. Botswana, N.W. and S.W. Africa with Caprivi Strip, S.E. Angola. Introduced in Adelaide district of Cape Province and in Orange Free State. 4 ssp. (1). Bangweolo or Black Lechwe (*smithemani*), Bangweolo Lake region (N. Zambia), earlier also extended N.E. to the R. Chambeshi, 1975 reintroduced there. Total population 1976 25,000. (2). Zambesi or Red Lechwe (*leche*), Upper Zambesi from Victoria Falls as well as lower course of the Zambesi tributaries the R. Kuando, Okavango including Delta and Chobe, locally extinct. 1976 total *c.* 30,000. (3). Kafue or Brown Lechwe (*kafuensis*), Kafue, mid-S. Zambia; area greatly reduced though still not endangered. Stock in 1976 *c.* 40,000. (4). Kawambwa Lechwe (*robertsi*), Kawambwa District between Lakes Mweru and Bangweolo, W. North Zambia; extinct. HABITAT: inundated marshes, rivers, swamps and lakes, normally 5–50cm deep and marsh borders at the water's edge (at least 100m broad at low water). Strong association with water fodder sources (grasses particularly) in still water up to 50cm deep, also other activities principally for flight from predators and man, only rest and calving on dry land. TERRITORY: locally diverse, in part territorial, part not, if yes, partly small, partly large breeding areas of ♂♂ (resembling Kob, p. 73). Very local, so in cases of local extermination no immigration. *Map p. 73.*
Habits. DAILY RHYTHM: active mostly in early morning and late afternoon to nightfall. Where much hunted by man, survivors entirely nocturnal, hiding in reed beds. TOILET: nothing known. VOICE: unimportant; in excitement varied mixture of coughing, grunts or whistling as in Kob but softer. ♂ sometimes snorts when suddenly disturbed, calves bleat. SENSES: sight and hearing good, scent not especially so. ENEMIES: lion, leopard, cheetah, spotted hyaena, hunting dog, crocodile, python; for young calves also eagles. Takes flight in leaping bounds or fast trot. Flattens itself on ground for protection like Reedbuck (see p. 78). Rapid decrease in last decade, however only due to man. FOOD: grasses and plants, also vegetation of flooded river marshes. Drinks daily. SOCIABILITY: highly social in large loose herds of ♂♂, ♀♀

and young, earlier in many thousands, today mostly only some hundreds. Large herds sub-divided into mixed troops varying locally and seasonally.

Reproduction. No strict seasonal limits, pairing, birth possible in every month, though in all locations distinct increases in fixed periods of year, the time of flooding and height of influx. Old ♂♂ occupy in rutting season small patches of higher ground as breeding sites, courting ♀♀ there and driving off other ♂♂. Gestation 7–8 months, not known exactly. 1 active young. Wt at birth *c*.5. Suckling time 3–4 months. Young lie up in tall grass and are suckled early morning and evening. SEXUAL MATURITY: ♀♀ about 1½, ♂♂ 2–2½ years, fully adult ♀♀ at 3–4, ♂♂ at 4–5 years. LONGEVITY: up to 15 years recorded.

NILE LECHWE or MRS GRAY's LECHWE,   Pl. 12
Kobus (Hydrotragus) megaceros (Fitzinger, 1855)
G. Weissnackenmoorantilope   F. Le Cobe de Mrs Gray

Identification. Very like Lechwe in size and form. Horns only in ♂ as in Lechwe, though rising more steeply from base, 20–30 rings. Inner hoofs long and narrow, outer hoofs long and robust, pasterns naked. 2 inguinal glands. 4 teats. Old ♂♂ above golden-brown to reddish-brownish-black or blackish-brown, head and neck darker than back with white nape stripe and shoulder saddle patch. ♀♀ above yellowish to chestnut-brown, light facial pattern weaker, nape stripe and shoulder saddle patch absent. Young like ♀♀. MEASUREMENTS: HB ♂ *c*.165, ♀ *c*.135, TL ♂ *c*.50, ♀ *c*.45, Ht ♂ *c*.100–105, ♀ *c*.80–85, Wt ♂ *c*.90–120, ♀ *c*. 60–90, H 45–87.

Distribution. S. Sudan, between 6° and 10°N and 29° and 34°E. Swamps in region of White Nile (Bahr-el-Jebel, Bahr-el-Ghazal, Bahr-el-Chabal, Sobat, Pibor etc.) as well as in adjoining S.W. Ethiopia in Gambela district on R. Baro and Gilo. No ssp. HABITAT: swamps, dry and inundated grassy marshes and steppes regions, as well as grassy levels with tall reed and sedge thickets. TERRITORY: very local, territoriality not investigated. *Map* p. 73.

Habits. DAILY RHYTHM: active mostly morning, evening and at night; in the midday heat and glare of sun resting. TOILET: no details known. VOICE: unimportant. When excited ♂ has an alarm grunt, no other details known. SENSES: no data. ENEMIES: lion, leopard, hunting dog, though of little importance; the habitat is natural protection and Lechwes swim well. Main enemy man (hunting, habitat destruction). FOOD: grass, herbage, water plants. SOCIABILITY: form large herds from 50 up to several hundred or thousands in loose bands. ♂♂ often form separate troops on edge of main herd. Solitary animals not known.

Reproduction. 1 active young, Wt at birth, ♀ *c*.4.5, ♂ *c*.5.5, doubled at 4–5 weeks. Further details unknown, though probably all Lechwes are alike in their habits.

VAAL RHEBOK, *Pelea capreolus* (Forster, 1790)   Pl. 13
G. Rehbok or Rehantilope   F. Le Rhebouk   A. Vaalribbok

Identification. Roe-like in size and form. Horns only in ♂, round, thin and pointed, rather wide apart, upright, generally the whole horn slightly curved forward, lower part with 10–15 weak rings. Rhinarium swollen and glandular. Tail halfway to heel, lightly tufted. Inner hoofs small, triangular, lateral hoofs short and broad, basally close grown. No preorbital or inguinal glands. 4 teats. Front of tongue, prepuce and penis gland black. Pelage short, rabbit-like, soft, thick and woolly, plain and smooth on head and legs. Upperside of body pale grey to brownish-grey, lower part of legs and forehead and nose more yellowish-brown, underside whitish. Young resemble adults. MEASUREMENTS: HB 105–125, TL 10–20, Ht 70–80, Wt 18–30, H 15–29.

Distribution. Mainly in east of Union of S. Africa; northern limit in E. about the tropic of Capricorn in W. Orange Free State, in Griqualand and S. to S.E. Botswana. Absent from S.W. Cape. Introduced in Addo and Bontebok National Park. No ssp. HABITAT: where undisturbed favours grassy valleys, hills and plateaux, besides also grassy hilltops and mountains with low bush and scattered trees; likes neighbourhood of water, however is independent of surface water. Area corresponds with the alpine pastures and bushy steppes of the Mediterranean Cape flora. TERRITORY: very local. ♂ holds home range for family group (several ♀ ♀ with young) and drives off all others of its species especially ♂ ♂. Territory marked by tongue clicking (see Voice), display postures from high points and latrines (which with the conspicuous display by tail waving of the white below the tail and on inside of thighs) mark the area. The urine is coloured blackish by the secretions of preputial gland, smells strongly and leaves black marking spots. Home range in summer (good feeding) 15–40 hectares, in winter (poor feeding) about double this size. *Map* p. 73.

Habits. DAILY RHYTHM: several feeding and resting periods spread over the day, in summer a 3-hour rest at midday, and in late afternoon a longer feeding session, in winter feeding sessions longer, resting periods reduced (also that of midday). At night feeding and drinking in valley bottoms. TOILET: as in Common Reedbuck (see p.78). VOICE: sharp clicking (possibly by expulsion of air through nose, varying in pitch and volume) as alarm, self expression or territorial establishment can last, with short pauses, up to $\frac{1}{2}$ hour; shrill long-drawn plaintive call in fear and distress and short soft hissing in sudden fright; ♂ in rut utters throaty sounds. SENSES: sight very good (movements recognised at 500m or more, shapes at 150m), scent and hearing excellent. ENEMIES: in the past, lion, leopard, cheetah, hunting dog, and for young also caracal, jackal, baboon and eagle. Now most large predators have disappeared from its haunts. Smaller enemies are attacked; flees from larger ones in a stretched out gallop (up to 65kph). FOOD: grass and herbage, with leaves of shrubs. Drinking (see HABITAT, TERRITORY). SOCIABILITY: (see TERRITORY). Young leave family at 1 year, ♂ ♂ then singly on fringe of locality until able to win territory.

Reproduction. Pairing only in territory with old ♂. ♂ ♂ in breeding season stage fierce mock fights without harm to each other, and pursue each other. Gestation $9\frac{1}{2}$ months. Parturition season in S. Cape Province Sep–Nov. 1, sometimes 2 active young. ♀ goes apart for the birth, young stays close for 6 weeks. ♀ suckles young morning and evening. Length of suckling time and details of growth not known (horns begin growth at 6 months). SEXUAL MATURITY: probably $1–1\frac{1}{2}$ years. LONGEVITY: not known.

MOUNTAIN REEDBUCK, *Redunca fulvorufula* (Afzelius, 1815)   Pl. 13
G. Bergriedbock   F. Le Redunca de montagne   A. Rooiribbok   S. Tohe

Identification. Form as in Bohor Reedbuck (p.77) but somewhat smaller. Differs from it in following: horns short and stocky, only 5–8 rings, slightly curved forward in upper part. Inner hoofs short. Gland below ear large and black-skinned. Tail reaching only $\frac{1}{2}$-way to heel, bushy. Pelage longer and woollier. Upperside of body greyish-brown, neck, head and upperside of tail more reddish-brown. In E. African form (ssp. *chanleri*), forehead, back of nose and outside of ears dark brown. Stripe above eye, lips, chin and throat yellow to greyish-white, underside of body and tail whitish. 4 inguinal glands. 4 teats. ♀ somewhat larger and greyer than ♂. MEASUREMENTS: HB 110–125, TL 17–26, Ht 60–80, Wt 20–30, H 13–23.

Distribution. E. Africa from S. Ethiopia to N. Tanzania and E. Uganda, S. Africa from Zambesi south to E. and mid-Cape Province; additionally in N. Cameroun. 3 ssp. HABITAT: grassy areas, open or with scattered bushes, stony or rocky knolls, hills and mountains, or high sloping river banks. Slopes and terraces preferred to summits and ridges. In mountain ranges to 4,200m. TERRITORY: very local; territory is marked and defended against adult ♂♂. TOILET, VOICE, SENSES, SEXUAL MATURITY, LONGEVITY: as Common Reedbuck (see p. 77), as also DAILY RHYTHM, but resting place also in thickets and between rocks and rocky outcrops; as also ENEMIES, but flight around hills or to steep slopes and when hunted lies low or skulks upwards. Obstacles up to 1.35m high are jumped over. FOOD: grasses and plants, also foliage of bushes. Can go without water for long time. SOCIABILITY: more sociable than Bohor Reedbuck, generally in loose herds from 1–3 dozen animals, usually 1 old ♂ with ♀♀ and young. *Map* p. 78.

Reproduction. Like Bohor Reedbuck, in S. Africa: births Nov–Mar, though young seen also in other months. Wt at birth ♀ *c*.2, ♂ *c*.2.5, doubled in 4–5 weeks. Sex ratio *c*. 1:1. LONGEVITY: 12 years recorded.

BOHOR REEDBUCK, *Redunca redunca* (Pallas, 1767) Pl. 13
G. Gemeiner Riedbock   F. Le Redunca   S. Tohe

Identification. Like Roe Deer in size and form. Horns only in ♂, lyre-shaped, tips inward and forward directed, 5–10 rings on lower half, horn base with fleshy, later hardening, pad-like bulge, horn angle and curvature subspecifically variable. Below base of ear a round scent gland, with small, dark and, in adult, naked skin surface, scent vaporises and is dispersed by ear movements. Pelage rather smooth and short, somewhat woolly or wispy; upperside of body isabelline to brownish-ochre. Fronts of legs with or without long dark stripe. Underside of body whitish-grey, as also stripe above eye, cheeks, lips, chin and throat. Albinos often occur, particularly in W. Tanzania. Young somewhat long-haired and often also darker than adults, forehead and nose especially brown to brownish-black. Tail a little more than half distance to heel, ending in thinly bushy tip, whitish underside conspicuous when exposed (in flight). Inner hoofs long and narrow. Lateral hoofs of foreleg nearly or wholly grown together at base. No preorbital or foot glands. 2 pairs inguinal. 4 teats. MEASUREMENTS: HB ♂ 125–145, ♀ 115–130, TL ♂ 20–25, ♀ 15–23, Ht ♂ 70–80, ♀ 65–80, Wt ♂ 45–65, ♀ 35–55, H 20–41.

Distribution. The Sudan zone from Gambia to Ethiopia, and E. Africa from N.W. Ethiopia to S.W. and N.E. Tanzania. 7 ssp. HABITAT: open plains or hilly or suitable regions in mountains interspersed with light cover, grassy or swampy with reeds, sedge or tall grass. Water in neighbourhood (not more than 5–8km distant) necessary. TERRITORY: very local. 1 old ♂ watches and defends 1–5 associated ♀ quarters, each of 15–40 hectares. Young and ♂♂ without territories live in young associations between the territories; young ♀♀ live near mothers gradually forming separate territories. *Map* p. 78.

Habits. DAILY RHYTHM: active morning and afternoon till evening, also in clear nights; midday rest in tall grass, reeds or bush. TOILET: details not known but probably like Common Reedbuck (see p.72). VOICE: shrill whistle when alarmed or put up. SENSES: sight, hearing and scent good. ENEMIES: lion, leopard, cheetah, hyaena, hunting dog and for young also jackal, serval, eagle and python. When disturbed lies flat with neck outstretched, only jumping up at last moment. Flight an uneven gallop, with waving hind legs and tail, generally away from water, but sometimes dives as far as the face. FOOD: almost only grass, but some herbage. SOCIABILITY: solitary, or in pairs, or in troops of 6–12 animals, of 1 ♂ with several ♀♀ and young, or with young ♂♂. Along Dinder River (Dinder National Park, Sudan) population very high (*c*. 15,000 per 50km) and predominantly in herds of 100 or more. In S. Tanzania (ssp. *wardi*) pairs either for season or for life, young with parents until sexual maturity.

Reproduction. Mating and calving seasons appear not to be seasonally fixed. ♂♂ fight, in part, vigorously in pairing time. In S. Tanzania (*wardi*) in courtship ♀♀ and following ♂♂ caper with outstretched legs and body. Growing young have circular 'dancing' places. Old animals look on. Gestation 7–7½ months. 1 active young, rarely 2. SEXUAL MATURITY: probably 1½ years. LONGEVITY: 10 years recorded in captivity.

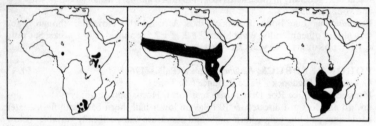

Mountain Reedbuck   Bohor Reedbuck   Common Reedbuck

COMMON REEDBUCK, *Redunca arundinum* (Boddaert, 1785)   **Pl. 13**
G. Grossriedbock   F. Le Redunca grande   A. Rietbok   S. Tohe
Identification. Form and horns as Bohor Reedbuck (p. 77) but under-ear scent gland somewhat larger. Other differences: more horn rings (10–15), lateral hoofs not united, tail only half reaching heel and thickly bushy; only 1 pair of inguinal glands (in ♀ sometimes 2), pelage of neck sometimes rather long. Upperside of body greyish-brown to brownish-grey or dark brown, seldom yellowish-brown to reddish-yellow. Nose and forehead sometimes darker. Front of legs usually with dark stripe. Stripe over eyes, lips, chin and underside of body and tail whitish. Adult ♂♂ have crescent-shaped greyish-white throat patch, in ♀ only slight, and yellowish-grey. Calf greyish-brown above, greyish-white below, back of ear and neck stripe dark, after 3 months yellowish-brown, assumes adult colour with dark back at 1 year. MEASUREMENTS: HB ♂ 130–160, ♀ 120–140, TL ♂ 18–30, ♀ 18–26, Ht ♂ 80–105, ♀ 65–95, Wt ♂ 60–95, ♀ 50–85; H 25–46.
Distribution. From mid-Zaire (*c.* 3°S), and S. Tanzania (*c.* 9°S) south to Cape of Good Hope, however widely absent today W. of 20°E, in S. of 25°E. 2 ssp. HABITAT: like Bohor Reedbuck (see p. 77). Water essential within 2km. TERRITORY: resident, a part of the range of adult (at least 3 year-olds) ♂♂ is defended and marked against other adult ♂♂. Territory marked by displaying the white throat patch by head raising, or reinforced by bouncing leaps with head raised; or whistling, and by secretions of under-ear and inguinal glands. 1 ♀ with young lives in a part of the territory. Latter about 30–60 hectares. Smallest at end of dry season owing to Reedbucks gathering in neighbourhood of the remaining watering places.
Habits. DAILY RHYTHM: active morning and afternoon to evening, but also at night. In dry season longer grazing necessary because of poor quality of fodder, up to and over midday, resting in early morning and late afternoon. TOILET: licking, nibbling, scratching and rubbing. Licking of body and hindquarters, nibbling on shoulders, body and legs, scratching with hind foot on head and neck, rubbing of cheeks on body

and forelegs, with horns on rump. No mutual licking or nibbling.   VOICE: whistle with closed mouth through nostrils (as in Chamois) when excited; depending on degree of excitement a little or as much as 150 times, one after another. Rattling sound at beginning of bouncing leap. Sharp sound before the whistling only in ♀, if excited only moderately. Smacking sound in flight said to be produced by high hind leg sudden opening of the inguinal glands. SENSES: sight, hearing and scent good. ENEMIES: principally lion, leopard, cheetah, hunting dog; also hyaena, crocodile and python; young preyed on by caracal, serval, jackal, baboon and large eagles. Flight in long leaps with raised neck and tail close to body, normally halts at 20–30m to look back. When disturbed may steal away with lowered head, or lie flat with outstretched neck. Only jumps up at last moment. Normal gallop uneven. Leaps over obstacles up to 1.35m high. FOOD: almost entirely grass, but also some plants. In dry season drinks daily. SOCIABILITY: singly (young ♂) or in pairs (♂ and ♀ or ♀ and young) or in families (♂ and ♀ with young), not in troops or herds; no troops of young ♂♂. Loose associations of up to 20 animals only subject to water and food conditions in dry season.

Reproduction. Seasons not clearly defined. Calves in all seasons with most in dry season. Gestation 7¾ months. 1 active young. Details of maturity not known; from 5 months ? Sex ratio c. 1:1. SEXUAL MATURITY: probably about 1½ years. LONGEVITY: up to 10 years in captivity.

HARTEBEESTES, ALCELAPHINAE

About size of Red Deer. Head long and narrow, back somewhat, or distinctly sloping. Horns in both sexes, crescentic, S-shaped, sharply angled and erect, or close and sharply hooked, with transverse bulges or smooth. Muzzle naked. Ears pointed, medium length, tail with end tuft reaching to heel or fetlocks. Hoofs narrow and pointed. Lateral hoofs rather large. Pelage short and smooth, in part with forehead, nape, lower neck, breast or throat manes. Preorbital and foot glands present; 2 teats. In grass and bush steppe or savannah outside the primeval forests in Africa as well as North Arabia and Palestine, though outside Africa and north of the Sahara exterminated between early historical times and today. 3 genera with altogether 5 species.

BONTEBOK or BLESBOK, *Damaliscus dorcas* (Pallas, 1766)   **Pl. 14**
G. Bunt and Blessbock   F. Le Bonte ou Blesbok   A. Bontebok, Blesbok.
Identification. Horns, skin glands, teats and form as in Sassaby though figure smaller and more graceful. Body colour grey-reddish brown to black, but body, upper legs and tail tuft dark, front of face, underside and lower legs white. In ssp. *phillipsi* front and mid body to rump reddish-brown, saddle (shoulders to rump) lighter. Face (apart from front), neck, flanks, lower throat, legs (apart from whitish axial area and groin, back of metacarpals and front of metatarsals) dark brown to brownish-black, hind parts and back of legs black, forehead and back of nose (often divided by narrow brown band between eyes) belly and underside of tail root white. Small area around tail root and breast yellowish-brown, back of ears greyish-white. Ssp. *dorcas* like *phillipsi*, only foreparts darker (dark reddish-brown), saddle lighter (reddish-yellow grey), dark areas of lower throat, flanks, thighs and legs blacker; belly white extending as far as breast, backs of thighs around tail root and these themselves white. Metacarpals white, front with narrow black stripe from hoof to middle of leg. Backs of ears brownish-grey.

Facial white becomes narrower above eyes. ♀ yellowish-brown with conspicuous white markings. Hoofs and horns greyish-black to black; in *phillipsi* dark grey to greyish-yellow, transverse rings yellowish-white. ♀ generally lighter than ♂. Calf uniformly light brown with greyish-black back of nose, without tail tuft, in *dorcas* darker tail tuft. Horn growth begins at 2 months, the curving and ridging in 8–9 months, the general colour pattern in 6 months. Full horn growth at 3 years in ♂. MEASUREMENTS: HB 140–160, TL 30–45, Ht 85–100, Wt ♂ 65–80, ♀ 55–70; H to 50.

Distribution. S. Africa. 2 ssp. (1). Blesbok (*phillipsi*); N. and E. Cape Province, Orange Free State, W. Transvaal, W. Natal, S. Botswana. Extinct in wild state. Now only in reserves and game farms where increasing, and further introduced more widely, so that at present good numbers in all States of the Union. (2). Bontebok (*dorcas*); S. Cape Province, coastal veld region W. and E. of Cape Agulhas, S. of Caledon Mts, and Little Karroo. In wild state reduced to 17. Then fully protected, and in Bontebok National Park near Swellendam (former Bredasdorp), on the de Hoop game farm near Bredasdorp, in Cape Point Nature Reserve, in Reserve of Cape University, and on the Van der Byl and Van Breda game farms, Bredasdorp region and other further localities, increasing further to about 1000. HABITAT: open grassland with or without small bushes and trees. Bontebok up to now also in macchia scrub reserves. TERRITORY: formerly local. ♂ at 4–6 years territorial and occupies in mating season (Blesbok), or whole year (Bontebok) areas from about 10–40 hectares, marked as Sassaby (see p. 81). Blesbok ♂ stands or lies a good deal by central large dung heap. Unattached ♂♂ are driven out, neighbouring occupiers are regularly seen off the border in ceremonial encounters. In territory several ♂♂ (Bontebok usually 3–6, Blesbok 8–10, though up to 25 possible) with calves (in Bontebok often yearlings) are free to wander anywhere. After breeding and up to beginning of rainy season small to large mixed herd (20–500, earlier many thousands).

Habits. DAILY RHYTHM: graze morning and afternoon, rest over midday, in hot weather probably lying in shade, at other times sleep standing, with sunken head, at night generally resting. Where disturbed, move upwind with head down. Obstacles up to 1.35m high are clambered over, or are crept under or through. TOILET: skin licking or scratching with hind foot. Earth scraping and lying by dung heaps (see TERRITORY). VOICE: snorting and grunting. Snorting when excited, grunting 'mboa' of mother to bleating calf (straying call), snorting of mother as call to calf to follow. Calf has contact and other calls. SENSES: sight and hearing very good, scent good. ENEMIES: earlier, lion, leopard, cheetah, hunting dog, large eagles (for calves), today these all exterminated, and only still black-backed jackal a threat to newborn calves. Bonte- and Blesbok in open range not aggressive to man. FOOD: only grass and herbage. Drink morning and evening, Bontebok also midday in summer. SOCIABILITY: harem troops around territorial ♂ (see TERRITORY), troops of young Blesbok of both sexes, about 8–10 months old. Mothers with newborn young, wander freely (up to 75). 2-year-old ♀♀ in troops, later seeking territorial ♂♂. Young ♂♂ establish their own territories at about 4–6 years. In Bontebok troops of young ♂♂ as in Blesbok, young ♀♀ live however with mother for 2 years, then with territorial ♂. Mixed herds (see TERRITORY).

Reproduction. Bontebok breeding season Jan–mid-Mar, parturition mid-Aug–mid-Dec (in Swellendam end of Feb), height of season Nov–Dec (in Swellendam Sep–Oct). Blesbok breeding season Mar–Apr, parturition Oct–Jan, most in Nov–Dec. Gestation $7\frac{1}{2}$ months, 1 active young. Birthplace in high grass. Mother eats afterbirth and licks calf dry. Wt at birth 6–7, at 8 months about 35. Sex ratio 1:1, later excess of ♀♀. First solid food at about 10 days, regular cud-chewing about 50 days. Suckling time 4 months. SEXUAL MATURITY: in ♂ and ♀ 2¼ years, ♀ rarely earlier; ♂ first becomes fully territorial at 4–6 years. LONGEVITY: in wild state ♀ to 14, ♂ to 16; in zoos up to 17 years.

SASSABY, KORRIGUM, TIANG, TOPI, HIROLA or HUNTER'S ANTELOPE, *Damaliscus lunatus* (Burchell, 1823) Pl. 15

G. Leier oder Halbmondantilope   F. Le Sassaby, Damalisque, L'Antilope Hirola
A. Basterhartebees   S. Nyamera

Identification. About size of Red Deer, though back rather sloping. Head rather long and narrow, muzzle naked, ears medium length, narrow. Horns in ♂ and ♀; in ♀ shorter and thinner than in ♂, weakly lyre-shaped, inclining backward and upward, with 10–20 widely spaced prominent ridges, only the tips smooth. Pelage short and smooth, in part glossy, hair in front of face from muzzle to horns reversed. Tail with tuft, reaching heel. Body colour chestnut-brown (ssp. *lunatus*, *jimela*, *phalius*), purplish red-brown (*lyra*, *tiang*, *topi*) to glowing reddish-brown (*korrigum*), reddish-yellow (*purpurescens*) and yellowish-brown (*hunteri*). Front of face and tail tuft black, lower arm and thigh and adjoining upper arm and thigh surface greyish, or bluish-black, lower legs and underside of body brownish-yellow to yellow (in *lunatus* belly white, in old *phallus* ♂♂ front of face light to brownish-white to white). *Hunteri* entirely yellow-brown, with only a narrow browband; breast, belly, tail tuft yellowish-white to white. Preorbital and foot glands present. 2 teats. MEASUREMENTS: HB 150–205, TL 40–60, Ht 100–130, Wt 75–160, H up to 72. ♂ rather larger and heavier than ♀.

Distribution. N.E. and northern S. Africa. 9 ssp.: (1). Western Korrigum (*korrigum*) from Senegambia to N. Nigeria, Lake Chad, and N.W. Darfur, between 11° or 14° and 19°N. (2). Cameroun Korrigum (*purpurescens*) E. Nigeria, N. Cameroun. (3). Shari Korrigum (*lyra*) Upper Shari region (Ubangi-Shari). (4). Tiang (*tiang*) Sudan and adjoining border region of Ethiopia, between 5° and 15°N. (5). Topi (*topi*), coastal region of E. Africa from S. Somalia (from about Mekka 2°N.) to S.E. Kenya (Malindi). (6). Hunter's Hartebeeste or Hirola (*hunteri*) west of the *topi* region, to S. Somalia (Jubaland) to Tana River in E. Kenya was seriously threatened, population now again up to 13,000. In 1963 30 animals introduced into Tsavo National Park. *Hunteri* is generally considered to be a distinct species. (7). Jimela (*jimela*), around Lake Victoria, Uganda, Ruanda-Urundi, Rutschuru, east border region of Zaire, W. and Mid Kenya, N. and Mid-Tanzania. (8). *Phallus*, Uasin Gishu Plateau, E. of Elgon, W. Kenya. (9). Sassaby or Tsesseby (*lunatus*) S.E. Katanga (Zaire) Zambia (earlier to S. border of Tanzania, now in northern part only still in Samfya, in S. part only still west of Zambesi), Malawi, W. and S. Mozambique, Rhodesia, E. Transvaal (now only still in

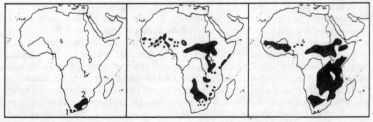

1 Bontebok   2 Blesbok   Sassaby   Hartebeestes

Kruger National Park and Percy Fife Game Reserve), N. Botswanaland, Caprivi Strip, northern S.W. Africa and S.E. Angola to about 15°E. HABITAT: completely open plains with scattered bush and light woodland or light to thick savannah, as well as inundated areas as in dry-semi deserts. Also found in grass fields. In plains and hilly districts. TERRITORY: where food is abundant is resident, then and in rutting season generally in small harems with an old ♂. Territory 10 hectares (2 sq km) with small central area specially well marked and defended against rivals. Often a few troops dispersed over the district. Marking by deposition of dung, preorbital glandular scent deposits on short stiff grass stems, by rubbing of horns and face on these stems and on ground or on termite hills, by forking up the ground in similar places, by scraping the ground with front hoofs (spreading scent from foot glands) by standing conspicuously on termite hills; head raising as threat gesture to rivals, and fighting on knees with horns.

Habits. DAILY RHYTHM: active mainly morning and evening, resting in shade at midday. Generally 2–3 rest periods daily. If little disturbed, rather curious, otherwise timid, but if cornered will defend itself. TOILET: head rubbing together, face rubbing on ground, rolling, at times after drinking stirs up mud with horns, smears mud on its foreparts with its hoofs. VOICE: snorts and grunts. ♂ bleats repeatedly if frightened from cover. Alarm calls of Klippspringer, Roan, Reedbuck and Guinea Fowl are responded to. SENSES: sight and hearing very good, scent good. ENEMIES: lion, leopard, cheetah, spotted hyaena, hunting dog, and also for calves, jackal, serval, caracal, python and large eagles. FOOD: almost entirely grass and herbage, rarely leaves. Normally drinks morning and evening, though can exist up to a month without water. SOCIABILITY: associate in small harems (½ to 2 dozen ♀♀ with calves), with 1 old ♂ (see TERRITORY), also troops of young animals and some solitary ♂♂. In dry season large herds form of some hundreds or (in *Topi*) thousands. Often associate with other antelopes particularly Wildebeestes as well as Zebras and ostriches.

Reproduction. Gestation 7½–8 months, calving season in Chad region Feb–Mar, in N. Cameroun Mar–May, in N.E.Zaire Feb–Mar, in S. Tanzania and Zambia Jun–Sep (mostly Sep as well as Jul–Aug), in Rhodesia Oct, in northern S.W. Africa and Caprivi Strip Sep–Dec, in Botswana Nov–Dec, in Transvaal Sep–Jan (chiefly end of Sep to end of Oct). 1 active young; Wt at birth 10–12, at ½ year ♂ *c*. 70, ♀ 45, at 1 year ♂ *c*. 90, ♀ *c*. 70, Ht *c*. 100, after 1½ years ♂ *c*. 110, ♀ *c*. 85, at 2 years ♂ *c*. 115, ♀ *c*. 95, Ht *c*. 110–120, at 3 years ♂ *c*. 140, ♀ *c*. 125. SEXUAL MATURITY: ♀ at 1½–2, ♂ at 3 years, ♂♂ begin to fight for territory at the earliest at 4 years. Sex ratio at first 1:1, though locally ♀♀ in excess through higher ♂ mortality. LONGEVITY: 12–15 years, about 9 recorded in captivity.

HARTEBEESTE, *Alcelaphus buselaphus* (Pallas, 1766)   **Pl. 16**
G. Kuhantilope   F. Le Bubale   A. Hartebees   S. Kongoni
Identification. Size and form as Sassaby (p. 81). Forehead of long narrow head generally narrow and high. Muzzle naked. Ears middle length, pointed. Horns in both sexes, somewhat shorter and thinner in ♀, bases in part wide and flat. Horns may be angular, with double curvature, the last bend at times like a kink; 12–15 prominent rings, only the tip smooth. Pelage short and smooth directed backwards or under, more or less wavy giving 'water-mark' effect. Scattered long hairs around nostrils and eyes. Tail with tuft reaches heel. Facial hair from crown to muzzle directed downwards, except in ssp. *caama* and *lichtensteini* where it grows upward from muzzle to eye, at eye level forming a short transverse ridge. Old ♂ often appears nearly naked on back. Colour isabelline (*tschadensis, lelwel, jacksoni*), yellowish-brown (*tora. cokii, lichten-*

steini), reddish-brown (*buselaphus*, *major*), lustrous chestnut reddish-brown (*caama*), dull reddish-brown (*modestus*), or pale chocolate brown with whitish hairtips (*swaynei*). Colour generally uniform, but *modestus* lighter in front than behind, and *caama* with white sides and back of thighs and sides of base of tail. Chin, tail and tail tassel nearly always dark brown to black. Forehead and back of nose dark (*major*, *tschadensis*), strong brown (*matschiei*, *invadens*, *lichtensteini*), brownish-black to black (*swaynei*, *caama*). In *swaynei* and *caama* transverse band between the eyes, in former brown as cheeks, in latter, yellowish-white interrupting the black of forehead. *Caama* has short, vertical, black stripe and black line from base of ears to shoulders. Underside of body slightly or distinctly paler than upperside, belly white in *caama*. Legs colour of body (*buselaphus*, *cokii*, *jacksoni*, *tora*) or metacarpals and feet with brownish-black stripe on front, in *swaynei* on upper front legs, in *caama* to hoofs, and from upper thigh to heel. Hoofs and horns pale horn colour (*buselaphus*) to blackish-brown. Iris yellow to brownish-yellow. *Swaynei* ♀ lighter than ♂, face not dark. Calves lighter than adults, without dark head, body or leg pattern, in *lichtensteini* however somewhat darker and with black neck stripe. Hoofs slender and sharp tipped. Lateral hoofs short and broad. Preorbital and foot glands present, no inguinal glands. 2 teats. MEASUREMENTS: HB 175–245, TL 45–70, Ht 120–145, Wt ♂ 135–200, ♀ 120–180 (♂ somewhat larger and heavier than ♀), H up to 70.

Distribution. Africa outside the forest zone, N. Arabia and Palestine. 13 ssp.: (1). North African (*buselaphus*); Atlas region to Egypt. N. Arabia and Palestine. In ancient Egypt kept half-domesticated in numbers as a sacrificial animal, in recent times exterminated in Egypt about 1850, in N. Arabia and Palestine about 1900, in the Atlas and Tripoli about 1920, in Rio de Oro about 1950. (2). Western H. (*major*); Gambia and Upper Senegal region between 10° and 14°N. Widely exterminated. (3). Togo H. (*matschiei*); Ivory Coast to N. Nigeria, between 8° and 12° – 14°N; threatened. (4). Nigerian H. (*invadens*); N.E. Nigeria to N. Cameroun. (5). Chad H. (*tschadensis*); Chad, Middle and Lower Shari region. (6). Ubangui-Shari H. (*modestus*); Upper Shari region (Ubangui Shari, Chad and Central African Republic). (7). Lelwel H. (*lelwel*); S. Sudan, N.E. Congo, S.W. Ethiopia west of R. Omo (Jamboland). (8). Jackson's H. (*jacksoni*); region around Lake Victoria, partly exterminated. (9). Tora H. (*tora*); N. and W. Ethiopia, Eritrea, S.E. Egypt, and E. Sudan, in many places threatened or exterminated. (10). Somali H. (*swaynei*); mid, S. and E. Ethiopia, Somalia W. of Berbera (formerly British Somaliland). In Ethiopia only 4 small remaining localities (Awash Valley, Javello, Senkele, Shashamanna) and Lake Chamo region; in Somalia extinct. Generally strongly threatened. (11). Cokes H. or Kongoni (*cokii*); M. and S. Kenya, N. Tanzania; extinct in M. Kenya. (12). Lichtenstein's H. or Konzi (*lichtensteini*); M. and S. Tanzania, S.E. Zaire, Zambia, Malawi, Mozambique, Rhodesia; S. borders Lundi and Save Rivers. Lichtenstein's H. is generally accepted as a distinct species, *Alcelaphus lichtensteini*. (13). S. African H. or Caama (*caama*); S. Africa, S. of a line from S. Angola to W. Rhodesia and W. Natal. In S.W. Africa still found only in East, in Botswana in Kalahari National Park, in S. Africa extinct in the wild state, though still found reintroduced in game reserves in Cape Province, Orange Free State and Transvaal (except in Kruger National Park, though once found in E. Transvaal). HABITAT: grassy plains sometimes with bush and trees, or dry savannah or bushveld, latter with scattered open areas; in plains and on hills. TERRITORY: generally local. 3–4 year old ♂♂ occupy mostly all the year round territories from ⅓–3 or 4 sq km in which 3–10 (15) ♀♀ with young, marked by scrapes on ground and scenting with facial glands, and also by boundary dung hills as well as by prominent watching posts on rising ground (sight marking), defends territory against neighbouring rivals (fighting methods as in Sassaby, see p. 81). Sometimes young ♂ troops occupy small territories and mark them by ground scraping. Sometimes in herds up to 200, or in dry season large herds of several hundred or thousands. *Map* p. 81.

Habits. DAILY RHYTHM: active mainly morning and evening, resting midday in shade. Generally 2–3 rest periods in day, harem ♂♂ rest the most. TOILET: mud stirring with forehead and horns then plastering body. VOICE: snorts when frightened. Fighting ♂♂ sometimes bark. SENSES: sight and hearing very good, scent good. ENEMIES: see Sassaby. FOOD: grasses and herbage, rarely leaves. Usually drinks daily morning or evening, but can go without for days or months. Salt and mineral licks eagerly used. SOCIABILITY: harem troops (see TERRITORY) young ♂ troops, sometimes also solitary ♂♂. Larger bands, see TERRITORY. Often associate with ostriches, zebras, wildebeeste and other antelopes.

Reproduction. Gestation 8 months. Calving in Kenya all year round, but 2 peaks in Feb–Mar and Jul–Aug, in Zambia Jun–Oct (mainly Jul–Aug), in N.E. Zaire Jan–Feb, in S. Zaire Jan–Feb, in S. Transvaal Oct–Nov, in Natal Sep–Oct, in Botswana Sep–Nov, in north Cape Province Aug–Oct (mainly Sep), in S.W. Africa Oct–Nov. 1 active young, twins rare. ♀ calves in cover alone, eats afterbirth (and embryonic envelope) and licks calf clean. Calf lies hidden 1–2 weeks. Wt at birth *c.* 13–15, HB *c.* 85, TL *c.* 18, Ht *c.* 80. Suckles about 4 months. Horns first grow straight: at 3 months about 15cm, at 1 year first curvature, in 2 years like adults. Wt at 1 year *c.* 100, 2 years ♂ *c.* 160, ♀ *c.* 130, 3 years ♂ *c.* 180, ♀ *c.* 165. SEXUAL MATURITY: usually at 2½ years, sometimes ♀ earlier (1½ years). ♀ mates again 1–4, usually 3, months after calving. Young ♂ lives with mother 10–30 months (young ♀ longer), at 20 months usually joins troop of young ♂♂, and at 3–4 years seeks to evict a harem ♂. Latter can hold territory usually up to 7 or 8 years of its life. Sex ratio at birth ♂:♀ *c.* 1:2, in adults 1:3. LONGEVITY: in captivity up to 19 years.

BLUE WILDEBEEST, BRINDLED GNU,   **Pl. 15**
Connochaetes taurinus (Burchell, 1823)
G. Weissbart, Streifengnu   F. Le Gnou bleu   A. Blouwildebees
S. Nyumbu ya montu

Identification. About cattle-sized. Head large, muzzle broad, neck short, legs slender, tail with long tassel reaching heel, back sloping, nostrils large, ears lancet-shaped, horns in both sexes, at base horizontal or somewhat depressed laterally, then curved outwards, inwards and slightly backwards, basally broad and rough. Body with vertical stripes, broader dark, narrower light, thicker from neck to front of body, fading out towards rump. Short hair pads on forehead, back of nose. Long manes on lower neck, nape to shoulders, hair long on shoulders mostly hanging. Body colour striped dark slatey-greyish blue (ssp. *taurinus*), or brownish-grey (*johnstoni*), or greyish-red (*cooksoni*), or light greyish-brown (*albojubatus*), the narrow stripes darker. Forehead and back of nose blackish-brown, in *johnstoni* with whitish transverse bands, in *mearnsi* upper forehead greyish-white. Chin blackish-brown. Lower neck mane blackish-brown (*taurinus, johnstoni*) or whitish-grey (*albojubatus*) or greyish-black grizzled (*mearnsi*). Neck mane brownish-black to black (*taurinus, johnstoni*) or greyish mixture (*albojubatus*). Tail tuft black to brownish-black. Occasional albinos. Calf brownish-yellow, underside whitish, front of face, back of ears neck mane and connected dorsal stripe as well as tail tip brownish-black to black. Adult colour at 2–2½ months. Hoofs pointed, lateral hoofs large. Preorbital and forefoot scent glands present. 2 teats. MEASUREMENTS: HB ♂ 180–240, ♀ 170–230, TL ♂ 65–100,

♀ 60–90, Ht ♂ 125–145, ♀ 115–142, Wt ♂ 165–290, ♀ 140–260; ♂ about ⅕ larger and heavier than ♀. H in ♂ up to 83, ♀ *c.* 30–40.

Distribution. E., S. and S.W. Africa; S. Kenya between Mara and Athi rivers, N. and S. Tanzania, S.W. Zambia, Mozambique, S. Malawi, S. and W. Rhodesia, Botswana, S. and S.E. Angola, N. and mid-S.W. Africa, N. Cape Province, N. Orange Free State, N. Natal and Transvaal. Extinct in Malawi and Union of S. Africa (except extreme N. of latter), in latter reintroduced in National Parks and game reserves. 5 ssp.: (1). Eastern Wildebeeste (*albojubatus*), S. Kenya and bordering N.E. Tanzania east of Rift Valley, S. to 5°S. (2). Western W. (*mearnsi*), N.W. Tanzania and S. Kenya west of Rift Valley to Lake Victoria region. (3). White-banded W. (*johnstoni*), S. Tanzania, S. Malawi (extinct) and Mozambique N. of Zambia. (4). Northern W. (*cooksoni*), E. Zambia (Luangwa Valley). (5). Southern W. (*taurinus*), general species region S. and W. of Zambesi, Union of S. Africa, Botswana, S.W. Africa and S. Angola (see above). A breeding herd established in S. Russia (Askania Nova) in 1910 (not capable of domestication). HABITAT: open grass and bush savannah in plains and hills, also at times in light woodland areas. TERRITORY: territorial where food and water sufficient. Old ♂♂ occupy territories of from 10–20 hectares with generally 6–10 (up to 30) ♀♀ with their young, and may remain there, circumstances permitting, for some years. Troops of young ♂♂ and ♂♂ without territories remain on the borders. Marking by voice and occupation; the centre used for stamping, scraping head stretching, head to tail striking, digging ground, rubbing face, prancing; has regular latrines and watch points. Occupied grounds may be marked by bare depressions often under isolated trees, whose trunks are marked by facial gland secretions. Intruding neighbours are threatened by standing broadside, caperings and head shaking; fighting (on knees with horn bases) and chasing rivals. Neighbouring territory occupiers practise a regular challenge ceremonial on the borderline. Where short grass plains and acacia thorn savannahs adjoin, wildebeeste favour the first during the rains, the latter in the dry season. At the beginning of the dry season usually a gathering of harem troops on the remaining pastures: after these are grazed off join up in large herds in further wanderings. With first rains and the abundant fresh grass, the herds split up again into troops and old ♂♂ establish territories. In the Serengeti-Mara plains of E. Africa enormous herds (up to 400,000) wander after the rains. At each halt the old bulls establish at once with much quarrelling closely adjoining small territories in which they try to enclose passing ♀♀. *Map* p. 89.

Habits. DAILY RHYTHM: active morning and afternoon, in midday heat rest, if possible in shade. When sky cloudy also active at noon, as also on moonlit nights. Normal gait ambling. TOILET: scratch body with horns, frequently with hind hoofs, rolling, face rubbing against ground, tree trunk or partner. VOICE: snorts when alarmed, sometimes stamping at same time, grunts when angry, ♀ lows, calves bleat; on territory may repeat a sharp metallic call, in morning, evening and also by night, in rutting season doubled or trebled, often ending with high squeal; ♀ calls like ♂ without the final squeal. Ssp. *albojubatus* the most vocal, others less noisy. SENSES: sight and hearing excellent, scent good. ENEMIES: lion, leopard, cheetah, spotted hyaena, wild dog; for calves newly born, black-backed jackal. On Serengeti-Mara Plains about 16% of deaths accidental (drowning, broken limbs, trampling) about 37% by predators (lion's share about 90%) and about 47% through disease (especially rinderpest in 6-month-old animals). When disturbed will form defensive circle or semi-circle, snorting, capering and brief fighting. In flight may gallop off in single file with head low, tail waving. When cornered will defend itself courageously. FOOD: close grazer, of up to 10cm, therefore the renewal of long grass by burning important.

Usually drinks morning and evening, though can do without 2–3 sometimes 5 days. SOCIABILITY: according to district and season varies from locally static harem and ♂ troops to migrating herds (see TERRITORY).

Reproduction. Gestation 8–8½ months. Calving season in Kenya and N. Tanzania Nov–Dec to Feb–Mar (peak Jan–Feb), in Zambia Aug–Nov (peak Sep–Oct), in Rhodesia Nov–Jan, in E. Transvaal Nov–Dec, in Botswana Sep–Nov (in the Kalahari following abnormal rains also Mar–Apr), in S.W. Africa Sep–Nov. 1 active young. In large herds calving in groups of 20 or more about the same time, the other ♀♀ chasing away jackals and solitary hyaenas. The ♀♀ do not (as in smaller groups) consume the foetal envelopes and afterbirth, which are consumed by the jackals, hyaenas and vultures. ♀ licks calf dry as it scrambles out of the foetal envelope; it stands within 3–5 minutes; follows mother closely. In large herds 80% of births within 2–3 weeks, calf losses about 15%; in small herds, on the contrary, loss of up to 50% of calves through predation and separation from their mother in herd confusion. Suckling period to 4 months occasionally up to 1 year, first solid food at 10–12 days. Wt at birth, ♂ c. 18, ♀ c. 14; Ht at birth ♂ c. 80, ♀ c. 73, at 1 year ♂ and ♀ c. 95, at 2 years ♂ c. 150, ♀ c. 120, at 3 years ♂ c. 190, ♀ c. 145, at 5 years ♂ c. 225, ♀ c. 160; horns at first straight, begin to curve in ½ year. Young ♀ lives with mother, young ♂♂ driven out of harem at 1 year, go into ♂ troops, fight for territory at 4–5 years, is only then capable of mating. SEXUAL MATURITY: young ♀♀ may mate at 1¼–1½ years, more often at 2¼ years and then up to 12 years of age produces annually 1 calf. Sex ratio at birth ♂:♀ 1:1–1.7, adults, 1:1–0.7. LONGEVITY: in wild state up to 18, in captivity up to 20 years.

WHITE-TAILED GNU, BLACK WILDEBEESTE, Pl. 15
Connochaetes gnou (Zimmermann, 1780)
G. Weisschwanzgnu   F. Le Gnou à queue blanche   A. Swartwildebees

Identification. Approximate size of Red Deer. Form as Blue Wildebeeste (p. 84) but back straight. Horns in both sexes, at first grow forward and downward then turn sharply upward, broad flat based. Pelage with wavy hair pattern (watered silk pattern). Back of nose, neck and shoulders with erect mane, in front forming a downward pointing forehead crest ridge below eyes. Chin and throat with shorter, breast with longer, manes. Body colour uniform dark brown (summer coat more brownish, winter coat more blackish), tail tassel whitish, neck mane hairs basally white, then brownish-black; facial and breast manes blackish-brown. Around eyes and mouth many individual white hairs. Calf pelage soft and somewhat woolly, longer on head and neck, light brownish-grey, lower muzzle, ear tips and upper part of short neck-mane brownish-black, legs and tail tufted. Adult colour acquired at 2–2½ months. Hoofs pointed, lateral hoofs large. Preorbital glands and front feet glands present. 2 teats. MEASUREMENTS: HB ♂ 185–220, ♀ 170–205, TL ♂ 90–100, ♀ 80–95, Ht ♂ 100–120, ♀ 90–105, Wt ♂ c. 180, ♀ c. 160; H ♂ up to 78, ♀ c. 45–60; ♂ about ⅕ larger and heavier than ♀.

Distribution. Formerly the high veld plains of Cape Province, S.W. Transvaal and W. Natal. S. border between 32° and 33°S. about along the line Beaufort-Bedford, north to Griqualand West, N.E. to the Vaal River. Extinct as a wild animal, still living as half wild animals on some large farms (particularly the De Beers Company farm in Griqualand West). From there reintroduced to reserves within former range and in N.E. also beyond. Also bred in various world zoos. Population at present over 3,500. No ssp. HABITAT: open grass and bush veld in plains and hills, also in the Karroo country. TERRITORY: adult ♂♂ occupy territories about 150–500m apart all the year, with usually 5–10 (up to 30) ♀♀ with young. Troops of young ♂♂ and ♂♂ without territories on the fringes. Occupied points in territory and their uses, as well as acoustic marking, ceremonial challenging, threats and fighting as in Blue Wildebeeste. Watch points are also used by ♀♀ and young for defecation and rolling.

Habits. DAILY RHYTHM: and TOILET: as Blue Wildebeeste (p. 84), as is ambling gait. VOICE: snorting and tail sideways waving with stamping when disturbed. Tail slapping produces a hissing sound that can be heard nearly ½km distant. Grunts when angry, ♀ lows, calf bleats. Basic sound in relation to threatening associates a 'mooing' becoming a loud cry afterwards when in great danger. Marking call of territorial occupier (if rivals or young ♂♂ are ejected) a disyllabic high-low (ge-nu) with head shaking. The first syllable carries a long distance. SENSES: as Blue Wildebeeste. ENEMIES: as Blue Wildebeeste though apart from jackal all of these once numerous large predators wholly or nearly extinct. Behaviour when threatened as Blue Wildebeeste. FOOD: as Blue Wildebeeste. SOCIABILITY: Locally static, no large seasonal migrations. *Map* p. 89.

Reproduction. Rutting Feb–Mar. Gestation 8–8½ months. Calving Nov–Jan. 1 active young. Habits of mother and young and growth rate as Blue Wildebeeste. Wt at birth rather less than Blue Wildebeeste. SEXUAL MATURITY: some ♀♀ at 1½, but most at 2¼ years. ♂♂ at 3 years. Young ♂♂ at 4–5 years can acquire territories and mate only then. Sex ratio *c.* 1:1. LONGEVITY: in captivity up to 20 years.

IMPALAS, AEPYCEROTINAE

About size of Fallow Deer. Horns only in ♂, S-shaped, with rings. Ears medium length, pointed. Tail lightly bushy, reaching half-way to hocks. Hoofs slender, pointed, no lateral hoofs. Pelage short and smooth. No preorbital, inguinal or foot glands, metatarsal glands with black hair tufts; 4 teats. Skull with large oval vacuity between premaxilla and maxillary bones. Sociable in troops and herds in E. and S. African savannahs. 1 genus with 1 species.

IMPALA, *Aepyceros melampus* (Lichtenstein, 1812)   **Pl. 17**
G. Schwarzfersenantilope   F. Le Pallah   A. Rooibok   S. Swala pala

Identification. Medium sized, slender and elegant, straight-backed. Muzzle a small triangle between nostrils. Ears pointed, medium length. Horns only in ♂ (though some cases of long-horned ♀♀ have been known), strongly lyre-shaped, curving back, sideways, then upwards, 16–26 strong ridges, terminal ¼ smooth. Tail average size but rather bushy, reaching about halfway to hocks. Hoofs narrow and pointed, no lateral hoofs, in their place small blackish-brown hair tufts. On hind legs large black hair tufts on metatarsal glands. On stern of ♂ a small bare glandular area with oily secretion. 4 teats. Coat short and smooth. Upperside of body and outside of legs brownish-yellow to light reddish-brown, lower edge of flanks lighter. Ends of ears, narrow dorsal stripe from middle of back to top of tail, a narrow vertical stripe on back of hindquarters, black. Front of metacarpals and metatarsal areas often with dark brown to blackish shadow stripe. Sometimes, or locally, crown or back of muzzle or all front of face dark or blackish-brown, in the ssp. *petersi* the latter is usual. Upper lip, chin, throat, breast, belly, inside of legs and underside of tail, white, as well as line above eyes and axillary region. Hocks yellowish-white to white, horns and hoofs brownish-black to black. Young lighter, edges of ears, thighs, dorsal line and metatarsal tufts only dark brown. MEASUREMENTS: HB ♂ 125–160, ♀ 120–150, TL ♂ 30–45, ♀ 30–40, Ht ♂

80–95, ♀ 75–90, Wt ♂ 45–80, ♀ 40–60; H to 91; ♂ about ¼ larger and heavier than ♀ (except in ssp. *petersi*, where ♂♂ only heavier but not larger).

Distribution. Ruanda, N.E. Uganda, N.W., Mid and S. Kenya, Tanzania, S.E. Zaire, Zambia, Mid and S. Malawi, Rhodesia, Mozambique, N. Natal, Transvaal, N. Cape Province (south to Kuruman), E. and N. Botswana, Caprivi Strip, Ovamboland (S. to Etosha Pan), Kaokoveld, S. Angola northwards to Nova Lisboa. In some parts extinct as in northern S.W. Africa and N. Cape Province, still in Union of S. Africa in some localities S. of original distribution widely established and introduced into Orange Free State. In Transvaal and Natal additionally established widely both inside and outside the natural distribution. 6 ssp. described, however not clearly distinguishable except (1). Angola Impala (*petersi*), S.W. Angola and bordering region of S.W. Africa to Etosha Pan, and (2). typical Impala (*melampus*) in rest of range.   HABITAT: parkland country, viz. light woodland with acacia thorns or dry savannahs (Miombo and Mopane woodland), gallery forest in plains and hills, edges of clearings preferred, nearby water essential.   TERRITORY: sedentary, area occupied by a herd 2.5–6 sq km but in dry season as food and water reduced, may wander more widely (usually 1–10km sometimes up to 20) to reach the nearest water and fresh grazing. In breeding season old ♂♂ establish territories of 0.2–0.9 sq km, which they mark by watch points (displaying a thickening of the neck), forehead rubbing on bushes and trees, dung hills (average up to 4m wide, 8cm high), bellowing and grunting. No ♂♂ more than ½ year old tolerated, and several ♀♀ (with young) forming the harem. In E. Africa, with 2 rainy seasons, there is nearly always sufficient food and water, therefore pairing and calving not limited. Territory occupied as long as herd stops in the neighbourhood. In Mid and S. Africa, with only 1 rainy season, territory usually only held in the 8–10-week breeding season.

Habits. DAILY RHYTHM: main grazing period early morning and late afternoon; rest periods midday and at night. ♂♂ holding territory graze little by day, rather at night when ♀♀ rest. During height of dry season when food is scanty old ♂♂ may give up territory to search for food.   TOILET: ♀ licks and nibbles coat of calf. Animals of the same sex engage in mutual grooming.   VOICE: old ♂♂ bellow and grunt in rutting time. Contact calls of mother and calf – soft call of mother, soft bleating of calf in reply; when lost the bleating is loud.   SENSES: sight not very good, hearing and scent very good.   ENEMIES: lion, leopard, cheetah, hunting dog, spotted hyaena and crocodile. For young calves also jackal, python and large eagles. Alarm cry loud snorting. In flight makes numerous high leaps (for orientation ?) up to 3m high and 10m long. In emergency leaps over 2½m high obstacles. All-out speed up to 60kph.   FOOD: short grass chief food in most areas (up to 95 %), also flowers, fruit and foliage of bushes and trees, and in Okavango region browsing on bushes and trees seasonally predominant. Normally drink daily in morning and evening, though can satisfy need for water for some time with dew.   SOCIABILITY: sociable, troops of ½–2 dozen animals, or herds of 30–50, rarely 100–200 or more. Small troops more usual in rainy season, large mixed herds mostly in second half of dry season. The smaller bands mostly ♀♀ with young and 1 old ♂, larger bands also with several old ♂♂, each of which (at least in rut) maintains separate territory. Young ♂♂, and ♂♂ without territory, usually in separate troops (youth clubs), with older animals in charge. Like ♀♀ troops they roam freely through the area, though usually near ♀ troops. Latter often spend much time in ♂ territory in breeding season. When changing location they follow (in *petersi* precede) the old ♂ troop. Impalas often associate with other species of antelope (up to 16).

Reproduction. Gestation 6⅓–7 months. Rut in southern Africa Feb–Jun; in Natal Mar–May, in Transvaal and Botswana Apr–May, in Rhodesia May–Jun, in northern

S.W. Africa and S.W. Angola Jan–Mar, in Zambia Sep–Nov in E. Africa all the year round with 2 peaks, Feb–Apr, and Aug–Oct. In E. Africa calving all the year round with 2 peaks Aug–Nov and Mar–May; in S. Africa usually Oct–Dec with peak generally in Nov. 1 active young. ♀ calves in thick cover about noon, when predators not active, licks calf dry and eats afterbirth, moves off in $1\frac{1}{2}$ hours, if calf active enough rejoins herd, otherwise leaves calf for some days lying hidden (regionally differing), 1–14 days after calving mates again. Wt at birth ♂ c. 5–5.5, ♀ c. 4–4.5; sex ratio at birth ♂:♀ 1:1 to 1:1.5; in adults on average 1:2. Suckle for 4–6 months. Wt increment in ♂ and ♀ at 1 month 7, 4 months 11, 8 months 18, 10 months 27, 15 months 40; ♀ over 18 months 45, ♂ 20 months 50, 30 months 60, 36 months and older 65. Horns begin to grow at 2–3 months, at $\frac{1}{2}$ year c. 15, 1 year c. 25 and first ridge, beginning of curve; at $1\frac{1}{2}$ years c. 30 and beginning of typical shape, at 2 years c. 50 and 9–13 ridges, at $2\frac{1}{2}$ years fully developed, from then on only length increases. Young ♂ ♂, at $\frac{1}{2}$ year in E. Africa, at $1\frac{1}{4}$ years in S. Africa, are turned out of adult troops and eventually join up with the 'youth clubs'. SEXUAL MATURITY: in both sexes usually about $1\frac{1}{2}$ years, in ♀ sometimes earlier, though earliest at 1 year. ♂ first comes in rut, if strong enough at $4\frac{1}{2}$–$6\frac{1}{2}$ years to hold territory. LONGEVITY: in wild state up to 12, in captivity up to 15 years.

1 Blue Wildebeeste
2 White-tailed Gnu

1 Impala
2 Soemmering's Gazelle

1 Grant's Gazelle
2 Dama Gazelle

GAZELLES, GAZELLINAE

Size variable, from water deer to llama-sized. Body slender and graceful. Horns sometimes only in ♂, partly also in ♀ (when however weaker), medium to long, thin to thick, smooth or ringed or twisted along axis, straight, or lyre- or S-shaped, or hooked. Muzzle absent or small and naked. Ears narrow, pointed or broad lancet shaped, short to medium length. Tail short to long, usually short-haired with terminal tassel. Inner hoofs narrow, pointed; lateral hoofs very small and flat to robust, pointed and of middle length, or short and broad. Skin glands such as preorbital, metacarpal, pedal, dorsal, unguinal or preputial. 2 or 4 teats. Coat short and smooth, only *Antidorcas* with dorsal gland and crest. In desert, semi-desert, grass, bush or woodland savannahs, or lightly to thickly bushy, or mountain forest from plains to mountain highlands. In Africa, Arabia, Near East, Middle and E. Asia. 6 genera with altogether 16 species, of which 4 genera with 12 species in Africa.

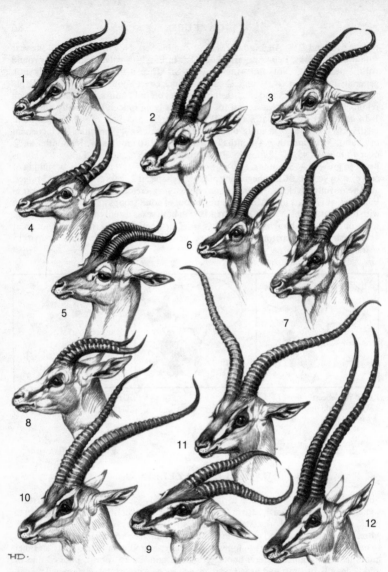

Gazelle horns. 1 Dorcas Gazelle, *Gazella dorcas*. 2 Thomson's Gazelle, *Gazella thomsoni*. 3 Heughlin's Gazelle, *Gazella rufifrons tilonura*. 4 Dibatag, *Ammodorcas clarkei*. 5 Gerenuk, *Litocranius walleri*. 6 Loder's Gazelle, *Gazella leptoceros*. 7 Springbuck, *Antidorcas marsupialis*. 8 Dama Gazelle, *Gazella dama*. 9 Soemmering's Gazelle, *Gazella soemmeringi*. 10 Typical Grant's Gazelle, *Gazella granti granti*. 11 Roberts Gazelle, *Gazella granti robertsi*. 12 Raineys Gazelle, *Gazella granti raineyi*.

SOEMMERING'S GAZELLE, *Gazella soemmeringi* (Cretzschmar, 1826) **Pl. 17**
G. Sömmeringgazelle   F. La Gazelle de Soemmering

Identification. ♂ with lyre-shaped horns, lying flat back and outwards, tips usually sharply turned outward and inward, lower ⅔ with 15–22 high ridges. Much variation (outward curving weak to strong, tips curved inward or outward or backwards). ♀ horns thinner, shorter, narrow, with little outward curve and with flatter ridges. Small naked muzzle between nostrils. Preorbital gland opening small, on naked area. Ears middle length, lancet shaped. Pelage short and smooth, tail with smaller, blacker upperside and tassel. Inner hoofs narrow and pointed, lateral hoofs short and broad. Preorbital, pedal, inguinal and metacarpal glands present (latter always recognised by white to roe-brown hair tuft). 2 teats. Upperside (crown, underpart of cheeks, neck, shoulders, back, flanks, thighs and outside of legs) pale to dark isabelline or light cinnamon to maize yellow, in S. Ethiopia narrow black stripe on posterior edge of thigh and distinct dark flank bank. Underside (lips, chin, underside of neck, front of breast, breast, belly, inside of legs), pygal area, tail apart from tip, white. Lower part of chin with sandy transverse band. Upper edge of stern patch straight, lateral edges projecting into the brown rump. Ears white outside, tips and edges dark. Back of nose and forehead blackish-brown (in central Ethiopia only the front of nose). Within the dark facial pattern whitish or whitish-yellow supraorbital stripe from horn bases to muzzle, separating the outer edge of mask from the dark eyestripe. Upper cheeks whitish grey, muzzle grey. MEASUREMENTS: HB 125–150, TL 18–28, Ht 85–92, Wt 35–45; H ♂ up to 58, ♀ up to 40. ♂ somewhat larger and heavier than ♀.

Distribution. From E. Nubia between Nile at Berber and Red Sea at Suakin, and Sennaar southward through E. Ethiopia (as far as S.E. border) Eritrea and Somalia (to S. border). In S. Somalia probably extinct. 6 ssp. described though only 3 distinguishable: (1). Sudanese S.G. (*soemmeringi*), facial pattern more brown than blackish-brown and horns shorter than in (2). (2). Somali S.G. (*berberana*). (3). S. Ethiopian S.G. (*butteri*), with narrow dark stripe on hind edge of thigh and distinct flank band.   HABITAT: open bush savannahs with acacia and light bush and thinly wooded grass steppes, in plains up to 1800m not in true mountain and hill country. In Sudan seasonal migration, in Mar–Apr from S. Nubia (between Rahat and Atbara rivers) northward, returning in Sep–Oct.   TERRITORY: old ♂ is in rutting season territorial, establishing a zone from which with vigorous threats and attacks rivals and young ♂♂ are driven, and in which ♀♀ are herded, and breeding takes place. Territory marked by dung heaps at fixed points, and by displaying (with horn presentation, craning of neck, head etc.), and scraping of ground, beating bushes (scraping also a displacement activity, on ground or bushes). Preorbital glands not used in marking. Whether territory is held after rutting is not known. Troops and herds usually all year in favourite localities, though details not known. *Map p. 89.*

Habits. DAILY RHYTHM: main grazing periods early morning and late afternoon. TOILET: licking, nibbling and scratching with hind feet of head, neck and breast, latter through the front legs. Cleans shoulders and withers by wiping with cheeks and horns. When resting may rub head and neck on ground. Repels insect pests by hoof and tail action, head shaking, ear flicking and twitching of skin. Mutual licking and nibbling as a contact activity among family. VOICE: nasal snoring as ♂ threat and driving sound. Loud bleating as cry of fear. Herd contact and alarm sounds not yet described. SENSES: sight and hearing very good, scent good enough. ENEMIES: cheetah, hunting dog, lion, leopard, and for young calves also hyaena, jackal, serval, caracal, ratel, python and eagles. When agitated and as warning reaction, snorting, stamping, skin shivering and bouncing leaps with head held high. ♀ with young calf will attack smaller predators up to jackal size, sometimes with another ♀. If possible, in danger also will lead the young to another hiding place. FOOD: mainly grass and leaves. Not known if it drinks daily. In very dry habitats can go a long time without open water. Salt or mineral licks are sought out. SOCIABILITY: in small family troops of 3–10 animals, but also in bands of 10–50 or herds of 50–150 or more, occasionally all ♂ or all ♀ (with young) troops or herds. The basic unit appears to be a troop of ♀ ♀ with young, guarded by a nearby adult ♂ who also keeps them together at rutting time. Often associate with oryx, topi, zebras etc.

Reproduction. Breeding season Sep–Nov. Old ♂ guards borders of occupied range (see TERRITORY). Mating is very quick, ♂ nearly upright on hind legs, forelegs angled, barely contacting ♀. Gestation 198–199 days. Wt at birth 3.5–4.5. Calving season Apr–May. 1 active young. ♀ lies up apart, licks young dry and eats afterbirth. Young lies up for a long time, ♀ comes to it 3–4 times a day, attracts it with a light call and repeatedly lowering its head to the hiding place, suckles and licks the calf, clearing up its excreta. Strange calves are not accepted. First solid food at 1 month, suckles for $\frac{1}{2}$ year. SEXUAL MATURITY: about $1\frac{1}{2}$ years. LONGEVITY: up to 14 years recorded.

GRANT'S GAZELLE, *Gazella granti* (Brook, 1872)   **Pl. 17**
G. Grantgazelle   F. La Gazelle de Grant   S. Swala granti
Identification. ♂ horns long and lyre-shaped, forming a weak S backwards and upwards, tips usually curving forward a little, oval in section at base, 20–30 rings. Tips smooth (in *robertsi* the wide-horned G.G. of N.W. Tanzania, first third of horn length bent nearly horizontally sideways, tips turned sideways, long axis rather twisted). ♀ horns similar but shorter, weaker ridges, smaller and fewer (15–20) and basal section roundish. Small naked muzzle between nostrils. Preorbital gland orifice small, in naked area. Ears of medium length, lancet-shaped. Coat short and smooth. Tail with small black tassel on upperside. Inner hoofs narrow, pointed, lateral hoofs short and broad. Preorbital, pedal and metacarpal glands present (latter indicated by white to brownish hair tufts), inguinal glands apparently absent, 2 teats. Upperside: cheeks, crown, neck, back, shoulders, front of thighs and outside of legs, isabelline to reddish-brown (in the Lorigi G.G. *notata*, west of Mt Kenya, dark brown croup). Underside: throat, breast, inside of legs, back of thighs, with pygal area and tail (less tassel), white. Thigh stripe light brown to black, short (then only in upper part) or long, sometimes absent. Flank band in young and ♀ ♀ pale to dark brown, disappears in ♀ between 2nd and 5th year, in ♂ between 1st and 2nd year (except in *notata*, when well marked). Upper edge of pygal area straight, at sides a strip projecting into the brown croup. In the Serengeti G.G. (Serengeti-Mara plains) a narrow and in Peters G. (*petersi* S.E. Kenya) a broader band of the croup brown reaching root of tail. Outside of ear tips dark brown, forehead and back of nose reddish-brown. Nose with brown to black triangular spot (tip above). Whitish supraorbital stripe from base of horns to muzzle. MEASUREMENTS: HB ♂ 130–150, ♀ 95–110, TL ♂ 25–35, ♀ 25–30, Ht ♂ 85–95, ♀ 80–85, Wt ♂ 55–80, ♀ 35–50; H ♂ 50–80, ♀ 30–43.
Distribution. From mid-Tanzania to Ugogo northward to S. Ethiopia and S.W. Somalia to Juba River, west to Lake Victoria, Lado Enclave and Karamoja districts of L. Rudolf, east to coast. 9 ssp. have been described though only *notata*, *petersi*, *robertsi* and *serengetae* (see above) are recognisable. HABITAT: open grass plain (in northern part of range also semi-desert) to loosely or thickly bushy savannahs in level or hilly districts; fond of grassy plain with large stands of bush and woodland (so-called Mbugas), never in high grass. TERRITORY: where grazing is good remain locally in large areas. In bush country old ♂ ♂ establish territory for several (up to 8) months,

of average size from $\frac{1}{2}$ to 1km, and there herd together 10–25 ♀♀ (5–45) seeking out and mating with those in rut, and driving off rivals. In open steppe inhabit area of about 5km on average, therein from time to time smaller or larger troops (harems, 'youth clubs', ♀ troops) or larger herds of 40–400 animals loosely in slowly wandering troops. Old ♂♂ establish territories of from $\frac{1}{2}$–1km on average, collecting, pairing and mating with passing ♀♀, chase other ♂♂ only out of the vicinity of ♀♀. In the transitional zone between steppe and savannah the inhabited area and herd size smaller (30–120 animals). In the dry season, particularly in N. of range, widespread wanderings of the groups. ♂ marks territory as in Soemmering's Gazelle (p. 91). *Map* p. 89.

Habits. DAILY RHYTHM and TOILET: as Soemmering's Gazelle (p. 91). VOICE: nasal bleat as threat, and driving call of ♂. Soft 'whoof' as ♀ call to young. Young bleating when straying. Cry of terror, loud bleat. Loud nasal grunts as alarm note. SENSES, ENEMIES: as Soemmering's Gazelle (p. 91). Also baboon as predator on young calves. FOOD: mainly leaves and grass according to habitat, normally does not drink, liquid needs obtained in food, hence not dependent on open water. SOCIABILITY: basic unit a troop of 1–3 dozen ♀♀ with young with 1 old ♂, besides 'youth clubs' and ♀♀ troops with young calves. According to habitat and season smaller or larger associations (see TERRITORY).

Reproduction. Breeding and calving times seasonally, not firmly fixed. Mating very quick, ♂ standing up with forelegs hanging; gestation, number of young, calving, rearing and development and SEXUAL MATURITY: as Soemmering's Gazelle (p. 92). Wt at birth ♂ 5.4–7.3, ♀ 5–5.5. LONGEVITY: could well be at least 12 years; in captivity recorded up to $8\frac{3}{4}$ years.

DAMA GAZELLE, ADDRA GAZELLE, *Gazella dama* (Pallas, 1766) **Pl. 17**
G. Damagazelle   F. La Gazelle Dama

Identification. ♂ horns lyre-shaped, flattish and curving strongly backwards, tips turn upwards, sometimes curved again forwards, section at base round to oval, 18–23 rings, end smooth. ♀ similar, but shorter, thinner and rings flatter. Narrow naked muzzle between nostrils. Small preorbital gland orifice on naked area. Ear medium length, lancet-shaped. Preorbital, pedal, metacarpal and inguinal glands present. 2 teats. Metacarpal glands indicated by small hair tufts. Coat short and smooth. Upperside of tail with weak tuft. Coat colour varies according to age, season or locality. 3 main stages: **1.** Dark form (*mhorr*): upperside of body and tail tuft brownish-yellow, underside, with supraorbital stripe and cheeks, white to whitish-yellow or whitish-red, pygal area upper edge laterally with projection into the brown croup, forehead and stripe from eye to muzzle blackish-brown to black. **2.** Light form (*ruficollis*): only neck (apart from round spot in front) light reddish-brown, forehead, back, fetlocks and front of forelegs from metacarpals upwards, light yellowish-brown, rest of body white. **3.** Intermediate form: in general colouring between 1 and 2. White of pygal area extends forward to front of croup, the brown of thigh only a narrow band. MEASUREMENTS: HB 140–165, TL 25–35, Ht 90–120, Wt 40–75, H 20–43.

Distribution. Whole of Sudan geographical zone from S. Morocco to Rio de Oro to north bank of Senegal R. and from Senegal (12°W) eastward through S. Sahara (in rainy season) northward to S. Hoggar, 22°N, and Sudan (political) to west bank of White Nile (Dongola, Kordofan). In Admer Plains S. of Tassili-Adjer absent, however was present in Air, Mouydir Plateau and Ahnet. South border partly to 12°N. In Morocco, Rio de Oro, Dongola, Darfur, practically extinct, in and from Senegambia in the Sahelian zone eastward threatened by man and greatly endangered by the latest catastrophic drought. Only still common in E. Chad. 9 ssp. described. Regarding the colour variations mentioned above, the descriptions are based on quite inadequate data. The only certainty is the transition from the north-western dark form (Moroccan Dama, *mhorr*) to the south-eastern pale form (Nubian or Red-necked Dama Gazelle, political Sudan, *ruficollis*). HABITAT: open bush or grass, semi-deserts and deserts. Seasonal wanderings at rainy season from Sudan (geographic) further northward into the Sahara, coming back to the south in dry season. TERRITORY: not known. *Map* p. 89.

Habits. DAILY RHYTHM: main grazing time early morning and late afternoon. TOILET: probably as in Soemmering's and Grant's Gazelles, though details not known. VOICE: not known. SENSES: sight, hearing and scent very good. FOOD: leaves of acacia and bushes, grass and foliage, often standing on hind legs to reach foliage. Drinks water, though may exist for long periods without open water. SOCIABILITY: small troops of $\frac{1}{2}$–2 dozen animals, usually several ♀♀ and young with 1 old ♂, non-territorial ♂♂ in separate troops. In wandering herds may number up to 500. Often in company of Dorcas Gazelles.

Reproduction. Pairing season in Sahara Mar–Jun, in Chad Apr–May, in Sudan (political) Oct–Nov. Gestation 198–199 days. 1 active young. Details of pairing, mating, calving, birth weight, rearing and development as well as SEXUAL MATURITY and LONGEVITY: not known, though probably resembling Soemmering's and Grant's Gazelles.

THOMSON'S GAZELLE, *Gazella thomsoni* (Gunther, 1884)   **Pl. 18**
G. Thomsongazelle   F. La Gazelle de Thomson   S. Swala tomi, Lala

Identification. ♂ horns lyre-shaped and weakly S-formed, curving back and up, tips curved upwards and inwards, basal section a thin oval, 15–18 rings, tips smooth. ♀ horns much weaker, only pencil thick, steep, widely separated, and nearly parallel, only tips slightly curved outward, usually not ringed, smooth, often dissimilar or crooked, or crossed or broken off on one or both sides, or wholly absent. Narrow naked muzzle between nostrils. Preorbital gland a vertical slit. Ears medium length, lancet-shaped. Coat short and smooth, under $\frac{2}{3}$ of tail has black tuft lengthening towards its tip. Inner hoofs narrow, pointed, lateral hoofs short and broad. Preorbital, pedal and metacarpal glands (latter indicated by hair tufts); no inguinal glands. 2 teats. Upperside (cheeks, neck, back, flanks, shoulders, thighs, outside of legs) light brown, flanks lighter with a broad flank band below as well as the narrow pygal stripe brown to black; underside (throat, breast, belly, inside of legs) white. Forehead and back of nose brown, blackish-brown spot on lower part of nose, forehead sometimes mixed with white, in the Mongalla-Thomson Gazelle (ssp. *albonotata* S. Sudan) with whitish spot. Whitish eye stripe from base of horns to muzzle, brownish-black stripe from front corner of eye to corner of mouth. MEASUREMENTS: HB ♂ 90–110, ♀ 80–105, TL ♂ 20–27, ♀ 19–26, Ht ♂ 60–65, ♀ 55–62, Wt ♂ 20–30, ♀ 15–22, H ♂ 25–43, ♀ 7–15: ♂ rather larger and heavier than ♀.

Distribution. From S. Sudan (Mongalla Province), N. border about 7°N. and N. Kenya (Lake Rudolf region) southwards to N. Tanzania, S. border *c.* 5°S, E. border about 38°E. Of the 15 described sub-species only 3 accepted, and only the Mongalla T.G. *albonotata* externally easily recognisable by the white forehead spot and inwardly curving horn tips. HABITAT: open short grass plains and only thin bush steppe regions in plains or hills up to 2000m. TERRITORY: old ♂ is territorial outside the migration season, holds an area of about 100–300m on average; guarded against rivals and young ♂♂ by threats and attacks, and in which ♀♀ are herded and mated. Marked by droppings and urination on particular spots, scraping of ground and nearby growth (usually a ritualised weaving). See Soemmering's Gazelle (p. 91) smearing plants and ♂ horns with preorbital gland secretion, and displaying by leaping, horn presentation, raising head high etc. *Map* p. 97.

Habits. DAILY RHYTHM: main feeding periods early morning and late afternoon. TOILET: see Soemmering's Gazelle (p. 91). VOICE: weak nasal contact call (mother–calf), nasal throat sound, a nasal, rather softer driving sound by ♂ 'whoof', loud bleating in terror. SENSES: sight, hearing and scent good. ENEMIES: cheetah, lion, leopard, hunting dog, spotted hyaena, serval, and for calves also jackal, ratel, baboon, eagle and python. When agitated, as warning signal stamps, skin shivering, tail waving and bouncing leaps with head high. FOOD: short grass (80–90%), sometimes foliage. When soft food sufficient, drinking not necessary, but where grazing is dry daily drinking necessary. SOCIABILITY: different groupings, open, loose and varying numerically in often changing bands. Harems (1 old ♂ with 5–65 ♀♀ and young), youth herds (5–500 ♂♂ without territories), mother groups (pregnant or freshly calved ♀♀). Where food is ample (as in the rains) sedentary, old ♂♂ hold territory (see TERRITORY) in dry season gather large herds, sometimes several thousands and roam around, mix with Grant's Gazelles, wildebeestes and zebras.

Reproduction. No fixed season, births throughout the year, though peak towards end of rainy season, in Serengeta-Mara region (N.W. Tanzania) Jan–Mar and Jun–Jul, in Sanya Plain (mid N. Tanzania), in central Kenya Nov–Apr. Mating; see Grant's Gazelle (p. 92). Gestation 187–188 days. 1 active young. Wt at birth 2.2–3. Birth, rearing and development of young see Soemmering's Gazelle (p. 92). 2 young a year possible. Sex ratio in young 1:1, in adults ♀♀ more numerous. SEXUAL MATURITY: ♀ 1, ♂ 1½ years. ♂ mates first after holding territory (at earliest at 2 years). LONGEVITY: 10½ years recorded.

SPEKE'S GAZELLE, *Gazella spekei* (Blyth, 1863)   Pl. 18
G. Spekegazelle   F. La Gazelle de Speke

Identification. ♂ horns strongly S-shaped backwards, tips curving upwards, not diverging strongly, outsides flatter than inside; 15–20 strong rings, terminal ¼ smooth. ♀ horns thinner, less S-shaped, therefore more erect and with only 10–12 weak rings. Muzzle, ears, hoofs, skin glands, teats and tail as in Thomson's Gazelle (see p. 94) though inguinal glands present and coat longer (up to 5cm). Back of nose above muzzle with 3–5 half tennis-ball sized inflatable skin protuberances. Upperside (cheeks, neck, shoulders, back, thighs, outside of legs) light brown, flank band dark brown, the brown of hind edge of thigh rather or markedly (in ♀) darker; underside (chin, breast, belly inside of legs) and back of thighs white. Back of nose greyish-brown, with black spot behind the swelling. A whitish supraorbital stripe from base of horns to muzzle, and from front corner of eye towards the corner of mouth a darker cheek band, black near the eye, from front to back dark and light brown, paling in ♂, in ♀ uniform. MEASUREMENTS: HB 95–105, TL 15–20, Ht 50–60, Wt 15–25; H ♂ 25–31, ♀ 15–25.

Distribution. Ogaden (E. Ethiopia) and Somalia, plateau south of Gulf of Aden behind Gulis Range, from there eastward to end of plateau near Indian Ocean and S. through Ogaden to Mogadiscio and Brava. No ssp. HABITAT: stony bush and grassy steppes and semi-deserts up to 2000m. TERRITORY: old ♂♂ probably territorial, details not known. *Map* p. 97.

Habits. DAILY RHYTHM: most activity early morning and late afternoon. TOILET: like Soemmering's Gazelle (p. 91) details unknown. VOICE: a loud alarm sound produced by expulsion of air from the inflated nasal sac. Other sounds not known. SENSES: sight, hearing and scent good to very good. ENEMIES: lion, cheetah, leopard, caracal, hyaena, and for fawns also kaffir cat, ratel, jackal, python and eagles. Behaviour in excitement, or in warning see Thomson's Gazelle (p. 95). FOOD: grass, herbage, foliage of bushes; water requirements not known and probably slight. SOCIABILITY: family parties of 5–10 or sometimes 20 animals; usually 1 old ♂ with ♀♀ and young. Further details not known.

Reproduction. Gestation c. 7 months, no other details known. LONGEVITY: not known.

DORCAS GAZELLE, *Gazella dorcas* (Linnaeus, 1758)   **Pl. 18**
G. Dorkasgazelle   F. La Gazelle dorcas

Identification. ♂ horns lyre-shaped, curving first backwards then upwards. Tips somewhat hooked up and inward, sometimes (especially in young ♂) strongly curved inwards, basal section narrow oval, 18–28 rings, terminal ⅓ smooth. ♀ horns shorter, thinner, rounder, more upright and straighter with few and weak ridges. Nostrils, ears, hoofs, skin glands, teats and arrangement of tail hair as in Thomson's Gazelle (p. 94) though inguinal glands present. Upperside (cheeks, crown, neck, back, shoulders, flanks, thighs, outer side of legs) pale light brown to strong reddish-brown, flanks lighter, lower edge generally with a brown to sepia flank band, and stripe on back of thighs brown to blackish-brown; underside (chin, breast, belly, inside of legs, back of thighs) white. Top of nose and forehead reddish-brown, sometimes a dark nose spot above muzzle. Whitish supraorbital stripe from base of horns to near muzzle. Blackish-brown stripe from front corner of eye to near corner of mouth. Summer coat pale with only weak flank band, winter coat darker with well marked flank band. MEASUREMENTS: HB 90–110, TL 15–20, Ht 55–65, Wt 15–20; H ♂ 25–38, ♀ 15–25.

Distribution. N. Africa between Atlantic, Mediterranean and Red Sea, S. to Senegambia, Chad, Darfur, Kordofan and N. Ethiopia (14°–12°N); in addition to Sinai, Palestine, Syria, Iraq and Arabia. 8 ssp. within the distribution. In the greater part of the range, above all in the Atlas country, Arabia and Near East, largely exterminated. Recently the following species have been considered to be ssp. of the Dorcas Gazelle: Pelzeln's Gazelle (*G. pelzelni*, N. Somalia, no ssp.) and the 3 ssp. of the typical Gazelle, *G. gazella*, in Near East, Baluchistan gazelle (*fuscifrons*, E. Iran, S. Afghanistan, Baluchistan). Indian Gazelle (*bennetti*, Upper India from Sind to Nepal and S. to c. 16°N), and Salt Range Gazelle (*monssalis*, Salt Range, Kashmir). HABITAT: Sahel savannahs, semi-deserts and deserts with scanty vegetation – grass, herbage, bushes. Prefers stony deserts (also with rock piles, erosion gullies) to sands, in the latter more at the edge where dune valleys have plant growth. TERRITORY: as in Thomson's Gazelle (p. 94), size of area however not known.

Habits. DAILY RHYTHM: main grazing periods early morning and late afternoon. Where persecuted (and on clear nights also) nocturnally active. TOILET: see Soemmering's Gazelle (p. 91). VOICE: contact calls, annoyed call a long growling 'rooo', threat and drive call of ♂, short nasal 'ro', terror cry loud resounding bleating. SENSES: sight, hearing, scent all good to very good. ENEMIES: cheetah, lion, leopard (these three largely exterminated throughout the range of the species) serval, caracal, hyaena; for fawns also kaffir cat, ratel, jackal and eagles. Agitation and warning signals as Thomson's Gazelle (p. 95). FOOD: grass, herbage, foliage of bushes, in dry season mainly latter. Needs little water, mostly supplied by food (leaves, succulents) as well as dew. SOCIABILITY: mostly in pairs in deserts, but where grazing good in family parties of 1 adult ♂ and several ♀♀ with young (5–12 animals) or in herds of 30–40. During seasonal migration also in herds up to 100 animals. Also associate with Dama Gazelles and grazing Camels.

Reproduction. Breeding season Apr–May, or Nov–Dec. Calving season in Chad region Nov–Dec, in N. Africa Apr–May, in Egypt Feb–Apr and Sep–Oct. Gestation *c*. 6 months (169–181 days), 2 births possible in 1 year. 1 active young, ♀ mates again 1–14 days after giving birth. Wt at birth 1.3–1.7; birth, rearing and development of young as in Soemmering's Gazelle (p. 91). SEXUAL MATURITY: about $1\frac{1}{2}$–$1\frac{3}{4}$ years in both sexes. LONGEVITY: up to $12\frac{1}{2}$ years recorded.

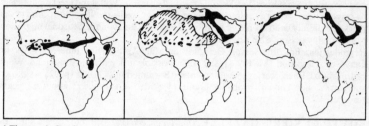

1 Thomson's Gazelle
2 Red-fronted Gazelle
3 Speke's Gazelle

Dorcas Gazelle

Edmi Gazelle

RED-FRONTED GAZELLE, *Gazella rufifrons* (Gray, 1846) Pl. 18
G. Rotstirngazelle F. La Gazelle à front roux

Identification. ♂ with horns weakly to strongly lyre-shaped, S-shaped backwards and forwards, tips curved upwards and inwards. Basal section round, 0–18 rings, terminal $\frac{1}{4}$ smooth. ♀ horns shorter, thinner, more upright, little curved, almost smooth, with not more than 13 weak rings, often dissimilar and crooked. Nostrils, ears, hoofs, scent glands, teats and tail structure as in Thomson's Gazelle (p. 94) though inguinal glands present, knee brushes (hair tufts on metacarpal glands) sometimes absent. Upperside (head, neck, shoulder, back, flanks, thighs, outside of legs) sandy to light-ochreous or reddish-brown (ssp. *rufina*), flanks rather lighter with lower edge with a brown (*kanuri*) to blackish-brown or black (*hasleri, rufina, tilonura*) band, 3–5cm broad (in old animals narrower than in young). *Hasleri* and *tilonura* with a further narrow band in same colour as flanks, below the dark band. Underside (chin, throat, breast, belly), sometimes fetlocks, also inside of legs and back of thighs white (latter brown in *tilonura*). Usually a darker nose spot above muzzle (in *hasleri* upper nasal area light brown) and usually a whitish supraorbital band from base of horns to muzzle (in *tilonura* only a whitish area round eyes), as well as a dark brown stripe from front of eyes to near corner of mouth. MEASUREMENTS: HB ♂ 110–120, ♀ 105–110, TL ♂ 19–25, ♀ 15–20, Ht ♂ 68–82, ♀ 65–70, Wt ♂ 25–35, ♀ 20–25; H ♂ 22–35, ♀ 15–25.
Distribution. The Sudan zone between 16° and 9°N from Senegambia to N. Eritrea, N. Ethiopia and N.E. Bahr el-Ghazal. 7 ssp., one of which, the Algerian Red-fronted or Red Gazelle (*rufina*, southwards of the Moroccan-Algerian borders, known only from 4 ♂, and no ♀, extinct, is considered by many authors to be a separate species): Nigerian Red (*hasleri*, N. Nigeria), Cameroun Red (*kanuri*, N. Cameroun to Lake Chad region), and Eritrean Red-fronted or Heuglin's Gazelle (*tilonura*, N. Eritrea, Meroe, Sennaar, N.E. Bahr-el-Ghazal, in S. part of range largely exterminated, was until recently considered a distinct species). HABITAT: grassy and open thorn bush steppes to savannahs and dune valleys where vegetation occurs. Cultivated fields

sought out. TERRITORY: as in Thomson's Gazelle (p. 94), size of range however not known.

Habits. DAILY RHYTHM: main grazing periods early morning and late afternoon, also where persecuted active on clear nights. TOILET: see Soemmering's Gazelle (p. 91). VOICE: details not known though probably like preceding species. SENSES: sight, hearing, scent good to very good. ENEMIES: see Dorcas Gazelle (p. 96). Behaviour in agitation, or as warning, see Thomson's Gazelle (p. 95). FOOD: grass, herbage, foliage of bushes, locally and seasonally varying. Will stand erect on hind legs to reach foliage. Water requirements as in Dorcas Gazelle (p. 96). SOCIABILITY: in pairs or in family bands (1 old ♂ with $\frac{1}{2}$–1 dozen ♀♀ and young). Seasonal migration to N. in rainy season, S. in dry season.

Reproduction. Breeding season Oct–Nov or Mar–Apr; calving time Mar–Apr or Oct–Nov. Gestation 184–189 days, 2 births possible in 1 year. 1 active young. Wt at birth 2.5–3.2. Birth, rearing, development see Soemmering's Gazelle (p. 92). SEXUAL MATURITY: not known, probably about $1\frac{1}{2}$ years. LONGEVITY: about 12 years recorded.

EDMI or CUVIER'S GAZELLE, *Gazella gazella* (Pallas, 1766) ⁓ Pl. 18
= (*cuvieri* (Ogilby, 1841))

G. Echtgazelle   F. L'Edmi, La Gazelle de Cuvier

Identification. ♂ horns weakly curved sideways, backwards and upwards, tips turned up and inwards, flattish-oval section at base, 12–17 rings, last $\frac{1}{4}$ smooth. ♀ horns shorter, thinner, rounder, more upright, straighter with a few weak rings. Nostrils, ears, hoofs, scent glands, teats and tail much as in Thomson's Gazelle (p. 94) but has inguinal glands. Upperside (cheeks, crown, neck, back, shoulders, flanks, thighs, outside of legs) dull roe-brown to dark, slaty, greyish-brown, flanks somewhat lighter, their lower band-like lower edge slightly to strongly darker, as well as a more or less well developed thigh stripe. Underside (breast, belly, inside of legs, back of thighs) white. Back of nose and forehead, dark roe-brown as well as a weakly or strongly developed nose spot above the muzzle. Whitish stripe above and in front of eye, dark brown stripe from under front corner of eye to muzzle. MEASUREMENTS: HB 95–105, TL 15–20, Ht 60–80, Wt ♂ 20–35, ♀ 15–20; H ♂ 25–37, ♀ 25–30.

Distribution. N.W. Africa from Morocco and Rio de Oro to Tunis, Cyrenaica(?), also in Sinai, Palestine, Syria, S. Iraq and Arabia as well as Farasan and Hanish Islands in Red Sea. 3 ssp. of which the African is Edmi Gazelle (*cuvieri*) in N.W. Africa. Extinct in wide regions. HABITAT: sandy or stony plains, mountains or hills with scanty grass and herbage or thin bush steppe or acacia thorn savannah. Seeks out cultivated fields. *Cuvieri* lives in macchia scrub or steppe-like slopes and valleys of hilly country, never in flat desert, often grazing at night in mountain valleys. TERRITORY: as in Thomson's Gazelle (p. 94). Size of area however not known. *Map* p. 97.

Habits. DAILY RHYTHM: feeds mainly in early morning and late afternoon. Feeds at night where persecuted or in clear nights. TOILET: see Soemmering's Gazelle (p. 91). VOICE: details not known, though probably resembling previous species. SENSES: sight, hearing, scent good to very good. ENEMIES: formerly cheetah, leopard, lion, serval, caracal: today these predators wholly or partly extinct in its range; at present still dangerous for fawns are ratel, kaffir cat, jackal and eagles. Agitation and warning, see Thomson's Gazelle (p. 95). FOOD: grasses, herbage and foliage of bushes according to availability locally or seasonally. Water needs are covered according to locality and season either by drinking or in green food, with dew. SOCIABILITY: pairs or family troops (1 old ♂ with several ♀♀ and young), in

Near East and Arabia seasonal migration in larger herds. Sometimes associates with Dorcas Gazelle.

Reproduction. In N.Africa and Palestine calving in Apr–May; in Arabia twice yearly in Jan and Jul–Aug. Gestation about 6 months, not known accurately. 1 active young, sometimes twins, in captivity one record of triplets. Wt at birth *c.* 2–3, not exactly known. Birth, rearing, development see Soemmering's Gazelle (p. 92). SEXUAL MATURITY: in captivity ♂ ½ year, in wild state may well be at least 1–1½ years. LONGEVITY: 12 years recorded.

RHIM or LODER'S GAZELLE, *Gazella leptoceros* (F. Cuvier, 1842)　　Pl. 18
G. Dünengazelle　F. La Rhim

Identification. ♂ horns like small Grant's Gazelle horns, lyre-shaped and forming a weak S curving backwards and upwards, rather upright, tips upturned, direction variable, section at base a long oval, 20–25 well-developed rings, terminal ¼ smooth. ♀ horns shorter, thinner, rounder, more weakly S-curved, more upright and parallel, 20–26 weaker rings, the 2 horns often dissimilar or in other ways irregular. Nostrils, scent glands, teats and tail structure as in Thomson's Gazelle (p. 94) though inguinal glands present and so-called knee tufts only weak. Ears very long and narrow, inner hoofs also long and narrow, lateral hoofs short and broad. Upperside (cheeks, neck, shoulders, back, flanks, thighs, outside of legs) light isabelline to whitish-yellow. Underside (chin, throat, breast, belly, inside of legs and back of thighs) white. ♂ back of nose below light greyish-yellow, above near forehead light brown; stripe above eye from base of horns to muzzle whitish-yellow, a light brown stripe from front corner of eye to muzzle. ♀ head, apart from whitish eye stripe, light isabelline. MEASUREMENTS: HB 100–110, TL 15–20, Ht 65–72, Wt 20–30; H ♂ 30–41 ♀ 20–28.

Distribution. N. Africa from mid-Algeria and Mid-Tunisia south of the Sahara Atlas east to Qattara Depression and the region west of Fayum (N.W. Egypt); S.E. and S. to Edeien (S. Libya), Tibesti and Ennedi (N. Chad). Not in Fezzan and Libyan Desert. 2 ssp. The Marica Gazelle (*G. marica*) in Arabia, S. Iraq and S. Khuzestan and the Goitred Gazelle (*G. subgutturosa*) in near and E. Asia, considered by some authors to be related to each other and to the Rhim are not recognised here.　HABITAT: true sand deserts with sparse vegetation.　TERRITORY: not known. *Map* p. 100.

Habits. DAILY RHYTHM: main feeding periods early morning and late afternoon to evening.　TOILET, VOICE: unknown. SENSES: sight, hearing and scent very good. ENEMIES: not known. FOOD: grasses, herbage, leaves of shrubs. Water requirements mostly through food and dew.　SOCIABILITY: pairs or family parties (1 old ♂ with several ♀♀ and young) exact details not known.

Reproduction. Pairing season in Libya May–Jun, calving Nov–Dec; in Egypt (Ghiza Zoo) Feb–Apr (Jun) and Oct, further details not known. Gestation 156–169 days, 1 active young. Wt at birth 1.8–2, birth, rearing, development, probably as in Soemmering's Gazelle (p. 92). SEXUAL MATURITY: ♂ in captivity ½ year, in wild probably *c.* 1–1½ years. LONGEVITY: 14 years recorded.

SPRING-BUCK, *Antidorcas marsupialis* (Zimmermann, 1780)　　Pl. 17
G. Springbock　F. L'Antidorcas　A. Springbok

Identification. Horns of ♂ lyre-shaped and lightly curving backwards and upwards towards the tips, directed outwards and then inwards, at base close together, thick, round in section, with 17–25 strong ridges, terminal ¼ smooth. Horns of ♀ of ssp. *angolensis* similar, rather shorter, thinner, weaker, more upright and further apart, 10–18 weak ridges. Bare part of muzzle only a narrow strip between nostrils. Ears narrow and pointed, lateral hoofs short and broad. Preorbital and digital glands present, no inguinal or metacarpal glands, 2–4 teats. Along spine from middle of back to just short of root of tail a double fold of the skin (only visible normally as a dark streak) enclosing a number of yellowish, sticky, sebaceous glands (the so-called dorsal gland) and densely laid with long white hairs (12–15cm long), erectile so that they can be spread in a wide fan. Tail of medium length, thin, underside naked to tip, upperside short-haired towards the end with tuft-like row of longer hairs. Pelage short and smooth. Upperside (crown, neck, shoulders, back, flanks, thighs, outside of legs) light to dark isabelline, broad flank band and narrow stripe on back of thigh, dark brown. Underside (throat to breast and belly, inside of legs and back of thighs) as well as head and ears, white. Narrow eye stripe, light to dark brown, from base of horns to corner of mouth, and a similar forehead patch in front of horns. Sometimes lower back of nose light brown. Tail tuft and back of fetlocks blackish-brown. Ssp. *marsupialis* has face all white or with sharply defined dark brown forehead patch, *hofmeyri* has gradual transition between forehead patch and white face and narrow flank band. Fawns yellowish-brown. Coat of immature like adult only forehead to back of nose brown, with eye stripe and flank band still not clearly defined. MEASUREMENTS: HB ♂ 125–150, ♀ 120–145, TL ♂ 25–30, ♀ 20–27, Ht ♂ 75–90, ♀ 68–80, Wt ♂ 25–45, ♀ 20–30; H ♂ 28–48, ♀ 16–28: ♂ about $\frac{1}{5}$ larger and heavier than ♀.

Distribution. S. Africa from S. bank of Limpopo (to about 30°E). N. Botswana in centre and S.W. Angola (coastal region from Benguella southwards). Absent in S.W. of Cape Province. Was to a large degree exterminated in the Union of South Africa, but has generally regained its former range by reintroduction. In S.W. Angola between Benguella and Mossamedes nearly exterminated. 3 ssp. (1). Cape Springbuck (*marsupialis*) Cape Province, Orange Free State, Transvaal. (2). Kalahari Springbuck (*hofmeyri*) Botswana, Great Namaqualand. (3). Angolan Springbuck (*angolensis*), S.W. Angola from Benguella region southwards to Kaokoveld and N. Namib in S. Africa. HABITAT: open, dry, hard or stony plains and hilly country with sparse vegetation, mainly thin bush and scrub. Avoids both high grass and pure desert; thicker bush cover only sought for shelter from winter cold or by ♀♀ for calving. TERRITORY: some adult ♂♂ set up territories in the breeding season, driving off neighbouring rivals and young by threats and attack, and form a harem to restrict and mate with the ♀♀. Territory marked by watching stations, latrines at selected scrapes (dunghills), beating of bushes, horn waving (see Soemmering's Gazelle, p. 91) and by their frequent grunting challenges. Territories are usually abandoned after breeding season, at the end of the dry season sometimes held longer.

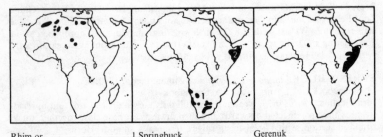

Rhim or   1 Springbuck   Gerenuk
Loder's Gazelle   2 Dibatag or Clarke's
                           Gazelle

Habits. DAILY RHYTHM: mainly active in early morning and late afternoon to evening, also on moonlit nights. TOILET: see Soemmering's Gazelle, (p. 91). VOICE: contact call a short grunting; in alarm a clear high whistling snore, a loud bleating cry of fear, and the loud grunting of breeding ♂. SENSES: sight, hearing and scent very good. ENEMIES: cheetah, leopard, lion, and for fawns also caracal, kaffir cat, ratel, black-backed jackal and eagles. When alarmed whistles and bouncing run, when frightened make high and wide leaps; in full flight an all-out gallop with leaps of up to 15m and speed up to 90kph. When agitated make bouncing leaps with head rising and falling, or high leaps (up to a dozen times) with back arched, fanned out dorsal gland hair and hanging legs and head. FOOD: grass and herbage, foliage of bushes (reaching up on hind legs) according to season. Dig out roots and bulbs. Drink regularly, but can go without for some time. Will drink saline water and search for mineral earths. SOCIABILITY: in breeding season harem (10–30 ♀ with young) in the adult ♂ territory, besides larger herds of numerous ♂♂ as well as young with non-territory holding adult ♂♂ and young form their own troops. In rainy season mixed large herds up to several thousand. Associate loosely with Black Wildebeeste, Hartebeeste, Blesbok, Oryx, Quagga (now extinct) and ostriches. In earlier times at irregular intervals of several years enormous collections of Springbuck (probably driven by food shortages) migrated by thousands, hundreds of thousands and millions (up to 100 million) for hundreds of kilometres (last great migration in 1896 occupied an area of 220 × 25km). In Namaqualand such treks could be seen at intervals of about 10 years; suddenly millions of these animals reached the coast, drank sea water eagerly and perished, their carcases littering the shore for up to 50km.

Reproduction. Possibly throughout the year, though locally main calving seasons (possibly varying from year to year): S.W. Angola Dec–Jan, Etosha Pan, Central Kalahari Dec, S. Kalahari, Orange Free State and Transvaal Aug–Nov (highest peak Sep–Oct), Great Namaqualand Aug. Gestation 167–171 days, 2 births in 1 year possible. 1 active young, twins very rarely. Wt at birth 4–5, doubled at 1 month, trebled at 2, quintupled at 10, sextupled at 18 months. Horn growth begins at 1 month; at 9 months ♂ c. 10, ♀ c. 3–5, at 12 months ♂ c. 15, ♀ c. 10, at 24 months ♂ c. 25, ♀ c. 16. Birth and rearing as in Soemmering's Gazelle (p. 92). SEXUAL MATURITY: ♀ 6–7 months, ♂ 1 year. LONGEVITY: 10 years recorded, though possibly double this figure.

DIBATAG or CLARKE'S GAZELLE,   Pl. 17
Ammodorcas clarkei (Thomas, 1891)
G. Lamagazelle   F. Le Dibatag
Identification. Graceful in shape, long legs and neck with small, narrow head. Lips very mobile, muzzle only a narrow naked strip between nostrils. Eyes large, ears long, broadly lancet-shaped. Only ♂ has horns, reedbuck-like, curved forward at top, tips only slightly diverging from each other, round in section at base, lower half with 6–10 well-developed rings, upper half smooth and pointed. Rounded tail reaches hocks, well haired and with distinct tassel. Inner hoofs narrow and pointed, lateral hoofs very small. Preorbital and carpal glands present, latter with hair tufts (knee brushes): pedal, interdigital and inguinal glands absent. 4 teats. Coat short and smooth. Upperside (crown, neck, shoulders, back, flanks, thighs, outside of legs and lower inside) and two stripes on front of breast, cinnamon brown; underside (chin, throat, breast, belly, upper inside of legs and back of thighs) white. Back of nose and forehead dark reddish-brown, whitish stripe above eye from base of horns to muzzle, reddish-brown stripe from front of eye to muzzle, whitish spot below eye; cheeks and backs of ears isabelline-grey. Root of tail coloured like back, rest of tail, tips of ears and knee tufts black, horns

and hoofs brownish-black. Immatures like adults.   MEASUREMENTS: HB 152–168, TL 30–36, Ht 80–88, Wt ♂ 28–35, ♀ 22–29; H 25–33: ♂ rather stronger and larger than ♀, neck especially thicker.

Distribution. Somalia and Ogaden, western R. Djerrer, eastward in part to coast, in north, south of Gulis Range (east of these mountains in places to the N. coast), in S. to near Equator. Locally exterminated by poaching and overgrazing by domestic livestock. No ssp.   HABITAT: sandy or grassy, loosely bushy plains with isolated trees and thickly or widely scattered thickets, interspersed bare patches of ground, at times with high grass. Grassy plains with small trees and low thickets are only used during and shortly after the rainy season: dense matted bushy areas on stony ground avoided. TERRITORY: seasonally, and according to food supply move around, only using any one place for limited time. Inhabited areas are recognised by well marked latrines (especially those of ♂). Nursing ♀♀ remain close to their fawn (1 or 2 weeks old) during dependence.

Habits DAILY RHYTHM: chief feeding time early morning and late afternoon; in midday heat stand still in shade of trees and bushes.   TOILET: groom body by licking and nibbling, scratching head, neck and breast with hind foot. Repels insects by hoof stamping, tail waving, head shaking, ear flicking and skin twitching.   VOICE: nasal alarm call and grunting snore. Other calls not known.   SENSES: hearing and scent very good, sight less keen.   ENEMIES: cheetah, leopard, lion, serval, caracal, hyaena, hunting dog; and for fawns also ratel and eagles, though principal predator leopard. Suddenly aroused, it flees with raised and backward bent head, erect ears and tail curved forward in an arch over the back.   FOOD: mainly foliage and young shoots of bushes and trees (often gathered while erect on hind legs), a little grass and herbage (particularly new grass after rain). Water requirements mainly met by food, so home in areas without open water possible.   SOCIABILITY: small family parties (1 adult ♂ with 3–5 ♀♀ with young) or in pairs, sometimes also solitary. Sometimes in loose association with Gerenuk or Soemmering's Gazelle or Swaynes Hartebeeste.

Reproduction. Not restricted seasonally, however it seems that in Mid-Somalia main breeding period Mar–May (rainy season). Gestation period not known exactly, 6–7 months, so 2 births a year quite possible. 1 active young, lies up (see TERRITORY). Details of birth, rearing and growing up not known.   LONGEVITY: not known, in wild could be 10–12 years.

GERENUK or WALLER'S GAZELLE,   Pl. 17
Litocranius walleri (Brooke, 1878)
G. Giraffengazelle   F. Le Gazelle de Waller   S. Swala twiga

Identification. Form graceful, legs and neck very long, with small and narrow head. Lips very mobile. Muzzle only as narrow naked strip between nostrils. Eyes large, ears long, broadly lancet-shaped. Horns only in ♂, thick and strong S-shaped to rear above, tips more or less hooked and curved upwards, forwards and inwards, position varies from narrow to widely-set, base section egg-shaped (oval) with pointed end in front, 25–35 strong ridges, terminal $\frac{1}{4}$ smooth. Roundish tail naked apart from hair band on upperside and all round tail tassel. Inner hoofs narrow, pointed, lateral hoofs very small. Preorbital, metacarpal and interdigital glands present, carpal glands with hair tufts (knee brushes) no inguinal glands. Pelage short and smooth. Dark chestnut-brown 'saddle' from neck to tail tuft, set off on flanks by narrow light-ochreous belt. Rest of upperside (neck, shoulders, flanks, thighs, outside and lower inside of legs) clear isabelline. The light-ochreous flank band becomes isabelline-brown like back at its lower edge. Underside (chin, throat, breast, belly, upper inside of legs and narrow strip on back of thighs) white. Face and forehead reddish-brown (in ♀ middle lighter and forehead blackish-brown), cheeks, crown and back of ears isabelline (in ♀ lower part of ear dark brown). Whitish area round eyes and base of ears, preorbital area dark brown, knee tufts brown to black, the white on back of thighs continued as narrow band on either side of root of tail. Horns and hoofs dark brown. Immature pelage as adult, only the saddle paler. MEASUREMENTS: HB ♂ 155–160, ♀ 140–155, TL 23–35, Ht ♂ 95–105, ♀ 90–100, Wt ♂ 35–50, ♀ 30–40; H 25–44. ♂ rather larger than ♀, neck especially thick.

Distribution. East Eritrea and Ethiopia (Danakil, Harar, Ogaden, Borana) and eastward including nearly all Somalia (apart from higher mountain ranges and coastal dunes) south through Kenya to N. Tanzania (to about 5°S.), western limit is the west border of the Great Rift Valley (about 37°E.). 2 or 3 ssp., classification uncertain. HABITAT: Sandy or stony bushy steppes (water not essential) with loose or dense thickets or islands of high dry grass in plains and hills up to 1,800m. TERRITORY: Sedentary and local. Home range of animals c. 2.5–6 sq km. Adult ♂ probably territorial, territory seems same as home range, with several ♀♀ and young, and marked by preorbital scent gland secretion and latrines. *Map* p. 100.

Habits. DAILY RHYTHM, TOILET: as Dibatag (p. 102). VOICE: alarm call soft short buzzing sound, or whistle when annoyed; when startled a short cry of fear. A loud bleat in extreme danger. SENSES, ENEMIES: as Dibatag. In headlong flight sometimes white stern displayed. FOOD: foliage of bushes and trees, including shoots, buds, flowers and fruit, climbing plants and lianas. No grass or herbage. With its long neck and legs reaches much food by standing erect on hind legs to browse. Water needs mainly derived from food, though will occasionally drink from pools and puddles. SOCIABILITY: lives in small family parties (1 adult ♂ with 2–5 ♀♀ with young), or in pairs, sometimes solitary; also occasionally small parties (2–4) of young ♂♂. Sometimes associate loosely with Dibatag or Grant's Gazelle or Oryx.

Reproduction. Gestation 203–210 days (c. 7 months). Calves throughout the year though most commonly in rainy season (N. Somalia Oct–Nov, S. Somalia Feb–Mar, Harar Apr–May, N. Tanzania Jan). Pairing takes place on the move, ♂ raises itself erect on hind legs with fore legs hanging. 1 active young which lies out in cover; 2 births in a year possible. Wt at birth c. 3; sex ratio c. 1:1. ♀ licks newborn calf dry and eats afterbirth. Further details of growth not known. SEXUAL MATURITY: ♀ 1 year, ♂ 1½ years. LONGEVITY: 6½ years in zoo recorded, in the wild perhaps 10–12 years.

IBEX and SHEEP, CAPRINAE

Horned animals of goat or sheep-size and appearance. Horns in both sexes, in ♀ much like those of ♂ but varying from a little to much weaker. Horns strongly curved either backwards or in a less or more upward direction, curving in a bow or screw-shaped, smooth or with prominent ridges. Tail short to medium, in part flattish with naked underside or round and well haired. Inner hoofs short and pointed, lateral hoofs small. Pelage smooth or woolly, commonly varying greatly in length in particular parts of the body, forming beards, mantles, manes, neck ridges or sleeves. Preorbital, post-horn, under tail, interdigital and inguinal glands present or absent; 2–4 teats. Generally sociable in troops or herds. Habitat wooded to bare mountains, high alpine pastures or steppes. Found in Eurasia, N. Africa and N. America. Domestic forms of almost world-wide distribution. 9 genera with altogether 12–20 species according to systematic opinions, of which 2 genera, each with 1 species, occur in northern Africa. The

Asiatic Tahr (*Hemitragus jemlahicus*), introduced on Table Mountain on the Cape, is not dealt with here, but is listed in the introduced species (p. 386).

ABYSSINIAN and NUBIAN IBEX, *Capra ibex* (Linnaeus, 1758)   **Pl. 19**
G. Steinbock   F. Le Bouquetin

Identification. Stocky build, head short, forehead swollen, ears short and pointed, muzzle only a narrow edge between nostrils, tail short, slightly tufted (reaching only $\frac{1}{4}$ way to hock). Adult ♂ with long beard on underside of lower jaw. Horns in both sexes, those of ♀ short, narrow and single, curving backwards in a bow-shape. Fully-developed horns of ♂ curved in a semi-circle (ssp. *walie*) or $\frac{3}{4}$ of a circle (ssp. *nubiana*) flattened from side to side, with prominent knobs on front edge (up to 20 in *walie*, up to 30 in *nubiana*). Colour in *nubiana* light brown, in *walie* dark chestnut-brown; in adult ♂ underside of neck, front of breast, under edge of flanks, front of legs, beard and tail dark to blackish-brown, belly, inside of legs, metacarpal area and fetlocks white. Kids light brown with dark brown to whitish legs. Inner hoofs short and pointed, lateral hoofs small. Scent glands under the tail. 2 teats. MEASUREMENTS: *nubiana* HB 140–150, TL 15–25, Ht ♂ 75–90, ♀ 65–80, Wt ♂ 60–80, ♀ 50–70; H (♂) up to 138; *walie* HB 150–170, TL 20–25, Ht ♂ 100–110, ♀ 90–100, Wt ♂ 100–125, ♀ 80–100; H (♂) up to 114: ♂ $\frac{1}{4}$ larger and heavier than ♀.

Distribution. Nile region from Lower Egypt (latitude of Suez) to N.E. Eritrea and to Simien and Gojjam mountains north-eastward of Lake Tana in N. Ethiopia, N.W., S. and S.E. Arabia, Sinai Peninsula, Israel and Jordan to north shore of Dead Sea and S. Syria. In the early Stone Age in N. Africa existed westward to the Atlas lands. Extinct in Egypt and large part of the Sudanese range, as well as in parts of Arabia and Syria and the Gojjam Mts. 2 ssp.: (1). Nubian Ibex (*nubiana*) distribution as above apart from Ethiopia, severely threatened, in Sudan only about 300 surviving. (2). Abyssian Ibex (*walie*), N. Ethiopia (see above), severely threatened, only about 150 surviving. HABITAT: *nubiana*; steppes, semi-deserts and deserts in mountain ranges between 200m and 2000m with boulder-strewn hillsides, ravines, steep slopes, high cliffs and high pleateaux, with sparse vegetation of grass, herbage and bushes: water only available during summer heat in a few places. *Walie*, high mountain-peak regions between 2500m and 4500m, usually between 3000m and 4000m with grass, herbage and bush clad slopes, sides of ravines, alpine meadows, home usually in upper forest zone with thickets under tree lobelias or conifers and birches. Food and water abundant, daily temperature range greater than seasonal. TERRITORY: sedentary and local, home range not divided into territories.

Habits. DAILY RHYTHM: main feeding activity morning and afternoon. Outstanding climbing ability among steepest rocks. TOILET: grooming by nibbling of coat, scratching with hoofs and horns. VOICE: alarm call a clear nasal whistling snort (usually uttered by ♂), kid bleat, cry of fear a far-reaching bleat. SENSES: sight, hearing and scent exceptionally good. ENEMIES: mainly leopard and serval, though in part greatly reduced, and for kids jackals, hyaenas and above all eagles; protection from the latter by mother. FOOD: grass, herbage, bushes, *nubiana* also foliage of trees (reaching up on hind legs to browse). SOCIABILITY: small troops of $\frac{1}{2}$–3 dozen animals, mixed, partly ♂♂, partly ♀♀ with young, also solitary: in *nubiana* calving ♀♀ go apart, in *walie* a group will combine to protect kids against eagles.

Reproduction. Breeding season mainly Sep–Oct; gestation 150–165 days, calving Mar–Apr; *walie* breeds all the year, though peak Mar–May, calving mainly from Jun–Aug, rainy season in Sep–Oct. Courtship and pairing not described, however probably as in Alpine Ibex (*ibex*). Usually 1 active young, though often twins; rarely

triplets. Wt at birth *c*. 2. Kids lie up at first in cover. Suckling period *c*. ½ year.
SEXUAL MATURITY: about 2½ years (in captivity 1½ years). LONGEVITY: in captivity
over 10 years recorded, in wild state probably 12 years.

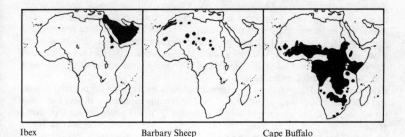

Ibex   Barbary Sheep   Cape Buffalo

BARBARY SHEEP or AOUDAD, *Ammotragus lervia* (Pallas, 1777)   Pl. 19
G. Mähnenschaf   F. Le Mufflon à manchettes

Identification. More goat-like than sheep-like (the genus stands between goats and
sheep), body narrow and high, croup sloping. Tail reaching half-way to hocks, rather
bushy. Underside of tail naked at root. Legs sturdy. Head long, ears small and pointed,
muzzle only a bare edge between slanting nostrils. Horns in both sexes, ♂ larger,
usually contiguous at the roots, in section triangular, with a corner at the back and
lightly-rounded front surface, usually with a weak central keel. Whole of the upper
surface of horns with narrowly spaced transverse folds, at front disappear with old age.
Horns curving to form segment of circle. Coat harsh and bristly, with soft underwool,
in summer short and smooth. Short hair ridge from neck to withers. Long mane along
lower neck and fore part of breast from chin backwards to forelimbs, elbows hidden by
long sleeves. General colour isabelline to reddish-brown. Chin, stripe along nose, part
of the breast-mane and lateral belly stripe often dark brown to black; mane, sleeves,
belly, inside of legs and sometimes stripe along nose light to white, ♀ like ♂ but
mane weak. Kids light brown, underside lighter, nose stripe and forehead darker. Only
the naked underside of tail with glands (♂ in rut with strong scent). 2 teats.
MEASUREMENTS: HB ♂ 155–165, ♀ 130–140, TL ♂ 20–25, ♀ 15–20, Ht ♂ 90–100,
♀ 75–90, Wt ♂ 100–140, ♀ 40–55; H ♂ up to 88, ♀ to 40.

Distribution. Formerly ranged in N. Africa from Sahara Atlas southern slopes, Tripolitania, Lower and Upper Egypt southwards to S.W. Sudan and Mid-Mauretania;
said also to have occurred from E. bank of Nile to the Dead Sea in Palestine, though no
certain evidence of this. 6 ssp. Extinct in Egypt, scarce in N. Sahara, very scarce other
localities, but still common occurrence in Darfur, Ennedi and N.W. Sudan, Tibesti,
Fessan, Air, Ahaggar (Hoggar), Tassili n'Azdjer, Adra and mid-Mauretania. Introduced in New Mexico, California, islands of L. Erie and many reserves in U.S.A.
HABITAT: rocky mountain ranges, or hills in deserts: outstanding climbing ability
also in rocky precipices. TERRITORY: size of home range unknown, or whether
territory is established at all. No particular latrine areas.

Habits. DAILY RHYTHM: early morning and late evening, resting in heat of day in
shade of overhanging rocks or in holes. TOILET: scratching with hind feet and horns,
self-grooming, rubbing against boughs and other solid objects between the horns,

rubbing on the ground. Bathes in damp sand, lying on belly and flanks including scattering sand over back with horns afterwards. In captivity will bathe in water. VOICE: young kids have clear sheep-like bleating in their first days (straying or uneasy calls); mother answers with deep grunts; the ♂ in rut utters similar but lighter grunts. SENSES: sight and hearing very good, scent good. ENEMIES: leopard, caracal, formerly lion (though now practically extinct). FOOD: grass, herbage, foliage of bushes and trees; will stand erect on hind legs to browse. From daytime resting place among rocks goes out at dusk to feed, also in neighbouring plains. Drinks at water holes where available, otherwise relies on moisture in food. SOCIABILITY: sociable in small family parties, 1 adult ♂ with several ♀♀ and young; at end of dry season a collecting together of several troops.

Reproduction. Adult ♂ follows ♀ in heat tenaciously for days, licking her anal region, and other actions, driving off other ♂♂ until ♀ is ready for mating; the act lasts only for seconds, with the ♂ upright with forelegs on ♀ hips. Pairing season Oct–Nov, gestation 150–165 days, lambing time Mar–Apr, 1–3 young, sex ratio at birth 1:1 in adults ♀♀ predominant. ♀ lies up with young for 1–2 days after birth, licks lamb dry after birth and eats the afterbirth. Wt at birth 1.5–3. Suckles for 3–4 months. SEXUAL MATURITY: about 1½ years. LONGEVITY: in captivity up to 24 years.

CATTLE, BOVINAE

Medium to large in size. Body generally muscular. Back with high withers and muscular ridge (especially in ♂), body barrel-shaped, tail short or long, tassel weak to strong. Usually large naked muzzle. Pelage plain, generally short and smooth, rarely woolly. Horns in both sexes, those of ♀ generally not much weaker than those of ♂. Horn direction simple, or curved in different species, horn section triangular to round. No scent glands. 4 teats. Range from 5000m high plains to tropical rain forest and swamps as well as savannahs. Very sociable in troops or herds. Eurasia, N. America, Africa. Domesticated forms practically world-wide in distribution. 8 genera with altogether 11–12 (according to classification) species, of which 1 genus with 1 species in Africa (Water Buffalo, p. 386, not counted).

AFRICAN BUFFALO, *Syncerus caffer* (Sparrman, 1779)　　**Pl. 19**
G. Kaffernbüffel　F. Le Buffle d'Afrique　A. Buffel　S. Mbogo, Nyati
Identification. Like cattle in size and shape. Snout with large naked muzzle. Ears large, pointed, with long fringes of hair. Withers with thick muscular ridge, tail round with large tassel, reaching to the hocks. Legs sturdy, inner and outer hoofs large. Pelage short, rough and scanty, in Forest Buffalo usually a short dorsal mane. Colour of coat from a clear reddish-brown through tobacco brown and dark brown to black. In Forest Buffalo and marginal forms partly ♂ and ♀ reddish-brown (some individuals also clear brownish-black to black) partly ♂ dark red, ♀ and calf light red, partly ♂ black, ♀ and calf reddish-brown, in typical savannah form ♂ and ♀ black, calf black to olive-brown, in a few months dirty yellowish-brown, in 1 year reddish to chocolate-brown (especially on hindquarters) at 3 years in ♀, up to 4 or 5 in ♂ and after, unicolour blackish-brown (♂) or black (♂). Old animals become partly hairless, face and neck hair become whitish. Red to dark brown animals with underside lighter than upperside. Face and neck often darker than back, often with neck mane, fringe on ears, tail tuft and lower part of leg, black, others have ear fringe orange to whitish yellow, individuals clear whitish, yellowish, or greyish red. Horns in both sexes, in ♂ barely to

distinctly stronger than in ♀. Form differs widely, in Forest Buffalo short, bases flattish, transverse ridges, clearly separate from each other, ends pointed, slanting to rear and upward. In Sudan Buffalo horns vary from unbroadened and separate to broad and touching each other at base (making together the so-called helmet) ridges from base to smooth terminal point strongly diminished, latter often with vertical curved tips. In Cape Buffalo bases very broad, in contact with one another, ridged and rough (powerful helmet). Terminal portion long, widely projecting laterally and with tips curved upwards and inwards. Between the 3 forms, all intermediates possible. No skin glands; 4 teats. MEASUREMENTS: HB 170–265, TL 50–80, Ht 106–165, Wt 250–800 (rarely more), ♂ markedly heavier than ♀ only in Sudan Buffalo. Forest Buffalo Ht 100–120, Wt 250–320; H 40–75; Sudan Buffalo Ht 120–150, Wt 320–600; H 75–117; Cape Buffalo Ht 150–165, Wt 500–800; H 117–150.

Distribution. From the north of the savannah zone of the Sudan (geographical) at about 14°N, south to Cape, except semi-deserts and deserts. Within this distribution, much reduced by man. Numerous forms described but only the W. African Forest and eastward to S. African plains Buffalo very distinct from each other; between them are the animals of the Sudan zone. Hence only 3 ssp. or subspecific groups distinguished here: (1). Forest, Red or Dwarf Buffalo (*nanus*), the primeval forest regions of W. Africa from Gambia to S. Zaire and N. Angola, east to Lakes Edward and Kivu and S.W. Ethiopia, exterminated in Fernando Poo. (2). Grass or Sudan Buffalo (*brachyceros*), Sudan Savannah from Mauretania and Senegambia to Bahr-el-Ghazal, further southward along the Western Rift (lake chain) from Mobuto (Lake Albert) to N. Tanzania (Lake Tanganyika). (3). Black or Cape Buffalo (*caffer*) from S. Somalia and S. Ethiopia to the Cape in the South and Cuanza (M-Angola) in the west. In the Union of South Africa is only now found in some reserves, in S.W. Africa only in extreme north. HABITAT: primary and secondary forests, thickets, swamps, reed beds, moist and dry savannah and grassy steppes in plains, and mountains up to 4000m. TERRITORY: not known in Forest Buffalo. In plains Buffalo each herd has a fixed home range, according to size of herd, up to 50km on average, in which they remain. In the rainy season they feed anywhere, in dry season prefer edge of water, the herd breaking up. No true territory in the home range. *Map* p. 105.

Habits. DAILY RHYTHM: little known about Forest Buffalo. In plains Buffalo most active in evening, night and morning; during heat of midday rest in shade of trees, bushes, reeds etc. TOILET: mainly wallowing in mud holes and rubbing on tree-trunks. VOICE: not noisy. Calves bleat, mother grunts to call calf; if calf gives danger cry all the animals in vicinity grunt. ♂♂ fighting in breeding season utter hoarse bellows, scrape ground, throw up the earth and roll in mud. SENSES: scent very good, hearing and sight less good. ENEMIES: principally lion, and in water crocodiles, and for calves also spotted hyaenas. Buffaloes defend themselves and their calves courageously; lions prefer to attack calves and old solitary animals, but are sometimes wounded or killed. A solitary old animal will, if angered, ambush men. FOOD: according to season and locality, grass, herbage, foliage all form part of the diet, generally the great part is grass (including coarse growth) though at times leaves and foliage predominant. Daily drinking (at times 30–40 litres) necessary, so hardly further than 15km from water. SOCIABILITY: Forest Buffaloes in small family troops of 3–12 (1 old ♂ with ♀♀ and young). Plains Buffalo in herds of 20–2000 animals, in dry season herds split up into troops of 2–20; basic herd consists of ♀♀ with young up to 3 years old. Young ♀♀ remain in herd longer; young ♂♂ after 3 years and old ♂♂ form bachelor groups (3–20) within or outside (only *c.* 15%) of the large herd. ♂♂ more than 10 years old usually solitary. Adult ♂♂ have an order of rank, 8–10 year olds the strongest, usually mate with the ♀ ♀. Members of a herd recognise it and keep apart from other herds.

Reproduction. Calving through the year in Cameroun, Zaire, Zambia and Rhodesia. In E. Transvaal calving Jan–Apr, in S.W. Africa Oct–Jan, in Uganda in both rainy seasons. Gestation 330–345 days, 1 active young, twins very rarely. Wt at birth ♂ 26–42, ♀ 26–36, Ht at birth 76–81. Wt increase ♂ 1 month 40, 2 months 50, 3 months 55, 6 months 135, 9 months 165, 18 months 270, $2\frac{1}{2}$ years 345, $3\frac{1}{2}$ years 400, $6\frac{1}{2}$ years 590, $7\frac{1}{2}$ years 614, $9\frac{1}{2}$ years 650. ♀ 1 month 44, 2 months 55, 3 months 65, 4 months 75, $7\frac{1}{2}$ months 120, 12 months 195, 2 years 360, $5\frac{1}{2}$ years 520, $9\frac{1}{2}$ years 550. Suckle for 5–6 months, sometimes for 1 year. SEXUAL MATURITY: ♂ $2\frac{1}{2}$–3 years, first able to breed at 7–8 years (♂ ♂ of this age fight furiously in rutting season, often to the death). ♀ at 3 years, first calving usually at $4\frac{1}{2}$–5 years, usually 1 calf every 2 years, rarely 3 calves in 2 years. Sex ratio about 1:1. LONGEVITY: in captivity up to 26, in the wild limit probably about 20 years.

Odd-toed Ungulates, Perissodactyla

ASSES, ZEBRAS, EQUIDAE

Medium to large animals (HB 180–240, TL 40–90, Ht 100–150) with large head, short to long pointed ears, strong neck with narrow mane, slender one hoofed legs with strong, round hoofs, and long-haired, tufted tail. Coat short, thick, smooth, at times in winter rougher with denser underwool, grey or light grey (Asses) or yellowish-brown to reddish-brown (Onagers, Wild Horses) or brown to black vertical stripes on light ground (Zebras). Dent.: 3/3 · 1/1 · 3/3 = 40–42. Incisors chisel-shaped, premolars and molar high-crowned with enamel folds; ♀ without canines. No skin glands. 2 teats. Chestnuts (coin-sized bare horny skin patches on inside of legs) in *Equus* on front and hind legs, in the other genera only on front legs. Grass and herbage feeders. Sociable, in troops or large herds. In savannahs, steppes, semi-deserts and deserts. East, Middle and Near Eastern Asia and Africa. 4 genera (Horses, *Equus*; Onagers, *Hemionus*; Asses, *Asinus*; Zebras, *Hippotigris*) with 8 species altogether, of which the Asses and Zebras have 4 species in Africa.

AFRICAN WILD ASS, *Asinus africanus* (Fitzinger, 1857)   **Pl. 20**
G. Afrikanischer Wildesel   F. L'Âne sauvage de l'Afrique   S. Punda
Identification. Head large, ears long and narrow, neck of medium length and sturdy; hoofs steeply sloping, tail with long tuft. Pelage short and smooth, short upright mane from crown to withers. Colour yellowish-brown to bluish-grey; inside of ears, ring round eyes, area round mouth, sometimes also roots of mane hairs, underside of body, inside of legs, whitish to yellowish-brown; lips, tips of ears, mane, narrow spinal stripe from shoulder to tail tuft, and transverse shoulder stripe (the cross), tail tuft and rings on legs, dark brown to black, tail tuft sometimes mixed with grey. Spp. *atlanticus* brownish-yellow to greyish-red, leg rings and shoulder cross stripe well developed; *africanus* grey to greyish-blue, otherwise as *atlanticus*; *somaliensis* greyish-red, usually without, sometimes with (small) shoulder cross, up to a dozen leg rings, always on fore and hind legs. MEASUREMENTS: no figures known for *atlanticus*. Ht in *africanus* 115–122, in *somaliensis* 120–125. No further details known.
Distribution. North Africa, 4 ssp.: (1). Atlas Wild Ass (*atlanticus*), formerly coast lands of the Mediterranean from Morocco to Cyrenaica, extinct by about AD 300. (2) Nubian Wild Ass (*africanus*) formerly the savannah zone, or in prehistoric times also in the Sahara including the geographic E. Sudan'from Kordofan and N. Eritrea through Nubia to N.E. Egypt. In Ancient Egypt domesticated about 4000 BC, source of domestic donkeys. A small remnant in Red Sea coast between Suakin and the Atbara R. (N. Eritrea), perhaps still some remaining north of Tibesti-Ennedi (Chad) and in Libyan-Egyptian border region near Giarabub north of Siwa Oasis (the latter have a dorsal stripe and 3 shoulder crosses and are perhaps survivors of *atlanticus*?). About 35 in zoos. (Meester and Setzer record the Saharan animals are probably feral or cross-breeds.) (3) Somali Wild Ass (*somaliensis*), Somalia from the Webbe Shebeli through Ogaden to the R. Hawash (E. Ethiopia). At the most 3000 animals in the Nogal R. region of N. Somalia and Danakil (N.E. Ethiopia). (4) Eritrean Wild Ass (*taeniopus*) (possibly a hybrid), from Hawash R. northwards to Tokar district of S. of Suakin. Extinct except for a small remnant. Within the former range of *africanus* are

isolated troops of fully wild-living feral Domestic Asses as also those found over many centuries on the island of Socotra in the Gulf of Aden. In N. Eritrea a small group of hybrids between *africanus* and *somaliensis*. HABITAT: grass steppes, semi-deserts and deserts, in plains and rugged regions. Exceptionally good climbing ability. TERRITORY: adult ♂♂ occupy territories 5–10 sq km, which also serve as home range for ♀♀ and young and hold it through rainy and dry seasons over the year, leaving it only in severe drought, wandering with others of the same species for some weeks until the first rains fall. Other ♂♂ are tolerated in the territory, so long as they keep away from the ♀♀ (especially those on heat). Other ♂♂ recognise the territorial ♂ as dominant. Borders of territory marked by display and voice. Large dung heaps (up to 1m square and 40cm high) at intervals along the boundary. Boundary only defended during presence of an oestrous ♀ near the border then neighbours fight and it is only within the territory that undisturbed mating takes place. *Map* p. 115.

Habits. DAILY RHYTHM: usually active at dusk and by night, as well as early morning and late afternoon; where shade can be found (under over-hanging rocks etc.), most of day spent resting.   TOILET: tail flicking, leg shaking and stamping, rubbing, scratching with hind hoofs, rolling (in dry soil or sand), skin twitching and general grooming (♀ and older young also groom mutually).   VOICE: squeal in fighting or in defence, snorting in attack, loud bray like 'hee-haw' of donkey as a general sound of excitement.   SENSES: sight and hearing very good, scent good.   ENEMIES: lion, leopard, spotted hyaena, hunting dog, but not important since they are scarce in today's Wild Ass range. When cornered defend themselves by kicking and biting, even against man.   FOOD: grass, herbage, occasionally foliage of bushes. The Danakil Wild Ass only grazes. Drinks regularly and daily or at the latest not more than 3 days. SOCIABILITY: ♂♂ solitary (usually territorial) or in ♂ troops, ♀♀ with young in separate troops or mixed ♂ and ♀ young troops, all troops impermanent, normal number ½–1 dozen animals, sometimes (in rainy season) herds of up to 50. Apart from the ♀-young relationship no close ties of animals with each other, in wanderings no active leader, territorial ♂♂ dominate all others, other animals without any rank order.

Reproduction. ♂ drives ♀ quietly, directs her by cutting off the track or threats, or lays his head and neck on her rump and shoulder and presses her shoulder from behind, left or right. Often mount without erection and sound; in high season commonly attempted mounting without erection. Thereafter mute mating, with light shoulder-bites, mating repeatedly over 1–2 hours for 1–2 days. Gestation 330–365 days. 1 active young, ♀ learns to recognise it by licking after birth, latter takes several days to recognise mother who drives all animals away from the neighbourhood to avoid the foal getting a false imprint. ♀ protects foal against small to medium-sized predators. In big droughts the mother will often leave the foal alone all day, while she goes up to 10km distant to drink, and comes back to nurse it. Foals may doze while standing, and having no flight or protective reaction are then very vulnerable to predators. Suckle up to ½ year, not sufficiently known. SEXUAL MATURITY: 1 year, full breeding capacity first at 2½ years. First birth *c*. 3–3½ years (only 1 in 3 survives). Young ♂♂ first come in rut, when at 5–7 years they can hold territory. LONGEVITY: up to 40 years and more, in wild state seldom 20.

MOUNTAIN ZEBRA, *Hippotigris (Hippotigris) zebra* (Linnaeus, 1758)   **Pl. 20**
G. Bergzebra   F. Le Zèbre de montagne   A. Bergkwagga
Identification. Head large, neck broad, with small dewlap, ears of medium length, pointed, short erect mane from crown to withers. Legs slender, hoofs sloping, tail with

well-developed tuft reaching below hocks. Snout black, above nostrils brown. Ground colour white to yellowish. Stripes black, of medium breadth, included in the mane, in part forked on back, on upper thighs broad and bow-shaped, on front of face and crown narrow and close together, on legs down to fetlocks transverse, on belly open. Tail root also with transverse stripes, upperpart of tail tuft somewhat mixed with grey. Spp. *zebra* distinguished from *hartmannae* by smaller and more ass-like form as well as broader and more narrowly spaced black rump stripes: whereas *hartmannae* is larger, more horse-like and with more widely spaced narrower rump stripes. MEASUREMENTS: *zebra*: HB 220–225, TL 75–80, Ht 120–125, Wt 230–250, *hartmannae*: HB ♂ and ♀ up to 260, TL ♂ to 55, ♀ to 51, Ht ♂ to 150, ♀ to 146, Wt ♂ to 386, ♀ to 322 (average of 7-year ♂♂ 300, 4-year ♀♀ 275).

Distribution. Coastal mountain areas (usually no more than 150km inland) from region *c*. 150km north of Mossamedes (Angola) south to S.W? and S. Cape Province (to Cathcart district *c*. 27°E). Earlier perhaps also in Gt Namaqualand though in past 150 years not further N. than Cedarberg so that at that time there was already a gap of about 1000km between the 2 ssp. *Zebra* (Cape Mountain Zebra) was originally widely distributed in Cape Province (but never out of it), from Kamiesberg in Little Namaqualand in the N.W. to Amatola Mts near Cathcart in E. and the Suur and Bamboosberg in the N. Only 75–100km from Cape Town Mountain Zebras lived on the Paardberg/Malmesberg, the Seronsberg near Riebeek Kasteel, the Paarl and Franschoekberg and the Hottentot-Holland mountain near Somerset West. Extinct except for a few dozen animals in Cradock district. Strictly protected since 1950, at present *c*. 170 animals, largest part in Mountain Zebra National Park near Cradock, smaller number in the De Hoop Wild Life Reserve not far from Cape Town, and *c*. 40 free but scattered in the Gamka, Kamanassie, Outeniqua and Kouga Mts in the S. of Cape Province. *Hartmannae* (Hartmanns Mountain Zebra) 25 years ago a good 100,000 in S.W. Africa and S. Angola from Mossamedes to the Orange River. Now only about 6000–6500 in 4 remaining locations: (1). From Iona Reserve on N. bank of Cunene R. S. to Ugab R. region; (2). Erongo Mountain region; (3). Kmoas Highland region (Swakop to Zarisberg); (4). Fish R. gorge region (S. of S.W. Africa). HABITAT: dry mountain and hill country. Hartmanns Zebra only in mountains between the high plateau in mid and eastern part of S.W. Africa and Namib in west (therefore the west slopes of the plateau region, which stretches from N. to S.). After good rains also in newly green deserts near the mountain ranges. TERRITORY: home range 5–20 sq km in rainy season smaller than in dry season, *zebra* only 3–5 sq km. Very local and resident. Not territorial, not even old ♂. *Map* p. 115.

Habits. DAILY RHYTHM: main feeding and activity periods early morning and late afternoon, resting in shade. Rest and sleep only while standing with lowered head, almost never lie down; only young foals lie down more often (5–35 minutes). Daily wandering (including going to drink), in rainy season up to 5km, in dry season further. TOILET: roll in moist sand or in dry dust. When lying down rubbing of head, neck and belly, while standing rubbing on prominent objects. No mutual grooming except young foals nibble neck and mane of mother. VOICE: *zebra* practically mute, *hartmannae* more vocal: snorting while grazing and resting, as contact call; similarly, a far-reaching (100m or more) and many times repeated high whistle, ending on a hoarse grunting; short, strong, sneezing snort, often repeated when suspicious; short, hoarse and generally double bark as alarm (can lead to flight of all zebras within range); 'heehaw' sound (emphasis on first syllable) breathing in and out (also a warning sound); squealing as a cry of pain, or submission (♀ to a courting ♂, young ♂ to old ♂, older foals to mares). Suckling foals mute; no contact call between mare and foal. SENSES:

sight (particularly for movement) good, hearing and scent good. ENEMIES: lion, leopard, cheetah, spotted hyaena, hunting dog: except lion and hunting dog, preying mostly on foals and young animals. In flight from predators normally go in close formation, with an old ♀ leading, old ♂ following keeping watch on the predator. In emergency defend themselves courageously, kicking with hind legs. Mare defends foal, especially in first 3 months. FOOD: grass, if necessary also leaves and bark. Drink daily, at any time of day, sometimes twice (morning and evening), therefore never far from water, but in emergency can go for 1–2 days, sometimes 3, without water. If a water hole is dry or muddied, they will excavate new ones in the river bed, up to 90cm deep. Other animals will also use these wells. SOCIABILITY: sociable in ♀ troops with foals and 1 adult ♂ (4–7, rarely 2–13 animals, of which 2–4, rarely 5 or 6, adult ♀ ♀). Old ♂ is highest in rank and drives other ♂ ♂ away, while the mares have their own ranking order; mares remain in the troop if the old stallion through age or disease is displaced by a strong one. ♀ foals stay with mare for 1 year, at most 2 years with the troop, then, sexually mature, will mate with a young ♂ and found a new family troop. ♂ foals leave the family troop before sexual maturity, join a ♂ troop (2–7, rarely 10) in which all bachelor ♂ ♂ between 1½–15 years live.

Reproduction. Only the harem stallion mates, following the oestrous mare closely until height of oestrus; in mounting lays head on mare's shoulder and ears; ♀ has special facial expression known as 'oestrus face'. Duration only a few seconds, repeated hourly over 1–2 days. Gestation 1 year (362–365 days) 1 active young. Wt at birth *c.* 25, HB *c.* 120. Suckles at most 2 months, weaned at 10 months although first grass eaten a few days after birth. Bone growth ends at 2½ years. SEXUAL MATURITY: ♀ at 2, ♂ at 3½ years: first foal at 3 years, most foaling in rainy season, Nov–Apr, occasional births also in other months. LONGEVITY: up to 25 years in captivity.

GREVY'S ZEBRA, *Hippotigris (Dolichohippus) grevyi* (Oustalet, 1882)   **Pl. 20**
G. Grevyzebra   F. Le Zèbre de Grévy

Identification. Largest of the equines, head long and narrow, ears notably long, broadly rounded, neck short and broad, erect mane from crown to withers, legs slender, hoofs upright, tail at first round, then a long terminal tuft to below the hocks. Ground colour white, transverse stripes black, narrow and close on head, on neck broad, continuing on to mane, narrow on shoulders and body, on latter sometimes forked, not reaching belly, on croup curved. Legs to hoofs closely transversely striped, mane hairtips brown, as also the spinal stripe from withers to beginning of tail, on croup separated by a white band from the transverse stripes. Muzzle black, brown above nose, and a white spot above that. Inside of ears densely haired, white edged black, tips white. Tail tuft commencing whitish, end part black. MEASUREMENTS: HB 250–260, TL 70–75, Ht 150–155, Wt 350–430.

Distribution. In west, from eastern wall of Great Rift Valley (a line from Lake Rudolf, Omo River, Lake Zwai, Hawash River) from N. Kenya (N. bank of Tana R.) and S. Somalia north to S. Danakil. In parts of Somalia partly exterminated or threatened. In N. Kenya still about 10,000 animals, also in Ethiopia still largely secure. Introduced to Tsavo National Park (S.E. Kenya) in 1963. No ssp. HABITAT: dry savannah to semi-desert. TERRITORY: as in African Wild Ass (p. 109). *Map* p. 115.

Habits. DAILY RHYTHM: principal periods of activity: first morning, second afternoon, midday (if possible in shade) rest standing closely together; also sleep while standing, only young foals lie down. TOILET: tail waving, leg movements, rubbing one another (forehead and shoulder on breast, underside of neck on back, or neck and back on lower jaw and throat of neighbour), scratching with hind foot, rolling in earth and sand, body shivering and skin twitching. No mutual nibbling. VOICE: grunt when disturbed, short warning snort, and longer snort of contentment, or contact call between mare and foal; a territory marking bray of the ♂, also used by ♂ driving ♀; and in repelling a young ♂ an ass-like repeated intermittent deep breath-expelling bray, and high inhaling whistle. SENSES: sight and hearing very good, scent good. ENEMIES: lion, leopard, spotted hyaena, hunting dog. No observations available on attack and defence. FOOD: almost solely grazers. Daily drinking customary, can go without at most 3 days. Like Mountain Zebra, Grevy's Zebra will dig for water (up to 60cm deep) in river beds. SOCIABILITY: like African Wild Ass (p. 110), ♂♂ single (mostly in territories) or in ♂ troops (½–1, rarely 1½ dozen). ♀♀ with foals in separate troops (size as in ♂ troops), also seasonally mixed herds (♂♂, ♀♀ and foals), up to 100–450 animals. Apart from mare-foal relationships no close contacts of animals with one another, in their wanderings from place to place no active leader, although territorial ♂♂ have precedence over all others; other animals without rank order. Often associate loosely with Burchell's Zebras, Giraffes, Oryxes and Elands.

Reproduction. Courtship, pairing, raising of young much as African Wild Ass (p. 110). Gestation 390 days ? (From only 1 observation, therefore unlikely: probably about 1 year as in the other equines). Suckle for about ½ year, but details not exactly known. Foals live 1½–2 years with mares. SEXUAL MATURITY: ♂ and ♀ 3½–4 years, first foal at 4½–5 years. Principal foaling season Jul–Aug, although births occur in all months. First mating 1½–3 weeks after foaling. LONGEVITY: about 21 years in captivity.

BURCHELL'S ZEBRA, *Hippotigris (Quagga) quagga* (Gmelin, 1788)   **Pl. 21**
G. Steppenzebra   F. Le Zèbre de steppe   A. Bontkwagga   S. Punda milia
Identification. Head medium-sized, neck short, broad, body rounded, legs slender, tail tassel reaching below hocks. Ears small, erect mane from forehead to withers, snout black, above nose a brown patch. Ground colour white to yellowish, head and legs to hoofs narrow close stripes, neck body and thighs with broader, wider spaced, sometimes forked (also including the mane) on belly stripes discontinuous. Foals with pelage rather woolly, stripes brownish. Animals with paler or without any stripes (yellows, albinos) or with more numerous stripes (black) or maneless animals sometimes met with in E. Africa. Great individual variation in pattern. Within the total range a lightening of the stripes on the hind parts of the body increases from north to south. 5 ssp.: (1) Grant's or Bohm's Zebra (*boehmi = granti*), ground colour white, striping black, legs striped to hoofs. (2) Selous Zebra (*selousi = wahlbergi*), ground colour white, stripes narrower and more numerous than in (1), legs as in (1). (3) Chapman's or Damara Zebra (*antiquorum = chapmani*), ground colour yellowish, often with shadow stripes between the blackish-brown main stripes, thigh stripes brownish, becoming weak, lower parts of legs only weakly striped. (4) Burchell's Zebra (*burchelli*), ground colour yellowish, belly and legs white, latter unstriped or with only few weak shadow stripes. Mane, tail tuft and stripes brown, stripes broad and widely spaced, with shadow stripes from the shoulder, hind part of thighs only weakly striped. (5) Quagga (*quagga*), separate species according to other authors: ground colour yellowish, belly and legs white, mane, tail tuft and stripes brown, only clearly defined on head and neck, (a) body uniform brown with weaker, rather darker, only half-length striping on fore-parts or (b) browner body with very broad, full length brown stripes, hind part of thighs beige with weak narrow shadow stripes. All gradations possible between (a) and (b).
Distribution. E. and S. Africa, 5 ssp.: (1). Grant's or Bohm's Zebra from Middle Zambesi, Luangwa, and Rovuma River N. to S.E. Sudan, S.W. to mid-Ethiopia (in the

Rift Valley from Boron to L. Zwai) and S. Somalia. Partly exterminated and in S. Somalia threatened. (2). Selous Zebra Mid- and N. Mozambique, E. Rhodesia, Zambia and Malawi. Locally exterminated otherwise little endangered. (3). Chapman's Zebra N. Transvaal, S. Mozambique, W. Rhodesia, S. and S.E. Angola. Locally exterminated otherwise little endangered. (4). Burchell's Zebra Zululand, S. Transvaal, Orange Free State, S. Botswana, N.E. Cape Province, S. Kaokoveld and Etosha Pan. In Orange Free State (the typical Burchell's Zebra, animal with the weakest striping, the typical form) exterminated by 1910, later the other subspecific representatives reintroduced, in Zululand only still in reserves in E. and N. Transvaal common, in W. Transvaal rare, in mid-Transvaal reintroduced, rare in Okavango region. (5). Quagga S.W. Cape region north to Great Namaqualand, east to Kei River, north to Vaal River (eastern border somewhere along the Orange Free State–Natal border). Extinct; the last 3 animals died in European Zoos; 1872 London, 1875 Berlin, 1883 Amsterdam. MEASUREMENTS: HB ♂ 200–245, ♀ 190–245, TL ♂ 43–51, ♀ 47–57, Ht ♂ 120–142, ♀ 106–125, Wt ♂ 220–355, ♀ 175–335. HABITAT: open and lightly wooded savannahs, as well as grass steppes, in plains, hills, in mountains up to 4500m. TERRITORY: home range of a family, shared with other families, 80–200km square, with seasonal migration and daily change of location (often by well trodden tracks) to sleep, graze, roll in dust, rubbing against trees, drinking and other purposes. No territory. The use of regular latrines by ♂♂ and ♀♀ does not mark a territory.

Habits. DAILY RHYTHM: generally active throughout the day. At sunrise leave sleeping place for the grazing areas (in single file) where eating, drinking, rolling, resting alternate. In late afternoon return to sleeping area. At night 3 rest periods with short grazing spells in between. In cold or rain stay near the sleeping area. TOILET: skin sucking, shivering, tail swishing, stamping, scratching with hind feet, skin grooming with teeth, rubbing against trees, termite hills etc., rolling in dry earth and sand, rarely on grass. Mutual grooming among all members of a family. Courting ♂♂ nibble ♀ on croup, tail root and hind legs. VOICE: warning double call 'ee-aa' or short loud snort; a long snort indicates content, short squeals from fighting ♂♂, long squeal of foal as distress call (alarming the family), neighing 'ee-aa' inhaling and exhaling breath (in repeated sequence) as contact call; the animals recognise each other by sound. SENSES: hearing good, sight not bad, scent moderate. ENEMIES: main predator lion, in many areas also spotted hyaena, as well as hunting dog; for foals leopard and cheetah. Single hyaenas are attacked, attacking lions and hyaenas are fought by kicking (eventually even disabled). When threatened the family closes up and eventually takes flight, with lead mare at the front and the old stallion as rear guard. At sleeping place one of the animals always on watch. FOOD: grass, in some places leaves, and bark also. Mineralized earths are eaten. In the first days young foals may eat their mother's droppings for the intestinal flora and bacilli. Drink regularly, can go no more than 3 days without water, also drink saline and soda water. SOCIABILITY: family consists of 1–6 mares with foals, and 1 old stallion who has the highest rank, after that the ♀♀ in order of age. ♀♀ live in the group until death, old ♂♂ to about 16–18 years, then are replaced without a fight by a 6–8 year old young ♂. Orphaned families are taken over by a young ♂, or old ♂ with a family, the two troops forming a new hierarchy in 2 weeks. Young ♀ in oestrus at 1¼ years, and is then abducted from the family by young ♂ to found a new family. A young ♂ leaves family at 1 year if mother has a new foal and then lives to its 4th year in bachelor troops (2–10 head) that range from 1¼ years to adults, and eventually provide new blood for the family. Relationship of old ♂ to young ♂♂ of the family good, the former does not drive away the latter. Very old, sick or wounded ♂♂ are solitary. Families joining in large herds recognise each other by

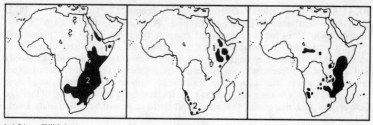

1 African Wild Ass   1 Grevy's Zebra   Black Rhinoceros
2 Burchell's Zebra   2 Mountain Zebra

stripe pattern, voice and scent. Sometimes associate with Mountain and/or Grevy's Zebra, oryx, eland, wildebeeste and giraffe.

Reproduction. Rival ♂♂ fight over ♀, using neck wrestling in a standing position, biting while standing or sitting (biting the legs), erect fighting with blows of fore-feet and biting, and running fights (the follower bites, the followed animal kicks out). No submission behaviour, flight likely; injuries are rarely serious. ♀ in oestrous allows close following by ♂, who smells, licks and grooms her. ♀ at height of ostrous is first to be ready. Mating lasts only a few seconds, ♂ lays head on ♀ withers. Mating takes place repeatedly at intervals of 1–2 hours throughout 1–2 days. Gestation about 1 year. Main foaling time in Tanzania Oct–Mar, Zambia Jun–Sep, Rhodesia Jul–Aug, N.W. Botswana Dec–Feb, E. Transvaal Sep–Mar. 1 active young, rarely twins. ♀ licks foal thus teaching it to recognise her, eats neither foetal sac nor afterbirth, and foals in neighbourhood of family with old ♂ watching. For the first days mare drives away the other animals from the foal which has an innate following reaction. Foal learns to recognise mother first after 3–4 days. Mare protects foal from small to medium-sized predators. Suckling period at least ½ year, first grass eaten after a few days. Independent at 1 year (see Sociability). SEXUAL MATURITY: ♀ at 1¼ years, first fully sexually capable at 2½ years, ♂ at 1½ years, fully capable of breeding at 2½–3 years and first capable of being a family stallion at 5–7 years. ♀ fertile up to 20 years, producing on average 1 foal yearly, of which only every second one survives. Sex ratio at birth and up to 2 years *c.* 1:1, in adults ♂:♀ = 1:1.25/3.25. LONGEVITY: in captivity up to 40 years; in the wild usually only 20.

RHINOCEROSES, RHINOCEROTIDAE

Large to very large (HB 200–420, TL 50–100, Ht 100–200) large-headed, large-bodied plant eaters with 1–2 horns of fibrous hair on the back of the nose. Eyes small, ears small to medium. Tail of medium length with tassel. Legs sturdy, each with 5 toes and hoofs on each foot and pliable sole pads under the toes. Body barrel-like, skin largely naked, sometimes with thick plate-like folds. Dent.: $0–1/0–1 \cdot 0/0–1 \cdot 3–4/3–4 \cdot 3/3 = 24–34$. Incisor teeth cone-shaped, sometimes absent, cheek teeth low to high-crowned with close transverse ridges. 2 teats. Solitary or in small parties, grazing or browsing in savannah and forests. 4 genera with 5 species in S. Asia and Africa, in the latter the 2 genera *Diceros* and *Ceratotherium* each with 1 species.

BLACK RHINOCEROS, *Diceros bicornis* (Linnaeus, 1758) **Pl. 22**
G. Spitzmaulnashorn F. Le Rhinocéros noir A. Swartrenoster S. Faru
Identification. Head long, with pointed grasping upper lip, small eyes placed well forward, mid-sized somewhat pointed funnel-shaped ears with fringe of hairs (In E. and S.E. Africa sometimes animals with congenital ear muscle loss, and half-tailed), and 2 horns, the front one usually longer (sometimes a third small horn). Neck muscular, however without a hump. Tail round, with small terminal bristle-haired tassel, reaches only to knee; skin with swollen folds on neck, breast and top of forelegs. Colour grey. Calf like adults, though without horns or pronounced skin folds. Dent.: $0–1 \cdot 0 \cdot 3–4 \cdot 3 = 24–32$. Incisors lost early. MEASUREMENTS: HB 295–360, TL 60–70, Ht 140–225, Wt 700–1600, H front horn up to 120 (average 50–80), rear up to 60 (average 35–40).
Distribution. Formerly from N.W. and S. banks of Lake Chad and N. Cameroun eastward through the Sudanese zone to W. S. and E. Ethiopia, Mid and S. Uganda, Kenya, Tanzania, S.E. Zaire, S. Angola, S.W. Africa, south to Orange Free State, N. Botswana, Rhodesia, E. and S.E. Zambia, Malawi, Mozambique and South African Republic to Cape Province. Today only in S. Chad, Central African Republic, S. Sudan, S. Ethiopia, S. Somalia, N. Uganda, Kenya, E. Tanzania, S.E. Zaire (only a few localities), Zambia, Malawi, N. Rhodesia, S. Angola, N.W. and S.W. Africa, N. and M. Mozambique and Natal. Reintroduced in Kagera National Park in Ruanda, in Wankie and Rhodes-Matoppo National Parks in Rhodesia, 7 ssp. have been distinguished according to body size and skull length, largest being the Cape Black Rhinoceros (*bicornis*) with Ht 202–224, the smallest the Somali B.R. (*brucii*) with Ht 137–142. HABITAT: usually dry thickly bushed country, with scattered trees or copses, but also met with in grassland with little cover, and in thickly wooded areas, such as mountain forest (up to 3500m). TERRITORY: home range size depends on the district's resources and on season, therefore varying from a few hectares in thick bush to 75sq km in semi-desert (S.W. Africa). Where sufficient food, water, shade, cover and wallows in vicinity, resident and local. Animals disperse pretty regularly over the landscape, so that individual home ranges often overlap, neighbours making their boundaries by dung heaps, thereby learning to recognise each other, whereas strangers to the area are driven off. Moreover (especially in dry season), mutual sharing of feeding grounds, water holes, wallows by animals of the whole district, up to 15km distant from water, sometimes up to a dozen animals at a time; or a region without a strong population may be visited by nomadic animals. Home ranges marked by main and secondary dung heaps about 50cm broad. After defecation the dung may be scattered by the hind feet, perhaps to ditribute better the scent. ♂ has a ritualised urination, with 1–4 sprays directed backwards against bushes up to 5m distant (urine showers) before and after encountering its sex partner. *Map p. 115.*
Habits. DAILY RHYTHM: mainly active morning and evening, during heat of day resting or sleeping in shade or sandy hollow, also nocturnal; interrupted by total of 6–7 hours rest. Where undisturbed, drinks and wallows at all times of day, where hunted, remains in cover. TOILET: mud wallows (often hour long) or (in dry season) sand bathing by rolling on both sides, but has difficulty in rolling over on its back. Sometimes rubs snout and base of horns against tree stump. VOICE: high-pitched sounds, squeals, grunts, bellows, snorts when disturbed, repeated snorts as alarm signal; grunting and bellowing in mating or fighting, squealing as contact call and high pitched sound as separated calf call. Also a low panting sound as call to calves by mother, in pairing, and nearing a water hole. SENSES: scent and hearing very good (scenting over several km), sight bad. ENEMIES: lion, spotted hyaena and elephant:

hyaenas sometimes attempt to bite a calf's hind legs. A cow will chase off or kill an attacker, unless she comes too late. Sometimes a leading cow elephant will attack the rhino, which in general has no fear of lion, hyaena or elephant. An attacking rhino lowers its head and snorts, breaks into a gallop (up to 50kph possible) and deals powerful blows with the horns. Sometimes only a mock attack with sudden halt before the target, an about-turn and flight. If faced by man on foot, behaviour according to age, experience and situation between flight and attack, the latter peculiar to self confident old ♂, where failure to scent man, and only sight of movement leads to attack. Cattle egrets, fork-tailed drongos and tick birds (absent from western S. Africa) often accompany rhinos, the first two catch insects disturbed by the rhinos, the latter seek out ticks and flies on the animal.   FOOD: predominantly leaves, buds and shoots of plants, bushes and trees, also acacias with long thorns and euphorbias; in latter branches broken off by horn leverage standing upright against tree, resulting often in the horn tip becoming broken. Some plants poisonous to man are eaten without harm. A very large variety of plants are eaten (in places up to 190 species), at certain times of the year a strong preference for leguminous plants, where these are not available will eat temporarily the droppings of other hoofed animals to remedy protein deficiency. Grass is only incidentally eaten, mainly in the rainy season. Browsing rhinos recognise particular plants for their nutritional value. Salt, or saline earth are favoured, and by dislodging earth with the horn large holes may be excavated. Drink daily, in dry season and emergencies where water may be distant may drink only every 2–3 days. Also in dry season may excavate a water hole with forefeet to a depth of 1m.   SOCIABILITY: solitary, only mother and young together, sometimes an older calf stays with cow. At pairing time ♂ and ♀ stay together for some days; at other times animals go their way alone, particularly old ♂♂; in an accidental meeting only a short contact (greeting ceremonial). Chance gatherings at drinking and watering places may occur (see TERRITORY).

Reproduction. ♀ coming on heat is closely followed by ♂ until ♀ is ready for mating (for vocal sound see Voice). Oestrous cycle 17–60, usually 26–30, days. Mating lasts 15–70, usually 20–60 minutes, with several ejaculations. Gestation 448–472 days, averaging 15 months. 1 young. Wt at birth 22–45, Ht c. 45, Ht at 4 months 83, 8 months 98, Wt at 1 month 70, at 2 months 100, at 3 months 140, at 4 months 165, at 5 months 205, adult at 6–7 years. ♀ may or may not lick the new-born calf or eat afterbirth. Suckling time c. 1 year. On 1st and 2nd days calf suckles every 1–2 hours for about 2–3 minutes, by 3rd day every 2–2½ hours, on 5th day every 3–4 hours, for 3–6 minutes. First attempt at solid food at 9 days, regular eating at 1 month. First drink of water at 3½ months. First wallow and dung scattering at 3 months. Horn development (first horn) begins at 4–5 months. Cow drives calf away from new birth but calf often returns, otherwise for the time being seeks company of older animals. Interval between 2 births 24–40 months, ♀ fertile to 30 years. First oestrous after a birth from 12 days, though first pregnancy in 3–7 months. Sex ratio c. 1:1.   SEXUAL MATURITY: ♂ and ♀ at 4–5½ years, first pregnancy not before 4½, generally first at 6–7 years.   LONGEVITY: up to 40 years.

WHITE RHINOCEROS, *Ceratotherium simum* (Burchell, 1817)   Pl. 22
G. Breitmaulnashorn   F. Le Rhinocéros blanc   A. Witrenoster

Identification. Form like Black Rhinoceros, but larger and with a conspicuous nuchal hump. Head usually carried low. Eyes, ears, horns and tail as in Black Rhinoceros though colour somewhat lighter grey, upper lip very wide, and front horn usually very long. Calf like adult, though without horns and the prominent skin folds. Dent.: 0–1 · 0

· 3.3 = 24–28, incisors are lost early.   MEASUREMENTS: HB 360–380, TL 90–100, Ht 175–205, Wt $3\frac{1}{2}$–$4\frac{3}{4}$ tons. H front up to 158 (average 90–110), rear usually considerably shorter (precise details lacking): ♀ longer and thinner than ♂.

Distribution. Two widely separated regions: (1). Northern W.R. (*cottoni*) S. Chad westward to L. Chad, E. Central African Republic, N.E. Zaire. S. Sudan, west of Nile and N.W. Uganda. Overall population greatly reduced by poaching for horns; altogether not more than 200–300 animals. Introduced in the Kabalega (Murchison Falls) National Park. (2). Southern W. R. (*simum*) formerly S. Africa south from S.E. Angola and Zambesi except West Cape Province, today extinct except a remnant in S.E. Angola and a good population (over 2000 animals) in Hluhluwe and Umfolozi Game Reserves in Natal. From both the latter, introductions in 4 further reserves in Natal: in the Kruger National Park in E. Transvaal, in the Chobe National Park and Motemi National Park in Botswana, in Cunene area in S.W. Africa, in Wankie National Park and Rhodes-Matoppo National Park in Rhodesia, in Meru National Park and Tsavo National Park in Kenya, as well as exported to zoos all over the world (up to 1973 over 500 exported).   HABITAT: bushy savannahs with thickets for cover, trees for shade, grass plains for grazing and watering places for drinking.   TERRITORY: suitable areas are divided up by old ♂♂ in territories of about 2sq km. These are for old ♂ also home ranges in which all activities take place. The old ♂ lives here all the year round only leaving it at the end of the dry season every 3–4 days to drink or wander. Borders between territories narrow, 20–30 dung heaps in territory and on borders. Old ♂♂ defecation, urination ceremonies for marking as in Black Rhinoceros (hind foot scattering of dung, urine spraying, see p. 116). Usually 1–3 younger bulls share territory with old ♂, are tolerated, and defecate and urinate without ceremony, as in ♀ defecate on same dung heaps without scattering, move in and out of territory. Home range of 1 old ♀ may take in territories of 6–7 old ♂♂, area *c*. 10–12sq km, home wherever sufficient food and water, otherwise may wander over 2–4 days for water in dry season or new grass after local rains, though always returns. In encounters between old ♂♂ over territorial boundaries or ♀♀, or between ♂♂ or young with old ♂♂ in the territory, ritual behaviour without fighting is usually sufficient, but if ♂ is strong enough, a real fight may follow, with fatal blows of the horns possible. The beaten ♂ may stay in the territory without ritual ceremonies.

Habits. DAILY RHYTHM: Grazing and resting at intervals of a few hours, at night, morning, late afternoon and evening; during heat of day long rests in shade of trees, often several in a group. Frequent mud wallowing by day and night, daily drinking, at end of dry season when some way to water, only every 2–3 days. Where persecuted drinking and wallowing only at night.   TOILET: mud wallowing.   VOICE: high pitched sounds, squeals, grunts, bellows, snorts and sneezes. High pitched sound as distress and straying call of calves; squeal as contact call and also at times distress call. ♂ grunts and snorts in courting, shrill trumpeting when repulsed, threatens rivals by bellowing, fighting ♂♂ roar and bellow. In contentment, sneezing and grunting. SENSES: as in Black Rhino (see p. 117).   ENEMIES: apart from man no enemies: attacks by lion, leopard, cheetah, hyaenas unknown.   FOOD: only grass, especially short grass. Drinking (see Territory).   SOCIABILITY: types of association. (1) ♀ with calf; (2) ♀ with young and previous calf (uncommon); (3) party of 2–6 young, usually of one sex, seldom of both; personal attachment between any two animals sometimes; (4) ♀ having lost her calf, tolerates union with 1–6 young animals, which are all bound to one ♀; (5) ♀ with calf tolerating several young animals; (6) 2 nursing ♀♀ keeping together; (7) 2 nursing ♀♀ tolerating several young close to their calves; (8) old ♂ always alone except at pairing time. Where the two species occur together they may use the same dung heaps. Tick birds, cattle egret and glossy starlings escort White Rhino; tick bird's alarm cry also serves to warn the rhino.

Reproduction. Adult ♂ follows ♀ coming into oestrus constantly, keeps ♀ within territory, if necessary drives her back with horn. Mating lasts 20–30 minutes, several ejaculations. Mating in S. Africa mainly in spring after new grass growth (Oct–Dec) therefore births commonly in Mar–May of the next year but one. Gestation 16 months, ♀ can be in oestrus any month. First oestrus ½ year after calving, births at intervals of 2–3 years, 1st birth at 6–7, last at 35–37 years. Sex ratio 1:1. ♀ calves alone in thickets, returns to old haunts in about 1 month. Wt at birth 80–90, HB at 22nd day 131, at 68th day 136, at 152nd day 148, H (front) at 22nd day 1.6, at 68th day 2.5, at 152nd day 6.3. First grass eaten in 2 months, suckling period at least 1 year, calf lives 2–3 years with cow but when next calf is born then leaves and associates with older animals or ♀ that has lost her calf. SEXUAL MATURITY: 4–5 years. LONGEVITY: up to 40 years.

White Rhinoceros

Tree Dassie
(text on p. 120)

Bruce's Dassie
(text on p. 121)

Hyraxes, Hyracoidea

HYRAXES or DASSIES, PROCAVIIDAE

Hoofed animals, rabbit-like in size and form, but with short rounded ears. Snout short, upper lip cleft. Eyes medium size with large nictitating membrane. Coat thick, short to medium length, with fine underwool, with light erect bristles and long guard hairs dispersed over the body. Uniformly coloured light grey to black. In centre of back a long and narrow naked scent gland with surrounding hair usually a conspicuous white to orange. No tail. Legs short. Feet with naked rubbery pads with sweat glands. Toes short and compact, number 4/3, flat nails projecting over top of toes, nail of inner toe of hind foot deeply cleft laterally to form a sharp-edged grooming nail. Dent.: $1/2 \cdot 1/1 \cdot 3/3 = 38$; upper incisors long, curved, triangular in section, rear surface without enamel, permanently growing; lower incisors inclined forward with 3 lobes on crown which may at times disappear during growth. P. and M. low- to high-crowned, roughly quadrangular, with 2 connected double tubercles. Small intestine with large bi-part appendix and a large sac at the hinder end. Testes internal. Teats 2–6. Live singly, in pairs or in groups, active by night or day. Vegetarian feeders living in trees or among rocks. Africa (apart from the Atlas and W. Sahara), Arabia, Palestine and Lebanon. 3 genera, each with 1 species, all 3 represented in Africa. *Note:* others consider 3 genera to include 11 species.

TREE DASSIE, *Dendrohyrax arboreus* (A. Smith, 1827)   **Pl. 23**
G. Baum or Waldschliefer   F. Le Daman d'arbre   A. Bosdas, Boomdassie   S. Perere
Identification. Fur rather long, thick, soft – woolly to silky (in *dorsalis* group straight) greyish-brown to blackish-brown or black (ssp. *emini* and *nigricans* north of the R. Zaire varying from black to white). Young like adults, sometimes lighter. Belly like back or lighter, sometimes ochreous to yellowish-white. Dorsal gland 2–7cm long, its border hairs white to yellow, lengthened in *dorsalis* group. *Dorsalis* group (W. and mid-African rain forests), with white spot behind chin and bare spot on nose (in young still hairy), other ssp. without spot, and with nose well haired. Ssp. *arboreus* (E. Africa and S.E. Cape coastal forests) with whitish supraorbital stripe, ear edge, spot below ear and edge of lips. Teats usually 2, in *arboreus* (Cape) and *ruwenzorii* (Ruwenzori) 4, in *mimus* (Malawi) 6. MEASUREMENTS: HB 40–60, Ht 25–30, Wt ♂ 2.5–4.5, ♀ 1.8–3.
Distribution. Rain forests of W. and mid-Africa from Sierra Leone to the Rift Valley, E. Katanga and N. Angola, further moist mixed and mountain forests in E. Africa (Kenya, Tanzania, Zambia, Malawi, Mozambique) and coastal rain forests of Natal and S.E. Cape Province. Also in Fernando Poo, Zanzibar, Pemba, Tumbatu, Mwana-Mwana, Wete and Fundu. 15 ssp. HABITAT: tropical rain forests in plains and mountains, up to 4000m, evergreen coastal forests (in Cape), moist savannah forests, mixed steppe woodlands, forest islands, gallery forests, tropical island forests (where forests destroyed by man, become rock dwellers). On Ruwenzori and the E. Zaire volcanoes, also in alpine regions above the forest zone, as rock dwellers. TERRITORY: resident, sedentary. Home range about 2–3 hectares, with living holes, food, water, latrines in trees or on ground (droppings about 1cm size green pills stuck together like little sausages, accumulating in large heaps). Living holes in trees (often at great

height), outside rain forests also between roots of trees or in holes in ground or rock crevices. Marking on trees by rubbing dorsal glands in strategic spots, also mark by sound (see VOICE). *Map* p. 119.

Habits. DAILY RHYTHM: in rain forests spends day resting in holes in trees, coming down at night to feed. Outstanding climbing ability, even to and fro on thin hanging lianas. Before leaving and entering tree hole both sexes call to mark their presence. Outside rain forests already wide awake in afternoon. Diurnal in alpine zone of high mountains. TOILET: coat scratching with grooming nail. VOICE: forest animals call daily to mark home range. Calling heard mainly at 9–11pm and 3–5am. Call begins as soft groaning and rises to (about 150 repeats at short intervals) an ear-splitting climax (heard up to 3km away) suddenly ending. Duration of calling 10–30 minutes, calls with lowered head outstretched. Distinct local differences in voice in ssp. within the whole rain forest region. Grunt when uneasy, grind teeth, shriek and scrape ground with forefeet in excitement. Also whistle in fear and emergency. Young have low sound, like guinea pig when lost, and twitter when satisfied. The dassies in savannah woodland call at beginning of dusk for ½–1 hour, performance begins with squeaking, becomes stronger as a whistling, rises to a pig-like squeal and ends like a child's scream. SENSES: sight, hearing and scent good. ENEMIES: leopard, large owls, outside rain forest also large diurnal birds of prey and python, as well as serval, caracal, kaffir cat and large civet. Protect themselves from smaller enemies by furious biting. FOOD: leaves, fruit, herbage, grass, ferns as well as insects, lizards and birds' eggs. Will descend to ground for feeding. Drinking water available all the year. SOCIABILITY: usually in pairs, sometimes old animals with young, individuals may be solitary. Associate with Rock Hyraxes on Mt Elgon in the 2000m high zone, and on the lava rocks north of Lake Kivu with baboons.

Reproduction. Gestation 8 months, no definite breeding season in rain forests, in alpine zone of Ruwenzori Jul–Sep. Young usually 1, often 2, rarely 3: Wt at birth *c*. 0.35–0.4, at 1 month 0.6, 2 months 0.8, 3 months 1.0, 4 months 1.1, 5 months 1.3. HB at birth 15–16, Ht *c*. 7. Young born fully haired with eyes open, at first day climb skilfully. Suckling period *c*. 3 months, first solid food at 2–3 days. SEXUAL MATURITY: about 16 months. LONGEVITY: 12 years reported.

ROCK HYRAX or BRUCE'S DASSIE, *Heterohyrax brucei* (Gray, 1868) **Pl. 60**

G. Busch or Steppenschliefer   F. Le daman de steppe   A. Geelkoldas   S. Pimbi

Identification. Coat short to rough. Upperside blackish-brown with yellow stippling or dark brown to light tan or whitish-yellow. Neck, shoulders, flanks and legs lighter than upperside, graduating to yellow or greyish-white underside. Face lighter than forehead and crown, sometimes chin, below back of ears, and feet white, sometimes feet brown or light ochreous or both mixed. Spot over eye, and hairs of the 2–5cm-long dorsal gland yellowish-white to white. Young like adults, in light ssp., however, darker. Back of nose hairy. Molar teeth low-crowned; 6 teats. MEASUREMENTS: HB 40–57, Ht 15–25, Wt ♂ 2.25–3.25, ♀ 2.15–2.85.

Distribution. E. Africa from Eritrea to Transvaal (Eritrea, Ethiopia, former French Somaliland, S. Sudan, Uganda, Kenya, Tanzania, Malawi, Rhodesia, Zambia, Mozambique, Transvaal), as well as W. and S. Angola and N. Botswana. 6 ssp. HABITAT: plains to mountains (up to 2500m), forests (gallery, savannah and mountain) savannahs and steppes. Home only in trees (mountain forest population) or rocks (isolated mountains) or termite hills, or in trees and among rocks on bush and tree-covered rocky kopjes, or only on cliffs along rivers, or on savannah. TERRITORY: live in colonies in forest or among rocks (resembling Cape Rock Hyrax p. 122). Living quarters holes in trees, under and between rocks as in Cape Rock Hyrax, or in holes in river banks. Latrines among rocks. Sedentary. *Map* p. 119.

Habits. DAILY RHYTHM: as Cape Dassie (below), active by day. Daily sequence includes sunning, grazing, shade-seeking, as well as temperature control of activity, strongly influenced by inactivity for a large part (*c.* 95%) of the 24 hours, as in Cape Dassie. Outstanding climber on trees and rocks.   TOILET: fur scratching with grooming nail, sand bathing.   VOICE: like Cape Dassie, whistling alarm call as in that form.   SENSES: as Cape Dassie. Nictitating membrane not recorded.   ENEMIES: as Cape Dassie. In danger a lightning-like bolt from trees to take refuge among rocks or holes in ground.   FOOD: predominantly leaves of trees, but also herbage and grass. Immunity to poisonous plants, and water requirements as in Cape Dassie. SOCIABILITY: as Cape Dassie, colonies usually not so large.

Reproduction. As Cape Dassie, but young 1–2, sometimes 3. Wt at birth, and development not known, though probably as in the other species. In E. Africa main litter period Feb–Mar.   SEXUAL MATURITY, LONGEVITY: as Cape Dassie.

CAPE DASSIE, CAPE ROCK HYRAX,   Pl. 60
Procavia capensis (Pallas, 1766)
G. Klipp- or Wüstenschliefer   F. Le Daman de rocher
A. Dassie, Klipdas,   Klipdassie   S. Pimbi

Identification. Coat short and rough (but long in ssp. *mackinderi* from Mt Kenya). Upperside dark reddish-brown to light-ochreous or greyish-yellow, often more or less sprinkled with black, often with posterior back over-washed with reddish-brown, sometimes with top of head chestnut-brown, in contrast with back, sometimes with a light neck band separating head and body coloration. Neck, shoulders and flank usually lighter than back, legs like latter. Belly lighter than flanks, yellowish to white. Sometimes a lighter or darker spot behind ear. Bordering hair of the 2–10cm long dorsal gland black, or orange to white, sometimes black or light in some ssp., or black mixed brown and yellow, or hardly different from the other dorsal hair. Colour often variable, sometimes dark and light animals together. Young resemble adults. Top of nose hairy, molars high-crowned; 6 teats.   MEASUREMENTS: HB 43–57, Ht 20–30, Wt 2.5–5.

Distribution. Africa apart from the Atlas, West Sahara, the rain forests of W. and mid-Africa, N. Malawi, Zambia and greater part of Botswana. Range also includes Robben and Dassen Islands in Table Bay at Cape of Good Hope. 16 ssp. The Hyrax of Sinai, *P. syriacus*, Syria and Arabia, is considered to represent this species.   HABITAT: rock piles, rocky hillsides, kopjes and isolated mountains in savannahs and plains, stony mountain sides, kloofs (rocky gorges), on Mt Kenya in alpine zone at 4000–5500m.   TERRITORY: colonial home ranges among rocks; in extensive rocky areas several or many colonies. Within home ranges are holes for individuals or groups, sun-bathing places, look-out points as observation posts, grazing grounds, sand-bathing places, drinking places, runways (30cm wide, up to several hundred metres long), latrine areas. Latter large heaps or level areas coloured yellowish-white by urine and easily seen. Droppings are 1cm long, linked like sausages. Musky scent 'hyraceum' used as medicine (by natives) or for perfumes. Entrance holes small enough to keep out leopard, jackal, serval and caracal, living quarters not too large for groups of animals to huddle together for warmth. *Map* p. 124.

Habits. DAILY RHYTHM: highly skilful climbers among rocks. Body temperature varying (35°–37°C when active outside holes) lower underground, maintained by limited activity and heat maintenance (by sunbathing, or in the cooler hours by groups huddling together). Usually sunbathing several hours in morning, followed by short feeding excursions and at dusk retiring to holes to sleep. In many places feed by night as protection against predators, though also sunning through the day, in other places from 3–4pm, active until dark. Alpine zone animals on Mt Kenya only active when sun or moon give good light, otherwise stay in holes (up to 3 days or more). TOILET: fur combing with special claw; sand bathing. VOICE: growling (with teeth gnashing) in threat; whistling warning and alarm calls, long-drawn piercing scream (carrying up to 1½km) as location indication (differs in tone-colour and tempo according to the ssp.). SENSES: hearing and scent good, sight very good; enemies recognised at more than 1km away. Upper edge of iris with extensible protuberance (umbraculum) or nictitating membrane, largely shielding the pupil and allowing vision direct into the sun, important in view of eagles' habit of attacking out of the low morning sun. ENEMIES: leopard, serval, caracal, kaffir cat, jackal, large civets, eagles and large snakes. An alarm whistle is sounded when predators are near which also alerts Rock Hyraxes. Defend themselves against smaller predators by vicious biting. Where leopard, jackal and eagle have been exterminated (e.g. in Cape Province) Cape Dassies have multiplied greatly, expanding into lowlands and damaging crops as a result. FOOD: grass, herbage, leaves, berries, fruit, in the height of dry season, bark of trees, in desert salt-loving plants, on Mt Kenya tufted grass, giant lobelias, moss and ferns. Highly poisonous plants eaten without harm. Sometimes insects and lizards as extras. Will stand erect on hind legs to reach food. When open water is lacking finds its liquid requirements in its food; in the economy of its bodily function (high heat tolerance, concentration of urine, urine economy, fat utilization etc.) by which life in waterless territory is possible. Feeding areas on or near the home rocks, if longer excursions are made to feeding place go in troops to ensure awareness of predators. SOCIABILITY: sociable in colonies of up to 50, sometimes also more than this. Divided into families (1 old ♂ and several ♀♀ with young). Kindergarten as play communities for many young. In alarm the dorsal gland hairs are ruffled up at 45°, in threat (with growling and teeth grinding) vertical, in close contact with one another the state of ruffling corresponds to rank order. Often associate with Rock Hyraxes on the same rocks, though each species has separate living holes, and the Rock Hyrax feeds in bushes and trees, the Cape Dassie on the ground. Also may associate with agamid lizards, banded mongooses and baboons.

Reproduction. Old ♂ at pairing time becomes aggressive, utters territory establishing call and bites rivals and young ♂♂ from separate troops. After pairing season sexes mix again. Pairing time in N. Africa Aug–Sep, in E. Africa depending on the varying rainy seasons, in S. Africa according to locality Feb–Mar, Mar–Apr, Apr–May, May–Jun. Gestation 7½–8 months. Litter may be 1–6 usually 2–3. Wt at birth c. 0.15–0.2, HB c. 20. Young born fully haired with eyes open, climb and jump already at 1 day very well. Often sit on mothers back. Suckling period 3 sometimes 5 months. First solid food at 2 weeks, leave hole after 3 months. Wt at 1 month c. 0.6, 2 months c. 0.8, 3 months c. 1.0, 4 months 1.1, 5 months 1.3, full adult weight at 3 years. SEXUAL MATURITY: usually at 16–17 months, some ♂ and ♀ already at 4–5 months. Sex ratio up to 2 years 1:1, later ♀♀ in excess since ♂♂ are driven out by mature ♂♂, and while searching or fighting for separate rocky quarters are greatly endangered. Last litter of ♀ at 9, rarely 10 years. LONGEVITY: 12 years recorded.

Trunked Mammals, Proboscidea

ELEPHANTS, ELEPHANTIDAE

Largest living land mammals. Head large, roundish. Nose lengthened to form a long, powerful trunk, serving for breathing, smelling, drinking, seizing and fighting. Eyes small, ears middle-sized to very large. Legs pillar-like, standing upright. Toes 5/5, though outer toes at times reduced so that not every toe carries at the tip a hoof-like nail. Hoofs therefore number 4–5/3–5. Bones of foot lie on elastic pad of connective tissue, forming the round sole fringed with the hoof-like nails. Tail medium length, naked, with terminal tuft of stiff bristle hairs. Skin grey, at birth covered thinly with dark hair, which is usually lost during growing up. Dent.: $1/0 \cdot 0/0 \cdot 3/3 \cdot 3/3 = 26$, upper incisors converted to long ever-growing tusks, without enamel (sometimes 1 or 2 supernumerary tusks and 7 molars). The dentine of the tusks is called ivory. Cheek teeth in a row of upright, cement-filled, enamel-crowned dentine plates that appear one after the other from back to front and are used consecutively. The first 3 to appear are the milk teeth or premolars. Stomach simple. Testicles internal. Penis remarkably mobile, at rest doubly curved (? folded) in a pouch; 2 teats on breast, on each side of head a temporal gland. Gregarious vegetarian feeders. Africa and S. Asia. 2 genera with together 3 species, of which 1 genus with 2 species in Africa. (Most workers accept only 1 species in Africa, the so-called Pygmy Elephant (*Loxodonta pumilio*) not being recognised as a distinct species.)

Cape Dassie
(text on p. 122)

African Elephant

African Pygmy Elephant
(see note in text)

AFRICAN ELEPHANT, *Loxodonta africana* (Blumenbach, 1797) **Pl. 23**
G. Afrikanischer Grosselefant   F. L'Eléphant d'Afrique   A. Olifant   S. Tembo, Ndovu

Identification. See Family above. Forehead smooth. Tip of trunk with two opposite grasping fingers or lips. Ears very large. Tusks rather long and large. Cheek teeth grinding surfaces with 4–8 flat, 3-corner shaped edged dentine plates (lamellae), number of lamellae of M_6 (largest back tooth) up to 15. Hoof-like nails number 5/4, sometimes 1st and 5th reduced or absent, sometimes some with deep central groove. ♂ larger and heavier than ♀, forehead broader and somewhat swollen, tusks longer and heavier. Skin colour light to dark grey, sometimes blackish, very rarely pinkish albinos. 2 main ecotypes: (1) Forest or Round-eared Elephant (*cyclotis*) in W. and mid-African rain forests, and (2) Bush or Large-eared Elephant (*africana*) in rest of range, which, bodily distinguishable, can produce intermediate forms in both regions. *Cyclotis*: middle sized (Ht 220–280), highest point of body behind middle of back, head carried rather down, skin finely wrinkled (sometimes visibly haired), ear roundish, lower part of front blunt-ended not reaching above neck when resting, tusks rather attenuated, usually pointing downwards, ivory whitish, strong and hard. *Africana*: very large (Ht 300–400), highest point of body in front of middle of back, head carried well up, skin heavily wrinkled, ear very large, lower part of front with angular end, reaches above neck when at rest. Tusks thick, usually curved forward, ivory yellowish and softer. Variations in individuals between ecotypes and mixed population large, so that status of earlier proposed ssp. uncertain. MEASUREMENTS: Bush Elephant: Ht ♂ 300–350, sometimes up to 400, ♀ 240–280, sometimes up to 300: Wt ♂ 4500–5000, sometimes up to 6000, ♀ 2200–2500, sometimes up to 3000: total length (trunk to tail tip) ♂ 700–730, ♀ 640–660; TL ♂ 130–150, ♀ 110–130: tail bristles up to 75 long; trunk length ♂ 200–220, ♀ 160–180; tusk length, ♂ to 345, ♀ to 75, Wt ♂ to 117, ♀ to 30. Forest Elephant: Ht ♂ 240–280, sometimes to 300, ♀ 210–240, sometimes to 260; Wt ♂ 2800–3200, sometimes to 3500, ♀ 1800–2500, sometimes to 3000: total length ♂ 500–550, ♀ 450–500, TL ♂ 100–120, ♀ 90–110; trunk length ♂ 120–150, ♀ 100–130: tusks, length ♂ to 180, ♀ to 80: Wt ♂ 6–25, ♀ 2–5.

Distribution. Formerly all Africa from Mediterranean and Red Sea coasts to the Cape of Good Hope, apart from deserts. Today extinct north of 13°N and south of the southern tropic extinct except for isolated pockets. Aouker Plateau, S. Mauretania, 60–100 small animals (Ht ♂ *c*. 240, ♀ *c*. 235); around Lake Chad; Knysna Forest near Port Elizabeth, Cape Province, *c*. 12; Addo National Park near last, *c*. 70; Kruger National Park, E. Transvaal, *c*. 8000. Within the limits referred to represented in Guinea–Bissau, Guinea, Sierra Leone, Liberia, Ivory Coast, Mali, Upper Volta, Ghana, Benin, N.E. Nigeria, S. Niger, S. Chad, Cameroun, Central African Republic, Gabon, Rio Muni, Congo, Zaire, Angola, S. Sudan, S. and W. Ethiopia, S. Somalia, Kenya, Uganda, Tanzania, Malawi, Mozambique, Zambia, Rhodesia, N. Botswana, northern S.W. Africa. In many open areas greatly reduced by human settlement and poaching; on the other hand many National Parks and Reserves over-populated by immigration and protection. Egypt, Carthage and Rome used North African elephants for military purposes; Rome also for circuses. In 1910 Leopold II of Belgium founded a training station on the Bomakandi near Bambili (later moved to Api) in the Belgian Congo (now Zaire) for domesticating Forest Elephants for work purposes; in 1925 removed to Gangala na Bodio in extreme N.E. Congo and still exists. HABITAT: rain forest to semi-desert in plains and mountains up to 5000m. Bush Elephant formerly an inhabitant of moist savannah and gallery forests, with migrations in rainy season into dry savannahs and plains, today through human reduction of habitat often confined all the year round to dry savannah regions. Forest Elephant an inhabitant of rain forests from Bissau to E. Zaire. HOME RANGE: Bush Elephant varies seasonally. In dry season home of families is moist savannah, forest edges, gallery forests etc., where food, water and mud wallows abound. Towards rainy season – rain detected at great distances – wanders (sometimes up to 500km at 5–7kph) often in herds of up to 1000 animals in dry savannah and plains in search of the newly blooming growth and fruiting food plants. Some adult ♂♂ with accompanying ♀♀ leave their families and establish there a new settlement, marking trees and bushes with temporal gland secretion and tolerating no other elephants. After rainy season all return and join the old family grouping. Migrations now severely restricted by human settlements. In the Tsavo National Park (Kenya) individual home ranges 400–3700sqkm according to district. Forest Elephants also roam seasonally in search of locally blooming and fruiting food plants, and also emerge at night from forest edge into open country wherein crops or plantations attract them. In the past both forms used long distance migration trails for generations, but now human settlements and disturbance make this no longer possible.

Habits. DAILY RHYTHM: Bush Elephant mainly active morning, afternoon, evening and at night; during noon heat rest in shade of bush or trees (body temperature depending on environment temperature 32.5°–37.5°C). At night 1–2 short rest periods (1–2 hours). Sleeps more often standing than lying down. Forest Elephants rest during the day in shady retreats, from late afternoon to end of night go in search for food with 1–2 short rest pauses between.   TOILET: Bush Elephants bathe daily if possible, usually after drinking. Mothers wash their small calves at the same time. After a bathe a mud or dust bath is favoured, and the body, especially forehead, neck and back, is covered with thick mud or a coat of dust for protection against sun and insects. Later the dry crusty mud-layer is rubbed off on tree trunks or termite mounds. The Forest Elephant too likes to bathe and wallow.   VOICE: in addition to the expression of feelings between associates by movements, position of trunk, ears and tail, also many utterances either through the trunk (blowing of air) or squealing (calves and young in play, adults when surprised or frightened) or trumpeting (as expression of anger or rage rising to a deafening sound) or as a commanding signal of the leading ♀♀, also rumblings apparently used as contact sounds, or in anger, or growling, bellowing and screaming when attacking. At close range an internal gurgle can be heard which *may* be produced by the stomach processes.   SENSES: scent and hearing very good, sight moderate, though better in dusk than in full daylight.   ENEMIES: lion, spotted hyaena, hunting dog and crocodile may attack weak young calves if they are unsupervised, otherwise cows and herd protect calves successfully.   FOOD: all food is grasped in trunk and put into the mouth. Select particular species of plant (well over 100 different kinds) and vegetation such as leaves, shoots, buds, twigs, branches, fruit, bark, roots, tubers etc., depending on season and locality, hence the wide roaming to particular places for flowers and fruit. Particularly likes over-ripe and fermenting fruit (where over-indulgence may lead to apparent drunkenness), as well as all cultivated plants, especially maize, manioc, cane sugar, bananas, paw-paws, mangoes, sweet potatoes and fruits, also aloes, sanseveria, borassus and oil palms, baobobs etc. Very wasteful feeders, often destroying as much as they eat, tearing up or breaking down trees up to 1m in diameter. Daily food requirements, depending on body size 100–200kg. Roots and tubers are dug out with the tusks, bark of trees torn off, the soft wood of the baobab torn to pieces, mineral salts dug out of the ground (often making deep holes) and eaten. Sometimes reach foliage by standing erect on hind legs. Bush Elephants were originally only partial feeders on grass and herbage, but as a result of habitat destruction and overcrowding, especially destruction of savannah woodland (especially also baobabs), have to make grass the main food. Earth on roots or torn up plants is shaken off before eating. Daily drinking is necessary, the water (at one drink 100–300 litres) is sucked up by the trunk and squirted into the mouth. Young calves suckle and drink water with the mouth.   SOCIABILITY: the kernel of a group is the mother-family, adult ♀ with calves of different ages (3–5). Young ♀♀ stay with or near cows, also in separate groups, young ♂♂ growing up leave the mother troop and form separate troops or become companions to an old ♂. ♂ troops are usually near ♀ troops, sometimes well away; old ♂♂ may become solitary. Family troops usually 10–20 head. In seasonal wanderings often a loose association of several troops as herds of 50–60 animals or several herds may form larger herds (some hundreds, earlier sometimes over 1000). Calves and young animals learn from their elders all the important details of living (food plants and their palatability, locations, blooming and fruiting seasons, drinking, resting, wallowing, trails, enemies and other dangers etc.), therefore the present overshooting of the old tuskers can have a harmful effect on the behaviour of the species. Friendly relations between animals usual, serious fighting (to the death) rare. In birth, injury or sickness, help each other; at the death of a companion, (if undisturbed) will remain on watch by the body (a cow may drag off the body of her small calf for a whole day), often covering a corpse with branches (sometimes likewise with human corpses). Cattle egrets, tick birds and piac piacs are common bird associates. Elephants drinking, mud bathing or otherwise, feeling themselves disturbed by other animals (antelope, buffalo, giraffe, hippo, rhino, zebra) drive them off, otherwise ignore them.

Reproduction. Births occur all the year round, however a relationship between the main or only rainy season and the maximum breeding time (following ample food, sex hormone stimulation) seems certain. ♀ oestrous cycle 2–3 weeks. ♀ coming into heat joins an adult ♂, drives off young ♂♂ from vicinity, lengthy love-play (pursuit, caressing etc.) hastens the beginning of actual mating. In mating ♂ rests front legs on back of ♀, the S-shaped penis finds the vagina in a curious spontaneous movement. Duration of mating 1–2 minutes over 1–2 days. Where there is no dominant herd bull, several ♂♂ share the mating without jealousy. Gestation about 22 months (650–660 days). 1 active young, twins very rare. ♀ seeks a shady place, which it cleans; birth in standing position, other ♀♀ may help. Afterbirth not usually eaten. Wt at birth 90–135, Ht 85–100, monthly weight increase 20–25, suckling period usually 2 years, though extension to 4–6 years possible. At birth first cheek tooth already usable, 2nd at 2–3 years, 3rd at 4–5, 4th at 10–14, 5th at 25, 6th at 30–35 years. Growth: Forest Elephant (first number Ht, second number Wt) 1 year 110/260, 2 years 135/500, 3 years 150/700, 4 years 165/900, 6 years 190/1300, 9 years 220/1900, 12 years 230/2300, 20 years 300/4500; Bush Elephant ♂ Ht 1 day 110, 1 year 130, 2 years 170, 4 years 200, 6 years 220, 7 years 230, 10 years 260, 20 years 300, 30 years 320; ♀ (not pregnant) Wt 10 years 1000–1300, 20 years 1800–2000, 30 years 2200–2500, 40 years 2200–2500, 50 years 2800–3000. Mostly growth ends at 25–30 years, afterwards little further growth, but tusks grow throughout life. Sex ratio at birth 1:1, in adults slight excess of ♀♀. SEXUAL MATURITY: Forest Elephant 8–10, Bush Elephant 10–12 years (in overcrowding retarded a year). First birth at 10–12 (Forest Elephant) or 12–14 years (Bush Elephant). Births occur every 2–2½ years (in overcrowding only 4 years or later). 1 ♀ has 10–12 calves in her lifetime. LONGEVITY: Average expectation of life in the wild 15 years. Duration of life of Bush Elephant up to 60 years, rarely more, in Forest Elephant 60–70, sometimes 80 years.

PYGMY ELEPHANT, *Loxodonta pumilio* (Noack, 1906)   **Pl. 23**
G. Afrikanischer Zwergelefant   F. L'Elephant pygmée
(Note: The existence of a species of pygmy elephant is not generally recognised; the animals described are believed to be small members of the Forest Elephant (*cyclotis*).)
Identification. See Family, p. 124. Body short, highest point behind middle of back. Skin greyish-brown to reddish-brown, in part violet overwash, in part smooth, finely wrinkled. Forehead flattened. Tip of trunk with two opposite grasping lips, upper notably longer than the lower. Ears large not resting on neck, round-elliptic front lower corner usually blunt, end rarely pointed. Tail round, thin, tuft of bristles. Nail-like hoofs 5/5. Tusks weak and short (Sierra Leone to S. Cameroon) or long, slender, pointing downwards (Gabon to S.E. Zaire). Cheek teeth as Bush Elephant, but only

about half the size.   MEASUREMENTS: Ht ♂ 170–205, ♀ 160–200, TL 50–70, trunk length 85–105, greatest length 400–490, Wt ♂ 1200–1500, ♀ 900–1100. Tusk length ♂ 60–125, ♀ 40–60, Wt ♂ 2–15, ♀ 1–5.

Distribution. Rain forests from Sierra Leone to N.E., S.E. and W. Zaire. Not found everywhere, from time to time only locally. Whether a ssp. (eg *fransseni* in W. Zaire) has no validity, is problematic. Habits not investigated (the last known large animal in Africa). In troops (10–20) and herds (50–70) of adults and young (smallest calves Ht only 60.5), in swampy forests. Locally remains apart from Forest Elephant (see African Elephant) (p. 125), said to be more aggressive; in some regions hunted by preference by pygmies whom it fears. *Map* p. 124.

Sea Cows, Sirenia

ROUND-TAILED SEA COWS, TRICHECHIDAE

Large, seal-like, cylindrical-bodied, aquatic. Skin wrinkled, almost completely naked, with thick layer of blubber. Bristly front of snout weakly curved downwards, upper lip deeply trilobed, laterally mobile. Nostrils can be closed by valve, eyes very small with nictitating membrane and oily tear ducts, no external ears. Forelimbs modified as fins, with 5 fingers, nails rudimentary. Hind limbs outwardly absent. In place of tail, a transverse, spade-shaped to round tail fin. The jaw parts of the sloping front of the muzzle with horny grinding plates, near them the incisors reduced to 2 functionless teeth in upper and lower jaw. Cheek teeth behind the grinding plates, low-crowned, enamel-covered, without cement, closed roots, proceeding regularly from back to front, where they fall out. Total number in lower and upper jaw 10 apiece, however at most 6 at a time in the jaw. Nasal bones present, 6 neck vertebrae, 2 teats on the breast (hence the name mermaid or siren). Gregarious, water plant eater in shallow coastal and fresh waters of the western and eastern mid-Atlantic coasts. 1 genus, 3 species, of which 1 in W. Africa.

AFRICAN MANATEE, *Trichechus senegalensis* (Link, 1795) **Pl. 24**
G. Afrikanischer Manati or Lamantin   F. Le Lamantin du Senégal
Identification. See Family, above. Skin colour brownish-grey to dark grey, belly lighter than back. Skin 5cm thick on back, to 1cm on belly, skin hairless apart from short bristles on sides of upper lip. In ♂, tail fin rear edge more obviously semi-circular, and front fin longer than in ♀. MEASUREMENTS: total length 250–365, of which tail *c.* 65–75, fin length 45–55, Wt 350–450.
Distribution. Coastal waters including lagoons and river mouths with inland lakes of W. Africa, from about 16°N to about 10°S, from Senegal to the Cuanza (principal rivers: Senegal, Gambia, Casamance, Corubal, Koukoure, St. Paul, St. John, Cess, Douobe, Sassandra, Bandama, Komoe, Tano, Volta, Mono, Niger, Benue, Lake Chad and Shari region, Sanaga, Nyong(a), Kouilou, Congo, said to be also in the river system of the middle Congo by a connection between the Ogowe in Gabon and Sanaga and Nyong(a) in Cameroun with Doume and Kadie, tributaries of the Congo-Lufunde, Loje, Kuanago, Kuanza). Because of its palatable meat greatly persecuted, in spite of local legal protection, and threatened with extermination. HABITAT: salt, brackish and fresh waters, viz, shallow coastal waters (1–12m) including lagoons and estuaries with rich sea-weed and aquatic vegetion growths as well as river creeks, and lakes with ample aquatic and riverside vegetation. Favourable water temperature 25°–35°C. HOME RANGE: size not known, but infrequent wanderer. Probably sedentary. *Map* p. 130.
Habits. DAILY RHYTHM: rests most of day, feeds at night, during which may ascend small tributaries. Rests floating in the water, or on the bottom, surfacing to breathe at regular intervals. Normal duration of dives 1–2, in emergency up to 15 minutes. Normal speed about 10kph in flight considerably faster. Propulsion is by vertical movement of the tail fin, front fins used for steering, partly as digging tools on the bottom, partly to convey food to mouth. Entirely aquatic (incapable of going ashore) at most may put its head out of water. VOICE: mute. Occasionally a loud breathing-

out sound. Ultrasonic communication and hearing. SENSES: sight bad, scent moderate, hearing good. ENEMIES: perhaps large sharks, details not known. In danger makes for deep water. Very shy where hunted by humans. FOOD: seaweed, marine grasses, fresh water vegetation and overhanging river bank plants. Of importance as destroyer of water hyacinths. Daily food intake 25–40kg. Front fins used to help gather food to mouth. Excreta potato-shaped balls. SOCIABILITY: associates in families (♂, ♀, 1–2 young of different ages), often several families in vicinity, young ♂♂ also solitary.

Reproduction. ♂ courts ♀ by snorting sounds, embracing and nestling together. Mating belly to belly in the water. Breeding over the whole year, also births, no restricted breeding season. Gestation 150–180 days (not exactly known). 1, rarely 2 young; born in the water. Mother helps young to surface. Total length at birth *c.* 100, Wt 20–30, skin pinkish. Suckles in water, for 1½ years, though first solid food after a few days. Both parents guard the young, which also rides on mother; lives 2 years with mother. ♀ mates again 1 week after calving. SEXUAL MATURITY: 3–4 years. LONGEVITY: 20–30 years possible, 11 years known in captivity.

FORK-TAILED SEA COWS, DUGONGIDAE

Form and habits as Round-tailed Sea Cows (Manatees, p. 129), with the following differences. Front of snout strongly curved downwards. Upper lip less deeply cleft. Between the mandibles 2 (in ♀ rudimentary, in ♂ tusk-like) upper incisors. Cheek teeth without enamel or roots, total number in upper and lower jaws always 6, however never more than 3 in each jaw at the same time. Tail fin 2-lobed, front flipper without nails. Nasal bones absent. 7 neck vertebrae, 2 teats on breast. 1 genus with 1 species from Red Sea and E. African coast eastward to Australia.

1 African Manatee
2 Dugong

DUGONG, *Dugong dugon* (P. L. S. Muller, 1776)   **Pl. 24**
G. Dugong   F. Le Dugong
Identification. See Family above. Skin brownish-grey above, flesh-coloured below, flanks grey. Body limbs and tail with fine hairs, sides of upper lips with short bristles. MEASUREMENTS: TL 250–320, Wt 150–200, ♂ larger and heavier than ♀.
Distribution. Red Sea and E. African coasts south to Delagoa Bay (25°S) as well as coasts of Madagascar, Comoros, Seychelles, Mauritius and other tropical islands,

Malabar, W. Ceylon, Gulf of Bengal, Andamans, Nicobars, Indochina, S. China to Formosa and S. Korea, S. Japan, Malayan Archipelago to S.E. Philippines, Moluccas, New Guinea, N. and N.E. Australia and further to Carolines, Solomons, Marshall Islands and New Caledonia. Owing to its palatable flesh (and in spite of legal protection) is hunted everywhere and in many areas is already extinct; greatly threatened. HABITAT: shallow coastal waters with abundant aquatic vegetation; not in fresh water. HOME RANGE: see Manatee (p. 129).

Habits. DAILY RHYTHM: by day in deeper water, at night (also where undisturbed, by day), in shallows to graze, no clear division of the day; in other ways see Manatee. VOICE: see Manatee. ENEMIES: large sharks. When in danger flees to deep water, where hunted is very shy. FOOD: predominantly marine grasses, preferring particular species. Some species are dug out of the sandy bottom by the snout and eaten with their roots. Before eating, shakes the food to get rid of the sand. Daily food intake 25–40kg. SOCIABILITY: families ($\male$, $\female$, and 1–2 young of different ages), often several families up to 80–100 animals together when feeding. Young $\male\male$ also may be solitary.

Reproduction. Courtship by $\male$ as Manatee. Pair belly to belly upright, partly above water. No limited breeding season, young in all months. Gestation said to be 11 months, see Manatee. Length at birth *c.* 100, Wt not known. Birth, rearing, suckling times and sexual maturity, see Manatee. LONGEVITY: not known, $6\frac{1}{2}$ years reported in captivity.

Pipe-toothed Animals, Tubulidentata

AARDVARKS, ORYCTEROPODIDAE

Size and form pig-like, with thick-set high backed figure, thick pinkish-grey skin and sparse (thicker on legs) stiff brownish-grey to blackish-brown hair. ♂ with dark, ♀ light, cheek hairs, whitish tail tip. Snout very elongated, tubular, broad muzzle with large nostrils protected by hair tufts. Ears very large, naked, spoon-shaped, can be folded and closed, normally upright. Eyes medium-sized. Limbs of medium length, strong, walks on half sole, half claw. Toes 4/5, with powerful claws, those of forefeet strong digging tools. Tail hangs down, medium length, thick at root, thin at tip, naked. Dent.: 0/0 · 0/0 · 2/2 · 3–2/3 = 18–20, milk teeth unerupted, molars all uniform, evergrowing, rootless; those at front coming first into use being replaced by successors as they fall out, each tooth consisting of 1000 to 1500 tubes of dentine cemented together. Tongue worm-like, sticky, stretching up to 30cm. Skin glands on elbows, hoofs and foreskin, 4 teats. Solitary, nocturnal insect eater in Africa south of Sahara. Only 1 genus.

AARDVARK, *Orycteropus afer* (Pallas, 1766) **Pl. 25**
G. Erdferkel   F. Le Fourmillier   A. Erdvark   S. Muhanga
Identification. See above. MEASUREMENTS: HB 120–140 (160), TL 45–60, Ht 60–65, Wt 50–80.
Distribution. Africa south of Sahara, northern limit from Senegambia to Air and Eritrea. Several ssp., however, number not clear. HABITAT: in all regions with sufficient termites, from dry savannah to rain forest; hard laterite soils unsuited for digging are avoided. HOME RANGE: self-excavated burrows in which they live form centre of range, roam nightly up to 30km in search of food. Burrows consist of several metre-long runs, about 40cm wide on average, with spacious living chamber at end, can also be more branching with several chambers. No individual territory marking, though the olive-shaped droppings are deposited in small pits near the entrance to the burrow and raked over. Aardvark holes serve many other animals as shelters; bats, ground squirrels, hares, cats, civets, hyaenas, jackals, porcupines, wart hogs, monitor lizards, owls and other birds.

Aardvark

Habits. DAILY RHYTHM: entirely nocturnal, but after a cold night may sun itself in front of burrow. If too far from home by end of night will excavate a temporary sleeping burrow. Entrance of an occupied hole is blocked with earth, leaving only an air vent.   TOILET: not known.   VOICE: snorting grunt on the move, grunting before entering hole, loud bleating in fright and terror.   SENSES: scent, hearing and tasting ability very good, sight less good.   ENEMIES: lion, leopard, cheetah, hyaena, hunting dog, python. In danger takes to nearest hole or rapidly excavates a refuge hole. If cornered defends itself with tail or shoulders, or sits erect and strikes with fore-claws, or lies on back and strikes with all four feet. If touched will somersault with loud bleat to frighten the enemy.   FOOD: mainly termites in above-ground columns, otherwise digs them out of ground. In dry season also the fungi from termite 'fungus gardens', besides ants, grasshoppers, grubs and other insects. Also soft wild cucumbers are eagerly eaten, their pips germinating only after passing through the intestines to the aardvark dung heaps.   SOCIABILITY: solitary, only ♀ with young (both younger and older) linger together. Where many aardvarks are found, sometimes several sleep in one burrow.

Reproduction. Gestation 7 months, births in mid-Africa mainly Oct–Nov, in S. Africa May–Aug. 1 (rarely 2) naked flesh-coloured young. Eyes open, stay 2 weeks in burrow, then follow ♀ in food searches, deposit droppings in separate pits. First solid food at 3 months, suckle for 4 months, at 6 months ♂ independent, young ♀ stays with mother until next young born. At birth Wt 1.8–2, TL 55; at 1 month Wt 3.5, TL 68; at 3 months Wt 9, TL 93; at 7 months Wt 33, TL *c.* 120.   SEXUAL MATURITY: 2 years.   LONGEVITY: in captivity 18 years recorded.

Scaled Animals, Pholidota

SCALY ANTEATERS or PANGOLINS, MANIDAE

Short-legged, size of marten to badger. Head, eyes and ears remarkably small, muzzle pointed. Upperside of body and both sides of tail covered with brown, tile-like, overlapping scales, growing from the leathery skin and capable of being closed up tightly in emergency. Underside of body and inside of legs naked or well haired, pale to dark. Hind legs longer than forelegs, toes 5/5, with claws, those of middle of hand especially large. Climbing species have naked pad on underside of tail tip, used as prehensile grasping organ. No teeth. Tongue elongated, very extensile, salivary glands very large, stomach muscular with horny surfaces for dealing with insect food. 2 axillary teats. Anal glands sometimes well developed. Solitary, nocturnal, borrowing or climbing ant and termite eaters. Africa except Madagascar, India with Ceylon, Burma, S. China, Formosa, Hainan, Malacca, Sumatra, Java, Bali, Borneo and Palawan. 1 genus, 7 species, 3 of which in Africa.

LONG-TAILED or BLACK-BELLIED PANGOLIN, Pl. 25
Manis (Uromanis) tetradactyla (Linnaeus, 1766)
G. Langschwanz or Schwarzbauchschuppentier   F. Le Pangolin à longue queue
Identification. Tail twice length of head and body. Under-tip of tail a naked pad. Upperside of front foot hairy, without scales. Face and underside of body blackish. Scales moderately large, keeled, 2 shoulder scales very large. Scales deep brown, edges lighter or sometimes yellowish, sometimes some whole scales light, free edge of scale with 1 (sometimes 3) point(s). On body 10–13 rows of scales.   MEASUREMENTS: HB 30–40, TL 60–80, Wt 2.5–3.25.
Distribution. Rain forests from Senegal to N.E. Zaire, extreme W. Uganda, from there S.W. to Mossamedes, S.W. Angola. No ssp.   HABITAT: rain forest, especially flooded forests.   HOME RANGE: adults are sedentary, with several feeding areas with holes for sleeping and trails marked by urine and anal scent glands. ♂ drives off sex partners.
Habits. DAILY RHYTHM: mainly nocturnal, though may also be seen in daytime. Sleeps rolled up in hole in tree. Good climber, hangs by tail tip and climbs up its own tail. Good swimmer.   TOILET: scratching between scales with claws of fore and hind feet.   VOICE: an audible snuffling while feeding. A loud hiss when rolling into a ball

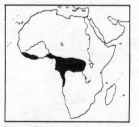
Long-tailed Pangolin

suddenly. SENSES: scent very good. Recognises by scent the sex, age, mood and condition of others of the species. Hearing good, sight bad. ENEMIES: the scaly armour and the rapid rolling up into a ball protect it from most predators. In emergency uses claws of forefoot in defence and the sharp edges of the tail scales; as well as spraying the offensive urine and ejecting a stinking anal gland secretion or droppings. FOOD: moving tree ants are licked up, nests of tree ants and termites torn open with fore claws and licked out (day's food 150–200g). SOCIABILITY: solitary, occupiers of neighbouring zones recognise each other, a loose ♂ and ♀ bond; when ♀ comes in heat sexes together until ready for mating, although each sleeps in separate holes.

Reproduction. In pairing ♂ moves sideways with pelvis under ♀, or latter lies on back, holding together with intertwined tails. Gestation 4½–5 months, 1 young at a birth, eyes open, clings with foreclaws on and under mother, who protects it by rolling up. Nursery a bare hole in tree, afterbirth eaten by ants. Wt at birth 100–150g, length 30–35, daily weight increment 4–6g. In first week ♀ goes to feed and leaves young in hole, afterwards young rides on root of tail of mother. First insect food at 14 days, weaned at 3 months, leaves mother at 4–5 months, roams around, becomes settled at about ¾ year. ♀ mates again 9–16 days after birth; 2 young in a year possible. LONGEVITY: not known in wild, in captivity over 3 years recorded.

WHITE-BELLIED or THREE-CUSPED PANGOLIN,   Pl. 25
Manis (Phataginus) tricuspis (Rafinesque, 1821)
G. Weissbauchschuppentier   F. Le Pangolin commun

Identification. Tail length about 1½ times head and body. Underside of tail tip with naked pad. Upperside of forefoot hairy, without scales. Underside of body, face and legs whitish-grey. Scales small, shoulder scales not notably larger than the rest. Scales brown, uppersides darker, sometimes some lighter. Free end of each scale with 3 points, middle one strongly keeled. 19–22 rows of scales on body. MEASUREMENTS: HB 33–43, TL 49–62, Wt 2.15–3.

Distribution. Rain forests from Senegal eastward to N.E. Zaire, Uganda, W. Kenya, N.W. Zambia, southwards to M. and S.W. Angola. Possibly N. Mozambique, also Fernando Poo. 2 ssp. HABITAT: rain forests, especially secondary forest, where ants and termites common; also in plantations. Only in lowlands, not in mountains. Commonest pangolin of rain forest regions. HOME RANGE: as Long-tailed Pangolin, above. Old ♂ range from 15–30 hectares, overlapping several ♀ ranges of 3–4 hectares. Young animals change their range and sleeping hole, wandering widely around. Sleeping places in self-excavated holes in ground (20–40cm deep) or in termite hills (with or without termites) or more frequently in holes in trees or in lianas around dead branches 10–15m high. *Map p. 137.*

Habits. DAILY RHYTHM: nocturnal. ♀ is only active for 3–4 hours at a time, covering a distance of 400–600m, ♂ 5–6 hours and about 700m, but in searching for the ♀ may travel 1.5–1.8km. Activity may begin between 7 and 11pm. Less activity in rainy season; in heavy rain, ♀ only goes short distance, leaving scent trails avoided by other ♀♀, and sleeps usually in the same hole. ♂ roams through ♀♀ range, making encounters easy, and often changing its sleeping holes. TOILET, SENSES, ENEMIES: as Long-tailed Pangolin. FOOD: searches for ants and termites on ground and in trees, under bark of dead branches. Fungus growing termite runs on surface and termite holes at foot of trees are opened, otherwise little digging. SOCIABILITY: as Long-tailed Pangolin.

Reproduction. Wt at birth 100–150, TL 30–35, weight increase 4–6g daily. ♀ stays in hole a week after giving birth, making only short food excursions. Young can ride on ♀ tail securely after 2 weeks, and are then taken around by mother; sleep with ♀ 4 months, independent at 4–5 months, living afterwards near mother with small range, grown up at 7–8 months, are then driven away by old ♂ and begin to roam. Other details as Long-tailed Pangolin. LONGEVITY: as Long-tailed Pangolin.

GIANT GROUND PANGOLIN, Pl. 25
Manis (Smutsia) gigantea (Illiger, 1815)
G. Riesenschuppentier   F. Le Pangolin géant

Identification. Tail shorter than HB. Tip of tail fully scaled, pointed. Upperside of front foot scaly. Face and underside of body naked, light brownish-grey, dense ring of short hair around eyes and base of ears. Claws brown, 1st and 5th very small, Scales very large, broadly rounded, posterior edge often irregular through damage, on upperside of body dark olive brown, flanks lighter, in newborn young amber yellowish. Body with 17 rows of scales, lateral edge of tail with 15–19 scales. Scales only grooved, never keeled, without noticeable pointed tips. MEASUREMENTS: HB 75–100, TL 50–70, Wt 30–35. ♂ rather larger and heavier than ♀.

Distribution. W. Africa from Senegal to mid-Gabon east to N.E. Zaire, Lake Mobutu (L. Albert), Uganda and perhaps also W. Kenya and W. Tanzania. No ssp. HABITAT: forests and nearby savannahs in areas of good rainfall and high humidity and without long dry season. Swamps and moist river valleys are favourite areas in plains, hills and lower mountains. HOME RANGE: sedentary, often living for months or a year in the same place, sleeping in the same hole, and wandering at night only a km away.

Habits. DAILY RHYTHM: nocturnal, mainly between midnight and dawn. Sleeps by day in Aardvark hole or self-dug hole up to 40m long and 5m deep. Walks on outside edge of hands, claws inward. Often erect on hind legs. Can swim if necessary. TOILET, VOICE, SENSES, ENEMIES: see Long-tailed Pangolin (p. 134). FOOD: terrestrial ants or termites in superficial runs are licked up, but principally their above and below ground colonies broken up by powerful digging claws of the front feet, and their inhabitants licked out (in 1 night 1½–2 litres). SOCIABILITY: as Long-tailed Pangolin.

Reproduction. Mating as Long-tailed Pangolin. Gestation about 5 months (not known exactly). Wt at birth *c*. 500g. TL *c*. 45. Soft scales of young harden in 2 days; ♀ leaves young in hole for a month, then takes it on base of tail while feeding. Young then begins to capture food. Weaning at 3 months (Wt then *c*. 6kg). Further details not known, however like Long-tailed Pangolin. LONGEVITY: not known in the wild; in captivity up to 4 years recorded.

TEMMINCKS GROUND PANGOLIN or CAPE PANGOLIN,
Manis (Smutsia) temmincki (Smuts, 1832)
G. Steppenschuppentier   F. Pangolin de Temminck   A. Ietermagog
S. Kaka, Kakakuona

Identification. Tail shorter than HB. Tail tip fully scaled, rounded. Upperside of forefoot scaly. Face and underside of body almost naked, whitish-grey, some short hair around eyes, bases of ears and on cheeks as well as sparse black hairs on underside. 1st and 5th claws of forefoot very reduced. Scales very large, broadly rounded, edges lighter, those of newborn young yellowish-grey with yellow spots on free edge. MEASUREMENTS: HB 50–60, TL 40–50, Wt 15–18.

Distribution. Central African Republic (Chad), S. Sudan, E. Uganda, W. Kenya, Tanzania, Malawi, Zambia, Rhodesia, Mozambique, N. and E. South Africa, Botswana, N.E. and S.W. Africa, Angola. No ssp. HABITAT: dry bush country, especially regions with light sandy soil. HOME RANGE: as Giant Ground Pangolin (p. 136).

Habits. DAILY RHYTHM: as in Giant Ground Pangolin. Holes not usually self-excavated. Can climb and swim if necessary. TOILET, VOICE, SENSES, ENEMIES: as Giant Ground Pangolin. FOOD: mainly surface ants, and termites in dung heaps, under or in rotten wood, also dug out from nests. At intervals stands up on hind legs to look around. SOCIABILITY: as Long-tailed Pangolin.

Reproduction. Pairing and gestation as in Long-tailed Pangolin. Wt at birth 330–450g. TL 15–18; at 3 months Wt *c.* 2000, after 1 year *c.* 3500. 1 month after birth ♀ carries young on base of tail while feeding, and young eat first solid food. Weaning begins at 3 months. Further details not known; probably as Long-tailed Pangolin. LONGEVITY: not known.

White-bellied Pangolin   Giant Ground Pangolin   Temminck's Ground Pangolin

Rodents, Rodentia

SQUIRRELS, SCIURIDAE

Animals from mouse to marmot in size, terrestrial, arboreal, or gliding. Often with hair tufts on ears and bushy tails. Dent: $1 \cdot 0 \cdot 1–2/1.3 = 20–22$, cheek teeth low, rooted, crowns with cusps. Toes 4/5. Most are diurnal, only flying squirrels nocturnal. Ground squirrels make burrows and do not usually climb. Arboreal and flying squirrels climb well and live in holes in trees, or in self-built nests. Live on vegetation, particularly nuts and conifer seeds, at times on insects, birds eggs and young as extras. Old and New Worlds apart from Arctic regions and Australasia. 46 genera, 245 species of which 10 genera and 29 species are African. The 10 African genera include 3 ground, 1 bush and 6 tree squirrels. The ground squirrels are earth- or sand-coloured, with or without a light flank stripe, have rough stiff short pelage with little undercoat, very short ears, a thinly haired bushy tail and live in burrows in open country. The bush squirrels are uniformly coloured, or striped with black, yellow or green, have a rather short but bushy tail and live in holes in trees or in nests in woodland savannah as well as in open light woodland. The tree squirrels are strongly and generally brightly coloured, with or without longitudinal stripes, and live in nests in light to heavy forest. Owing to space limitations only 4 species can be treated here in detail, but brief descriptions follow of all 29 African species.

| North African Ground Squirrel | 1 Western Ground Squirrel
2 Kaokoveld Ground Squirrel | 1 East African Ground Squirrel
2 Cape Ground Squirrel |

GROUND SQUIRRELS, *Xerini*
G. Erdhörnchen   F. L'Ecureuils foisseur
3 genera, 5 species, in N., W., E. and S. Africa.

1. *Atlantoxerus getulus* (Linnaeus 1758), only 1 species, Barbary Ground Squirrel, G. Nordafrikanisches Erdhörnchen; F. L'Écureuil de Barbarie. Morocco and Algeria in high to middle Atlas and Antiatlas (up to 4000m) to edge of Sahara. No ssp. Upperside greyish-brown with 3 whitish longitudinal stripes. Tail with light and dark rings. HB 16–22, TL 14–18.

2. *Euxerus erythropus* (E. Geoffroy 1803), only 1 species, Geoffroy's Ground Squirrel, G. West-Erdhörnchen; F. L'Écureuil foisseur de Sahel. From Senegal and S.W.

Morocco east to mid-Ethiopia and mid-Tanzania. 6 ssp. See p. 145 for full details.
Xerus (= *Geosciurus*) Bristly squirrel. 3 species in E. and S. Africa.

3. *rutilus* (Cretzschmar 1826). Unstriped Ground Squirrel. G: Ostafrikanisches Erdhörnchen; F. L'Écureuil unicouleur; S. Kindi, Kidiri. Eritrea, E. and S. Ethiopia, Somalia, W. Uganda, Kenya, N.W. Tanzania. 7 ssp. Upperside and tail reddish-brown to yellowish-grey, with white stippling. Underside beige-yellow. Tail tip white. HB 20–26, TL 18–23, Wt 300–350.

4. *inauris* (Zimmermann 1780) (= *capensis* Kerr 1792), Cape Ground Squirrel. G. Kap Erdhörnchen, F. L'Écureuil foisseur du Cap; A: Waaierstertmierkat. W. Transvaal, W. Orange Free State, N. and W. Cape Province, S. and M. Botswana, W. Rhodesia, S. and mid S.W. Africa. No ssp. See p. 144 for full details.

5. *princeps* (Thomas 1929), Kaokoveld Ground Squirrel. G. Kaokoveld Erdhörnchen; F. L'Écureuil foisseur de Kaokoveld. A. Waaierstert. Northern S.W. Africa and S. Angola. No ssp. Like *inauris* but tail hairs with 3 black rings and yellow front sides of incisors. HB 23–29, TL 21–28, Wt 700–1200.

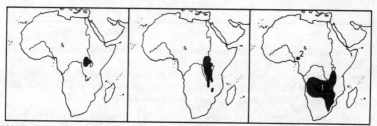

Alexander's Bush Squirrel

Boehm's Bush Squirrel

1 Smith's Bush Squirrel
2 Cooper's Green Squirrel

BUSH SQUIRRELS, *Paraxerus*
G. Buschhörnchen   F. L'Écureuil des bois
10 species in W., M., E. and S. Africa.

1. *alexandri* (Thomas and Wroughton 1907), Alexander's Bush Squirrel, G. Alexander Buschhörnchen; F. L'Écureuil d'Alexandre. N.E. Zaire and W. Uganda. No ssp. Upperside olive-greenish, a brown dorsal stripe with a black and white stripe on either side; underside whitish-yellow, edges of ears white. HB 9–12, TL 11–15, Wt 40–70.

2. *boehmi* (Reichenow 1886), Boehm's Bush Squirrel. G. Bohm-Buschhörnchen, F. L'Écureuil des bois de Boehm. N. and E. Zaire, S. Sudan, W. Uganda, W. Kenya, W. Tanzania, N. Zambia. 4 ssp. Dorsal central stripe olive green, on either side light yellowish to white lateral stripes, bordered on either side by a black stripe. Tail mixed black and greenish brown. Underside grey, sometimes whitish on breast. HB 10–15, TL 9–20, Wt 40–100.

3. *cepapi* (A. Smith, 1836). Smith's Bush Squirrel. G: Ockerfuss-Buschhörnchen, F. L'Écureuil des bois de Smith; A. Geelpooteekhoorntjie. W. Tanzania, S. Zaire, mid- and S. Angola, Zambia, Malawi, Rhodesia, western mid-Mozambique, Transvaal, E. and N. Botswana, N.E. S.W. Africa. 10 ssp. Upperside brownish yellow to yellowish

or olive grey, grizzled with darker shade, sometimes lower edge of flanks yellowish, hands and feet ochreous to greyish yellow, underside grey to yellowish white. Tail as back, with *c*.15 blackish rings. HB 13–20, TL 12–20, Wt 120–150.

4. *cooperi* (Hayman, 1950). Cooper's Green Squirrel. G. Cooper-Buschhörnchen; F. L'Ecureuil des bois de Cooper. Mountain forests (to 2400m and upward) in Kumba District, mid-W. Cameroun. No ssp. Upperside grizzled blackish yellow, underside greyish orange mixed; tail like back, but its underside with central yellowish longitudinal stripe; hands, feet and thighs deep red. HB and TL 19–21. *Map* p. 139.

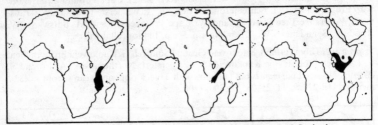

Striped Bush Squirrel   Black and Red Bush Squirrel   Huet's Bush Squirrel

5. *flavivittis* (Peters, 1852). Striped Bush Squirrel. G. Streifen-Buschhörnchen; F. L'Écureuil des bois raye. S.E. Kenya, E. and S. Tanzania, N. Mozambique. 4 ssp. Upperside light brown, darkly grizzled, whitish to yellowish flank stripes, sometimes with 1 additional blackish stripe above and below; underside whitish yellow, tail like back with about 7 indistinct dark rings in distal part. HB 16–20, TL 14–18.

6. *lucifer* (Thomas, 1897) (= *vexillarius* Kershaw 1923; *vincenti* Hayman 1950). Black and Red Bush Squirrel. G. Berg-Buschhörnchen; F. L'Écureuil des bois noir et rouge. 3 ssp. Mountains on N.W. shore of L. Tanganyika, N. Malawi (*lucifer*), N. and N.E. shore of L. Tanganyika, S.W. Tanzania (*laetus*) Udzungwe, Uluguru and Usambara Mts and Kilimanjaro, S., Mid- and N.E. Tanzania (*byatti*). Upperside orange red with black saddle, tail similar with several blackish rings (*lucifer*); head, legs and rump orange-red, rest of back olive, speckled with black, tail olive, with black rings (*laetus*); back olive, yellow speckled, tail yellowish, dark brown ringed, legs dull ochreous (*byatti*). Underside white, whitish grey or light grey. HB 20–32, TL 16–27, Wt 650–750.

7. *ochraceus* (Huet, 1880). Huet's Bush Squirrel. G. Ocker-Buschhörnchen; F. L'Écureuil des bois ocre. S. Sudan, Kenya, N.E. and mid-E. Tanzania. In mountains up to 2500m. 5 ssp. Upperside sandy-yellow, yellowish or greenish ochreous, speckled dark or black, sometimes a light flank stripe distinguishable. Underside white to yellow. Tail as upperside, with about 15 indistinct dark to blackish rings. HB 13.5–18.5, TL 13–19, Wt 80–100.

8. *palliatus* (Peters, 1852) (= *vincenti* Hayman, 1950). Red Bush Squirrel. G. Rotbauch-Buschhörnchen; F. L'Écureuil des bois à ventre rouge; A. Rovieekhoorntjie. Zululand, Mozambique, S.E. Rhodesia, S. Malawi, E. Tanzania, Zanzibar, Mafia Islands, coastal region of Kenya and S. Somalia. 11 ssp. Upperside mid to blackish brown, underside, legs and often also head pale to deep red, tail below red or yellowish, above coloured like back or like back at start, the rest light red. HB 17–25, TL 10–27, Wt *c*.200.

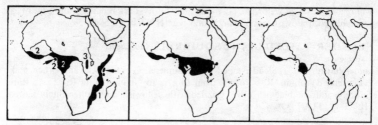

1 Red Bush Squirrel   Giant Forest Squirrel   Temminck's Giant Squirrel
2 Small Green Squirrel
3 Mountain Tree Squirrel

9. *poensis* (A. Smith, 1834). Small Green Squirrel. G. Grun-Buschhörnchen; F. L'Écureuil de Fernando-Poo. Sierra Leone to E. Ghana, E. Benin to Cameroun with Fernando Poo, Gabon, Congo (Brazzaville) and N. Zaire between N. bank of Congo and Ubangi, east to 25°E. No ssp. Upperside olive green, grizzled with black, tail similar though usually darker, underside greenish yellow like rest of underside of body, indistinctly black ringed. HB 14–18, TL 14–19.

10. *carruthersi* (Thomas, 1906). Mountain Tree Squirrel. G. Ruwenzori-Buschhörnchen; F. L'Écureuil des bois de Carruthers; Ruwenzori and mountain forests around Lakes Edward (Idi-Amin), Kivu and N. shore of L. Tanganyika. 4 ssp. Upperside olive green, speckled with black, tail similar with about 8 broad black rings. Underside greyish white, pale cream coloured ring round eyes. HB 19–26, TL 18–21, Wt 200–350.

GIANT FOREST SQUIRRELS, *Protoxerus*
1 species in W. M. and E. Africa.
stangeri (Waterhouse, 1842). Giant Forest Squirrel. G. Olpalmenhörnchen; F. Le Grand Écureuil de Stanger. Rain forests from Sierra Leone to W. Kenya, south to N. Angola, N. Katanga and western mid-Tanzania, also in Fernando Poo. 11 ssp. See p. 145 for full details.

TEMMINCK'S GIANT SQUIRREL, *Epixerus*
1 species in W. Africa.
ebii (Temminck, 1853). G. Nacktbauchhörnchen; F. L'Écureuil d'Ebi. Rain forests from E. Sierra Leone to R. Volta in Ghana, and S. Cameroun south of Sanaga River, southwards through Rio Muni, Gabon, and W. Congo (Brazzaville) almost to mouth of R. Congo. 3 ssp. Upperside reddish brown, overwashed with black, legs reddish brown, throat and breast orange, belly almost naked, finely haired with orange, tail blackish brown with 7–8 iron-grey rings, tip blackish brown. HB 24–30, TL 27–30.

PYGMY SQUIRREL, *Myosciurus*
1 species in W. Africa
pumilio (LeConte, 1857). Pygmy squirrel. G. Zwerghörnchen; F. L'Écureuil nain de l'Afrique. S.E. Nigeria, mid- and S. Cameroun and Fernando Poo, Gabon. Dormouse-like. Upperside reddish- or yellowish-grey overwashed with black, underside greyish

white, grey or faded yellowish, tail moderately bushy, dark reddish, inner edge of ear white-haired, yellowish-orange ring round eyes. HB 7–8, TL 5–6.

SLENDER-TAILED GIANT SQUIRREL, *Allosciurus*
1 species in W. Africa.
aubini (Gray, 1873). Slender-tailed Giant Squirrel. G. Dunnschwanzhörnchen; F. L'Écureuil d'Aubinn. Rain forests from Liberia to Ghana (Volta R.) 2 ssp. Rare. Entirely uniform blackish olive, grizzled with yellowish, tail rather thinly haired. HB 23–27, TL 27–33.

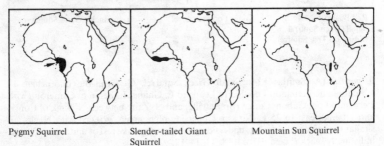

Pygmy Squirrel   Slender-tailed Giant   Mountain Sun Squirrel
                        Squirrel

SUN SQUIRRELS, *Heliosciurus*
G. Sonnenhörnchen   F. Les Heliosciures
3 species in W. M. and E. Africa.

1. *ruwenzorii* (Schwann, 1907). Mountain Sun Squirrel. G. Ruwenzori-Sonnenhörnchen; F. Le Héliosciure de Ruwenzori. Mountain forests around Lakes Mobutu (Albert), Idi Amin (Edward) Kivu and northern tip of Lake Tanganyika; border region of Zaire, Uganda, Ruanda-Urundi. 4 ssp. Dark grey, lightly speckled, underside lighter, white central stripe from chin to anus. Face and legs tan-coloured, tail bushy and flattened, upperside coloured as back, with c.13 black rings, underside whitish. HB 20–26, TL 22–28, Wt 200–380.

2. *gambianus* (Ogilby, 1822). Gambian Sun Squirrel. G. Gambia Sonnenhörnchen; F. Le Héliosciure de Gambie. Savannah woodlands and secondary forest regions from Senegambia to Darfur and Equatoria, Uganda, W. Kenya, W. Tanzania, Ethiopia, Zambia, S. and W. Zaire, Angola, S. Congo (Brazzaville). 22 ssp. Upper side dark olive, speckled with yellow or grey (black and white mixed) or light to greyish brown, underside orange, yellowish, grey or white. White ring round eyes, backs of feet pale. Tail like upperside, with 14 blackish rings. HB 17–27, TL 18–26, Wt 250–350.

3. *rufobrachium* (Waterhouse, 1842). Red-legged Sun Squirrel. G. Rotbein-Sonnenhörnchen; F. Le Héliosciure à jambes rousses. Rain forests from Senegambia to S.E. Sudan, Kenya, E. Tanzania with Zanzibar and Mafia Islands, N. Mozambique to Zambesi, S. Malawi, N. Zambia, in west south to Congo and Kasai lower reaches. Also Fernando Poo. 24 ssp. Upperside iron-grey, or grey to dark reddish-olive brown; inside of arms and thighs rust red or dirty ochreous, upper parts of hind feet rufous; underside fawn-olive brown to grey, greyish white or white. Light ring round eyes. Tail like upperside with about 18 narrow black rings. HB 20–27, TL 21–30, Wt 250–400.

Gambian Sun Squirrel   Red-legged Sun Squirrel   1 Le Conte's Four-striped
                                                      Tree Squirrel
                                                    2 Kuhl's Striped Tree
                                                      Squirrel

STRIPED TREE SQUIRRELS or ROPE SQUIRRELS, *Funisciurus*
G. Streifenhörnchen   F. Les Funisciures
7 species in W. M. and western E. Africa.

1. *lemniscatus* (LeConte, 1857) (= *isabella* Gray 1862). LeConte's 4-striped Tree Squirrel. G. Vierstreifenhörnchen; F. Le Funisciure rayé. Rain forests and montane forests up to 2100m, in Cameroun, Rio Muni, Gabon and Congo (Brazzaville), south to mouth of Congo, E. to Bangui (Central African Republic). Not on Fernando Poo. 3 ssp. Upperside yellowish olive-brown with 4 black longitudinal stripes and 3 intermediate light stripes, the 2 central stripes being blackest and strongest, underside greyish white, tail like flanks, dark rings can be distinctly seen. HB 15–18, TL 13–19, Wt 100–150.

2. *congicus* (Kuhl, 1820). Kuhl's Tree Squirrel. G. Kongo-Streifenhörnchen; F. Le Funisciure de Kuhl; A. Gestreepte Eekhoorntjie. Rain forests and savannah woodland from Congo R. south to N. S.W. Africa (Ovamboland), Katanga and N.E. Angola. No ssp recognised. Upperside yellowish brown, shoulders lighter, a whitish yellow longitudinal stripe on flanks bordered by a darker stripe, flanks and legs greyish-yellowish brown, underside greyish olive, tail like flanks with distinct dark brown rings. HB 16–19, TL 14–16.

3. *bayonii* (Bocage, 1890). Bocage's Tree Squirrel. G. Bocages Streifenhörnchen; F. Le Funisciure de Bocage. N.E. Angola to Kasai River, S.W. Zaire. No ssp. Upperside and tail brownish olive, latter with indistinct blackish rings, flanks with weak yellowish stripe, underside grey. HB 16–19, TL 17.

Bocage's Tree   De Winton's Tree   Orange-headed
Squirrel   squirrel   Squirrel

4. *substriatus* (De Winton, 1899). De Winton's Tree Squirrel. G. Togostreifen-hörnchen; F. Le Funisciure de Kintampo. In Guinea woodland from S. Ghana, Togo, Benin, S.W. Nigeria. No ssp. Upperside reddish black to olive-grey-brown, whitish or only weakly defined yellowish lateral stripe; underside reddish-grey to yellowish-grey. Tail like back with dark rings. HB 15–18, TL 14–20. *Map* p. 143.

5 *leucogenys* (Waterhouse, 1842). Orange-headed Tree Squirrel. G. Orangekopf-Streifenhörnchen; F. Le Funisciure à tete orange. Rain forests and montane forests from Ghana eastward to Rio Muni and Fernando Poo as well as Central African Republic. 4 ssp. Upperside dark to light olive brown, face brown to orange, flanks with stripe broken into a row of dirty yellowish to orange spots; underside greyish to whitish yellow, upperside of tail like back, black-ringed, underside mid-line brown to orange. HB 17–24, TL 13–20, Wt 200–300. *Map* p. 143.

6. *pyrrhopus* (F. Cuvier, 1842). Cuvier's Fire-Footed squirrel. G. Roteschenkel-hörnchen; F. Le Funisciure à pattes rousses. From Sierra Leone to E. Uganda. 9 ssp. See p. 146 for full details. *Map* p. 147.

7. *anerythrus* (Thomas, 1890). Thomas's Tree Squirrel. G. Thomas-Streifenhörnchen; F. Le Funisciure à dos rayé. S.W. Nigeria to W. Uganda, N.E. Katanga, S.W. Zaire and Gabon. 4 ssp. Upperside lighter or darker brownish-olive, on each side of dorsal area a whitish-yellow to nearly faded out brownish lateral stripe. Legs like back or over-washed with reddish. Underside light grey to pale orange. Tail like back, ringed with iron-grey or pale yellow, the underside sometimes reddish. HB 16–23, TL 14–20. Some authors unite 6 and 7 in one species.

CAPE GROUND SQUIRREL, *Xerus inauris* (Zimmermann, 1780)　　**Pl. 26**
G. Kap-Erdhörnchen　　F. L'Écureuil foisseur de Cap　　A. Waaierstertmeerkat
Identification. Form and body structure like Cuvier's Fire-footed Squirrel (p. 146), however pelage stiff. Eyes large, ears small, round, naked. Toes 4/5. Penis with bone, 4 teats. Upperside pale reddish brown or greyish brown, stippled with black. Underside, flank stripe and eye stripe white. Tail hairs bushy, two-toned, grey with lighter roots and blackish tips; end of tail with 2 black and white bands. ♂ and ♀ alike and young like adults. MEASUREMENTS: HB 20–29, Tl 18–25, Wt 500–1100, ♂ larger and heavier than ♀.
Distribution. S. and S.W. Africa, from northern S.W. Africa, N. Botswana, S.W. Rhodesia and W. Transvaal south to Cape. No ssp. HABITAT: open country; grassy plains, edges of salt pans, seasonally flooded flat, dry river beds, low bush growth, open acacia savannahs, bush. HOME RANGE: 100–150m around hole. *Map* p. 138.
Habits. DAILY RHYTHM: diurnal, most activity morning and late afternoon; in early morning will sunbathe near the hole. Lives in self-excavated burrows with several entrances and exits and a grass-lined den; each hole with 1 animal, or ♀ with young, in small colonies several holes together, usually 6–10, sometimes up to 30 in a colony. In inclement weather do not leave holes. Often sit erect like mannikins outside the hole with tail over back, or roam around with tail lightly arched. Go up to 150m in feeding. In alarm bolt back to the hole, tail level, and sit outside or stand erect on hind legs sniffing. VOICE: alarm call a long-drawn whining cry. SENSES: sight and hearing very good, scent moderate. ENEMIES: meerkats, mongooses, kaffir cats, black-footed cats, caracals, cape fox, black-backed jackal predatory birds, snakes. If cornered defend themselves with vigour. FOOD: herbage, grasses, seeds, fruit, bulbs, roots,

eggs and young birds, small reptiles, insects. SOCIABILITY: daily rhythm. Often associate with suricats, meerkats and other species of ground squirrel.

Reproduction. Whole year, 2–6 at a birth, usually 4, blind young in the central den. Further details not known. Dangerous as carrier of infectious diseases.

GEOFFROY'S GROUND SQUIRREL,   Pl. 26
Euxerus erythropus (E. Geoffrroy, 1803)
G. West-Erdhörnchen   F. L'Écureuil foisseur

Identification. Form and build like Giant Forest Squirrel and Cuvier's Fire-footed Squirrel (see p. 146), however pelage harsh, tail with hair flat on either side rather than bushy all round, P^3 very small, 6 teats. Hair lying flat and close, underside only thinly haired, axilla and groin naked. Upperside dark brown or sandy, underside white. Stripes over and under eye, and on flank, whitish. Crown like neck and back, cheeks and paws lighter, claws long and only slightly curved. White spot behind ear present or absent. Tail hairs bushy but in two rows, closely ringed with black and white, centrally coloured as back. Sexes and young alike, though pelage of young in nest very sparse. First hair change between 40 and 100 days, second at 5–6 months. MEASUREMENTS: HB 22–46, TL 18–27, Wt 500–950.

Distribution. from Senegal and S.W. Morocco (Sous) (about 30°N) to M. Ethiopia, Kenya and northern mid-Tanzania, northern border generally 15°N, also in Air, southernmost border in the west the Guinea coast, eastward from about 5°N to 3°S. 6 ssp. HABITAT: high forest to semi-desert; in the first only where in farmed clearings, in this way reaching to the coast of the Guinea countries. Common in farmland. HOME RANGE: about 100sq m around the hole. Solitary animals unknown. Living quarters either self-dug with many tunnels about 50cm long and perhaps a grass-lined den up to 1m deep, or in termite mounds, or in rock crevices and holes. Each animal has its own hole, but many holes may be grouped together. *Map* p. 138.

Habits. DAILY RHYTHM: diurnal, leaving holes after sunrise, in bad weather not before midday; in noon-day heat shelters under bushes or in holes; when going to sleep at dusk may close up the entrance from inside. During feeding may sit upright and watch its surroundings. Tail carried lightly curved, over the back in excitement, in flight runs quickly with tail horizontal. VOICE: several varying sounds, a squeak when annoyed, a soft 'chur' in courtship, in alarm or excitement 'chip-chip', with other sounds from the young. SENSES: sight very good, birds of prey recognised at a distance. Hearing very good, scent moderate. ENEMIES: ground predators (kaffir cat, serval, caracal, ratel, fox, jackal) birds of prey, snakes. Bolts rapidly to hole, but if caught bites savagely. FOOD: herbage of many kinds, leaves, seeds, fallen fruit, bulbs, roots, cultivated crops of all kinds, also hard-shelled nuts and seeds are gnawed: in addition insects, small reptiles, young birds, eggs. At times food may be stored underground. SOCIABILITY: See HOME RANGE.

Reproduction. Litter from 2–6, usually 4, births partly in all months, partly seasonal (in E. Africa Aug–Oct). Eyes open at 26–30 days, first solid food at 35 days, first excursion at 39 days, suckle $1\frac{1}{2}$–2 months. Wt at 2 weeks c.50, 1 month c.100, 2 months c.260. SEXUAL MATURITY: $\frac{1}{2}$ year. LONGEVITY: 6 years recorded in captivity.

GIANT FOREST SQUIRREL, *Protoxerus stangeri* (Waterhouse, 1843)   Pl. 27
G. Olpalmenhörnchen   F. Le Grand Écureuil de Stanger

Identification. Form and structure much as Cuvier's Fire-footed Squirrel (p. 146) but larger, snout blunter, tail bushier; P^3 as large as M^1. 8 teats. Upperside yellowish to olivaceous and reddish brown, sometimes crown white-speckled and yellow spot behind ear. Underside naked, skin yellowish brown, sometimes forehead, throat, sides of neck and breast with whitish hairs. Whitish dividing streak between flank and naked belly strong, weak or absent. Front legs coloured like back, hind legs yellowish to reddish brown. Base of tail coloured like back, the rest with 10–12 blackish rings on whitish ground. Sexes alike, young like adults, however tail apart from root is white, root with fine whitish rings and black medial band below. MEASUREMENTS: HB 22–40, TL 24–36, Wt 540–1000.

Distribution. Almost as Cuvier's Fire-footed Squirrel; forest belt from Sierra Leone eastward to W. Kenya and western Mid-Tanzania, with Fernando Poo, north boundary about 9°N in the west, about 5°N in the east, south boundary about 12°S in the west (mid-Angola) and about 4°S in the east. 11 ssp. HABITAT: high forest (rain, swamp, gallery) with clearings and not strongly closed canopy, also near settlements if forest, or forest remnants with large trees remain. HOME RANGE: size of area not known, see Cuvier's Fire-footed Squirrel, p. 146. *Map* p. 141.

Habits. DAILY RHYTHM: highest activity morning and afternoon; noisy on the move. Principally lives in highest tier of forest, now and then coming to the ground for fallen fruit in the forest or on grassland by the forest edge. Resting and sleeping place a large nest high in forked branches. VOICE: a scolding or growling chatter, in terror squeals and screams, but best known sound a deep booming contact call, far-reaching 'ku-ku-ku' or 'kom-kom-kom' especially heard in the morning. In alarm tail is waved fore and back. ♂ pursuing ♀ carries tail upright, in climbing the tail hangs. Tail normally curved backwards; in sitting, tail and back as in other forest squirrels. FOOD: oil palm fruits, nuts, fruits, seeds, leaves, bark, sometimes nestlings of birds. When food abundant may store some. SENSES: as Cuvier's Fire-footed Squirrel, but scenting ability poor. ENEMIES: as for other squirrels, particularly crowned eagle (*Stephanoaetes coronatus*). Dodges around tree-trunk on opposite side to the attacker. SOCIABILITY: in pairs.

Reproduction. 1–3 blind young at birth. Breeding season irregular.

CUVIER'S FIRE-FOOTED SQUIRREL, Pl. 27
Funisciurus pyrrhopus (F. Cuvier, 1842)
G. Rotschenkelhörnchen F. Le Funisciure à pattes rousses

Identification. Medium-sized to large. Pelage short, soft and smooth, long whiskers and sometimes also tactile cheek hairs. Tail uniformly bushy, rather shorter than HB. Muzzle sharp, eyes and ears small, latter rounded, naked. Arms and legs short, toes 4/5, thumb reduced. Dent: $1 \cdot 0 \cdot 2/1 \cdot 3 = 22$, P^3 very small. 4 teats, penis with bone, ♂ with large anal glands. Upperside light to dark olive grey, usually with middle of back darker, limbs and flanks to cheeks yellowish brown to dark red, underside yellow to whitish yellow or whitish grey to white. Behind ear a smaller or larger dark reddish-brown spot. On upper edge of flanks a yellowish-brown or whitish lateral stripe with a darker shadow stripe below it, or lateral stripe broken into spots. Tail with 10–15 dark greyish olive coloured rings on whitish grey ground; tip whitish grey or greyish black, underside with medium stripe coloured like flanks. Sexes alike. MEASUREMENTS: HB 13–27, TL 10–20, Wt 250–350.

Distribution. Sierra Leone, Liberia, Guinea, Ivory Coast, Ghana, Nigeria, Mid- and S. Cameroun, Gabon, Rio Muni, Congo (Brazzaville), S. Central African Republic, Cabinda, M. and N. Zaire to W. Uganda (Victoria Nile and Lake) Ruanda, Urundi, N. Angola. 9 ssp. HABITAT: high forest with undergrowth at edge and in clearings, secondary, gallery, coastal forests, mangrove and palm swamps, wooded grassland. HOME RANGE: size not known, however small, at most 1 hectare.

Habits. DAILY RHYTHM: mainly morning and late afternoon active; midday resting in nests built of leafy twigs or, regionally of palm leaf strips, in the lower branches or between tree roots. Lives in lower levels and often on ground. VOICE: a repeated chattering on descending scale as contact call. Also a mono-syllabic call which in excitement runs into a quick series. A buzzing during sexual excitement, and in fear or pain growling or squeaking. SENSES: sight and hearing very good, scent good. ENEMIES: genet, mongoose, snakes, birds of prey especially African Hawk Eagle (*Hieraaëtus fasciatus*), Cassins Hawk Eagle (*Cassinaëtus africanus*), and Longtailed Hawk (*Urotriorchis macrourus*). Take refuge by spiralling round tree trunk. FOOD: feeds mostly on the ground. Palm fruit (especially of Oil and Raffia Palms) the kernels being preferred to the flesh; also other fruits, nuts, seeds, insects, eggs of birds and reptiles. Insects, found mainly by scent, form a large part of the diet. SOCIABILITY: in pairs, sleeping in the same nest, or ♀ with young.

Reproduction. Tail position is used as a display or signal; in confrontation held trailing on the ground, in courtship by the ♂ circular shaped, curving like a cartwheel over the swollen testicles; in alarm flicks forward and backward quickly, normally carried with tip curved up. Time of births vary according to locality and season (1–2 blind young in nest). ♂ has cycles for maximum development of testicles and anal glands.

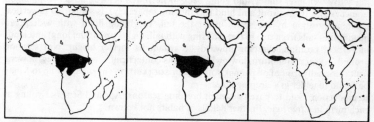

Cuvier's Fire-footed Squirrel   Thomas's Tree Squirrel   Pel's Flying Squirrel

SCALY-TAILED FLYING SQUIRRELS, ANOMALURIDAE

Squirrel-like forest animals from mouse- to cat-sized. Eyes and ears large, toes 4/5, tail long and bushy or with end tuft, underside of tail root with sharp-pointed horny scales or with file-like bare surface as climbing aids. Elbows with laterally directed cartilaginous spur about two-thirds of lower arm for spreading the gliding membrane, between neck, lower arm, base of toes and the first third of the tail (this membrane lacking in *Zenkerella*). Coat soft and thick. Dent: $1 \cdot 0 \cdot 1 \cdot 3 = 20$. 2–4 teats. Nocturnal, arboreal, gliding inhabitants of holes in trees from W., Central and E. Africa. 4 genera with 7 species.

PEL'S FLYING SQUIRREL,   Pl. 27
Anomalurus peli (Schlegel and Muller, 1845)
G. Pel-Dornschwanzhörnchen   F. L'Écureuil volant de Pel

Identification. Squirrel-like but cat-sized. Snout blunt, eyes rather small, ears naked, membranous, head extends beyond ears. Pelage dense, soft, rather long, underside shorter: long vibrissae, tufts of hair behind ears. Tail, nearly as long as HB, thickly haired with bushy tuft. Legs short, toes 4/5, thumb reduced, claws curved and very sharp. Elbows with lateral spur, for stretching the gliding membrane in flight. Gliding membrane from base of neck including arms, lateral spur, base of toes and first third of tail, like back above, scantily haired below, edged by a muscular strip enabling the membrane to be folded. Underside of tail root with 2 longitudinal rows of about 6 each sharp-edged and pointed horny scales as supports in climbing. Premolars and molars similar in size; 4 teats on breast, penis with bone. Upperside of body brownish-black; nose, hair tuft behind ear, upper edge of flight membrane from spur to tail, tail itself as well as rest of body underside and membrane underside, white. Chin sepia, upperside of hands and feet black-white mixed. Sexes alike, young similar except that the nose spot, ear tufts and tail (apart from the white root) are grey. Ssp *auzembergeri* (E. Liberia) whole upperside with tail brownish-black, underside whitish. MEASURE-MENTS: HB 40–46, TL 32–45, Wt 1.35–1.8.

Distribution. E. Liberia (ssp *auzembergeri*), Ivory Coast, Ghana (ssp. *peli*). 2 ssp. HABITAT: forest with outstanding giant trees, not linked by lianas and well separated, allowing unhindered flights from one to another. Also remaining trees on cleared ground, and burnt-out high stumps, rich in suitable sleeping holes. HOME RANGE: size not known, probably several hectares. *Map* p. 147.

Habits. DAILY RHYTHM: during day, sleeping, hanging on inside of tree hole, becoming active well after sunset, and going back to sleep well before sunrise. Hopping on branches and twigs (front and hind legs moving separately), is supported in vertical climbing position by the scales under the tail. In gliding flight with widespread membranes sails from tree to tree (steering with tail, flights up to 50m long) and lands in vertical position, climbing upwards to regain its former height. Not seen on ground. VOICE: a uniform low owl-like call as contact call. FOOD: leaves, flowers, fruit (especially fruit of oil palms), soft bark. SOCIABILITY: in pairs, but up to 6 may be found together in a sleeping hole.

Reproduction. Said to have two main breeding seasons, Apr and Sep. 1–3 young at each birth in a tree hole. Further details of habits not known.

LORD DERBY'S FLYING SQUIRREL, *Anomalurus derbianus* (Gray, 1842)
Syns: *fraseri* Waterhouse 1843, *erythronotus* Milne-Edwards 1879, *fulgens* Gray 1869, *jacksoni* De Winton 1898

G. Gemeines Dornschwanzhörnchen   F. L'Écureuil volant de Derby   S. Kipepeo

Identification. Form and build as Pel's Flying Squirrel (p. 148). Upperside dark or reddish, or orange or greyish brown, or dark grey with pale or whitish hair tips. Head usually grey to silver-grey, black hair round bases of ears, sometimes this black reaching to eyes. Gliding membrane between hands and feet with black hairs. Throat grey, rest of underside white, sometimes underside of membrane between hind legs brownish to blackish. Ssp. *erythronotus* (Cameroun to Congo) with red anterior back, *fulgens* (Gabon) has whole body reddish-brown, underside paler. Underside of gliding membrane almost naked. Anterior half of tail, like or lighter than back, hind part with black tuft, or whole tail black. Underside of tail root with 12–14 scales. 2 teats on breast, ♂ with penis bone, ♀ with 2 inguinal skin glands, seasonally active. MEASUREMENTS: HB 27–38, TL 22–30, WT 450–1100.

Distribution. Rain forest region from Sierra Leone to Cameroun, Fernando Poo, Gabon and N. Angola, and eastward to E. Zaire border and S. Uganda, S.W. Kenya, W. Zambia. Northern limit about 10°–7°N. in the west and 5°–3°N. in east, S. limit from 5°S. in west and 12°S. in east. Also in E. Kenya and E. Tanzania, with N. Mozambique and N. Malawi. 15 ssp. HABITAT: rain – gallery – montane forests, bush woodland and Miombo forests. In mountains up to 2400m. Is found hanging in tree holes so may be found in vicinity of villages in clearings where remnant trees, often dead or burnt out, nevertheless have many holes. HOME RANGE: sedentary, living in same hole all year, at times changing base when fruits ripen in neighbourhood.

Habits. DAILY RHYTHM: entirely nocturnal, though between 8–9 am may sun itself outside the hole. Rests all day and in middle of night. Sleeping position hanging on the inside of the hole. In evening starting from mouth of hole runs quickly up and in 4–5m opens the gliding membrane and takes off. In flight a right-angled turn is possible. Lengths of flight up to 250m. In 1 hour up to 70 flights, usually between 10 and 80m long. Rarely on ground though hops like a rabbit. Vertical climbing like a looper caterpillar, quick, goes down head first, also hangs from twigs by hind feet, as skilful as a squirrel in the branches. VOICE: growling, twittering, in fury hissing. SENSES: sight and hearing very good, scent good. Seasonally a strong monkey-like body smell. FOOD: fruit, bark, flowers, leaves, nuts, insects. Food is grasped and held in hands. SOCIABILITY: normally in pairs or ♀ with young, sometimes larger collections in sleeping holes.

Reproduction. In Guinea and Congo forests young in all months, in E. Africa at the end of rainy season. Gestation?, at each birth 1 large (HB *c*.16) fully haired young with eyes open, sometimes also 2–3 young. Young cling to inside of hole, feeding parents bring well-chewed food in mouth. Other details, of SEXUAL MATURITY and LONG-EVITY not known.

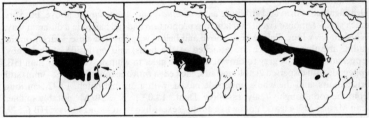

Lord Derby's Flying
Squirrel

Little Flying Squirrel

Beecroft's Flying
Squirrel

LITTLE FLYING SQUIRREL, *Anomalurus pusillus* (Thomas, 1887)
G. Zwergdornschwanzhörnchen   F. L'Écureuil volant pygmée
Identification. Form and structure as Lord Derby's Flying Squirrel (above), but smaller with shorter tail. Upperside olive brown with greyish crown, no black around ears and eyes, flying membrane between hind legs yellowish overwashed. Underside whitish-grey, yellowish in centre. Tail blackish-brown. Bristle hairs over claws of hind feet pale yellow (not blackish as Lord Derby's). MEASUREMENTS: HB 21–25, TL 13–16.
Distribution. Central African rain forest from Cameroun and Gabon to W. Uganda and N.W. shore of Lake Tanganyika. Otherwise only an isolated occurrence in West Liberia on the Du River. 2 ssp. Rare, up to present few specimens known. HABITAT: rain forest in plains and mountains up to 2000m. HOME RANGE: resembling Lord Derby's, details not known.

BEECROFT'S FLYING SQUIRREL, Pl. 27
Anomalurops beecrofti (Fraser, 1852)
G. Beecroft-Dornschwanzhörnchen   F. L'Écureuil volant de Beecroft

Identification. Form and structure resembling Pel's Flying Squirrel (p. 147), but muzzle sharper, ears shorter and rounder, pelage thick and fleecy, lightly waved. Tail shorter, at beginning smooth-haired, at the end only a slight tuft. Underside well-haired, membrane rather more lightly. Upperside dark brown or shining green or silver-grey with light olive-yellow wash over neck and back, often a whitish spot on crown and sides of neck, throat dark grey or reddish, breast reddish, belly yellow or golden yellow, tail coloured like back, 14–18 horny scales on underside at root. The green and golden-yellow of ssp. *argenteus* (Sierra Leone–Cameroun) fade quickly after death. MEASUREMENTS: HB 25–39, TL 16–24, Wt *c.*650.

Distribution. Forest regions (including Guinea woodland) from S. Senegal (Casamance), Guinea and Sierra Leone to mid-Cameroun, lower Congo and N.E. Zaire including western Uganda, N.W. Zambia. Also on Fernando Poo. 4 ssp.

Habits. DAILY RHYTHM: resembling Pel's. In mountains as far as 2500m. Rests by day either in a tree hole or clinging motionless on the trunk, where its camouflage colour conceals it from view. Contact call an ascending series of loud trilling, ending abruptly. Lives in small parties. Eats leaves and fruits, especially those of oil palms.

ZENKER'S FLYING SQUIRREL, Pl. 27
Idiurus zenkeri (Matschie, 1894)
G. Zenker-Gleitbilch   F. L'Écureuil volant de Zenker

Identification. Form and structure as *Anomalurus* and *Anomalurops*, above, but very much smaller, mouse-sized, ears larger in proportion and tail haired in a different way. Whiskers very long. Pelage both above and below very fine and close, sparser on the gliding membranes (which are attached at the heels) and on inside of the limbs. Upperside uniformly grey to brown, underside paler to whitish. Tail longer than HB, upperside with dispersed 2cm-long hairs, each edge with one row of short (2–3mm) stiff bristle hairs, and the whole underside naked, with a distinct patch, 1.5–2.5cm long from the root, roughly scaly, rasp-like. Dent.: $1 \cdot 0 \cdot 1 \cdot 3 = 20$. M^3 notably smaller than M^1 and M^2. 4 teats. Young like adults, sexes alike. MEASUREMENTS: HB 6.5–9, TL 7–13, Wt 14–17.5.

Distribution. Upper Cameroun to Rio Muni and N.W. Gabon, as well as N.E. and E. Zaire east of the Lualaba to Lake Kivu and West Uganda. 2 ssp.

Habits. Lives in primary high forest. By day hangs in groups or crowds (up to 100) in holes in large trees or behind old peeling bark, hanging thickly clustered on the inside, often sharing with other flying squirrels and bats. Climb dexterously and quickly on smooth trunks, jumping from the branches and skilfully avoiding obstacles, gliding

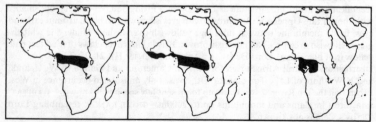

Zenker's Flying Squirrel

Long-eared Flying Squirrel

Flightless Scaly-tailed Squirrel

almost without losing height up to 3m from tree to tree. See as well by day as at night. In feeding may travel around several km. FOOD: oil palm fruits, nuts, insects; may occur in palm plantations. Mouse-like squeaking when disturbed. Probably 1 young; no further details of habits known.

LONG-EARED FLYING SQUIRREL, *Idiurus macrotis* (Miller, 1898)
G. Grossohrgleitbilch F. L'Anomalure nain

Identification. Form and structure as Zenker's Flying Squirrel (p. 150), only overall size and particularly ears, larger. Upperside mouse-grey, underside whitish to dark grey, both with slight brownish overwash. Upperside of tail with long soft hairs and underside with short stiff hairs, at the root light, at tips dark brown. MEASUREMENTS: HB 8–11, TL 13–19, Wt?

Distribution. Rain forest regions of W. and Central Africa from Sierra Leone to Cameroun and Gabon, and further east through Zaire to Ituri Forest and Lake Kivu. From Cameroun and Gabon to east, range coincides with that of Zenker's. 2 ssp.

Habits. Resembling Zenker's, few details known.

FLIGHTLESS SCALY-TAILED SQUIRREL, Pl. 27
Zenkerella insignis (Matschie, 1898)
G. Dornschwanzbilch F. L'Anomalure aptère

Identification. Dormouse-sized. Pointed snout, ears naked, rounded, medium-sized. Eyes rather small, toes 4/5, tail long ending with a conspicuous bushy tuft. On underside of tail near root 13 horny scales in two rows. No gliding membrane. Upperside and base of tail ashy to brownish-grey, underside light grey, silvery to light beige. Tail except root, black. Ankles with black hair tuft over a skin gland. Teats? MEASUREMENTS: HB *c*.20–23, TL *c*.16–17, Wt?

Distribution. Cameroun (S. of R. Sanaga), Rio Muni, Gabon to W. and Mid-Zaire. No ssp.

Habits. Unknown.

PORCUPINES, HYSTRICIDAE

Marten to badger-sized. Head roundish, snout blunt, eyes and ears small. Upperside of body with more or less erectile, short to very long quills. Tail short with spiny tuft or long with terminal tuft of soft flattened bristles. Body colour brown to blackish, spines and hair often banded with white. Toes 5/5, though thumb, and sometimes also great toe, reduced. Toes equipped with powerful claws. 4–6 lateral teats. Dent.: $1 \cdot 0 \cdot 1 \cdot 3 = 20$. Predominantly nocturnal ground-living animals of the Old World subtropical and tropical regions. (Africa, Near and S.E. Asia to Flores, Celebes, Hainan and Philippines; introduced into Italy in ancient times.) 5 genera, 15 species, of which 3 are in Africa.

AFRICAN BRUSH-TAILED PORCUPINE, Pl. 25
Atherurus africanus (Gray, 1842)
G. Afrikanischer Quastenstachler F. L'Atherure africain

Identification. Body slender, forehead somewhat swollen, snout short, with very long vibrissae. Eyes small, ears rather short, roundish. Legs short and sturdy, feet with sole pads and powerful claws, thumb and great toe reduced. 4 teats. Upperside of body greyish-brown to brownish-black. Underside grey to whitish. Underside of body hairy, upperside also with stiff hair, between which lie short, strong, in middle of back lengthened (up to 6cm) quills, flattened and keeled. In middle of back are supplementary longer, thicker round spines, up to a dozen and up to 14cm long. Tail about ⅓ HB length, round, almost naked in middle, ending in a tuft of soft flattened bristles. MEASUREMENTS: HB 40–60, TL 15–23, Ht 20–25, Wt 2–4.

Distribution. Rain forest regions of W. and Central Africa from Senegambia to W. Uganda and W. Tanzania, including Fernando Poo, southern limit in mid-Africa about 5°S; also an isolated occurrence N.E. of Lake Victoria (W. Kenya) and another near the N.W. shores of L. Rudolf (extreme S.E. Sudan). 3 ssp. HABITAT: forests (primeval, gallery, riverine, relicts) also in neighbourhood of plantations. HOME RANGE: about 2–5 hectares for a family party, with distinct living holes, trails and latrines.

Habits. DAILY RHYTHM: nocturnal, between sunset and sunrise, with a ½–2 hours rest at midnight. By day rest in holes in ground (in bushy river banks, between tree roots, in rock crevices, under boulders or fallen trees, in termite mounds etc.). Although clearly terrestrial, it climbs, jumps and swims well. VOICE: mute, in alarm drums on the ground with hind feet and rattles the tail tuft. SENSES: sight, hearing and scent good. ENEMIES: terrestrial predators up to leopard, also large owls (for young animals) and occasionally large snakes. In alarm (see VOICE), when attacked by enemies, erects spines and presents the hinder part of body. The conspicuous white tail tuft distracts from the unprotected head, and easily breaks off. FOOD: all parts of plants, digs out tubers and roots, eats fallen fruit, and does much damage to plantations and gardens. SOCIABILITY: family parties of 3–8 animals, all in same hole, in favourable places several parties in neighbourhood.

Reproduction. No seasonal breeding, gestation 100–110 days, as a rule 2 litters annually, 3 possible. Birthplace in hole lined with leaves and mould, 1–4 young born with eyes open and soft short spines in double rows, after a month the spines have grown hard; tail tuft still short. Wt at birth 140–175, suckling for about 2 months, first solid food after 2–3 weeks. SEXUAL MATURITY: 2 years. LONGEVITY: up to 15 years.

SOUTH AFRICAN CRESTED PORCUPINE,   Pl. 25
Hystrix africae-australis (Peters, 1852)
G. Südafrika-Stachelschwein   F. Le Porc-épique de l'Afrique du Sud
A. Ystervark   S. Nungu

Identification. Body thickset, head domed, muzzle short with long vibrissae, eyes and ears small, tail thick and short, legs short and sturdy, feet with large sole pads and

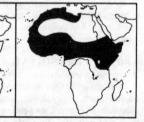

African Bush-tailed Porcupine

South African Crested Porcupine

North African Crested Porcupine

strong claws. Thumb greatly reduced, great toe less so, 4 (sometimes 6) teats. Upperside of body dark brown, underside blackish brown, white throat band. On head thin, on neck, shoulders, legs and underside thick grooved bristles 2–4.5cm long. On centre line of neck a white erectile mane of up to 30cm long wiry bristle-hairs. Hinder part of back with flanks and upper side of tail with black and white ringed quills up to 30cm long. End of tail with hollow bristles open at end, the 'rattle-quills'. Differences from the next species, *cristata*: nuchal crest, dorsal line on back, middle and underside of tail white, 'rattle-quills' thick and more than 6cm long. MEASUREMENTS: HB 65–85, TL 12–17, Ht *c*.25, Wt 15–27.

Distribution. Southern Africa northwards to S. Kenya in the east and to M. Gabon in the west; northern border, the Equator. Also on Zanzibar. In S. Kenya and N. to mid-Tanzania meets *Hystrix cristata*. No ssp. HABITAT: general, wherever cover and food available, not in moist rain forests, or in completely dry regions. In mountains to 3500m upwards. HOME RANGE: resident, in permanent roomy, taken over or self-excavated burrows (also in rock cavities, under boulder heaps, in river bank thickets etc.) with several exits. Well-worn trails lead to the feeding grounds, up to 15km wide.

Habits. DAILY RHYTHM: active only at dusk and by night, by day in burrow, sometimes sunbathes outside. VOICE: grunts in excitement, when threatened stamps hind feet and rattles tail quills. SENSES: hearing and scent good, sight not good. ENEMIES: occasionally ground predators up to leopard and lion (if hungry), though usually protected by its quills. In danger (see VOICE), when attacked erects quills and spines and jumps backward to drive the points into the attacker. If pursued may suddenly stop, allowing the attacker to run into the quills. The quills are not shot out, but fall out easily. FOOD: as African Brush-tailed Porcupine (p. 152). Ivory and bones are gnawed for the calcium, skeletal remains may be taken into the hole and eaten; carrion is not rejected. SOCIABILITY: as African Brush-tailed Porcupine, feed singly or in pairs, except when leading young.

Reproduction. In mating the ♀ erects tail and lays quills flat; act short. Gestation 7–8 weeks, breeds in summer in S. Africa, in mid-Africa Jul–Dec. 2 litters a year possible. At each birth 1–4, usually 2 active young (in a grass-lined chamber in the burrow), with open eyes and soft short quills. Wt at birth 300–400, HB 24–27, TL 4–5; Wt at 1 month 700, 2 months 1.3, 3 months 2.3. May leave hole at 1 week, suckling period 1½–2 months. First solid food at 2–3 weeks, adult and sexually mature at 2 years. LONGEVITY: up to 20 years.

NORTH AFRICAN CRESTED PORCUPINE,
Hystrix cristata (Linnaeus, 1758)

G. Nordafrika-Stachelschwein   F. Le Porc-épique de l'Afrique du Nord   S. Nungu

Identification. Like the previous species. Head to shoulders yellowish-grey, neck crest brown below, greyish-white above, quills blackish-brown with 5–10 whitish rings, legs, flanks and underside blackish-brown. Throat with incomplete whitish-yellow transverse band. Distinctions from previous species: nuchal crest brown and greyish-white, mid back, tail middle and underside black or sprinkled black and white, 'rattle quills' short (under 5cm). MEASUREMENTS: as previous species.

Distribution. West side of Africa from Rio Muni, in east Lake Mobuto (Albert) in Central Africa and mid-Tanzania. In S. Kenya and N. to mid-Tanzania overlaps with *Hystrix africae-australis*. 3 ssp. HABITAT: rain forest to dry bush and semi-desert. Up to 2000m in mountains. General habits as previous species.

CRICETINE RODENTS, CRICETIDAE

Vole-like rodents with muzzle often blunt, small eyes and ears, short tail, in size from dwarf hamster to musk rat, though form variable; sometimes with cheek pouches. Dent.: $1 \cdot 0 \cdot 0 \cdot 3 = 16$. In all types of habitat from plains to high mountains and primeval forests to deserts. New and Old Worlds (with Madagascar and Malaysian Archipelago) except Australasia. About 575 species of which about 250 occur in Africa and Madagascar; however, because of space limitations only the 3 largest are dealt with.

GIANT GAMBIAN RAT, *Cricetomys gambianus* (Waterhouse, 1840)
G. Buschhamsterratte   F. Le Rat géant de Gambia   A. Gambia Reuserot   S. Buku
Identification. Rat-like in form, but large, body long, muzzle with long vibrissae, large cheek pouches, small eyes, ears spoon-shaped, sides of back haired, toes 5/5, thumb small with flat nail, great toe short, tail round, naked, longer than head and body. Dent.: $1 \cdot 0 \cdot 0 \cdot 3 = 16$. 8 teats. Pelage harsh and rather loose, 1–1.5cm long, dark ring around eyes weak to strong, pelage grey, brownish grey or brown (savannah animals) or dark grey (forest animals), flanks a little paler than back, underside sometimes like flanks but paler, sometimes greyish-white to white, well or poorly defined from flanks. First part of tail like back, terminal part ($\frac{1}{4}$–$\frac{1}{2}$ tail length) white, hind feet wholly or partly white. MEASUREMENTS: HB 35–50, TL 37–52, Wt 1–2. ♂ distinctly larger and heavier than ♀.
Distribution. Africa south of Sahara from Senegambia to Lake Chad, Bahr-el-Ghazal, N. Uganda and mid-Kenya, southern limit from Ovamboland to N. Transvaal and Zululand. Ssp. question not clear.   HABITAT: woodland to dry savannah, in mountains to 3500m upwards, frequently in settlements and in buildings.   HOME RANGE: self-excavated or adopted holes in ground or in termite mounds, many-chambered and with several entrances, under fallen or in hollow trees, in rock crevices, boulder heaps, buildings etc., as central homes. From their tracks to feeding places, ♂ marks tracks with drops of urine, deposits faecal pellets in handstand, and rubs the upturned buttocks on adjoining objects as marking. Changes holes about every 2 weeks.
Habits. DAILY RHYTHM: nocturnal (10.30pm–5am) with a rest in the small hours. Seldom out by day, long exposure to direct sunlight fatal. Jumps, climbs and swims well.   TOILET: Daily cleaning of pelage up to $\frac{1}{2}$ hour (washing with licked paws) and licking mouse fashion.   VOICE: short sharp contact call commonly heard at night. Courting ♂ has a loud whistle, the ♀ a high whistle; high squeaking in irritation, and

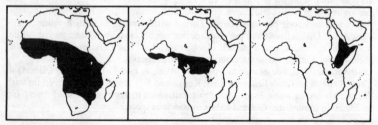

Giant Gambian Rat   Emin's Giant Rat   Maned Rat

as call for help from the young, ultrasonic squeaking. SENSES: hearing very sharp (ultrasonic hearing), dusk vision good, scent sharp, tactile sense very good. ENEMIES: terrestrial predators, large birds of prey, large snakes. FOOD: all parts of plants but especially fruit; snails, termites and other small creatures. Often in plantations and gardens. Drinks water frequently. Subsidiary use of cheek pouches to collect unpalatable objects (nails, coins, bottle tops, ballpoint pens etc.) for storing in a chamber below ground. SOCIABILITY: solitary; ♀ with young in breeding season, sometimes several ♀ ♀ with young sharing 1 hole.

Reproduction. Courting by persistent following by ♂, licking the ♀, back nibbling. Pairing only in the hole, gestation 31–32 days, litter size 2–4, young naked and blind in grass-lined nesting chamber; first hair at 5 days, fully haired, ears open and first solid food at 17 days, eyes open and first leaves nest at 19–23 days, leaves hole at 7 weeks and leaves mother at 11 weeks. Suckling period 1 month. SEXUAL MATURITY: About $\frac{1}{2}$ year. Birth Wt 22–23, HB 9–10, at 3 weeks HB 16–17, Wt 117–125, at 8 weeks HB 28, Wt 700, at 11 weeks HB 32, Wt 950. LONGEVITY: in captivity up to $5\frac{1}{2}$ years.

EMIN'S GIANT RAT, *Cricetomys emini* (Wroughton, 1910)
G. Waldhamsterratte   F. Le Rat géant d'Emin

Identification. Like previous species *gambianus*, differences as follows: form more slender, face narrower, ears thinner, longer and hairless. Pelage smooth, soft 0.5–1cm long. Colour sepia-brown to reddish-brown, flanks lighter than back (orange-reddish) underside usually pure white and sharply separate from dorsal colour. No dark eye ring. MEASUREMENTS: as previous species.

Distribution. Rain forests of Guinea and middle Africa. Northern border from Sierra Leone to N. Uganda (in Uganda overlaps *gambianus*). In west, southwards to Zaire (Congo) mouth, in E. to N.W. shore of Lake Tanganyika. Subspecific situation unclear. HABITAT: closed rain forests, not associating with villages.

Habits. DAILY RHYTHM: as in *gambianus*, but contact call a longer melodic call, and nocturnal activity between 6.30pm and 5.30am, with rest from 12.30 to 4.00am.

MANED RAT, *Lophiomys imhausi* (Milne Edwards, 1867)   Pl. 26
G. Mahnenratte   F. Le Rat de Imhause.

Identification. Size and stumpy build of guinea pig, short-legged. Head short, snout rather blunt, eyes and ears small, latter with backs densely haired. Toes 5/5, pollex reduced, hallux short, both opposable, toes with pads and feet with sole pads, claws short and pointed; tail length about $\frac{1}{2}$ HB. Face, limbs and broad skin band from ear to hips short-haired, head, body and tail long-haired (short dense under wool, long overhairs). Flank skin band with many small skin glands, whose secretion is absorbed by the short hairs. Snout and limbs black with white tips; forehead, cheek stripe, edge of ear, broad area edging the brownish flank, glandular area and tail tip, white. Dent.: $1 \cdot 0 \cdot 0 \cdot 3 = 16$. Bones of roof of skull remarkably expanded, very hard, granular surfaced. MEASUREMENTS: HB 25–36, TL 14–22, Wt 590–920.

Distribution. Eritrea, Ethiopia, N. Somalia, S.E. Sudan, E. Uganda, W. and mid-Kenya as well as isolated in middle E. side of L. Tanganyika in Tanzania. No ssp. Within its range not common. HABITAT: forests and woodland between 1200 and 2700m; in Somalia and Ogaden also in lower ground. HOME RANGE: extent not known. Shelters in hollow trees, rock crevices, thick undergrowth.

Habits. DAILY RHYTHM: active at dusk and by night. Moves slowly, climbs well, even head downwards. VOICE: in excitement single or double hiss with accompanying growls. ENEMIES: if attacked raises dorsal mane, exposes flank band (whereby the attacker is always confronted by the flank), hisses, growls and bites. The raised mane and exposed flank stripe together exhibit a remarkable black, white and brown warning coloration, of the toxic flank gland secretion (a dog biting this may die with slime on mouth). Hence this slow-moving animal is shunned by predators. FOOD: leaves, fruit, shoots, tubers, roots, field and garden crops (maize, sweet potato, ground nuts etc). Food is eaten held in hands while sitting upright. Water needs met by consumption of juicy food. SOCIABILITY: solitary. Seasonally in pairs, or ♀ with young. Good natured when meeting others.

Reproduction. 2–3 active young at birth (fully haired, mobile, eyes open). No further details known.

JUMPING HARES, PEDETIDAE

Only 1 genus and species in Africa; see following species description.

SPRING HARE, *Pedetes capensis* (Forster, 1778)   **Pl. 26**
(= *cafer* Pallas, 1779; *surdaster* Thomas, 1902)
G. Springhase   F. Le Lièvre sauteur   A. Springhaas   S. Kamendegere

Identification. Rabbit-sized, kangaroo-like. Head short, snout high, eyes large, ears large, hare-like spoon-shaped, closable. Front legs greatly shortened, toes with 5 digits with very long powerful digging claws, hind legs lengthened, especially the feet, in which the 4 toes (1st toe absent), the middle two the longest, end with pointed hoof-like claws. Tail as long as HB, thickly bushy from the root. Penis long, with bone, glans penis with many small horny spines. 4 pectoral teats. Dent.: $1 \cdot 0 \cdot 1 \cdot 3 = 20$. In the skull the auditory bones (bullae) greatly expanded. Pelage long, soft, rather thin, without distinct underfur. Upperside yellowish, cinnamon – or reddish-brown, or sandy yellowish-grey, stippled with black and white; crown, forehead and nose brownish-black. Underside whitish-yellowish or white, as also inside of legs and a stripe from upper thigh to hip. Front half of tail as back above, white below, the white sometimes extending to upperside, end half of tail brownish-black or black. MEASUREMENTS: HB 35–43, TL 34–49, Wt 3–4.

Distribution. Africa south of Sahara. 2 regions. (1). Kenya, S.W. Somalia, N. and mid-Tanzania. (2) From mid-Angola, S. Zaire, W. Zambia, Rhodesia and S. Mozambique, south to Orange River and Orange Free State as well as south coast of E. Cape Province. 12 ssp.   HABITAT: sandy plains, grassy or with thin bush or open wooded savannahs on sandy soil. Easy excavation essential.   HOME RANGE: plains within 300–400m radius of burrow; during food scarcity through drought also some km wider-ranging for food and water. Holes are very quickly dug, has several runs averaging 20–23cm diameter and several metres long, with nest chamber usually no more than 1m below surface. Excavated earth is built up as a ramp in front of entrance. Usually only 1–2 entrances, when going to rest these are stopped up from inside with sand. One or a pair has several holes useful as inconspicuous refuges for escape from predators. Neighbouring burrows are often linked.

Habits. DAILY RHYTHM: active only at dusk or by night, staying in hole in wet weather. Leaving the hole, takes great care to check the surroundings before going in search of food. In unhurried locomotion hops along on all fours, but at speed only on hind legs, making leaps of several metres long (2–8) with horizontal body, front legs together and sideways fanning tail. Sleeps sitting with hind legs stretched forward, with down-curved fore part of body between, head to ground facilitating detection of ground vibrations of approaching enemies. VOICE: silent, grunting as contact call. In great danger a loud bleat, soft piping when uneasy. SENSES: sight, hearing and scent very good. ENEMIES: ratel, striped weasel, serval, caracal, kaffir cat, genet, mongoose, jackals, snakes, monitor lizards, large owls. In danger always flees to particular hole. Does not defend itself if cornered. FOOD: particularly grass roots (rhizomes), as well as grass, herbage, leaves of low bushes, berries of bushes and in cultivated areas seeks ground nuts, sweet potatoes, maize, wheat, gourds, and incidentally insects. SOCIABILITY: each burrow 1 animal or pair with young, several burrows often adjoining so that on feeding grounds 1–3 dozen animals may be met with. Pacific in captivity, several may sleep in a heap.

Reproduction. In Kenya no fixed season, in Zambia and Rhodesia Nov–Feb, in rest of S. Africa to Apr. ♀ on heat presents posterior to ♂. Gestation *c*.2 months. Wt at birth 240–280. Daily weight increment 10–15, weight at 1 week 315, at 2 weeks 440, at 3 weeks 520. 1, rarely 2 at a birth, only 1 birth a year. Underside of young flesh pink, upper-side with fine sandy hair, end of tail black or brownish black, ears drooping. Young can sit on hind legs after birth, run after 2 days, when eyes open, suckle sitting between hind legs of ♀. ♀ licks it clean and eats afterbirth. Young live in hole until half-grown. SEXUAL MATURITY: not known. LONGEVITY: 7½ years reported in captivity.

Spring Hare   Cane Rat   Lesser Cane Rat

CANE RATS, THRYONOMYIDAE

Only 1 genus with 2 species in Africa, see following species descriptions.

CANE RAT, *Thryonomys swinderianus* (Temminck, 1827)   **Pl. 26**
G. Grosse Rohrratte   F. L'Aulacode grand   A. Groote Rietmuis
S. Ndezi, Nkungusi

Identification. Rounded, heavy, large head, muzzle high and short, eyes and ears small, latter naked, rounded almost hidden in fur. Tail short, scaly like tail of rat and tapering to tip. Legs short and sturdy, fore foot with 5 toes but 1st small and 5th rudimentary. Hind foot with 4 toes, 1st absent. Teats 4–6, on upper sides of edge of belly. Penis with bone. Dent: $1 \cdot 0 \cdot 1 \cdot 3 = 20$. Incisors very wide and powerful, upper ones with 3 deep grooves on inner half of outside, milk premolars remain, no permanent premolars. Hair of medium length, rough, bristly, hair standing in distinct rows. Upperside brown, yellowish or grey stippled, chin and throat white, rest of underside same or whitish grey. Young like adults, skin, limbs and tail tear off easily. MEASUREMENTS: HB 43–60, TL 17–26, Wt 4.5–9.

Distribution. Africa south of Sahara, from about 15°N. in west (Senegambia) and 10°–8°N. in east (mid-Ethiopia and mid-Somalia) south to mid S.W. Africa (20°S) in west and eastern Cape Province (Port Elizabeth) in S.E. 5 ssp, but number uncertain. HABITAT: dense grass up to elephant-grass height, reed beds, rushes and sedges in moist regions (marshes, watersides, swamps) and in thick undergrowth layers in forests. Only in lowlands and hills. HOME RANGE: size not known, probably 3000–3500 sq m. Home consists of runs (often tunnels) between resting places (grass-lined hollows or scraped-out lined 'forms') in thickest undergrowth, feeding areas (easily recognised by cut grass stems and droppings – hence common name Cutting-grass), and close to water. *Map* p. 157.

Habits. DAILY RHYTHM: active in mornings 1 hr before to 1 hr after sunrise, and evenings (at times also active day and night) rest of day resting in cover; may also live in rock crevices, termite mounds or aardvark holes. Runs quickly and adroitly, swims well and readily. VOICE: low staccato whistle as contact call, grunts, in alarm thumps with hind feet like rabbits. SENSES: hearing and scent good, sight moderate. ENEMIES: serval, kaffir cat, large civet, jackal, ratel, diurnal and nocturnal birds of prey, snakes. FOOD: roots, shoots and stems of grass, reeds and rushes; stalks bitten off at ground, cut up into sections, then consumed sitting up, holding food in forepaws. Does great harm to field crops of millet, sugar cane, maize and yams, sweet potatoes, cassava and ground nuts. Also eats bark, fallen fruit and allegedly small mammals. Likes to gnaw bones, ivory and soft stone. SOCIABILITY: in family parties (♂♂, ♀♀ and young) up to a dozen; in dry season large ♀♀ groups, ♂♂ separate.

Reproduction. ♂ shakes tail when courting. Gestation *c.*3 months; 2–6 usually 4, fully haired active young at a birth, eyes open and mobile. Wt at birth 150–180. In S. Africa young born from spring to summer, elsewhere in all months. SEXUAL MATURITY: 1 year. LONGEVITY: in captivity up to 4 years.

LESSER CANE RAT, *Thryonomys gregorianus* (Thomas, 1922)
G. Kleine Rohrratte   F. L'Aulacode petit   A. Kleine Rietmuis   S. Ndezi, Nkungusi
Identification. Form and body structure as Cane Rat (see p. 157) however, smaller, tail shorter (only half as long), the 3 deep grooves of incisors dividing up the front face of incisors equally. Pelage on upperside as Cane Rat, sometimes longer and softer, underside whitish-yellow, yellowish or brownish, sometimes also upper part of thigh and anal region reddish-brown. MEASUREMENTS: HB 35–51, TL 6–15, Wt 2.5–7.5.
Distribution. From N. Cameroun south to N.W. Angola, east to S. Sudan and coastal mid-Kenya, thence south to M. Mozambique, S. Malawi, S. Rhodesia and S. Zaire. No ssp. *Map* p. 157.
Habits. In moist savannahs with regular rainy seasons, in plains, hills and mountains (up to 2600m) in family parties. Tail wagged in appeasement and in courting, in latter also treadle the hind legs, mutually stand erect and rub muzzles. Ritual fighting with mutual blows of muzzle, as well as swinging rump sideways to overturn the opponent. A loser not quick enough to escape may be bitten on the body. The victor scratches the ground, empties its anal glands, and rubs cheeks on the spot. Habits otherwise much as Cane Rat.

GUNDIS, CTENODACTYLIDAE

Guinea-pig-like rodents with large eyes, small round ears, short legs and tail. Toes 4/4, ends of digits, palms and soles with thick rounded pads, claws strongly curved; on fingers and toes several rows of long curved bristles, and on both inner toes a transverse row of horny tips as cleaning brush and comb. Pelage thick and soft. Dent: $1 \cdot 0 \cdot 1–2 \cdot 3 = 20$ or 24. 4 teats. Diurnal rock dwellers in semi-deserts and deserts of N. Africa. 4 genera each with 1 species.

GUNDI, *Ctenodactylus gundi* (Rothmann, 1776) **Pl. 26**
G. Gundi, Kammfinger F. Le Goundi
Identification. Like guinea-pig in size and form; ears, legs and tail short, head flattened, broad, eyes medium-sized, nostrils naked, upper lip with upright median fork. Ears small, round, naked and stiff, but outer edge and front of inner edge with border of white hair, and backs finely haired. Digits 4/4, thumb and great toe absent, digits and soles with thick rubbery pads, claws strong and curved. On fingers and toes rows of stiff curving bristles and on both inner toes above the claws a transverse row of horny points as cleaning brush and comb, bristles on fingers shorter than on hind toes. 4 teats, 2 axillary, 2 on flanks. P^3 falls out earlier at same time as M^3 erupts, incisors without grooves. Coat long and fine, silky, thick with longer guard hairs, vibrissae very long. Root of tail short-haired, rest of tail with long stiff hairs. Colour above beige-brown, sandy or stone-coloured, below whitish grey, not well separated from upperside. Ears dark brown inside. Young like adults. MEASUREMENTS: HB 15–21, TL 3–5.
Distribution. N.W. Africa: E. Morocco, east and south to Middle Atlas (south as far as Beni Ounif on edge of Sahara), east through Algerian Atlas (south to Laghouat on edge of Sahara) and Tunisia and south of Gulf of Gabes through Jebel Nsufa east to Beni Ulid and Bondjem in N.W. Tripolitania. 2 ssp. HABITAT: rocky country with ledges, crevices, holes and boulder piles in semi-desert and deserts in hills and mountain ranges. HOME RANGE: not territorial, gregarious in family troops close together. From rock homes go no further than 100m around to feed.
Habits. DAILY RHYTHM: diurnal, appear at mouth of holes about 5am testing the surroundings (sitting upright on hind legs with outstretched body and hanging forelegs) for *c*.1hr. Feed in vicinity of hole, then sunbathe (stretched out flat on belly or side) until about 10.30, then back to rest in hole; 5pm to dusk feeding; night in the hole. When unhurried, move with underside almost on ground, tail curved upwards, in a hurry body high off ground. Dexterous, climb steep rocks, in danger disappear like lightning into hole. Likes to sit under overhanging rocks as protection from birds of prey. Do not dig, or gnaw wood. TOILET: head and fore-quarters cleaned on each side with the appropriate forefoot, belly and flanks combed with hind feet, passing a

1 Gundi
2 Speke's Gundi
3 Mzab Gundi
4 Felou Gundi

foot under belly to scratch or comb the fur of opposite side. VOICE: whistle in morning when alert before leaving hole, short whistle in alarm, a distinctive chirping whistle as warning. SENSES: sight and hearing very good, scent average. ENEMIES: birds of prey, also four-footed predators, details not known. Warning signal given and rapid flight to hole; if disturbed frequently may change quarters. If caught may appear dead (lying on side with outstretched legs, mouth and eyes open, breathing only once a minute; then after a while panting starts, the body relaxes. The duration of the apparent paralysis may be seconds, minutes or hours according to the degree of fright). FOOD: Grass and leaves, no water. Droppings are scattered about. SOCIABILITY: In family parties, many also alone. REPRODUCTION: 2–4 active young born in spring (haired, eyes open, capable of movement) in the hole. Further details of growth, sexual maturity, and longevity not known.

SPEKE'S GUNDI, *Pectinator spekei* (Blyth, 1856)
G. Buschschwanzgundi or Speke-Kammfinger   F. Le Gundi à queue touffue
Identification. Form and size as Gundi (p. 159) but tail longer in relation to body, and bushy, and outer and inner edges of ears without hair border. Upperside ash-grey to greyish-brown, sometimes suffused with blackish, tail beginning brownish-grey, then dark brown. Hands and feet whitish-grey, underside of body greyish-white to whitish-yellow. MEASUREMENTS: HB *c.*17, TL 4–5.
Distribution. E. Eritrea, E. Ethiopia south to Dolo, French Somaliland and N. and Mid-Somalia. 3 ssp. *Map* p. 159.
Habits. Like Gundi, in plains and mountains, in latter up to 2000m. Often associating with Rock Hyraxes. Further details of habits not known.

MZAB GUNDI, *Massoutiera mzabi* (Lataste 1881)
G. Langhaargundi or Saharakammfinger   F. Le Goundi du Sahara
Identification. Form, structure, size as Gundi (p. 159) but pelage notably longer. Upperside yellowish-brownish, underside lighter. MEASUREMENTS: HB 17–24, TL *c.*3.5.
Distribution. Mid-Sahara from Gardaia in N. to Tassili n'Adjer, Hoggar, Air, Djado and Tibesti in the south. 3 ssps. *Map* p. 159.
Habits. Probably as Gundi, details not known.

FELOU GUNDI, *Felovia vae* (Lataste 1886)
G. Senegalgundi   F. Le Goundi de Felou
Identification. Form, structure, size as Gundi, but fur nearly as long as Mzab Gundi, ears as Gundi but smaller and with small white tuft at base; tail somewhat longer and bushier. Incisors with weak groove on front. Hind foot combs short. Upperside dark reddish-yellow, underside reddish. MEASUREMENTS: HB 17–23, TL *c.*5.
Distribution. Only found in the rocky hills in the Felou Falls region of the middle Senegal River near Medine in W. Mali near the Senegal border. No ssp. *Map* p. 159.
Habits. Probably like Gundi, details not known.

Hares and Rabbits, Lagomorpha

HARES & RABBITS, LEPORIDAE

Hind legs slightly or much longer than fore legs, soles hairy, toes 5/5, though 1st digits very small, toes with claws. Tail absent or short. Ears medium length to very long, eyes medium-sized, upper lip deeply cleft. Pelage thick and soft, or sometimes harsh, plainly coloured (except in Sumatran Hare *Nesolagus*). Dent: $2/1 \cdot 0/0 \cdot 3/2 \cdot 3/3 = 28$ (only the Riukiu Rabbit, *Pentalagus*, with M $2/3 = 26$). Immediately behind upper pair of incisors lie 2 little functionless ones. Pigment glands on nose and cheeks, anal glands present, 6–10 teats. Vegetarian, but sometimes eat small creatures. 2 distinct types of droppings; beside the hard dry normal pellets are soft, vitamin-rich faecal pellets which are eaten again direct from the anus (reingestion). Most are nocturnal. Solitary (hares) or sociable (rabbits), terrestrial. Originally distributed over Old and New Worlds including Arctic regions, but absent from southern S. America, African rain forests, Madagascar, Malayan Archipelago (except Sumatra), Australasia and Polynesia. Both hares and rabbits widely distributed by human agency, the first to Scandinavia, Siberia, N. and S. America, and New Zealand; the second from its post Ice Age localities in N.W. Africa and Iberia introduced by man to Europe, Australia, New Zealand, S. America and many islands. 9 genera, *c.*36 species, of which 11 are African.

EUROPEAN RABBIT, *Oryctolagus cuniculus* (Linnaeus, 1758) **Pl. 28**
G. Europäisches Wildkaninchen F. Le Lapin de garenne
Identification. Head rounded, eyes large, ears shorter than head (stand upright), hind legs only a little longer than fore legs, tail short and woolly. Pelage thick and woolly, upperside greyish-brown, flanks lighter, rusty-red nape patch, underside (throat to tail) pale grey to white, ear upper edge, and upper side of tail, black. Colour variations not infrequent (white, yellowish, foxy red, bluish-grey, black). 6–10 teats. MEASUREMENTS: HB 35–45, TL 4–8, ear 6–7.5, Ht 16–18, Wt 1.3–3.
Distribution. Europe from Iberia to the Vistula in Poland, Danube in Hungary, Drau in Yugoslavia, as well as in the Rumanian Carpathian basin, and Ukraine; in Great Britain, Ireland, Corsica, Sardinia, Sicily, Crete and some Greek islands, S. Sweden, Gotland, also in N.W. Africa (Morocco, Algeria), on Madeira and Azores and some other islands (also Robben Island in Table Bay near Cape Town). Also in Australia, New Zealand and S. America. 6 ssp. in Europe and N.W. Africa. HABITAT: dry region with abundant cover, light easily excavated soil preferred, avoids mountains, large forests and loose sands. Very adaptable, if necessary lives entirely above ground with refuges in dense ground cover. TERRITORY: a few hectares, main burrow in centre, with runs, latrines, sun-bathing places; marked by urine, individual kinships marked by scent of droppings on the latrines near the borders. Chin gland scents also used. Strange animals are driven away. Burrow has several angular shafts, covered entrance, living quarters and adjoining occasional nest chamber. On edge of territory breeding burrows for low-ranking ♀♀. *Map* p. 163.
Habits. DAILY RHYTHM: main activity in evening and in first light of dawn, sometimes also at night and during day (sunning). TOILET: fur licking, and brushing with feet. VOICE: usually silent, in fear a rising scream. Alarm signal repeated drumming on ground with hind feet. SENSES: hearing very good, scent good, sight good for

lateral vision on the run, wide field of view. Practically no colour sense. ENEMIES: predators of musteline family, civets, wild cats and dogs, large diurnal and nocturnal birds of prey. Young sometimes defended. FOOD: grass, herbage, field crops of all kinds: occasionally animal food. SOCIABILITY: sociable in families as well as kin of up to 2 dozen. Animals with individual territories are dominated by an old ♂ (warren buck) whose favourite ♀♀ rear their young in the main burrow. Old ♂ watches over and marks (using urine and chin scent gland) his kindred, and covers most of the ♀♀.
Reproduction. ♂ courts by parading around, driving, spraying urine and leaping over ♀. Actual mating below ground, short but repeated. 5–6 litters from Mar to Nov. Gestation 28–31 days, births usually in isolated holes, 1.5m long, 40cm deep, with entrance plugged. Litter size 1–15, usually 3–4. Wt at birth 30–40, at 1 month 300; young born naked, blind, eyes open after 10 days, suckling period (♀ suckles only once in 24 hours, at night) 3–4 weeks, young independent at 4 weeks. SEXUAL MATURITY: 8–10 months. LONGEVITY: average 1½ years, up to 10 on record.

CAPE HARE, BROWN HARE, *Lepus capensis* (Linnaeus, 1758)   Pl. 28
G. Kaphase, Feldhase   F. Le Lièvre du Cap   A. Kaapse Vlakhaas   S. Sungura

Identification. Ears usually longer than head (though at times in African forms shorter), hind legs notably longer than fore legs. Upperside brown to yellowish, grizzled with black. Flanks and legs reddish-brown, throat and breast lighter, belly, inside of legs and underside of tail, white. Upperside of tail, and ear-tips, black (ssp. *starcki*, Ethiopia, has whole tail white, ssp. *arabicus*, Arabia, has ears and back very dark brown). Animals darker in moist climate, paler in dry climate; Plate shows Namib animal). 6 teats. MEASUREMENTS: HB 44–76, TL 7–11, HT 22–30, ear 8.5–13. Wt 1–7 (lower figures for Africa, higher for Mid and E. Europe).

Distribution. Cape and Brown Hares belong to same species, therefore distribution very wide. S., E. and N. Africa, Europe (apart from S. Ireland and M. and N. Scandinavia), Asia Minor and across temperate Asia to China. Many ssp, number not clear. European Brown Hare introduced in U.S.A. (1912), Barbados and Guadeloupe, Argentine (1880), Mauritius, Victoria (Australia, about 1870), New Zealand (1867). HABITAT: usually open country of all types from sea coast to high ranges (2000m, in Asia sometimes to 4500m). In Europe common in cultivated plains, but also occurs in forests.

Habits. Sedentary, size of home range several (up to 20) sq km, according to type of country. Range includes runs, sun and sand bathing places, and forms (these are flat well-hidden depressions on the ground, sometimes under bushes, where an animal may lie hidden for hours.) DAILY RHYTHM: active at dusk and in night, in breeding season also by day. TOILET: pelage is cleaned several times a day, also takes sand baths. VOICE: mostly mute. A shrill scream of fear. ♂ growls when courting, or fighting rivals. Small young squeak and growl, and if touched jump like frogs. ♀ calls young with a soft piping. Gnash teeth in threat; stamp with forefeet in anger. SENSES: hearing very good, scent good, sight moderate, but good for moving objects. ENEMIES: numerous predators from weasel to wolf, lynx and cheetah, as well as large birds of prey, crows and gulls, storks etc, for young. ♀ defends young from small to mid-sized predators. FOOD: vegetarian, wide range, twigs, buds, bark, roots, berries, fruit, fungi, sometimes as extra, small animals (e.g. mouse). Faeces in pellet form. SOCIABILITY: basically solitary, though tolerates neighbours of same species. In pairing time several ♂♂ with 1 ♀.

Reproduction. No pairing ties: in Europe breeding season Jan–Jul, births Mar–Oct. In E. Africa breeds all year round, in S. Africa from spring to beginning of summer.

Gestation 42 days, in Europe superfoetation common, viz., a pregnant ♀, towards the end of gestation, is ready to be mated again. At each birth 1–6, usually 2–4, fully haired active young with eyes open, hidden in thick vegetation. ♀ suckles usually only once in 24 hours, by night, suckling period 3 weeks, 1st solid food at 2 weeks, leave mother at 3–4 weeks. In Africa 1–2 litters annually, in Europe 3–4. Wt at birth in Europe c.130, at 6 months 3500, fully grown at 12 months. In E. Africa Wt at birth c.90, at 2 months 610. SEXUAL MATURITY: at 6–8 months. LONGEVITY: 10–12 years.

SCRUB HARE, *Lepus saxatilis* (F. Cuvier, 1823)   **Pl. 28**
G. Buschhase   F. Le Lièvre des buissons   A. Ribbokhaas   S. Sungura
Identification. Like Cape Hare, with long ears and comparatively long tail. Upperside brownish-yellow to brownish-grey, strongly brindled with black, flanks and legs rather lighter. Neck alone, or also front of shoulders, reddish-brown to reddish, underside of body and tail white, upperside of tail black. Light ring round eyes. Extreme tips of ears black or dark. Frequently a whitish forehead spot. Animals lighter or darker according to climate.   MEASUREMENTS: HB 45–58, TL 8–15, Ht 22–28, Ear 10–16, Wt 2–3.
Distribution. S. Africa south of the Cunene and Zambesi Rivers. 6 ssp.   HABITAT: in all regions outside forests, but especially in bush-clad stony hills; also in cultivated areas. In mountains up to 1500m.
Habits. Few details known, probably like Cape Hare. In southern localities 2 litters a year, in north 3. 1–3 active young at a birth, among thick undergrowth. Sexually mature at 1½ years, longevity unknown.

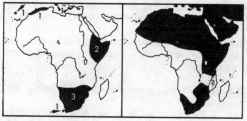

1 European Rabbit   Cape Hare
2 Abyssinian Hare
3 Scrub Hare

ABYSSINIAN HARE, *Lepus habessinicus* (Hemprich & Ehrenberg, 1832)
G. Äethiopienhase   F. Le Lièvre éthiopien
Identification. Form as Brown Hare, highland animals larger and longer-eared than lowland. Upperside brownish-yellow to yellowish-grey, brindled with black, neck sometimes cinnamon to pale reddish, ear tip spots small, black to dark grey or paler, sides of body lighter than back, outside of legs earth-brown to reddish-brown, underside of body and tail white, upperside of tail black.   MEASUREMENTS: HB 50–55, TL 8.5–10, Ht 25–28, Ear 11–12, Wt 2–3.
Distribution. Eritrea, Ethiopia, Somalia, N.E. Kenya. 4 ssp.   HABITAT: open country, deserts, semi-deserts, dry bush, hills and mountains up to 2500m.   HABITS: not known in detail, probably as in Cape Hare.

WHYTE'S HARE, *Lepus whytei* (Thomas, 1894)   **Pl. 28**
(= *crawshayi* De Winton, 1899)
G. Whyte-Hase   F. Le Lièvre de Whyte   A. Whytehaas   S. Sungura
Identification. Like a smaller Brown Hare, ears longer than head. Upperside
yellowish-grey to brownish-grey, brindled with black, rump darker than forepart of
body, neck grey, often a dark flank band; underside including that of tail, white;
upperside of tail, and ear tips, black. Light ring round eye. MEASUREMENTS:
HB 42–48, TL 7.5–13, Ear 10.5–13, Ht 22–25, Wt 1.5–2.5.
Distribution. Sudanese zone from W. Mauretania and Senegambia to Kordofan,
thence south between the Ethiopian highlands and the Congo rain forests to Uganda,
Kenya, Tanzania, further in all middle and southern Africa south of the Congo forests,
absent only in Cape Province, western S.W. Africa, and western S. Angola. 18 ssp, in
part dubious. HABITAT: savannah, dry bush, plains, semi-desert and desert; open,
dry and sandy regions preferred, in plains and hills. HABITS: no details known,
probably like Cape Hare.

BUSHMAN HARE, *Bunolagus monticularis* (Thomas, 1903)   **Pl. 28**
G. Buschmannhase   F. Le Lièvre de boshismane   A. Vleihaas
Identification. Rather like a smaller Brown Hare. Ears longer than head. Hind foot
rather short, woolly-haired. Pelage fine and soft. Upperside of head and back dirty
grey, brindled with black. Ears light grey to yellowish-grey, neck and throat reddish-
brown. Chin, lips and lower cheeks whitish, separated from upper cheeks by a blackish
stripe. Breast, belly and inside of legs light grey to brownish-grey, outside of legs
reddish-brown, soles smoke-grey. Tail thick, round, bushy, uniformly reddish-brown,
extreme tip sometimes black. MEASUREMENTS: HB 35–42, TL 7.5–9, Ht 18–22,
Ear 11–12, Wt 1–2.5.
Distribution. In central Cape Province on south edge of Bushmanland from Calvinia
in the west to Deelfontein in the east. HABITAT: bush-clad ravines in mountains.
Details of habits not known.

NATAL RED HARE, *Pronolagus crassicaudatus* (I. Geoffroy, 1832)   **Pl. 28**
(= *randensis* Jameson, 1907)
G. Natal-Rothase   F. Le Lièvre roux de Natal   A. Natalse Rooihaas
Identification. Rabbit-like in build, ears not longer than head, hind legs only slightly
longer than fore legs, feet woolly-haired, tail rather short, very bushy. Back and sides
brownish-grey to brownish-yellow, brindled with black. Head and ears grey, light ring
round eyes. Top of nose, nape, neck, breast, outside of legs, hinder back and all of tail
reddish-brown, latter sometimes with extreme tip black. Inside of legs, and belly,
whitish-grey. Pelage usually very soft (sometimes harsher). Hairs lie very loosely. The
reddish-brown of back of nose may be absent, that of the rest lengthened or shortened,
the dorsal colour may be darker or lighter, and tail may be blackish brown. 6
teats. MEASUREMENTS: HB 42–50, TL 6–14, Ht 22–25, Ear 7.5–8.5, Wt 1.5–2.5.
Distribution. S.W. Africa from Kaokoveld south, with adjoining Little Namaqualand
(extreme N.W. of Cape Province), also in eastern part of Cape Province from Beaufort
West eastward to Pondoland, Griqualand West, Orange Free State, Natal, Zululand,
Transvaal, S. and E. Botswana, Mozambique, M. and S. Rhodesia. Many ssp., number
not clear. HABITAT: stony and rocky regions with bush cover and scattered trees, in
plains, hills and mountains to 2500m or more. In Natal also on edge of large forests,
going at night into the fields. TERRITORY: not large; animals sedentary, have forms
under clumps of grass or bushes; in emergency bolts to rock crevices and holes

(including dassie holes etc) possibly with 2 exits. Prominent rocks and boulders used as sunning or watch points, marked by large heaps of droppings between the rocks.

Habits. DAILY RHYTHM: active at dusk and in night, where undisturbed, also in late afternoon. VOICE: noisy at night; if frightened and running away a series of penetrating screams. SENSES: sight and hearing very good, scent good. ENEMIES: as Cape Hare (p. 162). If cornered may escape by springing at enemy. In stony areas bolts very skilfully and fast among the rocks. FOOD: grasses and herbage. SOCIABILITY: solitary. Several may occur in favourable places but without pair associations. Often with dassies or in their holes.

Reproduction. Gestation said to be 1 month. 1–2 fully-haired young at each birth in a hidden place lined with belly hair of the ♀. Details of growth and longevity not known.

1 Whyte's Hare
2 Bushman Hare

1 Natal Red Hare
2 Uganda Grass Hare

Smith's Red Hare

SMITH'S RED HARE, *Pronolagus rupestris* (A. Smith, 1834)   Pl. 28
G: Smith-Rothase   F: Le Lièvre roux de Smith   A: Smithse Rooihaas
Identification. Form as Natal Red Hare. Upperside reddish-brown, brindled with black. Underside and upper legs reddish, speckled with greyish-white, lips white, chin and throat pale reddish, feet and tail dark reddish-brown, tail tip brownish-black to black, sometimes whole tail black. Colour may be lighter or darker, sometimes with a greyish tinge (desert animals), sometimes red very pronounced (ssp. *melanurus*, Little Namaqualand). MEASUREMENTS: HB 40–50, TH 6–16, Ht 20–25, Ear 6–11, Wt 1.5–2.5.

Distribution. S.W. Africa, Union of S. Africa, Rhodesia, E. Zambia, Malawi, and a narrow strip through Tanzania into Mid Kenya. 10 ssp. though some dubious. Habits not known in any detail, probably similar to Natal Red Hare.

UGANDA GRASS HARE, or BUNYORO RABBIT,   Pl. 62
Poelagus marjorita (St. Leger, 1932)
G. Uganda-Grashase   F. Le Lapin sauvage d'Afrique
Identification. Rabbit-like in form, ears shorter than head, hind legs only a little longer than fore legs. Pelage short and rather stiff. Upperside greyish-brown; flanks somewhat paler, yellowish, underside white suffused with grey, tail coloured above like back, white below, feet creamy yellow. Both sexes with glandular slits on either side of sex organs. MEASUREMENTS: HB 44–50, TL 4–5, Ht 22–25, Ear 6–7, Wt 2–3.
Distribution. Uganda, N.W. Kenya, S. Sudan, N.E. Zaire southward to northern tip of Lake Tanganyika, eastern Central African Republic, as well as, in the west, Mid-

Angola. 3 ssps.   HABITAT: stony, rocky grass plains, especially grassy hills with bushy eroded hollows, also in neighbourhood of woodlands. Uses forms under bushes, makes tunnel-like runs in long grass. Lives also in rock crevices and boulder piles, often with Rock Dassies. For grazing, prefers short grass plains, so sometimes associates with Cape Buffaloes, which help to create such conditions.   HOME RANGE: small, a few hectares; resident.

Habits: DAILY RHYTHM: active mostly at dusk and in night, resting under cover by day.   VOICE: silent; gnashes teeth in threat.   SENSES: hearing, scent and sight good.   ENEMIES: serval, kaffir cat, genets, jackals, baboons, large birds of prey, snakes. In danger bolts rapidly to cover.   FOOD: grasses, plants, shoots of low bushes.   SOCIABILITY: in pairs or family parties (♀ with young), common in suitable areas, though not gregarious.

Reproduction. Young in all months. Gestation 5 weeks, 1–2 naked blind young with very short black ears born in a grass-lined hollow. No details of growth or longevity.

Seals and Sea Lions, Pinnipedia

SEALS, PHOCIDAE

Torpedo-like shape. Limbs shortened and digits webbed to form fins. Tail a stump. Thick layer of blubber under the skin. Pelage short and thick. Limbs small, digits 5/5, claws usually well-developed, tips of toes with cartilaginous development forming swimming webs. Hind limbs not capable of movement on land. Locomotion on land by humping body. Soles hairy. Nasal and ear openings can be closed; no external ear. Dent: $2-3/1-2 \cdot 1/1 \cdot 4-6/4 \cdot 5 = 26-36$. Canines well developed, cheek teeth uniform with several cusps. Solitary or gregarious, living on fish, cuttlefish and small crustaceans. Found in north and south polar regions as well as in boreal, tropical and subtropical seas; in the Holarctic also in some freshwater lakes. 13 genera with altogether 18 species; one on African coasts.

MEDITERRANEAN MONK SEAL, Pl. 24
Monachus monachus (Hermann, 1779)
G. Mittelmeer – Mönchsrobbe   F. Le Phoque moine mediterranéen
Identification. Nose broad, hairy up to the narrow edge of nostrils, with short median slit. Eyes large. Whiskers straight, soft, not especially long. Tail a short stump. Front fins short, finger length decreasing from 1st to 5th, claws flat, reaching edge of fin. Hind fins rather long, outer toes reaching well beyond inner, claws only weak nails, skin between digits hairy. 4 teats. Dent: $2 \cdot 1 \cdot 5 = 32$. Hair short (0.5cm), sturdy, close-lying. Upperside of ♂ brownish-black, underside greyish-yellow, a fine sprinkling of blackish-brown on underside, and yellowish on upperside, as well as a large, irregular whitish-grey belly patch. Old ♂ suffused silvery. Black Sea animals greyer. ♀ and young have hair of upperside dark brown with yellow tips, underside light greyish-yellow. Sprinkling (when present) as in ♂; ♀ without belly patch. Young in first 4 weeks have soft, 1.5cm long, woolly coat, upperside blackish-brown, underside somewhat lighter; ♂ has large dirty yellowish belly patch. MEASUREMENTS: greatest length ♂ 230–250, ♀ 270–300; Wt ♂ *c*.280, ♀ *c*.320.
Distribution. Formerly the whole of Black Sea and Mediterranean coasts as well as Atlantic coast of N.W. Africa south to Cape Blanc; additionally the waters of Madeira and Canary Is. Today only in small parties or single animals in Black Sea (*c*.100), Lebanon (*c*.20), in the Dodecanese (*c*.200), in Cyrenaica (20–30), near Port Etienne, Cape Blanc (*c*.50), with perhaps 20–30 in Madeira and Canary Is. Perhaps altogether at the most 400 animals; extinction before long is feared.   HABITAT: at home on land on isolated sandy, pebbly or low stony coasts, today, because of continued persecution, may spend the day in caves only reached from the sea. Resident. *Map* p. 168.
Habits: DAILY RHYTHM: where undisturbed, sun-bathing and fishing during day, otherwise active at night.   TOILET: scratching with front fins.   VOICE: usually mute, but when agitated a dog-like whine, howling or braying. In threat gnashes teeth.   SENSES: scent moderate, hearing and underwater sight good, less so above water, but good enough to detect movement.   ENEMIES: large sharks, killer whales, but above all man, still pursuing the species without thought.   FOOD: fish as available, but mainly mackerel, sea-bream, sea perch, bonitos, sardines, anchovies, flat fish, eels; also lobsters and especially squids. Daily requirement 10–12kg.   SOCIABILITY: solitary or in small groups, no details known.

Reproduction. Gestation 11 months, young born Sep–Oct, 1 young born on land. Wt at birth 20–30, length 90–100. Pelage changes at 4–6 weeks, weaning at 6 weeks (Wt then 80–100); from then young swimming independently, but lives with mother for 2–3 years. She breeds only every second year. ♀ pairs again (in water) only 2 weeks after giving birth. SEXUAL MATURITY: at 4 years. LONGEVITY: of 30 years possible, but details not known.

EARED SEALS OR SEA LIONS, OTARIIDAE

Form, limbs, tail and blubber layer, see also Seals, p. 167. Coat short and thick (sometimes ♂ with short neck mane), with or without underfur (hair or fur seals). External ear present though small. Fore and hind limbs rather long, flexible, capable of active movement on land. Dent: $3/2 \cdot 1/1 \cdot 4/4 \cdot 1–3/1 = 34–38$. Canines well developed, cheek teeth uniform, with several cusps. ♂ larger than ♀. Gregarious, feeding on fish, squids, crustaceans. On coasts of cold and warm seas. 6 genera with altogether 12 species, of which 1 is on the coast of Africa.

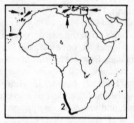

1 Mediterranean Monk Seal
2 Cape Fur Seal

CAPE FUR SEAL, *Arctocephalus pusillus* (Schreber, 1776)   **Pl. 24**
G. Zwergseebär, Sudafrikanische Pelzrobbe   F. L'Otarie de l'Afrique de Sud
A. Seeleeu, Rob.
Identification. Head round, nose sharp, whiskers long (30–33cm), stiff, external ears small, depressed. Tail a short stump. Undersides of all 4 fins naked, digits of hind fins about the same length, 1st and 5th without, 2nd to 4th with only small nail-like claws. Front fins with digits graduated in length from 1st to 5th, all without claws. Fingers and toes markedly extending beyond nails or nail positions. 2 teats. Dent: $3–1–6 = 36$. Pelage with thick underwool. Newborn have black woolly hair, at 4–5 weeks change to second coat with browner underfur under blackish stiff hairs with whitish tips. Whiskers black, pelage gives overall impression of olive-green. At 16–17 months change to 3rd coat, silver-grey. Afterwards throughout life annual coat change in Jan–Feb. Adult ♂♂ are blackish, brindled grey, with coarse pelage, adult ♀♀ brownish-grey to brownish-yellow, underside lighter in both sexes. Whiskers white. MEASUREMENTS: HB 220–240, ♀ 150–180, Wt according to season, ♂ 200–310, ♀ 90–115.
Distribution. Coasts and coastal islands of S.W. Africa and Cape Province, from Cape Cross (21°S), south to Cape of Good Hope and east to about Birds Island in Algoa Bay (34°S., 26°E). HABITAT: sandy, stony or low rocky coasts, convenient for fishing in

coastal waters, seldom goes far out (occasionally up to 150km distant). HOME RANGE: resident, young animals usually wandering within the general area, often return to birth place at sexual maturity. TERRITORY: see Sexual Maturity.

Habits. DAILY RHYTHM: active by day, at night sleeping on shore, or in water if far out. TOILET: scratching with fins. VOICE: noisy according to circumstances. Growling, snorting, belling, barking. SENSES: scent moderate, hearing good, underwater sight good, above water short-sighted but can detect movement. ENEMIES: sharks and killer whales. FOOD: Fish and crustaceans. Horse mackerel, sardines, pipe fish, squids, crabs. Each meal normally 2–3kg, exceptionally 10kg.

Reproduction. SOCIABILITY: at end of October (southern spring), old ♂♂ established territories on shore from 10–50 sq m in size (according to strength of ♂), and maintain them against other ♂♂ by threat and fighting; shortly after, the ♀♀ arrive and are grouped in harems (2–20) in the territories, and at same time give birth to their young (at birth HB 60–70, Wt 6–7). Young ♂♂, injured, sick or aged ♂♂ settle away from the harems. ♀♀ suckle the single young (very rarely twins) for 1 week, then go fishing for 1–2 days, return to suckle their young (recognition by sound and scent) and thereafter go at shorter intervals for longer periods away fishing. Young explore their surroundings, venture into the water, eat crabs, and also swallow stones. Milk teeth replaced at 6 months by permanent teeth. Although the mothers suckle young for a year they catch small fish and squid at 6 months. A week after giving birth the ♀♀ are mated again (pairing on land or in water); the blastocyst (early embryonic stage) remains unattached in the uterus until March–April. Gestation up to 11 months. The harems break up after about 6 weeks, and fishing expeditions occupy two-thirds of the month, enabling the ♂♂ to build up their depleted fat again. SEXUAL MATURITY: ♀ at 2 years, ♂ at 3 years, but does not become a fully active herd bull until 5–6 years. LONGEVITY: 20 years recorded.

Flesheaters, Carnivora

DOG FAMILY, CANIDAE

Short- or long-legged digitigrade animals. Toes 5/4–4, first finger reduced, absent in Hunting Dog (*Lycaon*) and Bat-eared Fox (*Otocyon*). 1st toe absent. Muzzle more or less pointed, eyes middle-sized, ears small to large. Tail of medium length, bushy. Dent.: $3/3 \cdot 1/1 \cdot 4/4 \cdot 1\text{–}4/2\text{–}4 = 38\text{–}48$. All African genera have $3/3 \cdot 1/1 \cdot 4/4 \cdot 2/3 = 42$, except *Otocyon* with $3/3 \cdot 1/1 \cdot 4/4 \cdot 4/4 = 48$, the back teeth being small. Anal and tail root scent glands present, and penis bone. 6–14 teats. Solitary or sociable active hunters, often of great endurance, some with mixed diet, some entirely flesh-eating. Diurnal, nocturnal or crepuscular. In all parts of the world except Australasia (where it first arrived with man) 4 subfamilies, 14 genera, 31 species, of which 11 occur in Africa.

DOGS & FOXES, CANINAE

Thumb present. Dent.: $3 \cdot 1 \cdot 4 \cdot 2/3$; short- or long-legged; ears small to large; tail of medium length, bushy. 4–14 teats. Include wolves, jackals, foxes and intermediate forms of the New and Old Worlds except Australasia (where introduced). True foxes are here separated under the genus *Vulpes* (as commonly recognised) from *Canis* (dogs and jackals).

RED FOX, *Vulpes vulpes* (Linnaeus, 1758)　　　　　　　　　　　　　**Pl. 29**
G. Rotfuchs　F. Le Renard
Identification. 3 ssp. in N. Africa: (1) Barbary Red Fox (G. Berber–R.; F. Le Renard de Barbarie), *barbarus* Shaw, 1800.
Back foxy-red, flanks pale yellowish, tips of ears black, back of feet ochreous, underside and tail tip white. (2) Atlantic Red Fox. (G. Atlantische R; F. Le Renard atlantique), *atlanticus* Wagner, 1841. Back suffused with grey, otherwise like *barbarus*; (3) Egyptian Red Fox (G. Ägyptische R.; F. Le Renard d'Egypte), *niloticus* E. Geoffroy St. Hilaire, 1803. Back with dark reddish-brown spinal stripe, flanks pale yellowish, tips of ears black, back of feet reddish-brown, underside whitish-grey, throat, chin, lower cheeks and tail tip white. 8 teats.　MEASUREMENTS: (1). HB 50–55, TL 33–40, Ht 30, Wt 4–8 (♂ averaging heavier than ♀). (2) HB 58–60, TL *c*.40, Ht and Wt as (1). (3) as (2).
Distribution. (1). Coastal regions of N.W. Africa. (2) Atlas region. (3) N. Libya, Egypt and N.E. Sudan. Overall distribution of species, most of Europe and temperate Asia, S. to Himalayas; nearly all N. America S. to Florida, W. to California. Introduced into Australia and some Pacific islands. 47 ssp.　HABITAT: all types of country from sea level to high mountains (4500m); semi-desert to forest. Very adaptable.　TERRITORY: resident. Territory hardly more than 100 hectares, with main and secondary holes (earths), runs, marking places (urine and faecal marking), food storing places, sunning spots etc.
Habits. DAILY RHYTHM: mainly active at dusk and at night. Spends day in the earth, or where undisturbed sleeping in open in cover. During mating and whelping season

also active by day. TOILET: coat licking, scratching with hind feet. VOICE: numerous calls (7 for cubs, 38 for adults recorded). In rut ♂ has a husky triple bark, more softly from ♀ as cry of fear or warning to distant young. Furious chatter when fighting, dog-like whining and cat-like mewing of cubs playing or begging for food. SENSES: hearing, scent and sight very good. ENEMIES: Wolf, lynx, puma, bear, wolverine, eagle, eagle owl, formerly leopard in N. Africa. FOOD: omnivorous; insects, eggs, young birds, young game animals, hares, rabbits, birds up to size of capercaillie and goose, poultry, rats and mice, as well as berries and fruit. Daily requirement ½–1kg. SOCIABILITY: generally solitary, in mating season several ♂♂ harass 1♀. ♂ lives with ♀ until birth of cubs and brings food for them (seasonal pairing). A life attachment possible but not confirmed.

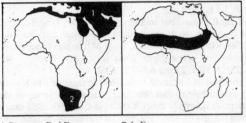

1 Common Red Fox
2 Cape Fox

Pale Fox

Reproduction. Mating may take 15–25 minutes. Pairing season in N. Africa Dec–Jan, in mid-Europe Jan–Feb, in N. Europe Feb–Mar. Gestation 49–55, usually 51–52 days, litter size 3–12, usually 3–5. Cubs born in chamber of den blind, with grey woolly pelage. Eyes open at 12–14 days, suckle for 4 weeks, first food brought by parents at 2 weeks, first venture outside earth at 4 weeks, independent at 3–4 months. SEXUAL MATURITY: at 9 months. Wt at birth 50–150, at 6 months 4000–5000. LONGEVITY: 10–12 years.

CAPE FOX, *Vulpes chama* (A. Smith, 1833)   Pl. 30
G. Kapfuchs   F. Le Renard du Cap   A. Silverjakkals

Identification. Like Red Fox but more elegant, tail bushier, ears larger. Head, back of ears, legs, reddish-brown; neck, back, thighs and tail except tip yellowish-brown with black and white grizzling which gives silvery appearance to the pelage but is weaker on flanks and tail. Tip of tail, chin, hind edge of upper lips as well as stripe on upper hind leg black. Some animals paler and more silvery. Body scent very weak. 6 teats. MEASUREMENTS: HB 54–62, TL 30–39, Ht *c.* 30, ear *c.* 9–10. Wt 2.5–4.0

Distribution. Nearly all S. Africa south of a line from S.W. Angola to S. Rhodesia, not in S. Mozambique, Kruger National Park, or coastal Natal. No ssp. Only open country, preferably sandy or rocky, bush-clad, with crevices, holes or overhanging rocks for refuge, especially at foot of kopjes. HOME RANGE: not large, details not known. Sedentary. Central point is the adopted or self-dug hole in ground.

Habits. DAILY RHYTHM: only active at dusk and in night, by day resting hidden in burrow or rock cavity. TOILET: as in Fennec Fox, but details not known. VOICE: drawn-out but not very loud scream with 2–3 yaps at end (contact call). No howling.

Further details not known. SENSES: hearing and sight outstanding, scent good. ENEMIES: details not known, but very alert and sharp-sighted. In flight doubles very sharply, runs very quickly through bush and ravines. FOOD: mainly small animals, insects, lizards, small mammals and others up to hare-size, ground-nesting birds and eggs, berries, fruit. Domestic poultry and lambs only rarely taken. SOCIABILITY: pair for life, parents with young form family troop.

Reproduction. Gestation 51–52 days, litter of 3–5 in Sep–Oct, usually in burrow. Parents rear young on surplus food which they bring near the burrow. Growth details not known. SEXUAL MATURITY: probably about 9 months. LONGEVITY: unknown.

PALE or SAND FOX, *Vulpes pallida* (Cretzschmar, 1826)   Pl. 30
G. Blassfuch   F. Le Renard pâlé

Identification. Like Red Fox, but smaller, more slender, longer-legged, larger-eared. Pale brown to flaxen, neck, back, upperside of tail, darker, dirty greyish-red; underside pale yellowish, feet whitish, tail tip black, front of fore legs sometimes blackish. Paler or darker animals may occur. Body scent very weak. 6 teats. MEASUREMENTS: HB 38–45, TL 23–28, Ht *c.* 25, ear 6.5–7.2. Wt 2–3.6.

Distribution. Sahel belt of Sudanese zone from Senegambia to Kordofan as well as Nubian deserts east of Nile to Red Sea. 5 ssp.   HABITAT: sandy or sandy and stony plains, semi-deserts or deserts.   HOME RANGE: as Cape Fox. Self-excavated burrows, 2.5–3m deep, with tunnels 10–15m long, with several grass-lined chambers, often under sandy tracks or in neighbourhood of villages. *Map* p. 171.

Habits. DAILY RHYTHM: active from dusk into night, sleeping in hole by day.   TOILET: as Fennec; details not known. Few details of habits known, but pairs for life, with family parties as in Fennec and Cape Fox.   FOOD: mostly small, including berries, fruit, sometimes poultry. 3–4 young at birth.

RUPPELL'S SAND FOX, *Vulpes ruppelli* (Schinz, 1825)   Pl. 30
G. Sandfuchs, Rüppellfuchs   F. Le Renard du desert

Identification. Like Red Fox, though smaller, more graceful, ears longer, tail bushier. Coat very thick and soft. Upperside, with backs of ears, reddish-brown, with individual guard hairs giving a silvery to steel-blue sheen. Middle of back darker than flanks, latter yellowish-grey. Face usually lighter, light yellowish-brown. Dark brown to blackish brown ring round eyes with same coloured stripe from eye to corner of mouth. Underside whitish-grey, outside of legs as back, at times with a dark wash, feet whitish, at times reddish above heels. Tail yellowish-brown, upperside intermixed with black hairs, tip white. Body scent weak. 6 teats. MEASUREMENTS: HB 40–48, TL 30–39, Ht *c.* 30, Ear 9.12. Wt 2–4.5.

Distribution. Mid and E. Sahara, from Hoggar and Air through Tibesti to Libyan, Nubian and Arabian deserts, Cyrenaica, Egypt, Nubia, Eritrea E. to Red Sea, S. to Berbera on Gulf of Aden (N. Somalia), Sinai Peninsula, Arabian Peninsula, N. to Dead Sea and Baghdad, E. through Persia to W. Afghanistan. 5 ssp.   HABITAT: sandy or stony semi-deserts and deserts.   TERRITORY: home range. Details not known.

Habits. VOICE: low chattering and long moans when content, barking and yelping in anger.   SENSES: sight and hearing exceptional, scent good.   ENEMIES: when threatened, humps back, raises tail, and sprays enemy with offensive secretion of anal gland.   LONGEVITY: $6\frac{1}{2}$ years in captivity. Further details of habits not known, but probably like Red and Cape Foxes.

FENNEC FOX, *Fennecus zerda* (Zimmermann, 1780)   **Pl. 30**
G. Fennek, Wüstenfuchs   F. Le Fennec

Identification. Red-Fox-like, but considerably smaller, ears extraordinarily large, eyes large, muzzle narrow and pointed. Pelage thick and soft. Soles densely haired, tail bushy. Upperside light sandy (isabelline). Back and outside of ears tinged with reddish-brown, flanks paler; underside, inside of legs, outside of feet, insides of ears, face, whitish. Tail reddish-brown, a dark scent gland patch near root above; tip of tail black. 6 teats.   MEASUREMENTS: HB 37–41, TL 19–21, Ht 19–21, ear *c.* 10, Wt 1.

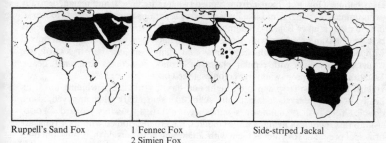

Ruppell's Sand Fox   1 Fennec Fox   Side-striped Jackal
                          2 Simien Fox

Distribution. Deserts of N. Africa (Sahara and Libyan deserts), in Morocco, Algeria, Tunisia, Libya, Egypt and Sudan, south to about 17°N (N. Mauretania, N. Mali, N. Niger, N. Chad), also in Sinai Peninsula and E. to Kuwait. No ssp.   HABITAT: semi-deserts and deserts with easily excavated sandy soil.   TERRITORY: not large, details not known. Resident. ♂ in mating season marks area with urine. Centre of territory is a self-dug burrow with grass-lined living chamber and many tunnels.

Habits. DAILY RHYTHM: nocturnal, from sundown to sunrise, resting in burrow during day.   TOILET: grooming with front feet, scratching with hind feet, fur licking, sand bathing.   VOICE: a wailing cry in distress (cubs whimper), growling and chattering in excitement. Contact call is a howling cry (melancholy – shuddering, lightly descending), lasting 1–2 seconds, oft-repeated. Is also a mating call or expression of hunger and cold. A shrill greeting call, a scream of agitation when hunted or in flight, and a scream indicating submission when lying on back. ♂ growls in mating, and alarm cry of cubs calls the parents.   SENSES: hearing exceptional, sight and scent good.   ENEMIES: details not known, but very courageous when attacked, parents defend young furiously.   FOOD: small prey (insects, desert snails, lizards, small mammals and birds, eggs, berries, fruit). Buries surplus food.   SOCIABILITY: mate for life. Live in family groups (parents and young). Very sociable.

Reproduction. Breeding season Jan–Mar, litters Mar–May, 1 litter a year, but if young are lost may breed again. Litter size 1–5, gestation 49–52 days. At birth HB 5, TL 5, Wt 42–45, at 4 weeks *c.*200, at 4 months size of adult. Tail and ears of newborn young short, but growing strongly from 3rd week. Coat at birth sandy (face, heels, spinal line blackish), after 2 weeks light beige, at 3 months like adult. Eyes open at 12–20 days, first solid food (not pre-masticated) at 3 weeks, first venture out of hole at 4 weeks, suckle for 2 months.   SEXUAL MATURITY: at about 6 months.   LONGEVITY: 11 years recorded in captivity.

SIMIEN FOX, Abyssinian Wolf, *Canis simensis* (Ruppell, 1835)   **Pl. 29**
G. Äethiopienfuchs   F. Le Chien sauvage d'Abyssinie
Identification. In build like coyote, in colour like Red Fox. Muzzle long and narrow, ears middle-sized, triangular to tips, legs long and slender, tail thickly bushy. Upperside, together with backs of ears, and two throat and breast transverse bands, fox-red; middle of back somewhat darker. Lips, chin, lower cheeks, throat, breast, belly, inside lower parts of legs as well as area under tail near base, white. Lower half of tail blackish. MEASUREMENTS: HB *c.*100, TL 25–30, Ht 50–55, Wt *c.*10.
Distribution. Only in Ethiopia, from Simien (where threatened) and region, centrally in mountains of Arussi E. of Lake Zwai, in E. in mountains from Garamuleta to Harar, in S. in mountains of Bale and Sidamo. Possibly 2 ssp.   HABITAT: mountain plateaux between 3000 and 45000m, with dense tree-heath and *Hypericum* thickets, intermixed with bogs and swamps with sedge grass and giant Lobelias.   HOME RANGE: see HABITAT: uses trails with regular places as latrines, sometimes with small heaps. Locations usually near swamp rat colonies. (See FOOD.) *Map* p. 173.
Habits. DAILY RHYTHM: active by night and day.   VOICE: high whining howl, repeated at short intervals (contact call). A fox-like sharp bark when annoyed, also a double 'Yeep' call of unknown significance.   ENEMIES: possibly leopard.   FOOD: swamp rats (*Otomys*), living in large colonies, the ground riddled with their runs, are principal prey. The fox catches them with a lightning grab outside their runs, but does not dig them out. Secondary food other small animals (hares, dassies and birds). SOCIABILITY: solitary, sometimes in pairs or ♀ with 2–3 young.
Reproduction. No details known.

SIDE-STRIPED JACKAL, *Canis adustus* (Sundevall, 1846)   **Pl. 29**
G. Streifenschakal   F. Le Chacal à flancs rayés   A. Vaaljakkals   S. Bweha
Identification. Long-legged, narrow-muzzled, ears large and pointed, bushy tail of medium length. Overall blackish, greyish-brown, back and flanks darker, lightly washed with brownish colour; head, thighs and outside of legs mixed with reddish, underside of body whitish-yellow. Flanks with more or less well-developed slanting stripe, from armpit to hips, blackish with upper edge light to whitish, also on thighs often a weak to strong blackish vertical stripe. Back of ears, and tail, coloured like body, tail tip black or white, in latter case middle of tail black. Cubs uniformly blackish, over-washed with brown, tail tip white. Adult colouring starts at 5–6 weeks.   MEASUREMENTS: HB 70–80, TL 35–45, Ht 45–50, Wt 6–13.5. ♂ rather larger and heavier than ♀.
Distribution. Africa between 15°N and 23°S (Tropic of Capricorn) but not in rain forests of W. and C. Africa. Ethiopia and Somalia, in S.E. south to S. Transvaal and Natal. 7 ssp.   HABITAT: savannahs and plains, prefers regions with plentiful cover of bush or open woodland. In hills up to 2000m.   TERRITORY: resident, territory not very large, a few sq km, containing tracks, sleeping places (thickets, holes in ground etc.), sun bathing places, all marked with urine and faeces by both sexes. *Map* p. 173.
Habits. DAILY RHYTHM: nocturnal or at dusk, resting most of day in bushy thickets, holes etc.   VOICE: a double bark, as contact call, repeated up to a dozen times, the head turning from side to side. Growls when disturbed.   SENSES: hearing and scent very good, sight good, especially for movement.   ENEMIES: leopard, possibly lion. Timid, hardly defends itself, easily overcome by dogs.   FOOD: small creatures of all kinds up to hare-size that can be pounced on (small mammals, ground-nesting birds, lizards, insects), also fruit and very eagerly carrion.   SOCIABILITY: pairs for life, joint rearing of young.

Reproduction. Breeding season varies locally; in N. Africa Jan–Feb, in S. Africa Apr–May, in E. Africa no fixed season. Gestation 57–60 days, litter size 1–4, cubs born in hidden den (usually a hole in ground, either taken over or self-dug). Wt at 5 days 280–290, eyes open at 8–11 days, first tooth at 14 days, feeds independently at 5 weeks. Further details of growth not known, probably like Black-backed Jackal. LONGEVITY: 10–12 years.

BLACK-BACKED JACKAL, *Canis mesomelas* (Schreber, 1775) Pl. 29

G. Schabrackenschakal F. Le Chacal à chabraque A. Rooijakkals S. Bweha

Identification. Form as in Side-striped Jackal, but ears somewhat larger and legs not so long. Back with blackish-grey saddle from neck to root of tail, sharply separated from yellowish-red of flanks. Head, sides, legs yellowish-red, throat, breast and belly white. Tail light brown, grizzled with black, end black. Strong body scent. Young at first uniformly grey-brown, back darker, then back reddish-yellow with sprinkling of blackish-grey. 8 teats. MEASUREMENTS: HB 70–100, TL 30–35, Ht 45–50, Wt 6.5–10. ♂ larger and heavier than ♀.

Distribution. In eastern Africa: Eritrea, Ethiopia, Somalia, S.E. Sudan, Uganda, Kenya, N. Tanzania; in southern Africa; Rhodesia, mid- & S. Mozambique south of Zambesi, S.W. Angola, S.W. Africa, Botswana, Union of S. Africa. 6 ssp. HABITAT: savannah, bush, light woodland with good cover preferred to open plains and semi-desert. Up to 2000m. TERRITORY: According to nature of ground and abundance of prey, size 2.5sq km (seldom more), protected by a pair against rivals. Contains tracks, sleeping places etc., marked by urine and faeces. *Map* p. 176.

Habits. DAILY RHYTHM: where undisturbed may be active day and night. TOILET: scratching, nibbling pelage, foot cleaning, skin shivering. Mutual grooming. VOICE: long-drawn clear howling, interrupted by short barks, as contact call on nocturnal hunts. A dog-like bark in alarm. In danger a fox-like chatter; when annoyed or fighting, a deep growling. ♀ warns cubs by a 'whoof', in rut has shrill hard chuckle, and ♂ at same time has a long howl. SENSES: as Side-striped Jackal. ENEMIES: leopard, cheetah, large birds of prey, pythons. Defends itself if cornered. FOOD: small animals of all kinds (mammals, birds, eggs, lizards, tortoises, insects, scorpions), fruit, berries, carrion, kills of large predators, afterbirth of antelopes and zebras; kills new-born (up to 14 days old) gazelles and small antelopes. Frequents settlements and takes lambs, young calves and foals, adult sheep, poultry; steals anything edible. Hunts adult antelopes up to reedbuck size. SOCIABILITY: pairs for life, parents rear young together; hunt in family parties.

Reproduction. Litter season in S. Africa Jun–Nov, in E. Africa Jun–Jul and Sep–Oct. Gestation 60–65 days. 2 litters a year possible but not the rule; over-population may occur. Young born usually in hole in ground, in a termite mound, rock crevice or bushy thicket. Litter size 5–7 (2–10). Eyes open at 8 days, first outside venture at 14 days, first solid food (premasticated) at 21 days (from the beginning the ♂ brings food for ♀ and young). Suckling period 8–10 weeks, then joins hunt with parents, leaving home finally at 2–2½ months. Adult coloration at 3 months, fully grown at 8–10 months. Family breaks up at 6 months. SEXUAL MATURITY: at 6–8 months. Sex ratio 1:1. LONGEVITY: normally 10–12 years, 14 recorded in captivity.

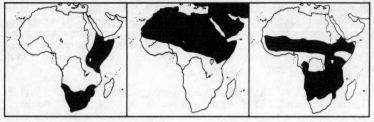

Black-backed Jackal   Asiatic Jackal   Hunting Dog

ASIATIC JACKAL, COMMON JACKAL,   Pl. 29
Canis aureus (Linnaeus, 1758)
G. Goldschakal   F. Le Chacal commun   S. Bweha

Identification. Much like Black-backed Jackal in build, but somewhat sturdier and
ears rather smaller. Upperside uniform dirty yellowish-grey with reddish overwash,
intermixed with black, sometimes with a light stripe forming a small shoulder saddle.
Tail like back, below half or tip black. Outside of legs, and backs of ears yellowish to
reddish brown. Lips, chin, lower cheeks, throat and front of breast whitish, breast,
belly and insides of legs yellowish-brown. Overall colour varies according to environment from reddish to dark fallow-brown. Young cubs uniformly greyish-brown. 8
teats. MEASUREMENTS: northern: HB 85–105, TL 22–27, Ht 45–50, Wt 10–15.
southern: HB 65–85, TL 18–25, Ht 40–45, Wt 6–10.

Distribution. S.E. Europe (S. of a line Dalmatia–Black Sea), in Middle East, India,
Ceylon, Burma, Siam. Arabia and N. Africa southwards to Senegal, Sudan, N.E.
Zaire, Ethiopia, Somalia, N. Kenya, N. Uganda. 19 ssp. HABITAT: open country
with good cover in form of trees, bushes, thickets, copses, high grass, rocks, ravines,
vineyards, gardens, fields. Follows human settlements. In mountains up to 2000m or
more. TERRITORY: like Black-backed Jackal. ♀ also marks with urine under raised
legs.

Habits. DAILY RHYTHM and TOILET: as Black-backed Jackal. VOICE: a complaining
howl, rising and repeated again and again, followed by short yelp, as contact call,
especially shortly after sunset and shortly before sunrise and towards rutting season.
When highly vigilant (before alarm or warning to young) a repeated sneezing, in rising
excitement barks, growls when annoyed, loud scream in pain (like domestic dog),
whine as expression of longing. ♀ warns young by deep 'chack-chack' with closed
mouth. SENSES: hearing and scent very good, sight good especially for movement.
Apparently colour blind. ENEMIES: wolf, leopard, python; large birds of prey for
cubs. Defends itself if cornered. FOOD: omnivorous. Also snakes, maize, sugar cane
and other green crops. May sham death to deceive possible prey. Has innate urge to
carry off unpalatable objects. SOCIABILITY: as Black-backed Jackal.

Reproduction. Pair formation begins some months before mating, through mutual
howling and mounting. Gestation 60–63 days. Litter size 3–8 (12), site and ♂ parent
behaviour as Black-backed Jackal. Eyes open at 10–14 days, first solid food at 4 weeks,
suckle for 6 weeks, change from woolly puppy coat between 2nd and 3rd months; other
development, and longevity, as Black-backed Jackal, but sexual maturity somewhat
later (10 months).

HUNTING DOGS, LYCAONINAE

First toe absent; Dent.: $3 \cdot 1 \cdot 4 \cdot 2/3 = 42$; M_3 very small. Size of wolf. Muzzle strong, rather short; ears large, legs slender, tail bushy. 12–14 teats. Live in packs in big game areas of Africa. 1 genus with 1 species.

HUNTING DOG, *Lycaon pictus* (Temminck, 1820) **Pl. 29**
G. Hyänenhund F. Le Cynhyène A. Wildehonde S. Mbwa mwitu
Identification. Long-legged, head broad, muzzle rather short and powerful, ears large and rounded without distinct tips. Tail bushy. Colour from black to blackish-brown, yellowish to brownish-yellow, with white areas, in no regular pattern, zones differing in size and pattern individually. All stages from nearly all yellow to nearly all black occur. No animal exactly like any other. Tail tip always white. 12–14 teats. Young pups black with irregular individual white patches, usually on legs; tail tip white. From 6th week the yellow tone appears. From the first day a penetrating unpleasant body scent. MEASUREMENTS: HB 80–108, TL 30–40, Ht 70–75; Wt 18–28. S. African animals average 5cm larger and 5kg heavier than E. African.
Distribution. Formerly all over Africa except deserts and forests, today found only S. of Sahara, from Senegambia to Eritrea, thence southwards through E. Africa to S. Mozambique, E. Transvaal, north of Cape Province and south of S.W. Africa on one side, and S. Zaire, N. Angola and S. Congo on the other. In many regions already extinct. 4 ssp. HABITAT: open savannahs, plains to semi-deserts, in mountains to 3000m. On Kilimanjaro has been met with up to 5000m. HOME RANGE: hunting area of a pack of up to a hundred ranging from hundreds or even a thousand sq km, in which they are nomadic; only sedentary at whelping time.
Habits. Hunt in early morning or late afternoon, also on moonlit nights. Otherwise resting in thickets, short or high grass, in burrows, or on knolls. VOICE: A soft howling, repeated up to 6 times, carrying for some distance, is a rally call among the pack: a deep bark or growling in fright or alarm: a high twittering in strong excitement (e.g. at beginning of a hunt): in high excitement a clear yelping; young whine when begging for food, adults also whine in appeasement: lost young yowl. ♀ calls young to suckle at the burrow with a soft yowl. SENSES: sight, hearing and scent very good. ENEMIES: hyaenas and eagles will prey on unguarded pups. FOOD: lives only in game-rich areas. Hunts by sight in packs. Principal prey medium-sized ungulates (gazelles, waterbuck, kobs, reedbuck, impalas, calves of larger antelopes, zebra foals), also more rarely large antelopes and zebras, also incidentally hares, spring hares, gazelle fawns etc. Selected prey is followed at first in the hunting trot, which in 5 or 10 minutes changes to the all-out racing hunt at 45/55km p h. By taking turns in the lead, and cutting off corners, the game is usually overtaken, brought down by a bite in the groin, and within minutes is torn to pieces and devoured by the pack. Daily food requirement 3–6kg of meat. SOCIABILITY: only found in groups or packs, from 4–6 or more, sometimes 20–40 animals: formerly large packs of up to 100 animals have been met with. Only a group of at least 4–6 can form a unit capable of successful hunting. Pack life is regulated by a few calls, gestures and bodily postures; no individual order of rank, but dominant animals may occur. Food sharing between all members.
Reproduction. Pairing season in the north and south in late winter, in the equatorial zone irregularly over the year. Mating without attachment. Gestation 69–72 days. Cubs mostly born in burrows (often aardvark or wart hog holes), lined with grass.

Often 2 ♀♀ in close company or sharing same hole. Litter size 2–16, average 7. Sex ratio ♂ to ♀ 2:1, in adults often 4:6. Eyes open at 2 weeks, with first venture outside hole. Suckle for 10–12 weeks. First premasticated food at 2 weeks, final abandonment of burrow and full hunting apprenticeship of young at 6 months. SEXUAL MATURITY 1½ years. LONGEVITY: 10–12 years.

BAT-EARED FOX, OTOCYONINAE

First toe present; Dent.: 3 · 1 · 4 · 3–4/4–5 = 46–50. Fox-like in appearance, muzzle pointed, ears very large, tail very bushy. 6 teats. Live in pairs in Africa south of Sahara; diet small animals and mixed foods. 1 genus with 1 species.

BAT-EARED FOX, *Otocyon megalotis* (Desmarest, 1822)   **Pl. 30**
G. Löffelhund   F. L'Otocyon   A. Bakoorjakkals   S. Bweha masigio

Identification. Like a long-legged fox with large ears. Muzzle short and pointed, eyes large, ears very large, broad and long-oval with tips inconspicuous. Body short, tail long and very bushy. Body rather uniform dark grey-fallow-yellow, sometimes with a rather greenish shimmer, flanks paler, underside greyish-yellow. Outside of ears dark brown with black edge, tail upperside and end half, as well as feet, black, rest of tail grey. Upperside of muzzle light brown, chin, lips, eyelids and surroundings black. In middle of back a glandular hairy slit. Body scent remarkable. 6 teats. MEASURE-MENTS: HB 60–70, TL 23–35, Ht 35–40, ear *c*.10, Wt 2.5–5.0.

Distribution. In E. Africa; Somalia, S. Ethiopia, S.E. Sudan, Uganda, Kenya, N. and Mid W. Tanzania. In S. Africa; S. Angola, S.W. Africa, Botswana, S.W. Rhodesia, Zambia, N. of Cape Province, Orange Free State, W. and N.E. Transvaal. 3 ssp. HABITAT: sandy country, grass and bush steppes, savannahs. HOME RANGE: not large (details not known); a central burrow either adopted or self-dug, with several entrances and chambers. Both sexes (only during rut) mark around the hole with urine, otherwise latrines some distance away mark the area.

Habits. DAILY RHYTHM: active mainly at dusk or in night; during day resting in hole, or sun bathing outside. TOILET: mutual grooming, mainly on the head. Rolls on back. Further details not known. VOICE: call a thin fox-like cry, though a more whining bark as contact call; in anger growls, chatters in excitement, shrill twittering as expression of unrest. ♀ has soft call for small young. SENSES: hearing and sight exceptional, scent good. ENEMIES: large birds of prey; sometimes spotted hyaenas. FOOD: small animals (earthworms, insects, scorpions, snakes, lizards, small mammals), ground-nesting birds and eggs, fruit, berries, soft tubers and roots. Mice and grubs are also dug out. SOCIABILITY: mate for life, parents and offspring form family parties.

Reproduction. In mating no attachment. Gestation 2 months, litter season Nov–Apr, litter size 3–4 (2–6), birth chamber in burrow. Newborn coat woolly, sandy, ears and tail short, feet and end of tail black. Wt at 1 week *c*.150, at 6 months (when adult) ♂ 3600, ♀ 3000. Eyes open at 2 weeks, first venture outside burrow 2½ weeks, first solid food at 3 weeks, suckling time 4–5 weeks. SEXUAL MATURITY: 9 months. LONGEVITY: 5½ years in captivity.

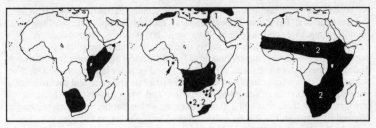

Bat-eared Fox

1 Weasel
2 White-naped Weasel

1 European Polecat
2 Striped Polecat

MARTENS & WEASELS, MUSTELIDAE

Range in size from Pygmy Weasel to Giant Otter, slender to unwieldy, short-legged. Muzzle short and broad to long and narrow. Eyes and ears usually small. Tail short or long and bushy. Toes with short or long claws, which in otters are sometimes reduced or absent and with swimming webs between the toes; digits 5/5. Dent: $3/2–3 \cdot 1/1 \cdot 2–4/2–4 \cdot 1/1–2 = 28–38$. Molars broad-crowned and low-cusped. Pelage short to long, soft or harsh. Pregenital, anal and circumanal glands (latter with foul-scented secretion) present. 4–8 teats. ♂ with penis bone. Solitary, sociable, nocturnal or diurnal animals. Mixed diet, mainly small animals, also fish, crustacea, molluscs. In New and Old Worlds except Madagascar and Australasia. 5 subfamilies, 24 genera, about 65 species, of which 10 are African.

WEASELS, MUSTELINAE

Size ranging from weasel to wolverine. Dent: $3 \cdot 1 \cdot 3 \cdot 1/2 = 34$. 6–8 teats. Diurnal or nocturnal, terrestrial or arboreal animals of open or wooded country. New and Old Worlds apart from Madagascar and Australasia. 11 genera, 33 species, of which 4 genera and 5 species in Africa.

WEASEL, *Mustela nivalis* (Linnaeus, 1766)   **Pl. 31**
G. Mauswiesel   F. La Belette
Identification. 2 ssp. in Africa. (1) Numidian Weasel *numidica* (Pucheran, 1855). G. Numidische Mauswiesel; F. La Belette de Numidie. Upperside, with legs and tail, light brown, underside with edge of upper lip, insides of legs and feet white to cream-coloured. (2) Egyptian weasel *subpalmata* Hemprich and Ehrenberg, 1833, G. Agyptisches Mauswiesel; F. La Belette d'Egypte. Upperside, with legs, feet and tail chestnut to umber-brown; chin, throat, breast and part of belly white to cream-coloured. Brown of back sometimes extending on to belly or forming a transverse band. Dent.: $3/3 \cdot 1/\% \cdot 3/3 \cdot 1/2 = 34$. 8 teats.   MEASUREMENTS: (1) HB ♂ 22–27, ♀ 20–24, TL ♂ 9.12, ♀ 7–8. (2) HB ♂ 26–29, ♀ 23–24, TL ♂ 11–13, ♀ 8–9. Ht (1 & 2) *c*.315–4. Wt (1 & 2) *c*.125–250. ♂ about a third larger and heavier than ♀.
Distribution. (1) Morocco (southward to northern side of Atlas), Algeria. Introduced to Malta, Azores and Sao Thome (Gulf of Guinea). (2) Lower Egypt; Nile Delta from

Alexandria and Port Said to Cairo, and in settled country further river-wards as far as Fayum Province. Total distribution of species most of Europe, with Mediterranean islands, temperate and northern Asia and N. America. Introduced in New Zealand. HABITAT: all types of country with enough cover to support a good rodent population. Avoids wet country and large forests, prefers agricultural land with field drains, hedges, thickets, bushes, farmsteads, found in mountains up to 3000m. *Subpalmata* is said to be commensal in villages, hunting rats and mice and cockroaches in buildings. TERRITORY: according to habitat and prey density, 1–5 hectares. ♂ territory larger than that of ♀ (latter may lie within former). Borders defended. Marked by urine and faeces on outstanding or new objects; in rut uses whole body scent from pregenital glands.

Habits. DAILY RHYTHM: mainly active at dusk or by day, each 24 hours divided into several resting and active periods. TOILET: scratching with hind feet, washing with spittle on fore feet, head cleaning after eating by rubbing on convenient objects. Bathes in water. VOICE: over a dozen calls according to situation. In rage or fear a sharp explosive threat cry against enemies; in increasing excitement a chatter or scream accompanied by scent gland activity; in decreasing excitement whining, spitting and snorting. Pair in mating play have further vocabulary. Young in nest pipe and whine softly if neglected. SENSES: sight and hearing very good, scent good (main hunting sense). Sense of touch in narrow spaces outstanding. ENEMIES: all predators from stoat upward; all large birds of prey, including crows, storks etc. Stinking scent glands used in defence. Defends itself to the death when attacked. FOOD: main prey mice and voles, also other rodents up to rabbit size; frogs, small birds and eggs, lizards, insects. SOCIABILITY: ♂ a polygamous but solitary animal, in rut in ♀ company, does not help rear the young. Mother and family stay together about 3 months.

Reproduction. First litter Feb–Mar, 2–3 litters a year likely, mating lasts $\frac{3}{4}$–3 hours, 3–5 matings in 3–4 days. Gestation 33–37 days; 4–9 (12) blind naked young in hidden well-lined nest. Wt at birth 2–4, at 60 days ♂ 200–210, ♀ 90–95, at 90 days ♂ 300, ♀ 95. First full pelage (white) at 1 week, at 3 weeks upperside brown, canines appear at 2 weeks, first solid food taken at 2–3 weeks. Eyes open at 3–5 weeks. First prey captured at 6–7 weeks, suckling for 6–8 weeks, independent at 8–12 weeks. SEXUAL MATURITY: ♂ 1 year, ♀ $\frac{1}{2}$ year. LONGEVITY: 7–8 years.

EUROPEAN POLECAT, *Mustela putorius* (Linnaeus, 1758)   **Pl. 31**
G. Iltis   F. Le Putois

Identification. 1 ssp. in N. Africa (African Polecat, *furo* Linnaeus, 1758, G. Iltis, F. Le Putois de Berberie.) Upperside pale sepia. Face with edges of ears whitish up to the sepia 'spectacles' round and under eyes. Underside, with tail and limbs, blackish brown to black. Pelage thick, with long dark guard hairs, and finer, thicker, yellowish underfur showing through. Eyes and ears small, tail of medium length and rather bushy. Dental formula and number of teats as in Weasel. MEASUREMENTS: HB 35–45, TL 12–16, Ht 4.5–6, Wt 700–1500. ♂ larger and heavier than ♀.

Distribution. N. Morocco, W. of the Rif between Tangier and Algerian border. Also widely in Europe (the species) and Asia. 6 ssp. The domesticated form, the Ferret, feral on Sardinia and Sicily as well as having been introduced with Polecat-Ferrets in New Zealand (both known there as 'New Zealand Fitch'). HABITAT: in all districts with dense cover, also in large closed woodlands, agricultural land with varied habitats, including hedgerows, bushes, overgrown banks of rivers and lakes and meadows with deep ditches. May be found near villages, in barns, stables, stacks etc. In mountains to 2000m. HOME RANGE: sedentary, range size, according to district, of some sq km.

Marked by anal gland secretions particularly near burrow; prominent points marked by urine and faeces. Uses burrows, sometimes of fox, badger, or rabbit, or crevices among rocks, holes in walls, under wood piles and similar places. *Map* p. 179.

Habits. DAILY RHYTHM: hides during day, hunts at dusk and by night. TOILET: as in Weasel. VOICE: whimpering of young in nest, whining in disquiet or straying, at 3 weeks old a piping. Chatter in anger or pain. In extreme fright a staccato shrill threat cry, often with stink gland discharge. SENSES: scent and hearing very good, sight best for moving objects; colour conscious for red and blue, limited for yellow and green. Sense of touch in narrow spaces well developed. ENEMIES: all predators from wild cat and fox to jackal and wolf, as well as the larger birds of prey. Has good protection in its very offensive anal gland secretions and its courageous defence. FOOD: mainly small mammals (mice, shrews, moles, hamsters, rats, water voles, muskrats, rabbits, leverets) ground nesting birds, eggs, lizards, snakes, frogs, fish, insects, fruit. Stores dead or crippled prey underground. SOCIABILITY: solitary, though generally pacific with others (except ♂♂ in rut). ♂ takes no part in rearing young.

Reproduction. Breeding season Feb–Mar, duration of mating 1–2 hours. Gestation 41–42 days. Litter of 1–12 (usually 4–8) finely grey-haired, blind young in hidden well-lined nest. Birth measurements: HB 6–7, TL 1.4–1.5, Wt 9–10. First solid food, and beginning of adult coat, at 3 weeks, eyes open at 1 week, first venture out of nest at 4 weeks, weaned at 6–7 weeks. Independent at 3 months. SEXUAL MATURITY: 9 months. LONGEVITY: 5–6 years, in captivity up to 10, even 18 reported.

WHITE-NAPED WEASEL, *Poecilogale albinucha* (Gray, 1864)   Pl. 31

G. Weissnackenwiesel   F. Le Poecilogale a nuque blanche   A. Slangmuishond

Identification. Like Polecat but with striped pattern. Eyes and ears small, legs short, tail rather bushy. Pelage short, silky-smooth, from neck on either side of the black spinal stripe 2 parallel yellowish-white to white stripes to root of tail, tail white. The white parts can also be cream or orange in colour, and lower lip can be white; breadth of lateral stripes variable. Dental formula as Weasel. 4–6 teats. MEASUREMENTS: HB ♂ 30–35, ♀ 27–32, TL ♂ 18–24, ♀ 14–18, Ht 7–8. Wt ♂ 300–350, ♀ 230–250. ♂ on average a third larger and heavier than ♀.

Distribution. W. Africa from S. Gabon to S. Angola, E. to Uganda, W. Kenya and W. Tanzania, southward between 22° and 32°–35°E, south to coast of Cape Province, probably Mozambique, S.W. Botswana and Mid S.W. Africa. 6 ssp. HABITAT: open woodland and bush savannahs, plains and semi-plains, in mountains to 1500m. TERRITORY: apparently territorial, marking by faeces on upright objects with raised hind-quarters. *Map* p. 179.

Habits. DAILY RHYTHM: mainly nocturnal, sometimes out at dusk, rests by day in hiding place (burrow, rock crevices etc.). TOILET: fur-licking and grooming, scratching with hind feet. VOICE: growls when angry, in rage loud scream, threat display jumping up and down on front legs with tail fluffed out; if further threatened sprays offensive secretion up to 1m. Whines softly while sniffing around. In rut a staccato purring. SENSES: sight, hearing and scent good. Hunts by scent and sight equally. ENEMIES: defends itself with anal gland secretions, warning in advance by erection and fluffing out of tail. Yawns widely and repeatedly when annoyed. FOOD: small mammals and ground birds. Apparently no eggs, reptiles or insects. SOCIABILITY: as Libyan Striped Weasel.

Reproduction. 2–4 young at a birth, showing already the colour pattern of adult. Further details not known. LONGEVITY: up to 5 years recorded in captivity.

LIBYAN STRIPED WEASEL,   **Pl. 31**
Poecilictis libyca (Hemprich & Ehrenberg, 1833)
(G. Streifenwiesel   F. Le Zorille

Identification. Form like polecat, smaller. Eyes and ears small, tail moderately to strongly bushy. Underfur fine and soft, overhair long to very long, can be fluffed out in excitement to increase apparent bodily size. Head, underside and legs blackish-brown to black, head with whitish forehead bands to chin, and partly white ear tips. Upperside white with longitudinal dark stripes, consisting of a dorsal line widening and dividing on the rump, and on either side parallel flank stripes, diverging from the dorsal stripe at the neck, and sometimes reuniting with it at root of tail. Tail preponderately either white or black. Soles hairy, digital pads naked. Pelage pattern variable individually and geographically. Dentition and number of teats as in Weasel. MEASUREMENTS: HB 22–30, TL 12–19, Ht 6–9. Wt 500–750.

Distribution. N. Africa, roughly from 12°N, between Atlantic and Red Sea on the one hand, and between Senegambia – N. Nigeria – Eritrea and the Mediterranean on the other. 7 ssp. HABITAT: dry, sandy, and particularly stony or rocky country.

Habits. DAILY RHYTHM: active at dusk and by night, during day hidden in rock crevices, burrows of other animals or self-excavated simple holes in dune slopes etc. VOICE: up to now only spitting and growling in anger known. ENEMIES: rather slow-moving, relying for protection on warning coloration, and operation of the nausea-inducing stink gland secretion. If attacked, the rear is presented and tail is erected (as in skunk) as a warning before spraying the liquid. FOOD: small mammals, birds, eggs, reptiles, insects. SOCIABILITY: as polecat.

Reproduction. Gestation uncertain, 7–11 weeks, litters in Mar–Apr. Usually 2–3 blind young, with fine white hair, in a simple burrow on bare ground. At birth HB *c*.5.5, TL *c*.1.8, Wt 2–3. At 3 weeks general colour as in adult, eyes open at $3\frac{1}{2}$ weeks. Further details not known. LONGEVITY: 6 years recorded in captivity.

STRIPED POLECAT, *Ictonyx striata* (Perry, 1810)   **Pl. 31**
G. Streifeniltis, Zorilla F. Le Zorille commun A. Stinkmuishond S. Kicheche, Kanu

Identification. Form and size as polecat. Eyes and ears small, claws of front feet very long and strong, tail rather bushy. Pelage dorsally longer and looser than the short breast and belly fur. Head, underside, legs and the 3 long stripes on back from neck to root of tail brownish-black to black. Broad forehead stripe to lower edge of cheeks (sometimes in 3 parts), and upperside of body, white. Tail black and white mixed, sometimes white, sometimes black, predominant. Width of dorsal stripes variable. Albinos may occur. Dentition as weasel. 6 teats. MEASUREMENTS: HB 30–38, TL 22–30, Ht 10–13, Wt ♂ 0.7–1.4, ♀ 0–5 – 0.8.

Distribution. Africa south of Sahara, except the Guinea and Central African rain forests. N. border between Senegambia and Eritrea about 15°N. 21 ssp. HABITAT: open country, in mountains up to 3000m, not in closed forest or densely bushy country. *Map* p. 179.

Habits. DAILY RHYTHM: hunts at dusk and by night; by day rests in burrows (taken over or self-dug), rock crevices, under piles of stones, barns or stables etc. VOICE: a shrill scream in threat. ENEMIES: behaviour as in striped Weasel; courageous. May sham death if surprised by larger predator. FOOD: small mammals up to hare size, birds, eggs, reptiles and insects. Will kill fair-sized snakes and take poultry. SOCIABILITY: as in Polecat.

Reproduction. 2–3 young with adult pattern. No further details. LONGEVITY: $5\frac{1}{2}$ years in captivity.

Striped Weasel   Ratel   1 Common Otter
    2 Spotted-necked Otter

RATELS, MELLIVORINAE

Badger-like. Dent: $3 \cdot 1 \cdot 3 \cdot 1 = 32$. 4 teats. Usually nocturnal, terrestrial predators of mostly open country. 1 genus with 1 species, in Africa, Arabia and India.

RATEL, or HONEY BADGER, *Mellivora capensis* (Schreber, 1776)   **Pl. 31**
G. Honigdachs   F. Le Ratel   A. Ratel   S. Nyegere, Kinyegale

Identification. Build and size as European Badger. Head brown, eyes small, ears small and round, legs short and sturdy, claws of front feet very long and powerful, tail short and bushy. Pelage short and coarse. Upperside from forehead to root of tail (the saddle) whitish-grey, rest of body black. Saddle separated by a narrow white edge from the black underside. Rump sometimes grey, yellowish or brown. Saddle sometimes extends to the front half of the tail, or up to the neck and crown; sometimes saddle absent (all-black forms). Skin itself very thick, but also very loose on the body, so that this very strong aggressive fighter is difficult to grasp and hold. 2 anal glands secrete an offensive fluid. 4 teats.   MEASUREMENTS: HB 65–75, TL 18–25, Ht 23–28, Wt 8–16. ♂ larger and heavier than ♀.

Distribution. Africa south of Sahara to Cape. N. border about 15°–20°N (occurs in Ennedi, Tibesti, Air and Adrar des Iforas), in the W. northwards to S. Morocco, in E. northwards to N. Sudan (formerly also in Egypt). In Union of S. Africa only locally. Elsewhere occurs from Arabian Peninsula to Iran and India south of Himalayas.15 ssp.   HABITAT: from deserts to rain forests, and in mountains up to 3000m.   HOME RANGE: several sq kms, details not known, roams widely in feeding. Tracks and particular places marked with anal gland secretion, stamped in. Within home range has an underground refuge in adopted or self-dug burrow (latter about 1–3m long, $\frac{1}{4}$ to $1\frac{1}{2}$m deep single tunnel with unlined chamber) or in rock crevices, holes among tree roots etc.

Habits. DAILY RHYTHM: active at dusk or by night, also by day where undisturbed. VOICE: grunting, growling and yowling. SENSES: scent very good, hearing good, sight moderate. ENEMIES: few enemies; itself often attacks intruders (even up to buffalo-size) furiously; its strong jaws give a powerful biting ability, so that it is seldom interfered with. May feign death if surprised with no escape possible. FOOD: great variety; insects, scorpions, spiders, fish, frogs, reptiles (including poisonous snakes and tortoises), ground birds, eggs, small mammals, young game animals (including young antelope calves), carrion, roots, tubers, berries, fruit. Investigates refuse bins at safari lodges. Climbs trees to open wild bee nests and eats grubs as well as honey. Allows itself to be led to hives by the wax-eating honey guide (*Indicator indicator*). SOCIABILITY: like Polecat.

Reproduction. Gestation 6–7 months, 1–2 young at a birth. Further details not known. LONGEVITY: up to 24 years in captivity.

OTTERS, LUTRINAE

Variable in size, medium to large. Dent: $3 \cdot 1 \cdot 4/3 \cdot 1/2 = 36$. 4–6 teats. Diurnal or nocturnal aquatic animals, living in inland waters, sometimes seacoasts, diet mainly fish, crustacea and molluscs. Toes webbed for swimming. Claws present, reduced or absent. In New and Old Worlds except Australasia and Madagascar. 6 genera with 13 species, of which 2 genera and 4 species occur in Africa.

SPOTTED-NECKED OTTER,   Pl. 31
Lutra (Hydrictis) maculicollis (Lichtenstein, 1835)
G. Fleckenhalsotter   F. La Loutre à cou tacheté   A. Kleinotter   S. Fisimaji
Identification. Form and dentition as Common Otter. 4 teats. Body light chestnut to dark brown. Chin, throat, fore part of breast and usually also belly, white to orange, with irregular brownish spots. White areas and spot sizes very variable, may be completely lacking on belly.   MEASUREMENTS: HB 60–65, TL 35–40, Ht *c*.30, Wt ♂ 4–6.5, ♀3.4.
Distribution. Africa S. of Sahara, in W. from about 10°N., in centre from Lake Chad (13°N), and in E. from S. Sudan and N. Ethiopia (10°–14°N), S. to E. Cape Province. Absent in Somalia, E. Kenya, E. Tanzania: and E. Transvaal as well as W. Cape Province (from about 23°S), S. Botswana, S. and Mid S.W. Africa (except Orange River). 6 ssp.   HABITAT: lakes, swamps and perennial rivers in plains and mountains. HOME RANGE: roam within a wide range; details not known. *Map p. 183.*
Habits. DAILY RHYTHM: where undisturbed, most activity from sunrise and before sunset. Where hunted is nocturnal.   TOILET: scratching, grooming of fur (also mutually), rarely only licking fur and brushing with fore feet. On leaving the water, only the head is shaken, rest of body may or may not be squeezed dry by rolling and rubbing on the ground.   VOICE: long-drawn mew as contact call, high trill when annoyed, when excited a squealing whistle, becoming louder and quicker with rising excitement.   SENSES: sight moderate, sharp up to 3m, recognises objects at 10m, good at detecting movement; scent good, smells water instantly. Hearing good; tactile sense outstanding.   ENEMIES: in water, crocodiles; nothing known of terrestrial enemies. In defence lies on back, fights with feet and teeth, squealing.   FOOD: mainly fish, as well as crabs, molluscs and frogs. Usual dive duration when fishing 15 seconds, sometimes up to 21, rarely up to 45 seconds.   SOCIABILITY: usually sociable in family or bachelor parties, up to 6 or 10 animals.
Reproduction. Details not known. On Lake Victoria pairing in July, births in September. Gestation presumably 2 months. Birthplace a hole in bank, or dense reed bed. Wt of a tame ♀; at 1½ months 1.36, at 7½ months 3.5, so fully grown.   SEXUAL MATURITY and LONGEVITY: not known.

COMMON OTTER, *Lutra (Lutra) lutra* (Linnaeus, 1758)   Pl. 31
G. Fischotter   F. La Loutre d'Europe
Identification. 1 ssp. in N. Africa, Common N. African Otter, *angustifrons* Lataste, 1885 (G. Afrikanische Fischotter; La Loutre de Berberie). (Possibly identical with European Otter). Upperside, with limbs and tail, dark brown to yellowish-brown, chin

and throat to whitish-grey, rest of underside brown to fallow. Pelage with very fine underwool and thick outer coat, water-resistant. Body cylindrical, legs short, all feet with claws, and webs between the toes. Head and muzzle broad and flat, strong vibrissae, eyes and ears small, latter barely projecting beyond the fur, like the nostrils, can be closed. Tail roundish, broad at the root, sharp-ended, furred like back. 2 anal glands with musky scent, usually 6 teats, sometimes 4. MEASUREMENTS: In N. Africa HB $c.65$, TL $c.42$, otherwise HB 60–95, TL 25–55, Ht $c.30$, Wt 6–16 (exceptionally to 27). ♂ larger and heavier than ♀.

Distribution. Morocco, from coast to Atlas Mts., and N. Algeria. The species of wide distribution; whole of Europe, temperate Asia north to about 70°N., east to Kamschatka, Japan, S. to Sumatra and Java, India. Near East to Palestine and Asia Minor. 10 ssp. HABITAT: open water with plentiful cover (reed beds, bushy or tree-clad banks) and good supply of fish; also on estuaries and sea coasts. In mountains up to 2500m. TERRITORY: adult ♂ holds a territory of 12–24km stretch of water, size changing according to country and season (largest in spring and autumn): marked by droppings on prominent points, and threat screams. Territory protected against other adult ♂♂. Within the overall territory are 1–3 smaller territories of ♀♀ with young. Essential features in territory are secure living quarters, runways, convenient eating places, latrines, sun-bathing and playing places (particularly slides on mud, snow or ice), holes with entrances and hidden exits, air holes.

Habits. DAILY RHYTHM: mainly active at dusk or in night; where undisturbed may be diurnal, usually swimming and diving (dive duration 1–2, possibly up to 10 minutes). Usually goes downstream first before returning. May wander overland and cross hill or mountain watersheds. TOILET: scratching with hind feet, grooming (also mutually), drying after swimming by rolling and rubbing on land. VOICE: soft whistle as contact call, trilling as danger signal, chittering as mating cry, a long rough mew as threat, and in play or other excitement hissing, growling and squeaking. SENSES: hearing and scent very good, sight particularly good for moving objects. Highly developed sense of touch and balance. ENEMIES: in northern countries wolf, bear, wolverine occasionally. FOOD: mainly fish, also crabs, molluscs, frogs, reptiles, birds and eggs, small mammals up to musk rat or hare size, insects, carrion, on coast also sea-urchins. Pair often hunt together. SOCIABILITY: mother with family, on good terms with the male. Ranking order adult ♂, ♀, or ♀♀, and young.

Reproduction. Breeding season uncertain. Cubs in all months. Pairing in water preferred, duration 1–1½ hours, gestation 59–63 days, litter size 1–5, usually 2–3. Wt of young at birth 225. Young born blind, at first with short silky hair, then longer woolly dark greyish-brown coat. Birthplace a burrow in the bank, with underwater entrance, air shaft, lined breeding chamber, but sometimes in a hollow tree, or in thick reed beds. Eyes open at 28–35 days, when first solid food. First swim at 1½ months, when the nest coat is replaced by the two-layered coat with underwool and guard hairs. First dive at about 2 months, weaned about same time. Young independent at ½–¾ year, fully grown at 1–1¼ years. SEXUAL MATURITY: four-fifths to one year. LONGEVITY: Up to 22 years in captivity.

CAPE CLAWLESS OTTER; *Aonyx (Aonyx) capensis* (Schinz, 1821) Pl. 31
G. Fingerotter, Kapfingerotter   F. La Loutre à joues blanches   A. Groototter
S. Fisi maji

Identification. Form, number of teeth and teats as in Spotted-neck Otter, but larger and much heavier. Fingers without claws or webs, hind toes also without webs, and with short pointed claws, usually only on 3rd and 4th toes, though these claws may also be absent. Upperside of body light greyish brown. Snout, cheeks, sides of neck, breast, throat and chin white to yellowish, sharply distinguished from the dark colour everywhere else on head and neck. Ears white-edged. Young like adults, though top of head and neck with white hairs giving a frosted appearance. Large rectangular blackish-brown preorbital spot on the white cheeks. MEASUREMENTS: HB 75–92, TL 40–57, Ht c.35, Wt 16–20, rarely up to 27.

Distribution. Africa south of Sahara (from Senegambia, Lake Chad, Ethiopia, c.15°N, south to Cape). 5 ssp. HABITAT: standing and running water in forests, savannahs, steppes, in plains and mountains up to 3000m. Also on sea coasts. HOME RANGE: details not known. Sometimes wanders far from water. *Map* p. 183.

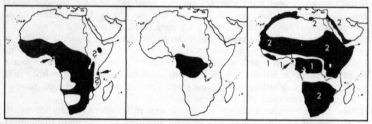

Cape Clawless Otter   Congo Clawless Otter   1 African Linsang
                                                                        2 Small-spotted Genet

Habits. DAILY RHYTHM and TOILET: as in Spotted-necked Otter. VOICE: contact call a high scream; when contented a purring growl; whines when displeased; in anger hisses and growls; loud scream in great fear or pain; in sudden alarm an explosive 'Ha'. Young in nest trill and squeak. SENSES and ENEMIES: as Spotted-necked Otter. FOOD: fish, crabs, molluscs, frogs, reptiles, small and medium-sized mammals, waterfowl, other bird's and crocodile eggs. SOCIABILITY: as Common Otter.

Reproduction. Details not known. Gestation probably 2 months, 2–3 young. Birthplace as in Spotted-necked Otter. LONGEVITY: not known.

CONGO CLAWLESS OTTER, *Aonyx (Paraonyx) congica* (Lonnberg, 1910)
G. Kleinzahn Fingerotter   F. La Loutre à joues blanches du Congo

Identification. Form, tooth formula, and number of teats as in Cape Clawless Otter. However, cheek teeth notably smaller and less specialised than in former. Fore feet also without claws, or with only small rudimentary claws on the middle fingers (unwebbed). Hind feet with small claws, and webbing up to half length of toes. Body upper- and underside dark chestnut-brown, inside of legs darker than back. Muzzle, cheeks, sides of neck, chin, throat and front of breast whitish-grey, or breast graduating to brown of body, otherwise sharply defined. Young like adults, though head, neck, shoulders and forepart of back silver-frosted by the white hair tips. Ear edges whitish, and larger, blackish-brown straight-edged preorbital spot on the white cheek. MEASUREMENTS: HB c.78–90, TL c.40–59, Ht c.35, Wt 15–25.

Distribution. Lower and Mid-Congo basin; extreme limits S.E. Nigeria, S. Cameroun, Gabon, Rio Muni, Congo, W., N. and M. Zaire, N.E. Angola, S. Central African Republic, E. to W. Uganda and Ruanda; N. and S. limits approximately between 5°N and 5°S. 3 ssp.

Habits. Little known. Lives along brooks and rivers, especially fond of swamps. Sometimes found well away from water. Rests in reeds, waterside vegetation, under tree roots or in holes in banks. More nocturnal than diurnal. Eats fish, crabs, frogs, lizards, birds and eggs, small mammals, and earthworms taken on muddy banks. Its smaller teeth indicate a perhaps more varied diet than the previous species. Lives singly, or in family party. Gestation *c*. 2 months, 2–3 young.

CIVETS & MONGOOSES, VIVERRIDAE

Size range from Dwarf Mongoose to Binturong. Muzzle sharp, eyes and ears small to large, legs short to medium length. Number of digits 4–5/4–5, thumb and great toe sometimes lacking. Claws partly or not retractile. Tail long, often bushy. Dent: $3/3 \cdot 1/1 \cdot 3/4 \cdot 1/3 = 32$–44. Molars broader than long, generally sharp-cusped. Penis bone usually well developed. 2–6 teats. Anal and perineal scent glands generally well developed. Diurnal or nocturnal, usually solitary, carnivorous predators or omnivorous, sometimes piscivorous. Found in S. Europe, Africa, Madagascar, Asia Minor, Near East and S. Asia to Indonesia. 6 subfamilies, 32 genera, 72 species, 36 of which occur in Africa and 7 in Madagascar.

GENETS, VIVERRINAE

Mostly cat-sized, some larger. Toes 5/5. 4 teats. Dent: $3 \cdot 1 \cdot 4 \cdot 1/2 - 1 = 38$–40. Mainly nocturnal, terrestrial or arboreal, in forests or savannahs. 6 genera with 15 species (1 genus and species in S. Europe, the rest in Africa and S. Asia). 4 genera with 12 species in Africa. 1 genus and species, *Viverricula malaccensis* from S. Asia, has been introduced to Madagascar (see Introduced Mammals, p. 389). The classification of the African genets is still not clear.

AFRICAN LINSANG, *Poiana richardsoni* (Thompson, 1842)   **Pl. 61**
(= *leightoni* Pocock, 1908)
G. Afrika-Linsang   F. La Poiane
Identification. Genet-like in size and form, but smaller and tail longer. Muzzle pointed, eyes and ears of medium size, latter rounded triangle. Body slender. Legs short, hind somewhat longer than fore; thumb and great toe small, soles hairy except for the digital pads; claws curved, sharply pointed, semi-retractile. 4 teats. Penis bone and anal glands present. Dent: $3/3 \cdot 1/1 \cdot 4/4 \cdot 1/2 = 38$, canines slender, premolars sharp-cusped, molars small, lower jaw weak. Pelage short and thick, tail very long and cylindrical, as long as HB or longer. Upperside pale yellowish- or brownish-grey to orange-brown, underside (chin, throat, breast, belly and inside of thighs) cream-coloured to white, as also front of upper lip, cheeks and supraorbital spot. Upperside with dark brown to black round to oval spots in 4 or 5 irregular rows on each side of body, and 2–4 rows of spots or stripes on the neck. The spots along shoulders and back often merging into stripes, otherwise becoming larger or smaller, more closely or more widely spaced, usually becoming more wide apart on thighs. Sometimes a thin, almost continuous, black dorsal stripe from back of nose to root of tail. Latter with 10–14 black rings, narrow or broad or varying. Tail tip black or light. Backs of hind feet black. MEASUREMENTS: HB 33–38, TL 35–40, Ht 15–18; Wt 500–700.
Distribution. Sierra Leone, Liberia, Ivory Coast, Mid and S. Cameroun with Fer-

nando Poo, Gabon, Congo, and N. Zaire east to about 28°E, south to about 6°S. 3 ssp. HABITAT: rain forest only.

Habits. Entirely nocturnal, good climber, living more in trees than on ground, sleeping in various self-built nests in the crowns, used for a few days from time to time. Eats insects, young birds, fruit etc. Gives birth once or twice a year to 2–3 young. No further details of habits.

SMALL-SPOTTED OR COMMON GENET,   Pl. 32
Genetta genetta (Linnaeus, 1758)
G. Gemeine Ginsterkatze   F. La Genette vulgaire   A. Kleinkol Muskejaallat
S. Kanu

Identification. Head small, body slender, legs short, tail long, eyes large, ears of medium size, triangular and rather blunt-tipped. Pelage rather rough, with short erect line of hair along the spinal line. Tail slender, nearly as long as HB, with long hair at root and pointed tip. Toes 5/5, soles hairy apart from digital pads, claws curved and sharp, semi-retractile. 2 anal and 2 perineal glands (latter produce a musky secretion), penis bone well developed, 4 teats. Dent: for the genus $3 \cdot 1 \cdot 4 \cdot 2 = 40$. P^2 and M^2 small. Pelage ground colour whitish-grey to grey or brownish-grey, underside lighter. White spot above and below eyes and on front of upper lip, back of upper lip black. Neck and back with round or longish brown to black spots, which form 5 long rows on either side of the dark spinal stripe; the upper two of these may run together, those below are usually imperfect. Tail with 8–10 black rings, tip white to black. Upper thighs and arms with separate spots. Upper side of fore feet pale, undersides dark grey, upper side of hind feet pale grey, undersides black, including heels. Newborn young well-haired, dark grey, spots suffused with grey, though much darker than in adults, tail with the rings weakly distinguished; on the head the dark upper lip and whitish suborbital spot clear. At $1\frac{1}{2}$–2 months the colour and pattern are as in adults. MEASUREMENTS: HB 40–55, TL 40–51, Ht 15–20, Wt 1–3 – 2.25. ♂ somewhat heavier and larger than ♀.

Distribution. France (south of Loire and west of Rhone, occasional animals from Normandy, Belgium, Alsace, W. Switzerland, W. French Alps), Iberia, Balearic Is., Morocco, Algeria, Tunisia, Cyrenaica, Spanish Sahara, Mauritania, S. Egypt, Nubia as well as Africa south of Sahara from about 20°N (outside the West and Central African rain forests), Also in Israel and W. Arabia. 11 ssp. (6 in Africa). HABITAT: open districts, from dry savannahs to semi-desert, with sufficient ground cover. In mountains up to 2500m. HOME RANGE: resident, ♀ more so than ♂, which wanders more widely (up to 30km). Probably territorial, limits marked by anal gland secretion (on elevated objects deposited in handstand), also droppings and urine in special places. *Map* p. 186.

Habits. DAILY RHYTHM: active at dusk and by night, usually from nightfall to midnight or later, resting by day in hole in ground, in tree, among rocks or other hiding places, rarely in thick bush. Good climber, including head downwards. TOILET: licking and grooming fur (also mutually), face washing with forepaws and spittle, scratching with hind feet, claw sharpening, rolling in favoured scents. Special defecation spots. VOICE: varied, 'uff – uff – uff' as contact call, growling in excitement, hissing as threat, spitting in extreme threat, purring by young in contentment, whining and mewing in mating, squeaking in pain. Young utter shrill call if lost or in danger, and keep up constant twittering in nest in absence of mother. SENSES: sight, especially at dusk or for movement (though colour blind), very good. Hearing very good, scent good. ENEMIES: as Kaffir Cat. Defends itself by cat-like arching of back,

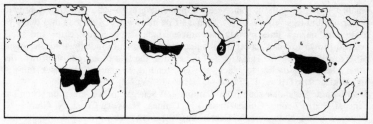

Angola Genet   1 Hausa Genet   Servaline Genet
                      2 Abyssinian Genet

erecting hair of tail and spinal crest, scratching and biting on its back; also ejects evil-smelling anal secretion. If hunted will take to trees.   FOOD: small animals up to size of hare, small birds up to guinea-fowl size, eggs, lizards, snakes, frogs, fish, insects, spiders, scorpions, millipedes, crabs, mussels, freshwater snails, sometimes fruit or carrion. Attacks poultry. Tames easily, kept in houses in ancient Egypt as mouse and rat killer.   SOCIABILITY: solitary.

Reproduction. Pairing as in Kaffir Cat. Duration of mating 3–5 minutes. Gestation 68–77 days. Births in Europe and N. Africa Mar–Apr, sometimes a second litter Aug–Sep, in E. Africa Oct–Dec, in W. Africa Mar–Jun and Sep–Dec (2 litters annually). Young born in holes in trees, in ground, among rocks etc. Litter 1–4, usually 2–3, blind, fully-haired but belly naked. Ears open 5th–8th day, eyes open 5th–12th. First solid food at $1\frac{1}{2}$ months, fully active at 2 months, weaned at 2–3 months; independent at $\frac{1}{2}$–$\frac{3}{4}$ year.   SEXUAL MATURITY: at 2 years. Wt at birth 60–80, at $\frac{3}{4}$ year c.1200, at 2 years c.2000. HB and TL at birth 17–18, at 2 months 20–25.   LONGEVITY: up to $14\frac{3}{4}$ years in captivity.

ANGOLA GENET, *Genetta angolensis* (Bocage, 1882)   Pl. 32
G. Angola-oder-Bürstenginsterkatze   F. La Genette d'Angola
Identification. Build, colour and pattern much as in *G. genetta*, but spinal hair crest (the brush) up to 6cm long, and tail thicker and more fully haired. Colour dark grey or dark reddish-grey with black to brownish-black spots arranged as in *genetta*. Underside paler grey. Underside of front feet, and hind feet as far as heel, greyish-black to black. Tail with about 8 black rings and light tip, or black on the underside with the last ring merging into the black tip. Face dark grey, supra-orbital spot only a little paler; suborbital spot, front of upper lip, and chin, white; back of upper lip, top of nose, and stripe on middle of forehead black. Very dark or entirely black animals not uncommon.   MEASUREMENTS: HB 44–48, TL 38–43, Ht 18–20, Wt 1.3–2.
Distribution. Zone between Atlantic and Indian Oceans between about 5° to 15°S (N. Angola, S. Zaire, N. Zambia, Malawi, N. Mozambique, S. and M. Tanzania). 3 ssp. (The classification of genets, and particularly the allocation to ssp., is still uncertain).   HABITAT: rain forests and moist savannahs.
Habits. Details not known, probably like *genetta*.

HAUSA GENET, *Genetta thierryi* (Matschie, 1902)   Pl. 32
(= *Pseudogenetta villiersi* Dekeyser, 1949, False Genet)
G. Haussa-Ginsterkatze   F. La Genette de Thierry
Identification. Form, colour and pattern much as in *genetta*, however somewhat

smaller and back without spinal crest. Upperside greyish-yellow to greyish-brown, underside and legs yellowish-grey. Spinal stripe narrow, often divided into two separate dark narrow lines by thin pale intermediate stripe. Spinal stripe and spots reddish-brown to black, spots on shoulder area sometimes indistinct, arrangement otherwise as in *genetta*. Tail with 7–9 dark rings, the first often reddish-brown, the others becoming darker to black, the last tending to merge into black tail-tip. MEASUREMENTS: HB 40–45, TL 40–45, Ht 15–18, Wt 1.3–1.5. *Map* p. 189.

Distribution. Savannah zone from Gambia and Senegal to N. Cameroun (Gambia, Senegal, Sierra Leone, Guinea-Bissau, N. Guinea, N. Ivory Coast, N. Ghana, N. Togo, N. Benin, N. Nigeria, N. Cameroun). HABITAT: moist to dry savannahs with woodland islands.

Habits. No details known, probably like *genetta*.

ABYSSINIAN GENET, *Genetta abyssinica* (Ruppell, 1836)   **Pl. 32**
G. Streifenginsterkatze   F. La Genette d'Ethiopie
Identification. Form, colour and basic pattern like *genetta* but with conspicuous stripes on back. Coat short, rather coarse, without spinal crest, upperside and legs light grey or light sandy-yellowish-grey. Underside, eye spots and front of upper lips white, feet whitish; hind part of upper lip, back of nose, body spots, the 7–8 tail rings and tail tip black. Pale grey narrow spinal stripe, on either side of which large elongated spots merge into 2 long stripes. Also the neck and shoulder rows of spots on each side tend to merge into long stripes. Flanks with two rows of long spots. MEASUREMENTS: HB 40–50, TL 40–45, Ht 18–20, Wt 1.3–2. *Map* p. 189.
Distribution. Highlands of Ethiopia. HABITAT: open dry country, with good ground cover, in plains and mountains; also near villages.
Habits. No details known.

SERVALINE GENET, *Genetta servalina* (Pucheran, 1855)   **Pl. 32**
G. Waldginsterkatze   F. La Genette servaline
Identification. Form as in *genetta*. Pelage velvety-soft, spinal crest along neck and back usually short, sometimes only on neck, sometimes only on back (with the greater part along the rump), sometimes absent. Upperside greyish-, creamy- or ochreous-yellow, sides lighter, lower part of legs brown to black. Underside yellowish-grey to brownish-black (in latter case chin and throat paler). No spinal stripe. Neck, back, flanks and upper parts of legs with numerous closely grouped small, usually rather angular, black spots; on underside weaker and more scattered. Spots on sides of body arranged in 6 or 7 longitudinal rows, which may tend to merge near the spine. Front upper lip and suborbital spot whitish, supraorbital spot weak yellowish. Tail with 8–12 blackish-brown rings, with yellowish to whitish spaces between. Tip whitish, yellowish or black. MEASUREMENTS: HB 45–60, TL 40–50, Ht *c*.20, Wt 1.3–2.
Distribution. West and Central African rain forests from S. Benin and Nigeria to S. Cameroun, S. Central African Republic, Gabon, Congo, Zaire (S. limit about 6°S), eastward to W. Uganda as well as some isolated forests in Kenya. 5 ssp. HABITAT: dense woodlands and primeval forests. Terrestrial and not arboreal. *Map* p. 189.
Habits. Details not known.

LARGE-SPOTTED GENET, RUSTY-SPOTTED GENET,
Genetta tigrina (Schreber, 1776) (= *rubiginosa* Pucheran, 1855)   **Pls. 32, 34**
G. Grossfleckginsterkatze   F. La Genette à grandes taches
A. Grootkolmuskejaatkat   S. Kanu

Identification. Like *genetta* in form. Pelage short, rather soft, no, or only indistinct, short spinal crest. Ears shorter and rounder than in *genetta*. Upperside yellowish-grey to yellow-ochre or brownish-red. Brownish-black to blackish spinal stripe, on either side two rows of large elongated chestnut-red or dark brown or blackish spots with paler centres; sometimes tending to merge. Below are 2–3 rows of smaller spots. Legs from elbows or knees brown, dark brown to blackish. Underside yellowish to whitish grey. Facial pattern as in *genetta*. Tail with 7–9 rusty red to brownish black or black rings, the broadest with lighter intermediate rings, and at end of tail merging into the black colour of the terminal $\frac{1}{4}$. Great variation in pattern; often partly or fully melanistic. Newborn young dark grey with darker grey spot pattern, dark upper lips and yellowish-white suborbital spot as in adults. Belly naked until hair growth begins at 4th day. Adult colour pattern reached at $1\frac{1}{2}$ months; in *rubiginosa* however the rust-red of the spots only fully developed at $\frac{3}{4}$ year. MEASUREMENTS: HB 40–55, TL 40–54, Ht *c*.18, Wt 1.2–3.1.

Distribution. Africa S. of Sahara; Ethiopia, Eritrea, Somalia, northern limit that of savannah zone from Senegambia eastward (*c*.13°N in west). Also on Fernando Poo. Absent in S. Africa from W. Transvaal, Orange Free State, Cape Province (apart from coastal strip), S. and M. Botswana, S. and M. S.W. Africa. About 14 ssp. HABITAT: forest edges, forest clearings, moist savannahs, bush country, agricultural regions, reed thickets, long grass. Favours water and swampy areas. Otherwise habitat as in *genetta*. *Map* p. 192.

Reproduction. Young eyes open at 5th–12th day, ears open at 8th–10th. Wt at 5 weeks 227, at 5 months 1000, at 12 months 1900. HB and TL at 5 weeks 28/20, at 10 months 46/42. LONGEVITY: in captivity $9\frac{1}{2}$ years.

GIANT GENET, *Genetta victoriae* (Thomas, 1901)   **Pl. 32**
G. Riesenginsterkatze   F. La Genette géante

Identification. The largest genet. Long-legged; pelage thick and soft, medium length spinal crest along neck and back. Upperside yellowish-grey to yellowish-ochre, underside paler or yellow or yellowish-white. Row of black spots along middle of back, and on either side 5–6 long rows of small to mid-sized, often angular, closely grouped black spots, dense also on shoulders and upper thighs; on neck often merging into 4 stripes. Legs dark brown to black. Facial pattern as in *genetta*, but with fore part of upper lip black. Tail rather thick, with usually 5–8 very broad black rings (on upperside these may be linked by median stripe), and with only narrow yellow to whitish intermediate bands; tip black. Total impression of a very dark animal. MEASUREMENTS: HB 55–60, TL 45–50, Ht 20–25, Wt 2.5–3.5.

Distribution. Dense forests between the Ubangui, Congo and W. Uganda (Bwamba Forest). *Map* p. 192.

Habits. Details not known.

PARDINE GENET, *Genetta pardina* (I. Geoffroy, 1832)   **Pl. 32**
(= *maculata* Gray, 1830).
G. Pantherginsterkatze   F. La Genette pardine. Probably only a forest form of *tigrina*.

Identification. Form as in *tigrina*. Pelage rather short, soft; a short spinal crest from shoulders to root of tail. Upperside greyish-yellow to yellowish-brown, black or rust-

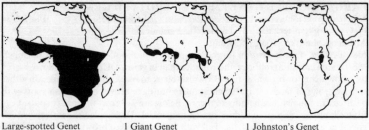

Large-spotted Genet   1 Giant Genet   1 Johnston's Genet
                           2 Pardine Genet   2 Water Civet

red spinal stripe, underside lighter. On each side of spinal stripe 4 rows of closely spaced, black to reddish-brown or black-edged reddish-brown spots, rounder or quadrilateral in shape, which at times may also tend to run together. Legs dark brown to black. Facial pattern as *genetta*. Tail rather thick, mainly black in appearance, the 8 dark rings being much broader than the light intermediate rings, and the last 3 almost wholly merged into the black tail tip. Gives a general dark impression; sometimes partial or complete melanos occur. MEASUREMENTS: as in *tigrina*.

Distribution. Guinea rain forest zone from Guinea to Ghana, as well as the forests of S. Nigeria and W. to S. Cameroon. HABITAT: primeval forests.

Habits. Few details known, probably like *tigrina*.

JOHNSTON'S GENET,   Pl. 61
Genetta (Paragenetta) johnstoni (Pocock, 1907) (= *lehmanni* Kuhn, 1960)
G. Liberia-Ginsterkatze   F. La Genette de Johnston

Identification. Form as in *pardina*. Coat thick and soft, with medium length crest along spinal line. Upperside yellowish-brown, underside paler, belly whitish. Black spinal stripe, with on either side 4 rows of blackish-brown to reddish-brown stippled spots: in the upper two rows the spots may in part or wholly merge as stripes. Below these 4 rows 2 further incomplete rows. Neck spots in rows or merging into stripes. Upper arms and thighs heavily spotted, legs and feet blackish brown. Tail thickly haired, with 7–8 black rings as broad as, or broader than, the whitish intermediate bands, and on upper surface linked by a black median line. Tail tip black. In the skull the jaws, cheek bones and molar teeth narrower and weaker than in other *Genetta* species, hence separated as a subgenus *Paragenetta*. MEASUREMENTS: as in *pardina* or *tigrina*.

Distribution. West Liberia. HABITAT: primeval forests.

Habits. Details not known. The tooth structure suggests a diet mainly of insects and arthropods.

AFRICAN CIVET, *Viverra civetta* (Schreber, 1776)   Pl. 33
G. Afrika-Zibetkatze   F. La Civette d'Afrique   A. Siwetkat   S. Fungo, Ngawa

Identification. Large, size of medium-sized dog. Head broad, muzzle pointed, eyes and ears small, latter rounded. Neck short and strong. Body laterally compressed, hind legs notably longer than fore, back sloping towards the front, head carried low. Toes 5/5, claws short, not retractile. Tail bushy, flattened laterally, pointed at end, about ½ HB length. Coat rough, hair loose, an erectile spinal mane from neck to end of tail, longest on rump and tail root. Dent.: $3 \cdot 1 \cdot 4 \cdot 2 = 40$. 4 teats. Upperside dark grey to yellowish-grey, lower half of face (apart from light orbital and upper lip spots), chin, throat, breast, legs, dorsal line (from forehead to tail tip) and pattern blackish-brown to black. Edges and tips of ears whitish, rest of backs black. Tail with 5–6 broad, or 5–9 narrow, black rings (linked above and below) and black tips. Pattern consists of 3 curved stripes on neck, 5–6 upright shoulder stripes, as many horizontal rump and upper thigh stripes, and large flank spots usually arranged in 6–8 upright rows. Pattern varies individually or regionally, can be close or well-spaced, darker (partly or fully melanistic), or reduced, with underside black invading the back, many spots absorbed in the grey neck and shoulder region; colour on sides of neck between the stripes varying from white to grey. Young resemble adults, though at 1 month the pattern still poorly defined. The abundantly produced oily anal gland secretion has been collected over the ages in many regions (e.g. Ethiopia and Zanzibar) from captive animals, to form the basis for perfumes. MEASUREMENTS: HB 80–95, TL 40–53, Ht 35–40, Wt 9–20. ♂ larger and heavier than ♀.

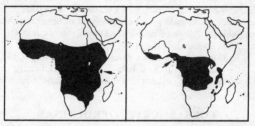

African Civet   Two-spotted Palm Civet

Distribution. Africa south of the Sahara (south of about 15°N). In west to S. Angola and northern S.W. Africa, in east to S. Mozambique, N. Zululand, E. Transvaal, E. and N. Botswana. Absent from Eritrea, Ogaden and Somalia, present in Zanzibar. 4 ssp. HABITAT: forest, moist and dry savannahs, also in farmland, in plains and hills, likes to be near water. HOME RANGE: size not known, probably territorial, marking with anal gland secretions on trees, stones etc, and droppings deposited in particular places, accumulating in neat piles.

Habits. DAILY RHYTHM: nocturnal, by day sleeping in high grass, thickets, burrows, rock piles, under tree roots and other hiding places. Terrestrial, only climbs trees in emergency (e.g. when hunted). TOILET: licking and grooming fur, also mutually. Face washing with fore feet, scratching with hind, skin shivering. Rubs neck and shoulders on fresh prey or pleasant scents. VOICE: growls in anger as threat, a deep spitting cough when alarmed (at same time erecting mane and jumping high on all four feet) or in extreme threat. In high excitement scream, young mew if left in the nest, as does ♀ in heat or mating; repeated short 'Ha' as contact call. ♂♂ fighting howl, pant and growl. SENSES: scent and hearing very good, sight outstanding and highly sensitive to dusk and for movement. ENEMIES: details not known, but young at risk from the smaller cats, genets, mongooses and hyenas. Adults defend themselves vigorously with hair ruffled up, and ♀ protects young bravely. FOOD: small to middle-sized mammals (also antelope calves and house cats), birds, eggs, domestic poultry, carrion, frogs and toads, reptiles, invertebrates, fruit, berries, vegetation. SOCIABILITY: solitary.

Reproduction. Litter season in N. Africa spring, in Kenya and Tanzania Mar–Oct, in southern Africa Aug–Oct, in tropical W. Africa all year. Cat-like pairing and mating, duration of latter 1–2 minutes. Gestation 63–68 days, rarely 72–82. Litter size 1–4, usually 2. 3 litters a year are possible. Eyes often open at birth or after 1–3 days. First solid food at 3 weeks, can leave nest at $3\frac{1}{2}$ weeks, weaned at 3 months. At birth HB 15, TL 9–10, Wt 315–335, at 6 months 6800. SEXUAL MATURITY: ♂ $\frac{3}{4}$–1, ♀ 1 year. LONGEVITY: up to 14 years in captivity.

AQUATIC GENET, *Osbornictis piscivora* (J. A. Allen, 1919)   Pl. 33
G. Wasserschleichkatze   F. La Genette aquatique

Identification. Genet-like in size and form. Sharp nose, eyes and ears middle-sized, latter triangular but somewhat rounded with distinct tips. Tail long and thickly bushy. Legs short, hind rather longer than fore. Thumb and great toe rather small and high set, claws curved and pointed, whole sole including pads naked. Skin glands and penis bone not yet investigated. Teats possibly 4. Dent.: $3 \cdot 1 \cdot 4 \cdot 2 = 40$, canines slender, molars narrow and sharp-cusped. Pelage rather long, with thick underfur; upperside brownish-red, spinal line, back of ears, and legs, darker: upperside of feet, and all of tail, black. Underside rather paler; throat, chin, front of upper lip, cheeks, and long spot above eye, whitish. Pelage of young not known. MEASUREMENTS: HB 45–50, TL 35–42, Ht *c*.22, Wt? (probably about 3).

Distribution. N.E. Zaire, south to Lowa River and S. Kivu. *Map* p. 192.

Habits. Very little known. Up to now only a few skins and skulls examined. The location, and bodily structure, indicate that it lives by streams in primeval rain forest and is piscivorous.

FOSSAS, CRYPTOPROCTINAE

Cat-like, toes 5/5, 6 teats; dent.: $3 \cdot 1 \cdot 3 \cdot 1 = 32$. Nocturnal terrestrial and arboreal predator in forests. 1 genus with 1 species in Madagascar. The largest carnivore in the island.

FOSSA, *Cryptoprocta ferox* (Bennett, 1833)   Pl. 33
G. Frettkatze   F. Le Foussa   MA Fosa, Kintsala, Tratraka

Identification. Cat-like in build. Head rounded and cat-like, but with muzzle somewhat longer, whiskers as long as head, eyes large, ears middle-sized, roundish. Neck short and thickset. Body long and slender. Legs rather short, hind longer than fore, thumb and great toe well developed, claws short, curved, sharp, retractile; soles naked and pads well developed. Usually semi-plantigrade, rarely digitigrade. Tail nearly as long as HB. Anal and preputial glands well developed, penis bone large (*c*.7cm long). 6 teats. Canines large, P^1 small, single-rooted, is lost early. Pelage short and thick, upperside reddish brown, darker along middle of back, underside rather lighter, palest on groin and inside of thighs. Sometimes melanistic. Young at first pale grey, almost white, then pearl grey. At $1\frac{1}{2}$ months the brown of the adults developing, beginning at the head, and complete at 3 months. MEASUREMENTS: HB 60–75, TL 55–70, Ht 36–40, Wt 7–12. ♂ somewhat larger and heavier than ♀.

Distribution. Whole of Madagascar, mostly in coastal areas, rarely in the central highlands. HABITAT: forests. HOME RANGE: several sq km according to country. ♂ marks upright objects with anal and preputial gland secretions. Probably territorial. *Map* p. 196.

Habits. DAILY RHYTHM: active at dusk and by night, in breeding season also diurnal. An outstanding climber, uses tail to help (but tail not prehensile), is as much at home in trees as on ground. TOILET: licking and grooming, scratching with hind feet, face washing with fore feet, neck rubbing on convenient objects.   VOICE: in threat, a short scream repeated 5–7 times. Pairing call of ♀ a long mew (up to 15 seconds); call of young sharp long whimpering. Young growl when beginning to suckle. Both sexes mew and growl in mating.   SENSES: hearing and sight very good, scent good. ENEMIES: no natural enemies: the most powerful predator in Madagascar.   FOOD: mammals up to size of lemurs, civets and young bush-pigs, birds up to guinea-fowl size, eggs, snakes, lizards, frogs, insects. Also poultry, domestic rabbits, sheep.   SOCIA-BILITY: solitary.

Reproduction. Breeding season Sep–Oct, young from Dec–Jan. Gestation 3 months, mates like Kaffir Cat, ♀ sitting, duration $\frac{3}{4}$–$1\frac{1}{2}$ hours. Young born in burrows, among rocks, in holes in trees or forks at base of large boughs. Litter 2–4, usually 2–3. ♀ alone rears the young. Eyes open at 12–15, sometimes up to 25 days. First milk tooth appears at $1\frac{1}{2}$ months (at first venture out of nest). Begins to climb at $2\frac{1}{2}$ months, first solid food at 3 months, weaned at 4 months, at 2 years fully grown and independent. At 4 years fully mature. Wt at birth 100, at 1 month 250–300; HB 20–22, TL 15; at 3 months Wt 800–875, HB 37, TL 30; at 1 year Wt 3.2–4.6, at 2 years c.7.   LONGEVITY: up to 17 years in captivity.

PALM CIVETS, PARADOXURINAE

Size range from genet to binturong. Toes 5/5, 4–6 teats. Dent.: $3 \cdot 1 \cdot 4 \cdot 2/1–2 = 38$–40. Nocturnal, mainly arboreal, forest animals. 6 genera with 9 species, in S. Asia and Africa; in latter 1 genus with 1 species.

TWO-SPOTTED PALM CIVET, *Nandinia binotata* (Gray, 1830)   **Pl. 33**
G. Pardelroller   F. La Nandinie   A. Palmsivet

Identification. Genet-like in build, but muzzle shorter and tail longer. Eyes medium size, ears short and round, whiskers very long, legs short. Thumb and great toe well developed, rather high set, claws curved and sharp, semi-retractile, pads of toes and soles naked, sole pads lengthened, on hind foot naked sole surface extends to heel. Plantigrade. Glandular sac with lateral slit on naked skin area in front of penis or vulva, producing a strong-smelling yellow fluid. Tactile vibrissae on wrist, chin, corner of mouth, and above eyes. Penis bone small (8–9mm), 4 teats. In the skull the posterior part of the tympanic bulla is cartilaginous or absent. Dent.: $3 \cdot 1 \cdot 4 \cdot 2 = 40$; canines stout, molars sharp-cusped, M^2 very small, often lost. Pelage short, woolly, very dense, rather tight, tail rather bushy. Upperside pale greyish-brown to dark reddish-brown, underside pale yellowish to dark olive-brown, spots dark brown to black. 1 spinal stripe or row of spots from forehead to root of tail; on either side a neck stripe, and on shoulders and flanks always 5–6 long rows of small round spots. These closely or widely spaced, sharp-edged or indistinct, neck stripes narrow or broad, continuous or interrupted, sometimes absent. Tail with 12–15 dark brown to black rings of variable breadth; in front and hind thirds of tail the rings may be broken up into spots. The rings are sometimes double or triple. Legs unspotted. On each shoulder a single whitish to yellowish spot usually present (hence the name 'Two-spotted') but these may be very pale or missing. A brownish-black spot behind each ear. Young like adults, but ground colour and shoulder spots paler, other spots black and indistinct, ground colour stippled with white.   MEASUREMENTS: HB 44–60, TL 48–62, Ht 22, Wt 2.3–3.2. ♂ rather larger and heavier than ♀.

Distribution. Rain forest regions of W. and mid-Africa from Guinea-Bissau and Sierra Leone to S.W. Sudan, W. and S. Uganda, and S.W. Kenya. Southern border from mid-

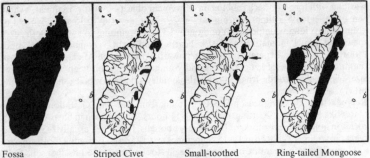

Fossa   Striped Civet   Small-toothed   Ring-tailed Mongoose
                          Mongoose (Falanouc)

Angola to mid-Mozambique (about 12°S in W, and 20°S in E.) Also on Fernando Poo.
4 ssp. HABITAT: rain forests in lowlands and mountains up to 2000m; gallery forests;
savannah woodlands. HOME RANGE: not known. *Map* p. 193.

Habits. DAILY RHYTHM: active at dusk or by night. Very good climber. In emergency
will leap from crown of tree, with widespread limbs, to the ground. TOILET: washes
face with licked fore feet like cat, scratches with hind feet, licks and grooms fur,
sharpens claws, rubs body on prominent objects. May rub neck and shoulders on flesh
food or other attractive scents, like a genet. VOICE: 'kwak-kwak' when satisfied, also
purring (both young and adults); growling and spitting in threat, a sharp short 'kraa'
when frightened, a dull grumbling in excitement, a shrill barking scream of rage, piping
as a begging sound, an ascending long mew as contact call. SENSES: sight, hearing and
scent good. ENEMIES: nothing known. FOOD: varied – insects, small mammals,
small birds, lizards, fruit of many kinds (may at times be sole diet), grass stems, tender
leaves. Will also eat carrion. SOCIABILITY: solitary.

Reproduction. Young born in any month. Litter size 2–3, gestation 64 days. Further
details not known. SEXUAL MATURITY: about 1 year. LONGEVITY: $11\frac{1}{4}$ years
recorded.

MADAGASCAN CIVETS, HEMIGALINAE (= FOSSINAE)

Mainly Palm Civet sized, mostly nocturnal, arboreal or partly terrestrial forest animals. Toes 5/5, 2–4 teats. Dent.: $3 \cdot 1 \cdot 4/3–4 \cdot 2 = 38–40$. 6 genera with 7 species, in
S. Asia and Madagascar; in the latter 2 genera, each with 1 species.

STRIPED CIVET, *Fossa fossana* (R. L. S. Muller, 1776)   **Pl. 34**
G. Fanaloka   F. La Civette fossane   MA. Fanaloka, Kavahy, Tomkasodina,
Tombosadina, Tombokatosody

Identification. Genet-sized, but rather long-legged and with shorter tail. Muzzle sharp
and rather lengthened, ears short and round. Legs slender, soles and digital pads
naked; thumb small, without claw; thumb and great toe set high, claws curved and
strong. Tail bushy, about $\frac{1}{2}$ of HB. 2 teats. Anal glandular sac absent, though a
prominent glandular ring around the anal opening present. 5 small glandular areas on
head, naked places with some long hairs (2 on each cheek, 1 on the chin). Penis bone
small ($c.\frac{1}{2}$cm). Dent.: $3 \cdot 1 \cdot 4 \cdot 2 = 40$; canines long and sturdy. Pelage short, soft and

thick. Upperside and tail light brown, underside light grey, over-washed with brownish. Supraorbital and eye-corner spots, narrow stripe on margin of ear, border of upper lip, chin and lower cheek, whitish. On upperside, on either side of spine, from behind head to root of tail, 2 dark brown longitudinal stripes, continuous at the front, interrupted at rear, and below them, on flanks, 2 similar rows of long spots. Upper arm and thigh with individual, usually round, spots. Upperside of tail with dark brown spots, arranged in about 8–10 transverse bands; tail tip dark brown. Young like adults, but spots more conspicuous. MEASUREMENTS: HB ♂ 48–56, ♀ 42–51, TL ♂ and ♀ 25–27, Wt ♂ 1.8–2.65, ♀ 1.4–1.74.

Distribution. Madagascar. Rain forest regions of E., N., and N.N.W. HABITAT: rain forests in lowlands and mountains up to 2000m. TERRITORY: each pair with 35–100 hectares according to nature of country. Territory may stretch 2–3km along a water-course, marked by secretions from anal gland and by head gland rubbing on prominent objects, and defended against neighbours of the same species. Territory has well-marked runs and refuges (rock crevices, stone heaps, hollow trees, adopted holes in ground, etc.)

Habits. DAILY RHYTHM: entirely nocturnal, terrestrial, seldom climbing, takes to water to capture prey, using its wide gape, not the feet. TOILET: nothing known. VOICE: usually mute, seldom vocal. Growls in threat, attack or rage; cries of fear a rough staccato mewing; rutting call in both sexes resembling threat and attack calls; contact call between adults and young up to about 5 months old a subdued 'chak-chak-chak'. SENSES: hearing, scent and sight good. ENEMIES: fossa. FOOD: prin-cipally aquatic, such as fish, eels, crabs, crayfish, amphibians and insects, as well as rodents, non-spiny Insectivora, small lemurs and birds. Tail root can store fat. Drinks large amounts of water, by lapping; cannot go without for more than 24 hours. SOCIABILITY: pairs for life.

Reproduction. Breeding season Aug–Sep, births in Nov-Dec. Breeding place an un-lined refuge (see TERRITORY). Mate standing like *Galidia* (p. 198), duration 3–5 min-utes. Gestation 3 months. 1 young, born fully-haired and with eyes open, but not fully capable of sight in first week. Milk teeth cut from 1st to 3rd months, permanent teeth from 11th to 14th months. First solid food at 1½ months, weaned at 2½ months. Active at 12 days. Catches small prey at 4 months, larger prey at 11, and is independent at 12 months. ♀ rejoins ♂ in the first week after young leaves. Wt at birth 60–70, at 1 month 230, at 12 months 1250–1350. SEXUAL MATURITY, and LONGEVITY: not known.

SMALL-TOOTHED MONGOOSE, *Eupleres goudoti* (Doyere, 1835)   **Pl. 33**
G. Ameisenschleichkatze   F. L'Euplère   MA. Amboa-Laola, Fanaloka, Fanaluk, Ridaridy

Identification. Muzzle pointed and narrow, eyes and ears middle-sized, latter roun-dish, body rounded, rear higher and more developed than fore parts, head small in proportion to body. Front legs shorter than hind, tail densely bushy, half HB length, and capable of fat-storing near the root. Thumb and great toe almost in same plane as the other toes, claws long, narrow and curved. Sole and toe pads naked, in ssp. *major* one extra sole pad on fore foot, and lengthened naked area with a central hair tuft behind the sole pad of hind foot. No prescrotal glands, anal glandular ring well developed. 5 small head glands as in Fossa (p. 194). Penis bone minute (3.5mm) 2 teats. In skull the rostrum, lower mandible and cheek bones narrow, tympanic bullae large. Dent.: $3 \cdot 1.4 \cdot 2 = 40$, canines and molars small, the latter sharp-cusped. Fur rather short, thick and woolly; upperside reddish-brown (in *major* stippled with grey), under-side light greyish-brown; tip of muzzle and spots below and above eyes, lighter. Young like adults, though blackish-brown instead of reddish-brown. MEASUREMENTS: HB, *goudoti* 46–50, *major* 52–65, TL. *goudoti* 22–24, *major* 24–25, Wt. *goudoti* 2–2.3, *major* 2.8–4.6.

Distribution. Ssp. (1) smaller, *goudoti* Doyere, 1835, rain forest region and swamps of E. coast; (2) larger, *major* Lavauden, 1929, same habitat in N. Both ssp. are now rare due to destruction of habitats. TERRITORY: size about that of *Fossa*, details not known. Both sexes scent mark with anal and head glands on tree trunks etc. May take refuge in dense grass and bush thickets.

Habits. DAILY RHYTHM: active at dusk and in night. Roams unhurriedly in slow hopping gait, does not climb, a poor jumper, goes belly in water fearlessly. TOILET: scratches fore part of body with hind feet, does not use fore feet. Fur licking frequent, as ♀ also with young. VOICE: very quiet. When threatened or attacked a soft hissing with wide-open mouth; in immediate danger a repeated spitting. Contact call between parents and young as in *Fossa*. Young mew. SENSES: as in *Fossa*. ENEMIES: fossa (*Cryptoprocta*). In danger may remain motionless for up to an hour. In defence strikes with fore claws from sitting position, and makes quick jabbing bites. FOOD: mainly earthworms, scraped up from leaves and soil, as well as frogs, water snails, insects, perhaps also small rodents and birds. Stores supply of fat under skin and in tail (500–800gms) for the June–July dry season when worms are scarce. SOCIABILITY: pairs for life.

Reproduction. Breeding season Aug–Sep (spring), litters in Oct–Dec. Gestation about 3 months. 1 young at a birth in an unprepared refuge on the ground. Young born fully-haired, dark to blackish-brown, mobile and with eyes open; can move quickly after 8 days. Lives for first month in hiding while ♀ goes out feeding, takes first solid food and is weaned at $5\frac{1}{2}$ months adult coloration and independent, leaving ♀ at next breeding season. In danger ♀ will carry young (up to $1\frac{1}{2}$ months old) in mouth. At birth, HB 15, TL 5, Wt 150. Wt at 6 months 2200. SEXUAL MATURITY and LONGEVITY: not known.

MADAGASCAN MONGOOSES, GALIDIINAE

Moderate sized; toes 5/5. 2 teats. Dent.: $3 \cdot 1 \cdot 3$–$4/3 \cdot 2/1$–$2 = 36$. Nocturnal, mainly terrestrial forest dwellers. 3 genera with 4 species in Madagascar.

RING-TAILED MONGOOSE,   Pl. 33
Galidia elegans (I. Geoffroy St. Hilaire, 1837)
G. Ringelschwanzmungo   F. La Galidea   MA. Vontsira, Kokia

Identification. Mongoose-like. Head elegant, muzzle narrow and pointed. Legs of medium length, hind longer than fore. Claws short, round, sharp, not retractile, soles with naked pads, short webbing between toes, thumb and great toe in same plane as other toes. 2 teats. Prescrotal, prevulval, anal and 5 head glands (latter small naked areas with some long hairs, 2 on each cheek, 1 on throat). Dent.: $3 \cdot 1 \cdot 3 \cdot 2 = 36$, canines moderately long, P^1 very small. Pelage short and rather rough, tail long and strongly bushy. Ears whitish yellow, pale subocular spot, entire body colour reddish-brown, tail with 5–7 broad black rings. Colour of the 3 ssp. (1) *elegans*; body red-brown, legs black, 6–7 tail rings; (2) *dambrensis*; body including legs light reddish-brown, throat and fore part of breast yellowish-grey, 5 tail rings; (3) *occidentalis*; back light reddish-brown, head greyish-red, sides of body, belly, thighs and legs black, 5 tail rings. Young like adults. MEASUREMENTS: HB 35–40, TL 23–30, Ht 18–20, Wt 850–1000.

Distribution. Madagascar. 3 ssp. (1) Eastern R., *elegans*, whole of E. coast, from sea to mountain crests; (2) Northern R., *dambrensis* Tate & Rand, 1941. Northern tip of the island, forested mountains from Ambres and Ankarana between Diego-Suarez and Ambilobe; (3) Western R., *occidentalis* Albignac, 1971; middle W. coastal region between Soalala in N., Bekopaka in the S., and Kelifely in W. HABITAT: forests and woodlands. Rain forest region on E. coast, dry woodland on limestone rocks with water holes in ravines and gorges in N. and W. In savannah only in gallery forests. Cover and shade essential, cannot endure full sun. TERRITORY: 1 family to 20–25 hectares, marked and strongly defended against rival neighbours; has numerous trails and hiding places. *Map* p. 196.

Habits. DAILY RHYTHM: diurnal, at all hours. Sleep at night in hole in ground or in tree, rolled up or sitting with head tucked below body. Climbs and swims well, uses its paws in agile cat-like fashion. VOICE: soft whistle as contact call (repeated 2–6 times at 4–5 second intervals), also heard from young a few hours after birth, intensified to a mewing whimper if neglected. Growls in bad temper, light scream in anger (2–3 times in 3 seconds). Muffled growl in threat, rising as danger draws near and followed by 4–5 spitting sounds. In attack, or when attacked, a clear sharp cry of 4–5 seconds. SENSES: hearing, scent and sight good. ENEMIES: only Fossa. FOOD: small mammals (rodents, insectivores, tenrecs, small lemurs), small birds and eggs, reptiles including snakes; amphibians, fish, crayfish, snails, insects, fruit. Eggs and large snails are opened by throwing with hind feet backwards against trees or stones. Drinks water freely, partly lapping with tongue, partly by licking a fore foot dipped in water. Can hardly go more than 24 hours without drinking. SOCIABILITY: pairs for life, accompanied by the latest young, sometimes also with the previous young. Family stays together, but after giving birth ♀ keeps ♂ away from the young for 1½ months.

Reproduction. Breeding season Jul–Nov, mainly Sep–Oct. Mate standing, ♂ lays head on back of ♀ and licks her neck: duration of 1st pairing *c*.40 minutes. Gestation 74–90 days, litter Sep–Apr, 1 young at a birth, in hidden refuge. Pelage of young, see Identification. Eyes open at 6–8 days, first activity at 21 days, first solid food at 30 days. Weaning at 2 months, permanent teeth from 8–12 months, catches prey independently at 14 months, leaves parents about 1½ years. Wt at birth *c*.50, HB 11–13, TL 7–8, Wt at 12 months 620–870. SEXUAL MATURITY: probably at 2 years. LONGEVITY: not known.

NARROW-STRIPED MONGOOSE, *Mungotictis decemlineata*   Pl. 34
(A. Grandidier, 1867) (= *Galidictis vittata* Gray, 1848)
G. Schmalstreifenmungo   F. La Galidie à bandes étroites
MA. Vontira, Votsotsoke, Bokiboki

Identification. Mongoose-like. Muzzle pointed, eyes medium, ears short, broadly triangular, body slender, legs short, hind longer than fore, tail bushy, about two-thirds of HB. Feet with naked toe and sole pads, the middle of underside of foot also naked; claws strong, short web between toes. Thumb and great toe low-set. 2 teats. Perineal glands present, anal glandular ring well developed. 5 small head glands as in *Galidia*. Dent.: 3 · 1 · 3 · 2 = 36, canines sturdy, molars sharp-cusped. Pelage short, tail hair rather harsh. Upperside and tail in ssp. *decemlineata* greyish-beige, with altogether 8–10 very narrow reddish-brown stripes on back and sides; underside paler. Upperside in ssp. *lineata* light grey with 8 narrow brown stripes on back and sides, underside and tail greyish-white. Pale spot above and below eye. Young like adults, somewhat paler, stripes still weak, at 1½ weeks colour darkening to adult hue. MEASUREMENTS: HB 30–35, TL 24–27, Ht 18–20, Wt 725–880.

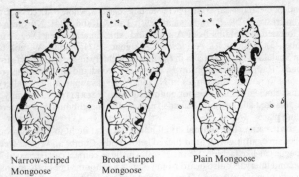

Narrow-striped   Broad-striped   Plain Mongoose
Mongoose   Mongoose

Distribution. 2 ssp: (1) *decemlineata* (A. Grandidier, 1867), Mid-W. Madagascar between Tsiribihina R. in N, and Mangoky R. in S. (2) *lineata* Pocock, 1915, S.W. Madagascar, north and south of Tulear. Both races seriously threatened by habitat destruction.   HABITAT: dry forest on sandy soil with deciduous trees (May–Sep), tall-stemmed trees 20–30m high (among them baobabs) or evergreen, thorny lower trees, 3–6m high, and bare ground carpeted with dry leaves.   TERRITORY: as *Galidia* (p. 198). Refuges mainly self-excavated burrows with 1 or 2 entrances, also hollow trees.

Habits. DAILY RHYTHM: diurnal only, not about much before midday, main activity in afternoon between 15.00 and 17.00. Mainly terrestrial, though good climber. TOILET: foot-licking and head washing, licking fur (also mutually).   VOICE: contact call a repeated 'buk-buk', young also use this on 1st day. Young mew in discomfort. A short clear cry indicates capture of small prey. Short growling (6–8 times) as threat with erect tail and fur standing on end, as well as head nodding. In nearer danger and territory defence a higher and higher growling. Tail and fur erection a useful signal. SENSES: sight, hearing and scent good.   ENEMIES: fossa.   FOOD: small animals; insects, crayfish, snails, amphibians, reptiles including snakes, small birds, eggs, small mammals including tenreks. Opens eggs and large snail shells as in *Galidia*. Further, in a crouching position uses the front feet to throw the object backwards between the hind feet as in some mongooses.   SOCIABILITY: pair for life.

Reproduction. Breeding season Jul–Dec, young born Oct–Mar; gestation 90–105 days, 1 young. Mating as in *Galidia*. ♀ keeps ♂ away from young for 1½ months. Eyes open at birth, can move about easily at 3 days, at 14 days jumps and climbs, at 15 days 1st solid food. Up to 1 month in danger carried in mother's mouth. Weaned at 2 months, at 3 months takes small prey, at 6–12 months also captures larger prey. Permanent teeth at 6–8 months, leaves parents at 1 year, sexually mature at 2 years. Wt at birth *c*.50, HB 12–13, TL 7–8, Wt at 12 months 510–540.   LONGEVITY: not known.

BROAD-STRIPED MONGOOSE, *Galidictis fasciata* (Gmelin, 1788)   **Pl. 34**
G. Bänder or Breitstreifen mungo   F. La Galidie rayée
MA. Vontsira fotsy;   Bakiaka bestaminea (*fasciata*), Bakiaka belomboka (*striata*)
Identification. Form as in *Galidia*, muzzle sharp, ears small and round, legs short, hind somewhat longer than fore, fingers and toes long, thumb and great toe well developed, claws strong. Tail longish, nearly ¾ of HB length, and bushy. 2 teats, anal sac, and penis bone present. Dent.: $3 \cdot 1 \cdot 3 \cdot 2 = 36$, 1^3 enlarged, caniniform, canines unusually

large and massive, premolars sharp-cusped, molars broad-crowned. Pelage short and thick. Ssp. *fasciata* light beige, almost white, with on either side of spinal line three 1–1.5cm. broad, dark brown, long bands from neck to tail root; upper arm and thigh also with matching stripes. Underside and tail (apart from root) white. Root of tail reddish-brown, lightly ringed. Ssp. *striata* yellowish-brown with 4 dark reddish-brown stripes on each side; underside and feet yellowish, tail wholly white. Pelage of young not known, probably resembling adult. Pattern variable. MEASUREMENTS: HB 30–33, TL 22–26, Ht *c*.18, Wt *c*.800.

Distribution. Madagascar. 2 ssp: (1) Broad-striped Mongoose, *fasciata* (Gmelin, 1788), S.E. Madagascar, rare (2) Banded Mongoose, *striata* (E. Geoffroy St. Hilaire, 1826), N.E. Madagascar, rare. HABITAT: rain forest. Live in self-dug burrows, hollow trees, among rocks etc. TERRITORY: resembles *Galidia*, details not known.

Habits. DAILY RHYTHM: nocturnal. Good climber. FOOD: rodents, lemurs, poultry; more carnivorous than *Galidia*. SOCIABILITY: pair for life.

Reproduction. 1 young born in spring. No further details known.

PLAIN MONGOOSE, *Salanoia concolor* (I. Geoffroy St. Hilaire, 1839)   **Pl. 34**
(= *Hemigalidia* Mivart, 1882). G. Schlichtmungo   F. La Galidie unicolore
MA. Salano, Vontsira

Identification. Form like *Galidia*, but tail shorter. Head slender, muzzle narrow and pointed, eyes and ears small, latter rounded. Legs rather short, feet powerful, the hind stronger than fore, claws long and strong. 2 teats, small penis bone, and anal glands present. Dent: $3/3 \cdot 1/1 \cdot 4/3 \cdot 2/1 = 36$, canines stout, premolars sharp-cusped, molars broad-crowned. Pelage short and thick, tail thickly bushy, about $\frac{1}{2}$ HB. Body and tail uniformly reddish-brown or brownish-olive. Young like adults. MEASUREMENTS: HB 35–38, TL 18–20, Wt *c*. 800.

Distribution. N.E. Madagascar. Rare. HABITAT: rain forests. TERRITORY: 1 family with at least 25–30 hectares.

Habits. DAILY RHYTHM: diurnal, at night in hiding place (self-excavated or adopted burrow, hollow tree etc.). TOILET, VOICE, SENSES, ENEMIES, not known. FOOD: predominantly insects, as well as amphibians, small reptiles, eggs (opened up as in *Galidia*), perhaps also small mammals and birds. SOCIABILITY: pairs for life.

Reproduction. 1 young at a birth, further details not known, but probably like *Galidia*.

MONGOOSES, HERPESTINAE

Sharp-faced, small-eared, short-legged, long-tailed. Toes 4–5/4–5, 2–6 teats; dent: $3 \cdot 1 \cdot 3–4/2 \cdot 4 \cdot 2 = 34$–40. Terrestrial, mostly diurnal, living in open or forested country in S.W. Europe, Africa, Further India and S. Asia. 11 genera with 31 species, of which 11 genera and 23 species occur in Africa.

EGYPTIAN MONGOOSE, Ichneumon, *Herpestes (Herpestes)*   **Pl. 35**
ichneumon (Linnaeus, 1758)
G. Eigentliches Ichneumon   F. La Mangouste ichneumon
A. Groot Grysmuishond   S. Nguchiro

Identification. Size of marten, rat-like in form with pointed head, long tail and short legs. Muzzle sharp, eyes and ears small, latter round and only projecting a little beyond the fur. Legs short, thumb and great toe small, high set. Digital and sole pads naked, naked sole of hind foot reaching to heel; claws long, slightly curved, not retractile, short web between 2nd and 3rd toes. Plantigrade. Scent gland on anal ring. Penis bone well developed. Usually 4 teats, sometimes 6. Dent: $3/3 \cdot 1/1 \cdot 4/3-4 \cdot 2/2 = 38-40$. Canines short and strong, P_1 very small, M^2 small. Pelage with thick underfur, covered on body by long, rather stiff, erectile guard hairs, longest on flanks, edges of thighs, and root of tail. Tail long and slender, thickly haired at root, at the tip a pencil-like tapering end tuft. Underfur usually yellowish to yellowish-brown, cover hair grizzled black and white, the whole effect a brownish-grey pepper and salt effect. Underside yellowish, in part naked, muzzle and legs dark brownish grey, tail tuft blackish. General colour varying according to ssp. between pale whitish-grey (with dark head, legs and tail tuft) in dry areas, and blackish reddish-brown in rain forest areas. Young like adults. MEASUREMENTS: HB 45–60, TL 35–38, Ht 19–21, Wt 1.9–4.0.

Distribution. S. Iberian Peninsula (in W. south of Tagus, in E. south of Guadalquivir), Palestine, Syria, E. Turkey, Morocco, Algeria, Tunisia, Egypt, Sudan, and in rest of Africa from about 15°N southward to northern S.W. Africa, N. Botswana, Transvaal, Natal, Zululand, and Cape Province coast west to Knysna Forest. Introduced into Madagascar, Dalmatia and Italy. 11 ssp. (10 in Africa). Although introduced into Madagascar has not been recently recorded. Was venerated in ancient Egypt. HABITAT: varies from rain forest to semi-deserts, moist and dry savannahs, steppes and mountains up to 2000m. Prefers vicinity of water, and does not avoid vicinity of villages. HOME RANGE: not known, probably family territories.

Habits. DAILY RHYTHM: depending on locality, predominantly diurnal, but sometimes active at dusk or by night. Sleeping place an adopted or self-dug burrow, rock crevice, hollow tree, stone heap, grass and reed thickets etc. Sleeps in sitting position with muzzle tucked in below. Swims well, jumps and climbs moderately well, going down tail first. ♂♂ show curiosity. TOILET: scratch with hind feet, clean out dirt by scratching with fore foot, picks teeth with fore claws, licks fur etc. VOICE: various contact and pairing calls, loud hickling of ♂ in mating and loud screaming of ♀; growl and hiss in threat, arch back and ruffle fur in defence, chatter and bite in defence, a low whining in contentment. Young have a querulous call. SENSES: scent, sight and hearing good – colour sensitive. ENEMIES: probably the larger carnivores, and large birds of prey. Details not known. In addition to defence attitudes and back-arching in threat, in extreme danger will lie on back to defend itself. FOOD: small mammals up to rat-size, birds up to guinea-fowl or poultry size, lizards, snakes (including large venomous species), insects, crabs, crayfish, fish, fruit. Digs up ground nuts; cleans frogs and toads of their distasteful slimy skins by rolling them on the ground. Poisonous snakes are overcome by the mongoose's quick reactions and mobility, the poison fangs are avoided by the coarse, ruffled protective hair. Poison sensitivity is reduced. SOCIABILITY: generally in pairs or family groups; in latter case often move in single file.

Reproduction. Breeding season in spring in temperate latitudes, but whether seasonally linked in the tropics is still not known. Mate standing up, duration of mating 3–5 minutes. Gestation 7–11 weeks, 2–3 young, rarely 4. ♂ helps to rear young. Fully grown at 1 year. SEXUAL MATURITY: 2 years. LONGEVITY: $12\frac{3}{4}$ years recorded in captivity.

SLENDER MONGOOSE, *Herpestes (Galerella) sanguineus*   Pl. 35
(Ruppell, 1835)

G. Rot- or Schlankichneumon   F. La Mangouste rouge   A. Rooimuishond

Identification. Form and bodily details as in *Herpestes ichneumon* (p. 201) however only half as large, sole of hind foot naked only for half distance to heel, claws curved and

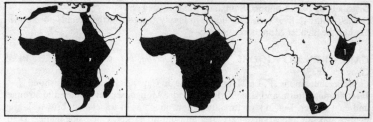

Egyptian Mongoose   Slender Mongoose   1 Yellow Mongoose
                                                     2 Cape Grey Mongoose

sharp. 4 teats. Dent: $3/3 \cdot 1/1 \cdot 4/3 \cdot 2/2 = 38$. P^1 and M^2 small. Cover hair not so long as in *ichneumon*, pelage therefore smoother. Upperside dark olive, olive-grey, ochreous, reddish, red-brown or dark greyish-brown according to ssp., owing to lighter or darker ringing of the individual hairs, giving finely speckled effect. Underside usually lighter, uniformly yellowish-grey to creamy, sometimes as upperside, however not speckled. Tail nearly as long as HB, uniformly coloured and with tip red to black. MEASUREMENTS: HB ♂ 27–40, ♀ 25–33, TL ♂ 24–36, ♀ 21–35, Ht 10–12, Wt ♂ 400–900, ♀ 350–500.

Distribution. Africa south of Sahara. Northern border from Senegal to Air and N. Sudan about between 15° and 18°N. Absent from N. Somalia and W. Cape Province. Islands of Cape Verde and Zanzibar. 43 ssp.   HABITAT: all types of country from deserts to rain forests, in mountains to about 3000m, dense cover and proximity to water preferred. Sometimes follows settlements, and may occur in villages and suburbs.   HOME RANGE not known.

Habits. DAILY RHYTHM: at night resting in thickets, hollow trees, termite hills, rock crevices, stone heaps, adopted burrows etc. Hunts by day and at dusk, also on moonlit nights, on ground and in trees. Climbs as well as squirrel, head first going down; takes refuge in trees. Carries tail upright when making for cover. When curious, will sit up on hind legs like a manikin to look around.   TOILET: not known, probably like *ichneumon*.   VOICE: not noisy, contact call a soft 'hoo'. No further details known. SENSES: sight, hearing and scent good.   ENEMIES: larger carnivores and birds of prey; they watch large flying birds closely. Defence and threat attitudes as in *ichneumon*. FOOD, and SOCIABILITY, as in *ichneumon*.

Reproduction. Usually 2 young at a birth, born in hiding places (see DAILY RHYTHM). Further details of growth and LONGEVITY not known.

YELLOW MONGOOSE, *Herpestes (Galerella) ochracea* (Gray, 1849)   **Pl. 35**
G. Gelbichneumon   F. La Mangouste d'Abyssinie
Identification. Very like Slender Mongoose (p. 202) in size and form. Distinguished by larger ears, bigger skull with larger tympanic bullae, stouter lower mandible with hinder edge of coronoid process nearly straight instead of curved. Teeth more closely grouped, larger M^2. Dental formula and number of teats as in Slender Mongoose. Upperside yellowish brown, greyish-ochre or yellowish-ochre, finely speckled by light or dark rings on cover hairs; underside greyish-white to creamy-white. Tail like upper side, somewhat darker, tip black.   MEASUREMENTS: HB 23–32, TL 21–27, Ht and Wt as in Slender Mongoose.

Distribution. N.E. Ethiopia, Somalia, N.E. Kenya. 4 ssp.

Habits. Diurnal, live alone, in pairs or in family groups. Further details not known, but like the Slender Mongoose.

CAPE GREY MONGOOSE, *Herpestes (Galerella) pulverulentus*   **Pl. 35**
(Wagner, 1839)

G. Kleinichneumon   F. La Mangouste grise du Cap   A. Klein Grysmuishond

Identification. Form and size nearly as Slender Mongoose, but stouter and stronger and coat longer. Fur in structure and colour much as in *ichneumon*, brownish-grey pepper and salt appearance. Face, feet and tail tip darker. Underside lighter. Dent: $3/3 \cdot 1/1 \cdot 4/3–4 \cdot 2/2 = 38–40$. P$_1$ usually absent, canines stout, molars sharp-cusped. 2–6 teats. Ssp. *shortridgei* in S. Angola light to dark reddish-brown with blacker tail tip; ssp. *nigratus* in Mid- and N. S.W. Africa with nearly black back and blackish-brown flanks as well as blacker tail tip. MEASUREMENTS: HB 28–37, TL 27–36, Ht and Wt as in Slender Mongoose.

Distribution. S. Africa: Orange Free State, Lesotho, Cape Province, S.W. Africa, and southern Angola. 5 ssp.   HABITAT: bush country and rocky districts. Favours kopjies and rocky hillsides, dry river beds and other cover-rich areas. *Map* p. 203.

Habits. DAILY RHYTHM: diurnal, terrestrial, but climbs trees if pursued.   FOOD: small mammals up to hare size, birds up to guinea fowl size, lizards, snakes (including poisonous), insects, crabs, worms, eggs. Latter, as well as snails, shellfish, nuts and rolled up wood lice, are broken open either by throwing on the ground, or by flinging between the hind legs against a stone or tree trunk.   SOCIABILITY: solitary, in pairs or in family groups.   LONGEVITY: $8\frac{3}{4}$ years recorded in captivity.

MARSH MONGOOSE, *Herpestes (Atilax) paludinosus* (G. Cuvier, 1829;   **Pl. 35**
G. Sumpfichneumon   F. La Mangouste des marais   A. Watermuishond
S. Nguchiro

Identification. Form as *ichneumon*, but head stronger, body stouter and tail shorter (two-thirds HB). Toes long, without webbing, claws strong, thumb and great toe small and high set, soles of feet (on hind foot as far as heel) completely naked. Plantigrade. Anal glands and penis bone well developed. 4 teats. Dent: $3/3 \cdot 1/1 \cdot 3–4/2–4 \cdot 2/2 = 34–40$. Canines and molars stout, P 1 and 2 small or absent. Coat rough like *ichneumon* but more coarsely haired, reddish-brown, dark brown, dark brownish-green or dark brownish-black, sometimes with faint transverse bands. Upperside sometimes has metallic sheen imparted by the varying individual hair bands. Back and legs darkest, head and underside paler, cheeks rather grizzled with grey, edges of lips pale to whitish. Wholly black animals occur. Young somewhat darker than adults.   MEASUREMENTS: HB 45–60, TL 25–40, Ht *c.* 18–20; Wt 2–4.

Distribution. Africa S. of Sahara, from about 12°N (in W. also in Senegal), southwards to Cape, also on Pemba I. off Tanzanian coast. Absent in E. Ethiopia and Somalia, Cape Province N. of Orange Free State, in S. and M. Botswana, and S. and M. S.W. Africa. 10 ssp.   HABITAT: swamps, marshes and other wet areas in savannah and forest, up to 2000m. Uses hiding places in holes in banks, hollow trees, thickets of tall grass, reeds and rushes and platforms of latter.   HOME RANGE: size not known. Probably territorial, marked by anal glands (also in hand stand) on prominent objects and particularly on defecation sites and trails.

Habits. DAILY RHYTHM: active at night, sometimes also by day. Spends much time by or in water, swims and dives well, but does not normally climb.   TOILET: licks fur and smooths it with fore feet. Rolls in shallow water, followed by drying and licking session. VOICE: purrs when content; in threat or defence growls, nasal snorting and spitting, in excitement a staccato rising bark, with fluffing up of fur expressing rage. SENSES: scent and hearing very good, sight good. FOOD: small mammals and birds, lizards, snakes, frogs, fish, insects, molluscs, crustaceans, eggs of birds and crocodiles, fruit. Uses fingers and hands skilfully in seeking and catching prey. Breaks open hard-shelled prey like Cape Grey Mongoose (p. 204). SOCIABILITY: solitary or in pair or family group.

Reproduction. 1–2 young at a birth, in South Africa in Nov–Dec. Details of breeding and development not known. LONGEVITY: 11½ years recorded in captivity.

Marsh Mongoose

1 Long-nosed Mongoose
2 Suricate

Banded Mongoose

LONG-NOSED MONGOOSE, Pl. 35
Herpestes (Xenogale) naso (De Winton, 1901) (= *microdon* J. A. Allen, 1919)
G. Langnasenichneumon   F. La Mangouste à long museau

Identification. Form and size as Marsh Mongoose, but snout longer, ears rather larger, tail longer (¾ instead of two-thirds HB) and thicker, legs somewhat longer. Pelage similarly long and rough and glossy brownish-black, so that superficially confusion with Marsh Mongoose likely. Pelage with fine stippling of greyish-brown to ochreous (due to banding of individual hairs), but on back this grizzling may be absent. Head suffused with grey, distinctly lighter than body. Underside rather lighter, legs darker than back. Soles up to the short hind high-set 1st digit fully haired. Fingers and claws thickset. Dent: $3 \cdot 1 \cdot 4 \cdot 2 = 40$, P1 very small, canines and molars stout. Immature like adults. Number of teats, glands and penis bone still undescribed. MEASUREMENTS: HB 52–59, TL 36–43, Ht *c*. 20, Wt 3–4.25.

Distribution. S.E. Nigeria, M. and S. Cameroun, Rio Muni, Gabon and N. Congo south to Equator, E. through N. Zaire to Uelle, Ituri and Kivu. S. of Congo R. to Shaba. Up to now only 30 specimens known, rare. 2 ssp. HABITAT: lives entirely in rain forests. No details of habits.

SURICATE, *Suricata suricatta* (Schreber, 1776) Pl. 35
G. Scharrtier   F. La Suricate   A. Graatjemierkat

Identification. Size of polecat. Stout-bodied, head rounded with short pointed snout. Eyes middle-sized, forward looking, so apparently close together. Ears low positioned, small, round, closable. Legs rather short, toes 4/4, the long slender claws of fore foot twice as long as those of hind foot. Soles naked. Tail about ¾ length of HB, from thick root tapering to tip. Anal glands only in ♂. 6 teats. Dent.: $3/3 \cdot 1/1 \cdot 3/3–4 \cdot 2/2 = 36–38$. Canines short and strong, molars sharp-cusped. Pelage rather long and soft, longest on flanks, edge of thighs, and tail root. Underside sparsely haired. Upperside greyish-brown to whitish-grey, back with about 10 transverse bands, shorter in front and behind, brown to indistinct black, becoming unclear on flanks. Head and throat whitish, nose, eye-ring, and ears, black. Underside pale yellowish, on belly darker, legs yellowish, tail yellowish-brown, last third or tip black. Young still thinly-haired on neck, belly and inside of legs, without stripes, the first appearing at 1 week, at 14 days coat denser, at 2 months as adults. MEASUREMENTS: HB 25–31, TL 19–24, Ht c.15, Wt 620–970.

Distribution. S. Africa: S. Transvaal, Orange Free State, Lesotho, W. Natal, Cape Province (except southern coastal region between East London and Cape Town), M. and S. Botswana, S. and M. S.W. Africa only in Kaokoveld north to Cunene R. (S.W. Angola). 6 ssp. HABITAT: open country, preferably stony or rocky with firm sandy or gravelly or other ground easily burrowed into, in dry savannahs or plains: in bush country in large clearings, also on sandy or gravelly banks of dry river beds or open pans; up to 1000m or more high. Sometimes kept half tame on farms. HOME RANGE: at times 10–30 animals live in a colony with several shelters, in rock crevices or more usually in burrows, each with several tunnels, averaging 10cm diameter and 150cm long, with a grass-lined chamber. The area for about 100–200m around the burrows forms the home and feeding range. The food supply only lasts a few weeks, and the colony moves several times annually to other sites $\frac{1}{2}$–2km distant. Burrows often shared with ground squirrels (*Geosciurus*), Spring Hares (*Pedetes*), or Meerkats (*Cynictis*). Entrances and conspicuous objects in the area are marked with anal secretions by males. Main latrines in front of burrow entrances. *Map* p. 205.

Habits. DAILY RHYTHM: entirely diurnal, in pairs or small parties feeding in region of burrows, frequently sitting up like manikins to keep watch. Good burrowers, quick runners over short distances, bad jumpers and climbers. Usually sleep with head tucked underneath. The thinly-haired underside serves as a thermostat. Sun themselves in groups sitting upright or lying on the warm ground (at night often several animals lying together). Reduce body heat by lying in the cool tunnels. TOILET: fur grooming (also mutually), tooth cleaning with claws of front feet. Urinating ♂ lifts a hind leg. VOICE: a wide variety of calls. Short growl as contact call when feeding (tame animals use a soft cooing as contact call with owner); grunting and whining in content (young growl for same reason), sharp repeated 'kroo' call when annoyed or in defence. Short repeated sharp bark as general alarm call; a clearer repeated note as specific warning (staccato for ground predators, long drawn for birds of prey); growling as threat when in danger from ground enemies, rising to a spitting sound. Nest young twitter like young genets, and when they become mobile have various calls to express moods. SENSES: sight very good, colour sensitive; scent and hearing good. ENEMIES: the larger carnivores (Kaffir cat, serval, jackal, ratel) the last digging out the burrows. Large birds of prey. When alarm is given they either bolt for burrow or nearest cover (in case of birds). At approach of smaller terrestrial predators they growl, erect their hair and make stiff-legged jumps as threat; in emergency a quick leap and a severe bite. Avian predators compel a constant sky-watch; can distinguish between harmless and dangerous flight. FOOD: insects, spiders, scorpions, centipedes and millipedes, small mammals and birds, eggs, lizards, snakes (including poisonous), snails, roots, tubers, young shoots, fruit, succulents; small prey is often dug out of ground. Resistance to scorpion or snake poison weak. SOCIABILITY: in families, usually several families form a colony of up to 30 animals.

Reproduction. Main breeding season Oct–Apr. Mate standing. Gestation 11 weeks, litter 2–5 (usually 2–3). Juvenile coat, see **Identification**. Young born in grass-lined chamber. Wt at birth 25–36, at 1 month 140–225, nearly fully grown at 6 months. Ears open at 8–10 days, eyes at 12–14. Weaned at 4–6 weeks, first solid food at 3–4 weeks, independent at 10 weeks. SEXUAL MATURITY at $\frac{3}{4}$ year; young ♀♀ are driven off, young ♂♂ stay near parents. LONGEVITY: $8\frac{1}{2}$ years in captivity.

BANDED MONGOOSE, *Mungos mungo* (Gmelin, 1788) **Pl. 36**
G. Zebramanguste   F. La Mangue rayée   A. Gebandenmuishond   S. Gitschiro
Identification. Typical mongoose build, but stouter, rather short-snouted and short-tailed, eyes and ears small, tail tapers to tip, about three-fifths length of HB. Toes 5/5, thumb and great toe small, high-set, short web between toes; claws of fore foot twice as long as those of hind foot. Entire sole naked. Anal glands in both sexes, penis bone *c.*1.5cm long, 6 teats. Dent: $3 \cdot 1 \cdot 3 \cdot 2 = 36$. Canines and molars strong. Pelage either without or with only a little underfur; guard hairs rather stiff and upright, longest on flanks, edge of thighs and tail root. Upperside grey, olive to brownish or reddish-grey, individual hairs ringed light and dark. Between shoulders and root of tail up to 35 alternately light and dark transverse bands of equal breadth, fading out on flanks. Head and underside like upperside, head sometimes darker, legs dark brown, feet and tail tip brownish-black. Pelage of young fine-haired, dark grey, with dark transverse bands, black legs and feet, long claws; at $1\frac{1}{2}$ months shows the grizzled hair annulation, and at 3 months has full adult coloration. MEASUREMENTS: HB 30–45, TL 20–30, Ht 18–20, Wt 0.6–1.5.
Distribution. Savannahs of Africa south of Sahara, northern limit from Senegambia to Lake Chad region, Kordofan and Eritrea; in the east southwards to N.E. Zaire, S. Sudan, E. Ethiopia, Somalia, Kenya, Uganda, Tanzania (recently introduced to Zanzibar), S.E. Zaire, Rhodesia, Mozambique, Zambia, N. and E. Botswana, Transvaal, Natal. In W. in Angola, N. and mid-S.W. Africa. Absent from the Guinea and Central African closed forests, Malawi, Cape Province and southern S.W. Africa. 17 ssp. HABITAT: dry and moist savannahs, prefers vicinity of water, avoids closed forests. HOME RANGE: family troops of 6–30 animals, roaming within a wide area, sometimes only for 1–2 days, sometimes also for 1–2 months (littering season) in one district, using various living quarters, such as adopted or self-dug burrows, hollow trees, holes among tree roots, rock crevices, stone piles etc. *Map* p. 205.
Habits. DAILY RHYTHM: diurnal, in cloudy weather active all day, in hot weather only early morning and late afternoon, also on moonlit nights. Like sun-bathing in morning. A large troop may divide for food searching, reuniting in evening at the burrows. Food search remarkable, travelling on a broad front without precautions, keeping in touch by continuous twittering. Climb well among rocks, in emergency also in trees, but not willingly. Swim if necessary, like vicinity of water. Often sleep in sitting posture with head tucked below. TOILET: pelage grooming, often mutually; also mutual scent gland marking of surrounding objects. Teeth cleaned with claws. VOICE: twittering as contact call. In threat and defence growling and spitting with arched back, neck hairs raised, jumping about on hind feet. A shrill warning cry, and a contented purring. SENSES: sight, hearing and scent very good. ENEMIES: larger carnivores and birds of prey. If cornered, courageous defence, spitting loudly. When attacked, may turn back on opponent and slash back with its canines over its shoulder. Joint defence by troop probable. Shows little fear. FOOD: snuffles and digs in ground or leaf litter, grass and stones, scattering dung heaps, for a varied diet (insects, spiders, scorpions, centipedes and millipedes). Also takes small mammals and birds, eggs, amphibians, lizards and snakes, fruit, roots and shoots. Snakes and larger prey may be overcome by the combined troop. Frogs are rolled in sand to get rid of skin slime.

Hard-shelled food may be opened by smashing on ground with forepaws, or throwing back between hind legs against stone or tree. SOCIABILITY see HOME RANGE.

Reproduction. Spring is breeding time in north of range, in S. Africa spring and summer, Oct–Mar. Mate standing. Gestation about 2 months. Litter size 2–6, in grass-lined chamber in burrow. Nest pelage, see **Identification**. Eyes open at 10 days, first venture outside at three weeks, well-grown at 3 months. SEXUAL MATURITY: ♀ at ¾ year, ♂ at 1 year. Wt at birth *c*.20, by 5 months rises to 1750–2250. Young may be cared for during day by 1 ♀, in evening after hunting party returns may be suckled by other ♀♀. LONGEVITY: up to 11 years in captivity.

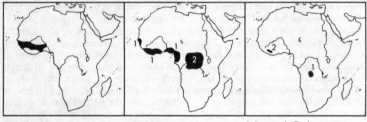

Gambian Mongoose

1 Cusimanse
2 Alexander's Cusimanse

1 Ansorge's Cusimanse
2 Liberian Mongoose

GAMBIAN MONGOOSE, *Mungos gambianus* (Ogilby, 1835)   **Pl. 36**
G. Gambiamanguste   F. La Mangue de Gambie
Identification. Form, foot structure, teeth, glands, teats and character of pelage as in Banded Mongoose (p. 207). Upperside brownish-grey, lightly sprinkled yellow. Individual hairs also ringed with light and dark, but there is no transverse stripe pattern. Underside more sparsely haired, reddish. Chin, throat, front of ear and edges, light yellowish. On each side of neck a narrow white and black band set off sharply from upper side of neck. Snout, ring round eyes, feet, and tail tip, black. Juvenile coat not known. MEASUREMENTS: HB 35, TL 21, Ht 18–20. Wt probably same as Banded Mongoose.
Distribution. Moist savannah and open woodland from Gambia to W. Nigeria.
Habits. Like Banded M., eats small animals, hunts by day in family groups. Further details not known.

CUSIMANSE, *Crossarchus obscurus* (F. Cuvier, 1825)   **Pl. 36**
G. Dunkelkusimanse   F. La Mangue brune
Identification. In form and size like Banded Mongoose (p. 207), however head and snout notably long and narrow. Latter with nose extending considerably beyond lower lip. Toe number and foot structure like Banded Mongoose, only sole of hind foot hairy in last third before the heel. Anal glands, penis bone, teats and teeth as in Banded Mongoose. Pelage with denser, finer underfur, and long, shaggy and rather stiff guard hairs. In contrast, head and throat very short-haired, belly thinly-haired but like back. Upperside dark brown to brownish-black, grizzled with yellow. Head and underside lighter brownish-grey, legs darker than back, blackish-brown. Tail like back, its tip like head. Young pelage fine woolly, without guard hairs, reddish-brown: nose still short. Guard hairs and snout lengthening after 1½ months. MEASUREMENTS: HB 30–40, TL 15–25, Ht *c*.18–20, Wt 1–1.5.

Distribution. Rain forests from Gambia and Sierra Leone to M. and S. Cameroun and Gabon. No ssp. HABITAT: rain forest only. Up to 2000m in mountains. HOME RANGE: not known. Uses hand-stand to mark vertical objects with scent gland secretion.

Habits. DAILY RHYTHM: diurnal. Spends night in self-dug burrow (often in old termite hill) with several entrances, or other hiding places. Terrestrial, only climbs in emergency. TOILET: nothing known. VOICE: a twittering contact call while hunting. Growls in threat while raising its pelage and arching back. Various calls indicate hunger, exhaustion, anger and fear. SENSES: sight, hearing and scent very good. ENEMIES: larger carnivores and birds of prey. Attacks large dogs fearlessly and is remarkably insensitive to pain. FOOD: small animals (worms, woodlice, myriapods, spiders, insects, snails) smelt out and scratched out of soil. Crabs, amphibians, reptiles (including poisonous snakes), small mammals and birds, fruit etc. Eggs and similar hard-shelled objects opened by throwing backwards against stones or trees. SOCIABILITY: in family parties (up to a dozen animals) roaming around. No further details known.

Reproduction. Mate standing. Gestation *c*.10 weeks, litter size 2–4 (usually 4). No distinct season. 2–3 litters a year possible. SEXUAL MATURITY: about $\frac{3}{4}$ year. LONGEVITY: $4\frac{1}{2}$ years recorded in captivity.

ALEXANDER'S CUSIMANSE, Pl. 36
Crossarchus alexandri (Thomas & Wroughton, 1907)
G. Kongokusimanse   F. La Mangue d'Alexandre

Identification. Very similar in most respects to Cusimanse (p. 208), but rather larger and additional short thick hair ridge from neck to root of tail. Upperside brownish-clay coloured with light grey grizzling, underside rather paler, head and throat light grey, chin, posterior upper lip and lower cheek whitish, feet blackish brown. Coat of young a short brown underfur with fine silvery white overhairs, head coloured like adult, underside dark brown, overwashed with red, spinal hair crest well-marked. Changes to adult pelage during milk-tooth stage. MEASUREMENTS: HB 36–44, TL 24–32, Ht and Wt not known.

Distribution. Rain forests of Congo (Zaire and adjoining regions of the Congo Republic and Central African Republic). No ssp.

Habits. Like Cusimanse, but details not known.

ANSORGE'S CUSIMANSE, *Crossarchus ansorgei* (Thomas, 1910) Pl. 36
G. Angolakusimanse   F. La Mangue d'Ansorge

Identification. Most details as in Cusimanse (p. 208), but smaller. Upper and undersides medium brown, snout, ear rims, feet and underside of tail blackish, face cinnamon, tail tip black. MEASUREMENTS: HB *c*.32, TL *c*.21.

Distribution. N.W. Angola and S. Congo. Little known.

Habits. Nothing known.

LIBERIAN MONGOOSE, *Liberiictis kuhni* (Hayman, 1958) Pl. 61
G. Liberia-Kusimanse   F. La Mangue de Libéria

Identification. Form resembling Cusimanse, but overall larger, more robust body, apparently longer legs, and with conspicuous neck stripe. Head slender, snout long and pointed, upper lip and snout projecting well beyond lower lip. Eyes and ears small, latter roundish. Toes 5/5, soles naked, claws long and strong, those of fore feet one-third longer than those of hind feet. Anal glands, penis bone, and number of teats at present not described. Dent: $3 \cdot 1 \cdot 4 \cdot 2 = 40$, canines and molars comparatively small and weak. Pelage like Cusimanse; short hair crest from shoulder to tail root; uniformly dark to blackish-brown, stippled lighter (pale ochreous), tail almost as back, more brindled, legs darker, feet black. Small spot in front of ear, lower cheeks, chin and throat pale ochreous. On each side of neck three longitudinal stripes, the middle one blackish-brown, from ear to shoulder, bordered above and below by two lightly-ochreous accompanying stripes. These stripes, in position and colour pattern, closely resemble those of the Gambian Mongoose (p. 208). Back of nose, and nostrils, black. Juvenile coat not known. MEASUREMENTS: HB 40–45, TL c.20, Ht c.20–25, Wt 2–2.3.

Distribution. N. and N.E. Liberia. HABITAT: Deciduous rain forest north of full rain forest on sandy soil, also secondary forest with impenetrable undergrowth. *Map* p. 208.

Habits. Hardly known, probably in small family parties, diurnal, terrestrial, living in burrows and other holes. FOOD: mainly small animals, above all worms, raked up with long snout and claws. The comparatively weak teeth and long claws suggest an insectivorous diet. The Cusimanse, *Crossarchus obscurus*, occurs at the same localities. Liberian name Bagou.

BLACK-FOOTED MONGOOSE, *Bdeogale (Galeriscus) nigripes*   Pl. 36
(Pucheran, 1855)

G. Schwarzfussichneumon   F. La Mangouste à pattes noirs   S. Nguchiro, Kitu

Identification. Large, powerful, with heavy head, muzzle broad, eyes and ears small, latter roundish. Legs sturdy, hind somewhat longer than fore, toes 4/4, thumb and great toe lacking, toes short and sturdy, claws robust, of equal length on fore and hind feet. Soles up to and between the pads naked, hairy behind. Dent: $3 \cdot 1 \cdot 4 \cdot 2 = 40$. Upper canines straight, laterally flattened, P1 very small, P^4 molariform. Anal glands well developed. Penis bone and number of teats not recorded. Pelage short and thick, tail rather long-haired. Head and throat whitish-grey, rest of upperside light greyish-brown to whitish-grey, finely grizzled; front of breast to front of belly, and lower legs, brownish-black. Posterior part of belly whitish-grey, tail whitish-grey to white. Ssp *jacksoni* has throat and sides of neck yellowish. Nearly adult juveniles much lighter down to the legs, and notably longer-haired on the body than full adults. Small young very woolly. MEASUREMENTS: HB 55–65, TL 35–40, Ht c.20. Wt?

Distribution. Rain forests from E. Nigeria (E. of Cross River), to N.E. Zaire on the one side and N. Angola on the other (*nigripes*); in addition, S.W. Kenya and S.E. Uganda (*jacksoni* (Thomas, 1894)). 2 ssp.

Habits. Lives in rain forests, up to 2000m in mountains, singly or in pairs, mainly nocturnal, lives in taken-over burrows and other holes. Terrestrial, only climbing in emergency. Voice a dog-like baying. Food small animals and fruit, can be trapped at flesh bait. 1 young at a birth. Has lived 11 years in captivity. No further details.

BUSHY-TAILED MONGOOSE,   Pl. 36
Bdeogale (Bdeogale) crassicauda (Peters, 1852)

G. Buschschwanzichneumon   F. La Mangouste à queue touffue
A. Dikstertmuishond   S. Kitu, Nguchiro

Identification. Form, foot structure, teeth and anal glands as in Black-footed Mongoose (p. 210), however somewhat smaller and tail shorter and bushier. Pelage with dense underfur and long, rather coarse, guard hairs. Colour according to ssp, medium to dark brown (with or without light stippling) to brownish-black and black. Face and underside rather lighter (throat golden-yellow to dark brown), lower legs darker to black, tail similarly mid-brown to black. Juvenile coat, and teats, ? MEASUREMENTS: HB 40–50, TL 20–30, Wt 0.9–1.6.

Distribution. East Africa from Zambezi valley in Mozambique, Malawi and Zambia through N. Mozambique, Shaba Province in S. Zaire, Rhodesia near Kariba; E. Tanzania including Zanzibar to coastal and inland Kenya. 5 ssp.

Habits. Shy, timid, nocturnal, by day hidden in adopted burrows and other holes. Lives on small animals including lizards and snakes. Inhabits coastal forests, acacia savannahs, rocky hills. Further details not known.

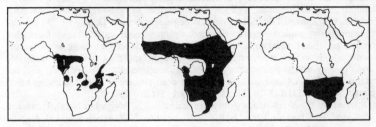

1 Black-footed Mongoose
2 Bushy-tailed Mongoose

White-tailed Mongoose

Southern Dwarf Mongoose

WHITE-TAILED MONGOOSE, *Ichneumia albicauda* (G. Cuvier, 1829) Pl. 36

G. Weisschwanzichneumon F. La Mangouste à queu blanche
A. Witstertmuishond S. Karambago, Nguchiro

Identification. In form like Egyptian Mongoose (p. 201) but longer-legged (hind legs longer than fore), and tail bushier; toes 5/5, thumb and great toe small, high set. Soles hairy up to pads. Claws of front and hind feet of medium length. Anal glands well developed, strongly scented secretion can be sprayed. Penis bone present, 4 teats. Dent: $3/3 \cdot 1/1 \cdot 3/4 \cdot 2/2 = 40$; canines strong, P^1 absent, P_1 very small, M2 comparatively large. Pelage with dense yellowish underfur, and long, coarse blackish guard hairs distinctly ringed with light bands. Head grey, silver or reddish-grey. Legs, feet, breast and belly dark brown, brownish-black, or black. Tail white, or black, or blackish-white or blackish-red mixed, with tip white or black. Rest of upperside dark yellowish-grey, reddish-grey, blackish-grey to black, with the pale underfur showing through the guard hairs. Young woolly, light brownish, without long guard hairs; underside and toes and also often tail tip dark brown to black. MEASUREMENTS: HB 47–69, TL 36–50, Ht 22–25, Wt 1.8–5.

Distribution. Africa south of Sahara, except rain forests and deserts. N. limit about 15°–18°N (Senegambia in W., N. Sudan in E.). Absent also in W. and M. African rain forests, as well as Orange Free State, Cape Province (apart from eastern coastal strip to Port Elizabeth), S. and M. Botswana and S.W. Africa. Occurs also in Oman, S. Arabia. 5 ssp. HABITAT: moist and dry savannahs, dense bush, forest edges, other areas rich in cover, often near water, sometimes near villages. Not in rain forests or deserts.

Habits. DAILY RHYTHM: mainly nocturnal; where undisturbed also active in late afternoon. Lives mainly in deserted burrows or holes of all kinds. Climbs badly and little, swims well but only when necessary. VOICE: alarm call like barking of small dogs. ENEMIES: main defence against attack is by ejecting the very offensive anal gland secretion. FOOD: small animals from insects to small mammals (up to hare size), and ground birds up to guinea fowl size, also mussels, snails, crabs, lizards, snakes (including venomous), eggs, berries, fruit. Eggs are opened in Banded Mongoose style (p. 208). SOCIABILITY: solitary or in pairs.

Reproduction. 2–3 young at a birth. LONGEVITY: 12½ years in captivity. No further details known.

SOUTHERN DWARF MONGOOSE, *Helogale parvula* (Sundevall, 1846) Pl. 37

G. Südliches Zwergichneumon   F. La Mangouste nain   A. Dwergmuishond

Identification. Form like a small Ichneumon, but with head proportionately shorter and rounder. Muzzle pointed, eyes and ears small, latter roundish, legs short. Toes 5/5, thumb and great toe small, high set, soles naked, claws mid-sized, plantigrade. Anal and cheek glands well developed, penis bone present, 6 teats. Dent: $3 \cdot 1 \cdot 3 \cdot 2 = 36$. Canines strong, molars simple cutting teeth. Pelage without underfur, cover hair rather coarse and thin, longest on tail root. Upperside reddish-brown to dark brown (sometimes wholly black), finely stippled with the light and dark hair rings; underside usually only a little lighter than upperside (sometimes also grizzled); legs and tail darker than back (some animals with light head and legs). Young naked at birth. MEASUREMENTS: HB 18–28, TL 14–19, Ht 7–8, Wt 210–350.

Distribution. Southern Africa from S. Tanzania and N. Malawi to Natal, Transvaal, Zululand, W. Rhodesia, E. and N. Botswana, northern S.W. Africa, S. and M. Angola, Zambia and S.E. Zaire. 6 ssp. HABITAT: savannah and bush country with termite and ant hills, burrows, fallen trees, stone heaps, rock piles and other hiding places as living quarters. HOME RANGE: size not known. Centre a deserted burrow with several entrances. Within the total range several such refuges, allowing a change of feeding areas. *Map* p. 211.

Habits. DAILY RHYTHM: diurnal from sunrise to sunset. Sunning outside the burrow, then a collective hunt for food; liveliest at midday, after returning in afternoon some playing before retiring. Sleep with head tucked under in sitting position, sometimes lying close together in burrow. May sit up in begging attitude. In emergency will climb trees, going downwards head first. Avoids water, but will swim only if necessary. Defecation sites near burrows. Urinates with raised hind leg. No scent marking of latrines. Head gland secretion serves as warning (effective for 3 weeks), anal gland secretions used for marking prominent objects (using hand stand sometimes) and kin (effective 2 days). The combined head and anal gland secretions convey to other members of the species the identity and state of the depositor, and the time of marking to within an hour. TOILET: tooth cleaning with claws, scratching with hind feet. No face washing or claw sharpening, though individual or mutual grooming or fur licking. VOICE: while hunting keep up continuous twittering contact call. Wide vocal range for various purposes. Growl in threat with arched back and erect neck hair against enemies, louder if threat nearer. SENSES: sight, hearing and scent very good. ENEMIES: larger carnivores and birds of prey. On account of its fearless curiosity is often in danger. FOOD: insects, varied invertebrates, lizards, snakes, small birds and mammals as well as eggs, fruit and berries. Main food apparently insects. Snakes (including poisonous) are killed by the pack, snails and eggs may be opened by catapulting backwards with fore feet between the hind legs against stones or trees. Slimy or spiny prey may be rolled on the ground; if hard-skinned or furry the skin is taken off. Drink daily where water is available (lapping, or immersing feet and licking them). SOCIABILITY: in families and packs, consisting of adult ♂ and ♀ with their offspring and relations. Usually 6–12, but also up to 30 or more possible. The highest ranking are the parents and young offspring, earlier young help in rearing the latest family. Young ♂♂ watch, and help defence against enemies. Old ♂ may impede the pairing off of young animals, only the old ♂♂ and ♀♀ produce young. Young are not fully grown until 3 years old, when they start families.

Reproduction. Duration of mating (standing) about 5 minutes. Gestation 50–54 days, litter 2–6, usually 3–4, nursery in unlined chamber in burrow. Newborn young naked and blind, HB *c*.4, TL *c*.2.5. When pelage begins, same as adults. Eyes open at 2 weeks, weaned at 3–4 weeks. First solid food at 7–10 days, independent at 2 months. 2–3 litters annually possible. SEXUAL MATURITY: in captivity already possible at 4 months, in wild usually at ¾ year. LONGEVITY not known.

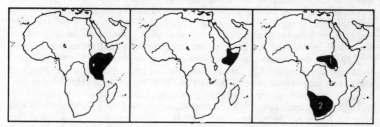

Eastern Dwarf Mongoose   Somali Dwarf Mongoose   1 Pousargue's Mongoose
2 Bush-tailed Meerkat

EASTERN DWARF MONGOOSE, *Helogale undulata* (Peters, 1852) **Pl. 37**
G. Östliches Zwergichneumon   F. as in *H. parvula*   S. Nguchiro
Identification. Much like *parvula* in build. Reddish-brown to dark greyish-brown, lightly grizzled, head and breast rather reddish. MEASUREMENTS: HB 20–25, TL 12–16, Ht 7–8, Wt 210–350.
Distribution. N.E. Mozambique, Tanzania, Kenya, Uganda, S. Somalia, S.W. and S.E. Ethiopia. 10 ssp. *Undulata* is very probably conspecific with *parvula*.
Habits. As *parvula*.

SOMALI DWARF MONGOOSE, *Helogale hirtula* (Thomas, 1904) **Pl. 37**
G. Somali-Zwergichneumon   F. La Mangouste velue
Identification. Form and build as Southern Dwarf Mongoose (p. 212), pelage longer and rougher. Smoky grey, lightly stippled, feet darker, lower cheeks lighter, underside suffused with ochreous. MEASUREMENTS: HB 20–27, HL 15–20, Ht 7–8, Wt ?
Distribution. N.E. Kenya, S. and M. Somalia, E. and S. Ethiopia. 5 ssp.
Habits. Not known, probably like *parvula*.

POUSARGUE'S MONGOOSE, *Dologale dybowskii* (Pousargues, 1893) **Pl. 37**
G. Listige Manguste   F. La Mangouste de Dybowski
Identification. Form and size much as in Southern Dwarf Mongoose (p. 212), but tail rather more bushy. Pelage rather short, but underfur present and guard hairs rather stiff. Dark brown, finely speckled with yellowish-grey, head rather darker than back and finely speckled with white, rump often suffused yellowish, tail like back, often with underside rather reddish, underside of body pale sepia, throat and lower cheeks grey. Feet brownish-black to black. Foot structure as in *Helogale*. Glands and teats not recorded, penis bone small (1cm). Dent.: 3/3 · 1/1 · 3–4/3 · 2/2 = 38; P¹ often absent,

otherwise tooth pattern as *Helogale*. Juvenile pelage unknown. Measurements. HB 22–29, TL 16–22, Ht *c*.7–8, Wt?

Distribution. N.E. Zaire, S.E. Central African Republic, M. and S. Sudan, N. Uganda. No ssp. *Map* p. 213.

Habits. Lives in savannahs. No details known.

BUSHY-TAILED MEERKAT, *Cynictis penicillata* (G. Cuvier, 1829)   Pl. 37
G. Fuchsmanguste   F. La Mangouse fauve   A. Geelmeerkat

Identification. Appearance rather like small fox. Slender, long-legged, bushy-tailed, muzzle short and pointed; eyes middle-sized, ears wide apart, short, rounded, but with rounded upper corner reaching past top of head. Legs slender, toes 5/4, thumb small and high-set, great toe absent, claws long, soles naked to thumb and site of great toe. Tail thickly bushy, anal glands well developed, penis bone small (¾cm). 6 teats. Dent: 3 · 1 · 4 · 2 = 40. Canines and molars strong, latter sharp-cusped. P1 very small, can be absent. Winter pelage with thicker under-fur and longer guard hairs, summer coat short and thin; winter coat paler than summer coat. Upperside and tail whitish-grey, yellowish-grey to brownish-yellow, orange or reddish, darkly stippled. Underside and feet lighter than back; lips, chin and throat white, vibrissae black. Front of body, with fore feet, sometimes lighter (to whitish-grey) than posterior parts. Tail usually darker in middle, tip white; sometimes white predominant. Juvenile pelage not described. MEASUREMENTS: HB 25–40, TL 18–30, Ht *c*.15–18, Wt 440–800.

Distribution. Southern Africa. Union of S. Africa west of Drakensberg Mts, (M. and W. Transvaal, W. Natal, N. Orange Free State, Cape Province, except the south between St. Helena Bay and Port Elizabeth), S.W. Rhodesia, Botswana, S. Angola from about 16°S between the Cubango and Cunene rivers, S.W. Africa. 12 ssp. HABITAT: prefers dry open plains with scanty grass and bush growth, hilly or higher ground, and rocky or stony regions. In the dry season, when there is no risk of flooding, and also on low-lying plains, on the edge of dried-up rivers and pans. HOME RANGE: usually pairs, families or in packs, forming colonies of up to 50 animals or more. Centre of area is a burrow, taken over from Spring Hares or ground squirrels and enlarged. A colony may stretch over 50sq m and can have up to 100 entrances. Refuges may also be under rock piles or in small sand dunes established by wind around acacia bush roots, ranging from 1–1.5m high and 10–20m long. Friendly association with ground squirrels and suricates, young may play together. Special latrine areas in vicinity of burrows. Food searches either singly or in pairs may range up to over 3km from burrow. When food is exhausted will move around to more distant colonies. *Map* p. 213.

Habits. DAILY RHYTHM: diurnal, at night only in neighbourhood of colony, then timid. Sun themselves in early morning sitting or standing upright like suricate. May also keep watch in this attitude. In the feeding sorties many small items scratched out of ground.   FOOD: small mammals of all kinds, snakes (including poisonous), lizards, small birds up to hen sized. Useful as rodent controller. As a colonial animal a dangerous carrier and spreader of rabies.

Reproduction. 2–4 (usually 2) young at a birth in unlined chamber in burrow. 2 litters a year possible.   LONGEVITY: up to 12 years in captivity.

SELOUS' MONGOOSE, *Paracynictis Selousi* (De Winton, 1896)   Pl. 37
G. Trugmanguste   F. La Mangouste de Selous   A. Selouse Mierkat

Identification. Ichneumon-like. Muzzle sharp, eyes small, ears short and roundish, wide apart. Legs rather short, toes 4/4, thumb and great toe absent. Soles, apart from pads, hairy, claws long and strong. Tail long, tapering towards tip. Anal glands well developed, 6 teats, ? penis bone. Pelage rather long, underfur dense, brownish, guard hairs rather stiff, ringed light and dark. Upperside dark yellowish-brown to yellowish grey, lightly speckled, underside whitish to yellowish. Sometimes forehead and cheeks whitish. Tail like back, becoming whitish towards tip. Feet dark brown to black. Juvenile coat not described. Dent.: $3 \cdot 1 \cdot 4 \cdot 2 = 40$; canines and molars powerful, latter sharp-cusped, Pl small. MEASUREMENTS: HB 35–48, TL 28–40, Ht c.15–18, Wt 1.3–2.7.

Distribution. Southern Africa: N.E. Natal, E. and N. Transvaal, Rhodesia, S. and N.W. Zambia, E. and N. Botswana, E. Caprivi, M. and S. Angola and perhaps N.E. S.W. Africa, Malawi, Maputo (Mozambique). 4 ssp. HABITAT: dry savannah, bush and open woodland with sandy or other easily excavated soil. HOME RANGE: size not known. Central point adopted or self-dug burrows (also under bushes or between tree roots) with branching tunnel system and several entrances.

Habits. DAILY RHYTHM: nocturnal or crepuscular, resting in hole by day. Little known of habits. FOOD: small animals of all kinds, from insects to frogs, lizards, small birds, mice.

Reproduction. Live singly or in pairs, breeding season Sep–Mar; usually 2 young.

MELLER'S MONGOOSE, *Rhynchogale melleri* (Gray, 1865)   Pl. 37
G. Maushund   F. La Mangouste de Meller   A. Mellerse Muishond   S. Nguchiro

Identification. Ichneumon-like. Sharp muzzle, eyes and ears small, latter roundish. Tail long, long-haired at root, tapering towards tip. Toes 5/5, thumb and great toe small, high set, soles hairy apart from pads, claws of medium length. 4 teats. Character of anal glands and penis bone not known. Dent: $3/3 \cdot 1/1 \cdot 4–5/4 \cdot 2/2 = 40–42$. Canines and molars sturdy, latter flat-crowned. Pl small. Pelage rather long and rough, with underfur. Throat hairs directed forward, making a lateral border line with neck hairs. Upperside reddish-brown, lightly speckled, head and underside lighter, back and feet darker, latter dark brown; tail coloured like back, the end black. Cheeks and chin light greyish-brown. Juvenile coat not known. MEASUREMENTS: HB 45–50, TL 35–40, Ht 15–18, Wt 1.5–2.7.

Distribution. Mid-Tanzania, M. and W. Mozambique, S. Malawi, M. and S. Zambia, S.E. Zaire, Rhodesia, E. Transvaal, Ngwana (Swaziland). 3 ssp. HABITAT: bush and lightly wooded savannah.

Habits. Largely unknown. Nocturnal, solitary, terrestrial, living on small animals and fruit, main food probably termites. By day hidden in burrows or among rocks.

Reproduction. Breeding season Sep–Mar. 2–3 young at a birth. LONGEVITY: not known.

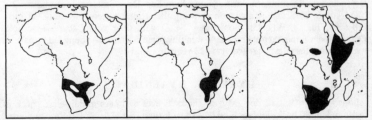

Selous's Mongoose   Meller's Mongoose   Aardwolf

AARDWOLF, PROTELIDAE

Hyaena-like, but much smaller, muzzle pointed, front and hind legs of same length, tail thickly bushy, long erectile crest along spine. Toes 5/4, 4 teats. Dent.: $3 \cdot 1 \cdot 3 \cdot 1 = 32$, cheek teeth rudimentary. Nocturnal insectivorous inhabitant of plains and savannahs of E. and S. Africa. 1 genus with 1 species. Generally considered to represent a distinct family separate from Hyaenas.

AARDWOLF, *Proteles cristatus* (Sparrman, 1783) **Pl. 38**
G. Erdwolf   F. Le Protèle   A. Erdwolf   S. Fisi ndogo, LeKimbu
Identification. In form and colour pattern rather like Striped Hyaena but much smaller. Muzzle rather pointed, ears rather large, pointed. Legs slender, 5 toes in front, 4 in hind feet. Back sloping. Neck and back with long erectile mane. Tail long and strongly bushy. Molars greatly reduced, sometimes deciduous. Tongue very long and mobile, covered with glutinous saliva. 4 teats. Body colour pale yellowish to reddish-brown, cheeks and throat yellowish-white; muzzle black and almost naked, back of forehead and crown greyish-black, mane with black stripes, tail nearly all, or only the tip, black; sides of body with 4–8 transverse black stripes, legs with 2–5 horizontal or slanting black stripes. Stripes variable, can be very prominent or reduced, sometimes only spots on legs. MEASUREMENTS: HB 65–80, TL 20–30, Ht 45–50, Wt 7–10.
Distribution. In eastern Africa from N.E. Sudan to Cape Province, from there to M. Angola and Zambia, recorded from Oubangui region of Central African Republic. 6 ssp. HABITAT: open mainly dry country, plains, thornbush, savannahs. Not in mountains. TERRITORY: about 1–1½sq km around the burrow, latter is usually an aardvark or spring hare burrow. In loose soil sometimes excavates a hole for itself, with a sunning hollow by the entrance. Territory marked by anal gland secretions on the ground; several large defecation sites (1–2sq m); faeces deposited in a scraped hollow. *Map p. 215.*
Habits. DAILY RHYTHM: only active at dusk and by night.   VOICE: rather quiet, only when threatened may growl, grunt or utter weak bark. Young whimper. SENSES: hearing very sharp (detects rustling of termites), scent and sight good.   ENEMIES: may be killed by lion, leopard, spotted hyaena, python. Fights dogs bravely. In defence the mane is erected and anal glands brought into use.   FOOD: mainly termites of the genus *Trinervitermes*, collected at night from ground and grass, located by sound and scent, and rapidly licked up. Each meal may be about 500gr. In eating termites also gathers other insects, will also eat birds eggs, small mammals, soft reptiles, and perhaps also soft carrion. SOCIABILITY: usually solitary, in pairs only when with young. ♂ helps to care for young.
Reproduction. In southern Africa young born Sep–Dec. Gestation not known. 2–4 blind young born in burrow, soon showing the striped pattern of adults. At birth HB *c.*9.5, TL *c.*8, Wt *c.*450. Sometimes 2 ♀♀ with their young share same hole. Details of development not known. At weaning (time not known) young fed by parents regurgitating termites. LONGEVITY: 13 years in captivity.

HYAENAS, HYAENIDAE

About size of Alsatian dog. Muzzle thickset, eyes and ears middle-sized, neck of medium length, back sloping, hind legs shorter than fore. Toes 4/4, thumb and great toe absent. Tail of medium length, bushy. Pelage short to middle length. Moderately long erectile mane on neck and back, in *Hyaena*. Dent: 3/3 · 1/1 · 4/3 · 1/1 = 34. Molar teeth extraordinarily powerful. 2 anal gland sacs in a pocket above rectum. No penis bone. 4–6 teats. Solitary or sociable, nocturnal carrion eaters or active predators. Open country in Africa, S.W. Asia and India, Arabia. 2 genera, 3 species, all in Africa.

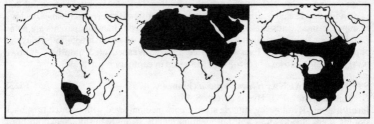

Brown Hyaena   Striped Hyaena   Spotted Hyaena

BROWN HYAENA, *Hyaena brunnea* (Thunberg, 1820)   Pl. 38
G. Braune Hyäne   F. L'Hyène brune   A. Strandwolf

Identification. Head bulky, muzzle broad and short, ears of medium size with pointed tips, back sloping rearwards, legs slender, toes 4/4, tail of medium length, strongly bushy. Pelage (apart from head and legs) rough and long-haired, lengthening to a mane on nape, sides of neck and shoulders. Teeth and external sexual organs as in Striped Hyaena. 4 teats. Head, underside of neck, whole of body and tail uniformly brownish-black, sometimes with 3–5 indistinct blackish transverse stripes on flanks. Mane whitish-yellow to yellowish-brown. Legs dark yellowish-brown, front with about 6, hind with 4–5 transverse black stripes; feet and forehead with light brown spots. Pups at first without mane, grey, with dark transverse stripes on body and legs, and a spinal stripe.   MEASUREMENTS: HB 110–125, TL 25–30, Ht 70–80, Wt 40–55.

Distribution. Southern Africa south of a line from S. Angola (about 15°S) to M. Mozambique (Zambesi the northern border). Previously in the whole of the region; absent now from Orange Free State, Natal, Cape Province (except NW), Malawi, Zambia, M. and E. Rhodesia, parts of Mozambique. No ssp.   HABITAT: dry savannahs, plains, semi-deserts and deserts as well as sea shores.   HOME RANGE: in feeding wanders over area up to 30km wide. Range large (in Kalahari up to 200sq km or more), marked at many points by scent glands and by defecation sites at particular trees (territory). Centre of range is the den, usually an old aardvark hole.

Habits. DAILY RHYTHM: nocturnal and crepuscular, rarely active by day, sleeping in burrow, rock fissures, thickets or tall grass.   VOICE: a loud, owl-like 'wah-wah-wah' at dusk and dawn, often repeated, as contact call. Does not laugh. Yowling, whining and growling when squabbling over carrion. Squeals when mating.   SENSES: scent and hearing very good, sight good.   ENEMIES: lions, spotted hyaenas in packs, and for pups also jackals, servals and caracals. Shy and cautious, at lion kills not as bold as Spotted Hyaenas and Jackals. In danger defends itself courageously.   FOOD: small prey of all kinds (rodents, birds, eggs, reptiles, even insects), also young game animals, wounded big game, carrion, poultry, fruit. On coast mussels, dead fish, squids, stranded corpses (birds, seals, whales). Takes lambs and kids, but is usually not so aggressive as Spotted Hyaenas, though, like these, in the Kruger National Park will attack large antelopes. Surplus food may be carried away and hidden. A burrow used by young is easily recognised by the food remains strewn about (bones, skulls, feathers). SOCIABILITY: solitary, but may gather at large carcases, or regionally in hunting troops. ♂ brings food to young, which stay with parents 1¼–1½ years.

Reproduction. In courting makes strong deposits of anal gland secretion on prominent objects, ♂ dances around ♀, rolls her on ground, growling and squealing. ♀ sits like a cat in mating, ♂ bites her in mane, both squealing. In Kalahari litter season Jul, not known for other regions. Birth place usually in burrow with narrow entrance, as long as pups are small, thus excluding jackals and other predators while parents are away searching for food. Gestation 92–98 days. Litter 2–4. Wt at birth 635–750. Pelage of pups, see **Identification.** Eyes open after 5 days. Weaned at 3 months. SEXUAL MATURITY: not known. LONGEVITY: 13 years in captivity.

STRIPED HYAENA, *Hyaena hyaena* (Linnaeus, 1758)   **Pl. 38**
G. Streifenhyäne   F. L'Hyène rayée   S. Fisi

Identification. Head bulky, muzzle strong, ears medium sized with pointed tips, back sloping. Legs slender, toes 4/4, tail medium length, strongly bushy. Neck and body pelage with long coarse guard hairs over thick underfur. Neck, shoulders and middle line of back with erectile mane of medium length. Dent: $3/3 \cdot 1/1 \cdot 4/3 \cdot 1/1 = 34$. 6 teats. External genital organs normal. Body colour grey to yellowish-grey. Sides with 8–11 black transverse stripes, varying from prominent to faded. Legs with 5–12 similar transverse stripes. Muzzle, 2 cheek stripes, and throat, black. Mane either with black hair tips or nearly all black. Tail colour uniform with body or partly striped black. Pups have close striping similar to adults, and black spinal stripe. MEASUREMENTS: HB 100–120 (exceptionally to 150), TL 25–35, Ht 65–80, Wt 25–45 (exceptionally to 55). In some areas ♂ on average 5kg heavier than ♀.

Distribution. Formerly most of N. Africa (today extinct in many districts) from Mediterranean coast to Guinea savannah (about 10°N); in E. from Egypt to M. Tanzania. Generally rare, especially where the more powerful Spotted Hyaenas also occur. Also in Near East, Arabia, S. Asia to India (S. to Nilgiris, 11°N). 6 ssp, 2 of which occur in Africa: (1) Berber Striped Hyaena, *H.h. barbara* De Blainville, 1884, in N.W. Africa; (2) Nubian Striped Hyaena, *H.h. dubbah* Meyer, 1793, in N.E. Africa. HABITAT: dry savannah, thornbush, plains, semi-deserts and deserts. In E. Africa acacia savannah, open grassland with medium height grass (up to 70cm), small bushes and scattered trees, also in dense bush country (annual rainfall always under 800mm). Thick cover essential. HOME RANGE: ♂ has wider range than ♀ (70–80sq km compared with 40–50). Numerous sleeping places (burrows, overhanging rocks and holes, under tree roots etc). No latrine marking, this is done instead by anal glands rubbed on grass, leaving a yellow streak 30–60cm long. *Map* p. 217.

Habits. DAILY RHYTHM: nocturnal only. Main activity from nightfall to midnight, then a rest, and a second active period before dawn. Searches for food in zig-zag course, covering about 2–4km an hour; going further trots at 8kmph. Average distance covered nightly about 19km (7–27). Uses temporary shelters if still out at daybreak. VOICE: has various calls when surprised, or hunting; a soft long-drawn howling in fear or pain. Growl when quarrelling over food; hungry pups whine. Normally quiet, calling only in meeting neighbours or when frightened. SENSES: hearing and scent very good, sight good. ENEMIES: no serious natural enemies, is shy and cautious, giving way to lions and avoided by others because of its offensive anal gland scent. May sometimes drive leopard or cheetah from prey, but may otherwise itself be driven off. Smaller predators are either ignored or taken as prey. Usually avoid the larger Spotted Hyaena. If they meet, the Striped Hyaena will circle suspiciously at a safe distance before going its way. Marked spots are respected. If cornered will defend itself furiously. FOOD: varied, largely medium to small mammals, birds, lizards, snakes, tortoises, insects and fruit (also robbing fields and gardens). Will eat antelope droppings, and near villages kitchen waste, pieces of leather etc. Has little success in hunting speedy prey (hares, spring hares etc); the hyaena does not run fast enough (highest speed 50kmph). Will eat carrion and remains of kills by lion, leopard, cheetah, hunting dog, also badly buried human remains. Bones of corpses are eaten (resulting droppings are chalky-white and dry). Young game animals, sheep, goats, dogs and unwatched babies may all be at risk. In rainy season drinks daily, in dry season seldom or not at all. In hunting, the mane is ruffled up. Surplus food may be hidden in thick grass or bushes, not buried. SOCIABILITY: usually solitary, in pairs at breeding season. At large carrion several may meet. In meeting neighbours, tail is upright; mutual smelling of noses, heads and anal region. Sometimes one animal may lie on its side, raising a hind leg to make investigation easier. In hunting or facing attack mane is ruffled and tail held horizontally; tail on back in food quarrelling.

Reproduction. In subtropics litters in spring; in tropics in all months. Gestation 3 months, 2–4 blind young in hole in ground or among rocks etc. ♂ helps to raise the young, ♀ suckles mostly at night. Weaned at about 1 year or earlier if much solid food is being taken. Young follow ♀ hunting at $\frac{1}{2}$ year, before that the ♀ has always brought the food. SEXUAL MATURITY: about 2–3 years. LONGEVITY: up to 24 years in captivity.

SPOTTED HYAENA, *Crocuta crocuta* (Erxleben, 1777)   Pl. 38
G. Fleckenhyäne   F. La Hyène tachetée   A. Tierwolf   S. Fisi

Identification. Head very massive and powerful, muzzle sturdy, ears middle-sized, roundish; back sloping, legs slender, toes 4/4, tail of medium length, bushy. Pelage short, nape and shoulders with short mane. Dent.: as Striped Hyaena. 4 teats (2 not functional). External genitalia of ♀ have superficial similarity to those of ♂ (hence much popular misconception). Body colour whitish-grey to yellowish red, head and feet darker brown; neck and underside of body as well as inside of legs whitish-grey; numerous irregular dark brown to blackish-brown spots (about size of penny) over body and upper part of legs. Colour and disposition of spots very variable. In Ethiopia albinos may occur. Pups woolly, uniformly dark- to blackish-brown. MEASUREMENTS: HB 120–180, TL 25–30, Ht 70–90, Wt 55–85, ♀ one-fifth bigger and heavier than ♂.

Distribution. Africa south of Sahara (in E. from N. Sudan) except in closed forest. Formerly southwards to the Cape, now only to S. Mozambique, Zululand, E. Transvaal, M. Botswana and M. S.W. Africa. 6 ssp. HABITAT: semi-desert to moist savannah, not in closed forest. In mountains to 4,500m. TERRITORY: usually resident in territories of several sq km; in the Serengeti over limited periods accompany the migrating herds of ungulates. In E. Africa at times in packs of 10–30, exceptionally up to 100 animals. Each troop has territory of 15–30sq km, marked by urination (dog-like with raised leg) and droppings on conspicuous sites of about 1000sq m, containing many heaps of white droppings (the chalk-like remains of bones). Marks grass stems and other points with anal gland secretions, and scratch up earth with fore feet (using the apparently strongly scented interdigital glands). The territory is guarded, regularly patrolled, and enemy packs ejected. Kin within the troop recognise each other by scent. *Map* p. 217.

Habits. DAILY RHYTHM: predominantly active at dusk and by night (in many areas also hunt by day). Sleep in adopted or self-dug burrows (up to 1.8m long and 1.5m high), or in tall grass, thick bush or among rocks.   TOILET: bathe in mud, roll in grass or carrion remains or stomach contents. Mutual licking and grooming.   VOICE: noisy, a great variety of vocalisations. Up to 17 different sounds have been listed. A succession of howling screams indicates gathering for the evening hunt; blood-curdling laughter when hunt is successful, high screams of anger when trying to drive off lions or other packs from prey; and many others.   SENSES: sight, hearing and scent very good.   ENEMIES: single animals may be killed by lions and hunting dogs, young pups sometimes attacked by old ♂♂ and strange packs. Mother defends them bravely.   FOOD: mainly carrion, often from lion kills. All parts of carcase, skin, hair and bones, are devoured. Young, sick and old animals are seized, even dead bodies of their own species (result of fights with lions or other packs) are not rejected. In many districts gazelles, antelopes and zebras are hunted and seized, the chosen victim being brought down by a bite on the fetlock and torn to pieces while still alive. Lions, leopards, cheetahs and hunting dogs may be driven off their prey by a pack of hyaenas (on the other hand lions may turn the tables). Also solitary humans may be threatened at night by the pack. Cattle kraals may be broken into, and sheep, goats, cattle, donkeys and horses seized. In villages anything edible may be stolen if not made secure. Subsidiary food includes small animals and vegetable matter; ungulate droppings are eaten perhaps for digestive purposes.   SOCIABILITY: rarely solitary, usually in pairs, family parties, or troops, in many areas in large troops (see TERRITORY). Within a troop the ♀♀ occupy the top-ranking order.

Reproduction. Courting as in Brown Hyaena, mating in sitting position like cats. Gestation 99–130 days, litter size 1–2, rarely 3. In all months. Birthplace in the burrow, Wt at birth 1.5; eyes open at birth with canines and incisor teeth already cut. After 1 week active, leave hole for first time at 2 weeks. Often several ♀♀ with young together in one or adjoining holes; young may be suckled by all of these ♀♀. After 2 weeks suckle outside the hole, duration often more than an hour. After 1–1½ months the young begin to show colour on head, after 4 months on body, at 1 year on legs. Weaning at 1–1½ years, thereafter the well-grown young are ready to take their place in the pack and help to catch prey. During suckling period the ♀ does not bring food or regurgitate semi-digested food.   SEXUAL MATURITY: ♂ at 2, ♀ usually at 3 years. LONGEVITY: up to 40 years recorded in captivity.

CATS, FELIDAE

In size from domestic cat to tiger. Muzzle short, eyes large, ears middle-sized, sometimes with terminal tuft. Legs medium to long, toes 5/4, claws (apart from cheetah) retractile. Tail short to very long, usually uniformly close-haired, sometimes with terminal tuft. Pelage soft, short or of medium length, sometimes with cheek ruff or a mane on neck, shoulders and belly. Dent: $3/3 \cdot 1/1 \cdot 2$–$3/2 \cdot 1/1 = 28$–30. Cheek-teeth narrow, with sharp cutting edge. Penis with either reduced bone or none. Circumanal glands and anal sac present; 4–8 teats. Generally solitary, unsociable, nocturnal small or large animals, some fish-eaters. New and Old Worlds apart from Madagascar and Australasia. 4 sub-families, 19 genera, and 35 species, 10 of which occur in Africa.

LARGE CATS, PANTHERINAE

Large, long-tailed, claws retractile. 4 teats. Dent.: $3 \cdot 1 \cdot 3/2 \cdot 1 = 30$, P^2 and M^1 small. Tongue bone (hyoid) with elastic connection, making roaring possible. Predominantly nocturnal inhabitants of open or forested country in plains and mountains. 2 genera with 5 species in New and Old Worlds, of which 1 genus with 2 species is African.

LION, *Panthera leo* (Linnaeus, 1758)   **Pl. 39**
G. Löwe   F. Le Lion   A. Leeu   S. Simba

Identification. Head broad and powerful, muzzle of medium length, ears short and round, legs thick and of medium length, tail long. Pelage short, but ♂ with neck mane, both sexes with short tuft on tip of tail, concealing a claw-like horny spine, 6–12mm long. Colour varying from tawny greyish yellow to dark reddish brown. Underside in ♂ somewhat, and in ♀ chin, breast and belly notably, paler, almost to white. Upper lips, chin and around eyes white, short dark vertical stripe over inner corner of eye. Back of ears black below, tawny above. Whitish and black variations extremely rare. Young lack mane and tail tuft, pelage woolly, with leopard-like rosette pattern of brownish-black spots, which are replaced during growth by the uniform adult colour, although on belly and legs remaining (especially in ♀) much longer. Mane of ♂ begins to grow at about 1½ years and is fully developed at 5–6 years, regionally varying in form from a short facial surround with a neck mane, to a longer (up to 25cm) mane on crown, cheeks, neck, elbows, shoulders, breast and belly. Colour of mane varies geographically from light yellow to black, in old age becoming darker from back to front. Tail tuft brown to black; penis bone present. 4 teats. MEASUREMENTS: HB 145–200, TL 67–102, Ht 75–112, Wt 120–200. ♂ larger and heavier than ♀.

Distribution. In early Pleistocene, Africa, Near East, India and Ceylon, Europe and northern Holarctic to Mid and N.W. South America; in historical times still in all Africa (apart from the rain forest belt), Sinai, Arabia, Iraq, Asia Minor, Greece, Iran, Baluchistan, N. and Mid India. Now extinct in Asia apart from about 200 in Gir Forest Reserve in Kathiawar (N.W. India), and in Africa except between 20°N and 23°S (in Natal to 27°S.). 9 ssp.; 7 in Africa. Of these, the most northern, the Atlas or Barbary Lion, *P.l. leo* (Linnaeus, 1758), and the southernmost, the Cape Lion, *P.l. melanochaita* (Smith, 1842), already extinct; elsewhere in part more or less threatened. HABITAT: open country from semi-desert to dry and moist savannahs, not in closed forests; in mountains up to snow-line (4500m). TERRITORY: occupied by 1–3 adult ♂♂ with their ♀♀ and young as the hunting ground or base: marked by scent (urination) and sound (roaring), and defended against intruders, particularly sexually mature ♂♂. Size of territory depends on nature of country, density of prey, and size of group; varies therefore between 20 and 400sq km. In the Serengeti Plains of E. Africa a large part of the lion population follows the big game herds on their seasonal migrations. *Map* p. 223.

Habits. DAILY RHYTHM: Lazy, resting for about 20 of the 24 hours; where undisturbed may be active by day (morning and late afternoon); where hunted is entirely nocturnal. Rets in shade of trees (sometimes well up in the trees), in thickets, in the shade of rocks etc. In addition to climbing, swims well in need. TOILET: fur licking (also mutually), scratching with paws, rubbing and rolling in loose soil. VOICE: roaring (for marking and claiming territory) very loud, can be heard for up to 8km, ♂ louder than ♀. Contact call a deep growling, also used as warning, coughing before attack; ♀ calls young with soft growl – they greet mother with high whimpering. ♂ moans when mating, ♀ purrs. Purring also when pleased. SENSES: sight very good (particularly for movement), hearing as in Leopard (p. 223), scent good. ENEMIES: unguarded young at risk from hyaenas, leopards and pythons, hyaena and hunting dog packs sometimes attack adults. FOOD: middle-sized to large mammals, principally gazelles, antelopes, zebras, whether adult or young. Sometimes combine in attack on adult buffalo, giraffe or hippopotamus. In emergency will also take small mammals, birds, snakes, crocodiles, or their own species (cannibalism). Rarely become man-eaters (usually when wounded or aged, making normal hunting difficult). In the Serengeti may be parasitic on spotted hyaenas, driving them off their kills. Hunting either solitary but more frequently jointly, in latter case usually by the ♀♀. Method, after choosing prey, is careful stalking to as short a distance as possible, then a rapid attack (up to 65kmph), to kill, when possible, by throat or neck bite. Drinks daily, but in emergency can go without for a month.   SOCIABILITY: rarely alone or in pairs; sometimes bachelor parties of 2–4 young ♂♂, but usually in family group of 1–3 old ♂♂ and several (up to 15) ♀♀ with young of various ages. Sometimes divided into several troops. Orphaned young may be cared for by other ♀♀. In feeding, the old ♂♂ have priority, then the ♀♀, the young last, often getting crowded out and going hungry. Young ♀♀ stay with the troop, young ♂♂ are driven out at 1½–2 years.

Reproduction. Not limited seasonally. ♀♀ on heat every 3 months for 4–8 days, and is mated repeatedly for several days by old ♂. Mate in sitting position like Kaffir cats. Gestation 102–113 days. Den hidden among rocks, in high grass, thickets etc. Litter size 1–6, usually 2–3; at birth weight 1–1.75, HB *c*.22, TL *c*.8; Wt at 6 weeks 3.5–6.3, at 6 months 18–20, at 20 months *c*.90. Coat of kitten, see **Identification**. Eyes open at 6–9 days, first teeth at 3 weeks, active at 6 weeks, first solid food at 8 weeks, first canine teeth, and black of tail tip, at 15 weeks. Weaned at 6 months, spots mostly lost at 10 months. Both sexes sexually mature at 18 months, hunting capability established at 2 years; fully grown at 5–6 years.   LONGEVITY: normally 13–15; in captivity 30 years recorded.

LEOPARD, *Panthera pardus* (Linnaeus, 1758)   **Pl. 40**
G. Leopard   F. La Panthère d'Afrique   A. Luiperd   S. Chui
Identification. Bodily structure well-balanced, build muscular but supple. Head broad, muzzle medium length, ears short and round, legs of medium length, sturdy; tail long. Fur soft, short and close, longer in cooler climates. Upperside from creamy-yellow and pale yellowish-grey varying from olive-grey, orange-yellow, olive-brown or brownish-grey; underside (chin, throat, breast, belly, inside of upper part of legs) white to whitish-grey or yellowish-white. Head, neck and underside with black solid spots, the rest of upperside with rosettes (2–4 black spots around body-coloured or darkened centre); on throat and breast the spots partly running into transverse stripes; on back partly arranged as 1–3 long rows; on end of tail spots fuse into several rings. Tail tip black. Individual and geographic colour and pattern variation considerable. In humid climates darkened on the back, and partly or wholly black animals may occur (name panther sometimes applied). Albinism very rare. Young like adults, but more grey, pattern very closely arranged, rosettes still solid, therefore look darker. Back of ears with white spot which grows larger and yellowish with age; only the lower and back edges remaining black. Penis bone present; 4 teats.   MEASUREMENTS: HB ♂ 130–190, ♀ 110–140, TL ♂ 70–100, ♀ 60–75, Ht ♂ 50–70, ♀ 45–60, Wt ♂ 45–85, ♀ 35–50. ♂ larger and heavier than ♀.

Distribution. Whole of Africa, with Zanzibar: north of about 20°N, as well as in Cape Province, Orange Free State, W. Transvaal, as well as the Sudanese zone, widely exterminated. Outside Africa, in Sinai, Near and Middle East, Asia Minor (everywhere widely exterminated), to Caucasus, Iran, S. Asia, whole of India, Malaysian Archi-pelago, China, Korea, Manchuria (everywhere threatened). 26 ssp, 12 in Africa. HABITAT: all types of country from deserts to primeval rain forests, and from lowland plains to snow line (4,500m) in the high mountains.   HOME RANGE: size according to food supply, 1–10sq km, usually 5–10 ♂♂ appear to set up territory in particular

Lion Leopard Cheetah

places, which may overlap, and are marked by calling and by spraying urine on bushes, boughs or tree trunks, as well as by scratching on ground or tree trunks.

Habits. DAILY RHYTHM: where undisturbed, active by day and night; where hunted, remains very secretive and nocturnal. Likes to sun itself on trees and rocks. Climbs and swims well. Sleeps in trees or among rocks and ground cover wherever suitable. TOILET: scratches with hind feet, licks and grooms fur. VOICE: rough sawing cough repeated up to a dozen times as territorial claiming or contact call ($\male$ call deeper than $\female$); short growl in greeting. Sometimes a short snarl when stalking prey, an explosive growl in alarm, and 2–3 short coughs at beginning of charge; in anger growling and spitting, in fury screaming roar; purring when content. $\female$ greets young with soft quickly repeated call. SENSES: hearing exceptional (range of 15- to 45,000 cycles), sight very good, scent good. ENEMIES: occasionally lion, hunting dogs, spotted hyaenas, crocodiles. Lions and spotted hyaenas sometimes drive a Leopard off its prey. Young may be endangered by hyaenas, jackals and similar-sized predators. FOOD: any mammals (including predators) up to reedbuck size, sometimes also larger antelopes, lion cubs, young apes, and particularly young baboons; any birds up to size of stork, and snakes, tortoises, fish, insects, as well as domestic stock (sheep, goats, calves, poultry). Domestic dogs, and all monkeys, are favourite prey. Carrion is not despised, also some large prey may be dragged up into a tree for temporary protection. Rarely a wounded Leopard, unable to hunt normal prey, may turn to man-eating. Where available, will drink daily, where not, may go a month without. SOCIABILITY: solitary.

Reproduction. In subtropics breeding season in spring, in tropics probably in all months. $\female$ on heat at 20–50 day intervals, usually 45, duration of heat 6–7 days. Several $\male\male$ may follow, and fight over, one $\female$. Mating as in Kaffir cat. Gestation 90–112 days, usually 95–98. Cubs born in rock crevices or holes, hollow trees, reedy nests, thickets etc. Litter 1–6 cubs, usually 2–3. Wt at birth c.430, HB c.20, TL c.15; Wt at 1 month c.1, at 6 months c.10, at 12 months c.30. Eyes open at 1 week, suckle for 3 months, independent at $1\frac{1}{2}$–2 years. SEXUAL MATURITY: at $2\frac{1}{2}$–3 years. LONGEVITY: 21 years in captivity.

CHEETAHS, ACINONYCHINAE

Leopard sized, but very long-legged, claws in adults non-retractile. Tail long. Hyoid bone of tongue without epihyale, hence incapable of roaring (see Pantherinae). 10–12 teats. Dent.: $3 \cdot 1 \cdot 2$–$3/2 \cdot 1 = 28$–30. Diurnal running hunter of gazelles in open plains in Africa, Arabia, Middle East and India, but now of doubtful occurrence outside Africa. 1 genus with 1 species.

CHEETAH or HUNTING LEOPARD,   Pl. 41
Acinonyx jubatus (Schreber, 1775)
G. Gepard   F. Le Guépard   A. Jagdluiperd   S. Msongo, Duma

Identification. About leopard-size in body, but shape greyhound-like (except head which is short-muzzled, small and rounded, with ears short and roundish). Body long, narrow, with deep chest and high abdomen, and high shoulders. Legs very long and slender, claws only retractile in young up to $\frac{1}{2}$ year. Tail long. Fur short and rather rough, neck and shoulders with short coarse mane, or mane-like middle stripe. Upperside light yellow or yellowish-grey to light reddish-brown; underside (chin, throat, breast, belly, inside of legs) whitish. Cheeks, forehead, crown, neck, body, limbs and first half of tail with numerous, small-sized blackish-brown to black spots, paler on fore part of breast, middle of belly and inside of legs. End half of tail with 3–6 black rings, last one broadest, tail tip white. Back of ears white below, body colour above. Black stripe from front of eye to corner of mouth. In some individuals in Rhodesia and other areas body spots enlarged and flowing together in stripes and blotches (the so-called King Cheetah, forma *rex*). Young coloured like adults, but with long yellowish-grey or whitish-grey erectile mane of mantle on neck and back, disappearing with growth. Penis bone? 10–12 teats. M^1 and P^2 very small, latter can be absent. MEASUREMENTS: HB 110–140, TL 65–80, Ht 75–85, Wt 40–60. ♂ rather larger and heavier than ♀.

Distribution. Africa except the closed forests, earlier from Mediterranean to the Cape of Good Hope; today extinct north of about 20°N and south of about 28°S; largely absent in Mozambique, M. Angola, S. Zaire and in the Sahel zone west of Lake Chad, threatened generally. Outside Africa extinct or very rare. 8 ssp., 6 in Africa. In former times Cheetahs were trained in India for gazelle hunting. HABITAT: mainly open country from desert to dry savannah, including open bush country, sometimes at edge of moist savannah; in highlands up to 2000m. HOME RANGE: size related to prey abundance, in open country usually 25–40sq km, but in National Parks and Reserves may need only $\frac{1}{4}$ of this area. ♂ marks conspicuous points by urine spraying (lasting about 24 hours), other cheetahs then avoid that area. Also avoid each other at sight and avoid fighting. *Map* p. 223.

Habits. DAILY RHYTHM: diurnal, hunts by sight, but sometimes on moonlit nights. Chief hunting time morning and late afternoon. TOILET: scratching with hind feet, fur licking and grooming (often mutual). VOICE: deep purring when contented, growling, hissing and spitting in anger, high twittering as contact call also used by young. A hunting ♀ uses a low 'ugh' to keep young away, then calls them to the kill with a high chirp. SENSES: sight outstanding, hearing very good, scent good. ENEMIES: lions, leopards and spotted hyaenas will kill and eat half-grown cheetahs, sometimes also adults. Cheetahs are peaceful and seldom fight, hence also easily tamed. FOOD: hares, jackals, porcupines, gazelles, dik-diks, oribis, common duiker, bushbuck, impalas, addax, young warthogs and young of large antelopes, guinea fowl and francolins, bustards, young ostriches. Before the hunt may gaze out from a termite hill or branches of a low tree; prey selected is then stalked carefully to within 100 yards if possible, then attacked at a gallop and pursued for up to 500 yards at about 80kmph, the strides up to 7m wide. The prey is caught and knocked over, then held with a throat grip lasting 5–10 minutes. The maximum speed in emergency is said to reach 110kmph. Several adults may combine to run down and kill larger antelopes and young zebras. Prey is often dragged to cover to avoid interference, is eaten on the spot and is not returned to if disturbed. Carrion is not eaten. Lions and hyaenas often drive cheetah from kill. Little water is needed; in emergency drink urine of prey and eat succulent desert melons (tsammahs). SOCIABILITY: solitary, in pairs, or in family parties, with ♀ and young of various ages. One ♂ in charge, ♀ brings up young alone, though ♂ brings prey when young are larger.

Reproduction. ♀ is in heat every 7–10 days for 2 weeks, and may be covered by the strongest ♂ after usually bloodless fighting between ♂♂. Mate in sitting position. Gestation 91–95 days. Birthplace in bushy thickets, rock cavities, adopted holes etc. Breeding period in S.W. Africa mainly Dec–Jan, in Transvaal Jun–Dec, in Rhodesia Mar–Apr, in E. Africa Mar–Dec. Litter size 1–6, usually 2–4. Wt at birth 250–300, daily increase about 50g. Wt at 1 year 25–28kg. Pelage of young, see **Identification**. Crawl at 2–3 days, eyes open at 4–14, first solid food at 21–28 days. Mane shedding (from back to front) at 2½ months. Suckle up to 2 months. SEXUAL MATURITY: ♀ at 9–10 months, ♂ at 14 months; leave mother at 15–17 months, but young have to learn hunting techniques over a long time, having much to learn. After giving birth, ♀ has first heat at 3½–4 months. LONGEVITY: up to 16 years in captivity.

LYNXES, LYNCINAE

Middle-sized, long-legged, tail short or stumpy, ear tips with hair pencils, claws retractile, tongue bone without epihyale, 6 teats. Dent.: $3 \cdot 1 \cdot 2 \cdot 1 = 28$. Essentially terrestrial, diurnal or nocturnal, of open or forested country in New and Old Worlds. 2 genera with 3 species, of which 1 genus and species occur in Africa.

CARACAL, *Caracal caracal* (Schreber, 1776)   **Pl. 43**
G. Wüstenluchs   F. Le caracal   A. Rooikat   S. Sibamangu
(Sometimes considered a subgenus or species of *Felis*.)
Identification. Lynx-like, head rather flat, ear tips triangular with long terminal tufts, legs long (hind rather longer than fore), tail only ⅓ HB (sometimes longer, up to ½ HB). Pelage thick and soft, upperside uniformly coloured, from light sandy through yellowish-red or light cinnamon to strong brownish-red, reddish-grey or wine red, variable, often with a suffusion of grey or black. Back darker than sides; underside (cheeks, chin, throat, breast, belly) whitish. Throat and front of breast sometimes also yellowish-red. Breast, belly and inside of legs with yellowish- to reddish-brown spots; sometimes a pale transverse stripe on back of upper thighs. Back of ears, vertical supraorbital stripe, stripe from eye to nose, spot at corner of mouth and vibrissae-root spots, greyish-brown to black. Ear tuft usually black, sometimes white. Melanistic animals sometimes occur. Young greyer and darker than adults; upper lip to eyes, and backs of ears, black; upper cheek stripe (behind eyes) usually indistinct. Teats 6. Penis bone present. MEASUREMENTS: HB 65–90, TL 20–30, Ht 40–50, Wt 8–18. ♂ usually larger and heavier than ♀.
Distribution. Whole of Africa except rain forest belt of W. and C. Africa. Also Sinai, Near and Mid-East as far as Central India. 9 ssp., 7 being African. This cat was formerly trained in Persia and India for catching hares and feathered game because of its extreme agility. HABITAT: open country (savannahs, plains, semi-deserts, sand deserts) in lowlands, hills and mountains. HOME RANGE: resident. A few or several sq km, according to food supply. Details not known. *Map* p. 227.
Habits. DAILY RHYTHM: crepuscular and nocturnal, but may be about by day. Patrols

widely, climbs well, sleeps in taken-over burrows, hollow trees, rock crevices, or in thick bush, sometimes in trees. VOICE: mostly non-vocal, growls and spits in anger. Calls its partner with a loud bark. SENSES: sight and hearing very good, scent moderate. ENEMIES: not known, though other predators may be a danger to the young. Takes refuge in trees. FOOD: all mammals from mouse to reedbuck size, all birds to greater bustard size. Catches birds on the wing by high jump. May attack sheep, goats, calves and poultry. Eats reptiles including poisonous snakes, taking these by surprise. May leap from trees or rocks on to prey. Will also eat some new grass, and fruit. SOCIABILITY: solitary.

Reproduction. Courting and pairing as in Kaffir Cat. Gestation 69–70 days. In subtropics breeds in spring, in tropics not restricted. Hidden den lined with fur and feathers. Litter 1–6, usually 2–3. Wt at birth $c.$ 300, at 12 days $\male$ $c.$ 560, $\female$ 500, at 2 months $\male$ $c.$ 1300, $\female$ $c.$ 1200. Eyes open at 6–9 days, leave den at 3 weeks, first solid food at 4 weeks, suckles for 6 months, independent at $\frac{3}{4}$–1 year. SEXUAL MATURITY: about 2 years. LONGEVITY: 17 years recorded.

SMALL CATS, FELINAE

Mostly domestic cat sized, but includes puma. Usually long-tailed, ears without tufts, claws retractile, tongue bone (hyoid) without epihyale. Dent.: $3 \cdot 1 \cdot 2 \cdot 3/2 \cdot 1 = 28$–30. 6–8 teats. Partly terrestrial, partly arboreal, nocturnal or diurnal predators on small animals or fish in open or forested areas. 14 genera, with 26 species, in New and Old Worlds apart from Australasia and Madagascar, of which 3 genera with 6 species are African.

SERVAL, *Leptailurus serval* (Schreber, 1776)   **Pl. 41**
G. Servalkatze F. Le Serval A. Tierboskat S. Mondo, Kisongo, Marara, Tschui mbara
Identification. Long-legged and size of Caracal, hind legs also longer than fore legs. Head comparatively small, ears large, broad at base, standing close together, high and pointed. Tail only $\frac{1}{3}$ HB. Upperside light ochreous to ochreous-brown or olive brown, underside white to whitish-grey or whitish-yellow. Light animals with large black spots in longitudinal rows; darker animals have numerous fine dots or blobs, giving a dusted nearly unicolorous effect on upperside. The pattern of light animals beginning on cheeks, forehead and neck, covering the body, fore breast and legs, and reaching to the belly. Tail with 6–7 brownish-black rings and black tip, backs of ears black, with a white spot. Dark stripe above eye and at corner of eye. In the dark animals a weak much reduced pattern on breast, belly, limbs and tail; spot on back of ear yellowish. The large-spotted, usually lighter type lives in dry savannah and steppe; the small-spotted to uniform, usually darker type (also known as Servaline Cat), lives in the moist savannah zones around the rain forests (the Guinea, Cameroun, Congo and Zaire closed forests). Intermediates of all stages between the two types. Melanos often occur (especially in the moist zones). Young coloured like adults, but pelage without underfur. Penis bone present; 8 teats. Dent.: $3 \cdot 1 \cdot 3/2 \cdot 1 = 30$, P^2 and M^1 small.
MEASUREMENTS: HB 65–90, TL 25–35, Ht 45–55, Wt 6–15.
Distribution. Africa south of 20°N, except the closed rain forests of W. and Central Africa. Formerly also in N.W. Africa, and S. to Cape Province, today extinct or very rare in N.W. Africa and S. of Orange Free State. 6 ssp. HABITAT: dry and moist savannahs, steppes, gallery forests, small woodlands, not in large forests. Vicinity of water and abundant cover (tall grass, reeds, bushes, rocky kloofs) necessary. Up to

3000m in mountains. HOME RANGE: resident. Range 1.5–3 sq km in area (exact details not known). Urine marking on bushes after capturing prey or meeting neighbours. Encounters usually peaceable. ♀♀ wander freely in ♂♂ territory.

Habits. DAILY RHYTHM: active by day, occasionally also at dusk or on moonlight nights. Main activity morning and afternoon, resting in shade during noonday heat. Occupies old burrows, thickets, rock crevices etc. VOICE: high-pitched repeated cry as call to partner; in annoyance or rage snarling, growling and spitting. When content purrs like domestic cat. SENSES: sight and hearing very good, scent moderate. ENEMIES: larger carnivora, and for young also smaller carnivora. Not very courageous. In emergency will take refuge in trees, climbs well. FOOD: hunts by sight and sound within its range; strong winds deter hunting. Prey is stalked and pounced on. Often plays with prey before eating it. Mammalian prey from mouse to oribi-sized, birds up to guinea fowl size. Grabs flying birds out of the air with a high leap; takes poultry, sometimes eats lizards, fish, insects, new grass and fruit. SOCIABILITY: solitary.

Reproduction. Mating as in Kaffir Cat. ♀ in heat for 1 day, gestation 67–77 days. Birthplace hidden among rocks, in thickets or burrows. Litter size 1–4, usually 2–3. Wt at birth c. 250, eyes open at 9–12 days, first solid food at 3 weeks, suckle for 6 months, independent at ¾–1 year. SEXUAL MATURITY: 2 years. LONGEVITY: up to 20 years in captivity.

Caracal   Serval   1 Sand Cat
                                                    2 Black-footed Cat

SAND CAT, *Felis (Otocolobus) margarita* (Loche, 1858)   **Pl. 42**
G. Sandkatze   F. Le Chat des sables

Identification. Form of Kaffir Cat, but rather smaller and stockier. Head broad, ears broad, wide apart, low set. Pelage soft and thick, soles of feet with long dark-brown to blackish fur, hiding the pads. Pelage lighter or darker yellowish-sandy colour, lower half of face, and underside, whitish. Stripe pattern as in Kaffir Cat, varying between distinctly obvious and nearly faded out. But also in latter case the dark brown ear-tips, cheeks, forehead, elbows, upper thigh stripes, sole hair pads, and a ring or spot in front of the black tail tip, remain. Young animals have a conspicuous pattern of dark to blackish-brown on the light fawn ground. As the sole pads grow, the body pattern becomes paler. External glands, penis bone, and dentition as in Kaffir Cat, but M^1 still smaller. In the skull the bony bullae (internal auditory structure) very large. The very low set ears and flat head enable stalking among rocks with minimum of exposure.
MEASUREMENTS: HB 43–52, TL 23–31, Ht 24–30, Wt ♂ 2.1–3.4, ♀ 1.5–3.1. ♂ somewhat larger and heavier than ♀.

Distribution. Deserts (including sand deserts) of North Africa (Saharan and Libyan deserts south to about 15°N); and across the Near East deserts to the Karakum and possibly Afghanistan. 4 ssp., one, the Sahara Sand Cat (*margarita* Loche, 1858) in Africa. Rare. HABITAT: see **Distribution**. HOME RANGE: not known, no doubt several sq km. Resident.

Habits. DAILY RHYTHM: wanders widely at dusk and by night, tirelessly, but does not climb willingly and is not a good jumper. On account of its very low population makes use of a loud mating call (see VOICE). By day avoiding the heat by lying up in old or new burrow (usually among dunes and under bushes) or among rocks in rock-strewn regions. TOILET: as in Kaffir Cat. VOICE: as in Kaffir Cat, but a very loud mewing mating or contact call, repeated more often. SENSES: hearing extremely good, sight very good, scent moderate. ENEMIES: poisonous snakes, jackals, large owls. Defence behaviour as in Kaffir Cat. FOOD: small mammals (above all desert rodents) which may be dug out of burrows, ground squirrels and other mammals up to size of hare; birds, reptiles, insects. SOCIABILITY: solitary.

Reproduction. Generally as in Kaffir Cat. Gestation 63 days, breeding season Mar–Apr, litter of 2–4, birthplace in burrow or among rocks. Wt at birth 50–60, HB *c.* 12, TL *c.* 6, Wt at 1 week *c.* 100, at 4 weeks over 300. Eyes open at 2 weeks, 1st venture outside at 3–3½ weeks, 1st solid food at 5 weeks, independent at 3–4 months. SEXUAL MATURITY: probably at 10–12 months. LONGEVITY: in captivity 8 years.

BLACK-FOOTED CAT, *Felis (Microfelis) nigripes* (Burchell, 1823)   **Pl. 42**

G. Schwarzfusskatze   F. Le Chat à pieds noirs   A. Swartpoot-Wildekat.

Identification. Build like Kaffir Cat, though about ⅓ smaller, with tail shorter. Ears rather rounded at the tip. General colour dark to light ochreous or sandy, in winter paler and more grey. Cheeks, throat, breast, belly and inside of legs whitish. Body pattern like Kaffir Cat, but spots larger and in part longish, brown to black, on shoulders also paler and with rusty suffusion. Throat with 3 dark brown to reddish unbroken stripes, cheeks with 2 reddish-brown stripes, forelegs with 3, hind legs with up to 5 black transverse stripes. Throat, breast and belly with transverse spots. Soles of feet black, with average length hairy pads. Tail above like back, fawn-ochreous below, tip black after 2–3 black rings following several incomplete dark brown transverse bands or spots. Pattern of ♀ distinctly more conspicuous and blacker than ♂. Young coloured like adults, but because of the closer pattern of spots seem much darker. External glands, penis bone and dentition as in Kaffir Cat, but P³ inner cusp reduced. Bony auditory bullae enlarged. MEASUREMENTS: HB ♂ 37–50, ♀ 34–37, TL ♂ 15–20, ♀ 16–18, Ht *c.* 25. Wt ♂ 2.5–2.75, ♀ 1.5–1.75.

Distribution. S. Africa from S. Angola and N. Botswana south through N. and M. S.W. Africa, Botswana, middle to S.E. Cape Province as well as Orange Free State and W. Transvaal, as well as northern part of Kruger National Park to southern Karroo. 2 ssp.: (1) *nigripes* Burchell, 1823; Cape Province. (2) *thomasi* Shortridge, 1931; rest of the species range. HABITAT: dry country (stony desert or Karroo, hard ground, sandy or semi-desert, steppes). HOME RANGE: like Sand Cat.

Habits. TOILET: like Kaffir Cat. VOICE: in relation to its thinly scattered population has a loud voice (like tiger but an octave higher) as call to mate. Young purr like domestic cats. SENSES: as Sand Cat. ENEMIES: as Sand Cat. At alarm young scatter and lie motionless until the mother gives the all clear (soft 'ah-ah-ah'). FOOD: small mammals up to ground-squirrel size, small birds, eggs, reptiles, insects. Some prey may be dug out. New grass sometimes eaten. SOCIABILITY: solitary.

Reproduction. ♀ heat lasts 5–10 hours, during which several matings, these as in

Kaffir Cat. Gestation 63–68 days. Litter size 1–2, born in burrow or other hiding place. Wt at birth 60–88, at 1 week *c*. 155, at 6 months ♂ *c*. 2500, ♀ *c*. 1500. Eyes open at 6–9 days, first solid food at 34–35 days, first capture of prey at 43–44 days. Independent at 3 months. LONGEVITY: 13 years in captivity.

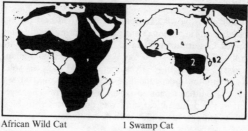

African Wild Cat

1 Swamp Cat
2 Golden Cat

AFRICAN WILD CAT, KAFFIR CAT,   Pl. 42
Felis (Felis) silvestris (Schreber, 1777) (= *libyca* Forster, 1780).
G. Falbkatze   F. Le Chat sauvage d'Afrique   A. Vaalboskat   S. Kimburu, Paka Pori

Identification. Form as domestic cat, but generally larger. Colour varies according to nature of environment between light sandy or light grey (in dry regions) to ochreous-brown (in moist areas). Underside (breast, belly, inside of legs) white to gold-cream colour. Spinal stripe weak or well developed. Sides of body with about 12 dark transverse bands, that may be reduced to spots, faded or entirely lost. In rain forest regions all-black varieties may occur. Below elbow and knee always 2 easily recognised pale brown to black transverse bands, tail with similar rings, tip black. Soles brownish to black. Forehead with 4 dark stripes or rows of small spots, cheeks with 2 horizontal pale brown to black stripes, and lower throat sometimes with 2 similar transverse stripes. Pelage of young like adults, seeming darker because of closer pattern. Dent.: 3 · 1 · 2–3/2 · 1 = 28–30. P^2 and M^1 set well back (the first can be absent). Circumanal gland in both sexes, 2 anal sacs in ♂, penis bone present. 6–8 teats. MEASUREMENTS: HB ♂ 50–73, ♀ 45–60, TL ♂ 25–33, ♀ 21–38, Ht 30–36, Wt ♂ 2.5–6, ♀ 1.5–4. ♂ somewhat larger and heavier than ♀.

Distribution. Whole of Africa apart from pure deserts, outside Africa to Mediterranean islands, all Europe except Scandinavia and Ireland (wild cats) (these considered by many authors to be distinct from the purely African *F. libyca* Forster, 1780). In Asia Minor, Near East, India (again possibly distinct). 23 ssp., of which 11 are in Africa. HABITAT: all types of country from semi-desert to rain forest, in mountains up to 4000m. Often near villages. Kittens reared become very tame house cats. HOME RANGE: resident. Range, according to food supply, several hectares or sq km (details not known). Area marked and defended by ♂.

Habits. DAILY RHYTHM: crepuscular and nocturnal; in cool cloudy weather also active by day. Normally during day hidden in tree, ground or rock holes and other refuges. TOILET: fur grooming by licking, washing face with forepaws, scratching with hind feet, claw sharpening on trunks or posts. VOICE: mewing, growling, spitting and hissing, screaming and purring as in domestic cats. SENSES: sight and hearing very good, scent average. ENEMIES: serval, caracal, golden cat, leopard, ratel, large owls. Kittens in den also in danger from jackals, civets, genets and other small carnivores as well as snakes. Climbs well, uses trees to escape. Defends its home with arched back and ruffled fur, growling, hissing and spitting, striking out with extended claws. FOOD: small to medium mammals and birds, reptiles, amphibians, fish, invertebrates, fruit. Can harm young game animals, lambs, kids, poultry. SOCIABILITY: solitary

Reproduction. Courting ♂ yowls like domestic cat. ♀ in heat for 2–3 days every 6 weeks, if not mated. ♀ sits in mating. Young born in spring in subtropics, all the years round in the tropics. Gestation 56–60 days. Litter 2–3 furred blind kittens in hidden den. Wt at birth 40–55, at 1 month c. 500, at 3½ months half adult weight, latter reached in ♀ at 1–1½ years, 1½–2 years in ♂. Eyes open at 9–11 days, 1st solid food about 1 month, suckle for 3 months, independent at 4–5 months. SEXUAL MATURITY: at 10 months (♀) – 12 (♂). 2 litters a year possible. LONGEVITY: 12–15 years. The Kaffir Cat is the origin of the domestic cat, and was domesticated in Mesopotamia and Palestine in 6000 BC. Interbreeds readily with domestic cats.

SWAMP CAT, *Felis (Chaus) chaus* (Guldenstaedt, 1776)   **Pl. 43**
G. Rohrkatze   F. Le Chat des marais

Identification. In build and appearance like a very large and noticeably long-legged Kaffir Cat with only a short tail (reaching only to hocks). Ears pointed, with small dark tuft. Colour sandy yellowish-brown to yellowish-red or yellowish-grey, the Kaffir Cat pattern only on head, legs and tail, faded and indistinct, tip of tail brownish-black to black. Body uniformly coloured or very finely speckled with darker colour, or with some washed-out indistinct spots. Underside yellowish. Middle of back, and backs of ears, darker brown. Young dark with distinct spotted pattern. External glands, penis bone and dentition as Kaffir Cat. MEASUREMENTS: HB ♂ 65–90, ♀ 60–85, TL ♂ 25–30, ♀ 20–28, Ht 40–48, Wt ♂ 5–12, ♀ 2.5–7.5. ♂ larger and heavier than ♀.

Distribution. Nile Delta and valley south of Quena Province (about 26°N), west to Mersa Matruh and Fayum (ssp. *nilotica* De Winton, 1898), as well as in A'Haggar and Tassili N'Adjer Mts., S. Algeria (ssp. not described). Outside Africa in Near and Middle East, S. Russia, India, and S.E. Asia to Indochina. 9 ssp., of which 1 or possibly 2 in Africa. HABITAT: swamps or moist regions with high grass, reed or rush beds, so prefers vicinity of water in woodland or on river banks. Frequents neighbourhood of villages, also fields of corn, sugar cane, cotton and maize, in gardens etc. HOME RANGE: resident. Range up to some km square (however details not known). *Map* p. 229.

Habits. DAILY RHYTHM: mainly crepuscular and nocturnal, but may be seen by day. Runs, climbs and swims well. Lies up in dry places among reeds etc., under thickets, or in old burrows (rarely self dug), or among rocks and ruins, abandoned buildings etc. TOILET: as Kaffir Cat. VOICE: as Kaffir Cat. Young purr like domestic cats, adults have repeated loud harsh mewing as mating call. SENSES: sight and hearing very good, scent moderate. ENEMIES: few; formerly principally leopard (no longer found in Egypt). Young may be at risk from jackals, civets etc. Courageous, ♀ defends kittens vigorously, if cornered will attack man. Defensive behaviour as in Kaffir Cat. FOOD: small to medium-sized mammals and birds, waterfowl, eggs, often raids poultry. May take lambs, kids and young game animals, sometimes also game up to roe or gazelle size. Eats snakes, lizards, frogs and fish. SOCIABILITY: solitary.

Reproduction. Much as in Kaffir Cat. Rutting time Feb–Mar, gestation 66 days, litter size 3–5, kittens born in hiding places. Wt at birth 45–55. Eyes open at 10–12 days, suckle for 2 months, independent at 5 months. SEXUAL MATURITY: 1½ years. LONGEVITY: 12–15 years.

GOLDEN CAT, *Profelis aurata* (Temminck, 1827)   **Pl. 43**
G. Goldkatze   F. Le Chat doré

Identification. Middle-sized (twice size of Kaffir Cat), legs rather short and sturdy, ears short and rounded, tail of medium length. Pelage short and soft, hair of neck from crown to shoulders directed forward. Ground colour of upperside varies from wine or brownish-red to dark slate-grey, underside (cheeks, chin, throat, breast, belly, inside of legs) white to greyish-white or light creamy. Back of ears black, spot at edge of eyes whitish. Broad zone on back more or less darkened. Pattern of large dark brown to black spots on upper and undersides or on neck and back, or, on upperside, smaller and less distinct or finely speckled spotting, which may be totally lacking on upperside and only found on underside. Tail with up to 12 conspicuous or weak rings; tail tip, like upperside, darkened. Conspicuous pattern of spots predominantly in the Western Golden Cat (*aurata*) from Gambia to Togo, merging into a dark base in the Congo or Eastern Golden Cat (*cottoni*), Cameroun to W. Kenya. Melanistic specimens in both not uncommon. Young coloured like adults. Penis bone present, number of teats not known. Dent.: as Kaffir Cat, M^1 very small, P^2 very small or absent. MEASUREMENTS: HB 72–93, TL 35–45, Ht *c.* 50, Wt 8–16.

Distribution. Equatorial Africa from Gambia to W. Kenya, absent from Nigeria. Northern limit about 8°N, southern about 5°–7°S. 2 ssp. (see **Identification**). HABITAT: Rain forests in lowlands and mountains, up to 2000m. Also on forest edges and in gallery forests.   HOME RANGE: not known. *Map* p. 229.

Habits. DAILY RHYTHM: active at dusk and at night; mainly arboreal, sleeping also in trees by day.   TOILET: as Kaffir Cat.   VOICE: young purr when contented, hiss and spit in anger.   SENSES and ENEMIES: not known.   FOOD: mammals up to size of small antelopes, birds up to guinea-fowl size, occasionally also poultry.   SOCIABILITY: solitary.

Reproduction. No details known, in fact one of least known animals. Young probably born in hole in tree.

Primates

Prosimians, Prosimii

LEMURS, LEMURIDAE

Mouse- to cat-sized monkey-like animals. Head roundish, muzzle more or less pointed, eyes large. Ears small to mid-sized. Pelage close, woolly. Limbs of medium length, hind legs rather longer than arms. Digits 5/5, finger and toe-tips rounded, first toe more or less opposable; 2nd toe of hind foot with claw-like nail (used for grooming), finger nails otherwise pointed. Tail long and furry like bottle brush. Dent.: $0-2/2 \cdot 1/1 \cdot 3/3 \cdot 3/3 = 32-36$. Lower incisors and canines strongly projecting forward, cheek teeth pointed, molars 3-cusped. 2–6 teats. Penis pendant, with bone (as in clitoris). Usually once, rarely twice a year, one or sometimes 2–3 young, born with eyes open after gestation of 54–150 days, and carried by mother. Usually nocturnal, some species also diurnal. Terrestrial or more often arboreal, mainly vegetarian but sometimes also eat small animals. Sociable, living in families or tribes, but partly also solitary, mother-child group. Except *Hapalemur*, are not swimmers. Very clean, without outer (nearly without internal) parasites or body scent. Fur-grooming done without hands, using teeth, tongue, and grooming claw on hind foot. 6 genera, with altogether 14 species, only in Madagascar.

BLACK LEMUR, *Lemur (Prosimia) macaco* (Linnaeus, 1766)　　　　**Pl. 44**
(= *fulvus* E. Geoffroy St Hilaire, 1812)
G. Mohrenmaki　F. Le Maki dimorphisme　MA. Akomba, Varika, Varikoy
Identification. Cat-sized. Pelage dense and soft, face short-haired, tail thickly bushy, longer than HB, legs longer than arms. Pointed fox-like muzzle, eyes large, ears small, roundish, with short or long marginal fringes. Cheeks with or without whiskers, when present long or short. Thumb and great toe short, widely opposable, latter twice as wide as the other toes; second toe with claw instead of flat nail. Tips of fingers and toes with broad sensitive pads, similarly the palms of hands and soles of feet, the skin between horny; heel hairy. Upper surface of hands and feet hairy, skin naked around anus and vagina. Both penis and clitoris with bone. Prepuce spiny, scrotum hairy and pendulous, clitoris narrow and pendulous, 2 pectoral teats. Long contact hairs on wrist. Dent.: $2 \cdot 1 \cdot 3 \cdot 3 = 36$. Upper incisors rudimentary, minute pegs; lower incisors and incisiform lower canines very narrow, long, projecting forward in comb-like way; upper canine long and sharp-edged, P_2 caniniform. Young of both sexes at first coloured alike, at 6 weeks have colour of adults. Latter vary from white to black and grey to orange or red or dark brown, sexes usually different .8 ssp.[1]: (1) Black Lemur, *macaco* Linnaeus, 1766, N.W. Madagascar, Ambanja district with Ampasindava Bay and Nossi-Be Island. With long ear fringes, ♂ entirely black, ♀ reddish-brown; ear fringes, whiskers and rump spot white, underside whitish-grey to cream, tail like back or yellowish-brown, yellowish-white or white. Young black, ♀ at 6 months generally brown. (2) Sanford's Lemur, *sanfordi* Archbold, 1932; Ambre Mts, N. Madagascar. Ear fringe short. ♂ with upperside brownish-grey, underside pale grey, nose and tail black, forehead and rump spot grey, ear fringe white; whiskers orange, tail tip white. ♀

1. Many authors consider *macaco* and *flavifrons* to be one species, *macaco*.

brownish-grey, without whiskers and rump spot. (3) Sclater's Lemur, *flavifrons* Gray, 1867, N.W. Madagascar, Maromandia district, nearly extinct. Like (1) but without ear fringes; short forehead crest. (4) White-fronted Lemur, *albifrons* E. Geoffroy St Hilaire, 1796. N.E. Madagascar, between Andapa and Mananara. No ear fringe. Upperside greyish-brown, underside greyish-white, muzzle and tip of tail black, around face (crown, ears, whiskers) white in ♂, greyish-white in ♀. Albinism not uncommon. (5) Brown Lemur, *fulvus* E. Geoffroy St Hilaire, 1812. E. Madagascar south of *albifrons* as far as Andovoranto. In ♂ top of head, ears, and muzzle, black; ear fringe white. (6) Collared Lemur, *collaris* E. Geoffroy St Hilaire, 1812. S.E. Madagascar, south of *fulvus*, south to Fort Dauphin. No ear fringe. Upperside dark brown, often a blackish spinal stripe, underside dirty whitish-grey to whitish-yellow, orange cheeks, light supraorbital spot, blackish face, reddish brown tail, suffused with black. (7) Red-fronted Lemur, *rufus* Audebert, 1800. Large part of W. Madagascar between Marindo Bay in N. and Fiherenana in S. No ear fringe. ♂ with grey upperside, washed with red, underside ochreous, muzzle black, whitish eye-rings. Top of head, and tail, red, tail tip black. ♀ with upperside reddish-brown, underside pale red, head grey, cheeks orange. (8) Mayotte Lemur, *mayottensis* Schlegel, 1886. Mayotte I., Comoros. No ear fringe. Upperside pale olive, underside lighter, face and pygal spot black, supraorbital spot white. MEASUREMENTS: HB 35–40, TL 45–50, Wt *c*. 2.

Distribution. Madagascar; and Mayotte I., Comoros. Ssp. (1), (2), (7) seriously endangered, (7) possibly extinct. HABITAT: forests, according to region either evergreen rain forests or seasonally deciduous forests. TERRITORY: each troop has area of about 5–40 hectares according to type of forest, in *fulvus* very small (0.75–1 hectare). Both sexes mark area with urine, and by ♂ with skin gland secretions of underarm and naked anal region. ♂ rubs flanks and forehead where ♀ has urinated. In *fulvus* strong overlapping of territory. Area defended against neighbouring troops by voice and threatening gestures. Groups separated in the territory during day may share common sleeping place at night. Population density in *fulvus* high, 900–1200 per sq km. *Map* p. 235.

Habits. DAILY RHYTHM: active morning, late afternoon and evening, in breeding season also at mid-day, sometimes also on clear nights. Arboreal (*fulvus*) and terrestrial. Very active in trees, very good jumper (up to 6m wide), landing on all fours on branches and twigs, balancing with tail: climbs upward hand over hand. In emergency leaps to ground and takes refuge in undergrowth. TOILET: fur grooming by licking and nibbling; where muzzle and comb-like lower incisors cannot reach, uses combing claw of second hind toe. Tail held in hands for grooming. Mutual grooming common. VOICE: short, coughing, many times repeated as contact call, or varying from deep to high, soft to loud, according to circumstances. Barks in threat, screeches in fear of enemies or under other tensions. Young purr like cats, whine if lost, squeal in fear. SENSES: hearing and sight very good, colour and definition ability outstanding (the retina with fovea centralis and many cones). Scent good, probably important for sexual and individual recognition. ENEMIES: in mammals, the fossa; in birds, the banded gymnogene (*Polyboroides radiatus*). FOOD: above all, leaves, shoots, fruits, berries. Whether animal food is included in the wild is uncertain, though in captivity lemurs eat meat gladly. Drink either dew or rain water, sometimes licking water from hands after dipping into water in tree holes. SOCIABILITY: in family troops of ♂♂, ♀♀ and young under leadership of an old ♂; up to about 17.

Reproduction. Pairing season Apr–Jun, gestation 120–133 days, young born Aug–Oct. Mate standing. Usually 1 young; twins not uncommon, triplets rare. Young born fully haired with eyes open, weigh about 80gm, cling tightly to mother's belly fur.

♀ licks young dry and eats the afterbirth. Young rides on mother's back at 3 weeks, at 1 month eats 1st solid food. 1st leaves the mother occasionally at 2 months, is weaned at 5 and is independent at 6 months. SEXUAL MATURITY: ♂ at 1½ years, first breeds at about 2½ years if strong enough to win a mate. LONGEVITY: up to 30 years in captivity.

RED-BELLIED LEMUR, Pl. 44
Lemur (Prosimia) rubriventer (I. Geoffroy St Hilaire, 1850)
G. Rotbauchmaki   F. Le Lĕmur à ventre rouge   MA. Soameria
Identification. Generally similar to *L. macaco*, but nails (apart from thumbs, great and second toes, which are as in *mongoz*) keeled and pointed. Perineal area hairy, a naked skin fold between anus and vulva, clitoris pendulous with acorn-like tip. Penis ?. ♂ almost entirely chestnut-brown, tail brownish-black, underside coppery-red, belly yellowish-red, scrotum brownish-black, hands and feet reddish, narrow ring round eye greyish-blue, sometimes whitish spot at inner corner of eye. ♀ with upperside umber, tail brownish-black, underside creamy, face and mid-forehead dark brown, cheeks yellowish-white. Young like adults, but with head coppery-red with black nose stripe. MEASUREMENTS: HB 40–45, TL 42–50, Wt 1.8–2.2.
Distribution. Rain forests of E. Madagascar. No ssp.
Habits. In most ways as *mongoz*, details however not known.

MONGOOSE LEMUR, *Lemur (Prosimia) mongoz* (Linnaeus, 1766)   Pl. 62
G. Mongozmaki   F. Le Lémur mongoz   MA. Akomba, Ankomba, Gidro
Identification. Form, pelage and most details as in *L. macaco*, only muzzle shorter and skin of perineal area hairy. Small circumanal skin glands. 2 ssp.: (1). True Mongoose Lemur, *mongoz* Linnaeus, 1766. W. Madagascar, south of Betsiboka R., a 15–90km broad strip from coast to Ankaratra mountains, and in Comoro Is., on Grand Comoro, Anjouan and Moheli. In ♂ crown, neck, shoulders dark grey, back, thighs, arms and outside of legs reddish-brown to brownish-grey, cheeks, upper throat and sides of neck reddish-brown; back of nose, lower throat, front of breast, hands and feet, whitish-grey: rest of underside reddish-yellow, first half of tail reddish-brown, remainder grey with darker tip. ♀ like ♂, only tail, hands, feet and face blackish, cheeks and underside of body white. (2). Crowned Mongoose Lemur, *coronatus* Gray, 1842. N. Madagascar, north of a line between Bombetoka Bay in west and Antongil Bay in east. In ♂, upperside brownish-grey to reddish-grey, underside greyish-white to pale red, scrotum brownish-black, tail reddish-brown, muzzle with area round eyes and ears, whitish-grey, black ring around light eye-ring, black triangle on crown, cheeks reddish. In ♀ upperside light to mid-grey, ears, back of nose, cheeks and underside of body whitish. Front edge of forehead light orange (the crown, hair lengthened). Young ♀ grey like mother, ♂ reddish-grey with dark crown. Ears and area around eyes light grey, nostrils and front of snout black, light nose-frontal stripe, dark spot above eye with long tactile hairs as on snout. On inside of lower arms small glands with 4 tactile hairs. MEASUREMENTS: HB 40–45, TL 40–45, Wt 1.8–2.2.
Distribution. Madagascar and Comoro Is. (see **Identification**). Threatened. HABITAT: dry forests and savannahs, in mountains to 800m, also in some districts with thick low bush. TERRITORY: no details known.
Habits. DAILY RHYTHM: mainly diurnal and arboreal, quieter and less conspicuous in behaviour than *L. macaco*. Very good climber and jumper, lands from jump on all fours, tail held upright in jumping, rolled up in threat. Both sexes mark with anal glands. VOICE: quickly repeated grunts as contact call, 'cru-cru-cru' cry in rising

excitement. Young squeak when uneasy, buzz when contented. TOILET, SENSES, ENEMIES: as *macaco*. SOCIABILITY: in family parties of 4–8 (1 old ♂, several ♀ and young).

Reproduction. Seasons as in *macaco*. Gestation 114–128 days, usually 1 young, 8% twins. Rearing of young as in *macaco*. Young ride on mother's back at 14 days, first leave her at 18–20 days; first solid food at 30 days, at 2 months independent, weaned at 5 months. SEXUAL MATURITY: about 1½ years. Wt at birth 55–61, HB 10–14, TL 13–14. LONGEVITY: 26 years recorded in captivity.

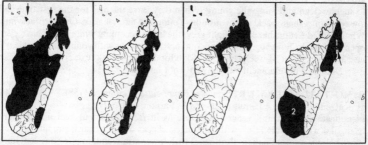

| Black Lemur | Red-bellied Lemur | Mongoose Lemur | 1 Ruffed Lemur |
| | | | 2 Ring-tailed Lemur |

RUFFED LEMUR, *Lemur (Varecia) variegatus* (Kerr, 1792)   **Pl. 44**
G. Vari   F. Le Maki vari   MA. Varikandra, Varimena, Varikossi

Identification. Form, fur, hands and feet, and teeth as in *L. macaco*, but larger and fur somewhat longer. Face, apart from forehead, with longer ruff, beginning above the ears and encircling them, as in *L. catta*. Perineal area short-haired. Penis bone *c.* 1cm, clitoris bone *c.* 0.3cm; prepuce without horny spines, 6 teats (2 on breast, 4 on belly). Wrist with long tactile hairs. Colour conspicuously black and white, or brownish-black and white, or brown and white, or foxy red and white. Usually face (in part without cheeks), hands, feet, underside and tail black or brownish-black; ruff, lower arms and legs white. 3 ssp.: (1) Black or Black and White Ruffed Lemur; *variegatus* Kerr, 1792 (Pl. 44/4) besides, in the same region, the red representative, Red-Ruffed Lemur (*ruber*, E. Geoffroy St Hilaire, 1812); face and hands, feet and tail brownish-black, ruff, body, arms and legs foxy-red, neck spot and heel ring white (Pl. 44/7). N.E. Madagascar, from Port Loki bay in N., south to Antongil Bay, in latter on Mangabe Is. (2) White-girdled Ruffed Lemur, *editorum* O. Hill, 1953; like Black and White Ruffed Lemur, however the black parts red to dark brown (Pl. 44/5); N.E. Madagascar west of (1) and (3), as far as the edge of the high plateau. (3) Brown Ruffed Lemur, *subcinctus* (A. Smith, 1833), resembling Black Ruffed Lemur but with back olive brown (Pl. 44/6). E. Madagascar from Antongil Bay south to Perinet (18°S). Interspecific colour variation great, so that ssp. still not certain. MEASUREMENTS: HB *c.* 60, TL *c.* 60, Wt 4–5.

Distribution. N.E. and E. Madagascar, details see above. HABITAT: rain forests. TERRITORY: little known, apart from voice (q.v.), no physical marking.

Habits. DAILY RHYTHM: most activity at dusk and first half of night; like to sunbathe in early morning, sitting up with spread-out arms and legs. Little activity by day, resting in noon heat. Agile leaper and climber among the boughs, rarely on ground. TOILET: grooming of fur by licking and nibbling. VOICE: grunting when watchful, often repeated, increasing with growing excitement. Young have piping call to mother, her answer in lower pitch. A far-reaching echoing howling, used as territorial marking, begun by ♂ with other members of the family joining in; neighbouring families reply in chorus, repeated over several seconds and abruptly broken off. Sometimes a very loud gurgle is interspersed in this chorus. SENSES, ENEMIES: not known. FOOD: fruit, leaves, bark. SOCIABILITY: live in families of 2–5 animals.

Reproduction. Gestation 99 days, births in Nov, 1–3 young (about 30% twins, about 30% triplets. ♀ lines a nest in hole in tree, or in fork of branches, or among epiphyte mould, with her own fur pulled out of flanks or thighs. Licks young dry and eats afterbirth. ♀ covers young with her body for the first days, thereafter comes regularly to suckle, clean and nurse the young. When they leave the nest for the first time she always brings them back in her mouth. Young are finely-haired (in the Black and White Ruffed Lemur black and light grey, the latter becoming white later), have eyes open and weigh about 50g. ♂ stays away at first, later plays with young, who first leave nest at 1 week, after 3½ weeks take first solid food, after 4 weeks exercise actively near nest. Details of development and longevity not known.

RING-TAILED LEMUR, *Lemur (Lemur) catta* (Linnaeus, 1758)　　**Pl. 44**
G. Katzenmaki　F. Le Lémur catta　MA. Varikia, Gidro, Hira

Identification. Form and general structure as in *L. macaco*, but heel naked. Ears triangular with rounded tips, without fringes, cheeks without beard, circumanal area short-haired, scrotum naked. Both sexes with lower arm gland, in ♂ about 2cm long and 1·8cm broad naked area of skin on the inside, with a lateral short horny spur and naked strip of skin as far as wrist; in ♀ gland only half this size and without the spur. ♂ with upper arm gland, a sunken sac and short-haired area in axillary region. Further glands by scrotum below root of penis; and chin gland; ♀ with vulva and clitoris glands. Nostrils, muzzle, ring round eyes, soles of hands and feet, scrotum, and the 12–14 tail rings as well as tail tip, black; rest of tail rings, rest of face, ears, upperside of hands and feet, and underside of body white. Neck, shoulders and upperside of body pearl grey. Young like adults. MEASUREMENTS: HB *c.* 45, TL *c.* 55, Wt 2.4–3.7.

Distribution. S.W. Madagascar from Morondava R. south to Cape St Marie and Fort Dauphin, east to foot of the high mountains. No ssp. HABITAT: dry woodland districts with 7–8 month dry season, and annual rainfall not more than 40 inches. Ground can be sandy or stony. TERRITORY: resembling *L. macaco*, each troop with 4–24 hectares. Population density can be 150–350 animals to each sq km, depending on food sufficiency. Territory marked by ♂♂ with underarm, scrotal, palm glands and loud 'uhu' calls; by ♀♀ with vulval glands (also placed, like ♂, in hand stands), with horizontally-forward-stretched tail on thin smooth stems, on ground or on low branches; the secretion mark up to 70cm long, clearly visible. ♂♂ rank highest, ♀♀ mark more or less as subjects. Any excitement leads to marking. The troop may live for some days in part of the territory, then move on to another part. Territorial boundary may remain unchanged for several years. *Map* p. 235.

Habits. DAILY RHYTHM: active mainly in early morning and late afternoon, resting mid-day in shade of crown foliage of trees. In dormitory tree in evening still active up to dark, sometimes also at night, calling frequently in pairing season. Occupies all tiers of the forest, and also much ground activity, with tail upright. Sometimes stands erect. Climbs very actively horizontally and vertically, makes wide leaps, landing hind feet first, can survive a 15m fall to ground without harm. Likes to sunbathe in morning sitting upright with outspread arms. Sleeps with head and arms between legs, and tail wrapped round. Daytime rest in lower tiers, sleeps in upper tiers of forest. TOILET: grooming, also mutually, scratching with fingers or with cleaning claw of second toe.

Tail rúbbing, see **Reproduction**. Urination and defecation on all fours (not marking) serves also to deter dogs and men from the neighbourhood. VOICE: short grunting as contact call within troop (rarely as in *macaco*), quickly following bark in excitement, also in choruses. Many other cries in varied circumstances, including the loud hoot of old ♂♂ as territorial marking (heard 1km distant). SENSES: sight good, especially at night (retina with cones and fovea centralis) for colour and sharpness definition. Hearing and scent also good. ENEMIES: large birds of prey, and fossas. FOOD: fruit, blooms, leaves, bark, grass, herbage. Water needs met by licking dew or rain drops, or by licking hands after dipping in tree hole rain water. May drink from river or may rely on fruit juices. SOCIABILITY: in families or kindred groups, usually 1–2 dozen, sometimes 4 dozen animals. ♀♀ with young form base of troop, ranking higher than ♂♂, stay lifelong in the troop, whereas ♂♂ change about. Neighbouring troops not considered as direct enemies.

Reproduction. Pairing time Apr–Jun. ♂♂ fight among themselves, making provocative leaping attacks. Use threatening gestures, staring and baring teeth, standing on hind legs rubbing tail with upper and lower arm glandular secretions: in all fours position with tail over back leap around each other and strike downwards with canine teeth. Heat of ♀ lasts ½ day, mating several times with 1 or more ♂♂, in standing position, duration 3 minutes. Gestation 132–136 days. Usually 1 well-haired young with eyes open, however about 15% twins, about the same triplets. ♀ eats afterbirth and licks young dry. Wt at birth 50–85, HB *c.* 15, TL *c.* 18. Young sits upright on mother's belly, after 2–3 weeks creeps on her back, at 3 weeks climbs about, first solid food after 4 weeks, at 6 months weaned and independent, at 1½ years fully grown and sexually mature, though ♂ mates first at 2½ years. LONGEVITY: in captivity 20 years.

WEASEL LEMUR, *Lepilemur mustelinus* (I. Geoffroy St Hilaire, 1851)   **Pl. 45**
G. Wieselmaki   F. Le Lepilémur mustélin
MA. Fitiliki, Hattock, Repahaka, Bohenglie

Identification. Like a Lemur, but smaller and muzzle shorter. Ears rather large, oval, bare-skinned, only in the ssp. *dorsalis* short, rounded and nearly hidden in fur. Tail as long as head and body, and thickly bushy, hind legs longer than fore legs, hand and foot structure much as in Red-bellied Lemur (p. 234). Whiskers and supraorbital tactile hairs well developed, wrist without tactile hairs, skin glands absent except on scrotum. Latter hairy up to the lower side glandular area and perineal area. Penis with bone, prepuce with small horny spines, clitoris leaf-shaped. 2 teats. Dent.: as in *Lemur*, permanent upper incisors usually absent, P^1 single, M^3 tri-cusped, P^2 spatulate, P^3 and P^4 single-cusped, lower molars narrow and 4-cusped. Fur thick and woolly, upperside brown, reddish-brown, or greyish-beige, sometimes with a darker spinal line, sometimes only on neck. In brown and reddish-brown animals, face light brown to greyish-beige, lower and insides of legs light grey, end of tail darker than base. Sometimes sides of neck to shoulders beige. In the greyish-beige animals, cheeks, eye-ring, lower and inside of legs white. Tail brownish to reddish, tip sometimes white. Young as in adults. MEASUREMENTS: HB 25–35, TL 20–30, Wt 600–800.

Distribution. Rain and dry forests of Madagascar. 5 ssp. (According to Rumpler and Albignac (1975), *Lepilemur* can be divided on chromosome study grounds into several (for the time being 7) species, including the following named ssp. and adding *rufescens* Lorenz-Liburnau, 1898, and *septentrionalis* Rumpler and Albignac 1974): (1) Greater Weasel Lemur, *mustelinus* I. Geoffroy St Hilaire, 1851; E. Madagascar from Tamatave to near Vohemar. (2) Light-necked Weasel Lemur, *microdon* Forsyth Major, 1894; south of (1), from Tamatave south to near Fort Dauphin. (3) Dry-bush Weasel Lemur, *leucopus* Forsyth Major, 1894; dry bush country wholly in south, between Fort Dauphin and Ambovombe. (4) Lesser Weasel Lemur, *ruficaudatus* Grandidier, 1867; all the west, from the extreme north southward to Tulear. (5). Island Weasel Lemur, *dorsalis* Gray, 1870; Island of Nosy Be on N.W. coast. Ssp. (3) and (4) seriously threatened, (5) rare. HABITAT: rain and dry forests, in mountains up to 1200m. TERRITORY: small, only some 10m around the sleeping hole. Each ♀ (usually with young) has its own territory, defended against other ♀♀. 1 ♂ has a territory of 0.2–0.5 hectares, overlapping 2–5 ♀ territories and defended against other ♂♂. Defence by threat calls, threat postures (boxing with forearms) and biting. ♂♂ often sit calling against each other. *Leucopus* population density in gallery forest may be as high as 400–450 to a sq km; in dry bush *c.* 200–300.

Habits. DAILY RHYTHM: nocturnal, most active after nightfall, calling usually at that time, however feeding period only short. Much display of territory watching, however, inactive for large part of the night. By day resting in tree holes (*dorsalis* in bush foliage). Sleep with head tucked between fore legs and tail wrapped round. In cool or wet weather little activity. Much screaming in pairing season. Entirely arboreal, going short distances on all fours, otherwise in a series of quick jumps on hind legs, also from tree to tree; usually sitting up. TOILET: not known. SENSES: sight very good both by day and night, large tapetum lucidum, ensuring safety in nocturnal leaps; probably colour sharp. Waking and sleeping periods are determined by a comparatively narrow range of light gradations: 4.30–4.45 in morning, and 18.20–18.23 evenings (in open bushland around 18.08, in thick forest about 18.16). Hearing very good, scent good. VOICE: territory marking and defence calls loud, suddenly broken off; often a duet or trio between ♂♂ sitting not far apart. Warning cry of anger, calls of ♀ to young. Meeting of sexes 'hiii'. Also growling and other sounds. Sometimes calls are subspecifically or specifically distinct. ENEMIES: fossas, and nocturnal birds of prey. SOCIABILITY: see TERRITORY. FOOD: mainly leaves and bark, also flowers and fruit. Refection (reingestion of foecal droppings as in some rodents and rabbits).

Reproduction. Pairing season May–Jul, litters Sep–Oct. Gestation 4½–5 months. Usually 1 hairy young, with eyes open, nestles in belly fur of mother, is left behind in tree hole while she is out feeding. In danger mother will carry young in mouth. First solid food at 1½ months, at 1 month can climb, at 2 months jump. Suckling period 4 months. Size at birth, HB 12, TL 8. Fully grown and sexually mature at 1½ years. Young stays with mother for 1 year. LONGEVITY: not known.

GREY GENTLE LEMUR, *Hapalemur griseus* (Link, 1795)   Pl. 45
G. Kleinerhalbmaki   F. Le Hapalémur gris   MA. Bokombouli

Identification. Thickset, short-legged, long-tailed, rather short-limbed. Head round, muzzle short, pug-like nostrils, depressed, with transverse fold. Eyes medium-sized, ears short, round, hairy. Tail bushy, longer than head and body. Hind legs only a little longer than arms. Hands and feet almost as in *Lemur macaco*, only nails pointed (second toe also with claw). Pelage thick and soft. Long whiskers, tactile hair tufts high above each eye, and on wrists; perineal region and scrotum hairy. Penis with bone, and without horny spines. Both sexes with stripe-like horny lower arm gland (0.5cm broad, 2–3cm long), ♂ with upper arm gland, near axilla (both like *Lemur catta*). 4 teats (2 breast, 2 axillary). Dent.: $2 \cdot 1 \cdot 3 \cdot 3 = 36$; upper small incisors persistent, lower incisors very narrow, strongly projecting forward (serving as scrapers), canines short and strong, hardly longer than P^2, premolars with serrated cutting edge. Upperside greyish-green to olive-brown; cheeks, ears, ring around eyes, and tail, grey; hands and feet blackish-brown, underside yellowish-grey to greyish-brown, belly. and inside of legs orange. Young like adults. MEASUREMENTS: HB 32–36, TL 32–36, Wt ?.

Distribution. 3 ssp.: (1) Western Grey Gentle Lemur, *occidentalis* Rumpler and Albignax, 1975; W. and N. Madagascar from Ampasindava Bay and Tsaratanana south to Cape St Marie and Fort Dauphin, east to the high mountain ridge. Endangered. (2) Eastern Grey Gentle Lemur, *griseus* (Link, 1795); S.E. Madagascar from high mountain ridge to the coast from Fort Dauphin north to Fianarantsoa. (3) Larger Grey Gentle Lemur, *alaotrensis* (Rumpler and Albignac, 1975). Lake Alaotra region (central E. Madagascar), larger than (1) and (2). In mountains up to 1000m or more. HABITAT: rain and dry forests, in the first prefers bamboo thickets. At Alaotra Lake in broad reed zone. TERRITORY: 1 troop (see SOCIABILITY) lives in 3–4 bamboo thickets; further details not known.

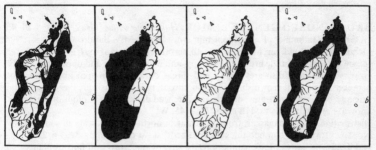

Weasel Lemur   Grey Gentle Lemur   Broad-nosed   Lesser Mouse Lemur
                                       Gentle Lemur

Habits. DAILY RHYTHM: in early morning climbing among the bamboo stem tops, which they eat. With rising of the sun they seek shade, where they rest until 16.00, then a further feeding period until nightfall, 20.00. Rest of night sleeping. Body temperature swings within a few days between 32°–36°C. In reed beds the same cycle. Sleeping position with head between legs, tail wrapped round. Frequently sits upright (also while feeding on the ground); agile climber, makes wide leaps in upright position like Indri. At Lake Alaotra leaps upright among the reeds, or runs quickly on all fours over the carpet of water plants, swims well. Both sexes mark all objects in neighbourhood with urine drops, ♀ presses sexual organs and belly on the ground; ♂ also rubs arm glands on ground, branches or tail. TOILET: as *Lemur macaco*. VOICE: purrs when contented, low grunting as contact call during diurnal activity, various other cries of threat, alarm, fear, pain or as territory marking. ♀ on heat whistles and cries in excitement, both sexes have sharp cry in mating. Aggressive ♀ bares teeth and screams. SENSES: sight and hearing very good (as in other nocturnal lemurs eyes adapted for night vision and colour). Scent sense valuable for near-orientation (sniffing at surroundings). ENEMIES: ring-tailed Lemurs, banded gymnogenes (hole kites), Madagascar buzzard, Death adders. Threatened, stands erect with ears laid back in threat, tail waving, and lower arm glands active; threat call. When hunted, may remain still for a long time in foliage, or leap from bough to bough in flight; in extreme danger will fall to ground and hide. Young 2 weeks old will fall off as mother flees. FOOD: bamboo shoots and leaves. Slender pieces are bitten off and leaves stripped off by passing with hands through mouth, afterwards shoots bitten and leaves eaten. At Lake Alaotra reed and papyrus shoots are handled the same way. SOCIABILITY: in small troops; 1 old ♂, 1–2 ♀♀ and 1–2 young live close together in 3–4 nearby bamboo thickets. Similarly in the Lake Alaotra reed beds, where, however, in the rainy season with high water levels, several troops unite to form a horde of 30–40, making a good deal of noise.

Reproduction. Pairing season Sep–Oct, at Lake Alaotra Oct–Nov. Mate in standing position, ♂ grasps ♀ legs with arms. Duration about 5 minutes. Gestation about 140 days. Births in Dec–Jan, or Jan–Feb. 1 young, fully-haired, chocolate-coloured, with open eyes and fully developed tail. Wt at birth *c*. 50. Young are born in nesthole or in dense foliage (in that case lying motionless and quiet) and only occasionally carried (at breast or on hips or across the back). ♀ licks young assiduously, and ♂ also helps, friendly to young. Suckling time ½ year. SEXUAL MATURITY: at 2 years. LONGEVITY: not known.

BROAD-NOSED GENTLE LEMUR, *Hapalemur simus* (Gray, 1870)   Pl. 45
G. Grosser Halbmaki   F. Le Hapalémur à nez large   MA. Bandro

Identification. Build, fur, hands, feet, teeth, scrotum and teats as in *H. griseus*, however somewhat larger, muzzle broad and stumpy, and without lower and upper arm glands. Upperside dark reddish-grey, rump and thighs darker, rump spot above tail root ochreous, end of tail brownish-black; chin, throat, breast whitish-grey; cheeks, orbital ring and belly yellowish-grey, muzzle and forehead dark brown. Colour of young not known. MEASUREMENTS: HB *c*. 45, TL *c*. 45, Wt ?.

Distribution. E. Madagascar, from Vohemar in north to Fianaranta in south. Rare. No ssp. HABITAT: bamboo thickets, reed beds, sugar cane stands. *Map* p. 239.

Habits. Little known. Eats bamboo, reeds, sugar cane, grass and fibrous plants. No fruit. Spends large part of day feeding unhurriedly. Normal voice a duck-like quacking. A loud scream in fear. One animal was kept in captivity for 12 years.

LESSER MOUSE-LEMUR, *Microcebus murinus* (J. F. Miller, 1777)   Pl. 46
G. Mausmaki   F. Le Chirogale nain   MA. Tilg, Tsidy, Kely-he-ohy.

Identification. Lemur-like, but not much larger than a mouse. Head round, muzzle short, eyes and ears large, latter nearly naked, tips rounded; in ssp. *smithi* ears shorter, half hidden by fur; legs longer than arms, with lengthened heels. Hands and feet resembling *Lemur macaco*, soles of hands and feet hairy between the tactile pads. Tail usually longer than HB, bushy, with pointed tip, at root less thickly haired. Perineal area hairy, scrotum small, reduced, but in breeding season, however, very large. Penis and clitoris long and thin, with isolated long hairs, the former forked. 6 teats (2 on breast, 4 on belly). Whiskers and tactile hair tufts over eyes, on cheeks, chin and wrist. Dent.: $2 \cdot 1 \cdot 3 \cdot 3 = 36$, teeth resembling *L. macaco*, but P^2 spatulate. Pelage thick and soft. Upperside grey or greyish-red (*murinus*) or reddish-brown (*smithi*) with white nose stripe (with blackish edge in *smithi*) and dark spinal line (indistinct in *smithi*). Cheeks brown (*murinus*) or white (*smithi*). Underside white, in *murinus* in part with grey tinge. Tail upperside as back (in *murinus* red-tinged, underside paler). Young like adults. MEASUREMENTS: HB 10–15, TL 12–17, Wt 40–75, if very fat up to 100.

Distribution. Coastal regions of Madagascar. 2 ssp.: (1) Western or Miller's Lesser Mouse-Lemur, *murinus* (J. F. Miller, 1777); W. and S. coastal regions from Bombetoka Bay in N. to Fort Dauphin in S. (2) Eastern or Smith's Lesser Mouse-Lemur, *smithii* (Gray, 1842); remainder of coastal regions. HABITAT: rain forests, dry forests and bushy woodlands (also in small isolated patches of forest), *viz*. large, secondary forests and high bush. TERRITORY: resembling *Lepilemur*. Size only up to about 50m around sleeping place. ♂ territory overlaps or separates ♀ territories. At times a single population of several dozen animals with central region and many sleeping places in which are the above-mentioned territories (many ♀♀, a few ♂♂), and a border region in which are the remainder of the ♂♂. Both sexes mark with urine (some drops in the hand are rubbed into soles of feet on same side of body, repeated with the other hand and foot). Build leaf nests as sleeping and breeding places, 17–20cm in section, at a height of 2–4m, or use leaf-lined tree holes; in E. Madagascan rain forests prefers the holes in the arching leaf stems of the 'Travellers Tree' (*Ravenala madagascariensis*) a tree related to and resembling a banana tree. *Map* p. 239.

Habits. DAILY RHYTHM: nocturnal, from nightfall. Quick and agile on all fours, or hopping and jumping up to 3m, or climbing, or hanging by hind feet: also sits upright. Sleeps rolled up like a ball. No aestivation in dry season, however body temperature varies within a few days between 25° and 34°C. TOILET: rubs head with both hands, licks and grooms fur (also mutually), scratches with cleaning toe. VOICE: series of long high screams, usually in ultrasonic range, as contact calls; duration of each 1 second, range 15–20m. 3–4 high, but still audible, cries in fright or warning. A series of much shorter, sharply increasing audible cries (18 per second) in greater excitement. High double note of ♂ following ♀ in heat. Chatter in anger or threat. Soft purring of contented young. Shrill high call of discontent. SENSES: sight and scent good, hearing very good, including ultrasonics from neighbours and insects, and location of precise sources; however, no echo-location as in bats. ENEMIES: mainly owls. FOOD: small sweet fruits, also leaves, blooms and insects. Western ssp. in rainy season (Dec–Apr) stores fat in skin and tail, using it up in the dry season (May–Nov). SOCIABILITY: see TERRITORY. Often solitary or in pairs, however, in nest or sleeping hole usually more (up to 15). ♂♂ quarrelsome in breeding season, with breeding ♀♀, or if strangers enter the territory.

Reproduction. ♂ marks in pairing season, rubbing scrotum in urine. ♀ cycle 35–108, usually 50–60 days. Breeding season end of Aug to beginning of Feb. ♀ comes on heat 2–4 times at intervals of about 50 days, if not fertilised. 1 ♀ can have young twice in 1 season at intervals of 71–75 days. Litter season end of Oct to beginning of Mar, principally in Jan. 1–3 young, usually 2, sex ratio 1:1. Suckling period 40–45 days. Young thick-headed, thinly-haired, with eyes closed, opening after 4 days. Young can soon cling to twigs. ♀ eats afterbirth, licks young dry, seldom leaves nest for first days. Young can jump at 12, climb at 15, run at 20, eat solid food at 21–25 days, and are independent at 2 months. SEXUAL MATURITY: at 7–10 months, leave mother at 1 year, and pair at 1¼ years. Measurements at birth: HB 3.7–5, TL 2.5–3.2, Wt 2.7–5g, at ½ year 35–48g. LONGEVITY: up to 6 years in captivity.

COQUEREL'S MOUSE LEMUR, Pl. 46

Microcebus coquereli (Grandidier, 1867)

G. Rattenmaki   F. Le Microcèbe de Coquerel   MA. Sisiba, Sietui, Setohy, Tsitsihy, Tsitilivaha

Identification. Form as in Lesser Mouse-Lemur but twice the size. Head round, muzzle short and pointed, eyes large, ears rather small, oval-roundish, naked; nails keeled and pointed (second toe with claw); dent. with smaller upper incisors and larger upper canines, tail also thickly bushy at the root: other characters as Lesser Mouse-Lemur. Upperside greyish-red, stippled with golden yellow, general impression olive-brownish, middle of back darker, tail grizzled with black, particularly towards the end. Around eyes and back of nose yellowish-grey, cheeks, chin, throat, breast, belly and

inside of legs greyish-whitish-yellow. Immature pelage not known.   MEASUREMENTS:
HB 23–25, TL 28–32, Wt 380–400.

Distribution. Southern West Madagascar between the rivers Onilahy, Fierenana and
Mahavavy, as well as N.W. Madagascar south of Ambanja. No ssp. Endangered.
HABITAT: dry forest, shedding its leaves in hottest part of dry season (Sep–Mid-Dec).
The larger trees 15m high, a medium layer, and thick bush below.   HOME RANGE:
area not known. No marking (lacking any scent-marking means). Centre of range
a nest, 25–30cm in diameter, built of leaves, usually hanging among lianas. Also uses
tree holes for nesting. Population density 250–300 animals per sq km.

Habits. DAILY RHYTHM: most active at dusk and by night from 18.15 to 5.00, mostly
in first half. Lives mainly in the lower tiers of foliage. Leaps upright from tree to
tree.   TOILET, SENSES, ENEMIES: not known.   VOICE: rather quiet; soft call while on
move, chattering when angry.   FOOD: fruit, leaves, insects; is fond of sap from trees.
For fat-storing, see Lesser Mouse-Lemur.   SOCIABILITY: not known.

Reproduction. 1–4 young in nest or tree hole in second half of Nov (beginning of rainy
season), no further details known.

GREATER DWARF LEMUR,   Pl. 46
Cheirogaleus (Cheirogaleus) major (E. Geoffroy St Hilaire, 1812)
G. Grosser Katzenmaki   F. Le Chirogale grand

Identification. Size, form, hands, feet, fur more or less as Coquerel's Mouse-Lemur.
Scrotum and perineal area hairy, clitoris and penis with bone. 4 teats (2 on breast, 2 on
belly). Dent.: as in Coquerel's Mouse-Lemur, but P^2 and P^3 pointed. Upperside
greyish-brown, brownish-grey or brownish-red, usually with hind part of body from
middle of back, with tail, darker than fore part; underside (chin and cheeks, throat,
breast, belly and inside of limbs) grey to yellowish-white, throat sometimes orange.
Nose stripe white to grey, sometimes absent, orbital ring black or reddish-brown or
indistinct, sometimes edge of ears blackish. Young dark greyish-brown with brownish-
black dorsal line.   MEASUREMENTS: HB 25–27, TL 23–25, Wt ?.

Distribution. E. Madagascar. 2 ssp.: (1) Typical Greater Dwarf-Lemur, *major* (E.
Geoffroy St Hilaire, 1812), northern part of E. Madagascar. (2) Crossley's Greater
Dwarf-Lemur, *crossleyi* (Grandidier, 1870); southern part of E. Madagascar. (These
ranges perhaps should be reversed, according to other sources.) Precise limits of range
not known.   HABITAT: rain forests.   HOME RANGE: size not known, no territorial
occupation, no marking, however, foecal rubbing with anal area on boughs, and
urinating on boughs and twigs, leaving distinctive scent.

Habits. DAILY RHYTHM: day spent in tree holes, sometimes also in nests of about 30cm
diameter as in *Microcebus*. Animals often lie closely together. In evening leave nest to
seek food in the trees, along horizontal boughs and twigs. Movement usually unhurried and skulking; not much jumping or sitting upright; sometimes sit quietly,
returning to sleeping place at end of night. Sleeps rolled up like a ball. Body temperature varies from 25° to 32°C, moreover in winter (Sep–Feb) often a period of dormancy
(2–3 days) with lowering of body temperature to near the environmental range. In
some regions also a winter sleep for several weeks in the ground or tree-trunk hole,
perhaps excavated in rotting wood of a tree stump. In the previous months fat has been
stored under skin and in tail.   TOILET: grooming (also mutually) and scratching with
cleaning claw.   VOICE: usually silent. Sometimes short grunts while on move. In
annoyance, defence or attack a series of quick rising grunts. Call 'kwe-kwe-kwe' in
excitement. Young have piercing chirp when uneasy. 'Grumbling' when content. ♂
twitters in mating.   SENSES: as *Hapalemur griseus* (p. 239).   ENEMIES: owls and

fossas. Uses teeth in defence.   FOOD: fruit, flowers, insects, small vertebrates, perhaps including young birds in nests.   SOCIABILITY: often alone or with young, seldom in pairs.

Reproduction. Pairing season Sep–Oct, births Dec–Jan, gestation 70 days. In mating, ♀ squats low, duration 2–3 minutes, repeated many times at 10-minute intervals. Birthplace leaf-lined hole in tree. 2–3 young, usually 2, hairy, blind (eyes open on second day), at 3 weeks can climb, first solid food at 3½ weeks, at 4 weeks following mother, weaned at 6 weeks. At birth HB 7.3–8.2, TL 6.7–7.5, Wt 17.2–19.5. At 8 weeks Wt 176–183. Further development data and sexual maturity knot known. LONGEVITY: 5 years reported in captivity.

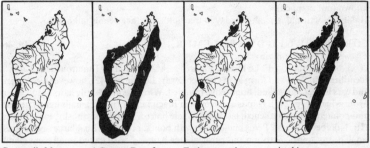

Coquerel's Mouse Lemur

1 Greater Dwarf Lemur
2 Fat-tailed Dwarf Lemur

Fork-crowned Dwarf Lemur

Avahi

FAT-TAILED DWARF LEMUR,   **Pl. 46**
Cheirogaleus (Opolemur) medius (E. Geoffroy St Hilaire, 1812)
G. Mittlerer Katzenmaki or Fettschwanzmaki F. Le Cheirogale à queue grasse
MA. Kely Behoy

Identification. Form and build as in *Cheirogaleus major* (above) but smaller. Upper-side grey with reddish suffusion, or greyish-brown, underside including root of tail white, whitish-yellow or orange. Nose stripe white, eye rings black. White of throat tends to extend behind head on both sides, leaving a wedge of brown on neck. Young like adults.   MEASUREMENTS: HB 19–24, TL 17–22, Wt ?.

Distribution. Coastal forests of all W. Madagascar, however nowhere common. En-dangered. 2 ssp.: (1) Southeastern Fat-tailed Dwarf Lemur, *medius* (E. Geoffroy St Hilaire, 1812), neighbourhood of Fort Dauphin, S. coast. (2) Western Fat-tailed Dwarf Lemur, *samati* (Grandidier, 1868); rest of W. Madagascar. Subspecific validity doubtful.   HABITAT: rain and dry forests.   HOME RANGE: size not known. No ter-ritory held, no marking.

Habits. DAILY RHYTHM: as in *C. major*. Sleep mainly in tree holes. In dry forests aestivate from Aug–Sep, in other forests a hibernation period from 1 week to 1 month in Sep–Feb. At other times body temperature normally between 21° and 32°C. Moreover large storage of fat, especially on legs, tail and below tail root.   TOILET, SENSES, ENEMIES, FOOD, SOCIABILITY and VOICE: as in *major*, but call sometimes still shorter, higher, louder, of uncertain significance.   LONGEVITY: 7½ years in captivity.

HAIRY-EARED DWARF LEMUR, Pl. 46
Cheirogaleus (Allocebus) trichotis (Gunther, 1875)

G. Buschelöhr-Katzenmaki   F. Le Cheirogale aux oreilles velues

Identification. Form and body characters as in *C. medius*, only smaller, and ears short with long hair. Upperside brownish-grey, hands and feet grey, tail brownish-red, underside grey, washed with white. Black eye rings; cheeks and back of nose white. Tail not as thickly bushy as in *major* and *medius*, however becoming thicker in last third. Nails (apart from great toe) pointed and narrowly keeled. Second toe with claw-like nail. Dent.: P^2 caniniform as in *Phaner* (below). MEASUREMENTS: HB 13.5–15, TL 15–17, Wt ?.

Distribution. E. Madagascar, further details lacking. Up to present only 4 examples known (not mapped).

Habits. Nocturnal, sleeping by day in tree holes. Further details unknown.

FORK-CROWNED DWARF LEMUR, Pl. 46
Phaner furcifer (De Blainville, 1841)

G. Gabelkatzenmaki   F. Le Phaner à fourche   MA. Walouvy, Tantaroue-lela, Tanta

Identification. Size and form as in Greater Dwarf Lemur (p. 242), however legs longer and ears longer and naked, upper edge rounded. Whiskers and tactile hairs as in Lesser Mouse-Lemur (p. 240). Hands and feet as in Black Lemur (p. 232), nails lightly keeled and pointed, foot lengthened, last third of sole haired. Tail thickly bushy, longer than HB. Number of teats ? Penis and clitoris with bones, prepuce with 4 large and several small horny spines. Scrotum and perineal area hairy. ♂ with naked small scent gland on throat. Dent.: like Greater Dwarf Lemur, however, I^1 large, strongly projecting forward and standing directly in front of long dagger-like canine; P^2 caniniform, $\frac{2}{3}$ length of canine, P_2 lancet-shaped. Upperside brownish-grey to yellowish-brown with black spinal stripe which forks on the crown to merge on each side with the black orbital ring. Limbs and tail darker, latter brownish-black, with tip black (sometimes tip or terminal third white). Underside yellowish-white, cheeks and back of nose to forehead greyish-yellow. Juvenile pelage not known. MEASUREMENTS: HB 22–28, TL 30–37, Wt 400–450.

Distribution. W. Madagascar north of Onihaly and Fierenana Rivers, up to northern tip, with Ambre Mt (up to 1000m or more) as well as in the N.E., the Masoala Peninsula north of Antongil Bay. Northern animals larger than others, perhaps a distinct ssp. Endangered. HABITAT: moist, dry, secondary or gallery forests. HOME RANGE: about 1 hectare, around sleeping and feeding trees. Mainly solitary, are apparently unsociable, mark territory by loud calling, ♂♂ also by rubbing throat gland on boughs. Pursue, scream at and fight if meeting others, although when feeding more than one may be in the same tree. In suitable areas population up to 850 animals to 1 sq km. *Map* p. 243.

Habits. DAILY RHYTHM: nocturnal from sunset according to light intensity up to first morning light. Most active in evening. Animals suddenly emerge from sleeping places, run 20–30m over the boughs, then start to call loudly. All do the same, resulting in a great noise. By day sleep in tree hole or a nest of Coquerel's Mouse-Lemur. Return to sleeping quarters about 4.15. Sleep sitting with head between legs and tail wrapped round. Will sit upright, run with tail vertical, leaps horizontally up to 5m very skilfully, climbs up and down (head first). TOILET: fur grooming, scratching with hind foot. VOICE: 'kui', singly or repeatedly, is contact call, threat, warning and general call when excited. Meeting of animals leads to duet, pursuit and squabbling, latter accompanied by other calls. SENSES: sight very good, large tapetum lucidum, enabling nocturnal leaping without harm. Periods of activity or sleeping within close light intensity limits. Hearing very good, scent good. ENEMIES: not known. FOOD: fruit, leaves, flowers, and especially nectar, sap of trees; the juicy secretions of plant aphids, as well as other insects.

Reproduction. 1 young at beginning of rainy season (mid-Nov), in a tree hole; carried at first by mother on her belly, later on her back. No further details known.

INDRIS, INDRIDAE

Ape-like, slender-limbed, legs about a third longer than arms, tail short or long, head rounded, muzzle short or medium length. Eyes large. Ears fairly large. Fur dense and woolly, face naked. Digits 5/5. Thumb and great toe very large, middle of hand and foot narrow and long. Ends of fingers broadened, with pointed nails. Second toe with claw. Dent.: $2/2 \cdot 1/0-1 \cdot 2/2 \cdot 3/3 = 30-32$. Upper incisors and canines large, lower incisors strongly projecting forward. Cheek-teeth cusps in V-formation. Penis pendulous, with bone, 2 teats on breast. 1 young, carried, born with eyes open after gestation of 120–130 days. Vegetarian; on ground and in climbing usually in upright attitude. Diurnal, except Avahi which is nocturnal. Usually in pairs or troops. 3 genera with 4 species, only in Madagascar.

AVAHI, *Avahi laniger* (Gmelin, 1789)   **Pl. 47**
G. Vliesmaki   F. L'Avahi   MA. Avahy, Ampongi, Fotsi-fe, Fotsiefaka, Vareka
Identification. Form as in *Lemur macaco*, but muzzle short and ears hidden in fur. Head short and round, eyes large with nictitating membrane and eye-lashes; pupils vertical slits when contracted. Face, except nostrils, covered with short hairs. Ears short and round, backs hairy, hidden in fur. Legs longer than arms, tail long. Hands and feet long and narrow, thumb short, great toe of medium length, twice as broad as the other toes. Thumb and great toe opposable, all digits ending in tactile pads, as also palms and soles with 3–4 narrow pads, with horny skin between. Second digit shortest, 4th longest, 3rd and 5th growing together for part way. Nails narrow, curved, lightly keeled, rather pointed. Second toe with claw. Hands and feet fully-haired above. Fur short, densely woolly, tail bushy. Whiskers short and small; tactile hair tufts on cheeks and above eyes, none on wrists. At corners of chin 2 small skin glands, white in ♀, reddish-brown in ♂, with short hairs directed inwards. Also a cutaneous gland at back of scrotum. Perineal area hairy, scrotum bifid, naked, penis pendulous, with bone and 4 large and several small horny spines; clitoris long and pendulous, with bone. 2 teats on breast. Angular process of mandible very large, rounded. Dent.: $2/2 \cdot 1/0 \cdot 2/2 \cdot 3/3 = 30$. Upper incisors small, upper canines short and strong, $M^3 \frac{1}{2}$ size of M^1 and M^2. Lower incisors very long and narrow, projecting strongly forward; no lower canines; M_1 and M_3 five-cusped. Upperside olive to light greyish-brown (ssp. *occidentalis*) or dark brown (ssp. *laniger*), underside whitish-grey to whitish-yellow, hands and feet yellowish-brown to brownish-red, back of upper thighs whitish or reddish, tail yellowish-red, forehead region whitish. A peculiarly short-haired rump spot pale reddish. Juvenile coat like adult. MEASUREMENTS: HB 30–45, TL 33–40, Wt ?.

Distribution. E. and N.W. Madagascar. 2 ssp.: (1). Eastern Avahi, *laniger* (Gmelin, 1788), E. Madagascar from Vohemar in N. to Fort Dauphin in S. (2). Western Avahi, *occidentalis* (Lorenz, 1898); N.W. Madagascar from Bombetopa Bay northward to region south of Ambre mountains. Endangered. HABITAT: mountain rain forests. HOME RANGE: not known, population low. *Map* p. 243.

Habits. DAILY RHYTHM: nocturnal, sleeping by day in dense foliage of trees and tall bushes, sitting with head tucked between legs and tail curled around, usually with a second or third all close together. Arboreal, good jumper, rarely on ground, where it goes upright. VOICE: weak grunting; a ringing whistling twitter when moderately excited; rising to a higher louder scream in higher excitement, and a short deep 'tuif' as contact call. TOILET, SENSES, ENEMIES: no data. FOOD: leaves, buds, bark, fruit. SOCIABILITY: pair for life.

Reproduction. Gestation ?. Young born Aug–Sep. 1 weakly-haired young with eyes open, clings at first to mother's belly, later rides on her back. ♂ also carries the young. Suckling time 6 months. No further data.

VERREAUX'S SIFAKA, *Propithecus verreauxi* (Grandidier, 1867)   **Pl. 47**
G. Larvenmaki   F. Le Propithèque de Verreaux   MA. Sifaka, Simpona

Identification. Form like Avahi (p. 245), but larger, and tail longer in proportion to body. Pelage thick and silky. Face, palms of hands and soles of feet naked and black; on back of nose fine white hairs. Whiskers small and short. Tactile hair tufts on cheeks and above eyes, none on wrist. ♂ with oval cutaneous glandular area on throat, about 8cm long. 2 axillary teats. Eyes large, with nictitating membrane. Ears of medium size, backs hairy, nearly concealed in fur. A web-like margin of skin, with long hair fringe, between axillary region and upper arm, and along the underarm. Hands and feet narrow and long, 2nd–5th digits united at base by small web; great toe twice as broad as the other toes, thumb and great toe opposable, ends of fingers with round tactile pads, hands and feet also with 5–6 tactile pads on palms and soles. 2nd toe with claw. Nails rounded, weakly keeled. Perineal area hairy, scrotum black, sparsely haired, penis pendulous, with bone, prepuce with small horny spines. Clitoris short, with large vulva, swollen like scrotum. Dent.: $2 \cdot 1 \cdot 2 \cdot 3 = 32$. Much as in Avahi, but upper canine long and dagger-like, lower canine like premolar, and lower molars 4-cusped. Colour mainly white: of the 4 ssp. Decken's Sifaka, *deckeni* (Peters, 1870) (middle W. Madagascar between Manhavavi R. in N. and Mania R. in S.) is wholly white. Coquerel's Sifaka, *coquereli* (A. Milne-Edwards, 1867) (northern W. Madagascar between Betsiboka R. in S. and Narinda Bay in N.) is white with brown arms and inside of upper thighs. The Crowned Sifaka, *coronatus* (A. Milne-Edwards, 1867) (between the 2 former) has crown and neck blackish-brown, back pearl grey, underside, or breast at least, rusty-red, rest of body and limbs white. Similarly coloured, though with whiter underside, is Verreaux's Sifaka, *verreauxi* (Grandidier, 1867) (south of W., and S. Madagascar from Mania R. in N. to Fort Dauphin in S.). A blackish variety of the latter occurs in the south (earlier considered to be a distinct ssp. *majori* (Rothschild, 1894) with crown, neck, back, insides of arms and legs chocolate brown to black, and rest of body white. The colour variations within the ssp. are great. Young are at first so thinly-haired on head and back that the black skin shows through. Within $1\frac{1}{2}$ months of birth the full subspecific pelage is beginning to appear. MEASUREMENTS: HB *c.* 45, TL *c.* 55, Wt 5.5–6.0.

Distribution. See Identification. Seriously endangered. HABITAT: rain and dry forests. TERRITORY: each troop (2–10 animals) has its own territory of from 0.5–2.5 hectares, according to the type of forest and population density. Territory borders may vary somewhat according to season or location; however, troops are generally resident and territory may exist for many years. Some overlapping with neighbouring troops, leading to threats and chases, in pairing time also to serious fighting. All the territory is used by the troop in rotation, changing every 2–3 days and covering whole area in 7–10 days. A territory usually combines growth consisting of tall trees (13–21m, up to 30m), lower trees 7–13m, and bush. ♂ marks branches with throat gland, and urinates from sitting position against upright trunks, sometimes rubs branches with back of scrotum and anal region. ♀ rubs vulva, and urinates, similarly. *Map* p. 243.

Habits. DAILY RHYTHM: little urgency in movements. After sunrise troop scatters over 20–50m wide sunning place (sunbathe sitting with outstretched arms and legs), afterwards moving on to feeding place perhaps 20–50m on. At midday rest in leafy shade of crowns of middle tier. In afternoon move on 20–50m to feeding place, and in late afternoon 50–100m to sleeping quarters. Sleep in forks of highest branches, singly or together. Most movement in the trees on the largest branches on all fours, on smaller branches sometimes hang for short while, otherwise bipedal with hands gripping the branches. Horizontal leaps from tree to tree up to 10m apart, landing upright, feet first. Sometimes search on ground for fallen fruit, progressing in wide hops with waving arms held at head height.   TOILET: fur grooming with lower comb-like incisors (see *Lemur macaco*) also mutually. Tail held in hands while combing it. Licking fur, scratching and ear-cleaning with toilet claw. VOICE: contact call soft 'koo' with closed mouth. Among other calls is a repeated warning grunt at second intervals, breathing in and out. The name Sifaka derives from the native word for another call 'shi-fak', a warning against ground enemies. A loud alarm call when birds of prey appear, with heads turned towards sky, repeated 3–4 times. Both calls acknowledged by members of the same group or by adjoining troop. When being hunted, a short 'mmm'. Young squeal when uneasy. SENSES: sight very good, flattish face allows stereoscopic vision, can recognise motionless objects. Scent good, permitting individual recognition by scent marking. Hearing good. ENEMIES: fossas, and large birds of prey. FOOD: leaves, buds, blooms, fruit. Do not drink. SOCIABILITY: in troops of 2–10, usually 4–6, generally equal sexes, or some ♂♂ forming bachelor troop. Normally only 1 young annually. An old ♂ or ♀ has priority in feeding. Usually sit close together or behind one another. Rub noses in greeting. Moderate quarrelling common, but only serious fighting is between ♂♂ in pairing season.

Reproduction. Breeding season end of Jan to beginning of Mar, births end of Jun to beginning of Aug. ♀ cycle 33–45 days, mating from standing position from behind, ♂ clasps ♀ thighs with feet. ♀ only allows best fighter among ♂♂ to mate. Duration 3–5 minutes. Gestation *c.* 130 days. 1 young born with eyes open, well-haired, clings tightly to mother's body. Length at birth (HB + TL) *c.* 13cm. ♀ licks young dry, after 2 weeks allows other members of the troop to help with rearing and cleaning. At 1 month the young one rides on mother's back; at 2 months is fully haired, takes 1st solid food at 3 months, suckles for 6 months, is carried for 6–7 months. SEXUAL MATURITY: at 2–2½ years. Wt at birth 35–40, at 6 months ⅔ Wt of adult. LONGEVITY: 7 years in captivity.

DIADEMED SIFAKA, *Propithecus diadema* (Bennett, 1832)   Pl. 47
G. Diademmaki   F. Le Propithèque diadème   MA. Sifaka, Simpona

Identification. Form and bodily details as in Verreaux's Sifaka (p. 246), but larger, fur silkier, back of nose naked, and tail shorter in relation to body. Colour, see Distribution. MEASUREMENTS: HB 50–53, TL 45–48, Wt?

Distribution. E. Madagascar, from N. to S. 5 ssp.: (1) Perrier's Diademed Sifaka, *perrieri* Lavauden, 1931; Analamera Forest, extreme N.E. Madagascar; wholly black. (2) Silky Diademed Sifaka, *candidus* A. Grandidier, 1871; N.E. Madagascar from Sahambave in N. to Antongil Bay in S.; silky white, sometimes lightly suffused with yellowish, and tail root rusty-red. Face black with fleshy spots. (3) Typical Diademed

Sifaka, *diadema* Bennett, 1832, middle E. Madagascar, from Antongil Bay in N. to Masora R. in S. Face, crown and hands black, white forehead band; neck, back, flanks and upper arms light to dark grey or dark brown. Legs, feet and lower arms yellow to orange, anal area reddish, tail root orange, middle yellow, tip greyish-white. Breast dark brown, belly yellowish-white. Young like adults, but paler and with yellowish forehead band. (4) Milne-Edwards Diademed Sifaka *edwardsi* A. Grandidier, 1871; middle E. Madagascar, south of (3), from Masora R. in N. to Matitanana R. in S. Upperside with flanks white or yellowish-white or reddish-white, underside greyish-white, rump dark brown, middle of back, arms, legs and tail black. (5) Black Diademed Sifaka, *holomelas* Gunther, 1875, middle of S.E. Madagascar, south of (4), southwards to Antandroy; wholly black, only rump patch brown, sometimes throat white and underside brown. Very strong colour variation within the ssp.

Habits. Details not known, but probably like Verreaux's Sifaka.

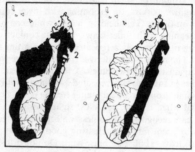

1 Verreaux's Sifaka
2 Indris

Diademed Sifaka

INDRIS, *Indri indri* (Gmelin, 1788)   Pl. 47
G. Indri   F. L'Indri   MA. Endrina, Babakota, Amboanala
Identification. Like the Sifakas in form, but larger, muzzle longer, and tail only a stump. Face naked and black, whiskers and tactile hairs rudimentary, ears short, rounded, largely hidden in fur, outsides hairy. Eyes with nictitating membrane and round pupils. Legs longer than arms, wrists without tactile hair tufts. Hands and feet long and narrow, structure as in Sifakas (above), but pads on palms of hands and soles of feet not sharply separated. ♂ with glandular cell spot on upper throat and probably also on scrotum. Perineal area and scrotum hairy. Penis with bone, pendulous, prepuce with about 28 medium-sized horny spines. Clitoris short, 2 breast teats. Dent.: $2/2 \cdot 1/0 \cdot 2/2 \cdot 3/3 = 30$. Upper incisors middle sized, upper canines strongly hooked. M^3 considerably smaller than M^1 and M^2, lower incisors very long and narrow, strongly projecting forward, no lower canines. Pelage dense and soft. Circle of hair around blackish-grey face, throat, lower arms, outside of legs, long narrow triangular rump patch reaching from pointed tip to haunches, and root of tail stump, whitish-grey. Crown, ear fringes, neck, shoulders, upper arms, back, front of thighs, hands and feet, black, as also band from shoulders over fore part of breast. Sometimes lower arms, rump patch and tail reddish or orange or browner flank stripe. Colour variations frequent, nearly all-white to nearly all-black animals likely. MEASUREMENTS: HB 61–71, TL 3–6, Wt?

Distribution. Northern half of E. Madagascar, from Masora R. in S. to Vohemar in N., in mountains to 1800m upwards. No ssp. Regionally extinct or threatened. HABITAT: Mountain rain forest. TERRITORY: each troop of adults and 1 (sometimes 1–2 older as well) young has a large area of about 17–18 hectares (about 8–16 animals to a sq km), and scent marks it with throat and scrotum glands, with a loud howling 'wei-wei-wei' which, thanks to the membraneous throat sac, carries a long way, is recognised by all troop members, and is eventually repeated many times as a long drawn sound. Very similar to howling of gibbons, may be heard at all hours of day, but mostly in morning, sometimes also at night, in good weather more often than in bad, mostly in Dec–Jan. Can be heard over a distance of 1km. TERRITORY: defended against neighbouring troops.

Habits. DAILY RHYTHM: home is all tiers of forest, from ground upward. Day's wanderings only up to 500m. Spend all day feeding without noon rest. Late afternoon grooming fur with teeth (also mutually) and cleaning claw. VOICE: warning call for birds of prey a loud, many times repeated scream, with head turned up. For terrestrial enemies another call. Soft grunting in neutral mood, spitting in anger. ENEMIES: fossas, birds of prey. FOOD: leaves, shoots, fruit.

Reproduction. Mate from rear without long preliminary play. Pairing season Jan–Feb. 1 young annually in May or Jun, after about 4½–5½ months gestation; young at first clings tightly to belly of ♀, rides on back at 4–5 months. Weaned at 9 months, independent at 6 months, but sleeps with mother for 1 year. SEXUAL MATURITY and LONGEVITY: no data.

AYE-AYE, DAUBENTONIIDAE

Only 1 genus and species, in Madagascar, see following species description.

AYE-AYE, *Daubentonia madagascariensis* (Gmelin, 1788)   **Pl. 47**
G. Fingertier   F. Aye-Aye   MA. Hai-Hai, Ahay, Aiay
Identification. Size of large squirrel. Head round, muzzle short, eyes large, with nictitating membrane, pupils vertical slits when contracted. Ears large, broadly spoon-shaped, naked, thin-skinned. Whiskers, and tactile hair tufts on cheeks and above eyes short, absent from wrists. Legs longer than arms. Hands and feet narrow, thumb and great toe twice as broad as the other digits, opposable. All finger tips with round tactile pads and with claws, only the great toe with flat nail. Palms of hands and soles of feet with only small tactile pads, the rest of soles and undersides of digits horny. 2nd and 5th digits thin and long, on hand 3rd and 4th fingers nearly twice as long as 2nd and 5th, 3rd especially thin with very long first joint. On hind feet the 2nd–5th toes about the same length. Dent.: $1/1 \cdot 0/0 \cdot 3/3 = 18$, rodent-like; incisors very large, especially lower, and chisel-shaped, no canines, premolars very small, molars rectangular, low, cusps little developed, wide gap between incisors and cheek teeth. Scrotum naked, penis with bone, pendulous, prepuce with many small horny spines, clitoris short, anal and perineal area hairy. 2 teats on abdomen. Scrotum, soles of hands and feet, and ears, black; nostrils and lips flesh-coloured. Pelage with short underfur and long rather stiff over hair. Hairs basally white, upper part black; white shows through on face, throat, breast and belly; the long hairs of crown and neck with white tips. Tail very long, thick and very bushy. Hairs 10–12cm long, black. Young like adults. MEASUREMENTS: HB 36–44, TL 50–60, Wt *c.* 2.
Distribution. Formerly northern E. Madagascar from about Mangoro R. in south to

Antongil Bay in north, as well as the region around Narinda Bay in N.W. Madagascar. No ssp. Today almost everywhere extinct, and still found only on the island reserve of Nosy-Mangabe in Antongil Bay, to which the last animals (at the most a dozen) were specially taken. In perhaps still historical times, between Mangoky R. in N. and Cape St Marie in S.W. Madagascar, another species, ⅓ larger, the Greater Aye-Aye, *D. robusta* (Lamberton, 1934) existed, only known through discovery of its teeth and bones.   HABITAT: rain forests with bamboo thickets of the coastal region up to about 200m.   HOME RANGE: rather large, up to 5km in circumference, containing several (2–5) nests, but overlapping the range of neighbouring animals. Both sexes mark branches or surroundings with urine in long bands (up to several metres).

1 Aye-Aye
2 Greater Aye-Aye

Habits.   DAILY RHYTHM: entirely nocturnal, leaving nest at dusk, first a thorough grooming, then feeding until about 23.00, then little activity until about 3.00, then active until 5.00. Moonlight increases activity, rain reduces it. Run and jump on all fours, tail carried lightly arched; is also often on ground, when tail is carried erect. Thanks to the clawed fingers climbs vertical trunks easily. May hang by hind feet. By day sleeping deeply (with lowered body temperature) in nest built of leaves and twigs, at height of 5–20m in the foliage of crowns of trees. C. 50–70cm diameter on average, with one entrance and a mossy lining. Each animal may have 2–5, older ones repaired with fresh twigs. Sleep rolled up and covered by tail.   TOILET: fur combing and scratching, corners of eyes, ears and nostrils cleaned with 3rd finger of hand.   VOICE: loud shrill cry as contact call, often repeated, and answered by other distant animals. Cry of anger or threat 'Ron-sit'. Piercing squeal as cry of pain.   SENSES: sight and hearing very good, scent good.   ENEMIES: fossas. Courageous, spits and bites in self-defence, and utters threat call if strangers come near.   FOOD: bamboo shoots and pith, sugar canes, tips of shoots, fruit of all kinds; shells (coconuts or birds eggs) are opened by the powerful incisor teeth, and the contents extracted by the long 3rd finger. Large beetle larvae are extracted from rotting wood in the same way and eaten eagerly. They drum on the wood with the 3rd finger, and when the grub is located by sound, the wood is bitten open. Adult insects are not eaten. Drink either directly by lapping with tongue or by dipping the elongated 3rd finger in the water and conveying it rapidly to the mouth.   SOCIABILITY: solitary, or ♀ with young, but may contact others.

Reproduction. 1 young, probably only every 2nd or 3rd year, in Oct–Nov. The young one HB 15–17, hairy, tail handsome with long hairs. At 6 months ⅓, at 12 months ⅔, adult size. Young lives in the nest with ♀ over a year, suckles probably for a year or longer. SEXUAL MATURITY: probably in 3rd year. LONGEVITY: 23 years recorded in captivity.

LORISES, LORISIDAE

Small to medium sized (HB 10–40cm) lemuroids, tailless, stump-tailed or with long tail, round head, small to large ears, large eyes, arms and legs of equal length, or with legs longer than arms. Digits 5/5, but in part fingers reduced or tarsus lengthened, digits with flat nails, second toe with claw. Penis bone present, or absent. Dent.: $2 \cdot 1 \cdot 3 \cdot 3 =$ 36, lower incisors projecting forward, canines long. Cheek teeth with 3–4 cusps. Gestation $3\frac{1}{2}$–$6\frac{1}{2}$ months. 1–3 young born with eyes open. Nocturnal, solitary or sociable, slow or rapid climbers. Mostly omnivorous. 2 subfamilies, 6 genera with 11 species in S. Asia and in Africa; 3 genera with 8 species in Africa.

GALAGOS OR BUSHBABIES, GALAGINAE

HB 10–40cm, tail long and bushy, head round, muzzle rather pointed, eyes and ears large, latter naked, skin-like, flexible. Legs longer than arms, tarsus lengthened, fingers slender, terminal pads broad, with flat nails, second toe with claw. Penis bone present, 4 teats. Gestation 108–146 days, 1–3 young born with eyes open, and carried by parent. Nocturnal, sociable jumpers and climbers, preying on small creatures or eating soft vegetation. 1 genus with 6 species, in Africa only.

GREATER BUSHBABY,   **Pl. 48**
Galago (Galago) crassicaudatus (E. Geoffroy St Hilaire, 1812)
G. Riesengalago   F. Le Galago à queue épaisse   A. Bosnaagaap   S. Komba
Identification. Rabbit-sized. Head round, muzzle of medium length. Strong build. Eyes large, forward looking, pupils a vertical slit when contracted. Ears large, spoon-shaped, naked, membraneous, individually flexible (the conch can be folded back-wards). Whiskers of medium length, tactile hair tufts over eyes and on cheeks, none on wrists. Legs longer than arms, tarsal bones elongated. Thumb and great toe opposable. Digits of medium length, all with terminal round tactile pads and with flat nails, except the 2nd toe which has a claw. Palms and soles with 6 tactile pads, that on base of great toe very large, the space between horny; haired behind. Scrotum furry, but naked behind, in rut rose coloured; perineal area hairy, penis with bone, pendulous, prepuce with many horny spines, clitoris short and thick. Teats variable in number; 2 pectoral, or 2 pectoral and 2 inguinal, or 2 axillary, 2 pectoral and 2 inguinal. In both sexes a glandular strip from middle of breast to throat. Dent.: $2 \cdot 1 \cdot 3 \cdot 3 = 36$. Upper incisors very small, upper canines strong, upper molars broader than long, lower incisors, with canine, long, narrow, strongly inclined forward, P_2 caniniform, lower molars longer than broad. Fur soft, thick and woolly, tail thickly bushy. Within the wide distribution the colour ranges from light silvery grey with whitish tail, to dark brown with black-tipped tail. Underside always lighter than upperside, varying from white through yellowish-white to grey. Tail uniformly coloured (white, creamy, grey, greyish-brown, dark brown) or upperside dark, underside lighter, or darkened in the terminal part. Hands and feet coloured like back, or light brown to brownish-black, or black. Face like crown or distinctly lighter (ochreous to white), with dark around eyes and on muzzle as well as light back of nose. Sometimes the grey upperside washed with

reddish-brown, or back of thighs orange, or ears black. Sometimes black examples occur in mountain forests. Young have upperside somewhat darker than adults, tail already bushy, and underside of body naked, beginning to show hair at 1 week. MEASUREMENTS: HB 27–47, TL 33–52, Wt 1–1.8.

Distribution. Africa between Equator and Tropic of Capricorn. In E. Africa from S. Somalia, S. Kenya and S. Uganda southwards to Zululand. In Mid and W. Africa the northern limit about 5°S (a line from north end of L. Tanganyika to mouth of R. Congo), south border from S. Angola, E. Caprivi, S. Rhodesia to E. Transvaal, Swaziland, Zululand. Also on islands of Pemba, Zanzibar and Mafia. 9 ssp. HABITAT: Forests of various types, from gallery to mountain rain forests, also wooded savannahs, bushveld, bamboo, thickets, eucalyptus plantations as well as cypress, gum, coffee and mango plantations, suburban gardens. etc. In mountains up to 3500m or more. TERRITORY: each animal or family has a territory of several hectares, with sleeping holes and well-used runs. Several territories may overlap, or several animals may sleep in one hole. Territories marked by both sexes by rubbing the breast gland on boughs and stems, as well as by anal and foot rubbing on ground. Sniffing and bark biting are part of the marking system. Size, shape and numbers of territories of a group varying seasonally. As young reach sexual maturity they start a territory. The strongest ♂♂ have the largest territory, with most territorial ♀♀; the weakest ♂♂ the smallest, on the edge of the range. Territory of 1 family about 7 hectares. Population density can be about 70–125 animals to a sq km. *Map* p. 255.

Habits. DAILY RHYTHM: sleep deeply by day in dense foliage, leafy thickets, or tree holes (5–12m high), rolled up with ears folded and tail wrapped round (vulnerable to grass and bush fires), becoming active at beginning of dusk. Up to 12 sleeping places in one territory. Most activity in first hours of night, then a rest period (dozing quietly), becoming active again towards end of night. Seldom venture out in wet, cold or windy conditions. Run on all fours, tail horizontal, leaping where necessary. At beginning of activity may moisten soles with urine, perhaps to improve suppleness and adhesion in climbing when natural humidity is low. In higher humidity such activities decrease; originally not part of territorial marking, but may perhaps help in nocturnal location of runs. In excitement augmented urine-washing and audible rubbing of feet on branches, often associated with rocking of body. On the ground carries tail upright, in quicker movement hops on hind legs like a kangaroo. TOILET: face washing with licked hands and forearms, fur combing with teeth, and fur licking (also mutual), ear cleaning with fingers. VOICE: in evening a loud child-like cry (hence name bushbaby) repeated 50–100 times in an hour, is contact call. Seasonally linked with breeding period, otherwise not so often heard. In addition, a cackling sound as threat, a scream as anger and alarm cry; young have high clicking when uneasy, mother replies with low growl. Adults also have similar clicking as expression of unease. ♂ also has crackling cry in sexual excitement. SENSES: sight and hearing very good (can make wide leaps in dark safely), scent good, very important in recognition of runs and neighbours. ENEMIES: nocturnal birds of prey, and arboreal predators (e.g. genets, snakes etc). FOOD: fruit, nuts, seeds, berries, leaves, buds, sap, insects, small reptiles, small birds and their eggs. Prey is caught in a lightning jump, killed by biting, and chewed up. Drinks either by lapping or by dipping hand in water and licking it. SOCIABILITY: partly solitary, otherwise ♀ with young, or young and ♂ (2–6). Family sleep together, disperse at waking, and come together again to sleep. Ranking order: old ♂, old ♀, then young ♂♂ and ♀♀. Lower ranks carry tail rolled under and ears not fully open. On meeting partners, touch noses and sniff, or investigate anal-genital region, going on to mutual fur grooming, when ♂ uses the crackling cry. In defence will strike with hands and bite viciously. Dominant animals may also chase a lower ranking animal. In the uncommon event of serious fighting (mainly between ♂♂), grappling, striking, biting of face, hands and feet, as well as biting out hair. Sometimes fatal finish.

Reproduction. Breeding season May–Oct, in S. Africa mainly Jul; births Aug–Nov, in S. Africa beginning of Nov. ♀ cycle 44 days, with 1 week in heat, 2nd and 3rd days most intense. Mating lasts several hours (♂ mounts from rear); gestation 126–136 days. Courting ♂ follows ♀ with the crackling cry, licks face and genital region, then mates if ♀ in heat. If she refuses, ♂ threatens her with open mouth, sometimes with spitting and screaming cries. 1–3 young at a birth, usually 1 or 2, with open eyes, hairy. Young may cling to belly hairs of mother, but are however usually left in nursery hole or the open nest built by ♀; in danger carried in mouth. First leave nest and climb on mother's back at 2 weeks; at 1 month free-moving and take 1st solid food, suckle for 3 months. Young stay with mother until the next birth (about 6 months). ♀ keeps ♂ away from young for only a few days after giving birth. MEASUREMENTS at birth: HB 10–12, TL 12–13, Wt 51–73, after 7 weeks 20/26/270. SEXUAL MATURITY: 1 year. LONGEVITY: 14 years recorded.

LESSER GALAGO, SENEGAL BUSHBABY, Pl. 48
Galago (Galago) senegalensis, (E. Geoffroy St Hilaire, 1796)
G. Steppengalago, Senegalgalago F. Le Galago du Sénégal A. Nagapie S. Komba

Identification. Shape and structure as in Greater Bushbaby, but only half the size, muzzle shorter (in the ssp. *zanzibaricus* nose upcurved 'snub-nosed'). Tail (longer than HB) short-haired at root, becoming thickly bushy in the last third; (or not, as in part, in ssp. *moholi*). Ears with upper edge rather pointed. Ears, palms and soles flesh-coloured. Clitoris (with bone) long and thin. 6 teats (2 pectoral, 4 inguinal). ♂ with naked triangular glandular area in middle of breast. Dent.: upper canines with small tubercle, M^3 triangular. Pelage close, soft, woolly, principal colour of upperside grey (light grey, dirty grey or dark bluish grey), sometimes crown and neck brownish or yellowish to cinnamon, suffusing the whole upperside. Tail usually as back, sometimes brownish towards end with tip black. Face grey, eye patches and sides of muzzle brown to black, back of nose to between eyes white. Underside white to creamy, sometimes throat and breast light brownish. Hands and feet grey, whitish grey, or white. Sometimes arms and thighs washed with yellow. Albinos are known. New-born young are covered above with long fine grey hairs, tail already well-haired, darker than upperside, facial pattern appearing, underside naked; hair growth beginning at 7–10 days. MEASUREMENTS. HB 14–21, TL 20–30, Wt 150–300.

Distribution. Africa south of the Sahara, except the Guinea and Central African rain forests as well as the region south of the Orange, Vaal, and Limpopo Rivers. Northern limit about 15°N (Senegambia to Ethiopia). Also in Zanzibar and Pemba. 9 ssp. HABITAT: savannah, bush, and light woodland (Acacia forest and bush, Mopane woodlands) in dryish regions; river banks, mountain and coastal forests preferred. Up to 2000m in mountains. TERRITORY: as in Greater Bushbaby, size 1·25–3 hectares, determined by old ♂. Overlapping with adjoining territories, but encounters between old ♂♂ limited by the marking calls. Marking also by breast-gland rubbing on boughs, nests, sleeping holes and tree trunks, similarly by muzzle rubbing with spittle, head rubbing, and deposition of urine drops, latter rubbed by belly. Marking ended by biting boughs. ♂ does more marking than ♀. Feeding area of an old ♂ in one night about 2km in which 500 trees may be searched. Population density according to type of country 100–500 animals per sq km. *Map 255*.

Habits. DAILY RHYTHM: as in Greater Bushbaby. A more active jumper (up to 7m), and more agile in general, running around, leaping from tree to tree, feeding, resting, grooming, mixing with neighbours. In flight tail carried over back. Sleeps in forked branches, holes in trees, self-built shelters or open nests according to type of country, and the season. Will also shelter under roofs. Nests and shelters are lined with leaves and small twigs. Entrance to shelter or hole closed before sleeping. Up to 12 sleeping places in one territory. Families sleep together (up to 9), but during breeding season in pairs; shortly before giving birth the ♀ is alone or sleeping with young. Sleep in sitting position, head between legs (ears folded), or lying on side, always with tail over head. Sleeping places, runways, special feeding places, females, and territory boundaries are all marked with urine, either directly or by rubbing with moistened palms and soles, and rubbing of feet on boughs (see Greater Bushbaby). TOILET: after waking, and again before sleeping, the fur is cleaned, using grooming claw; tail included. No face-washing with hands. Mutual grooming of fur with fingers of one hand is common; the other hand holds firmly the back of companion. ♂ also holds ♀ with both hands while using the grooming claw of the hind foot. VOICE: loud chattering as contact call, cackling and shrill whistle in anger, and soft clicking on meeting strangers. ♂ has loud scream while pursuing ♀ at pairing time. A territorial border call as in Greater Bushbaby; twittering to express various moods; shrill cry of fear, soft grunting in contentment. Young have high clicking call when uneasy, soft grunting while suckling and grooming. Young also click and croak in strange surroundings. ♀ calls young softly, and they answer. SENSES and ENEMIES, as Greater Bushbaby. FOOD: spiders, scorpions, insects, young birds, lizards, nectar, petals, sap, fruit, seeds. Catches prey like Greater Bushbaby. Water lapped up with tongue. SOCIABILITY: as in Greater Bushbaby. Partly solitary, partly in family parties. Family sleep together, disperse after waking, come together again to sleep. Ranking order as in the larger species. Old ♂ is aggressive to strange ♂♂ and sexually mature younger ♂♂, especially at pairing time; ♀ is aggressive shortly before and after giving birth. Greet strangers by touching noses, followed by short snuffling and fur scratching on chin and head, or a quarrel. In latter case, sit up with eyes and mouth wide open, ears folded back, hands raised to strike. In light encounters, boxing, wrestling and rolling over each other, but without biting. In the uncommon serious fighting fatal outcome possible. Submissive attitude flat on ground, head drawn back, ears laid back, mouth and eyes almost closed.

Reproduction. In the Sudanese zone litters in Mar–Jun, and Dec. In S. Tanzania and Zambia Aug–Sep, mainly Sep–Oct, in N. Uganda Mar–Jun, and Dec–Feb. In Rhodesia and Botswana young in nearly all months, in S. Africa Nov, Dec, and May. Where there is only 1 rainy season, usually only 1 birth annually, with frequent twins: where there are 2 rainy seasons, usually 2 litters, with normally 1 young at a birth. The ♀ cycle is varied by environment, varying from N. to S. between 40 and 20 days. ♀ on heat for 3–5 days. Mating duration 3–10 minutes, sometimes 1 ♀ mates with several ♂♂. Gestation in the northern ssp. *senegalensis* and *braccatus* 144–146 or 136–142 days; in the southern *moholi* 120–126 days; 1–2 young at a birth, eyes open and hairy. ♀ mates again soon after birth. ♀ licks and cleans young zealously, stays in birth place for first 3 days, afterwards leaves young in hole or carries it on belly, later on her back, when going to feed places it on a bough, returning to it at short intervals. If disturbed, the ♀ changes the nest or hole, carrying the young in her mouth. After 4 days the young one can scramble about, leaves hole for 1st time at 10 days, 1st solid food at 20 days, at 30 days (already two-thirds of adult size) jumps and climbs well, weaned at 6 weeks, is fully grown at 4 months, and at 7–9 months is sexually mature. Wt at birth of *braccatus* 15.6–22.6, *senegalensis* on average 11.5, *moholi* 8.5–13. LONGEVITY: 14 years in captivity.

DEMIDOFF'S GALAGO OR DWARF GALAGO,   Pl. 48

Galago (Galagoides) demidovii (G. Fischer, 1808)/
G. Urwaldgalago   F. Le Galago de Demidoff   S. Komba

Identification. Form and build as in Greater Bushbaby, only much smaller ($\frac{1}{3}$), muzzle short, pug-nosed, ears of medium length, conical; tail like bottle-brush, hands and feet narrower, digits more slender, skin between pads on palms and soles finely pleated. Dent.; upper canines short, barely longer than P^2 and P^3, P_2 and P_3 long, caniniform, upper molars broader than long, lower on the contrary. Penis with bone, long, prepuce with horny spines, clitoris of medium length, with bone. Teats? Upperside dark grey or greyish-brown to brownish-red, tail sometimes greyish-black; underside greyish-white to yellow. Eye patches and spot on side of muzzle dark brown to black, back of nose white. Palms of hands and feet, naked heel spot and region of genital organs in young animals particularly yellow (sniffing areas on meeting). Young cinnamon to dark brown, otherwise like Lesser Galago (p. 253). MEASUREMENTS: HB 11–16, TL 14–22, Wt ♂ 50–90, sometimes up to 120, ♀ 50–80, sometimes up to 95.

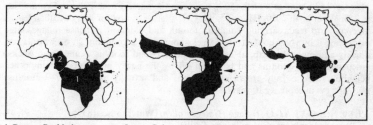

1 Greater Bushbaby   Lesser Galago   Demidoff's Galago
2 Allen's Galago

Distribution. Guinea rain forest to W. Nigeria, central African rain forests from E. Nigeria to E. Zaire and N. Uganda, N. limit about 10°N in west, 5°N in east; south to mouth of Congo and N.E. Angola (6°–11°S), and further east 3°–10°S, in Kenya, Tanzania and N. Malawi. Also on Fernando Póo. 7 ssp. HABITAT: primary, secondary, flooded and gallery forests, also around human settlements and in plantations. From lowest levels of growth to crowns of tall trees (from 2–40m in height), everywhere that foliage is most dense. TERRITORY: size, for ♀♀, 0.–1.5 hectares, sometimes overlapping; for old ♂♂ 1.5–3 hectares (1♂ territory may include 2–5 ♀♀ territories); middle-aged ♂♂ 0.5–2 hectares; their territories lie on the edge of the total population (the larger) or within (the smaller); these animals have no ♀♀, but eventually take the place of the older ♂♂. Younger ♂♂, sexually unripe, live at edge of total population, without territory, wandering around, young ♀♀ establish individual small territories. Between separate populations (10–50 animals) wide intervals. Population density between 50–300 per sq km according to character of the forest.

Habits. DAILY RHYTHM: like Greater Bushbaby. Run, climb and jump with great agility and speed, clearing up to 2m. Spend day among dense foliage, in self-built nests of leaves in forks of boughs or among networks of lianas. Nests are used for 2–3 weeks, fresh leaves being added daily. Usually ♀ with young, sometimes a pair, if ♂ usually alone. Urinate on hands and feet (as in Greater and Lesser Bushbabies) 4–8 times an hour, thus marking all used ways in trees. Marking by strangers is recognised and avoided. In breeding season marking by rubbing ano-genital region on twigs. TOILET: Fur licking, combing with teeth (also mutually), mainly in morning and evening. VOICE: contact call, a high 'yaah', repeated up to 10 times every 5–10 minutes, mostly in evening after going out, as the animals disperse to feeding areas (dispersal call). Threat or alarm cry, high, short, loud and piercing. Growling and twittering if disturbed by man. Cooing when sexes meet. Soft growling of ♀. Clicking call of unattended young. Deep growling in anger when quarrelling. Cry of fear in great danger, shrill and loud. Chattering when quarrelling. Gathering call at end of night (a rising series of sharp cries of 2–3 second duration), calling all to return to the nest, perhaps moving in single file. Also call of neglected young or old animals. SENSES: as in Greater Bushbaby. FOOD. At least 4/5ths part is insects, 1/5th sap of trees, fruit, tender shoots and buds. Catches prey by sudden pounce. SOCIABILITY: as in Lesser Galago.

Reproduction. Births all year round, but main season Dec–Feb. Mating duration 3–15 minutes. 1–2 young at a birth (50% twins), in the nursery nest. Pelage of young, see p. 255. Wt at birth 7–10, HB c. 7·5, TL c. 9. ♀ stays in nest for first day, then leaves in evening to feed, carrying young in mouth and hiding it in dense foliage, later recovering it by vocal contact. At 2 weeks young can accompany ♀, at 3 weeks run quickly and make 1st leap, at 3½ weeks eats 1st solid food, is weaned at 6 weeks, independent at 3 months and is driven off by the newly pregnant ♀; joins other neighbours and is fully grown at 6 months and sexually mature at 7–9 months. LONGEVITY: in captivity 10 years.

ALLEN'S GALAGO, *Galago (Galago) alleni* (Waterhouse, 1837) **Pl. 48**
G. Buschwaldgalago   F. Le Galago d'Allen

Identification. Form and build as Lesser Galago (p. 253) but somewhat larger, muzzle rather sharper and longer, tail evenly bushy, fingers and tails longer. Penis long and narrow, with bone. Prepuce with horny spines. Vulva swollen, like scrotum; perineal area naked. 6 teats (2 axillary, 2 pectoral, 2 inguinal). Dent.: P^2 long, separated by a space from P^3, M^3 as large as M^2. Fur thick, soft and woolly. Upperside light brown to dark reddish-brown, usually arms and outside of legs leather to rust-coloured, tail brown to black or at root dark slate grey and black at tip, sometimes extreme tip white. Hands and feet slate grey to greyish-black, palms and soles flesh-coloured. Underside greyish-white to yellow, sometimes with a reddish breast stripe. Face grey, with blackish eye patches, and light grey stripe from nose to forehead. Juvenile coat not known. MEASUREMENTS: HB 20–28, TL 22–28, Wt 260–410.

Distribution. Western Central Africa from Niger east to S. Chad, W. Central African Republic and E. Congo (Brazzaville), and along the Congo and Ubangui river basins to about 15°–18°E. Southward to mouth of Congo. Also on Fernando Póo. 2 ssp. *Map* p. 255.

Habits. Lives in primary forest, mostly in the undergrowth up to 2m high, also often on ground searching for fallen fruit. Jumps usually in upright attitude. Sleeps in tree holes. Population density about 15 per sq km. Births noted all year round. ♀ carries young in mouth, as in Demidoff's Galago. FOOD: about 70% insects, 30% vegetable matter.

Rather slow in movement, washes with urine as in Demidoff's Galago. Contact call a long-drawn 'ooo', often repeated many times. Further details not known.

WESTERN NEEDLE-CLAWED GALAGO,   Pl. 48
Galago (Euoticus) elegantulus (Le Conte, 1857)
G. Westlicher Kielnagelgalago   F. Le Galago mignon

Identification. Size, form and build as in Allen's Galago, only muzzle short. Ears long, narrow, rounded. Tail thickly bushy, longer than HB. Finger and toe nails (apart from thumb and 1st and 2nd toes) with central keel, and ending in a sharp point. Scrotum hairy above, naked below, cone-shaped, skin grained. Teats? Penis with bone, prepuce triangular, with many small horny spines. Dent.: canines long and pointed, P^2 lengthened and caniniform, P^3 molar-like; upper molars broader than long, lower conversely. Pelage thick, soft, woolly; tail thickly bushy. Upperside pale grey-cinnamon coloured to pale cinnamon, mid-line of back darker, eye rings dark brown to black, nose stripe light brown or grey to black, face greyish-brown; arms and legs rust-coloured, hands and feet brown, tail coloured like back, sometimes towards the tip darker or greyer, sometimes white-tipped. Underside slate-grey to grey, sometimes washed with yellow. Juvenile coat not known. MEASUREMENTS. HB 17–24, TL 26–32, Wt 200–350.

Distribution. As Allen's Galago. 2 ssp.

Habits. Much as in Allen's Galago. On Mt Cameroon to over 1000m. Runs, climbs and jumps very skilfully. Lives in the forest crowns up to 50m high or more, sometimes in feeding 3–4m more. Rarely on ground. Uses strong boughs and lianas in climbing, the pointed nails helping to grip smooth trunks. Also goes head down. Sleeps in dense foliage and among lianas. Population density *c*. 15 animals per sq km. Feeds largely on tree sap (75%), as well as insects (20%) and fruit (5%). Apparently 2 principal breeding seasons; Nov–Jan and Jun–Jul. ♀ carries young in mouth for about a month, afterwards on back. Further details not known.

EASTERN NEEDLE-CLAWED GALAGO,   Pl. 48
Galago (Euoticus) inustus (Schwarz, 1930)
G. Östlicher Kielnagelgalago   F. Le Galago mignon sombre

Identification. Form and structure as in Western Needle-clawed Galago, only smaller, ears larger, and tail towards end becoming progressively more thickly haired. Dent. P^2 not like canine. Upperside dark brown, black eye-rings, light nose-stripe, underside greyish-brown, tail becoming darker towards the tip. Juvenile pelage not known. MEASUREMENTS. HB 16–20, TL 19–26, Wt 170–250.

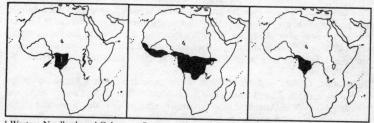

1 Western Needle-clawed Galago   Potto
2 Eastern Needle-clawed Galago   Angwantibo

Distribution. E. Zaire border region from Lake Mobuto (Albert) to Lake Tanganyika as well as possibly W. Uganda. Details not fully established.   HABITAT: as Western Needle-clawed Galago, and Demidoff's Galago, but apparently outside the closed forests.

Habits. Resembling both latter, very quiet, further details not known. Main litter season apparently Nov–Dec.

SLOW LORISES, LORISINAE

HB 17–40cm. Arms and legs of equal length, tail a mere stump or absent, head round, eyes very large, ears very small and round, 2nd finger (sometimes also 3rd) greatly reduced or a mere stump. Second toe with claw, other digits with broad terminal pads and flat nails. 4–6 teats: with or without penis bone. Gestation $3\frac{1}{2}$–$6\frac{1}{2}$ months. 1 (rarely 2), young. Fur dense and woolly. Solitary, nocturnal, slow-climbing omnivorous feeders, soft plant food incidental. 4 genera with altogether 5 species in Africa and S. Asia, of which in Africa are 2 genera, each with 1 species.

POTTO, *Perodicticus potto* (P. L. S. Muller, 1766)   **Pl. 48**
G. Potto   F. le Potto de Bosman
Identification. Form thickset. Head round, muzzle short, eyes large, ears short, rounded, half hidden in fur. On the back of the neck are 4 horny points, consisting of processes of the last 2 cervical vertebrae and the first two thoracic vertebrae, projecting through the surrounding naked, sensitive neck skin. A few short whiskers, and long tactile hairs on neck, which is very muscular and thick-skinned. Arms and legs same length. Hands and feet short and sturdy. Thumb wide-angled, great toe opposable through 180°; both are short and broad. 2nd finger only a stump, 3rd and 5th the same length, united at base. Skin between the 6 tactile pads of soles naked. Flat nails, only the second toe with long claw-like nail. The stumpy tail thick-haired in bottle-brush style. Penis short, with bone, prepuce without horny spines, lower part of scrotum with horny skin, and adjoining skin gland with a scrotum-like swelling. The gland encloses base of clitoris, latter long, with bone. 6 teats (2 pectoral, 4 inguinal). Dent.: $2 \cdot 1 \cdot 3 \cdot 3 = 36$; upper incisors mere pegs, lower incisors, together with lower canines, long and narrow, strongly projecting forward (grooming comb). Upper canines long and sturdy, P_2 caniniform, upper molars broader than long, lower similar. Fur, dense, soft, woolly, with projecting guard hairs. Upperside slate-grey, cinnamon-, reddish-, mahogany-brown, to brownish-black, usually with darker spinal stripe and eye rings. Hands and feet lighter or darker than back. Underside light to slate-grey or beige. Sometimes fore part of body brownish-black, hind part greyish-brown. Newborn thinly haired, skin flesh coloured, ears yellowish, nose brown. Young lighter or darker than adults, pale whitish, whitish-grey, cinnamon coloured, or dark reddish-brown; underside whitish, grey or creamy. Whitish animals, after 4 days, others after 7 weeks, coloured grey to silvery-grey, spinal stripe appearing; after 8 weeks general colouring as in adults, completed at about $\frac{1}{2}$ year, when also the slight crest that marks the young disappears. The neck bone processes appear at 1 month.   MEASUREMENTS. HB 30–40, TL 5–10, Wt 0.6–1.6.
Distribution. Guinea and Mid-African forest zone from Sierra Leone in W. to W. Kenya in the N.E., and from mid-Zaire (about 25°E) south to Lower Congo and mouth. Also in N.E. Angola. 5 ssp.   HABITAT: primary (10–30m high), and secondary forests (5–15m high); favours clearings and forest edges, particularly with individual high trees, as well as shade trees in plantations. In mountains up to 2000m or

more. TERRITORY: ♀ territory averaging 7.5 hectares, old ♂ averaging 12 (7.5–15). 1 old ♂ territory may cover several ♀♀ areas. Old ♂ usually controls the ♀ territories; will follow 1 ♀ for a day or a week until it is in heat, then mates. Drives off other sexually mature ♂♂ from his territory. ♀♀ avoid meeting each other. Urination marks territory, defining the sex, sexual state, and identity of the marker; made at intervals by spraying urine on branches and screaming. Each territory has favourite sleeping and feeding places. Population density may be 8–10 animals per sq km. *Map* p. 257.

Habits: DAILY RHYTHM: active only at night. Arboreal. Movements very deliberate, without shaking branches, thus avoiding enemies or disturbing prey. Goes on all fours, sometimes hangs under boughs to reach fruit, may hang by hind feet. In great danger may let itself fall to ground. Otherwise seldom on ground, perhaps when other trees are not easily accessible. Sleeps sitting in lianas, thick foliage or in forks of boughs, holding tightly with hands and feet, or rolled up in a tree hole. A rough surface inside a tree hole may be smoothed by the horny neck processes. Body temperature may vary between 30°–35°C within a few days. TOILET: fur grooming and licking, scratching with toilet claw. At pairing time mutual grooming of the sexes, also ♀ and young. Mutual cleaning of the sensitive area around the horny neck processes. VOICE: very quiet. Young have a high clicking call when uneasy, mother answers in same way, and adults use it as a contact call. Also used by ♂ following oestrous ♀. Growling and screaming when fighting or attacked. SENSES: scent and hearing very good, sight good. ENEMIES: Palm civets, genets, large owls, snakes, monitor lizards. Defends itself by putting head between arms, the thorny neck processes towards enemy, may suddenly strike with head and teeth, growling and twittering. In extremity may drop to ground. Rarely fights in the wild, only with same sex, clasping, rolling, biting, squealing and chattering. Fighting ♂♂ strike each other with the horny neck processes. In fear the genital glands emit 'fear scent.' FOOD: fruit, leaves, buds, sap of trees, moss, lichens, fungi, insects, birds, lizards, eggs, snails. About 80% of food vegetarian, the rest of animal extraction. Prey is approached very deliberately, then grabbed suddenly with both hands and killed with a bite. The scent of its glands attracts flies. Small birds will mob a sleeping potto. It seems that feeding may take place only every second day. SOCIABILITY: each animal lives alone in its territory; old ♂ will search regularly for a ♀. A young ♂ will wander around on sexual maturity, but young ♀♀ stay near mother. An intruder finding itself in enemy territory near the occupant will stay motionless to avoid detection.

Reproduction. In E. Zaire, Uganda and Kenya litter period Nov–Feb and Apr–Jun; in Gabon Aug–Jan. Only 1 young annually. Strong scent of scrotum and clitoris skin glands especially noticeable at pairing time. ♀ secretions excite ♂. The two sexes may sit with the sensitive neck processes in a position to rub mutually the sex organs and release the strong secretions. ♀ cycle 34–48 days. Mating either from behind or from front. Gestation 6–6½ months. Birth may be induced by previous mating. Usually 1, rarely 2 young. ♀ eats foetal sac and afterbirth and licks young. All 6 teats are used by the young which clambers about actively. ♀ cleans and guards young. After 1 week she may take young outside, leaving it clinging to branches while she goes off to feed. On return the ♀ finds the young by the clicking hunger call. At 1 month the young rides on mother's back, at 2 months follows her cautiously, at 5–6 months goes feeding alone, finding mother again in the morning. First solid food at 2–3 months, suckling period 2–3 months. At 9 months fully grown. Hair development (see **Identification**); independence (see SOCIABILITY). Wt at birth 35–50, at 3 months 500. Total length at birth 9–11, at 3 months 42. LONGEVITY: 11 years in captivity.

ANGWANTIBO, *Arctocebus calabarensis* (A. Smith, 1860)   **Pl. 48**
G. Bärenmaki   F. Le Potto de Calabar

Identification. Resembling Potto in form, but smaller, nose and ears rather more slender, eyes larger and closer together, no horny cervical processes; 1st finger and external tail absent. Edge of ears with fringe of hair. Thumb and great toe widely opposed, considerably longer and nearly twice as broad as the other digits. Index finger missing, 2nd hind toe reduced, with claw. Of the other digits the 4th is longest; the 3rd–5th fingers, and 2nd–5th toes are united at the base. Tactile pads on thumb and great toe very large, all pads without papillae. Penis with bone, prepuce without horny spines, with papillae only, scrotum hairy as far as the small glandular horny surface at base. Clitoris long and thick, root thickened and turnip-shaped; in corner of vulva a small horny plate holding a scent gland. 6 teats (2 axillary, 2 pectoral, 2 inguinal). Dent. as Potto, P^2 longer, upper molars rectangular. Fur like Potto, without spinal stripe. Upperside yellowish-brown to light brown or reddish-gold; underside light grey to ash grey, greyish-brown or yellow, in part chin and throat whitish. Tail stump with or without black tip. Eye rings and muzzle faded or distinctly darker than face. Young much darker than adults, hair long and shaggy, with white tips. Within 9 months attains adult colour. MEASUREMENTS. HB 25–40, TL 1–1·8, Wt 200–470.

Distribution. S. Nigeria (E. of Cross River), Mid and S. Cameroun including Mt Cameroon, E. to Sanaga R, Rio Muni, Gabon, E. to Ubangui and Congo Rivers in E. and S. 2 ssp. HABITAT: primary and secondary forests; the lower denser growth preferred (also found in tree nurseries and plantations). Usually in low trees (up to 5m) sometimes also in the higher storeys (up to 10m or more). TERRITORY: probably territorial, marking with drops of urine. Details not known. Population density about 2 per sq km. *Map* p. 257.

Habits. DAILY RHYTHM: nocturnal, rather slow moving, but can also run and climb quickly among the branches, but does not jump. Always takes flight upwards in trees. Sometimes goes on ground, e.g. to eat fallen fruit or to go from one tree to another. By day sleeps lethargically. Sleeping position like Potto, sitting with head between legs in dense foliage or creepers. TOILET: after waking spends $\frac{1}{2}$ hour grooming with teeth and claw. VOICE: very quiet; growls when angry. Young have a clicking call. SENSES and ENEMIES: not known. In defence position stands up on hind legs, growling open-mouthed with head turned under an arm. FOOD: up to 90% insects (especially caterpillars and other grubs) as well as snails, lizards, fruit. SOCIABILITY: mainly solitary, at breeding time in pairs, and ♀ with young.

Reproduction. ♂ marks ♀ by creeping over her lengthwise from behind (sometimes from front) pressing scrotum on her back. Adult ♀ ♀ also mark each other in the same way, but not with ♂. Genital glands in both sexes produce a strong liquid secretion in unrest or danger, with a 'fear scent' as in Potto. ♀ cycle 36–45 days. Gestation 131–136 days. 1 young at a birth, hairy and with eyes open, climbs slowly into mother's fur and usually clings to her belly. ♀ licks young clean. At 11 days the young first leaves mother and hangs in twigs, at 17 days is more active, at $1\frac{1}{2}$ months catches and eats insects, is weaned at 4 months, is fully grown at $7\frac{1}{2}$ months and is driven off by the ♀ shortly before her next birth. From 2 weeks the mother lets young go alone among the branches while she feeds, and locates it on her return by the clicking call. Wt at birth 24–30, at 1 month 60, at $7\frac{1}{2}$ months 235, when fully grown. SEXUAL MATURITY not known. LONGEVITY: $4\frac{1}{2}$ years in captivity.

Apes & Monkeys, Anthropoidea

MONKEYS & BABOONS, CERCOPITHECIDAE

Small to middle-sized; HB 30–110cm, TL 0–100cm, Wt 1·5–50kgm. Nostrils close together. Number of digits 5/5, nails flat, thumb and great toe opposable; (in Colobinae thumb small or absent). Dent.: $2 \cdot 1 \cdot 2 \cdot 3 = 32$, upper canines long, M^3 5-cusped. 2 pectoral teats. Penis pendulous, with bone. Gestation 5–9 months. 1 active young born with eyes open. Sociable, arboreal and/or terrestrial, mainly herbivorous and diurnal. In the subtropical and tropical regions of the Old World from Africa and Arabia through India, Ceylon, China and Japan, and the Indo–Malayan archipelago. 3 subfamilies, 20 genera, 62 species, of which 8 genera with 32 species are African.

BABOONS, PAPIINAE

HB 40–110cm, tail absent, stumpy, or long (20–80cm). Head rounded, muzzle moderately or strongly projecting. Eyes close together. Ears naked, small to medium sized; large part of face naked, sometimes swollen. Cheek pouches present. Fur short to medium length, soft or harsh, often with peculiar outgrowths (especially in $\male\male$): crown or temporal crest, beard or shoulder mane. Tail with or without tuft, in part breast and buttocks naked, latter with ischial callosities. Face, breast, buttocks and/or genital region often vividly coloured, especially in $\male\male$. Arms and legs about same length, or only slightly different; in mangabeys the fingers partly joined basally. Predominantly terrestrial; for security sleep in trees or among rocks. Sociable in troops or packs. Omnivorous, but largest part of diet vegetarian, locally occasionally carnivorous. DISTRIBUTION, see Family. 10 genera with 22 species, of which Africa has 3 genera with 10 species.

BABOON, *Papio (Papio) cynocephalus* (Linnaeus, 1766)   **Pl. 50**
G. Steppenpavian   F. Le Babouin   A. Bavian   S. Nyani
Identification. The largest, terrestrial, on all fours, dog-headed monkey with long muzzle and medium or long tail. Muzzle sharply angled from braincase. Ears small, naked, rounded, with indistinct or slightly elongated tips, high set, though sometimes hidden in fur. Eyes small, close set under prominent supraorbital swellings. Large cheek pouches. Body with deep chest and high abdomen. Back more or less sloping from front to rear. Tail short-haired, with more or less prominent tuft, carried evenly arched or sharply angled at the first third of length. Arms longer than legs. Walks mainly on fingers of hands and on soles of hind feet. Hands and feet narrow, thumbs and great toes reduced. All digits with nails. Tactile pads, with papillae, on all digits and soles of hands and feet. Buttock area naked, with 2 small or large kidney-shaped ischial callosities. Scrotum and penis pendulous, latter with bone and large prepuce. Vulva prominent, clitoris well developed but not prominent. In $\female$ large genital swelling when in heat. 2 pectoral teats. Dent.: $2 \cdot 1 \cdot 2 \cdot 3 = 32$, incisors large and powerful, canines long and dagger-like, P_1 with long narrow cutting cusp. Molars with 4 or 5 cusps. Face naked, with numerous tactile hairs. Pelage thick and harsh, sometimes in $\male\male$ with side-whiskers and neck or shoulder mane. Underside thinly haired, some-

times almost naked. Upperside olive-yellow, reddish-brown, olive-grey, or olive-brown to blackish. Sometimes face, hands and feet blackish. Underside like upperside or lighter, or creamy to whitish. Ischial callosities slate-grey, purplish-grey or purplish-red. Young blackish with pink face; after 4 months grey to brown, face darker; at 1 year full adult pelage. MEASUREMENTS. HB ♂ 65–110, ♀ 50–80; TL ♂ 45–75, ♀ 35–50. Ht ♂ 50–75, ♀ 40–60; Wt ♂ 25–30, ♀ 10–30.

Distribution. Africa south of Sahara except the Guinea and Central African rain forests; south to Cape. In N. Africa still occurring also in the remote Air, Tibesti and Ennedi mountains, otherwise northern limit about 15°N. Absent in N.E. (Ethiopia, Eritrea, Ogaden, N. Somalia) and in S. and S.W. (W. Transvaal, Orange Free State, northern Cape Province). About 30 ssp. have been described, and 7 are here considered valid (these mix in their boundary regions and therefore are not full species. (Other authors, however, recognise at least 4 as full species): (1) Guinea Baboon *papio* (Desmarest, 1820) (G. Guineapavian F. Le Babuin de Guinée). HB up to 75, reddish-brown, well developed mane, tail curved, reddish broad ischial callosities; western Senegal region (E. Senegal, E. Gambia, N. Guinea, W. Mali, S. Mauretania). Threatened. (2) Olive Baboon, *anubis* (Lesson, 1827) (G. Anubispavian F. Le Papion anubis). HB up to 100, olive-green brownish, with mane, tail angled, face and callosities blackish-grey, the latter broad; eastwards connection from (1), from Senegal east through N. Zaire to Ethiopia, Kenya, Uganda and N. Tanzania. (3) Yellow Baboon, *cynocephalus* (Linnaeus, 1766) (G. Babuin F. Le Babouin cyno-céphale). HB up to 100; yellowish-brown to grey, without mane, limbs slender, tail angled, ischial callosities broad, purplish grey: E. Africa coastal regions from mid-Somalia south to Zambesi (E. Kenya, E. Tanzania, Malawi, N. Mozambique). (4) Kinda Yellow Baboon, *kindae* (Lonnberg, 1919) (G. Zwergpavian F. Le Babouin de Kinda). HB up to 65, the smallest baboon; Zambia, Katanga, N. Angola. (5) Kalahari Chacma, *ruacana* (Shortridge, 1942) (G. Kalahari Barenpavian F. Le Chacma de Damara). HB up to 85; ochreous-greenish to brownish, long hair crest on shoulders, tail angled; callosities small, grey. S. Angola, S.W. Africa, W. and N. Botswana. (6) Rhodesian Chacma, *griseipes* (Pocock, 1911) (G. Grosser Tschakma F. Le Chacma grand A. Boombobbejaan). HB up to 110, brownish-yellow, darker than (5); feet grey, otherwise like (5); approximately between Zambesi and Limpopo (Rhodesia, Mozambique, S. Zambia, N.E. Transvaal). (7) Cape Chacma, *ursinus* (Kerr, 1792) (G. Schwarzer Tschakma F. Le Chacma de Cap A. Kaapse Bavian). HB up to 100, blackish-brown, hands and feet black, otherwise like (5). Union of S. Africa (see **Distribution**). HABITAT: open country (semi-desert, steppe, savannahs), gallery forests, open woodland, locally in closed forest (in Zaire, N. of Congo R.), broken country with rocky ravines, lava fields, kopjies etc. In mountains up to 3000m or more. Must have access to water always. HOME RANGE: each troop (depending on type of country) has home range of about 2–30sq km. Neighbouring troops may have overlapping ranges, but rarely intrude on essential central features (sleeping, drinking and feeding zones). In dry season tolerate neighbours at the water holes. While the troop remains in one place, old ♂♂ stay on watch for intruders, although direct encounters are not frequent, and no part of the range is defended like a strict territory. *Map* p. 265.

Habits. DAILY RHYTHM: sleep at night in trees or among rocks. In the morning the troop goes out to feed, within a radius of 1–2km around sleeping quarters; however, wanderings up to 10km possible. Mid-day rest in shade, in afternoon another feeding period (may last 2–3 hours), then return to sleeping place. As the troop wanders, the older juveniles are in the lead, followed by ♀♀ and juveniles, then the old ♂♂ with mothers and babies. In face of danger, the old ♂♂, aided by all other adult ♂♂ in the troop, take up defensive positions. The long powerful canine teeth and fierce fighting ability make baboons very dangerous adversaries. TOILET: grooming with fingers and teeth, whether separately or mutually, is an important feature of troop life as a means of communication, indicating befriending, comforting, rewarding etc. VOICE: noisy, with wide range of vocal sounds, e.g. Barking, very common, single or polysyllabic, in warning or excitement, increasing in intensity with rising excitement. Grunting, a common general contact call, in satisfaction, but also as warning (e.g. old ♂ to a straying ♀), in excitement rising to a sharp snore. 'Wah-wah' with head rocking and tail waving indicates great pleasure. 'Ooo–ooo' in young if hungry, or in play, or in old animals when anxious or angry. Chattering in alarm. Soft 'eek-eek' or buzzing sound when surprised. Lip smacking in a friendly way when grooming. Scream or yell in fear or suffering. SENSES: sight and hearing very good (can distinguish colours). Scent good. ENEMIES: principally leopard, capable of killing a solitary ♂, but usually snatches a young one from edge of troop. Other occasional killers of baboons are lion, hunting dog, crocodile, python, Cape eagle. Not uncommonly associate with antelopes. On farms in S.W. Africa a single tamed ♀ has been known to guard isolated flocks of sheep like watchdog. FOOD: omnivorous. Grass (usually the greatest part of the vegetarian diet), herbs, seeds, roots, tubers, bulbs, leaves, buds, fruit, bark and sap of trees, lichens, beside field crops in farming areas. Also insects at all stages, honeycombs, molluscs, worms, crabs, spiders, scorpions, eggs and young of ground-nesting birds, lizards, new-born gazelles and antelopes and young hares, as well as lambs. Occasional cannibalism (when an old ♂ may kill and eat a young one of the same troop); even known to have killed young children (several cases in the Transvaal). SOCIABILITY: associate in herds of 10–150 animals, depending on country and food supply. On the plains of E. and S. Africa usually 20–80, in the semi-deserts of S.W. Africa up to 150 animals (dividing up during the day into several foraging troops). Within a troop more ♂♂ than ♀♀ (the first mature earlier). Each troop has marked ranking order: ♂♂ always precede ♀♀, within the ♂♂ according to strength, within the ♀♀ according to age (however ♀♀ with small sucklings rank high). The highest ranking ♂ or ♀♀ (in large herds usually 2–4) lead and defend the troop, and in return expect the best in food or in personal attention.

Reproduction. ♀♀ have oestrous cycle of 23–42 days (usually 30–35). At beginning the perineal and anal skin swells, reaching maximum intensity within a week, remains at peak for a week, followed by ovulation (18th–19th days), and thereafter quick return to normal. At peak of ovulation only the highest ranking ♂ may mate and fertilise the ♀; thereafter other ♂♂ may mate with her. Mate from behind, standing, feet of ♂ holding ♀ thighs. Gestation averages 187 (173–193) days. No definite breeding season, in E. and S.E. Africa most births in Oct–Dec. 1 young, twins very uncommon, born hairy and with eyes open. ♀ licks young clean and eats afterbirth. At first young clings tightly to mother's belly fur, at 5 weeks begins to ride on her back. At 3 months begins to explore for itself and plays with others of same age. First solid food at 5–6 months, weaned at 8 months and independent, is still guarded by mother up to 2 years; at 2½ years is established in ranking position. M^1 cut at 1½ years in ♂, in ♀ at 2 years (up to that age considered juvenile): upper permanent canine in ♂ at 4¾ years, in ♀ at 4 years (from that time reckoned to be adult). Wt of young ♂ 1–4, ♀ 1–3·5, immature ♂ 3·5–14, immature ♀ 3·2–9. SEXUAL MATURITY: 3½–4 years in ♀, 4–6 years in ♂. LONGEVITY: in captivity several records of 30 years or more, once 45 years.

HAMADRYAS, *Papio (Papio) hamadryas* (Linnaeus, 1758)   **Pl. 49**
G. Mantelpavian   F. L'Hamadryas
Identification. Form, body structure and dentition as in Baboon (p. 261). Back rather sloping, muzzle less sharply angled to front of cranium. Ears round with small points. Tail about two-thirds HB length, with tuft, usually arched. ♂ with well developed cheek whiskers, strong neck and shoulder mane (hair length up to 25cm). Callosities moderately broad, forming transverse band with wider ends; in ♂ surrounded by prominent naked skin swellings. ♀ with larger swellings around the callosities during oestrous cycle (as in Baboon). In ♂, face, callosities, scrotum and penis flesh coloured to red, skin of breast and belly with bluish overwash, palms and soles dark brown with upperside blackish-brown. In ♀ soles of hands and feet, callosities and face dark brown. ♂ pelage ash-grey with brownish suffusion, in ♀ grey- to olive-brown, with greenish suffusion. Newborn black-haired, pink-faced, at 4 months begins to assume ♀ colour, at 12 months the complete ♂ coat at sexual maturity. Blackish, silver-grey or white animals sometimes occur.   MEASUREMENTS: HB ♂, 70–95, ♀ 50–65, TL ♂ 42–60, ♀ 37–41. Ht ♂ 50–65, ♀ 40–50. Wt ♂ 15–20, ♀ 10–15.
Distribution. N.E. Africa and S.W. Arabia. Red Sea coasts from Suakin southwards, Eritrea, N.E. and E. Ethiopia with Ogaden, N. and Mid-Somalia. S.W. and S. coastal regions of Arabia about 20°N to about 50°E. No ssp. In bordering regions may mix with Baboons. The Hamadryas was honoured in ancient Egypt as representing Thoth, the scribe of the gods.   HABITAT: savannahs, semi-deserts, dry rocky regions, rocky cliffs and steep mountain sides, valuable as sleeping places.
Habits. As Baboon. The sociable troop consists of 1 old ♂, several ♀♀, and their young. The old ♂ keeps the ♀♀ close together, discouraging them from roaming widely by neck-bites with incisors. Several troops may make a pack, numbering 20–50, sometimes 200–300 animals. Adult young ♂♂ stay near the troop, watching for a chance to steal a ♀ from the old harem leader (the pasha), to start their own harems.
Reproduction. Oestrous cycle *c.* 33 days. Gestation 154–185, usually 170–175 days. LONGEVITY: up to 33 years in captivity.

DRILL, *Papio (Mandrillus) leucophaeus* (F. Cuvier, 1807)   **Pl. 49**
G. Drill   F. Le Drill
Identification. Much like Hamadryas (above), but head larger in relation to body, and tail only a short stump, pointed, carried vertically. Sides of nostrils large, erectile, back of nose with distinct ridges, and on either side similar cheek swellings. Callosities rather longish, coalescing, perineal area broad, naked. In ♀ in oestrus perineal skin and clitoris strongly swollen. Dent. as Baboon (p. 261), P_1 however considerably longer. Thumb and great toe widespread, latter very long and strong. ♂ with loose muzzle beard, chin beard and ruff, narrow crest on forehead and crown, and mane on neck and shoulders. In ♂ face, ears and perineal area black, forehead crest brownish-black, beard, ruff and spot behind ear whitish, lower lip with transverse red bands, callosities pink on bluish-violet buttocks. Upperside of body olive-brownish-grey, underside greyish-white. Palms and soles reddish brown. Middle of breast with tuft of greyish-brown hair over a skin gland. Genitalia and back of ears pink-spotted. In ♀, face and ears black, surroundings of teats violet, callosities fleshy, vulva and clitoris reddish, oestrous swellings red. Upperside greenish-grey, underside and sides of head whitish. Newborn: skin (face, ears, soles) fleshy, crest black, back, arms and legs silvery-grey, flanks and tail greyish-white, underside and front of shoulders thinly-haired white.   MEASUREMENTS. HB ♂ 75–90, ♀ 45–60, TL ♂ and ♀ 6–12, Ht ♂ 55–60, ♀ 45–50. Wt ♂ 15–20, ♀ 10–15.

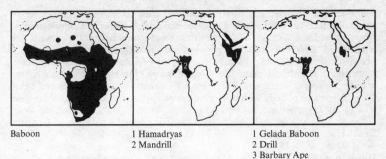

Baboon

1 Hamadryas
2 Mandrill

1 Gelada Baboon
2 Drill
3 Barbary Ape

Distribution. W. Africa from Cross R. in S.E. Nigeria eastward through Mid-Cameroun and Fernando Póo, Gabon (except N. and E.), Congo (Brazzaville) and Cabinda, as well as western Congo south to the lower Congo, north to about 7°N., east to about 13°–15°E. 3 ssp.: (1) Northern Drill, *mundamensis* (Hilzheimer, 1906); north of Sanaga R. (2) Southern Drill, *leucophaeus* (F. Cuvier, 1807); other mainland localities south of Sanaga R. (3) Fernando Póo Drill, *poensis* (Zukowsky, 1922); Fernando Póo.   HABITAT: Mainly rain forest with little ground cover, occasionally in forested rocky territory, sometimes in plantations. Up to 1000m in mountains.   HOME RANGE: only a few sq km in size; forages slowly.

Habits.   DAILY RHYTHM: by day feeding on ground in forest, at night sleeping in lower branches of forest trees. Moves on all fours. Climbs well.   TOILET: as Baboon.   VOICE: deep grunts, often repeated many times only if troop is on the move, presumably close contact call; rapid grunting of old ♂ pursuing young animals, the latter screaming. A kind of crow-like call as long-range contact (about every 4 minutes) and when reunited with the troop. A sharp warning and alarm cry. Loud 'err-err-err' of young when astray.   SENSES: as Baboon.   ENEMIES: mainly leopard.   FOOD: small animals (spiders, snails, worms, ants, termites, small vertebrates on ground, also grass, herbage, shoots, roots, bark, tubers, fruit. Hard-shelled fruit broken open by smashing on ground.   SOCIABILITY: family troop consists of 1 old ♂, several ♀♀ and their young, may be as many as 20 animals. Supernumerary sexually mature ♂♂ may be solitary. Several troops may join to form hordes of up to 200 animals, dividing up into feeding parties. Old ♂♂ guard the troop, as in Hamadryas. Threat gestures consist of abrupt up and down movements of head and neck, staring eyes and mouth closed, or by seizing and shaking branches. Friendship expressed by lateral head movements with canines exposed.

Reproduction. Young at all times of year. Gestation 7 months. Mating as in Baboon. 1 young at a birth. ♀ cycle about 33 days.   SEXUAL MATURITY: as Baboon.   LONGEVITY: 28½ years in captivity.

MANDRILL, *Papio (Mandrillus) sphinx* (Linnaeus, 1758)   **Pl. 49**
G. Mandrill   F. Le Mandrill

Identification. Form, size and structure as in Drill (above), but with cheek ridges broader with longitudinal grooves (in ♂ up to 11 grooves on each side). ♂: upper eyelids, spot behind ears, and muzzle beard whitish. Back of nose, nostrils, transverse stripe on lower lip, buttocks above callosities, and penis, red. Cheek swellings, lower buttocks and scrotum blue. Chin and side whiskers yellowish-orange. Ears pink, callosities rose to violet. Crest on forehead and crown, shoulders and upper arms brownish-black. Cheeks, neck- and shoulder-mane, back, flanks and outside of limbs olive-brown. Underside grey with yellowish wash. Pectoral hair tuft with black and white mixed. ♀: face blackish, back of nose slightly reddish, cheek ridges only slightly bluish. Buttocks dark red, swellings violet, cyclic swellings pink with violet spots. Underside of tail white. Upperside of body with dark olive-brown, underside lighter, greyish. Newborn young: naked skin areas (face, ears, buttocks, palms and soles) fleshy. Upperside of body with dark olive-brown hair; underside thinly haired, pale. Cheeks already grooved. At 11 weeks coloured as in ♀, only the nose still flesh-coloured. ♂ attains full adult coloration at sexual maturity, 5–6 years. MEASUREMENTS: HB ♂ 70–95, ♀ 55–70, TL ♂ and ♀ 7–10; Ht ♂ 55–60, ♀ 45–50, Wt ♂ 20–30, ♀ 10–15.

Distribution. As in Drill, with in addition an outlying occurrence E. of Volta R. (Togo, Benin, S.W. Nigeria). S. border about 4°S (Lower Congo not reached). Not on Fernando Póo (but this is disputed). 2 ssp: (1) Northern Mandrill, *sphinx* (Linnaeus, 1758); N. of Sanaga R. (2) Southern Mandrill, *madarogaster* (Zimmermann, 1780); S. of Sanaga River. *Map* p. 265.

Habits. As Drill, habitat dense rain-, secondary- and mountain forests, in dry season in plantations. Sleep in crowns of trees. Grunting contact call or in contentment, shriek when excited (mainly ♀♀ with young). Births at all times of year, however mainly Dec–Feb. Gestation 7½ months. LONGEVITY: 46 years in captivity.

GELADA BABOON, *Papio (Theropithecus) gelada* (Ruppell, 1835)   **Pl. 49**
G. Blutbrust Pavian   F. Le Gelada

Identification. Form as in Hamadryas, thickset, tail of medium length, with terminal tuft, carried arched. ♂ with longer mane, muzzle high, rounded in front, back of nose convex, on each side several (5–6) cheek folds and grooves. Nostrils small, well back from muzzle, upturned; cheeks below the folds deeply hollowed. Ears small, rounded, naked, tips indistinct. Hands, feet and teeth almost as in Hamadryas. Buttocks naked, callosities separate, rounded or rectangular; in ♂ in 4 parts. Naked skin patch on throat, almond-shaped, 2 similar ones on breast, usually triangular, pointed at top, linked narrowly or broadly with throat patch. 2 teats, close together on middle edge of breast patches. In ♀ on heat a line of blister-like spots on throat, breast and upper buttocks. ♂ with brown to light yellowish whiskers (hair long, sickle-shaped, directed backwards), light to blackish-brown or partly black nape, neck and shoulder mane (hair up to 40cm). Face naked, reddish or dark brown to blackish, upper eyelids white. Rest of body greyish to dark brown, front of arms, hands and feet uppersides brownish-black, tail brown, tuft black, callosities purplish-grey, scrotum, throat and breast patches red. Breast and inside of limbs whitish grey, belly pale brown, soles of hands and feet black. Newborn smoky grey to black-haired, mane development and skin gland colouring reached with sexual maturity. MEASUREMENTS: HB ♂ 70–75, ♀ 50–65, TL ♂ 45–55, ♀ 40–50; Ht ♂ 55–65, ♀ 40–50; Wt ♂ 15–20, ♀ 10–15.

Distribution. Mid-Ethiopia, mountains around Lake Tana, northward to about 14°N., southward to about 9°N. 2 ssp.: (1) Northern Gelada, *gelada* (Ruppell, 1835); mountains N. of Lake Tana. (2) Southern Gelada, *obscurus* (Heuglin, 1863), mountains west, east and south of L. Tana. HABITAT: mountains between 2000 and 5000m, upwards to alpine meadows; favours gorges, steep slopes and precipices on border of grassy plateaux, tree-less and with little vegetation. HOME RANGE: One troop may roam 3–7km each day along the plateau borders. No definite territory is held. *Map* p. 265.

Habits. DAILY RHYTHM: each morning leave sleeping quarters on cliffs or rocks with grassy ledges, to forage on the plateaux meadows at edge of gorges (♀♀ and young on edge of gorges, ♂♂ scattered about on guard). Always retreat to the cliffs in danger. At evening return to the old, or seek out new, sleeping places. TOILET: as Hamadryas. VOICE: grunting as contact call or when contented. Very high sharp bark of adults when excited. Chatter and screech in fear or anger; young in play scream, yowl and bark; if lost have long-drawn complaining cry. In alarm a bisyllabic warning call. Mating ♂ has deep grunt. SENSES: sight and hearing very good, scent good. ENEMIES: perhaps leopard, otherwise only man. FOOD: grasses and seeds, fruit, herbage. Additionally small animals, especially insects. In dry season (Sep–Jun) also dig up roots and bulbs. At that time little nutritive value in food, so longer feeding periods necessary. Cultivated crops sometimes raided. SOCIABILITY: basically family groups of old ♂, several ♀♀, and young; sometimes bachelor parties. Now and then family troops join to form large herds of up to 300 or more. Old ♂ keeps family together by voice and gestures (threat includes eyebrow lifting, head movements, glaring and mouth opening). Greeting and friendliness are shown by curling up the upper lip and displaying the red mucous membrane. They may sometimes encounter Hamadryas and Anubis Baboons without any animosity, sometimes even mixing in the troops by day.

Reproduction. ♀ cycle of 32–36 days, mating by old ♂ (as in Baboon). Gestation 147–192 days. 1 young at a birth, rarely 2. Young born mainly Feb–Apr, and carried as in other baboons. Suckle for 1½–2 years. ♀ has first oestrus 1–1½ years after giving birth. SEXUAL MATURITY: ♀ 5, ♂ 6–7 years. LONGEVITY: 22 years in captivity.

BARBARY APE, *Macaca sylvana* (Linnaeus, 1758)   **Pl. 51**
G. Berberaffe or Magot   F. Le Magot

Identification. Thick-bodied, sturdy, tailless. Head round, muzzle and neck short, ears small, rounded, tips indistinct. Large cheek pouches. Arms somewhat longer than legs. Thumb short, great toe rather longer and thicker, 3rd finger and toe longest. Palms and soles naked. Dent. as in *Papio*, ♂ also with long canines, P$_2$ however shorter. Callosities in ♂ rounded, contiguous at lower edge; scrotum and penis as in *Papio*, penis bone short and thick. Clitoris projecting forward. ♀ callosities narrowly rounded, separated by vulva; usual oestral swelling of circumanal skin. Pelage dense on upperside, with short under fur and long harsh guard hair; hair on crown rather elongated. ♂ with bushy cheeks and short chin beard. Underside thinly haired, showing the bluish skin, arms and insides of legs flesh coloured. Upperside yellowish-brown, crown ochreous, upper side of hands and feet brownish-black. Underside yellowish-grey to yellowish-white. Sexual skin, penis, scrotum, 2 teats, palms and soles, pink; callosities brownish in ♂, slate-grey in ♀; face naked, dark pink. ♀ like ♂, but hair of crown not lengthened. Upperside of newborn young black, underside only thinly haired, chin beard indistinct, skin pale pink. Adult colour at 6 months. MEASUREMENTS: HB ♂ 65–75, ♀ 55–65, Ht ♂ c. 50, ♀ c. 45. Wt ♂ 7–10, ♀ 4–7.

Distribution. In Pleistocene occurred in S.W. Europe and N.W. Africa. Of the former European range now only a remnant population on Gibraltar, where, since the British occupation (1704) they have been reinforced with N. African animals. In N.W. Africa extinct in Libya and Tunisia; in Algeria now only in the mountains between Algiers and Constantine; in Morocco in the Er-Rif region of Spanish Morocco, and in the Middle and High Atlas, south as far as the R. Sous in S.W. Morocco. Present population now only 1200–2000, largely because of habitat destruction. HABITAT: plains and mountains up to 2000m. Persecuted in the plains because of damage to crops in fields and gardens. In the mountains lives in forests with clearings and sparse undergrowth.

Partial to rocky areas, with gorges and rock shelters. Must always be near water. HOME RANGE: range of each troop includes feeding and various sleeping places, and may be of several sq km. Neighbouring troops may overlap; in dry season all will use the same watering place. Troops are friendly to each other. When troops meet the old ♂♂ mutually pacify the younger ones. *Map* p. 265.

Habits. DAILY RHYTHM: sleep among rocks or in trees, with head between knees or lying on side. Generally go on all fours, only stand up on hind legs when reconnoitering. Climb and jump well. Daily wandering from ½–3km. TOILET and SENSES, as *Papio*. VOICE: grunting as contact call or expression of satisfaction; scream in excitement, fear or anger. Young chatter when uneasy. ENEMIES: formerly leopard, now extinct, large eagles, eagle owl (now rare). Keep keen watch for danger. Old ♂♂ deal with attackers courageously, killing dogs, for instance. FOOD: grasses, herbage, berries, fruit, leaves, shoots, roots, bulbs and tubers, insects and spiders. Very partial to garden and farm crops. SOCIABILITY: troops of 10–30 animals, with several adult ♂♂, ♀♀ and their young; old ♂♂ friendly to each other and to young, are allowed to help ♀ to look after and carry young in the first 14 days. Submission is shown by lowering front of body, baring the teeth, and high screaming. If at ease, retract corner of mouth and wrinkle lower eyelids. Teeth chattering is a sign of desire to approach for grooming, etc. Cries of fear are accompanied by up and down movements of lower jaw. Other mimicry and gestures as in *Papio*.

Reproduction. Mating as in *Papio*. Oestrous cycle of ♀ recurrent, every 27–33 days, menstruation 3–4 days, pairing mainly in Nov–Mar. Gestation about 7 months, parturition not restricted, but mainly May–Sep. 1 young (rarely 2), Wt about 400g. Carried as in *Papio*. Between 4th and 8th day, young learns from old ♂ to run, and to ride on parent's back. Suckling period 3 months, stays with mother 6 months, then independent. SEXUAL MATURITY: 3–4 years. LONGEVITY: 20 years or more reported.

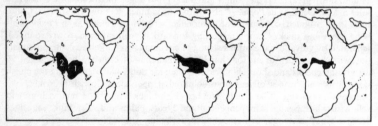

1 Black Mangabey   Crested Mangabey   Grey-cheeked Mangabey
2 Collared Mangabey

BLACK MANGABEY, *Cercocebus aterrimus* (Oudemans, 1890)   **Pl. 51**
G. Schopfmangabe   F. Le Mangabé noir

Identification. Form, dentition and structure as in Collared Mangabey (below). Crown with high pointed hair crest. Long backward-directed cheek whiskers. Fur, face, ears, palms and soles black, callosities and sex organs pink. Near each callosity a small colourless spot. Young black, fur soft, no crest. Albinism in various stages not uncommon. 2 ssp.: (1) Typical Black Mangabey, *aterrimus* (Oudemans, 1890); crest high and pointed, tip somewhat inclined forward. Cheek whiskers directed forward, outward and upwards, sepia in colour like sides of neck; underside brownish-black to black, otherwise all black. (2) Opdenbosch's Black Mangabey, *opdenboschi*, Schouteden, 1944. Black. Crest rises over eyebrows, inclining backwards as a median crest. Cheek whiskers long, directed outwards and backwards. MEASUREMENTS: HB 60–65, TL 80–85, Wt 4–11.

Distribution. Congo basin, S. of R. Congo. 2 ssp. (see **Identification**). (1) *aterrimus*, from Kasai junction with R. Congo in W. to Upper Congo (Lualaba) in E. S. limit around 5°S. (2) *opdenboschi*, between Kasai and Kwango Rivers, south to N. Angola, southern limit about 9°S.

Habits. Entirely arboreal inhabitant of closed forests; habits and voice as in Collared Mangabey. Tail upright or in curve forward.

COLLARED MANGABEY, *Cercocebus torquatus* (Kerr, 1792)   Pl. 51
F. Halsbandmangabe   F. Le Mangabe enfumé

Identification. Slender build, back curved, tail longer than HB. Muzzle of medium length, rounded, a deep hollow in each cheek, large cheek pouches. Face and ears naked, latter small and rounded. Eyes deep set, with short nictitating membrane. Fingers rather shorter than palms, thumb very short. Foot long and narrow, toes short, 2nd and 3rd united at base, great toe large, widely opposable. Short web between all fingers and toes. Nails narrow, only broad on thumb and great toe. Ischial callosities broad, semi-circular, the opening above, united in ♂, separated in ♀ by vulva. In ♀ the swelling of sexual skin high, in two zones, the upper part around anus circular, the lower around vulva more rectangular. Penis long and pendulous, with bone, scrotum large. Dent.: as in Baboon, upper canines very large, upper incisors larger, projecting forwards, molars 4-cusped except M_3 which is 5-cusped. Fur of medium length, silky, underside only thinly haired, the pink skin showing through. Short whiskers in three rows, lower lips and chin with short tactile hairs. Tail short-haired. 2 pectoral teats, no skin glands. 3 ssp.: (1) Sooty Mangabey, *atys* (Audebert, 1797) (G. Mohren Mangabe   F. Le Mangabé enfumé). Upperside dark slate grey, often with dark spinal stripe, underside lighter; lower arms and front of thighs and upperside of tail blackish-grey, palms and soles black; face, buttocks with callosities, scrotum and penis flesh-coloured, ears grey, upper eyelids white, whiskers light grey. Temporal band and neck spot black. Young like adults. (2) White-crowned Mangabey, *lunulatus* (Temminck, 1853) (G. Weissscheitelmangabe   F. Le Mangabé couronné). Upperside light slate grey, darker spinal line, underside white, sharp edge between upper and underside colours. Crown blackish-brown, behind yellowish-white to white, black temporal band present or absent. Young with a yellowish-red suffusion on underside, crown rusty. (3) Collared Mangabey, *torquatus* (Kerr, 1792) (G. Rotkopfmangabe   F. Le Mangabé à collier blanc). Upperside as in *atys*, underside as in *lunulatus*, tail nearly black, with white tip. Arms and legs darker. Crown reddish-chestnut brown, cheek whiskers whitish-grey, narrow temporal band and broad neck-band white. Face and ears black, upper eyelids white; callosities flesh-coloured. Young without the coloured cap, first appears after some months. MEASUREMENTS: HB ♂ 47–67, ♀ 46–59, TL ♂ 52–79, ♀ 40–65, Ht ♂ 40–45, ♀ 38–42; Wt ♂ 7–12.5, ♀ 4.5–7.

Distribution. W. Africa from S. Guinea to mouth of Congo: (1) *atys*, S. Guinea to Sassandra R., W. Ivory Coast. (2) *lunulatus*, Sassandra R. to Afram and Volta Rivers, E. Ghana. (3) *torquatus*, Cross R. (S.E. Nigeria) to Ubangui and Congo Rivers to mouth of Congo (northern limit between 7° and 5°N). HABITAT: primary, secondary and swampy forests, palm swamps, rice fields, plantations and cultivated gardens near forest edge. HOME RANGE: each troop has range with permanent favourite sleeping trees and feeding areas. Ranges can overlap (size of range some sq km but no details available) but the noise made by a troop makes direct encounters easily avoidable. *Map* p. 268.

Habits. DAILY RHYTHM: active by day (also through noon-day), and in morning and evening dusk. Very active and inquisitive. Normal locomotion on all fours, on flat of hands and feet. Tail carried at sharp angle over back, in *torquatus* the white tip is valuable signal to associates, indicating mood according to its height above head. When sitting on a bough the tail may be draped about it, but it is not prehensile. Travels both on the ground and in the trees (mainly in the lower tiers). TOILET: grooming as in *Papio*. VOICE: a wide variety of calls; grunting, cackling, screaming, barking and rumbling, some as contact calls or to attract attention. The cackling is an alarm call. Scream and bark when fighting or chasing. ♂ has a throat sac to increase vocal sounds. An attacker barks, the attacked animal screams. The staccato barking and grumbling indicate territory marking not only by old ♂♂ but also by the rest of the troop. Gestures and mimicry include glaring, wide yawning, eyelid flickering, and baring of teeth. SENSES: sight very good, including colour sensitivity and crepuscular vision, hearing very good, scent good. ENEMIES: leopard, eagles, large owls for young. In danger become silent, motionless and watchful, then bolt down the tree to the ground and thence probably to a swamp. FOOD: mainly fruit and nuts, including coconuts (powerful teeth useful for dealing with hard nuts and fruit kernels); also leaves and shoots; particularly farm crops, including ground nuts. SOCIABILITY: live in troops of about 12–20 animals, with 2–3 old ♂♂, a series of sexually mature ♀♀, and young of varied ages. Friendly in troop behaviour, old ♂♂ care for young. Often associate in mixed troops with guenons (*Cercopithecus cephus, nictitans, pogonias* and rarely *talapoin*).

Reproduction. No particular season. ♀ cycle 24–46 days, average 33. Mating as in *Papio*. Gestation 7 months. 1 young, clinging tightly at first to belly of mother, using its tail to help hold on. Further details not known. LONGEVITY: over 20 years in captivity.

CRESTED MANGABEY, *Cercocebus galeritus* (Peters, 1879)   **Pl. 51**
G. Kappenmangabe   F. Le Mangabé ou Cercocèbe à crête

Identification. Form and bodily structure as in Collared Mangabey. 3 ssp.: (1) Tana River Mangabey, *galeritus* (Peters, 1879) (G. Tana-M. F. Le Cercocèbe de la fleuve Tana). Fur of medium length, rather rough. Hairs of upperside ringed, resulting in yellowish-brown-olive appearance. Crown with a mat of smooth hair, radiating in a whorl from centre and almost concealing ears. Lower arms blackish-brown, face and ears bluish black. Cheeks, throat and underside yellowish-white. ♀ like ♂ but with neck and shoulders paler, hairs unringed. Juvenile coat not known. (2) Agile Mangabey, *agilis* (Riviere, 1886) (G. Olivm. F. Le cercocèbe agile). Pelage shorter than in *galeritus*, whiskers short, hair whorl only on front of crown. Upperside dark greyish-brown to dark olive, speckled with golden-yellow. Palms and soles, face and ears, black; feet brown. Upper eyelids whitish, callosities flesh-coloured. Underside greyish-white, suffused with brownish-red on belly, yellowish-brown skin showing through. ♀ like ♂. Young like ♀, pelage thinner, paler, softer, crown tinged with red. Both *galeritus* and *agilis* variable in colour, occasional albinos. (3) Golden-bellied Mangabey, *chrysogaster* (Lydekker, 1900) (G. Goldbauch-M. F. Le Mangabé à ventre doré). ♂ very sturdy. No frontal hair whorl. Upper lids whitish, whiskers golden yellow. Crown, neck, back, golden brown, black speckled (overall impression somewhat greenish). Arms and legs darker than back. Hands, feet and back of tail brownish-black. Underside, from the chin, gold-ochreous. Callosities pink, penis scarlet, scrotum blue. ♀ like ♂, teats coral red. Juvenile pelage not known. MEASUREMENTS: HB ♂ 51–65, ♀ 44–55, TL ♂ 56–79, ♀ 45–70, Ht ♂ 40–45, ♀ 37–42; Wt ♂ 7–13, ♀ 4·5–7.

Distribution. Middle African rain forest belt from S.E. Nigeria to Lake Mobuto (Albert) in E. Congo, and in E. Kenya. 3 ssp. (see **Identification**): (1) *galeritus*, gallery forest for about 75km along the lower Tana R., in N.E. Kenya. Was seriously threatened by habitat destruction, now has a 'Tana River Primate Reserve' of 175 sq km. (2) *agilis*, closed forest zone from S.E. Nigeria (E. of Cross R.) to Lake Mobuto (Albert), E. Congo, between about 5°N and 1°S in the west, and 2°N in the east. (3) *chrysogaster*, forest zone south of R. Congo, southward to Lukenie, east to Lomami R. HABITAT: Rain, gallery and swamp forests; favours river banks; in mountains up to 1000m or more. *Map* p. 268.

Habits. Few details known, probably like Collared Mangabey (composition of troops, times of activity, terrestrial and flight habits, sleeping places, voice). FOOD: leaves, shoots, fruit, insects, field and garden crops. Tail usually carried arched backwards, in *agilis* sometimes at a sharp angle over the back, in *chrysogaster* sometimes upright and arched above like a handle. Main season for births in Gabon Dec–Feb.

GREY-CHEEKED MANGABEY, *Cercocebus albigena* (Gray, 1850) Pl. 51
G. Mantelmangabe F. Le Mangabé à gorge blanche

Identification. Form, structure and teeth as in Collared Mangabey (p. 269). Fur rather long and rough. Back of head with crest strongly directed backwards. Eyebrow tufts conspicuous, hair of nape, neck, breast and shoulders lengthened to form a shortish mantle (10–15cm-long hairs). Tail long, hair rather long and shaggy like a bottle-brush, shorter at the tip. Face naked as far as ears. Face, ears, hands, soles and scrotum black; callosities, penis and oestrous swelling of buttocks pink or flesh-coloured. Breast and teats of nursing ♀ long. General colour black, no white on upper eyelids. The mane grey or sepia coloured according to subspecies. Albinos sometimes occur. 3 ssp.: (1) Grey-cheeked Mangabey, *albigena* (Gray, 1850) (G. Grauwangen M. F. Le Mangabé à joues grises). Throat greyish-white, underside smoky grey, lower arms brown, mane and cheeks grey. (2) Zenker's Mangabey, *zenkeri* (Schwarz, 1910) (G. Zenker-M. F. Le Mangabé de Zenker). Mantle long, brownish-grey, crest brown, lower arms grey. (3) Johnston's Mangabey, *johnstoni* (Lydekker, 1910) (G. Johnston M F. Le Mangabé de Johnston). Crest up to 10cm, mane mid-brown to dark sepia, underside sometimes sepia. ♀ like ♂. Juveniles: naked areas flesh-coloured, fur black; underside thinly haired, crest and mantle indistinct, sepia-coloured in *johnstoni*, appearing after some months. MEASUREMENTS: HB ♂ 54–73, ♀ 44–61, TL ♂ 73–100, ♀ 73–93; Ht ♂ 40–45, ♀ 38–43. Wt ♂ 6–11, ♀ 4–7.

Distribution. Similar to Crested Mangabey. Mid-African rain forests from mid-Cameroon to W. Uganda, W. Kenya and W. Tanzania. 3 ssp. (see **Identification**). (1) *albigena*, S. Gabon and W. Congo (Brazzaville). (2) *zenkeri*, Mid-Cameroun. (3) *johnstoni*, N. Zaire between Ubangui and Uelle Rivers in N. and Congo R. in south; in the East southwards to 3°S., east as far as Kioga (Lake Victoria), Kisumu, W. Kenya, and Bukoba, W. Tanzania. HABITAT: primary and secondary forest, thick liana-festooned forests, swampy forests; vicinity of lakes and rivers preferred. Only occasionally in plantations. In mountains up to 1500m. HOME RANGE: Size for each troop *c*. 100–200 hectares. In favourable areas 80–150 animals per sq km. Neighbouring troops keep their distance by sound. Short seasonal roaming to places with ripening fruit trees. *Map* p. 268.

Habits. DAILY RHYTHM: as Collared Mangabey, feeding times early morning, midday, late afternoon and evening. Sleep 15–20m up in branches. Entirely arboreal, rarely on ground. Stretch legs forward when sitting. When standing or moving, tail upright, tip lightly curved forward, otherwise held downwards. The tail can grip branches and twigs and so is semi-prehensile, the gripping part being short-haired. TOILET: mutual grooming. VOICE: noisy, with wide range of calls for keeping in touch, passing information etc. Also grunting in unusual circumstances and as further contact call. Old ♂♂ warn of danger with loud repeated call. Old ♂♂ mark territory by staccato barking with a deep giggling ending, although this is also used by other members of troop. During quarrels barking, screaming and howling. Mimicry and gestures are used: in threat staring with raised eyebrows, yawning and lip smacking: in submission present rear of body while lowering fore parts. SENSES: as Collared Mangabey. ENEMIES: leopard, golden cat, crowned eagle. Take refuge in densest foliage and crowns of highest forest trees with loud calls. FOOD: fruit and hard fruit kernels, nuts, leaves, buds, bark; insect grubs in rotting wood. SOCIABILITY: troops of 10–30 animals; in small troops 1, in larger troops 2–3 adult ♂♂, the rest ♀♀ and young. Adults have little tolerance for others of same sex; usually in pairs, with no strong ranking order. Old ♂♂ friendly to ♀♀ and young. Young ♂♂ may form their own small groups. Threaten by glaring and yawning; submissiveness expressed by head-shaking and teeth baring. Often seen in company with guenons (*Cercopithecus*).
Reproduction. Usually no marked breeding season, but in Gabon most births in Dec–Feb. Mating as in *Papio*. ♀ cycle of 30 days, with greatest swelling 8th, 10th, 13th, 15th days. Gestation 174–180 days. Young clings tightly to mother's breast fur, after 2 months climbs onto her back. Suckles for 8–10 months. SEXUAL MATURITY: ♀ about 4, ♂ about 5 years. LONGEVITY: over 20 years in captivity.

LONG-TAILED MONKEYS or GUENONS, CERCOPITHECINAE

HB 30–90cm, long-tailed. Head round, muzzle short, ears naked, of medium size, eyes close together, cheek pouches present. Legs usually somewhat longer than arms. Fur close, soft, only the eye and nasal region naked. Distinctive patterns of hair growth on head, in the form of crests, side-whiskers, moustaches, beards; often in addition to bright colours of these adornments (penis and scrotum often brightly coloured). Sociable, highly agile runners and jumpers, excellent climbers completely at home in the trees. Only the Patas Monkey is a notably terrestrial animal. Mainly frugivorous, sometimes including small animals in the diet. Africa south of the Sahara, with Fernando Póo, Zanzibar, Mafia and Pemba Is. 4 genera with altogether 18 species.

TALAPOIN, *Miopithecus talapoin* (Schreber, 1774)   **Pl. 52**
G. Zwergmeerkatze   F. Le Talapoin
Identification. Very small, not much more than squirrel-sized (the smallest African true monkey). Head round, large in proportion to body, muzzle short, legs longer than arms, tail longer than HB. Ears round, large. Eyes large, with small nictitating membrane. Cheek pouches small. Hands small, fingers of medium length, thumb short; feet long and narrow, toes rather short, great toe short and deep-set, like thumb is widely opposable. Nails narrow, arched, on first digit short and broad. Scrotum large, penis pendulous, with large prepuce; callosities small, oval, clitoris large, rounded, projecting forward; in oestrus swelling of the naked narrow perineal region from underside of tail over anus to vulva. 2 pectoral teats. Dent.: number of teeth as *Papio*, incisors well developed, upper projecting forward, P_1 short, molars 4-cusped, only M^3

three-cusped. Face round eyes whitish, mouth yellowish. Nose with short black hairs, or whole of nose, and area between and under eyes, black. Ears flesh-coloured to black, perineal area violet to grey, scrotum bluish, penis purple, callosities rose-pink, nails, palms and soles colourless. Whiskers golden yellow, directed backwards or downwards, in part radiating in front of ear, at times covering the ears, and with upper edge with narrow black temporal band. Upperside (crown, neck, back, flanks) olive-yellow, middle of back darker (individual hairs grey at base, yellow in middle, black at tip), outside of legs, upper sides of hands and feet golden-yellow, upperside of tail olive-yellow or ash-grey, tip darker or yellow, or with first third blackish-brown and rest brown, and underside yellow to golden yellow. Underside of body white, in part suffused with yellow. ♀ paler than ♂, young like ♀, sometimes with callosities blackish. MEASUREMENTS: HB ♂ 30–40, ♀ 25–37, TL ♂ 36–53, ♀ 26–46, Wt ♂ 1·2–1·9, ♀ 0·8–1·2.

Distribution. Central African rain forests from S. Cameroun to mid-Angola, and ? by Ruwenzori (see note under ssp. *pilettei*). 4 (?) ssp.: (1) Gabon Talapoin, *talapoin* (Schreber, 1774); Cameroun south of Sanaga R, southward to S. Gabon, eastward to about east border of Cameroun and Gabon. Introduced to Fernando Póo and Canary Is. (2) Zaire Talapoin, *vleeschowersi* (Poll, 1940); S. bank of Lower Congo in W. Zaire between Congo, Kasai and Kwango rivers, south to Angolan border. (3) Angolan Talapoin, *ansorgei* (Pocock, 1907); N.W. Angola, south to about 12°S, east to about 15°E. (4) Ruwenzori Talapoin, *pilettei* (Lonnberg, 1919); Congo side of Ruwenzori at 2500m. Up to now known only from one specimen. (Recent studies suggest that *pilettei* is of doubtful location, and that both this and *vleeschowersi* are not distinguishable from the typical form. See Meester & Setzer, 1974). HABITAT: swampy or seasonally flooded forests, mangrove swamps, gallery and secondary forests, often near human settlements (plantations, gardens); always near water. HOME RANGE: each troop in about 6 sq km, with well-used trails in the trees, and sleeping places in bushes and mangroves. On good terms with neighbouring troops. *Map* p. 274.

Habits. DAILY RHYTHM: diurnal, feeding time early morning and afternoon; run and climb actively, sometimes moving backward. In emergency to escape danger will fall into water and dive deeply. Sits upright. Swims freely, and dives in play. TOILET: fur grooming (also mutually) as in *Papio*, scratches with hand or foot. VOICE: rather quiet, various chirping or chattering calls in fear, as alarm cries or in unrest, or to keep contact between other members of troop moving to fresh places, going to sleeping quarters, or if lost. ♀ has sharp cry during mating. SENSES: sight and hearing very good, scent moderate. ENEMIES: leopard, golden cat, genets, large birds of prey, large snakes, Nile monitors. FOOD: leaves, seeds, fruit, water plants, insects, grubs, eggs, small vertebrates; fond of raiding plantations, but shy and hard to catch (in Gabon and Rio Muni can be a pest). Will wash manioc roots in water. Soft fruits may be rolled by hand on the ground and further softened to enable the edible kernel to be got at. SOCIABILITY: family troops of 12–20; sometimes several troops uniting in a herd of 60–80, regrouping as families at the sleeping places (♀♀ with smaller and older young). Often associate with other monkeys, e.g. Moustached and Mona Monkeys. No strict ranking order. Display by lowering head and forequarters, swinging head to and fro and up and down; threat similar with wide open mouth. When angry the tip of tail twitches like a cat's.

Reproduction. Pairing in May–Sep. Gestation 6½ months, births Nov–Mar; 1 young, well-haired and with eyes open. Wt at birth 150–175g. ♀ cycle 27–43 days, with menstruation of 1–4 days. Mating as in Baboon, but duration ¼–½ hour. Young develop very quickly, from 3rd day is aware of its environment, in 2 weeks leaves its mother's body for first time, eats 1st solid food at 3 weeks and from 6 weeks is largely dependent on solid food, though suckles up to 4–5 months. At an early age plays at hunting or scenting. At 3 months largely independent, and, if ♂, joins a troop of bachelors at 6 months. LONGEVITY: has lived 28 years in captivity.

BLACKISH-GREEN GUENON, Pl. 52
Allenopithecus nigroviridis (Pocock, 1907)
G. Sumpfmeerkatze   F. Cercopithèque noir et vert

Identification. Macaque-like, thick set, mid-sized, sturdy, arms, legs and tail rather short, latter only a little longer than HB, thickened at root, somewhat stiff. Head round, muzzle projecting as in macaque, with cheek pouches. Ears round, with short tips. Eyes with nictitating membrane. Palms and fingers moderately long, thumb short, opposable. Feet long and narrow, great toe deeply set, large, widely opposable, toes moderately long. Short web between 2nd and 5th digits. Nails narrow, arched, on the 1st digit short and broad. Callosities longish, in ♂ nearly or wholly contiguous, cushion-like; that of ♀ swelling in oestrus. Scrotum large, naked, penis with large prepuce, clitoris small. 2 closely adjoining teats. Dent.: as in *Papio*, P_1 however with short crown. Fur rather rough on upperside, below softer and thinner. Face, ears, scrotum and sacral pads rosy-red, callosities horn-coloured, scrotum light blue, penis purple. Chin whitish-grey, cheek whiskers greyish-green, bordered above by black, directed backwards, with vertical central ridge. Eyebrows black. Upperside dark olive-green (individual hairs dark with 2 golden-yellow rings), underside from chin to belly whitish-grey, edge of belly with reddish wash, breast spot (over skin gland) with whitish stiff hairs, flanks rather lighter, thighs rather more golden than back. Tail above and below like body. Newborn young like adults, only front of crown whitish-grey and general tone somewhat yellowish, hair soft, tail tip black, sharp division between flanks and belly. After 10 weeks the change to full adult colour complete.
MEASUREMENTS: HB ♂ 45–50, ♀ 40–45, TL ♂ 50–55, ♀ 45–50; Wt 2.5–5.

Distribution. E. Congo (Brazzaville), and M. and N. Zaire between Congo, Ubangui and Uelle Rivers in N., and Kasai, Fini and Lukenyi Rivers in S. E. border between 26° and 27°E. No ssp.   HABITAT: swampy forests.

Habits. Little known. Lives in troops, climbs, jumps and swims well. Eats leaves, fruit, nuts, but also snails, freshwater crabs, fish and insects.

Reproduction. 1 fully-haired young at a birth, clings to mother's belly fur, at 2 weeks leaves her for 1st time, at 5 weeks takes 1st solid food, weaned at 2½ months. Wt at birth *c.* 200, HB + TL 15. Old ♂ helps look after young.   LONGEVITY: 15 years in captivity.

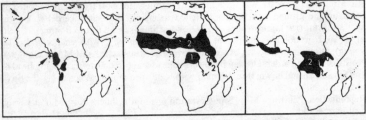

Talapoin

1 Blackish-green Guenon
2 Patas Monkey

1 Lesser White-nosed Guenon
2 Black-cheeked White-nosed Monkey

PATAS MONKEY, *Erythrocebus patas* (Schreber, 1775)   **Pl. 52**
G. Husarenaffe F. Le Singe rouge

Identification. Very slender, long-legged and with long tail. Head round, muzzle short to roundish, prominent eyebrows, eyes deep-set, close together. Nose narrow and flat, ears small, roundish, high set. Hands longer than broad, fingers shorter than palms; feet long and narrow, toes rather short. Thumb and great toe very short, barely reaching beginning of 2nd digit. Nails longish, broad on thumb and great toe. Callosities oval, scrotum naked, penis pendulous, with large prepuce. Vulva and clitoris small. Dent. as in *Cercocebus*. Pelage rough-haired, eyebrows lengthened, nose short-haired, face and ears naked, pink. Cheek whiskers strongly directed backwards. Tail short-haired. Callosities yellowish to greyish-white. Scrotum pale blue, penis pink. On underside the bluish skin shows through the sparse hair. Eyebrows black, produced as a black band to ears. Nose hairs black (*patas, villiersi*) or white (*pyrrhonotus, baumstarki*). Whiskers greyish-white to yellowish-white, front edge black (*patas, villiersi*) or white (*pyrrhonotus, baumstarki*). Crown reddish-orange in front, reddish-brown behind, blackish-brown band separating front and hind crown (*pyrrhonotus*) or not (other ssp.). Neck and shoulders reddish-grey (*pyrrhonotus*), iron-grey (*patas, villiersi*), or greyish white (*baumstarki*). Rest of upperside brick red, underside, arms and thighs greyish to yellowish-white (in ♂♂ limbs pure white). Tail reddish above, yellowish-white to white below. Juveniles: at first dark brown, later head and upper arms dark grey, rest of upperside yellowish, underside greyish-white, with bluish skin showing through; callosities dark blue. MEASUREMENTS: HB ♂ 60–75, ♀ 50–60, TL ♂ 62–74, ♀ 50–60. Wt ♂ 7.5–13, ♀ 4–7.5. ♂ nearly twice as large and heavy as ♀.

Distribution. Sudanese zone from Senegal and Mauretania to the Nile and Atbara in the east; north border between 18° and 15°N., southern limit in west and centre about 10°N, in east about 3°S. 4 ssp.: (1) West African Patas, *patas* (Schreber, 1775); Sudanese zone, as the species, to W. Kordofan, north limit as species, south limit N. border of Guinea and Central African forest zone. (2) Air Patas, *villiersi* (Dekeyser, 1950); Air Massif region, Niger. (3) Nile Patas or Nisnas, *pyrrhonotus* (Hemprich and Ehrenberg, 1829); W. Kordofan to Nile and Atbara, in west southwards to Uelle R., in east to west border of Ethiopia and mid-Kenya. (4) Ikoma Patas, *baumstarki* (Matschie, 1905); N. Tanzania, S.E. of Lake Victoria; southern limit about 3°S. HABITAT: High grassy plains, savannahs and open river banks; sometimes at edge of patches of forest (for sleeping and drinking places), sometimes on open rocky plateaus (*villiersi*), sometimes in fields near settlements. Not shy of water, since in rainy season territory may be flooded. HOME RANGE: each troop may occupy 20–30, sometimes up to 80 sq km, wandering widely (a day's travel from ½ to 12km). Neighbouring troops rarely overlap.

Habits. DAILY RHYTHM: main activity morning and late afternoon; in mid-day heat resting close together in shade. At night sleeping in trees (preferring edges of forest) widely dispersed (up to 400m). Otherwise almost entirely terrestrial. In morning all move off searching for food in open grassland. During feeding period an old ♂ keeps a look-out for danger from a termite hill or low tree, warns the troop and all flee with the old ♂ as rearguard. In great danger the slower young hide in high grass, and are recovered later. Running speed high (up to 50km/ph). Tail normally carried curved over back. Feet wholly, hands partly, flat on ground. Climbs well, though trees are used only for watching and resting. To reconnoitre may stand on hind legs; can run bipedally if carrying food in hands. Uses tail as support when sitting up. When excited make bounding leaps up and down, swinging to land on hands or feet. TOILET: individual and mutual fur-grooming with fingers, lips and teeth. Where hands cannot reach, scratch with toes. VOICE: in the wild normally silent, and usually call with closed mouth. Calls range from shrill scream or explosive sounds in fear; twittering or whistling or long undulating call when pleased; a soft contact call. Scream or chatter when uneasy or afraid. Warning note is a high bark; threat by adult ♂ a series of barks. Expressive gestures; in fear, raising of eyebrows and drawing down corners of mouth; in great fear, crouching, flattening ears; in threat lifting chin, opening mouth wide, bracing the body, and striking with hands. Bared canines and snarling indicate fear. SENSES: sight and hearing very good, scent mediocre. ENEMIES: principally cheetah, leopard, hyaenas, hunting dogs (first and last of these largely extinct in some Patas regions); crowned eagles for young. FOOD: fruit, seeds, leaves, roots, in plantations ground nuts, insects, small lizards and birds, eggs, mineral-impregnated earth. Needs little water. SOCIABILITY: live in troops of 1 old ♂ and up to a dozen ♀ ♀ and their young, usually 6–20, sometimes up to 30 animals; sometimes several troops may come together at a watering place. Troops mix easily. Old ♂ scouts around the wandering troop in new territory, as vanguard; in known areas acts as rear guard; watches in all directions when the troop disperses in search of food, and if necessary diverts enemy attack away from ♀ ♀ and young, giving them time to escape. The old ♂ thus keeps on edge of troop, which is led directly by the top-ranking ♀ at the front. Supernumerary ♂ ♂ may form separate troops, or stay apart; the old ♂ drives off sexually maturing young ♂ ♂.

Reproduction. Pairing in Uganda Jul–Aug. ♀ is without sexual swelling, cycle of 30 days. Presents hindquarters to ♂, blows cheeks out and hisses, mates only with the old ♂. Standing position with ♂ feet on ground. Gestation about 170 days. Births mainly Dec–Feb. 1 young (HB 21–25, TL 24–27) clings tightly to mother, begins to explore surroundings at 2 weeks, but is carried by mother for 3 months; after this takes 1st solid food. SEXUAL MATURITY: ♀ 3, ♂ 3½ years. LONGEVITY: 20 years in captivity.

GUENONS, *Cercopithecus*

G. Eigentliche Meerkatzen   F. Cercopithèques.

Identification. Slender, tail longer than HB, legs longer than arms. Head rounded, muzzle short and round. Ears small, round, naked. Cheek pouches of medium size. Teats, hands, feet, dent. as in *Miopithecus*, only P_1 like *Papio*, scrotum naked, penis pendulous, with bone and large prepuce; clitoris small, ♀ without sexual swelling of sacral region. Ischial callosities small, roundish-oval to pear-shaped. No cutaneous glands. Pelage thick and smooth; often with cheek whiskers and/or full beard. Individual hairs ringed light and dark (agouti-coloured). 15 species, only in Africa south of the Sahara, of which 14 are forest inhabitants (Forest Guenons), 1 species in savannahs and plains.

Habits of Forest Guenons

HABITAT: tropical forest zone. Mainly arboreal, except for *l'hoesti*, seldom on ground. In the forests in all tiers according to species, e.g. *erythrotis, nictitans, mitis* and *diana* in the crowns; *cephus, petaurista, pogonias* in the lowest tiers; *mona* in lower and middle tiers. In all forms of forest, e.g. *cephus* and *mona* in primary, secondary and gallery forests, *mitis, nictitans, pogonias, wolfi* and *diana* in primary forest, *ascanius* in secondary forest, *l'hoesti* in mountain forest, *neglectus* (like *Allenopithecus* and *Miopithecus*) in swampy forest and mangroves, *mona* occurring in latter. In mountains up to 4000m. TERRITORY: each family party resident in ½–2 sq km area, with established arboreal routes, sleeping and feeding places. Old ♂ ♂ use voice to indicate their territory; neighbouring troops keep to a distance of usually 200–1000m: are usually hostile. DAILY RHYTHM: diurnal, 1st feeding session from sunrise to 9·00–10·00; then a rest, and a second feeding period from 15·00–16·00 until sunset. Only *hamlyni* appears to be also active by night. TOILET: fur grooming (also mutual), with fingers, lips and teeth, scratching with hands and feet. No licking except in drying new-born young. VOICE: sometimes noisy; piercing screams, barking, croaking, twittering etc. according to species and situation. In both sexes a small throat sac for increasing vocal powers. The old ♂ territorial marking call differs with the species, serves also to keep the troop together. SENSES: sight and hearing very good (colour sensitive), scent moderate. ENEMIES: mainly crowned eagle, also python, sometimes leopard and golden cat. Warning call usually given by ♀♀ and young, not often by old ♂. Enemies may be threatened by screaming, tail raising, head ducking, shaking or throwing of small branches, urination or defecation on enemy. Small young in the conspicuous first juvenile pelage are protected (if mother is dead may be adopted), but with the change to 2nd juvenile coat (between 2 and 4 months) this ends. FOOD: leaves, shoots, fruit, flowers, berries, seeds, sap of trees, occasionally insects. Field crops and fruit plantations etc. are eagerly raided; with the frequent assembly of several troops into large herds (100–200) can cause havoc. Drinking not necessary because of the juicy diet. SOCIABILITY: usually in family parties of 1 ♂, several ♀♀ and young (6–10, in *ascanius* up to 15, in *erythrotis* up to 30); in *neglectus* and *l'hoesti* only one pair of adults and 1–2 young. No strict ranking order. The troop forms a strong sleeping association. During the day several troops may combine to raid a plantation. In primary forest frequent association of several species in mixed troops, often staying together for a month (e.g. *cephus* with *nictitans* and/or *mona, mona* with *nictitans*) giving better protection all round against crowned eagles (more eyes to watch, and higher numbers of animals confusing the attacker). Also frequently associate with Mangabeys and Colobus monkeys. Near family troops are sometimes found solitary animals (of both sexes, healthy, not driven out of the troop). In addition to voice, information also conveyed by gesture and mimicry (eyebrow movements, head tossing or shaking, mouth opening in threat etc.).

Reproduction: not limited seasonally. Mate in sleeping tree, usually at night, rarely by day, without preliminary play, in style of Baboons. ♀ cycle about 30 days, no menstruation. Gestation 7–7½ months. 1 young at a birth, hairy, eyes open. Rarely 2. ♀ eats afterbirth and licks young dry. The young clings tightly to mother's belly hair, helped by her hand. Weight at birth *c.* 300g. Pelage, see ENEMIES. 1st movement at 1 week, running and climbing at 4 weeks. 1st solid food at 2 months, weaning and independence at 6 months. SEXUAL MATURITY: At 2–3¼ years. LONGEVITY: up to 31 years in captivity.

LESSER WHITE-NOSED GUENON, Pl. 52
Cercopithecus petaurista (Schreber, 1775)
G. Helle or Kleine Weisnase   F. Le Hocheur blanc-nez

Identification. Rather small, with backward directed whiskers. ♂: face, ears and scrotum bluish, muzzle pink, hands and feet black. Black stripe from eyebrows and forehead to ears, and further onto neck where both sides unite (in *buttikoferi* only to ears). From the black eyebrow stripe an offshoot to middle of back of nose and around lower edge of eyes, in *buttikoferi* above the black edge a yellow crescent under eyes. On front of nose a more or less heart-shaped white patch; whiskers and underside of body white; in underside the bluish skin showing through. Upper edge of whiskers to ears black; lower part of latter covered by whiskers. Upperside of body dark greenish,

Heads of Guenons in frontal aspect showing their distinctive specific characters in the head and face hair arrangement and pattern. 1 Mona Monkey, *Cercopithecus mona*. 2 Crowned Guenon, *C. pogonias*. 3 White-nosed G., *C. nictitans*. 4 Moustached Monkey, *C. cephus*. 5 Hamlyn's G., *C. hamlyni*. 6 Buttikofer's Lesser White-nosed G., *C. petaurista buttikoferi*. 7 De Brazza's Monkey, *C. neglectus*. 8 Green Monkey, *C. aethiops sabaeus*. 9 Tantalus Monkey, *C. aethiops tantalus*. 10 Vervet, *C. aethiops pygerythrus*. 11 Malbrouck's Green Monkey, *C. aethiops cynosuros*. 12 Grivet, *C. aethiops aethions*.

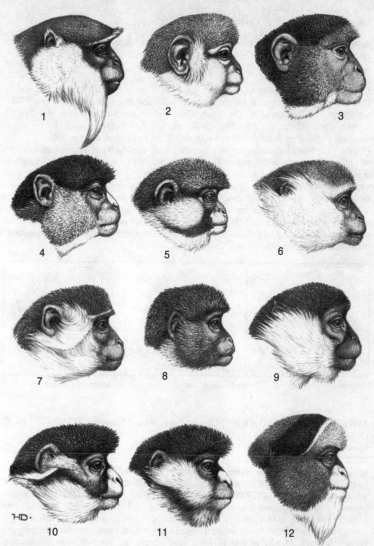

Heads of Guenons in lateral aspect showing their distinctive specific characters in the head and face hair arrangement and pattern. 1 Diana Monkey, *Cercopithecus diana*. 2 Talapoin, *Miopithecus talapoin*. 3 Blue Monkey, *C. mitis doggetti*. 4 Martin's Greater White-nosed Monkey, *C. nictitans martini*. 5 Russet-eared Guenon, *C. erythrotis*. 6 Tantalus Monkey, *C. aethiops tantalus*. 7 Green Monkey, *C. aethiops sabaeus*. 8 Blackish-Green Guenon, *Allenopithecus nigroviridis.*. 9 L'Hoest's Monkey, *C. l'hoesti*. 10 Buttikofer's Lesser White-nosed G., *C. petaurista buttikoferi*. 11 Schmidt's Black-cheeked White-nosed Monkey, *C. ascanius schmidti*. 12 De Brazza's Monkey, *C. neglectus*.

partly over-washed with brownish. Outside of lower arm blackish. Tail brownish above, with black tip, whitish below. Sexes alike. Juvenile pelage paler, otherwise as in adults. MEASUREMENTS: HB ♂ 44–48, ♀ 40–44, TL ♂ 60–68, ♀ 57–66, Wt ♂ 2.5–3.5, ♀ 2–3.1.

Distribution. Rain forests of West Africa from Guinea Bissau (Casamance R.) to E. Ghana. 2 ssp.: (1) Typical Lesser White-nosed Guenon, *petaurista* (Schreber, 1775); Casamance to Sassandra R. (W. Ivory Coast). Also on Bubaque I. in the Bijagos Archipelago, off the coast of Guinea-Bissau. (2) Buttikofer's Lesser White-nosed Guenon, *buttikoferi* Jentink, 1886; Sassandra R. to E. Ghana. *Map* p. 274.

Habits. Frequents secondary forest, swampy forest, coastal bush, young forest, forest clearings with thick undergrowth, forest edges, as well as woodlands and thickets in moist savannahs. Lives mainly in the lower tiers of the trees. Diet includes a wide variety of plants and fruits. Climbs and leaps with great agility. Tail carried horizontally with tip curved downward. In wild state rather silent, however they have a vocabulary; best known is the territorial call of the old ♂ 'kjurr, kjurr' staccato, repeated often. Display and throat gestures: fore part of body bowed down, arms widespread, quick up-and-down head movements to emphasize the white nose-spot; mouth opening with interrupted 'Tschirr' call.

| Moustached Monkey | Red-bellied Guenon | Russet-eared Guenon |

MOUSTACHED MONKEY, *Cercopithecus cephus* (Linnaeus, 1758)   **Pl. 52**
G. Blaumaulkatze   F. Le Moustac

Identification. Medium-sized, whiskers bushy, directed downward and backward; often a noticeable hair tuft on ears. ♂: face bluish-grey to violet, upper lip whitish blue to light blue, black margin on lower edge separate from the black cheek spot and stripe to below the ear. Edge of ear black, conch blue, ear fringe yellow to yellowish-white, whiskers egg-yolk yellow. Black stripe from forehead to ears. Upperside greenish-brown, crown lighter, outsides of legs darker, hands and feet blackish. Underside ash-grey. Tail coppery red (*cephus*) or olive-brown above and greyish-yellow below (*cephodes*). Ischial callosities black, perineal region and scrotum azure, penis cobalt, prepuce brownish-black. ♀ like ♂ but perineal area purple. 1st juvenile coat not known. MEASUREMENTS. HB ♂ 50–58, ♀ 44–50, TL ♂ 70–99, ♀ 66–80; Wt ♂ 4–5, ♀ 3–4.

Distribution. S. Cameroun, Rio Muni, Gabon, and Congo (Brazzaville); N. border Sanaga R., E. and S. border Ubangui and Lower Congo. 2 ssp.: (1) Red-tailed Moustached Monkey, *cephus* (Linnaeus, 1758); Gabon S. of Ogowe R. (2) Grey-tailed Moustached Monkey, *cephodes* Pocock, 1917; rest of the distribution.

Habits. In primary, secondary or gallery forests, widely linked with the distribution of the Oil Palm (*Elaeis*) whose fruit seems essential. Makes home in thick shelter of dense foliage. Leaps from tree to tree up to 20m apart. Each troop 6–10 animals. They use recognized routes along the boughs in follow-my-leader style. ♂ territorial call a sharp, often repeated 'ho-ho', ♀ warning call 'ke-ke', chatter of fear 'ke-ke-ke'. A whistle and other calls by both sexes, significance not known. White-crested hornbills (*Tropicranus albocristatus*) often accompany the monkeys, and both benefit from the joint food-seeking. Also association with *Cercopithecus nictitans* and *mona* not uncommon. In Gabon births in Dec–Feb.

BLACK-CHEEKED WHITE-NOSED MONKEY, Pl. 54
Cercopithecus ascanius (Audebert, 1799)
G. Kongo-Weissnase   F. Le Cercopithèque ascagne
Identification. Middle-sized. 5 ssp.: (1) Black-cheeked White-nosed Monkey, *ascanius* (Audebert, 1799) (G. Kongo-Weissnase). ♂ face bluish, nose spot heart-shaped, white; moustache black, cheek whiskers white, lower edge broad, black, narrowly produced to ear, forehead stripe narrow, black; hair whorl under ear yellow, ear flesh-coloured. Upperside of body dark olive with reddish wash, lower thigh, feet and hands black. Underside of body white. Tail coppery at root, the remainder red. Scrotum and perineal area blue, penis blue-grey. Sexes alike. (2) Katanga Black-cheeked White-nosed Monkey, *katangae* (Lonnberg, 1919). ♂: black forehead band absent, black cheek-band very broad in front, becoming abruptly very narrow. Nose spot white below, washed with yellow above. Crown yellowish-brown, rest of upperside reddish-brown washed, lower arms and hands black, lower thigh and feet greyish-black. Underside white. Tail at base coloured like body, then black. Sexes alike. (3) Yellow-nosed Monkey, *whitesidei* (Thomas, 1909) (G. Gelbnase). ♂ upperside brownish-olive, underside yellowish white; lower arms, lower thighs, hands and feet greyish-black; tail with 4 colours (at beginning coloured like the back, in middle dark brown, terminal portion red with black tip). No forehead band; cheek band narrow, nose spot and under-ear hair whorl orange-red. Sexes alike. (4) Black-nosed Monkey, *atrinasus* (Machado, 1965) (G. Schwarznase). ♂ forehead band, broad cheek band and nose spot black, light blue around eyes, hair whorl below ears orange, upperside olive-green-grey, lower parts of limbs black, underside grey, base of tail copper-coloured, middle reddish-brown, end dark brown, tip blackish. Sexes alike. (5) Uganda Red-tailed Guenon, *schmidti* (Matschie, 1892) (G. Schmidt Congo Weissnase). ♂ Upperside very dark-brown olive, lower parts of limbs black, underside grey; base of tail copper coloured, remainder reddish-brown. Upper edge of ear with small white hair tuft, nose spot white, whiskers greyish-white between the blackish forehead and cheek bands, muzzle pink, face bluish. Scrotum and penis as in (1). Mountain animals have thicker and longer fur, and forehead band extending to nape. Sexes alike. 1st juvenile coat soft, uniformly dark grey, back darker, crown and spinal line black, underside and cheeks lighter, tail dark grey, grizzled with yellowish, nose spot indistinct. Coloration begins at 3 weeks, completed at 3 months; young then like adults but somewhat paler and duller.   MEASUREMENTS: HB ♂ 43–63, ♀ 34–49, TL ♂ 60–92, ♀ 54–79, Wt ♂ 3.2–14, ♀ 1.8–8.5.
Distribution. Zaire (except N. of Congo mouth, S.E. Katanga, and N. Zaire north of Congo and Uelle Rivers); N. Angola south to 9°S in west and 11°S in east, Uganda, S.W. Kenya, N.W. Zambia. 5 ssp. (see **Identification**). (1) *ascanius*, N. Angola and W. Zaire, east to Kasai R. (2) *katangae*, Katanga east to Lualaba R. and N.W. Zambia, S. limit about 11°S. (3) *whitesidei*, S. Congo to Lukenie R. (4) *atrinasus*, N.E. Angola and neighbouring Zaire (distribution area small). (5) *schmidti*, N.E. Congo to Uganda and S.W. Kenya, and mountains west of N. Tanzania to Lake

Edward. HABITAT: secondary, gallery, swamp and mountain forests, forest edges and clearings, sometimes in thick bush. In middle tier in forest, sometimes in upper tier. HOME RANGE: in Uganda about 130 hectares. *Map* p. 274.

Habits. FOOD: leaves, shoots, flowers, fruit, sap. Also ants and grasshoppers. Each meal ½–1kg. Likes to raid native plantations. VOICE: chirping (♀♀ and young in alarm), twittering (young in submission). ♀♀ call young with clear whistle; young scream when frightened; old ♂ warning sound an explosive coughing. A call serving as territorial marking as well as contact with troop a repeated 'heck', also at evening. Much grunting among troop on the move. ENEMIES: crowned eagle, leopard, where much hunted by man, become secretive, otherwise at alarm rushing flight through the trees, sometimes also on the ground. SOCIABILITY: in family troops (1 old ♂, 1–2 ♀♀ with young, all sleep together. At favourable feeding places several troops together, building up to packs of up to 200 where plantations offer abundant food. Pacific, no inter-troop clashes. Some may be solitary. In threat, bob forequarters, rapid up and down head movement, with staccato chirping. Often associate daily with other species, as *Cercopithecus mona, mitis, albogularis* and *aethiops, Cercocebus albigena, Colobus polykomos, guereza* or *badius*. White-crested hornbills (*Tropicranus albocristatus*) and turacous often join the throng.

Reproduction. In E. Africa most births Dec–Apr. Weight at birth *c.* 230: 1st activity at 1 week, 1st solid food at 2 months; weaning, completion of milk dent., and independence at 6 months. During the 1st 5 months the young use their tails for holding on.

RED-BELLIED GUENON, *Cercopithecus erythrogaster* (Gray, 1866) **Pl. 54**
G. Rotbauchmeerkatze F. Le Cercopithèque à ventre rouge

Identification. Size of Lesser White-nosed Guenon (*petaurista*). ♂: area around eyes blue, muzzle greyish-pink, upper part of back of nose black, lower nose white or black, cheek stripes from corner of mouth as far as ears black below, grey above. Crown golden-green, black forehead bands broaden to nape where the 2 sides unite. Whiskers (directed backwards) and throat white or whitish-yellow, front of breast, arms and inside of legs greyish-white, breast and belly rusty-red, sometimes (individually) grey. Upperside olive-brown, arms to hands approaching black, hands and feet black. Upperside of tail like back, darker at the end, below greyish-white, the two sides sharply separated. ♀ like ♂, except that arms and legs are grey, and underside greyish-white. Young: nose black, with white surround. MEASUREMENTS: HB *c.* 45, TL *c.* 60, Wt *c.* 2–3.

Distribution. W. Africa, probably S.W. Nigeria. However, there is uncertainty as to the origins of the very few specimens known, having come in trade. *Map* p. 274.
Habits unknown.

RUSSET-EARED GUENON, **Pl. 54/1**
Cercopithecus erythrotis (Waterhouse, 1838)
G. Rotnase F. Le Moustac à oreilles rousses
Some authors consider this to be a subspecies of *C. cephus.*

Identification. Size of Lesser White-nosed Guenon (*petaurista*). ♂: region round eyes blue, muzzle pink, chin and throat white, in *camerunensis* greyish white. Nose spot triangular, brick red (but in *sclateri* white). Whiskers yellowish-white, yellow in *camerunensis*. Forehead temporal band and lower edge of whiskers black. Ears pink, hair fringe red, in *sclateri* whitish. Upperside of body dark olive-green, in *camerunensis* hands and feet black; in *sclateri* rump reddish-brown, lower arms and hands black, lower thighs grey. Underside greyish-white, perineal area and scrotum red, penis pink, vulva blue, callosities brown. Tail red, with black middle line above (the latter short in *camerunensis*), in *sclateri* upper and underside sharply separated, upper side at first red, then yellowish, the end greyish-black, tip black; under side first red, then grey. Sexes alike. 1st juvenile pelage not known. MEASUREMENTS: HB ♂ 45–55, ♀ 40–45, TL ♂ 56–77, ♀ 46–65. Wt ♂ 3–4.25, ♀ 2.25–3.5.

Distribution. Fernando Póo and adjoining mainland. 3 ssp.: (1) Fernando Póo Russet-eared Guenon, *erythrotis* (Waterhouse, 1838) (G. Fernando Póo Rotnase). Fernando Póo. (2) Cameroun Russet-eared Guenon, *camerunensis* (Hayman, 1940) (G. Kamerun Rotnase), N. Cameroun between the Sanaga and Benue Rivers, exact distribution unknown. (3) Sclater's Russet-eared Guenon, *sclateri* (Pocock, 1904) (G. Nigeria Rotnase), S. Nigeria; Niger delta and surroundings and Lower Niger about to the Benue confluence. HABITAT: rain, gallery and mountain forests, to upper forest edge at about 2400m; forest edges, forest islands outside the main blocks. Troops of 4–30, with 1 old ♂. LONGEVITY: up to 18½ years. *Map p. 280.*

GREATER WHITE-NOSED MONKEY,   **Pl. 54**
Cercopithecus nictitans(Linnaeus, 1766)
G. Grosse Weissnase   F. Le Hocheur

Identification. Large, sturdy. 3 ssp.: (1) Typical Greater White-nosed Monkey, *nictitans* (Linnaeus, 1766) (G. Grosse Weissnase). Face greyish black, white oval nose spot, upper eyelids flesh-coloured, the backward-directed whiskers, top of head, and upperside of body dark olive-green. Forehead-temporal band, arms, hands, legs, feet, tail and callosities black, chin and throat light-grey, rest of underside black. (2) Martin's Greater White-nosed Monkey, *martini* (Waterhouse, 1838) (G. Martin's G. W.). Like (1), but with body somewhat suffused with red. Arms, hands, feet black, legs blackish-olive; chin, throat, breast and insides of arms whitish-grey, greyish-black transverse band between throat and breast, belly and inside of legs smoky-grey. (3) Stampfli's Greater White-nosed Monkey, *stampflii* (Jentink, 1888) (G. Stampflis G. W.). As (1), forehead, cheeks and flanks rather suffused with red; chin, throat, breast and inside of arms white. Juvenile coat faded, nose spot barely distinguishable. MEASUREMENTS: HB ♂ 55–70, ♀ 43–53, TL ♂ 95–100, ♀ 56–72. Wt ♂ 5.5–8, ♀ 2.7–4.1.

Distribution. Upper and Lower Guinea forests. (1) *nictitans*: from Lower and Middle Congo north to Central African Republic, S. W. Chad and N. Cameroun, middle Ubangui valley in E. and Benue Valley in W. N. border about 10°N, most eastern point about 22°E. (2) *martini*: Fernando Póo and neighbouring W. Cameroun (E. limit about 10°E), and S. Nigeria to Benin (N. border about 8°N). (3) *stampflii*: Ivory Coast westward from Bandama R., and Liberia. HABITAT: for *nictitans* secondary forest and bush, for *martini* secondary forest, bush, high forest, mountain forest and forest islands north of the main forest block; for *stampflii* upper tiers of primary forest. Troop ranges do not overlap, distances maintained. *Map p. 285.*

Habits. Active in morning to 10·00 and in afternoon from 15·00 to 16·00, resting in shade mid-day. ENEMIES: leopard, golden cat, crowned eagle, python. FOOD: leaves, shoots, fruit, occasionally ants. Often raids plantations, has been known to steal and eat poultry. VOICE: old ♂ marks territory by rough 'ho-ho'; has special alarm 'hon-hon-hon' for appearance of crowned eagle (other members of troop seem paralysed with fear). Another alarm call, in both sexes, a sharp metallic whistle. Threat gesture a deep bowing of forequarters and shaking of head (hence the French name Hocheur 'the shaker') emphasizing the white nose-spot as recognition mark.

SOCIABILITY: in troops of 7–20, with 1 old ♂, sometimes in large troops of up to 60 or more. Often in company with Grey-cheeked Mangabeys.
Reproduction. Most births Dec–Feb in Gabon.

DIADEMED GUENON OR BLUE MONKEY, Pl. 52
Cercopithecus mitis (Wolf, 1822)
G. Diademmeerkatze   F. Le Cercopithèque à diadème   S. Kima
Considered by many authors to form a superspecies together with *albogularis*.
Identification. Large, sturdy, fur close and thick, sometimes rather long; eyebrow and forehead hair projecting forward (hence the name Diademed). Whiskers rather close-lying, directed backwards and upwards. Tail long, carried slightly arched with tip about height of heels; in rapid movement carried higher than back. 8 ssp.: (1) Angolan Diademed Guenon, *mitis* (Wolf, 1822) (G. Angola D.). Face blackish-blue, lighter round eyes, nose and muzzle finely haired, white; diadem whitish-yellow, ear with whitish hair tuft, whiskers greyish-black, crown, nape, shoulders, arms, hands, legs, feet, tail, callosities and underside black, back and rump greyish-black. (2) Congo Diademed Guenon, *maesi* (Lonnberg, 1919) (G. Kongo D.). Black, posterior back and flanks greyish over-washed, tail reddish-brown at root, the rest grey; throat white, the rest of underside slate-grey, diadem narrow, black speckled with yellow. (3) Stuhlmann's Diademed Guenon, *stuhlmanni* (Matschie, 1893) (G. Uganda D.). Diadem not distinct, whitish ear tuft, chin and throat white, black breast band, otherwise like (1). (4) Doggett's Guenon, *doggetti* (Pocock, 1907) (G. Silbermeerkatze). Diadem black, speckled olive-grey, crown, nape, shoulders black, forepart of body greenish-black, flanks grey, rump and root of tail washed with reddish-brown. Arms, legs and end of tail black, throat white, underside slate-grey. (5) Golden Monkey, *kandti* (Matschie, 1905) (G. Goldmeerkatze). Fur long; diadem, whiskers, sides of neck, and shoulders, olive-greyish-black. Crown, nape, arms, legs and end of tail black. Back a mixture of grey-green reddish-yellow, back of thighs, tail root and underside of body rusty red. Very variable. (6) Schouteden's Diademed Guenon, *schouteden* (Schwarz, 1928) (G. Kwidji D.). Fur long, like *kandti*, but without all the red; underside mouse-grey. (7) Rump-spotted Guenon, *opisthostictus* (Sclater, 1894) (G. Katanga D.). Diadem, whiskers and sides of neck grey; crown, nape, shoulders, arms, legs and end of tail black, underside black, tail root greyish-black. (8) Boutourlini's Guenon, *boutourlinii* (Giglioli, 1887) (G. Äethiopien D.). Fur long, diadem indistinct, crown and nape blackish-yellow, shoulders, arms, legs, tail and underside black; back black with greyish-yellow speckling. Sexes alike. 1st juvenile coat: skin of body, palms and soles, scrotum and callosities still pink, body with thin dark grey or blackish hair, ear tuft (where present) white. MEASUREMENTS: HB ♂ 48–67, ♀ 44–52, TL ♂ 55–109, ♀ 64–102. Wt ♂ 5–7, ♀ 3.5–4.5.
Distribution. From N.W. Angola eastward through Congo basin to S. Sudan, W. Ethiopia, Uganda and W. Kenya on one side, and to Katanga and N. Zambia on the other. 8 ssp. (see **Identification**): (1) *mitis*, N.W. Angola. (2) *maesi*, Zaire between R. Congo in W. and N., Lomami R. in E., and Lukenie R. in S. (3) *stuhlmanni*, N.E. Zaire, Uganda and W. Kenya. (4) *doggetti*, S. Uganda, Ruanda-Urundi, W. Tanzania eastward to Lake Victoria. (5) *kandti*, mountain forests around Lake Kivu. (6) *schouteden*, Kwidji I., Lake Kivu, and northern shores of lake. (7) *opisthostictus*, Katanga and N.W. Zambia. (8) *boutourlinii*, W. Ethiopia, between Lakes Tana and Rudolf. HABITAT: rain-, gallery-, savannah-, swamp-, and mountain forests. *Stuhlmanni* in deciduous mountain forests, *kandti* in the bamboo zone of mountain forests, *doggetti* in swampy hollows with papyrus stands. In mountain forests up to

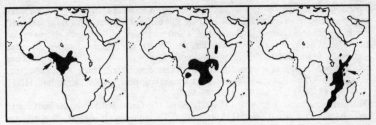

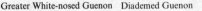

Greater White-nosed Guenon   Diademed Guenon   White-throated Guenon

3,300m. Prefer shade, avoid strong sunlight.   HOME RANGE: resident; a troop may range over $\frac{1}{4}$ to $2\frac{1}{2}$ sq km, with well-used trails and favoured sleeping places.

Habits.   DAILY RHYTHM: feed in morning and late afternoon in the higher tiers of forest, descend for shade in the heat of the day into the lower tiers, sometimes also on the ground. Quieter on the move than smaller monkeys.   TOILET: invite grooming by half-creeping approach with head turned away, and tail held over back.   VOICE: alarm call of old ♂ a rough coughing; ♀ and young chirp.   TERRITORY: marked by repeated loud 'peoo', especially at sunrise and sunset. Soft grunts of unknown purpose. Juveniles trill in submission or appeasement. *Kandti* has a constant twittering as contact call when feeding in thick cover (as in the dwarf mongoose, *Helogale*). Gestures include threat, shown by staring and eyebrow movements, mouth opening and lowering of head.   ENEMIES: leopard, golden cat, crowned eagle, python.   FOOD: leaves, shoots, flowers, fruit, berries, bark, young birds, eggs, insects; in mountain forests bamboo shoots, grass, herbage, fungi, lichens, moss: in swamps the soft papyrus stalks. Sometimes raid plantations, occasionally take hens and young chicks.   SOCIABILITY: family troops, usually 4–6, often up to a dozen animals; sometimes larger troops, depending on the subspecies and environment. Not uncommonly associates with other species, depending on locality, with Green Monkey (*aethiops*), L'Hoest's Guenon (*l'hoesti*), Black-cheeked White-nosed Monkey (*ascanius*), Guereza (*Colobus abyssinicus*), Mantled Mangabey (*Cercocebus albigena*), Chimpanzee (*Pan troglodytes*).

Reproduction. Breeding season usually not restricted, in Uganda Jul–Nov. Gestation 120–130 days. Weight at birth *c.* 400, HB *c.* 20, TL *c.* 23. Young grow more slowly than in other species. First leaves mother at 1 month, when the pelage colouring begins (see **Identification**).

WHITE-THROATED GUENON,   **Pl. 62**
Cercopithecus albogularis (Sykes, 1831)
G. Weisskehlmeerkatze   F. Le Cercopithèque à collier blanc   A. Samangoaap
S. Kima
Considered by many authors to form a superspecies with *mitis*.
Identification. Form as *mitis*. Face, callosities and scrotum grey, but in *schwarzi* and *samango* black, upper eyelids lighter. Muzzle with short, ear tuft with long, white hairs; ear tufts yellowish-white in *erythrarchus*, red in *francescae*. Whiskers directed rearward. No diadem. Head, nape, back, flanks, upper part of limbs, olive-green or pale olive-green (*erythrarchus*), or yellowish olive-grey (*monoides*), or black (*schwarzi*,

samango). Rump golden-yellow (*albotorquatus*) or reddish brown (*phylax*) or dark brown (*moloneyi*) overwashed. Lower arms, thighs, hands, feet, tail (or its hinder half) black. Upper arms, upper thighs, tail root and underside of body grey. Chin, throat and sides of neck, in *kolbi* also shoulders ánd breast, in *phylax* and *erthrarchus* also underside, white. Sexes alike. 1st juvenile coat; face pink, whiskers and eyebrows not yet developed, tail still apparently short, upperside, with tail, black, underside from chin, white. After 4 days the 1st grey cheek whiskers appear. MEASUREMENTS: HB ♂ 50–62, ♀ 45–60, TL ♂ 66–94, ♀ 62–83. Wt ♂ 5–7, ♀ 3.5–5.

Distribution. E. and S.E. Africa (usually E. of the Great Rift) from S. Somalia to eastern Cape Province. 12 ssp.: (1) Pousargues' White-throated Guenon, *albotorquatus* (Pousargues, 1896) (G. Somalia-W.). S. Somalia between Webi-Shebeli and Juba rivers. (2) Maritime White-throated Guenon, *monoides* (I. Geoffroy St Hilaire, 1841) (G. Tanzania-W.). Southern Somalia to Rovuma R. (border of Tanzania and Mozambique) westwards to Great Rift and mid-Zambia. (3) Patta I. White-throated Guenon, *phylax* (Schwarz, 1927) (G. Patta-W.) Patta I. off N.E. Kenya coast. (4) Mt Kenya White-throated Guenon, *kolbi* (Neumann, 1902) (G. Keniaberg-W.). E. slope of Mt Kenya to Aberdares, up to 3,300m. (5) Kilimanjaro Blue Monkey, *kibonotensis* (Lonnberg, 1908) (G. Kilimandjaro-W.). Kilimanjaro, Meru, Pare and Usambara Mts, east to S. Tsavo and Tanga. (6) Syke's Monkey, Zanzibar White-throated Guenon, *albogularis* (Sykes, 1831) (G. Sansibar-W.). Zanzibar, Mafia and Tumbatu. (7) Moloney's Monkey, *moloneyi* (Sclater, 1893) (G. Sambia-W.). N.E. Zambia. (8) North Malawi Blue Monkey, *francescae* (Thomas, 1902) (G. Malawi-W.). Malawi except south. (9) Nyasa White-throated Guenon, *nyasae* (Schwarz, 1928) (G. Nyassa W.). S. Malawi, south of Lake Nyasa. (10) Mozambique Monkey, *erythrarchus* (Peters, 1852) (G. Mozambique-W.). Mid-Mozambique. (11) Transvaal White-throated Guenon, *schwarzi* (Roberts, 1931) (G. Transvaal-W.). S. Rhodesia and Transvaal. (12) Samango Monkey, *samango* (I. Geoffroy St Hilaire) (G. Pondoland-W.). Pondoland, eastern Cape Province (Natal and Pondoland westward to Great Fish River). HABITAT: rain-, gallery-, coastal-, and mountain forests, to 3,300m.

Habits. Resemble Diademed Guenon (p. 285).

DE BRAZZA'S MONKEY, CHESTNUT-BROWED GUENON, Pl. 62
Cercopithecus neglectus (Schlegel, 1876)

G. Brazza Meerkatze   F. Le Cercopithèque de Brazza   S. Kalasinga

Identification. Middle-sized, thickset, back sloping up to hind part, tail rather thick, only a little longer than HB, carried curved downwards, hanging down when walking. Face hairy, apart from the narrow area around eyes, the bare skin light blue. Brow and forehead hair make a broad frontal diadem. Fur fine and soft. Whiskers and the long chin and throat beard join, directed downwards. Upper eyelids brownish-red, lower lids slate grey, upper part of top of nose, broad band on head behind the diadem, lower arms, stripe from the top of arm to forehead band, hands, feet and tail, black. Lower part of nose, muzzle, chin, throat, inside of legs, buttocks and the sloping stripe on side of thighs, white. Diadem light ochreous to reddish. Whiskers, crown, nape, back, upper arms, flanks and legs, olive-grey. Breast and belly sooty-grey. Perineal region cobalt blue, scrotum dark blue, penis pink. ♀ like ♂, but perineal area reddish brown. Newborn: face, palms and soles naked, pink, chin with small white hair spot, body gold-or yellowish-brown to brown, legs and underside yellow. At 2–3 weeks begins to develop the general colouring, where first the brows, cheeks, nape, body and base of tail appear nut-brown, followed by the development of the white beard and diadem, darker diadem edges, and whitish thigh stripes. The last step to completion of the adult coat is the black of the lower arm. At about 14 months the full adult colour is reached; however, the general colour gradations in the ♂ are unrelated to the size and age of the animal, so that young still with the milk dentition may have the nearly full adult coat, and on the other hand an adult may still have the immature coat. MEASUREMENTS: HB ♂ 50–60, ♀ 40–50, TL ♂ 63–85, ♀ 53–63, Wt ♂ 5–8, ♀ 4–5.

Distribution. Congo basin. From S.E. Cameroun and E. Gabon (between Nyong R. in N. and Ogowe R. in S.), eastward to Uganda, western mid-Kenya, extreme S. Sudan and S.W. Ethiopia to middle course of R. Omo (the overall northern limit between 3° and 7°N.). Further south, the east border on the lower Lualaba and upper Lomami rivers. South border about 11°S. Lower W. border about 17°E along the Kwango R., upper about 14°E. No ssp. HABITAT: rain, mountain and swampy forests, especially bamboo growths and palm swamps; in dry mountain forests keep near rivers. Up to 2000m in the mountains. *Map* p. 288.

Habits. DAILY RHYTHM: diurnal, especially active in morning and afternoon. Good climber and swimmer, and runs well on ground. ENEMIES: leopard, golden cat, crowned eagle, python. Flees on ground, uttering 'hoon-hoon' call. Sometimes seems paralysed and dumb when in danger. FOOD: leaves, shoots, fruit, berries, roots, insects, lizards, geckos. Raids plantations, and spends a large part of feeding time on the ground. Will go a good distance over open land to reach plantations. VOICE: quiet, not often noisy. Grunt when pleased. Old ♂ has chattering alarm call followed by separate barks. Other calls indicate threat or excitement, while young have a weak call expressing loneliness, as well as chattering, twittering or screaming when annoyed or frightened. ♂ has peculiar threat gestures; in milder forms sits with legs apart to expose the blue scrotum and red penis, as well as the white inside of thighs and the prominent white beard. In stronger form he opens the mouth widely and exposes most of the white areas, namely beard, throat and inside of legs, standing on hind legs and displaying the beard in up and down movement. Submission of young ♂ to old ♂: lies on elbows, head and breast (hiding the beard); hind parts and tail raised, reversing in this attitude and, with hind parts and tail shaking, lying flat on its side and displaying to old ♂ the neutral colour of the back. The invitation for fur grooming is a sideways timorous approach (also by old ♂), displaying the neutral colour of back and hiding the aggressive white of the undersides, then lying down with back to partner. SOCIABILITY: family troops of 1 old ♂ and several ♀♀ with young, also larger troops of sometimes up to 3 dozen animals. Old ♂♂ sometimes solitary. Size of troop determined by strength of old ♂ in relation to younger ♂♂, which may split off to form a separate small troop. Frequently associate with Green Monkeys (*aethiops*) and Mantled Mangabeys (*Cercocebus albigena*).

Reproduction. Usually not linked with season, but in Gabon main parturition time Dec–Feb. Gestation 177–187 days. Weight at birth *c.* 250; HB *c.* 11, TL *c.* 22. At 1 week first separation from mother's body, and at 3 weeks first attempts to climb, run and jump.

L'HOEST'S MONKEY, *Cercopithecus l'hoesti* (Sclater, 1898)   **Pl. 53**
G. Vollbartmeerkatze   F. Le Cercopithèque de l'Hoest

Identification. Middle-sized, slender, back sloping upwards at rear; tail, as in Collared Mangabey (*Cercocebus torquatus*), partly prehensile, normally carried upright with handle-like tip curving downwards. In *insularis* tail barely as long as HB. Fur rather long, soft and thick. Face black (grey in *preussi*), lighter around eyes, ears black (grey in *preussi*), nose and muzzle black. Whiskers directed backwards and upwards to behind ears (these partly hidden) lower edge merging into the long throat and fore-breast fur.

Whiskers and throat hair white (in *preussi* dark grey), upperside dark grey, as also root of tail; end of tail black, limbs black, underside blackish-grey to black, callosities blackish brown, scrotum pale violet. *L'hoesti* has a distinctive saddle of orange-red, black-speckled, long-oval in shape on hind part of back from shoulders to root of tail. ♀ like ♂, but clitoris red, perineal area bluish grey. Newborn young uniformly brown, adult coat reached after 2–3 months.   MEASUREMENTS: HB ♂ 54–70; ♀ 45–55, TL ♂ 50–76, ♀ 46–67. Wt ♂ 6–8, ♀ 3–4.5.

Distribution. 3 ssp.: (1) E. Congo L'Hoest's Monkey, *l'hoesti* (Sclater, 1898) (G. Vollbartmeerkatze   F. Le Cercopithèque de l'Hoest). N.E. Congo in Uelle and Kivu districts, eastward from Lualaba R., southward to 4°S., north to 3°N. Also in S.W. Uganda and Ruanda-Urundi. (2) Preuss's Monkey, *preussi* (Matschie, 1898) (G. Westafrika V.   F. Le Cercopithèque de Preuss). S.E. Nigeria from Cross R. and adjoining N.W. Cameroun with Mt Cameroun, south to Sanaga R. (3) Fernando Póo L'Hoest's Monkey, *insularis* (Thomas, 1910) (G. Fernando Póo V.). Northern mountains of Fernando Poo. *Insularis* is not accepted as a distinct form by some authors.   HABITAT: mountain forests (in Cameroun up to 1800m, in Central Africa up to 2,500m), especially dense secondary forest with clearings, similarly in lowland forest. Often come close to or on ground. Raids plantations, descending from high sleeping places to the valleys and crossing open areas on the ground.   HOME RANGE: according to locality a troop may have a range of 5–15 sq km, over which it roams widely. Favourite sleeping trees high on mountains.

Habits.   FOOD: leaves, shoots, fruit, grass, plants, lichens, fungi, occasionally insects, cultivated crops.   VOICE: rather quiet; old ♂ at evening calls 'uooo', probably marking territory, otherwise a deep murmuring call when meeting, a sharp barking alarm call, also a low chirping.   TOILET: a favourite activity is mutual grooming of the fur, particularly on chin, cheeks, nape and shoulders.   ENEMIES: leopard, golden cat, crowned eagle, python. Very vigilant, keeping a keen watch from high vantage point. On an alarm the old ♂ acts as rear guard.   SOCIABILITY: in small troops, $\frac{1}{2}$–$1\frac{1}{2}$ dozen animals, with 1, rarely 2, old ♂♂ living at the edge of the troop. Solitary ♂♂ not uncommon. Generally of friendly nature. The conspicuous display of the white whiskers and throat acts as a threat symbol. Sometimes associate with Greater White-nosed Monkeys (*C. ascanius*) and Colobus monkeys (*Colobus abyssinicus*).

Reproduction. Breeding season not limited, in C. Africa most births in February. The young at first clings tightly to mother's belly, curling its tail around hers as in the Collared Mangabey, later rides on her back. First juvenile coat, see **Identification**.   LONGEVITY: up to $16\frac{1}{2}$ years in captivity.

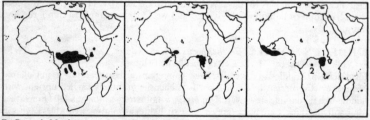

De Brazza's Monkey   L'Hoest's Monkey   1 Hamlyn's Guenon
                                            2 Diana Monkey

HAMLYN'S GUENON, OWL-FACED MONKEY, Pl. 53
Cercopithecus hamlyni (Pocock, 1907)
G. Eulenkopfmeerkatze   F. Le Cercopithèque de Hamlyn
Identification. Middle-sized, sturdy, bulky head with flattish face, tail barely longer than HB, thickened at base, at end rather tufted, carried curved downwards and used in a semi-prehensile way as in L'Hoest's Monkey (*C. l'hoesti*) and Collared Mangabey (*Cercocebus torquatus*). Face triangular with tip of nose as point, plum-coloured, with large owl-like eyes and narrow vertical white nose-stripe from eyebrows to tip of nose. Whole face enclosed by long, thick backward-directed hair concealing the dark brown ears. Narrow yellow forehead band. Head barn-owl like. Head and upperside of body, with upper arms, dark olive-green; tip of tail, underside of body from chin, inside of thighs, lower arms, lower thighs, hands and feet, black: rump, ⅔ of tail and back of thighs grey. Callosities blackish-brown, growing together in ♂, buttocks greenish-blue, scrotum malachite green, penis flesh-coloured, teats pink with whitish aureoles. Newborn young uniform golden yellow, face fawn, hair surrounding face not yet developed. After some weeks the slow change to adult pelage begins. MEASUREMENTS: HB *c.* 55, TL *c.* 57.
Distribution. E. Congo basin, E. Zaire, from Lualaba River eastward to E. border of the area, north to Aruwimi R. (*c.* 2°N.), south to upper Elila and Kindi Rivers (*c.* 3°S.). No ssp.
Habits. Lives in rain forests in plains and on mountains up to 4,200m. Main home in mountain forests is in the bamboo zone. Eats bamboo shoots by preference. Often terrestrial, and said to be nocturnal.

DIANA MONKEY, *Cercopithecus diana* (Linnaeus, 1758) Pl. 53
G. Dianameerkatze   F. Le Cercopithèque diane
Identification. Middle-sized, slender build, legs longer than arms, tail long, carried in a tight curve upward and downwards. Face brownish-black to black, ears dark grey, hair of browband and forehead (diadem) directed forwards, diadem ridge white, lower and upper edges (latter with crown) blackish, similarly back of arms, hands, lower breast and belly, lower thighs, feet and tail black. Whiskers (directed backwards, almost hiding ears), shorter or longer chin beard, sides of neck, throat, front and inside of arms, inside of thighs, buttocks, upper thigh stripe (sloping forward and downward), white. Nape, shoulders, flanks and outside of upper thighs greyish-black. From shoulders to root of tail a long triangular (point on shoulder) bright chestnut-red saddle. The inside of the thighs, and the buttocks, may be either yellowish or red. Callosities brownish-black, teats pink. Sexes alike. Newborn young have upperside light grey or brownish with yellowish tint, underside naked, at 1–1½ months white throat and breast hairs, white diadem complete, beginning at 2 months the change to the immature coat (resembling the adult) begins, and is completed at 4–5 months. 3 (?) ssp.: (1) Typical Diana Monkey, *diana* (Linnaeus, 1758) (G. Dianameerkatze). Beard short, with black base, white ear tuft, inside of thighs and buttocks reddish brown, diadem suffused with yellow. (2) Roloway Monkey, *roloway* (Schreber, 1774) (G. Roloway D.). Beard long and pointed, ears without hair tuft, diadem white, insides of thighs and buttocks, orange yellow. (3(?)). Congo Diana Monkey, *dryas* (Schwarz, 1932) (G. Congo D.). (This is regarded as highly doubtful, and certainly not a member of the *diana* species.) Diadem white, joining white upward and backward-directed whiskers, chin beard short and broad, ears with white hair tuft, no white upper thigh stripe. Nape, shoulders, flanks, outside of upper thighs and first half of tail greenish-

grey, hands and feet greyish-black, end of tail black.   MEASUREMENTS: HB ♂ 50–57, ♀ 40–48, TL ♂ 76–82, ♀ 52–60. Wt ♂ 3.5–7.5, ♀ 2.2–3.5.

Distribution. West Africa (and ? Congo basin). 3 (?) ssp. (see **Identification**): (1) *diana*, Sierra Leone, Liberia, and W. Ivory Coast to Sassandra R. (2) *roloway*, Sassandra R. (W. Ivory Coast) to E. Ghana (up to 60km from the R. Volta). (3) *dryas* (?), Lomela on upper Lomela or Tshuapa R., central Zaire. Only 1 example known (see notes above in **Identification**).   HABITAT: primary rain forests; entirely arboreal, in middle and upper, never in lower, tiers.

Habits. Troops of up to 30, home range ½ to 1 sq km. Inquisitive, very active, noisy; beside the chirruping and screaming of other guenons, the old ♂ has a long, piercing territorial call 'ki-ki-ki-ki'. Displays by exhibiting the glossy rear and underside by hanging from a branch, with hands between the feet, and tail hanging.

Reproduction. Young at 2 weeks weigh *c*. 140; HB *c*. 9, TL *c*. 18. Suckle for 6 months, milk dentition complete at 20 months, permanent dentition at 3¼ years.   SEXUAL MATURITY: 4½ years.   LONGEVITY: 19 years recorded.

MONA MONKEY, *Cercopithecus mona* (Schreber, 1774)   **Pls 53, 54**
G. Monameerkatze   F. Le Cercopithèque mona
Identification. Middle-sized, sturdy, long thin tail, often carried over back, thick backward-directed whiskers, largely hiding the ears. 7 ssp. (Note: other authors consider 2 of these, *campbelli* and *wolfi*, to be distinct species): (1) Campbell's Guenon, *campbelli* (Waterhouse, 1838) (G. Campbellmeerkatze). Face blue, muzzle pink, ears bluish-black, broad white forehead band, whiskers whitish-grey, hair tuft in front of ears yellow, crown black, speckled with yellow, nape, shoulders, back, gold-green, rump dark grey, arms and legs grey outside, becoming black lower to hands and feet; chin, throat, breast, belly, insides of limbs white, sharply separated from outsides. Tail black at root and tip, dark grey in middle. Callosities dark grey, scrotum blue, penis pink. (2) Lowe's Guenon, *lowei* (Thomas, 1923) (G. Lowemeerkatze). Like (1), only forehead band yellow to yellowish-green, whiskers dark grey, rump and thighs blackish grey, arms black, tail dark grey above, middle grey below. (3) Typical Mona Monkey, *mona* (Schreber, 1774) (G. Monameerkatze). As (1), but broad black temporal band from white forehead band to ear, crown, nape and shoulders yellowish green, back and flanks rust-red, tail root and upperside black, underside grey; on each side of tail root an oval white spot, whose shape and size varies; arms and legs outside almost or completely black. Perineal region bluish-green. (4) Wolf's Guenon, *wolfi* (Meyer, 1891) (G. Wolfmeerkatze). As (1), only tail with slight end tuft, white forehead band, with projecting brows (diadem), reaching to ears; upper and underside colouring sharply separated by orange-red flank stripe; upperside slate-grey, flanks bluish-grey, rump greyish-brown, whiskers and spinal line yellowish brown, shoulders and arms black, hind legs reddish brown. (5) Red-bellied Guenon, *pyrogaster* (Lonnberg, 1919) (G. Feuerbauchmeerkatze). As (4), ear tuft red, diadem mixed black and white, crown, nape, shoulders, outside of arms, hands, and end half of tail black, forepart greyish-brown, spinal line nut-brown, hind legs rust-red, chin and throat light reddish-yellow, rest of underside bright rust-red. (6) Elegant Mona Monkey, *elegans* (Dubois and Matschie, 1912) (G. Lomamimeerkatze). As (4), only whiskers and ear tufts white, and upper thighs light grey. (7) Dent's Guenon, *denti* (Thomas 1907) (G. Dentmeerkatze). Like (1), only ear tuft yellow, crown and nape olive-grey, back nut-brown, lower arms, hands and feet, tail root and tufted tip, black, middle of tail grey, hind legs yellowish-olive, lower side and insides of hind legs whitish yellow. Sexes alike. 1st juvenile coat

not known; when half-grown already has adult coat. MEASUREMENTS: HB ♂ 48–60, ♀ 40–50, TL ♂ 70–80, ♀ 54–70. Ht ♂ c. 35, ♀ c. 32, Wt ♂ 4.5–7.5, ♀ 2.5–4.

Distribution. West and Central Africa; Upper and Lower Guinea and Congo forests. 7 ssp. (see **Identification**): (1) *campbelli*, from Casamance R. in S. Senegal east through Gambia, Guinea-Bissau, Guinea and Sierra Leone to E. border of Liberia (Cavally R.). (2) *lowei*, from Cavally R. eastward through Ivory Coast to Volta R. (E. Ghana). (3) *mona*, from E. Ghana east to Nyong R., mid-Cameroun except Niger delta region. Introduced in St Kitts and Grenada, Lesser Antilles. (4) *wolfi*, W. Zaire east of Congo R., between Congo and Kasai Rivers, east to about 22°E. (5) *pyrogaster*, W. Zaire south of (4), between Kasai and Kwango Rivers, south to N.E. Angola. (6) *elegans*, E. Zaire between Lomami and Lualaba Rivers, south to 6°S. (7) *denti*, E. Zaire, north of Congo R. to S.E. Central African Republic and S.W. Sudan, east to Upper Bahr-el-Jebel and the lake region (Mobuto or Albert, Idi-Amin or Edward, and Kivu) south to 6°S. Habitat. Primary-, lower mountain-, secondary-, gallery-, and coastal forests. Partly in mangroves.

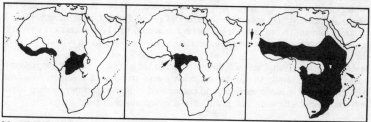

Mona Monkeys   Crowned Guenon   Green Monkeys

Habits. FOOD: leaves, shoots, fruit, sometimes also in plantations. VOICE: old ♂ barks morning and evening, as territory marking; also deep loud grumbling. A common contact call 'oooo', additionally at times a melodious call. SOCIABILITY: family troops from 3–18 animals, during day several troops may come together, but some animals may be solitary. Associate at times with *Cercopithecus ascanius*. Mainly in lower and middle tiers of forest. Move very quickly in the branches, jumping long distances. Old ♂ is watcher and overseer, always in a commanding position; is attended by ♀♀ for grooming. No particular ranking order.

Reproduction. Gestation about 6 months. Breeding season not defined; in Gabon births mainly Dec–Feb. Young are cared for in 1st year by 'aunts'; suckling period 1 year. At 2 weeks leave mother for 1st time, 1st jumping at 1 month, also 1st solid food. Sexually mature ♂♂ set up separate troops, marking their own territory by voice.

CROWNED GUENON, *Cercopithecus pogonias* (Bennett, 1833) **Pl. 54**
G. Kronenmeerkatze   F. Le Cercopithèque pogonias
Identification. In form like Mona Monkey. 4 ssp.: (1) Crowned Guenon, *pogonias* (Bennett, 1833) (G. Fernando Póo K.). Face black, muzzle thinly haired yellow. Whiskers directed backwards, light yellow, ear tufts yellow, narrow black brow stripe, forehead and crown olive-green, 3 broad black bands from brow over crown to nape, central one forming a crest. Upperside yellowish-green, with broad black spinal stripe

from shoulders to rump, broadening towards the tail. End of tail black, proximal part of tail with underside olive. Upper arms and upper thighs lighter than back, lower arms and thighs darker, hands and feet black. Buttocks and scrotum blue, callosities dark grey, insides of limbs golden-yellow. Sexes alike. 1st juvenile coat not known. (2) Gray's Guenon, *grayi* (Fraser, 1850) (G. Gray K.). Like (1), but face flesh-coloured, crown yellowish, ear tufts orange, upperside chestnut brown without spinal stripe. (3) Black-footed Guenon, *nigripes* (du Chaillu, 1860) (G. Graue K.). Like (1), however whiskers yellowish-red, crown yellowish-white, upperside iron grey, rump black. (4) Schwarz's Black-footed Guenon, *schwarzianus* (Schouteden, 1946) (G. Schwarz-K.). Like 2, but back darker and underside whitish-yellow. MEASUREMENTS: HB ♂ 50–66, ♀ 38–46, TL ♂ 60–87, ♀ 50–68, Ht ♂ c. 35, ♀ c. 32. Wt ♂ 3–6, ♀ 1.8–3.

Distribution. West Cameroun with Fernando Póo, south to mouth of R. Congo, eastward to 25°E., northern limit a line from northern Mamfe district to Sanaga R. and Ubangui R., southern limit Middle Congo to Ubangui confluence and westward to Gabon. 4 ssp. (see **Identification**). (1) *pogonias*, Fernando Póo (south part), and adjoining W. Cameroun south to Sanaga R. (2) *grayi*, distribution of the species apart from (1), (3) and (4). (3) *nigripes*, W. Gabon between Ogowe R. in north and Chiloanao R. in south. (4) *schwarzianus*, south of (3), as far as Congo mouth. Only 1 example known. (Note: considered to be a synonym of (3)). HABITAT: primary, secondary, lowland and mountain forests (up to 1000m or more). In primary forest in the topmost tier.

Habits. FOOD: fruit, leaves, shoots, insects; also raids nearby plantations. SOCIABILITY: in family troops, by day often several troops join together. Associate with *Cercopithecus mona, nictitans* and *cephus*. Old ♂ marks territory by deep barking; contact call a lapwing-like 'piwitt', also a melodious twittering.

GREEN MONKEY, TANTALUS MONKEY, GRIVET, VERVET, Pl. 53
Cercopithecus aethiops (Linnaeus, 1758)

G. Grünmeerkatze　F. Le Grivet　A. Blauaap　S. Tumbili, Ngedere

Identification. Middle-sized to large. Arms and legs usually same length, tail long, when running in branches held upwards with down-curving tip; on ground held nearly vertically. Whiskers short to long. Hair tufts below root of tail; sometimes with hair ridge along back of upper thighs. Face, ears, callosities black, in *pygerythrus* brownish-black, in *cynosurus* flesh-coloured. Scrotum white to light blue. 21 ssp. (but other authors divide these between 4 species, *sabaeus, aethiops, tantalus* and *pygerythrus*: see Meester & Setzer). (1) Green Monkey, *sabaeus* (Linnaeus, 1766) (G. Gelb grünmeerkatze　F. Le Singe vert). Whiskers yellowish, forming temporal whorl in front of ears, no white forehead band. Upperside golden-green, lower arms, thighs, hands and feet greyer, back of upper thighs with yellowish hair ridge, underside, and inside of limbs, whitish-grey, scrotum pale blue, tail like back above, yellow below, no hair tufts under root of tail. (2) Ethiopian Grivet, *aethiops* (Linnaeus, 1758) (G. Äethiopien G.　F. Le Grivet d'Ethiopie). Narrow forehead band, long whiskers, underside of body and tail, including tufts below tail root, and tip of tail, white; upperside greyish-green, outside of hind legs mouse-grey, hands and feet light grey. (3) Abyssinian Grivet, *hilgerti* (Neumann, 1902) (G. Galla G.　F. Le Grivet de Neumann). As (2), but upperside redder, hands and feet dark brown, under tail tufts reddish brown. (4) Matschie's Grivet, *ellenbecki* (Neumann, 1902) (G. Zwai G.　F. Le Grivet de Matschie). As (2), but upperside dark chestnut-brown, under tail tufts reddish-brown. (5) De Beaux's Grivet, *zavattarii* (De Beaux, 1943) (G. Omo G.　F. Le Grivet de Zavattari). As (2), but upperside olive-reddish, arms and legs mouse-grey, hands and feet black, under tail tufts whitish-red. (6) Tantalus Monkey, *tantalus* (Ogilby, 1841) (G. Tantalusmeerkatze F. Le Cercopithèque tantale). As (2), but black temporal band on upper border of whiskers, upperside gold-green, hind legs mouse-grey, under tail tufts white, buttock spot rust red. (7) Jebel Marra Tantalus, *marrensis* (Thomas & Wroughton, 1923) (G. Dschebel-Mara-G. F. Le Grivet de Darfur). As (6), upperside gold-olive, whiskers yellowish-white, end of tail light yellow. (8) Budgett's Tantalus, *budgetti* (Pocock, 1907) (G. Budgett-G. F. Le Grivet de Budgett). As (7), upperside brownish-green, red buttock spot. (9) Black-faced Vervet, *centralis* (Neumann, 1900) (G. Uganda G. F. Le Vervet de Bukoba). Whiskers short, not covering ears. Face, ears, hands, feet, tip of tail, and callosities, black; forehead band, whiskers, underside, white, upperside greenish-olive, hind legs grey, under tail tufts reddish, scrotum turquoise-blue, tail grey above, white below. (10) North-eastern Vervet, *arenarius* (Heller, 1913) (G. Marsabit G. F. Le Vervet de Heller). As (9), but under tail tufts brown, and tail tip black. (11) Naivasha Vervet, *callidus* (Hollister, 1912) (G. Naivasha G. F. Le Vervet de Naivasha). As (10), but with upperside pale olive-green. (12) East African Vervet, *johnstoni* (Pocock, 1907) (G. Moshi G. F. Le Vervet de Moshi). Like (10), but fur longer, upperside yellowish-grey, underside greyish-white. (13) Manda Vervet, *excubitor* (Schwarz, 1926) (G. Manda G.). Like (9), but upperside ochreous-brown, underside yellowish-white, forehead band and whiskers greyish-brownish-white, black chin spot, hands and feet brownish-black, tail tip black, callosities as well as root of tail rusty-red. (14) Pemba Vervet, *nesiotes* (Schwarz, 1926) (G. Pemba G. F. Le Vervet de Pemba). As (13), but upperside darker, whiskers light brown, chin spot, hands and feet black. (15) Russet-green Vervet, *rufoviridis* (I. Geoffroy St Hilaire, 1842) (G. Mozambique G. F. Le Vervet de Mocambique). As (13), however upperside reddish-brown, underside whitish-yellow. (16) Whyte's Vervet, *whytei* (Pocock, 1907) (G. Nyassa G. F. Le Vervet du Mont Chiradzulu). As (9), but underside reddish-white, and rusty-red spot below root of tail. (17) Cloet's Vervet, *cloeti* (Roberts, 1931) (G. Mariepskop G. F. Le Vervet de Mariepskop). Like (9), only smaller. (18) Okavango Vervet, *ngamiensis* (Roberts, 1932) (G. Okawango G. F. Le Vervet de la fleuve Okavango). Upperside yellow, underside white, limbs pale grey. (19) Namaqualand Vervet, *marjoriae* (Bradfield, 1936) (G. Kuruman G. F. Le Vervet de Kuruman). Like (17), but paler. (20) South African Vervet, *pygerythrus* (F. Cuvier, 1821) (G. Sudafrika G. F. Le Vervet bleu). Like (9), but whiskers long and upperside greyish olive. (21) Malbrouck Monkey, *cynosurus* (Scopoli, 1786) (G. Malbrouck G. F. Le Malbruck). Face, ears, palms and soles and callosities, pink; forehead band and shorter whiskers white, upperside olive-green, legs grey, hands, feet and tail tip black, underside greyish-white, scrotum azure blue to violet. Sexes alike. Newborn young uniformly thinly-haired grey to brownish-black, limbs lighter, face, ears, palms, soles and callosities pink, underside sparsely haired, the blue skin showing through. Beginning of general adult coloration at 3–4 months, completed at 16–17 months. MEASUREMENTS: HB ♂ 45–83, ♀ 40–61, TL ♂ 55–114, ♀ 50–65. Wt ♂ 3.5–7.7, ♀ 2.5–5.3.

Distribution. African savannahs and steppes south of Sahara from about 18°–15°N., apart from a large part of S.W., S. and S.E. Africa. 21 ssp. (see Identification). (1) *sabaeus*, western Sahel zone from Atlantic coast to about 2°W. (Mid Niger and Volta River), northern limit about 18°N. S. border the rain forest bloc. Introduced in the Cape Verde Is. and in the West Indies (St Kitts and Barbados). (2) *aethiops*, region of White and Blue Niles and Atbara (E. Sudan, W. Ethiopia). (3) *hilgerti*, middle E. Ethiopia. (4) *ellenbecki*, W. Ethiopia south of Lake Tana to Lake Zwai. (5) *zavattari*, Omo R. region, S.W. Ethiopia. (6) *tantalus*, geographical Sudanese zone from

Volta R. in west to W. border of Mid-Ethiopia. (7) *marrensis*, Jebel Marra, Darfur. (8) *budgetti*, S.W. Sudan and N.W. Uganda with extreme N.E. Zaire. (9) *centralis*, Uganda west of Lake Victoria. (10) *arenarius*, S.W. Somalia, west of Juba R., and N.E. Kenya. (11) *callidus*, region around Lake Victoria except west side. (12) *johnstoni*, S.E. Kenya and N. Tanzania between Tana and Rufiji Rivers. (13) *excubitor*, islands of Manda and Patta, N. Kenya coast (14) *nesiotes*, Pemba and Fundu Is., N. of Zanzibar. (15) *rufoviridis*, eastern S. Tanzania and N. and Mid-Mozambique. (16) *whytei*, Mt Chiradzulu, south shore of Lake Nyasa. Only 1 specimen known. (17) *cloeti*, Mozambique and E. Rhodesia between Zambesi and Limpopo. (18) *ngamiensis*, Okavango region, N. Botswana, and N.E. Southwest Africa. (19) *marjoriae*, Kuruman region, north of Orange R., north of Cape Province. (20) *pygerythrus*, coastal region S. of Drakensberg Mts, from Zululand to Cape Agulhas. (21) *cynosurus*, Angola, Zaire, Zambia and Rhodesia; between Congo and Kasai Rivers, N.W. Lake Tanganyika, Lake Bangweolo, and Cunene R. HABITAT: open parkland regions, moist and dry savannahs, bush regions, gallery forest, bush-clad rock piles and kopjies. Not in rain forest or semi-desert. Neighbourhood of water necessary. In mountains up to 4000m. HOME RANGE: size varies according to strength of troop and nature of country; $\frac{1}{2}$ to several sq km. *Map* p. 291.

Habits. DAILY RHYTHM: diurnal, sleep in trees, feed often on the ground, sometimes some distance to feeding places. Eagerly raid gardens, fields and plantations, often becoming a major pest. Climbs well, jumps widely from tree to tree, swims well. VOICE: in wild state not very noisy, rather quiet. ♂ has a hard 'kek-kek-kek' for territory marking. Various chirping and twittering calls from the troop, scream when frightened. Lively mimics, eyebrow and lip movements much in use. Old ♂ threatens ♀ and young with bared teeth, sideways jaw movements, or tooth snapping. If aware of being watched, will swing head and shoulders sideways. In heat shakes the branches. ♂ displays by sitting upright with erected penis, or standing upright with erected penis in up and down movements. The blue scrotum and red penis in front of the white belly and thighs are together important in display. May also strut about with uplifted tail, presenting the blue scrotum. A ♀ on heat presents the blue perineal region and red clitoris. FOOD: fruit, berries, flowers, buds, shoots, bark, sap, grass seed, cultivated crops, insects, spiders, lizards, bird's eggs, young birds. ENEMIES: leopard, caracal, serval, baboon, large eagles, crocodile, python. SOCIABILITY: in troops of 6–60; usual family troop of 1 old ♂, several ♀ ♀ and young. Daytime gatherings of several troops, on average 20–30, though in Guinea and Sudan savannahs larger packs of up to 100 animals. Any animosity more likely between rather than within troops.

Reproduction. Breed all the year round, locally at certain seasons (Uganda, e.g. Apr–Oct). ♀ cycle 31 days. Gestation 175–203 days. Weight at birth 300–400. ♀ licks young dry, eats the afterbirth, and bites off the umbilical cord. Young clings tightly to mother's belly; she holds it also with one hand for first 10 days. Young separates from mother for first time at 3 weeks, and begins to climb at 4 weeks. First solid food at 2 months. Juvenile coat, see Identification. Suckling period 6 months. SEXUAL MATURITY: 2–2$\frac{1}{2}$ years. LONGEVITY: up to 24 years in captivity.

THUMBLESS MONKEYS, COLOBINAE

HB 40–85cm, long-tailed. Head roundish, muzzle short, face and ears naked, latter small. In part snub-nosed, or with large fleshy nose. Limbs long and slender, fingers and toes lengthened, great toe short. Thumb reduced to a stump, or absent. Tail with small to very large terminal tuft. Fur close, short to middle-length, sometimes with crown crest, whiskers, shoulder or flank manes. Sociable, arboreal (in part also terrestrial) leaf and fruit-eaters with chambered stomachs. Africa and South Asia from India to Ceylon, W. China with Hainan and Lombok. 6 genera with altogether 22 species, of which 1 genus and 4 species are African.

WESTERN BLACK-AND-WHITE COLOBUS,   Pls 55, 56
Colobus (Colobus)polykomos (Zimmermann, 1780)
G. Weissbartstummelaffe, Bärenstummelaffe, Mantelaffe
F. Le Colobe blanc et noir d'Afrique occidentale.   S. Mbega, Kuluzu

Identification. Large, slender but sturdy, long-tailed, hind legs notably longer than arms, face and ears naked, latter small and rounded. Nose somewhat raised and broad, tip projecting over upper lip. Digits of hands and feet long and slender. Thumb reduced to a short stump (hence specific German name). Great toe short, opposable. Dent.: as in *Cercopithecus*, but with a 5th cusp on back of M_3. No cheek pouches. Stomach very large, complex. Air sac below hyoid bone. Callosities medium-sized. Penis with small bone. Fur long, silky, hair of crown not lengthened as a crest. Facial surroundings (forehead band, whiskers, beard) short to long. Shoulders without or with narrow or broad mane or mantle, tail with or without terminal tuft. Naked skin areas (face, ears, palms and soles, callosities, scrotum) black. Fur black. Beard and whiskers white or grey; forehead band, mane and tail white to yellowish-white, latter also may be grey or black, end tuft white. Thighs black or narrowly or broadly white on hinder half. Newborn young white, ears, face, palms and soles pink, after 1 day dark grey, after 1 week black. At 14 days fur grey, from 2–3 months adult coloration. 10 ssp.: (1) Ursine Colobus, *polykomos* (Zimmermann, 1780). Gambia to western Ivory Coast to Sassandra R.; facial surroundings loose and of medium length, together with front of shoulders grey, thighs all black, tail white, without tuft. (2) Dollman's Black and White Colobus, *dollmani* (Schwarz, 1927). Sassandra to Bandama R. region, Ivory Coast: facial surroundings long, thick, white, mantle small and white, thighs as well as tail root and tail white, latter without tuft. (3) White-thighed Colobus, *vellerosus* (I. Geoffroy St Hilaire, 1834). Bandama R. region, middle Ivory Coast, to W. Nigeria, west of Lower Niger; like (2), but with mantle only a few white hairs, and whole of upper half of thighs white. (4) Black Colobus, *satanas* (Waterhouse, 1838). Fernando Póo, Cameroun, Gabon, and part of Congo (Brazzaville); longer whiskers and mantle, tail without tuft; entirely black. (5) Mantled Colobus, *angolensis* (Sclater, 1860). Zaire, south of the middle and Lower Congo, as well as N. Angola south to Cuanza R. and about 10°S.; whiskers and beard very long and crescent-shaped, white mantle very broad and long, no white forehead band, back of thigh with white stripe, tail black with white tuft. (6) Cordier's Colobus, *cordieri* (Rahm, 1959). Manyema region, middle E. Zaire: mantle thinly white, thighs black, tail grey without tuft. (7) Cotton's Colobus, *cottoni* (Lydekker, 1905). Uelle, Ituri and Aruwimi districts of N.E. Zaire; like (6), however tail black. (8) Prigogine's Colobus, *prigoginei* (Verheyen, 1959). Mt Kabobo, west wide of Lake Tanganyika, S.E. Zaire; like (6), but tail white. (9) Ruwenzori Colobus, *ruwenzorii* (Thomas, 1901) (= *adolfi-friederici* Matschie, 1904). Ruwenzori (West Uganda and E. Zaire), and W. Ruanda-Urundi. Fur and whiskers very long, latter crescentic, mantle white and small, hind edge of thighs broadly white, tail black with short whitish tip, without tuft. (1) Tanzanian Black Colobus, *palliatus* (Peters, 1868) (= *sharpei* Thomas, 1902). S.W. Tanzania with N. Malawi, through mid-Tanzania to N.E. Tanzania (Uluguru and Usambara Mts), and S.E. Kenya

(Kwale District). Like (5) MEASUREMENTS: HB ♂ 50–67, ♀ 50–61, TL ♂ 65–90, ♀ 63–88; Wt 9–20.

Distribution. From Gambia to W. Nigeria, Zaire to E. border, W. Ruanda-Urundi, N. Angola south to Cuanza R. and about 10°S. Also mountain forests from N. of Malawi and N.E. shore of Lake Tanganyika in S.W. to Uluguru and Usambara Mts of N.E. Tanzania (as well as extreme S.E. coastal corner of Kenya). HABITAT: rain-, mountain rain-, bamboo-, gallery-, swamp-, and coastal forests; forest islands, moist savannahs. In mountains up to 3000m or more. TERRITORY: resident; each troop has territory of 8–15 hectares; size of territory related to food supply and number in troop. Well-marked routes and favourite sleeping trees, latter in middle of area. Territory defended against neighbouring troops by movement and voice.

Habits. DAILY RHYTHM: diurnal. Wake at sunrise, then bask in sun, later go off to feeding places. At midday to about 15.00, they rest, groom or sleep. Afterwards they feed until evening, then return to sleeping tree. Daily foraging usually only over 80–150m. Live mainly in the forest canopy, in danger flee to the lower tiers; rarely on ground. Run quickly along the boughs, and make fantastic leaps from tree to tree, using the elasticity of the boughs in catapult fashion, landing feet first among the foliage. Occasionally swing by the hands. In display or in danger will make wide leaps with head forward, allowing the mantle and tail tuft to flutter. TOILET: as in *Cercopithecus*, much mutual grooming, especially in the midday rest, and after storms. Tail tuft receives special attention. VOICE: adults, especially ♂♂, utter far-reaching howls as territory marking and contact calls. Uttered for 15–20 minutes at a time 3 or 4 times a day: from dawn to sunrise, from the dormitory tree: neighbouring troops join in; on arrival at the feeding place, at the same time running and leaping in remarkable activity among the highest branches, neighbouring troops join in on hearing this, activity at reduced level if no neighbours are to be seen; in afternoon at end of midday rest; in evening on return to sleeping tree. Silent in bad weather. If 2 troops meet on the border there is much display and threat activity, staring, head nodding, false chewing, hand clapping. Old ♂♂ start to roar, jump around, allow themselves to fall and climb up again. The troop furthest away from its own territorial centre usually retreats, with a roaring old ♂ as rearguard. In threat or alarm an old ♂ snorts. Soft grunting while troop is on the move; soft croaking when uneasy. Quarrelling young squeal and scream. SENSES: sight and hearing very good, scent moderate. ENEMIES: mainly large eagles. Alarm call a goat-like bleating; take refuge in lower tiers of forest. Give alarm of ground enemies by hand-slapping on branches, and other demonstrations. FOOD: green leaves, fruit, palm nuts, bark, beard moss (in mountain forests), grass seeds, insects, mineralised earth. Lick dew from branches or drink from hollows in trees. In feeding, the hands draw a bunch of twigs together, and the lips strip off the foliage. SOCIABILITY: family troops of 1 old ♂ and several ♀♀ with young. Supernumerary adult ♂♂ either solitary, or found new separate troops. Normally 3–12, or 18, in a family troop; sometimes troops join up to a large party of 50 or so. The old ♂ is sentry, alarm-giver, rear guard and territory marker. Animals usually friendly together, no serious fighting, relieve false tension by apparent chewing with closed mouth.

Reproduction. Breed all year round. ♀ in heat has no perineal swelling, carries tail over back, and may be mated by an old ♂ and younger ♂♂. ♀ giving birth stays away from ♂ for 1 day. Gestation 147–178 days. Young white (see Identification); weight at birth *c.* 450, clings tightly to mother's body (helped at first by mother with one hand); becomes active at 1 week, begins to climb and jump at 3 weeks, and at 6 months can leap from tree to tree, but if scared still clings to mother up to a year or longer. Suckles up to 1¼ years or longer, although 1st solid food taken at ⅓–½ year. Other ♀♀, and also ♂♂, seem to have an urge to nurse and carry the young, even to steal it. At 3 weeks the young one recognises its mother and rejects strangers by kicking and screaming. A ♀ will also suckle other young (a valuable habit in case of the death of the mother. SEXUAL MATURITY: ♀ 2 years, ♂ 4. LONGEVITY: 20 years recorded in captivity.

GUEREZA, OR EASTERN BLACK & WHITE COLOBUS, Pls 55, 56
Colobus (Colobus) guereza (Ruppell, 1835) (= *abyssinicus* Oken, 1816, invalid)
G. Guereza or Seidenaffe   F. Le Colobe Guereza   S. Mbega, Kuluzu

Identification. Form, structure and juvenile pelage as in Western Black and White Colobus. Fur of crown forming a short crest; shoulders, flanks and rump with long mantle or cloak, tail with terminal tuft. Body black, but facial surroundings, mantle, tail tuft, broad hair ring round callosities, and indistinct thigh spot, white. Tail tuft varying in length and degree of bushiness, from a simple terminal tuft to a long flowing brush ¾ the length of the tail. Sexes alike. Skin of newborn young reddish under the white fur, becoming pink at 3rd day. The full adult coat is acquired at 4–7 months. A small population of pure albinos on Mt Kenya, near Nanyuki. 6 ssp.: (1) Typical Guereza, *guereza* (Ruppell, 1835) (= *poliurus* Thomas, 1901: *dodingae* Matschie, 1912). W. and S. Ethiopia west of R. Hawash; white mantle very well developed, root of tail black, mixed with white, rest of tail bushy, white. (2) Neumann's Colobus, *gallarum* (Neumann, 1902). E. Ethiopia, E. of R. Hawash; like (1), but base of tail entirely black. (3) Matschie's Colobus, *matschiei* (Neumann, 1899). Kenya, W. of Rift Valley; like (1), however basal half of tail black, rest white. (4) Mt Kenya Colobus, *kikuyuensis* (Lonnberg, 1912) (= *percivali* Heller, 1913). Kenya E. of the Rift Valley; like (1), but only short part of the tail root black, four-fifths of the rest of tail very bushy, white. (5) Kilimanjaro Colobus, *caudatus* (Thomas, 1885). Kilimanjaro – Meru region. Like (4), but tail entirely white and bushy from base. (6) Congo Guereza, *occidentalis* (Rochebrune, 1886) (= *uellensis* Matschie, 1913). From E. Nigeria and Cameroun through Ubangui–Shari region and N. Zaire, north of Congo R. to Lado Enclave, S. Sudan, and W. Uganda to Lake Victoria; mantle only moderately long, tail black, long, with well-developed white tuft ¼ of total tail length. MEASUREMENTS: HB ♂ 54–70, ♀ 48–65, TL ♂ 67–90, ♀ 72–83. Wt 10–23.

Distribution. Eastern Mid-Nigeria, N. and E. Cameroun (south to Sanaga R.), S.W. Chad, Central African Republic, N. and N.E. Zaire north of Congo R., S. Sudan, S. Ethiopia, Uganda, W. Kenya, N.W. Tanzania eastward to Meru and Kilimanjaro (see ssp.)

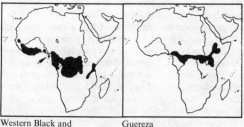

Western Black and   Guereza
White Colobus

Habits. Like Western Black and White Colobus. Introduction to fur grooming often by a playful mutual biting on arms, shoulders and nape. Urinating ♀ often scents its tail strongly, ♂ not.   VOICE: also like the Western species, however in troop meetings additionally a tongue-clicking.   LONGEVITY: 24 years reported in captivity.

OLIVE COLOBUS, *Colobus (Procolobus) verus* (Van Beneden, 1838)   **Pl. 55**
G. Grüner Stummelaffe   F. Le Colobe de Van Beneden
Identification. Slender, small, long-tailed, legs longer than arms. Head small, rounded, muzzle short, back of nose straight. Nostrils half-sideways slits, separated by septum. Otherwise structure as in Western Black and White Colobus; M_3 however often with 6 cusps, and thumb still further reduced. Lower edge of forehead with 2 whorls of stiff hairs, middle of crown with short crest, whiskers long and directed backwards. Tail without tuft. Face flesh-coloured, blue-grey around eyes; palms, soles and callosities slate-grey, forehead whorls light grey; whiskers, underside of body, inside of legs, backs of thighs, scrotum, lower arms, hands, feet and underside of tail ashy-grey. Upperside from crown to and including tail, upper arms and thighs olivaceous, crown, nape and back with a brownish suffusion, lower thighs weak olive. ♀ like ♂, but without crown crest. Anal and perennial region can be swollen, but swelling unrelated to monthly oestrus, however during gestation and suckling it is nearly always reduced. Newborn young have adult colouration.   MEASUREMENTS: HB ♂ 43–50, ♀ 44–50, TL ♂ 57–64, ♀ 57–64. Wt ♂ 3.3–5.4, ♀ 2.9–4.4.
Distribution. From Guinea and Sierra Leone to left bank of R. Volta, Ghana. No ssp. Endangered.   HABITAT: lowest tier of rain forest up to about 10m high, thickets, secondary forests by rivers, swampy forests, palm swamps, but also in drier forest regions.
Habits. Flees from enemies into the middle tier (10–30m high), also sleeps at that level, but does not climb into highest tier. Only rarely on the ground. Diurnal.   FOOD: leaves, sometimes flowers.   SOCIABILITY: family troops of 1 old ♂, several ♀♀ and young, usually 6–10 animals, sometimes up to 20, with more than 1 old ♂ in the troop. Friendly among themselves, no particular ranking order. Rather silent and secretive, no separate warning call, but they respond to the calls of the common Guenons (*mona* and *petaurista*) with which they often associate. In danger sit still with head on breast, trusting to merging of colour with its surroundings. Apart from grunts, no other sound known, except a scream in great danger.
Reproduction. Details not known. Young are carried in her mouth by the mother, as in the lemurs, *Lemur variegatus, Galago demidovii, alleni* and *elegantulus*, for about a month, and are then carried on her belly.

RED COLOBUS, *Colobus (Piliocolobus) badius* (Kerr, 1792)   **Pls 55, 56**
G. Roter Stummelaffe   F. Le Colobe bai
Identification. Large, slender, long-tailed, hind legs longer than arms. Head small, round, muzzle short, nose straight (in *badius* and *temmincki* somewhat curved in profile), nostrils half-sideways slits, separated by a septum. Otherwise in structure like Western Black & White Colobus, however stump of thumb very small or lacking. ♀♀ with more or less genital swellings according to the subspecies or individually. ♂♂ also with permanent swelling of anal and perineal region between the oval callosities. Fur on upperside somewhat lengthened, loose and silky, longest in *kirki*. Whiskers medium to long, directed backwards; hair of forehead and crown sometimes rather tufted (*tephrosceles*), or forming a longer forehead crest (*foai, kirki*). Tail without tuft. General colour orange to dark red upperside, partly or wholly darkened, to blackish

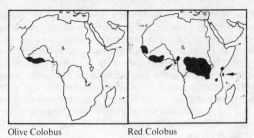

Olive Colobus   Red Colobus

back, and with lighter reddish-yellow to whitish underside according to subspecies. Forms from the west of the distribution have more black than those of Central and E. Africa, in which any black of the upperside is widely mixed with brown or reddish-brown. Face bluish to black, with flesh-coloured 'spectacle' pattern on nose and lips. Wide colour variation in some of the 13 ssp. (other authors consider several of these to be distinct species): (1) *temmincki* (Kuhl, 1820). S. Senegal, Gambia, Guinea–Bissau, N.W. Guinea; upperside greyish-black, rest of body orange. (2) *badius* (Kerr, 1792). S. Sierra Leone, Liberia, Ivory Coast to Bandama R.; upperside black, rest of body reddish-brown, tail reddish black. (3) *waldroni* (Hayman, 1936). Ivory Coast eastward from Bandama R. to W. Ghana; forehead and thighs dark red, back and tail black. (4) *pennanti* (Waterhouse, 1838). Fernando Póo: upperside reddish-brown, crown, nape and shoulders washed with black, whiskers white, underside yellowish-red. (5) *preussi* (Matschie, 1900). W. Cameroun opposite Fernando Póo, with Mt Cameroun; back dark brown, crown black, whiskers white, flanks orange red, underside creamy white, first ⅔ of tail red, the remainder black. (6) *oustaleti* (Troussart, 1906). From S.W. Cameroun and N. Congo (Brazzaville) to N.E. Zaire north of Congo R.; whiskers grey, crown and back dark brown, otherwise like (5). (7) *tholloni* (Riviere, 1886). Zaire, south of Congo R., between Congo, Kasai and Sankuru Rivers, E. to Lualaba R. (Upper Congo); bright reddish-brown, above darker, below lighter. (8) *ellioti* (Dollman, 1909). Ituri region, E. Zaire, to W. Uganda; front part of body reddish, hind part dark brown. (9) *foai* (Pousargues, 1899). E. of Upper Congo (Lualaba) to Lake Tanganyika; red forehead crest, otherwise like (7) or (8), extremely variable. (10) *tephrosceles* (Elliot, 1907). Ruwenzori to S.E. and S.W. of Lake Tanganyika; E. Zaire, W. Uganda, W. Tanzania; crown reddish-brown, back dark or light brown, arms and legs greyish brown, hands and feet black. Tail like back. Very variable. (11) *gordonorum* (Matschie, 1900). Iringa region, S.W. Tanzania: seriously threatened. Very variable, upperside black to shoulders, from there forward reddish-brown, crown usually reddish-brown, arms and hands black to brownish-black, hind legs to feet light grey, though feet remain dark to black; whiskers and underside white or grey. (12) *kirki* (Gray, 1868). Jozani Forest on Zanzibar, is now protected but is still threatened; crown, back and tail reddish-brown; whiskers, forehead crest, underside and tail whitish; shoulders, arms, hands and feet black. (13) *rufomitratus* (Peters, 1879). Lower Tana R., and coastal forests southward, S.E. Kenya. Seriously threatened. Crown reddish-brown, back and tail black, arms, hands, hind legs and feet, whiskers, grey; underside whitish. Sexes alike. Young with upperside black, underside grey, fur silky. Reach adult colouring at 1½–3½ months. MEASUREMENTS: HB ♂ 46–70, ♀ 47–62, TL ♂ 55–80, ♀ 42–80. Wt ♂ 9–13, ♀ 7–9.

Distribution. From Senegambia to W. Uganda, S.E. Kenya, S.W. Tanzania and mid-Zaire, also on Zanzibar and Fernando Póo. Distribution only partly continuous. 13 ssp. Details, see Identification. HABITAT: rain-, gallery-, swamp-, mountain-, and secondary forests; in places deciduous forests and forest islands. Permanent water nearby is necessary. Up to 1500m in mountains. In W. Africa its home is usually in the highest tiers of the forest, in Uganda also occurs in the lower tiers, sometimes also in dense secondary forest undergrowth and on ground; *temmincki* and *tephrosceles* often on the ground. TERRITORY: according to size of troop and nature of forest, an area of 25–150 hectares. Very resident. Has well-marked sleeping, sunning and feeding places, with connecting routes. Territories may overlap. Marked by sound, as in *C. polykomos* but voice not so far-reaching.

Habits. DAILY RHYTHM: activity during day as in *C. polykomos*, 30 % of day feeding, 60 % inactive. Feeding periods mainly morning and afternoon, and short midday session. Powerful jumpers from tree to tree. TOILET: as in *Cercopithecus*; largely mutual grooming. VOICE: usually quiet. Old ♂ has a high warning and contact call, another call when quarrelling or as warning of danger, as well as a shrill 'yow' as warning of attack by crowned eagle. Scream in great danger. FOOD: flowers, buds, shoots, soft fruits, leaves. During the course of the day feeds in many different species of tree. SOCIABILITY: troops of 50–100 animals, each ♂ with about 3 ♀ ♀ and their young. In feeding, the troop scatters; for resting, sleeping, in heavy rain or in alarm divide up into small family groups again. Old ♂ ♂ sociable and friendly, but small squabbles between members of the troop, perhaps to work off stresses, are common. In alarm the ♂ ♂ use threat to deter an enemy while the family crouch together; in flight the ♂ ♂ form a rearguard.

Reproduction. Mating usually at night. ♂ stands on branch, or holds the ♀ ♀ ankles with foot, according to the subspecies, ♀ mute or twittering. In rain forest breeding season not restricted, in other habitats seasonal. Gestation 5–5½ months; in E. Africa main parturition season Mar–May and Jul–Nov. Young is carried clinging to mother's belly and is nursed only by its own mother; no 'aunts'. Leaves mother for first time at 2–3½ months, is weaned at 9–12 months. SEXUAL MATURITY: ♀ 2, ♂ 3–3½ years. LONGEVITY: in captivity up to 2 years only; difficult to keep because of specialized diet.

ANTHROPOID APES, PONGIDAE

Height at crown, standing erect, 100–180cm, weight 30–300kg, ♂ usually much larger and heavier than ♀. No tail. Head and muzzle rounded, latter projecting. Ears naked, small to middle-sized. Face, and in part upper breast naked. ♂ Orang with cheek folds and large throat sac; Gorilla ♂ with helmet-like crown and nape sagittal crest. Arms longer than legs. Dent.: $2 \cdot 1 \cdot 2 \cdot 3 = 32$, canines larger than incisors and premolars. Arm span 150–275cm; thumb short, fingers sometimes lengthened. Great toe opposable. Pelage short to long, dense or thin. 2 pectoral teats, scrotum and penis small. Gestation 7–10 months, 1 active young with eyes open; sexually mature at 7–10 years, fully adult at 10–12 years. Longevity up to 30 years or more. Sociable, terrestrial and arboreal (or only arboreal-Orang). Vegetarian, but Chimpanzee also omnivorous and will even prey on other animals. Primeval forests of Borneo and Sumatra (Orang-Utan, *Pongo pygmaeus*) as well as in Africa (Gorilla, Chimpanzee, Dwarf Chimpanzee). Altogether 3 genera with 4 species, of which 2 genera with 3 species are African.

GORILLA, *Gorilla gorilla* (Savage and Wyman, 1847)　　　　**Pl. 58**
G. Gorilla　F. Le Gorilla　S. Makaku

Identification. Form heavy and thick, trunk short and broad, arms longer than legs, no tail. Head large and massive, low forehead, eyebrow swelling notable, eyes close together, small and deep set. Nose flat and broad, with large flat nostrils (in *gorilla* the nasal septum projects as flat swelling to edge of lips), projecting beyond the swollen muzzle. Ears small, rounded, lying close to head. Skull of old ♂ with high crown and posterior ridge as base for powerful neck and chewing muscles. Crown externally has a high keel formed by muscle and fat. Arms very muscular, hands broad, fingers short, thumbs weak and short, not reaching base of index finger. Skin of middle fingers thickened. Legs short and thick, whole of soles used in walking, heel long, toes short, bound together at base, great toe deeply set, short, widely opposable. Scrotum and penis remarkably small. Sometimes has small callosities. Top of throat with air sac. Dent.: incisors broad, canines of old ♂♂ specially powerful and conical; upper molars 4-cusped, lower 5-cusped, lower increasing in size from M_1 to M_3. Skin black, as also naked face, ears, palms and soles and upper breast. Fur short, thick and rough in the lowland animals, longer and thicker (especially on lower arms and thighs) in the mountain form. Young at birth pinkish grey to greyish-black, head, nape, back and outside of limbs black to brownish grey, breast, belly and inside of limbs only sparsely haired; ears, face, palms and soles naked. In a few days the skin has brownish-grey hair becoming black as the animal grows up; small white hair tuft on buttocks disappearing in 4th year. With growth the belly and sides become grey; in the ♂ at about 10 years the back is light to silvery grey (the saddle) hence the old ♂ may be known as a silverback. In *gorilla* the crown is sometimes brownish-black to rust coloured, or the fur light-coloured, with occasional partial or complete albinos. MEASUREMENTS: body size, standing erect: ♂ 170–180, ♀ 140–150, Wt in wild, ♂ 140–200, ♀ 70–110; Wt in captivity ♂ up to 340, ♀ up to 125.

Distribution. 2 separate areas; one in the west around the Gulf of Guinea; the other in the east, in E. Zaire to W. Uganda and W. Ruanda. 3 ssp.: (1) Western Lowland Gorilla, *gorilla* (Savage and Wyman, 1847). Uniformly greyish-brown, silver saddle reaches to buttocks and upper thighs; flared nasal swellings with irregular borders. Cameroun, Rio Muni, Gabon, Congo (Brazzaville) and Central African Republic, south to mouth of Congo, eastward to Sanga R., northern limit Sanaga R. Also a population on the upper Cross R. on the Nigeria–Cameroun border. (2) Eastern Lowland Gorilla, *graueri* (Matschie, 1903) (= *mayema* Alix and Bouvier, 1877). Silver saddle on the short-haired surface of back reduced. Body broader and trunk-like, face longer, nose slender, the nasal swellings regularly bordered, jaws and teeth longer than (1). Eastern Congo basin from Lualaba R. eastward to mountains west of Lake Edward (L. Idi Amin) in the north, and northern tip of Lake Tanganyika in the south (Mitumba Mts with Mt Tshiaberimi in the north and Itombwe Mts in the south). A former population from Bondo on the Uelle R. extinct. (3) Mountain Gorilla, *beringei* (Matschie, 1903). Colour black to bluish-black, saddle as in (1), however hair longer, especially on head and arms, jaws and teeth larger, face shorter and broader, nose smaller, the border swellings nearly semicircular and regular, arms distinctly shorter than in (1) and (2). The high mountains north and east of Lake Kivu (Birunga volcanoes in E. Zaire and W. Ruanda). Also in Kayonsa Forest in Kigezi, S.W. Uganda). Population greatly threatened, only about 500 animals still existing. HABITAT: rain forests with dense herbage and bushy undergrowth, also in secondary forest and in vicinity of plantations. *Graueri* up to 1500m, *beringei* to 4,100m, the latter in the Birunga region in the bamboo zone between 2,500 and 3,000m, and in the tree heath zone and the densely bushy slopes to around 4,100m; from Kayonsa Forest up to 2,500m, in Kigezi in bamboo zone between 2,500 and 3,000m. HOME RANGE: depending on nature of country and size of troop, 10–40 sq km. No holding of territory, no defending or marking; if neighbouring troop overlaps they may disregard each other or mix in a friendly manner for a short time. No fighting. Troop wanders casually, changing sleeping quarters daily. Usually cover only 1–2km daily. Population density in the lowlands about 1 per sq km, in the Birunga region about 3·5.

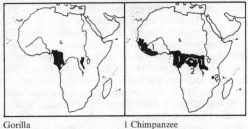

Gorilla

1 Chimpanzee
2 Dwarf Chimpanzee

Habits. DAILY RHYTHM: 6.00–8.00 waking and rising, 8.00–10.00 feeding, 10.00–14.00 resting, 14.00–17.30 feeding and roaming. Go in single file when changing locations. Sleeping place is a simple construction of twigs and foliage on the ground at the foot of a tree, or a tree nest of twigs and boughs collected together. Each animal makes its own bed, but young up to 3 years old sleep with mother. Nests irregularly distributed. In the bamboo and Birunga tree-heath zones all nests are on the ground; in the western and eastern lowlands only old ♂♂ have ground nests, the others use trees; in the Kayonsa region all build high tree nests. Each used for only one night. Frequently also use nests for mid-day rest, in the east more often than in the west. Eastern Gorillas defecate and urinate in their nests. On the ground they travel usually on all fours, with head erect, hind feet with whole of sole flat on the ground, arms supported by the outside of the middle fingers, 'knuckle walking'. An old ♂ will stand erect when chest beating, but bipedal locomotion of adults in the wild uncommon. Young and ♀♀ climb commonly, old ♂♂ rarely. Cannot swim. TOILET: occasional scratching, not mutual, mostly by mother with young. VOICE: information conveyed to each other by behaviour, gestures, mimicry and voice. About 21 distinct sounds are known. Contact call is a grunting; a loud deep bark (like a bushbuck) is the alarm. Breast drumming of ♂ may be a relief from excitement or a prelude to 8 forms of ritualised behaviour: screaming, with inflation of throat sac; grabbing foliage and placing it in the mouth; standing erect on hind legs; tearing up and throwing plants; drumming on the chest with clenched fists, and stamping feet; lowering on to hands and a 4-footed diagonal gallop (mock attack); tearing up plants; and striking the ground with the flat of the hands. These sounds serve also as contacts with other troops (audible up to 1½km distant), whose ♂♂ are alerted and drum in reply. By this means direct confrontation with other troops, with possibility of clashes, is avoided. Young ♂♂ at 1 year already drum. Altercations between old ♂♂ begin with yawning, staring (the latter is a direct challenge, since normally face to face vision is avoided, eyeing from the corner of the eyes is usual) followed then by barking and roaring (also used against strange animals or men), and chest drumming. Serious fighting between old ♂♂, which may last for days and can end fatally, is rare. SENSES: sight and hearing very good, scent exceptional (man can be scented at distance of 20m). ENEMIES: only leopard, which may occasionally overpower adults. FOOD: purely vegetarian (over 100 distinct species of food plants known). Mainly leaves, buds, shoots, stalks, roots, tubers, bark, fruits, ferns etc. Banana and sugar-cane plantations are sought out, and owing to their wasteful feeding habits much damage may be done. Insects, bird's eggs etc are not eaten, although in captivity flesh is taken willingly. Because of the juicy diet drinking is not necessary. Owing to the great bulk of food eaten, numerous droppings at regular intervals, rather like horse dung. SOCIABILITY: sociable, in small to large family groups. In the Cameroun–Gabon coastal region usually only 1 ♂, 1 ♀ and 1–3 youngsters; in the highlands of that region and in E. Zaire usually 1 old ♂, 3–4 ♀♀ and their young; in the Mountain Gorilla 2–3 old ♂♂, several young ♂♂, and up to 10 females with their young (altogether 15–30 animals). An old ♂ may sometimes be solitary. In general the composition of a troop changes only with births and deaths, sometimes by addition of a solitary ♂. Adult sex ratio in troop, of ♂♂ to ♀♀, 1:2. The old ♂ is leader and protector of the family, but does not exploit his dominance; young ♂♂ come next in linear ranking order, ♀♀ next with suckling young, according to size. Meetings between outside troops, see Home Range.

Reproduction. No marked breeding season. Mate from front or behind. ♀ has a 25–38 day cycle, with no genital swelling during heat. In the height of oestrus (3 day period), offers herself to several nearby ♂♂; old ♂ not possessive. Gestation 236–296 days, twins rare (see Chimpanzee, below). Births at intervals of 3½–4½ years. Mother dries the young and eats afterbirth. Young one clings tightly to mother's belly fur. Gripping ability in some young weak at first, and ♀ supports it with one hand. First crawling by young at 1¼–1¾ months, sits upright at 3–4 months, can stand upright with a hand-hold at 4–4½ months. Goes on all fours and climbs at 3½–5 months, first free upright locomotion at 8½ months, first solid food at 4–5 months, milk dentition developed between 1 month and 1½ years, permanent dentition completed between ½ and 11 years. Young lives with mother for 3 years. Suckles for about 1 year. Weight at birth 1.8–2.5, HB at birth 28–32. Weight development, 1 month 2.8, 5 months c. 8, 1 year 15.6, 6 years c. 70, 10 years 140–190. SEXUAL MATURITY: ♂ 7–11, ♀ 6–9 years. LONGEVITY: in wild 25–30, in captivity 38 years recorded.

CHIMPANZEE, *Pan troglodytes* (Blumenbach, 1779)   **Pl. 57**
G. Grossschimpanse   F. Le Chimpanzé   S. Soko, Soko motu
Identification. Form like Gorilla, but much smaller. Body thickset, shoulders and breast broad, arms longer than legs, neck short, no tail. Forehead low, eyebrow ridges prominent, eyes deep-set and close together. Nose flat, broad below, lips narrow and mobile. Hands and feet long and narrow, fingers long, outer skin of middle fingers thickened (for knuckle-walking), thumbs short, great toes deeply set, short, like thumbs opposable, nails curved. Dent.: I¹ broadly spatulate, ♂ canine conical, powerful, twice as long as incisors, ♀ canine shorter; upper molars 4-cusped, decreasing from 1st to 3rd, lower molars 5-cusped. Skull of old ♂ with sagittal and occipital ridges. Large throat air sac. Scrotum and penis small, latter longish, thin and without prepuce. ♀ with greatly enlarged cyclical genital swellings. Skin of face black, or dark to black-spotted on a bronze-coloured ground, ears in part light, palms and soles dark, body skin of young flesh- to bronze coloured, becoming black. Fur long and sparse, predominantly black, adults with blackish grey mixture on hips and thighs, chin, in

part, with white beard. Some adults may become bald-headed. Young up to 3 years old have white hair tufts above buttocks. 4 ssp.:[1]. (1) True Chimpanzee, *verus* (Schwarz, 1934). Senegambia, Sierra Leone and Guinea to W. bank of Lower Niger; northern limit about 10°N. Head high and narrow, muzzle projecting strongly, ears large and prominent, palms and soles flesh-coloured with some dark spots; face of young flesh-coloured, dark bluish mask around eyes and above nose, hair of head with central parting, in older animals darker, spotted, becoming matt-black, but facial spots still distinguishable; ears becoming bronze-coloured, old ♂♂ with whitish beard, both sexes becoming bald, beginning in ♂ as triangular spot above forehead, in ♀ further back. (2) Tschego, *troglodytes* (Blumenbach, 1779). East of Lower Niger to Ubangui and Lower Congo R. in E. and S. head flatter and broader, ears smaller than in (1): face in young flesh-coloured without spots, hair of head without parting, face freckled, merging later as brown, later black; also ears, palms and soles and body skin black, narrow whiskers, early balding in both sexes, eventually affecting half or all the head. (3) Koolokamba, *koolakomba* (Du Chaillu, 1860). Mountain rain forests of S.E. Cameroun and E. Gabon, east to Sanga R., south perhaps to Congo R.; like (2) but eyebrow swellings and muzzle strongly projecting forward, nostril openings gorilla-like in breadth, great toe longer than in (1) and (2); fur long and rough, whiskers present, skin and fur black. Many authors consider this only a variant of *troglodytes*. (4) Schweinfurth's, Eastern or Long-haired Chimpanzee, *schweinfurthi* (Giglioli, 1872). Zaire between Ubangui and Congo rivers, as well as east of Lualaba R. to W. Uganda and both shores of Lake Tanganyika (E. side now the Gombe National Park). On the N.E. shore of Lake Nyasa around Nkata Bay lives (or lived – may well be extinct) a relic population, completely black, with grey rump saddle in adults, as an undescribed ssp.; known to natives as Ufiti. (*Note.* This record seems to be due to a lone female chimpanzee that had probably escaped from captivity.) MEASUREMENTS: HB ♂ 77–94, ♀ 64–85, Ht 120–170, Wt ♂ 45–55, ♀ 40–55 in wild state, in captivity ♂ up to 90, ♀ up to 80.

Distribution. Senegal, S. Mali, Gambia, Guinea–Bissau, Guinea, Sierra Leone, Liberia, Ivory Coast, Ghana, ? Togo and Benin, S. Nigeria, Cameroun, Rio Muni, Gabon, Cabinda, Central African Republic, Congo (Brazzaville), Zaire, S. Sudan, W. Uganda, Ruanda, Burundi, W. Tanzania (E. shore of Lake Tanganyika). In Congo basin only on right side of Congo R. 4 ssp. (see Identification and footnote). In W. Africa widely exterminated between Senegal and Ivory Coast, in eastern part of range also seriously threatened by human settlements, poaching, and the capture of young animals for the animal trade. HABITAT: rain forests, savannah with forest, gallery forests, deciduous forests in hilly country, secondary forest, mountain forest to 3,300m (where Mountain Gorillas live, Chimpanzees remain at lower levels). The prerequisite for a Chimpanzee location is a rich all the year round food supply. HOME RANGE: size depends on the food supply. In the rich Budongo Forest in W. Uganda each troop has about 20 sq km (*c.* 3 animals per sq km); in the tree savannahs of the Gombe National Park (E. shore of Lake Tanganyika), each troop needs 40–60 sq km (about 1 animal per sq km). Each range has well-marked trails, often used by big game. Within the range they roam from one food source to another, according to season, so are assured of a food supply over the year. Ranges can overlap; if 2 troops meet there is much uproar, but on the whole behaviour is friendly. The Koolokamba is more solitary, less friendly, aggressive. *Map* p. 203.

1. Reynolds and Luscombe (1971) consider the differences between the four subspecies are founded only on individual and age variations, and that subspecies in the chimpanzee cannot be maintained.

Habits. DAILY RHYTHM: rise at dawn, using their nests as latrines, and go off gradually on the first feed, having first a quick stomach-filling snack, afterwards a more selective feeding. Satisfied after 3–4 hours. Mid-day rest for several hours, in part in self-built sleeping nests in trees or on the ground. Such nests are built in a few minutes by bending branches and twigs together into a platform with a rim. Feed again 16.00–18.00. At dusk make for the tree nests (6–20m high), where the troop stays for the night. Each animal builds its nest, young up to 3 years-old sleep with mother. May sleep sideways with drawn-up knees, or outstretched on back or belly. Move around partly on ground (on all fours, feet flat, arms supported by outer edge of middle digits of hand on ground, the so-called knuckle walk), partly in the trees, running or hanging, also leaping up to 10m from branch to branch. Bipedal erect position on the ground when on the look-out. If arms loaded with fruit, may run bipedally for a short distance. Streams are crossed by the overhanging boughs; rivers usually form barriers, since Chimpanzees do not swim. They use tools in the form of grass stems, or twigs stripped of leaves, to get termites and ants out of their tunnels, or honey out of hollow trees or ground nests. They will crumple leaves together and use them like a sponge to get water out of a hole in a tree. Hard nuts may be wedged between tree roots and broken open with a stone. Sticks may be used, either as clubs or thrown, as weapons against enemies. TOILET: little obvious, mainly between mother and young. VOICE: very noisy, main call 'hoo-hoo-hoo' in various inflexions. Loud calling mostly by day, sometimes also at night, can be heard up to 3km away. Often accompanied by drumming with the flat of the hands on hollow or other trees or on board-like roots. In group encounters, loud calls of ♂♂, drumming, bough shaking, and beating the ground. At a major food discovery calling may last up to 10 minutes, with other groups answering. Also call in morning on rising and in evening before retiring. Parts of the group withdrawing to a new region call and drum. Sometimes a sort of carnival lasting for hours, with calling, screaming and a concert of drumming and ground stamping, by day and sometimes by night. The cause may be the meeting of 2 groups, a distant thunderstorm or earth tremors, or perhaps spontaneous and without any obvious instigation. SENSES: sight and hearing very good, scent good. ENEMIES: apart from man, only leopard, whose appearance gives rise to screams of fury as the adults band together, throwing branches or even striking with them. At the appearance of man the short low warning cry of the scouts warns all the troop to remain motionless. If discovered they make a quick descent to the ground and flee silently in the undergrowth. FOOD: mainly plants and their products; above all fruits, then leaves, flowers, shoots, bark, stalks, seeds, palm- and coconuts. Hard fruits or nuts are beaten against a tree trunk or opened by hitting with a stone. 30–80 different food plants have been identified. Supplementary foods include termites, ants, insect larvae and pupae, honey, fish, kids, young antelopes, young guenons, baboons or colobus monkeys; even young of their own species, and (reportedly) human babies. Kids and young monkeys are hunted by a joint party. Seasonally the monotony of the diet (particularly in woodland savannah) may lead to a craving for protein, hence hunting for animals and eating flesh, sometimes even leading to cannibalism by old ♂♂. Captured young animals are picked up by the hind legs and killed by striking the head on the ground: the old ♂♂ get the best of the feast. SOCIABILITY: in tribes of up to 60, sometimes even 80, animals, splitting up during the day into small groups, so that the whole tribe is seldom together. In rain forests groups have differing compositions, either all adult ♂♂ and ♀♀, or only adult ♂♂, or adult ♀♀ with their young, or both sexes and young together. Some ♂♂ may be solitary. Group composition commonly changes. In woodland savannahs almost only mixed groups of 1 or more adult ♂♂, several ♀♀

and their young; group consistency, and nomadism, more evident than in rain forest population. Adults finding a valuable food source will call neighbouring animals by howling, screaming and drumming. No particular ranking order within a group, old, especially if greying, are respected by young, ♂♂ by ♀♀ of a similar age, and mothers by their children. In an altercation the opponents may stamp, shake branches as intimidation: sometimes a short and harmless attack. ♀♀ on heat are often quarrelsome. In threat, plants are torn up, arms and legs agitated and hair erected, serving as demonstration of dominance, maintenance of home range and intimidation of possible enemies. A submissive animal greets an old ♂ by touching his head, shoulder, belly, hip or penis, adopting an obsequious attitude with open hands (begging behaviour). Other gestures of appeasement: ♀ stretches towards rear of old ♂; young ♂ goes to old ♂ and touches his lips or penis. In various other ways members of a group communicate with each other by their rich vocalisation, gestures and mimicry.

Reproduction. No marked breeding season, but in Gombe National Park (W. Tanzania) most births in Aug–Nov. ♀ oestrous cycle of 35–41 days, usually 37; of which 7 days preliminary swelling, 18 the pink main swelling of the anogenital region, 10 days decreasing, 3 days bleeding; ovulation during last week of main swelling. ♀♀ in heat may be mated by all the sexually mature ♂♂ of the group in succession. In mating the ♂ sits upright or half bent over ♀. Mating lasts only a few seconds, with ♂ grunting and ♀ squealing and screaming. Gestation 201–266 days, average 227–232. Usually 1 young at a birth; twins not very rare, but either through abortion or postnatal death of 1, seldom survive. In captivity triplets reported once. ♀ cleans young carefully, bites off the umbilical cord and eats afterbirth. Eyes of young open after 20 minutes as young clings tightly to mother's breast, suckles for 1st time before 1 day old. ♀ sometimes puts young on her back, or, while feeding or nest building, on a convenient branch. Young sits upright at 5 months, stands, with support, at 6 months, goes independently at 1 year, lives closely with mother up to 2 years, still sleeps in nest with mother at 2½–3 years, to end of suckling period and end of childhood. Separates completely from mother at 4 years and joins other juveniles. ♀, on average, gives birth every 3 years, has a menstrual cycle to end of her life, and can still breed at 30 years. SEXUAL MATURITY: ♂ 8–10, fully adult at 11–13, ♀ at 8–9 years. Milk teeth complete between 2½–3 and 14½–15 months, the permanent teeth between 3 and 11 years. Wt at birth 1·5–2, HB 28–30. Wt increments 1 month 2·5, 1 year c. 7·5, 5 years c. 21, 10 years c. 37, 15 years 47–50. LONGEVITY: up to 50 years recorded in captivity.

PYGMY CHIMPANZEE OR BONOBO, Pl. 57
Pan paniscus (Schwarz, 1929)
G. Zwergschimpanse   F. Le Chimpanzé pygmée ou nain, Le Bonobo

Identification. In form and structure closely resembling Chimpanzee, but with the following differences: body structure more elegant, trunk narrower and more slender, arms and legs proportionately longer, hind legs more slender and attenuated, feet narrower, great toe larger, second and third toes united at base, vulva more forwardly directed, eyebrow swellings weaker, forehead somewhat arched, skull not developing sagittal crest, ears usually smaller, nostrils strongly swollen. Pelage close-lying, sparse on breast, belly, axillary region and inside of thighs; also whiskers longer, no balding. Young at birth black, apart from the flesh-coloured eye surrounds, ears, muzzle, palms and soles of hands and feet. Sometimes a few white hairs on buttocks. Lips dirty reddish. Later the ears, face and the other named parts becoming black. MEASUREMENTS: HB 55–60, Ht 90–100, Wt 25–45, ♂ a little larger and heavier than ♀.

Distribution. Zaire, in southern part of the great Congo basin, i.e. between the Middle and Upper Congo (latter = Lualaba) on the one hand, and the Kasai and its southern Congo tributaries on the other. Earlier everywhere common, today, following the increase of settlement, restricted or rare. No ssp. HABITAT: primary, secondary and swampy forests (outside the flooding season). HOME RANGE: size not known. In light high forest numerous well-trodden paths, indicating much movement on ground. *Map* p. 302.

Habits. DAILY RHYTHM: in morning and late afternoon their home is in the top layer of the crowns, 30–50m high, where they collect and eat the fruits of particular trees, moving rapidly and with considerable agility, at times hanging by the hands. At noon, if heat in the canopy is great, descend to ground to pick up and eat any fallen fruit. Sleeping nests as in Chimpanzee, but on average higher, from about 27m. There is no association on the ground with baboons, chimpanzees or gorillas, none of which occur in the Bonobo range. In the forest canopy slight association with guenons and colobus monkeys; as a terrestrial animal the Bonobo easily reaches the scattered fruiting trees. VOICE: in wild state quiet, no far-reaching calls or territorial calls, no noisy behaviour as in the Chimpanzee, no noise on meeting of families. Sometimes a high alarm call can be heard clearly. In captivity, on the other hand, full of movement and use a wide range of sounds, particularly the high vowel sounds 'ah' and 'eh', often accompanied by arm-stretching and quick shaking of the hands. They scream in fear or fright. TOILET and SENSES: as in Chimpanzee. ENEMIES: essentially only man; not known whether leopard is a serious predator. In the forest crowns monkey-eating eagles may be a danger to young. At the sight of men or dogs a warning call is followed by silent flight, at first through the forest canopy, then on the ground. FOOD: principally fruit, then leaves and shoots. SOCIABILITY: in families, parents with 1–2 young: in good feeding areas, above all in secondary forest, occasional gatherings of several families. Active nature, sensitive and excitable. In altercations in captivity seldom any blows, biting or scratching, rather a few well-aimed kicks.

Reproduction. ♂ has no display before the ♀, who, as in the Chimpanzee, offers herself to the ♂, but sits near her making friendly sounds, then clasps her with hands on neck and back, and mates from the front. Wt at birth 1.2–1.5. Gestation, development and longevity, see Chimpanzee.

Insect-eaters, Insectivora

HEDGEHOGS, ERINACEIDAE

Rat- or hedgehog-like in appearance and size; insect-eaters with hairy or spiny upper-sides, long or short tail, small eyes, small to large ears and sharp muzzle. Digits 5/5 (*Erinaceus albiventris* sometimes 5/4). Dent.: $2-3/3 \cdot 1 \cdot 3-4/2-4 \cdot 3 = 36-44$. 4 to 10 teats. Usually crepuscular or nocturnal feeders on small creatures, or omnivorous. Temperate regions of Palaearctic and S. Asia to Sumatra, Java, Borneo, Hainan and Mindanao as well as in Africa. 2 subfamilies, 8 genera, 13 species, of which 1 subfamily (Erinaceinae, True Hedgehogs) and 3 genera with 5 species are found in Africa.

FOUR-TOED HEDGEHOG, *Erinaceus albiventris* (Wagner, 1841)   **Pl. 59**
(= *pruneri* Wagner, 1841: *sclateri* Anderson, 1895).
G. Weissbauchigel   F. Le Hérisson à ventre blanc   S. Kalungujeje
Identification. Size and form of European Hedgehog (*E. europaeus*), but most animals lack a great toe or hallux (digit number 4–5/4, and I³ is single instead of double-rooted). Dent.: $3/2 \cdot 1/1 \cdot 3/2 \cdot 3/3 = 36$. 10 teats, penis long. Muzzle pointed, ears shorter than spines of head, rounded, thinly haired, becoming naked. Tail short, a thinly-haired stump. Legs short, toes with well-developed claws. Upperside to tail and upper thighs thickly covered with stout grooved spines, 1·5–2·5cm long. Spines white with brown or blackish-brown band. General colour speckled black and white. No darker dorsal stripe. Spines of head continuous, not divided medially into 2 sections. Muzzle brownish, rest of face, legs and underside white. Juvenile coat, see Reproduction.
MEASUREMENTS: HB 17–23, TL 2–5, Wt 500–700.

Distribution. From Senegambia eastward through the Sudanese zone to Somalia, Kenya and Tanzania, as well as Zambia and Malawi. No certain ssp.   HABITAT: well covered country with dry soils (not in damp or marshy land). Woodland-, bush-, grass-savannahs; thickets, agricultural land (plantations, fields, gardens) in plains, hills and mountains up to 2,000m. Locally common, though absent from large areas.   HOME RANGE: small; usually within a radius of 200–300m around the inhabited hole. May live in termite hills, holes in the ground, among rocks or heaps of stones, in thick bush, in stables, food stores and other buildings.

Habits. DAILY RHYTHM: active at dusk and by night, most active at dusk and dawn. Wanders around with unsteady gait, but can run quickly. Swims well. In dry season may aestivate (sleeping through the hot weather), living on its stored fat. Body temperature before going out 36·78°C, during wakefulness 32·9°-35·4°C.   TOILET: scratching with hind feet, licks muzzle after eating, and self-spitting (see FOOD). VOICE: snuffling and growling in excitement; in unease or in strange surroundings a weak high twittering (barely audible to humans) with mouth closed; often with panting. Intrusion of strange animal into territory results in hissing and spitting (rather like the spitting of a cat; in greater excitement is louder, with more spitting than hissing; in lower excitement more growling in a regular continuous series (like the ticking over of a car engine). Chatter in anger or fighting, screams in terror and pain. ♂ courting twitters (followed by whistling and squealing); ♀ answers by hissing, spitting and turning away.   SENSES: scent and hearing very good, can locate prey 4cm deep in soil. Sight moderate, however has a limited colour vision.   ENEMIES: owls, ratel, jackal, striped hyaena, village dogs. When in danger rolls itself into ball. FOOD: earthworms, insects, snails, frogs, lizards, snakes, eggs and young of ground-nesting birds, small mammals, fruit, fungi, roots, ground nuts, carrion. Can eat ⅓ of its own weight daily. Nose and ears mainly used for food finding. Lizards and small mammals are killed by biting and shaking, snakes are pressed on the ground by the erected forehead spines and the backbone is bitten (40 times less sensitive to poison than a guinea-pig). Low sensitivity to insecticides, prussic acid, chloroform, arsenic, opium and mercury. Substances unfamiliar by taste or scent are investigated by taking into the mouth, where a large amount of saliva is produced (connected with Jacobson's organ, an additional tasting organ behind the palate) until the excess is distributed by the tongue over the flank and body spines. This is the so-called self-anointing – purpose unknown.

Reproduction. ♂ courts ♀ by persistent following. Mates from behind, ♀ lays spines flat and presses hindquarters out. ♂ has long penis. Young born in rainy season, nest a lined cavity, well hidden. Gestation 35–40 days, young 2–10, usually 5, born blind and naked except for a few soft white spines. Wt at birth 12–18, HB 4–7. ♀ licks young dry and eats afterbirth. After 2–3 days the first dark juvenile spines appear between the white; the latter are lost after 1 month, when the first adult spines appear. Eyes open at 8–18 days. After a month look like miniature adults and accompany the feeding ♀, and begin to eat solid food. At 40 days are weaned and are capable of rolling into a ball for defence. Leave mother at 1½–2 months. SEXUAL MATURITY: 1 year. LONGEVITY: 8–10 years in captivity probable.

1 Four-toed Hedgehog   Desert Hedgehog   Long-eared Hedgehog
2 Algerian Hedgehog
3 South African Hedgehog

ALGERIAN HEDGEHOG, *Erinaceus algirus* (Duvernoy & Lereboullet, 1842)
G. Wanderigel   F. Le Hérisson d'Algérie
Identification. Form and structure as in Four-toed Hedgehog (above), but ears larger, toes 5/5, legs longer, and head spines divided into 2 parts by a median parting. Spines banded black and white, general appearance paler than in Four-toed Hedgehog. Muzzle, cheeks, ears and paws brown; forehead, underside and legs white, sometimes brown underside. MEASUREMENTS: HB 20–25, TL 2–4; Wt 900–1600.
Distribution. N.W. African coastal region from Morocco to Cyrenaica (Benghazi); coastal strip of E. Spain from Gibraltar to Pyrenees, as well as coastal strip of S. France east of Rhone (Charente Maritime). Possibly introduced in Europe. Also on the Balearic Is. of Majorca and Minorca, and on Fuerteventura in the Canary Is., and Djerba I. off Tunisia. 3 ssp., of which *algirus* is African.

Habits. As in Four-toed Hedgehog. Found near villages. In Europe hibernates.
Reproduction. Gestation 35–48 days. Young 3–7, 2 litters a year possible. Body temperature 36·9°C.

SOUTH AFRICAN HEDGEHOG, *Erinaceus frontalis* (A. Smith, 1831)
G. Kap-Igel   F. Le Hérisson du Cap   A. Krimpvarkie
Identification. Form and structure as Four-toed Hedgehog (p. 308). Toes 5/5, teats 4–8. Spines white with broad brown band, head spines not parted. Muzzle dark brown, forehead with white transverse band that may extend over shoulders before or behind arms to throat and breast. Legs and underside greyish-brown to dark brown. Colour variation not uncommon; albinism also occurs. MEASUREMENTS: HB 15–20, TL 1.5–2.8, Wt 250–600.
Distribution. S. Africa northwards to S.W. Angola, W. and E. Botswana, Rhodesia (probably restricted to S. of the Zambesi), possibly S. Malawi and Mozambique. Distribution uneven, annual rainfall of at least 300mm necessary; regionally absent. No ssp. HABITAT: open grassland, bush, Mopane woodland, wooded savannahs, bush-clad kopjies, fields, gardens. *Map* p. 309.
Habits. As in Four-toed Hedgehog, but more mobile, sleeping each day in a different place (heaps of grass, bush, termite hills, holes in ground, rock crevices etc). In winter (May–Aug) lethargic or hibernating.
Reproduction. Gestation *c.* 40 days. Litters in Oct–Mar, 4–9 young, usually 4. Wt at birth 9–12.

DESERT HEDGEHOG, *Paraechinus aethiópicus*   Pl. 59
(Ehrenberg, 1833)
G. Wüstenigel   F. Le Hérisson du désert
Identification. Form and structure as in Four-toed and Long-eared Hedgehogs (p. 311). 8 teats. Toes 5/5, great toe very small. Ears large, however somewhat shorter although basally broader than in Long-eared Hedgehogs. Dent.: $3/2 \cdot 1/1 \cdot 2 - 3/2 \cdot 3/3 = 34$–36. Spine structure and colour as in Long-eared Hedgehog. Spines of head divided into two zones by a 3cm-long bare strip. Spines of back about 2·7cm long. Middle of back usually dark brownish-black, the spines without cream-coloured tips and bands; flank spines speckled light and dark. Face dark brown; forehead, ears, chin, throat, front of breast, white; front and hind legs, hind part of belly, and tail, brownish-black, belly spotted dark brown and white. Many individuals almost entirely brownish-black, others nearly all white (apart from legs and tail, these brownish-black). MEASUREMENTS: HB 14–23, TL 1·3–4, Wt ?
Distribution. Morocco, Algeria, Libya, Egypt, Sudan, Eritrea, N. Ethiopia, N. Somalia, in Sahara south to Timbuctoo and Air, in Libya to Fezzan, in Sudan to Sennaar. Also in Sinai, Arabian Peninsula, Israel, Jordan and S. Iraq. 4 ssp. HABITAT: steppes, semi-deserts, deserts. *Map* p. 309.
Habits. As in Long-eared and Four-toed Hedgehog. Like 1st, makes its own burrows, stores food underground.
Reproduction. Once a year has litter of 1–4 (rarely 6) young in the burrow or hidden in soil litter. Mother licks belly and anal region of young to promote cleanliness; defends young by raising her head spines and attacking the enemy, screaming at the same time. Suckles for about 2 months. First solid food at about 40 days (♀ brings food); at 2 months half size of adult. At birth HB *c.* 5·5, Wt 8–9; Wt at 4 weeks *c.* 57, at 10 weeks *c.* 160.

LONG-EARED HEDGEHOG, *Hemiechinus auritus* (Gmelin, 1770)   **Pl. 59**
(= *megalotis* Blyth, 1845)
G. Grossohrigel   F. Le Hérisson à grandes oreilles
Identification. Shape and structure as in Four-toed Hedgehog, but more slender, long-legged, muzzle sharper, ears considerably longer (projecting well above the head spines). Head spines not divided medially. Spines longitudinally grooved, edges of grooves finely thickened. Spines of back about 1·5cm long, each spine cream-coloured with 2 dark slate-grey bands. Upperside speckled light and dark; face, ears, underside, legs, claws and tail, white. Face suffused with brown. Middle of back without dark stripe. Toes 5/5. Dent.: as in Four-toed Hedgehog, but I[1] strongly projecting forward. 10 teats, penis long. Young as in Four-toed Hedgehog.   MEASUREMENTS: HB 14–27, TL 1.3–5. Wt?
Distribution. Cyrenaica, Egypt (Nile Valley south to Fayoum). Also Near and Middle East and all S.W. Asia, Cyprus, southern U.S.S.R. to India and Mongolia. 17 ssp., of which one, *aegyptiacus* (Fischer, 1829) in Africa. *Map* p. 309.
Habits. Nocturnal, excavates burrows 60–100cm long, as permanent homes. Does not roll into a ball completely when in danger. ♀ enlarges end of tunnel for a nest chamber when young are due. 1 birth a year, with from 2–7 (usually 4) young. Otherwise habits as in Four-toed Hedgehog.

OTTER SHREWS, POTAMOGALIDAE

Insectivores ranging in size from large mouse to large rat, with long flattened head, small eyes, smallish ears, long sensitive whiskers, short legs, partly webbed hands and feet and long tail, either flattened laterally or roundish. Toes: 5/5. Dent.: $3 \cdot 1 \cdot 3 \cdot 3 = 40$. 2 teats, penis with bone. Fur very dense and soft. Active at dusk or by night on water's edge in lowland and mountains. Good swimmers and divers. Live on crustaceans, fish, worms and insects. 2 genera with altogether 3 species in West and Central Africa.

GIANT OTTER SHREW, *Potamogale velox* (Du Chaillu, 1860)   **Pl. 59**
G. Grossotterspitzmaus   F. Le Potamogale
Identification. Otter-like in shape. Head long, flat and broad. Nostrils closable, with heart-shaped horny plate with vertical median groove. Eyes very small. Ears of medium size, projecting noticeably above head, closable. Muzzle and head with numerous very long sensitive vibrissae, 3 pairs also on throat. Legs short, hands and feet long and narrow. Thumb and great toe short, 2nd and 3rd toes united for half their length. Outer edge of hands without comb of bristles, outer edge of hind feet with marginal skin fold. Tail very thick and muscular, laterally compressed, no obvious basal distinction from body, dorsally keeled, with pointed tip. 2 teats, penis with bone. Fur otter-like, underfur short and very close, continued from rump over base of tail, rest of tail very finely short-haired. Upperside dark chestnut-brown, underside white to creamy. Young like adults.   MEASUREMENTS: HB 30–35, TL 25–30, Wt *c.* 300.
Distribution. From Cross R. in Nigeria eastwards to west border of the Western Rift Valley (Lake Mobuto or Albert, to Lake Tanganyika) northwards to Ubangui and Uelle Rivers in Zaire, northern limit between 8°N in west and 3°N in east, southward to S.E. Katanga and Zambia (Bangweolo Lake and Mwinilunga) in east, and N. Angola in west, southern limit about 14°S. No ssp.   HABITAT: watersides (mountain streams to slow-flowing rivers, swamps and pools in rain forest regions or marginally outside in hilly regions). Up to 2000m in mountains.   HOME RANGE: size not known. *Map* p. 309.

Habits. DAILY RHYTHM: active at dusk and by night. Moves on land with humping gait like otter, very active in water, swimming with lateral strokes of hindquarters and tail; arms and legs lie alongside. Dive duration often quite short. VOICE: when hunting hisses and growls, if captured hisses like a snake. SENSES: scent and touch strongly developed, sight moderate. ENEMIES: unknown. FOOD: preferably fresh-water crustacea, also fish, frogs, molluscs and insects. Crabs are taken to land, turned on bank, killed by quick bites, and their soft parts (also from the claws) extracted and eaten. May take 20–25 crabs in a night. SOCIABILITY: solitary so far as is known.
Reproduction. No details known.

RUWENZORI OTTER SHREW, *Micropotamogale ruwenzorii* Pl. 59
(De Witte & Frechkop, 1955)
G. Mittelotterspitzmaus F. Le Micropotamogale du Mont Ruwenzori.
Identification. Shrew-like in form. Head and muzzle flat and broad as in Giant Otter Shrew. Nostrils closable by heart-shaped horny shield as in latter. Eyes very small. Ears small and rounded, projecting only slightly above fur, closable. Dent.: as in Giant Otter Shrew. Tactile vibrissae on muzzle and head numerous and very long as in the latter. Legs short, 1st and 5th digits equal in length, notably shorter than 2nd and 4th, all fingers and toes joined by short webbing, 2nd and 3rd toes united, outer edge of hands and feet with ridge of stiff bristle hairs, as well as on inner edge of hands. Tail shrew-like, with pointed tip, in section high oval, weakly keeled above and below, thinly clad with short hair. Fur desman-like with very dense underfur and short stiff guard hairs. Upperside dark brown, washed with grey, underside grey, front of breast with light brown spot. Upperside of tail like body, underside like belly. Young like adults. MEASUREMENTS: HB 16–17, TL 13–15. Wt ?
Distribution. Mt Ruwenzori, western slopes in Zaire, also west side of Lake Edward and Lake Kivu, and further westward. HABITAT: small streams in mountain forests (up to 2200m), lowland forests, savannahs and cultivated land. Builds runways in banks with grass-lined chamber. Water temperature limits 12°–21°C. HOME RANGE: unknown.
Habits. DAILY RHYTHM: leaves burrow between 19·30 and 20·30, then during night alternates between activity and resting; in the burrow all day. Defecation and urination on special places. In fast swimming uses all four legs, in slow swimming front and hind legs alternate. Also swims on surface with head and upper back out of the water. Duration of dives short. TOILET: much time devoted to grooming, scratching with hind feet. Walls of burrow are used to absorb surplus water squeezed from the fur. VOICE, SENSES, ENEMIES: no data. FOOD: earthworms, insect larvae, fresh-water crustaceans, fish, toads, frogs. Crabs (only up to 5cm broad in shell are taken – larger ones too dangerous because of the claws) are bitten from behind, taken on land, turned over and eaten from underside. Fish also are eaten on land, small items in the water, worms and grubs are sucked up. Daily food requirement up to 80gm. Solitary.
Reproduction. 1 female had 2 embryos, otherwise nothing known.

LESSER OTTER SHREW, *Micropotamogale lamottei* Pl. 59
(Heim de Balsac, 1954)
G. Kleinotterspitzmaus F. Le Micropotamogale de Lamotte
Identification. Shape and structure as in Ruwenzori Otter Shrew, but with tail rounded, hands and feet as in Giant Otter Shrew (p. 311), however, feet without skin lobe. Fur greyish-brown, underside not lighter than upperside. MEASUREMENTS: HB 12–15, TL 10–12, Wt ?

Distribution. Mt Nimba region on borders of N. Liberia, S.E. Guinea, and middle W. Ivory Coast. No ssp. HABITAT: ditches, brooks, swamps in the lowland, gallery and mountain forests, up to 1000m.

Habits. Resembles Ruwenzori Otter Shrew. FOOD: freshwater crustacea, fish. Good swimmer, up to 15 minutes in the water.

Reproduction. Gestation at least 51 days, most young born in dry season, when streams are low and prey more easily taken. Several litters annually possible. Young 1–4, naked and blind in well-hidden nest. 1st hair at 11 days, full pelage at 20, eyes open at 23, nest left and animal independent at 40 days. SEXUAL MATURITY, and LONGEVITY, not known.

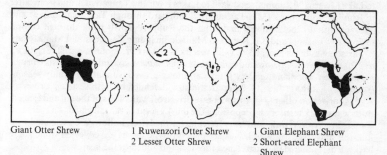

Giant Otter Shrew

1 Ruwenzori Otter Shrew
2 Lesser Otter Shrew

1 Giant Elephant Shrew
2 Short-eared Elephant
Shrew

ELEPHANT SHREWS, MACROSCELIDIDAE

Mouse- to rat-sized, with legs slim and long, usually soft-furred animals, feeding on insects and other small creatures, diet mixed, with trunk-like elongated mobile snout, large eyes, mid-sized to large ears, hind legs with elongated tibia and metatarsal bones. Toes 4–5/4–5. Tail naked, of medium length or long. Dent.: $1-3/3 \cdot 1 \cdot 4 \cdot 2-3 = 36-44$. 4–6 teats. Usually diurnal, rarely nocturnal, quick runners in deserts, steppes, savannahs, bush or forested districts. 2 subfamilies with altogether 5 genera and 12 species, only in Africa.

GIANT ELEPHANT SHREW, *Rhynchocyon cirnei* (Peters, 1847)   Pl. 59
G. Rüsselhundchen   F. Le Rhynchocyon   S. Njule

Identification. Sharp-headed, long-legged, long-tailed. Head long and pointed, nose very long, thin, pointed and mobile. Mouth opening set well back below. Tongue long, extensile. Eyes large, ears of medium length, long oval, naked, projecting distinctly above head. Legs long and thin, hands and feet very narrow, strongly lengthened, hind legs longer than fore legs. Tibia and fibula united at lower end. Fingers and toes with long, flat, strong claws. Digits 4/4; hand, 1st digit (thumb) absent, 2nd–4th about equal length, 5th very small. Foot: 1st digit (great toe) absent, 2nd–5th about equal. Tail rat-like, almost naked, pointed at tip. Fur short, rather coarse. Nose and muzzle with long tactile hairs, three more as a tuft on cheeks. Dent.: $1(0)/3 \cdot 1 \cdot 4 \cdot 2 = 36$; upper incisor rudimentary or absent, upper canine dagger-like, twice as long as P[1]. End of penis trilobed. 4 teats. Underside of tail root with skin gland. Pelage colour very variable according to the subspecies and their composition. Upperside light (*reichardi*) or dark, olive-green (*shirensis*), or light- (*stuhlmanni*) or middle- (*hendersoni*) or dark-brown (*stuhlmanni*), or the fore part of the body yellowish-olive, middle part dark reddish-brown, rump yellowish-orange (*chrysopygus*), or fore part yellowish to reddish-orange, posterior half black (*petersi*). The latter two are unspotted, the others with 6 long rows of large, rectangular, whitish to light brown spots between 6 long dark brown stripes. Spots may be indistinct or may coalesce. $\frac{1}{5}$–$\frac{1}{3}$ of tail dark from root, the end white, with extreme tip dark. Hybrid populations occur with variety of intermixed colours and patterns. Underside white to creamy. Young are like adults. MEASUREMENTS: HB 23–32, TL 19–27, Wt 400–450.

Distribution. Middle and E.Africa. N.Zaire between Congo, Ubangui and Uelle Rivers; in the N. eastward to Lake Victoria, east of the Upper Congo (Lualaba), south to Lake Mweru (N.Zambia), eastward to Lakes Kivu and Tanganyika, and from latter to Rufiji R. south bank (Mid-Tanzania). Southward through Tanzania, Malawi and Mozambique to the Zambesi, and from the Rufiji R. north bank through coastal regions of Tanzania and S.E.Kenya to Malindi, including Zanzibar and Mafia. 6 ssp. (*Note*: some authors accept 3 as valid species.) HABITAT: mountain rain forests, up to 2,300m (*hendersoni*), lowland rain forests (*stuhlmanni*), coastal bush forests (*chrysopygus*), open woodland, gallery forest, and long grass savannahs (in rainy season) (*reichardi*). TERRITORY: 1$\frac{1}{2}$–2 hectares in size, defended by both sexes. ♂ drives off ♂♂, ♀ drives off other ♀♀. Intruders are driven off with blows of the tail and ejected. Both sexes mark territory by depositing the musky scent of the tail glands on twigs and stones. In territory, trails and leafy retreats, for the latter, hollows are excavated with fore-feet and large heaps of leaves are piled up. The leaves are collected while going backwards, gathered in outstretched fore feet and added to the heap.

Habits. DAILY RHYTHM: active all day, exceptionally in mid-day heat. In gait like little antelopes, can run very fast or trot along sniffing the ground on its beat; sometimes gallops in a circle or makes high bounding jumps before trotting on. In evening seeks out its leafy nest, examines the surroundings carefully, then creeps under the pile of leaves and goes to sleep. VOICE: usually quiet. In excitement or when hunted, tooth clapping, chattering and loud squeal; in alarm tail beating and soft squealing. SENSES: scent and touch capability the main senses, hearing good, sight good for movement. ENEMIES: snakes, birds of prey, small carnivores. In defence strike and kick with hind legs, do not bite. FOOD: mostly licked up from ground with tongue, or, if scented, scratched up; prey off the ground, as on twigs etc., is not noticed. Ants and termites are the main food, as well as beetles, spiders, worms, millipedes, woodlice, small lizards. Confined largely to areas where food supply is plentiful all the year, with thick ground cover and nearby water supply. The black droppings include much earth licked up with the food. SOCIABILITY: in pairs, usually with 1 young. Sometimes a loose association of small family parties together in good feeding area.

Reproduction. Gestation 2 months, 2 – rarely 1 – young, suckled for 3 weeks in the nest, then joins mother for a week on her feeding forays, and eats first solid food. After a further 6 weeks with the mother is sexually mature, and seeks an area for itself. 4–5 litters a year. Young carry tail high, lowered in adults. LONGEVITY: 3–4 years, in captivity over 4 years reported.

FOUR-TOED ELEPHANT SHREW, *Petrodromus tetradactylus* **Pl. 59** (Peters, 1846)

G.Rüsselratte F.Le Petrodromus A.Bosklaasmuis S.Isanje, Ssanga

Identification. Sharp-headed, round-bodied, long legs and tail. Head long and pointed, large in relation to body, nose very long, thin, pointed and mobile; opening of mouth set well back below muzzle, tongue long, extensile. Eyes and ears large, latter naked, tips rounded. Legs long and thin, hind legs longer than fore, tibia and fibula united at base; metatarsal strongly, metacarpals moderately elongated. Hands and feet long and narrow, claws long and flat, thumb very small, great toe absent, digits 5/4. Tail rat-like, round, nearly naked, tip pointed. Underside of root of tail in ssp. *sultan* with skin gland, from which arise scattered bristle-hairs with knobbed tips. Dent.: $3 \cdot 1 \cdot 4 \cdot 2 = 40$, I^3 2-rooted, C short and weak. 4 teats. Fur very thick and soft, tactile hairs very long. Upperside sandy-brown, washed with yellowish or orange, or mid-brown overwashed with reddish; white ring round eyes, surrounding area with chestnut red tint. Often a greyish or brownish flank stripe. Underside white to light ochreous. ♀ warmer colour than ♂. Young like adults. MEASUREMENTS: HB 16–22, TL 13–18, Wt 150–220.

Distribution. From Natal northwards to Mid-Kenya, with Zanzibar and Mafia Is. From Mid-Kenya to W. Zaire (only S. of Congo R.), in neighbourhood of Kinshasa to N.E. Angola, from there S.E. to E. bank of the upper and N. bank of the middle Zambesi to Lake Kariba, from there S. to Natal. 9 ssp. HABITAT: thickets and dense growth in rocky areas, around and on kopjies, in *Brachystegia* woodland, by water's edge, in dry mountain and coastal forest, and, to a limited extent, in rain forest regions. HOME RANGE: resembling Giant Elephant Shrew, also territorial, though range smaller, threaded by trails, with plenty of hidden cover such as ant-hills, gerbil holes and holes in fallen trees, among rocks etc. *Map* p. 317.

Habits. DAILY RHYTHM: active partly by day, partly mornings, evenings and nights. Trots high on all fours, with tail held high; if pursued makes wide leaps. VOICE: commonly a shrill squeal in excitement, soft growling when content, gurgling and chirping if caught; contact signal drumming on ground with hind feet, besides tail beating. SENSES and ENEMIES, as Giant Elephant Shrew. FOOD: scrapes in the leaves with hind feet to uncover insect food. Principal food termites and ants, also beetles, bugs, cicadas, crickets, grasshoppers etc. SOCIABILITY: single or in pairs.

Reproduction. All year round; 1 young at a birth (HB *c.* 7·5), further details not known. SEXUAL MATURITY and LONGEVITY not known, only record in captivity is of $1\frac{1}{4}$ years.

SHORT-EARED ELEPHANT SHREW,   Pl. 59
Macroscelides proboscideus (Shaw, 1800)
G. Rüsselspringer   F. Le Macroscélide de l'Afrique de Sud
A. Swartoor-Skeerbekmuis

Identification. Mouse-like in form and size, body rounded, otherwise as in Four-toed Elephant Shrew (above), however head (not nose) and ears longer. Latter almost triangular with rounded tips, hairy inside. Digits 5/5, thumb small, great toe very high set, small and without claw. Underside of tail at base with naked black-skinned glandular area, with musky scented secretion. Dent.: $3 \cdot 1 \cdot 4 \cdot 2 = 40$, I^2 and I^3 bilobed, I^3 single-rooted, C small. Bony auditory bullae in skull extraordinarily large. Cheek pouches present. Penis very long, with tip tri-lobed. 6 teats. Fur soft and thick, tactile hairs very long. Upperside beige (sandy) to orange-brownish, suffused with reddish or dark brown or blackish. No white ring round eyes. Outside of ears, and mobile proboscis, blackish. Underside white to greyish-white. Adults lighter than young. Only the tips of the hairs are light, the rest being dark grey to black. MEASUREMENTS: HB 9.5–13, TL 8.3–14. Wt 35–45.

Distribution. Cape Province (apart from S.E., east of Grahamstown), S.W. Africa (apart from N., north of Omaruru R.), extreme S.W. Botswana. 10 ssp., but validity uncertain. HABITAT: desert, semi-desert, rocky country with low bushes, open thorn bush, gravelly or sandy plains with bushes or fragmented rocks. HOME RANGE:

depending on land and population density, $\frac{1}{10}$ to 1 sq km. Each animal has several shelters in its so-called living area, with well-marked trails linking shelters and feeding areas. In deserts, interval between neighbouring quarters 200–800m, in thickly populated areas much less. Refuges may be self-dug holes under bushes, with main entrance and hidden vertical escape emergency holes, or abandoned holes of gerbils, suricates, or vlei-rats, or small holes under rocks and scree. The animals can dig themselves in very quickly. Holes are cleaned of small stones, twigs etc. but are not lined. *Map* p. 313.

Habits. DAILY RHYTHM: diurnal or nocturnal according to region and type of enemy. In deserts usually nocturnal, going out at dusk hunting (up to 1km distant), usually for several nights; if food becomes short, then looks for new hunting range; after feeding, may check on the refuges in the area. Towards end of night seeks shelter. Change of regular shelters induced by disturbance, weather changes, breeding time. When going slowly has a sniffling trot, in a hurry runs very quickly on all fours, in flight long running leaps at speed of up to 20kph. May travel several kilometres, a ♀ caring for young may go up to 15km. In excitement the tail is carried in a high curve, otherwise horizontally. At sunrise may sun-bathe, doze, sleep or groom. If the shelter goes over 58°C then changes to a cooler site (trunk and tail act as thermostat). TOILET: wash face with fore feet, lick anal region, scratch fur with hind feet, clean sides and belly by rubbing along the ground. VOICE: generally silent, a thin squeak. Young chirp. SENSES: hearing very good, can hear flying owls (barn and spotted eagle owls), and even in sleep can recognise significant sounds (creeping of insects, which are then eaten) or crawling of snakes (producing immediate flight) as distinct from unimportant sounds. Sight and scent very good. Orientation ability and sense of direction unerring, even on a dark night. Temperature regulation ability very good, can cope within 1 day with outside temperature range from 10°–58°C. ENEMIES: small predators, diurnal and nocturnal birds of prey, also occasionally raven, ostrich, black-backed jackal. In case of bigger enemies will squeeze into nearest hole, or in case of smaller predators and snakes will flee even in the mid-day heat. If predation severe, or disturbance frequent, may change from diurnal to nocturnal habits. FOOD: ants, termites, spiders, other small invertebrates, reptile eggs, young lizards and geckos, soft shoots and roots as well as berries and fruit. In food searching has a jerky zig-zag run. Stores food in cheek pouches, stops to eat it when convenient. Does not drink; liquid requirements met by soft insect diet. SOCIABILITY: solitary. Neighbours normally keep a distance of normal vision; if they meet, show unconcern; a short chase only occurs if one animal comes too near. During breeding season pair formation for a few days, or a ♀ with 1–2 young for a few weeks, or twins in the nursery area for 2–3 weeks. In Great Namaqualand may occur together with the Elephant Shrew (*Elephantulus*) in the same areas, the two genera indistinguishable in the field.

Reproduction. 1–2 very large and active young at a birth, in Sep–Nov, gestation of about 2 months. ♂ courts by pursuing and sniffing the ♀, which has an oestrous cycle every 2½ months. ♀ rears young alone, if necessary may move it or them by carrying in her mouth. Nest chamber is any out of the way hiding place. ♀ leaves young alone and returns several times a day to suckle it. From 5th day feeds it on insect mash from its cheek pouches. Suckling period 1 week. Young soon learn to go outside shelter for toilet purposes, gradually going longer and further, exploring new hiding places and sleeping apart, returning to ♀ only to suckle. At 2½–4 weeks is independent and looks for its own home range. SEXUAL MATURITY: 5–6 weeks. LONGEVITY: in the wild 1–1½ years, in captivity up to 3¼ years.

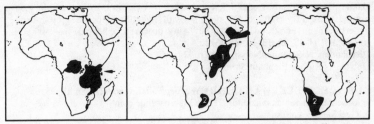

Four-toed Elephant Shrew

1 Rufous Elephant Shrew
2 Cliff Elephant Shrew

1 Somali Elephant Shrew
2 Bushveld Elephant Shrew

RUFOUS ELEPHANT SHREW, *Elephantulus rufescens* (Peters, 1878)   **Pl. 59**
G. Rote Elefantenspitzmaus   F. Le Macroscélide rouge   S. Sange mdogo
Identification. Form and structure as in Short-eared Elephant Shrew (p. 315) but eyes and ears large, latter long – oval and naked. Underside of trunk hairy. Digits 5/5, thumb small, great toe very small and high set. Dent.: $3\cdot1\cdot4\cdot2 = 40$; I^2 much smaller than I^1, I^3 single-rooted, C small. Bony auditory bullae not greatly enlarged. 6 teats. Scent gland below base of tail reduced, gland over breastbone well developed. TL = HB length, tail sharp-tipped. Pelage thick and soft. Upperside greyish yellow or beige, or light brown dark brown or glossy reddish brown. Underside whitish, grey or beige. White ring round eyes, brown stripe behind eyes. Young like adults. MEASUREMENTS: HB 10–15, TL 10–16.5, Wt 25–50.
Distribution. Steppe and savannah regions of eastern Africa from (in N.–S. direction) Mid-Ethiopia from 10°N., N.W. and S. Somalia, Kenya, mid- and E. Uganda, mid-Tanzania to near northern tip of Lake Malawi or Nyasa, and near the S.W. shore of Lake Tanganyika. 6 ssp.   HABITAT: dry bush country (usually over 300m).   HOME RANGE: small, each pair in 20 sqm to $\frac{1}{4}$ hectare. Most important is plentiful green growth of fire-resistant character, with dense thickets offering secure refuge against predators; termite hills, hollows, thorn hedges round cattle kraals and farms, permanent growths of aloes, Sanseveira, Euphorbia, sisal etc. Take refuge in abandoned holes, among rocks, in termite hills and rodent burrows, between bush roots etc. Do not make their own burrows. Shelters and feeding places linked by well-used runs.
Habits.   DAILY RHYTHM: diurnal, but sometimes still active up to nightfall. Moves on all fours like Short-eared Elephant Shrew, does not hop.   TOILET: as latter.   VOICE: twittering squeaking in anger, shrill squeak in fear and danger; sounds alarm by drumming with hind feet on ground.   SENSES: as in Short-eared Elephant Shrew. ENEMIES: small carnivores, diurnal and nocturnal birds of prey, snakes. When caught does not bite.   FOOD: as in Short-toed Elephant Shrew. Does not drink.   SOCIABILITY: in pairs, at feeding grounds perhaps several pairs. Often associate with field rats (*Arvicanthis*), gerbils, and hyraxes.
Reproduction. Probably seasonal, most young born May–July. Gestation 50 days. 1 active young (rarely 2) at a birth; suckle for 1 month; fully grown and independent at 2 months.   LONGEVITY: $1\frac{1}{2}$–3 years.

SOMALI ELEPHANT SHREW, *Elephantulus revoili* (Huet, 1881)
G. Somali-elefantenspitzmaus   F. Le Macroscélide de Revoil
Identification. Like Rufous Elephant Shrew (above). Underside of trunk hairy, skin

gland on breast. 6 teats. Dent.: $3 \cdot 1 \cdot 4 \cdot 2 = 40$, I^1–I^3 equal in size; bony auditory bulla normal in size. TL = 120 % of HB, tip of tail with slight tuft. Upperside greyish-brown, underside, hands and feet white. White eye-ring, brown stripe behind eye. MEASUREMENTS: HB 11–12, TL 13–14, Wt 25–40.

Distribution. N. Somalia. No ssp. *Map* p. 317.

Habits. As Rufous Elephant Shrew.

BUSHVELD ELEPHANT SHREW, *Elephantulus intufi* (A. Smith, 1836)
G. Buschfeld-Elefantenspitzmaus   F. Le Macroscélide jaune
A. Geel Skeerbekmuis

Identification. Like Rufous Elephant Shrew (p. 317). Underside of trunk naked, no breast skin gland, gland under tail root. 6 teats. Dent.: $3 \cdot 1 \cdot 4 \cdot 2 = 40$, I^2 bi-lobed, P^1 with 1 lingual cusp, P^2 with 2. Bony auditory bullae normal. TL 105 % of HB, thinly haired. Upperside yellowish-brown to greyish-yellow, underside paler to white, soles of hind feet light brown. White eye-ring complete, no brown stripe behind eye. MEASUREMENTS: HB 10–14, TL 11–15, Wt 40–55.

Distribution. S. Rhodesia, W. Transvaal, northern and western Cape Province, S.W. Africa, S. Angola, Mid and S. Botswana. 10 ssp., but validity uncertain. HABITAT: sandy and stony regions with bushes, bushveld, woodland savannahs. *Map* p. 317.

Habits. Like Rufous Elephant Shrew. Diurnal. Uses abandoned or self-excavated burrows under bushes, thorn hedges, among stones or rocks. Holes and feeding grounds linked by runways. FOOD: insects. ENEMIES: gives alarm signal by drumming on ground with hind feet. VOICE: thin squeaks.

Reproduction. Litters born Aug–Feb. 2 (rarely 1 or 3) active young at a birth. No further details known.

ROCK ELEPHANT SHREW, *Elephantulus rupestris* (A. Smith, 1831)
G. Felsen-Elefantenspitzmaus   F. Le Macroscélide des roches   A. Klipklaasmuis
Distribution. S.W. Africa, W. and Mid Cape Province (Little Namaqualand, Upington, Cradock, Grahamstown). Number of ssp. uncertain.

CLIFF ELEPHANT SHREW, *Elephantulus myurus* (Thomas & Schwann, 1906)
G. Klippen-Elefantenspitzmaus   F. and A., as in *rupestris*
Distribution. S. Rhodesia, Transvaal, Orange Free State, mid-E and S.E. Botswana, Richmond district in Mid-Cape Province. Number of ssp. uncertain. *Map* p. 317.

CAPE ELEPHANT SHREW, *Elephantulus edwardi* (A. Smith, 1839)
G. Kap-Elefantenspitzmaus   F. Le Macroscélide du Cap   A. Kap-Klaasmuis
Identification. Form and structure as in Bushveld Elephant Shrew (above). Underside of trunk naked. No skin gland over breast zone, but gland present under base of tail. 6 teats. Dent.: $3 \cdot 1 \cdot 4 \cdot 2 = 40$. I^2 one-cusped (*myurus, edwardi*), 2-cusped (*rupestris*), P^1 without lingual cusp (*my., ed.*) with (*rup.*), P^2 without lingual cusps (*ed.*), with 1 (*my.*), with 2 (*rup.*). On the tragus of ear, the upper part (Supratragus) very large and thin (*rup.*), small and little thickened (*my.*), large and thin (*ed.*). Whitish eye ring incomplete or whole, no darker post-orbital stripe, tail terminal hairs somewhat lengthened. Tail bicolored for all its length (*rup., my.*), or with whole of end half black (*ed.*). Soles of hind feet black (*my.*) or dark brown (*rup., ed*). Upperside lighter or darker greyish-brownish, yellow-brownish or reddish-brownish; underside white, whitish grey or sandy white. MEASUREMENTS: HB 10–14, TL 12–16.5, Wt 40–70.

Distribution. West coastal and Richmond district of Cape Province. No subspecies. These three species are very much alike outwardly and in habits.

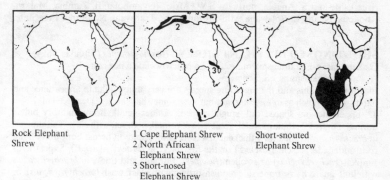

Rock Elephant
Shrew

1 Cape Elephant Shrew
2 North African
  Elephant Shrew
3 Short-nosed
  Elephant Shrew

Short-snouted
Elephant Shrew

Habits. HABITAT: rock and stone heaps, kopjies with bushes and scattered trees with cracks and holes at ground level as refuges. Also sandy and gravelly plains with scattered bushes, under which the holes may be found (either taken over or freshly dug). Well-used runs link holes with feeding grounds. Live alone or in loose family parties. Diurnal or nocturnal according to type of country. Other habits as in Bushveld Elephant Shrew.

NORTH AFRICAN ELEPHANT SHREW, *Elephantulus rozeti*
(Duvernoy, 1830)

G. Nordafrika-Elefantenspitzmaus   F. Le Macroscélide de l'Afrique du Nord

Identification. Form and structure as in Rufous, Rock and Bushveld Elephant Shrews. Gland on underside of tail root, not on breast. Underside of trunk naked. 6 teats. Dent.: $3 \cdot 1 \cdot 4 \cdot 2 = 40$, I^2 one-cusped, I_2 larger than I_1 and I^3, P^1 without lingual cusp, P^2 with 1 lingual cusp. Narrow white eye-ring, no brown postorbital spot. Upperside reddish-brown, over-washed with blackish (except behind ears and on lower flanks). Underside whitish. Upperside of tail brown, underside white. Young like adults, but at first still without black hair tips.   MEASUREMENTS: HB 10–12, TL 9–11, Wt ?

Distribution. Mediterranean- and desert-bordering regions of N.W. Africa, from S.W. Morocco to W. Libya, with ssp. *rozeti* north of the Atlas, and *deserti* south of the range.

Habits. Like other species. Lives in sandy or rocky districts, in holes under stones or in rock crevices. Solitary in loose colonies. Diurnal. Usually 2 young, seldom 1, at a birth.   LONGEVITY: over 3 years in captivity.

SHORT-SNOUTED ELEPHANT SHREW, *Nasilio brachyrhynchus*
(A. Smith, 1836)

G. Kurzrüssel-Elefantenspitzmaus   F. Le Macroscélide à museau court
A. Kortbekklaasmuis   S. Sengi. (*Note*: Nasilio is now considered to be a synonym of *Elephantulus*).

Identification. This and next species very much alike in appearance and habits (see below).

Distribution. Mid and S. Kenya, W. Uganda, Ruanda-Urundi, Tanzania (only a few scattered localities), S. and S.E. Zaire (south of Sankuru and east of upper Kasai rivers), M. and S. Angola, northern S.W. Africa (Ovamboland), Zambia, Malawi, Rhodesia, N. and E. Botswana, Mid-Mozambique, Transvaal, N. Orange Free State. 9 ssp.

SHORT-NOSED ELEPHANT SHREW, *Nasilio fuscipes* (Thomas, 1894)

G. Kurznasen-Elefantenspitzmaus   F. Le Macroscélide à nez court
A. Kortneusklaasmuis   S. Sengi

Identification. This and the preceding species are very much alike in appearance and habits. Form much as in *Elephantulus*, but nose somewhat shorter. Dent.: $3 \cdot 1 \cdot 4 \cdot 2/3 =$ 42, upper incisors spaced out, single cusped, canines small. Bony auditory bullae normal. Digits 5/5, thumbs small, great toe very small, high set, with claw. Tail shorter, in *brachyrhynchus* the first $\frac{2}{3}$ thickened. 4 teats. Skin gland on breast bone and on tail root underside present (*fuscipes*) or the first lacking (*brachyrhynchus*). Supratragus simple (*brachyrhynchus*) or swollen (*fuscipes*). Fur soft and thick, in *brachyrhynchus* with long guard hairs; upperside reddish-brown with black wash (*brachyrhynchus*), or mid to yellowish-brown, in part washed with grey (*fuscipes*). Underside white to whitish-grey, yellowish or brownish. Whitish eye-ring, no brown post-orbital stripe. MEASUREMENTS: HB 10–14, TL 8–13, Wt 30–55.

Distribution. Extreme N.E. Congo, extreme S. Sudan, E. Uganda. No ssp. *Map* p. 319.

Habits. Almost as in *Eelephantulus* (but see note above). HABITAT: sandy plains with sparse grass and bush, grassy steppes, thorn bush, light woodland with dense undergrowth, sometimes in stony or rocky areas. Home may be in termite hills, or in burrows either adopted or self-excavated under bushes or stones. Diurnal. Solitary, in loose family colonies. FOOD: as in *Elephantulus*, insects, soft parts of plants, also fruit and berries. Tail carried curved up in running. Alarm signal given by hind feet drumming on the ground; otherwise only squeaking, soft or loud, according to situation. Season for births: Mozambique, Jan; Angola, Apr; Rhodesia, May; Botswana, Jun; East Africa, Jun and Nov; Zambia, Feb and Oct. 2 litters a year probable. Usually 2 young at a birth, rarely 1. Active at birth. HB at birth 6.8, TL 4.5; after 2 weeks 7.2 and 5.8.

Colour plates

Plate 1

1 Red River Hog, p. 29. 2 Bush pig, p. 29. 3 E. African Warthog (♂ with young), p. 31. 4 Eastern Forest Hog, p. 30. (♂)

Plate 2

323

1 Water Chevrotain, p. 35.   2 Barbary or Atlas Deer, p. 36.   3 Pygmy Hippopotamus, p.34.   4 E. African Hippopotamus, p. 33.

Plate 3

1 Okapi, p. 38.   2 Reticulated Giraffe, p. 37.   3 Masai Giraffe, p. 37.   4 Uganda Giraffe, p. 37.

Plate 4 325

1 Red-flanked Duiker, p. 40. 2 Maxwell's Duiker, p.40. 3 Blue Duiker, p. 40.
4 Zebra Duiker, p. 41. 5 Bay Duiker, p. 41.

HELMUT DILLER

1 Peter's or Harvey's Duiker, p. 42.   2 Gaboon or White-bellied Duiker, p. 43.
3 Red Duiker, p. 42.   4 Black-fronted Duiker, p. 43.   5 Black Duiker, p. 44.

Plate 6

327

1 Ogilby's Duiker, p. 42.   2 Abbott's Duiker, p.44.   3 Crowned or Common
Duiker, p. 46.   4 Yellow-backed Duiker (young), p. 44.   5 Yellow-backed Duiker
(adult), p. 44.   6 Jentink's Duiker, p. 45.

1 Salt's Dikdik, p. 49.   2 Royal Antelope, p. 47.   3 Phillip's Dikdik, p. 50.
4 Kirk's Dikdik, p. 51.   5 Swayne's Dikdik, p. 50.   6 Gunther's Dikdik, p. 50.
7 Steinbock, p. 52.   8 Grysbok, p. 53.   9 Beira, p. 55.   10 Oribi, p. 54.
11 Klippspringer, p. 56.

Plate 8 329

HELMUT DILLER

1 and 2 Cameroon Bushbuck, p. 57. (1 = ♂, 2 = ♀)   3 Limpopo Bushbuck,
p. 57.   4 Masai Bushbuck, p. 57.   5 Northern Ethiopian Bushbuck, p. 57.

1 and 2 Nyala, p. 58. (1 = ♀, 2 = ♂) 3 and 4 W. African Sitatunga, p. 60.
(3 = ♀, 4 = ♂) 5 Mountain Nyala, p. 61.

Plate 10 331

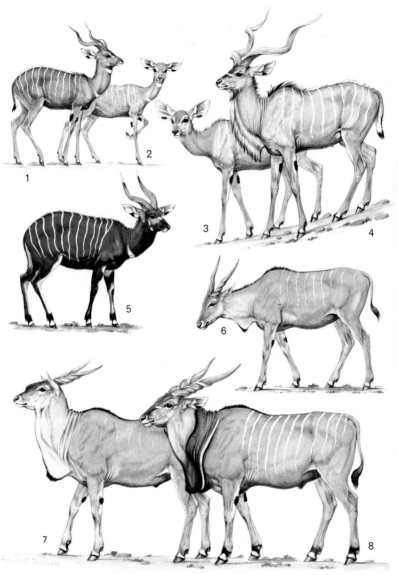

1 and 2 Lesser Kudu, p. 62. (1 = ♂, 2 = ♀) 3 and 4 Greater Kudu, p. 63.
(3 = ♀, 4 = ♂) 5 Bongo, p. 64. 6 and 7 Eland, p. 65. (6 = ♀, 7 = ♂)
8 Giant Eland, p. 65. (♂)

Plate 11

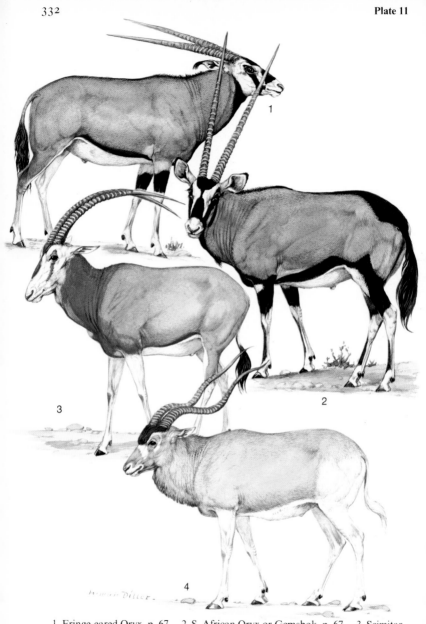

1 Fringe-eared Oryx, p. 67.   2 S. African Oryx or Gemsbok, p. 67.   3 Scimitar-horned Oryx, p. 67. (winter coat)   4 Addax, p. 68. (winter coat)

Plate 12

333

1 and 2 Waterbuck, p. 72. (1 = ♂, 2 = ♀)   3 Defassa Waterbuck, p. 72.
4 White-eared Kob, p. 73.   5 Uganda Kob, p. 73.   6 Bangweolo Lechwe, p. 74.
7 Zambesi Lechwe, p. 74.   8 Nile Lechwe, p. 75.

Plate 13

1 Vaal Rhebok, p. 75.   2 Mountain Reedbuck, p. 76.   3 Bohor Reedbuck, p. 77.
4 Common Reedbuck, p. 78.

Plate 14

335

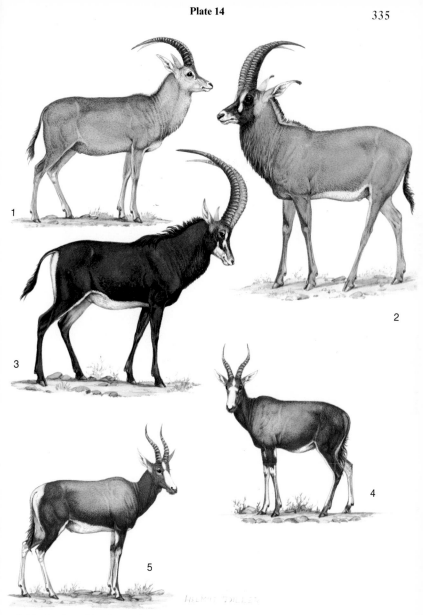

1 Bluebuck, p. 69.   2 E. African Roan Antelope, p. 69.   3 Sable Antelope, p. 71.
4 Blesbok, p. 79.   5 Bontebok, p. 79.

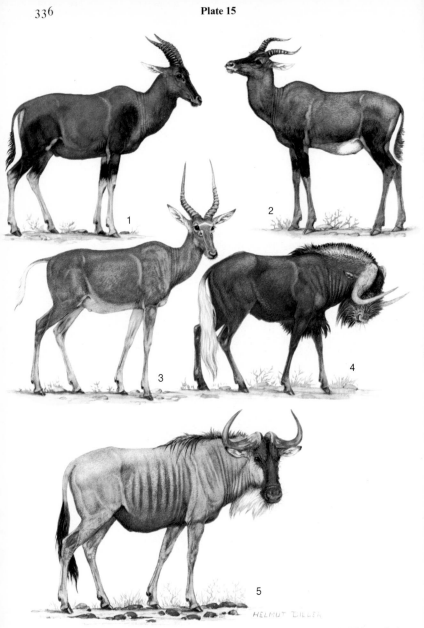

1 Topi, p. 81. 2 Sassaby, p. 81. 3 Hunter's Hartebeeste, p. 81. 4 White-tailed Gnu, p. 86. 5 White-bearded Wildebeeste, p. 84.

Plate 16 337

1 Tora Hartebeeste, p. 82.   2 Lichtenstein's Hartebeeste, p. 82.   3 Jackson's Hartebeeste, p. 82.   4 Swayne's Hartebeeste, p. 82.   5 Caama Hartebeeste, p. 82. 6 Kongoni or Coke's Hartebeeste, p. 82.

1 Soemmering's Gazelle, p. 91. 2 Grant's Gazelle, p. 92. 3 Dama Gazelle (pale form), p. 93. 4 Angolan Impala, p. 87. 5 Springbuck, p. 99. 6 Dibatag or Clarke's Gazelle, p. 101. 7 Gerenuk, p. 102.

Plate 18

339

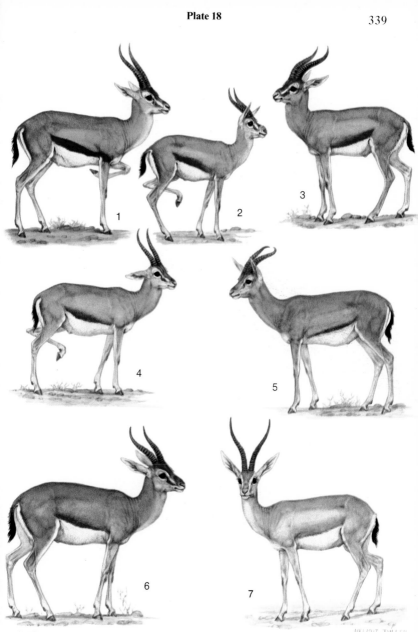

1 Thomson's Gazelle, p. 94. 2 Speke's Gazelle, p. 95. 3 Dorcas Gazelle, p. 96.
4 Pelzeln's Gazelle, p. 96. 5 Heuglin's Gazelle, p. 97. 6 True Gazelle, p. 98.
7 Rhim or Loder's Gazelle, p. 99.

1   Barbary Sheep, p. 105.   2   Nubian Ibex, p. 104.   3   Forest Buffalo, p. 106.
4   Cape Buffalo, p. 106.

Plate 20

341

1 Somali Wild Ass, p. 109. 2 Nubian Wild Ass (not to scale), p. 109.
3 Mountain Zebra, p. 110. 4 Grevy's Zebra, p. 112.

1 Grant's Zebra, p. 113. 2 Burchell's Zebra, p. 113. 3 and 4 Quagga, p. 113.
(3 = Munich specimen, 4 = Vienna specimen)

Plate 22

343

1 Black Rhinoceros, p. 116.   2 White Rhinoceros, p. 117.

Plate 23

1 Mountain Tree Hyrax, p. 120. 2 Dwarf Elephant, p. 127. (but see note in text) 3 African Elephant, p. 124.

Plate 24

345

HELMUT DILLER

1 Monk Seal, p. 167.   2 and 3 Cape Fur Seal, p. 168. (2 = ♂, 3 = ♀)
4 African Manatee, p. 129.   5 Dugong, p. 130.

Plate 25

1 Longtailed Pangolin, p. 134.   2 White-bellied Pangolin, p. 135.   3 Giant
Ground Pangolin, p. 136.   4 African Brush-tailed Porcupine, p. 151.   5 S. African
Crested Porcupine, p. 152.   6 Giant Gambian Rat, p. 154.   7 Aardvark, p. 132.

Plate 26 347

1 Maned Rat, p. 155.   2 Spring Hare, p. 156.   3 Gundi, p. 159.   4 Cane Rat, p. 157.   5 Cape Ground Squirrel, p. 139, 144.   6 Western Ground Squirrel, p. 138, 145.

Plate 27

1 Sierra Leone Red-footed Squirrel, p. 144, 146.   2 Giant Forest Squirrel, p. 141, 145.   3 Flightless Scaly-tailed Squirrel, p. 151.   4 Zenker's Flying Squirrel, p. 150.   5 Pel's Flying Squirrel, p. 147.   6 Beecroft's Flying Squirrel, p. 150.

Plate 28

349

HELMUT DILLER

1 European Rabbit, p. 161. 2 S.W. African Cape Hare, p. 162. 3 Red Hare, p. 165. 4 Scrub Hare, p. 163. 5 Abyssinian Hare, p. 163. 6 Bushman Hare, p. 164. 7 Whyte's Hare, p. 164. 8 Natal Red Hare, p. 164.

Plate 29

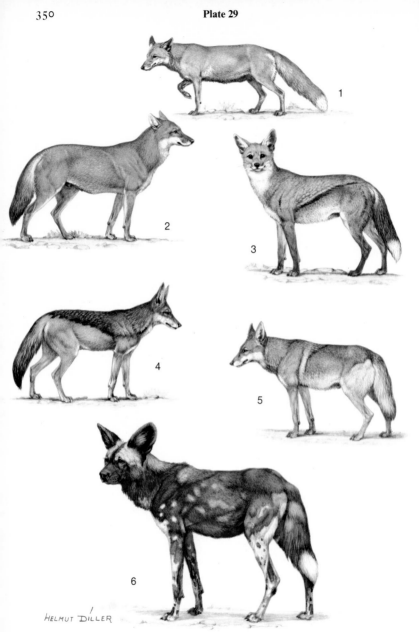

1 Red Fox, p. 170.   2 Simien Fox, p. 174.   3 Side-striped Jackal, p. 174.
4 Black-backed Jackal, p. 175.   5 Asiatic Jackal, p. 176.   6 Hunting Dog, p. 177.

Plate 30

35**1**

1 Fennec Fox, p. 173. 2 Cape Fox, p. 171. 3 Pale or Sand Fox, p. 172. 4 Bat-eared Fox, p. 178. 5 Ruppell's Sand Fox, p. 172.

352 Plate 31

1 Weasel, p. 179.   2 European Polecat, p. 180.   3 White-naped Weasel, p. 181.
4 Libyan Striped Weasel, p. 182.   5 Striped Polecat, p. 182.   6 Ratel or Honey
Badger, p. 183.   7 Spotted-necked Otter, p. 184.   8 Common Otter, p. 184.
9 Cape Clawless Otter, p. 185.

Plate 32

1 Common Genet, p. 188.   2 Angola Genet, p. 189.   3 Hausa Genet, p. 189.
4 Abyssinian Genet, p. 190.   5 Servaline Genet, p. 190.   6 Large-spotted
Genet, p. 191.   7 Giant Genet, p. 191.   8 Pardine Genet, p. 191.

HELMUT DILLER

1 African Civet, p. 192.   2 Fossa, p. 194.   3 Ring-tailed Mongoose, p. 198.
4 Two-spotted Palm Civet, p. 195.   5 Aquatic Genet, p. 194.   6 Small-toothed
Mongoose, p. 197.

Plate 34

355

HELMUT DILLER

1 Large-spotted Genet (Dark phase), p. 191.   2 Plain Mongoose, p. 201.
3 Narrow-striped Mongoose, p. 199.   4 Broad-striped Mongoose, p. 200.
5 Striped Civet or Fanaloka, p. 196.

Plate 35

1 Cape Grey Mongoose, p. 204. 2 Suricate, p. 205. 3 Slender Mongoose, p. 202. 4 Yellow Mongoose, p. 203. 5 Marsh Mongoose, p. 204. 6 Long-nosed Mongoose, p. 205. 7 Ichneumon or Egyptian Mongoose, p. 201.

Plate 36

357

HELMUT DILLER.

1 Banded Mongoose, p. 207.   2 Cusimanse, p. 208.   3 Gambian Mongoose,
p. 208.   4 Ansorge's Cusimanse, p. 209.   5 Alexander's Cusimanse, p. 209.
6 Black-footed Mongoose, p. 210.   7 White-tailed Mongoose, p. 211.
8 Bushy-tailed Mongoose, p. 210.

HELMUT DILLER

1 Southern Dwarf Mongoose, p. 212.   2 Eastern Dwarf Mongoose, p. 213.
3 Somali Dwarf Mongoose, p. 213.   4 Pousargue's Mongoose, p. 213.
5 Bushy-tailed Meerkat, p. 214.   6 Selous' Mongoose, p. 214.   7 Meller's
Mongoose, p. 215.

Plate 38

359

HELMUT DILLER

1 Aardwolf, p. 216.   2 Brown Hyaena, p. 217.   3 Striped Hyaena, p. 218.
4 Spotted Hyaena, p. 219.

HELMUT DILLER

1 and 2 Masai Lion, p. 221. (1 = ♂, 2 = ♀ with young)   3 Barbary Lion, p. 221.

Plate 40

361

HELMUT DILLER

1 S. African Leopard, p. 222. 2 East African Leopard, p. 222.

HELMUT DILLER

1 E. African Serval, p. 226.   2 Servaline Cat, p. 226.   3 S. African Cheetah, p. 224.   4 King Cheetah, p. 224.

Plate 42 363

HELMUT DILLER

1 Sand Cat, p. 227.   2 Black-footed Cat, p. 228.   3 N. African Kaffir Cat,
p. 229.   4 Kaffir Cat, p. 229.

Plate 43

1 Caracal, p. 225.   2 Jungle Cat, p. 230.   3 W. African Golden Cat, p. 231.
4 Eastern Golden Cat, p. 231.

Plate 44

365

1 and 2 Black Lemur, p. 232. (1 = ♀, 2 = ♂) 3 Ring-tailed Lemur, p. 236.
4 Ruffed Lemur, p. 235. 5 White-girdled Ruffed Lemur, p. 235. 6 Brown
Ruffed Lemur, p. 235. 7 Red Ruffed Lemur, p. 235. 8 White-fronted Lemur,
p. 233. 9 Red-fronted Lemur, p. 233. 10 Brown Lemur, p. 233. 11 Red-bellied
Lemur, p. 234.

1 Greater Weasel Lemur, p. 237.   2 Lesser Weasel Lemur, p. 237.   3 Grey Gentle Lemur, p. 238.   4 Broad-nosed Gentle Lemur, p. 240.

Plate 46

367

1 Coquerel's Mouse Lemur, p. 241.   2 Lesser Mouse Lemur, p. 240.   3 Fat-tailed
Dwarf Lemur, p. 243.   4 Greater Dwarf Lemur, p. 242.   5 Hairy-eared Dwarf
Lemur, p. 244.   6 Fork-crowned Dwarf Lemur, p. 244.

Plate 47

1 Aye-Aye, p. 249.   2 Avahi, p. 245.   3 Verreaux's Sifaka, p. 246.   4 Diademed Sifaka, p. 247.   5 Indris, p. 248.

Plate 48 369

HELMUT DILLER

1 Senegal Galago, p. 253.   2 Allen's Galago, p. 256.   3 Demidoff's Galago, p. 255.   4 Eastern Needle-clawed Galago, p. 257.   5 Western Needle-clawed Galago, p. 257.   6 Angwantibo, p. 260.   7 Greater Bushbaby, p. 251.   8 Potto, p. 258.

HELMUT DILLER

1 and 2 Drill, p. 264. (1 = ♀, 2 = ♂) 3 Mandrill, p. 265. ♂ 4 Gelada
Baboon, p. 266. ♂ 5 and 6 Hamadryas, p. 264. (5 = ♀ with young, 6 = ♂)

Plate 50

37^I

1 Chacma Baboon, p. 261. 2 Guinea Baboon, p. 261. 3 Olive Baboon, p. 261.
4 Yellow Baboon, p. 261.

Plate 51

HELMUT DILLER

1 Barbary Ape, p. 267.   2 Black Mangabey, p. 268.   3 Collared Mangabey,
p. 269.   4 Crested Mangabey, p. 270.   5 Grey-cheeked Mangabey, p. 271.

Plate 52

373

HELMUT DILLER

Patas Monkey, p. 275.   2 Blackish-green Guenon, p. 274.   3 Lesser White-
osed Guenon, p. 277.   4 Moustached Monkey, p. 280.   5 Talapoin, p. 272.
Doggett's Guenon, p. 284.

1 Diana Monkey, p. 289. 2 Tantalus Monkey, p. 292. 3 Owl-faced Monkey, p. 289. 4 Wolf's Guenon, p. 290. 5 L'Hoest's Monkey, p. 287.

Plate 54

375

1 Russet-eared Guenon, p. 282.   2 Dark White-nosed Monkey, p. 283.   3 Black-nosed Monkey, p. 281.   4 Yellow-nosed Monkey, p. 281.   5 Red-bellied Guenon, p. 282.   6 Golden Monkey, p. 284.   7 Congo Diademed Monkey, p. 284. 8 Crowned Guenon, p. 291.   9 Mona Monkey, p. 290.   10 Campbell's Guenon, p. 290.

HELMUT DILLER

1 Olive Colobus, p. 298. 2 Guereza, p. 297. 3 Black Colobus, p. 295.
4 Typical Red Colobus, p. 298.

Plate 56

377

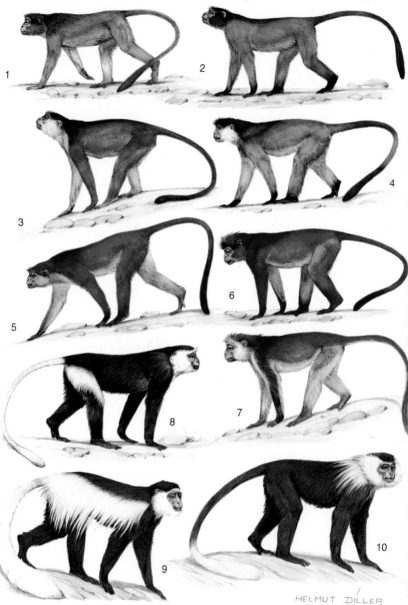

HELMUT DILLER

1 Temminck's Bay Colobus, p. 298.   2 Oustalet's Bay Colobus, p. 298.
3 Pennant's Bay Colobus, p. 298.   4 Black-handed Bay Colobus, p. 298.
5 Powell's Bay Colobus, p. 298.   6 Grauer's Bay Colobus, p. 298.   7 Kirk's Bay
Colobus, p. 298.   8 White-thighed Colobus, p. 295.   9 Kilimanjaro Colobus,
p. 297.   10 Angolan Colobus, p. 295.

Plate 57

1 Typical Chimpanzee, p. 303. 2 Eastern Chimpanzee, p. 303. 3 Bonobo, p. 306. 4 and 5 Tschego, p. 303. (4 = ♀, 5 = young).

Plate 58

379

1 Mountain Gorilla, p. 301.   2 Western Lowland Gorilla, p. 301.

Plate 59

1 Short-eared Elephant Shrew, p. 315.   2 Four-toed Elephant Shrew, p. 314.
3 Rufous Elephant Shrew, p. 317.   4 Ruwenzori Otter Shrew, p. 312.
5 Giant Otter Shrew, p. 311.   6 Lesser Otter Shrew, p. 312.   7 Giant
Elephant Shrew, p. 313.   8 Four-toed Hedgehog, p. 308.   9 Long-eared
Hedgehog, p. 311.   10 Desert Hedgehog, p. 310.

Plate 60 381

1 Cape Dassie, p. 122.   2 Rock Hyrax, p. 121.   3 Bate's Dwarf Antelope,
p. 47.   4 Suni, p. 48.   5 Rasse, p. 389.   6 Barbary Wild Boar (♀ with young),
p. 30.   7 Abyssinian Ibex, p. 104.

1 African Linsang, p. 187.   2 Johnston's Genet, p. 192.   3 Small Indian Mongoose, p. 389.   4 Liberian Mongoose, p. 209.

Plate 62   383

1 Mongoose Lemur, p. 234.   2 Uganda Grass Hare, p. 165.   3 Chestnut-browed Guenon, p. 286.   4 White-throated Guenon, p. 285.

1 Himalayan Tahr, p. 386.   2 Javan Rusa, p. 385.   3 Water Buffalo, p. 386.

Introduced Mammals
(Africa, Madagascar and adjacent islands)

DEER, CERVIDAE

SPANISH RED DEER, *Cervus elaphus hispanicus* (Hilzheimer, 1909)
G. Spanischer Rothirsch   F. Le Cerf de l'Espagne
Identification and **Habits.** See Barbary Stag. Adults without light spots; antlers with more than 8 points.
Distribution. Middle and S. Spain with adjoining S.E. Portugal. Introduced in 1952 in Morocco between Ceuta and Tangier, and in 1954 in Fernando Poo.

JAVAN RUSA, *Cervus timoriensis russa* (Muller & Schlegel, 1839–44)   **Pl. 63**
G. Java-Mähnenhirsch   F. Le Cerf Rusa de Java
Identification. Smaller than Barbary Stag, tail well developed, antlers with total of 6 tines (on each side brow, middle and end), terminal tine of the main beam very well developed, longer than brow or middle tines, forming continuation of main beam. Body hair thick, rather long and shaggy, ♂ in rut has conspicuous neck mane. Upperside dark to reddish-brown, underside paler. ♀♀ lighter than ♂♂, young like ♀♀, unspotted. Preorbital, metacarpal and reduced toe glands on hind feet present. 4 teats. Dent.: as Barbary Stag.   MEASUREMENTS: HB ♂ *c.* 180, ♀ *c.* 170; TL ♂ *c.* 25, ♀ *c.* 20; Ht ♂ *c.* 110, ♀ *c.* 100. Wt ♂ 100–120, ♀ 60–70. H up to 85cm.
Distribution. Sunda Isles and Moluccas from Java to Celebes and N.W. New Guinea (8 ssp.). Ssp. *russa*, Java (where threatened), introduced in S.E. Borneo, Ambon, Celebes, Mauritius (1639), Anjouan in Comoro Is. (1870), and Madagascar (1930).   HABITAT: prefers savannahs, grassy plains and park lands, also lives in swamps, rain forest, bushy rocky mountains, conifer forests, eucalyptus woods and plantations. Diurnal. HABITS: lives on grass, herbage, leaves, sugar cane shoots etc. Separates into ♂ and ♀ parties from 6 to several dozen head.
Reproduction. Sexes come together in rut in Jul–Sept, no harem stag, all the stronger ♂♂ fighting together. ♂♂ in rut have deep passionate roar. Gestation 8 months, births Apr–May, 1 active young, suckle for 3 months. ♂ Wt at 1 year 40–50, at 5 years up to 120. Antlers shed Dec–Jan, newly cleaned May–Jun. 4 tines at 2 years, 6 on and after 3rd year.   SEXUALLY MATURE: ♀ at 1¼, ♂ at 2 years.   LONGEVITY: 8–10 years.

FALLOW DEER, *Cervus dama* (Linnaeus, 1758)
G. Damhirsch   F. Le Daim   A. Damhert
Identification. Smaller than Javan Rusa, tail well developed; antlers with brow and middle tines and with upper part broadened and shovel-like. Pelage in summer short and glossy, in winter thick and rough with dense underwool. Upperside light to dark brown with black spinal stripe and white-spotted flanks. Stern 'mirror' or pygal area narrowly white, edged with black, tail black above, white below. Underside whitish-grey. Coat colour very variable, from white, isabelline, dark brown to black, spots absent or conspicuous. Also palmation of antlers very variable. Young brownish-red, closely spotted with white. Scent glands present (preorbital, metacarpal and inter-digital). 4 teats. Dent.: $0/3 \cdot 0/1 \cdot 3 \cdot 3 = 32$.   MEASUREMENTS: HB 130–150, TL 15–20, Ht 80–100; Wt ♂ 85–100, ♀ 35–50. Ht 65–78.

Distribution. Asia Minor (nearly extinct), brought by man to Europe, N. America (USA, Canada), S. America (Chile, Argentine), Australia, Tasmania, New Zealand, Madagascar and S. Africa. Introduced in Madagascar 1932, a population in forested highlands about 60km S. of Tananarive, to S. Africa in 1897 on Groote Schuur Farm at foot of Table Mt (population at present 400), to Middelburg, Sutherland, Bedford, Somerset East, Bredasdorp, Paarl and Colesberg in Cape Province (present population over 1000), on Vereenigung Farm in Harrismith district in Orange Free State as well as in the Transvaal. Further distribution taking place by feral animals in Union of S. Africa. An old population in N. Africa in the wooded coastal region from La Calle on the Algerian–Tunisian border near Tripoli is apparently gone. *Map* p. 388.

Habits. Lives in wooded parkland areas, diurnal when not disturbed. FOOD: grass, herbage, also leaves, buds, shoots. Sociable, in small to large herds.

Reproduction. In northern hemisphere rut at end of October, parturition end of June, in southern hemisphere altered correspondingly. Breeding challenge of bucks a high monotonous grunting. Gestation 7½–8 months, 1 active young, rarely 2, still more rarely 3. Wt at birth 2.5–3.2; suckle for 8 months. ♀ sexually mature at 1¼ years, ♂ at 2¼ years. LONGEVITY: normally 8–10, in captivity up to 16 years.

HOLLOW-HORNED RUMINANTS, BOVIDAE

HIMALAYAN TAHR, *Hemitragus jemlahicus jemlahicus* (H. Smith, 1826) **Pl. 63**
G. Himalaja-Tahr F. Le Tahr de l'Himalaya A. Himalaya Thar

Identification. Goat-like in form and size. Ears small, neck short, shoulders higher than rump, tail short with naked underside. Both sexes with thick short horns, curved backwards. Coat thick and rather long. ♂ with well-developed cape-like mane on neck, shoulders and breast. Upperside blackish-brown, underside rather paler, front of mane light yellowish. ♀ like ♂, but without mane; young greyish-brown. Underside of tail with glands, interdigital glands on hind feet rather reduced. 4 teats. Dent.: $0/3 \cdot 0/1 \cdot 3 \cdot 3 = 32$. MEASUREMENTS: HB ♂ 150–175, ♀ 140–150; TL 15–20. Ht ♂ 90–105, ♀ 80–90. Wt ♂ 80–90, ♀ 60–70. H, ♂ 30–42, ♀ 20–25.

Distribution. S.E. Arabia, Himalaya, S. India (4 ssp.), *jemlahicus*: Himalaya (Pir Panjal, Kashmir, Punjab, Kumaon, Nepal). Introduced in New Zealand 1904 and about 1930 on Groote Schuur Farm near Cape Town. From here a pair in 1937 escaped to Table Mountain, on whose slopes there is now a population of about 100. HABITAT: high wooded mountain slopes, with steep cliffs. *Map* p. 388.

Habits. ♀♀ in summer frequent the open summit zones, ♂♂ prefer woodland cover below. Remarkable climbing ability on the roughest rocks. Sociable in large groups, ♂♂ remain apart in the summer. FOOD: grass, herbage, foliage of bushes. Active in morning and afternoon, resting mid-day.

Reproduction. In the Himalayas breeding season in Dec, births in Jul; at the Cape altered accordingly. ♂ silent when mating, remains with 1 ♀ as long as she is in heat. No fighting between rivals. Gestation 7 months, 1, rarely 2, active young. Suckle for 6 months. SEXUAL MATURITY: ♀ 1¼, ♂ 2¼ years, then ♂ joins ♂ troop, and ♀ lives with party of mothers. LONGEVITY: 10–14, rarely to 16 years.

WATER BUFFALO, *Bubalus bubalis* (Linnaeus, 1758) **Pl. 63**
G. Wasserbüffel F. Le Buffle d'eau

Identification. Large and heavy. Ht to 160, Wt 400–550, pelage black, in winter 10cm long, tail with large tuft reaching hocks, tuft sometimes white. Ears large with long hair fringes, large muzzle. Horns light grey, curving backwards in a semicircle, flat triangle in section, with transverse ribbing. Length to 60cm. Legs sturdy, inner and outer hoofs large. 4 teats. No skin glands.

Distribution. Very probably already established since Roman times as a wild-living herd and royal hunting quarry at Lake Ischkeul, at foot of Ischkeul mountains not far from Bizerta, N. Tunisia, with varying fortunes. In 1957 all but 3 calves were shot; from these a new herd has been built up which now has its own special reserve at Ischkeul. For 2000 years has lived in the wild, but original descent unknown. *Map* p. 388.

Habitat. Tall grass, reed beds, swamps, mud holes, water courses.

Reproduction. Cows have 1–2 young after a 10-month gestation. Calves are born with eyes open and are fully haired. Weaned at 6 months. SEXUAL MATURITY: can breed in second year, fully adult at 3–4 years.

SQUIRRELS, SCIURIDAE

GREY SQUIRREL, *Sciurus carolinensis* (Gmelin, 1788)
G. Grauhörnchen   F. L'Écureuil canadien   A. Grijze Eekhoorn

Identification. Larger than Red Squirrel (*Sciurus vulgaris*), tail bushy as in latter, however ears also in winter without tufts. Upperside grey, underside whitish, light ring round eye, legs and lower edge of flanks washed with red (more distinctly in summer than in winter). Melanistic examples occur. Dent.: $1 \cdot 0 \cdot 2/1 \cdot 3 = 22$. ♂ with penis bone. 8 teats. MEASUREMENTS: HB 24–30, TL 19–25, Ht 6–7·5. Wt 340–750.

Distribution. Eastern U.S.A., from 98°–96°W., eastward to S. border of E. Canada. Introduced into Saskatoon (Saskatchewan), Vancouver (British Columbia), Seattle (Washington), England and Ireland. Introduced in Cape Town about 1900, now in Cape Town district and western Cape Province.

Habits. Resembles Red Squirrel. Active by day in parks, gardens and leafy woods. Sleeping place a hole in tree or sometimes on the ground, or in a loose nest of twigs in fork of tree. Does not hibernate. FOOD: nuts, fruit, buds, leaves, flowers, fungi; also insects, bird's eggs and nestlings. VOICE: in excitement a rasping whickering, with tail jerking, ending with a harsh chatter. Not unsocial, often in groups at feeding places.

Reproduction. Gestation 44 days, 1–6 young, usually 2–4; 2 litters a year probable. Wt at birth 15–18, and total length 11–12. Born naked and blind. Upperside furred at 3 weeks, ears open at 4, eyes at 5, weaned at 5–6 weeks, independent at 8. SEXUALLY MATURE: 8–9 months. LONGEVITY: 8–10 years.

CAVY-LIKE RODENTS, CAPROMYIDAE

COYPU OR NUTRIA, *Myocastor coypus* (Molina, 1782)
G. Nutria, Biberratte   F. Le Ragondin
Identification. Size and form of beaver, but tail round and rat-like, almost naked, long; eyes and ears small, toes 5/5. 1st to 4th toes of hind feet webbed for swimming. Fur with long guard hairs and fine dense underfur. Upperside dark, light or reddish-brown (underfur slate-grey), underside lighter, tip of muzzle white. Young resemble adults. Dent.: $1 \cdot 1/0 \cdot 0/1 \cdot 3 = 20$. 8 teats. ♂ with penis bone.   MEASUREMENTS: HB ♂ 50–60, ♀ 40–50; TL ♂ 30–40, ♀ 25–35. Ht 12·5–14. Wt ♂ 6–9, ♀ 4–7.

Distribution. S. America from Patagonia and S. Chile north to Bolivia, Paraguay, S. Brazil and Uruguay as well as in N. Venezuela. 4 ssp. Introduced in the present century as a fur-farm animal in S. U.S.A., Europe (Germany, Switzerland, Holland, France, England, Denmark and S. Soviet Union), Japan and E. Africa. In the latter area from 1960 has gone feral in the coastal swamps in Tanzania, and in Kenya in Lake Naivasha.
Habits. Sociable, living by and in plant-rich waters, also in brackish or salt-water lagoons. Makes burrows in banks. Active at dusk and by day. Swims and dives well. FOOD: vegetation on banks and in water, will also eat mussels.   VOICE: low grunting, spitting, mewing, courting ♂ hums.
Reproduction. ♀ has 28-day cycle, with 2–3 days on heat. Gestation 110–140, usually 128–132 days. From 4–13 young in litter, usually 5–6, fully haired and active with eyes open, suckle for 2 months. The teats are high along the lower side of back.   SEXUALLY MATURE: at 7–8 months, independent at $\frac{1}{4}$ year, fully grown at $1\frac{1}{4}$–$1\frac{1}{2}$ years. 2 litters annually.   LONGEVITY: 8–10 years.

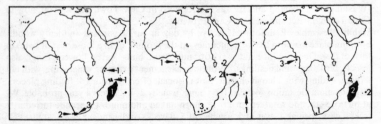

1 Indian Rasse	1 Small Indian Mongoose	1 Himalayan Tahr
2 European Rabbit	2 Coypu 3 Fallow Deer	2 Javan Rusa
3 Grey Squirrel	4 Water Buffalo	3 Spanish Red Deer

HARES & RABBITS, LEPORIDAE

EUROPEAN RABBIT, *Oryctolagus cuniculus,* see text, p. 161.

CIVETS & MONGOOSES, VIVERRIDAE

INDIAN RASSE, *Viverricula malaccensis indica* (Desmarest, 1817)   **Pl. 60**
G. Indien Rasse   F. La Civette rasse   MA. Jaboady, Alazy
Identification. Like genet in form and size, but rather stouter, muzzle not so sharp, ears rather short. Fur thick and soft, tail long and bushy, upperside of body yellowish-brown with 6 rows of dark brown to brownish black spots, the uppermost 3 rows with spots usually coalescing in lines. Eye and nose spots, cheeks, throat, breast and belly as well as tail-ring interspaces white. 3 rows of spots on cheeks, and 1–2 throat bands, dark like the body spots. Tail with 7–9 blackish rings. Young like adults, but colours still not contrasting well. Digits 5/5, thumb and great toe very small. Perineal and anal glands present. 4 teats. Penis with bone. Dent.: $3 \cdot 1 \cdot 4 \cdot 2 = 40$.   MEASUREMENTS: ♂ & ♀, HB 51–57, TL 34–37, Wt 1.8–2.2.
Distribution of the species. Upper India and Ceylon, Further India and Malayan Peninsula, S. China to Yangtse, and all S.E. Asian archipelago, 10ssp. Ssp. *indica* (Desmarest, 1817), from S. India, introduced into Philippines, Comoros, Madagascar, Zanzibar, Pemba and Socotra. In Madagascar arrived with the first Indo–Malayan invaders, date on other islands not known.
Habits. Found in all open areas, moist or dry, in mountains up to 2000m; not in closed rain forest, favours vicinity of villages. In Madagascar shelters well hidden on ground in thick bush, not in burrows. Active at dusk and by night, entirely terrestrial, does not climb, silent except for growl in excitement, solitary or ♀ with young.   FOOD: earthworms, insects, crustaceans, fish, amphibians, reptiles, birds and eggs, small mammals, fruit. Will take domestic fowls readily.
Reproduction. Breeding season in Madagascar late winter (Jul–Aug), gestation 8–9 weeks, litter size 1–4, born in spring (Sep–Dec). Development of young, SEXUAL MATURITY and LONGEVITY probably like African Civet, but details not known.

SMALL INDIAN MONGOOSE, *Herpestes javanicus auropunctatus*   **Pl. 61**
(Hodgson, 1836)
G. Indisches Javaichneumon   F. La petite mangouste des Indes.
Identification. Structure and appearance as in Ichneumon (p.000), but smaller. Upperside olive-grey to brownish-grey or light brownish-grey, closely speckled with yellow to golden-yellow (individual hairs brown to dark brown with 2 cream-coloured to golden yellow rings), underside paler, feet rather darker, tail like back. Digits 5/5, thumb and great toe small, penis bone present, 4 teats, a pair of anal glands present. Dent.: $3 \cdot 1 \cdot 4 \cdot 2 = 40$. Young at first naked and dark brown, but when hairy at 3 weeks are like adults.   MEASUREMENTS: HB 30–35, TL 25–30, Wt ♂ 500–1300, ♀ 350–600.
Distribution. Wide range from Iraq to N. Indian plains, Assam, Burma, Indo–Malayan archipelago, S. China, Canton, Hainan (8 ssp.) Ssp. *auropunctatus* from India introduced on Mafia (off coast of Tanzania), Mauritius, Trinidad (1870), Jamaica (1872), Martinique and St Lucia (after 1872), and later on all the larger Antilles and Guyana, also to Ambon or Amboina by Ceram, and on Hawaii (1883, from Jamaica).

Habits. Like the true Ichneumon. HABITAT: preferably open, dry bush and savannah districts with plentiful cover. Avoids thick forest, likes to be near villages, and goes up to over 3000m in mountains. Active by day, terrestrial but climbs well when necessary, but rarely, swims well but not willingly. VOICE: growls and hisses, raises fur and humps back as threat in defiance, sharp 'chack' as threat, anxious young have querulous call. Nights spent in abandoned holes, or in self-excavated burrows, in rock crevices, holes in lava and other hiding places. Solitary, in pairs, or mother with young. FOOD: omnivorous; insects, scorpions, centipedes, crustaceans, fish, amphibians, reptiles (including snakes and tortoises), birds up to size of goose, eggs, rats and mice and other small mammals. In emergency will prey on young domestic stock (kids, lambs, puppies, kittens) as well as hens and other poultry, carrion, fruit, milky grain, tender sugar-cane shoots etc.

Reproduction. 2 litters a year, gestation 43–49 days, 1–5 (usually 2) young, in hole. Eyes open at 16–17 days. Leaves hole first at 3 weeks. ♀ alone rears the young. SEXUALLY MATURE: at 1 year. LONGEVITY: up to 7 years in captivity.

It may be mentioned that in Mauritius (outside the scope of this book), in addition to the Javan Rusa (p. 385), the Small Indian Mongoose (p. 389), and the Brown Hare (p. 162) further introductions have also been made: the Indian Grey Mongoose (*Herpestes edwardsi*), the Javan macaque (*Macaca irus*), and the Tenrec (*Tenrec ecaudatus*), as well as domestic pigs in the feral state. Additionally, from the Shrew family (Soricidae), not included in this book, the S. Asiatic Musk Shrew (*Suncus murinus*) has come to Zanzibar and Pemba.

Bibliography

The original list of useful reference works or background material has been revised with the needs of the English-speaking reader in mind.

ALLEN, G. M. *A Checklist of African Mammals*, Bull. Mus. Comp. Zool., Cambridge (Mass.) *83*, 1939.

ANSELL, W. F. H. *Mammals of Northern Rhodesia*, Lusaka, Govt. Printer, 1960.

BEST, A. & RAW, M. (EDITORS) *Rowland Ward's Records of Big Game*, Africa. 16th Edition, Rowland Ward Publ. Ltd., London, 1975.

CABRERA, A. *Los mamiferos de Marruecos*, Trab. Mus. Cienc. Nat. Madrid. *57*, 1932.

CLARK, J. *The Prehistory of Africa*, Thames & Hudson, London, 1970.

DORST, J. & DANDELOT, P. *A Field Guide to the Larger Mammals of Africa*, Collins, London, 1976. (*Note*: This book does not include North Africa or Madagascar).

ELLERMAN, J. R. & MORRISON-SCOTT, T. C. S. *A Checklist of Palaearctic and Indian Mammals, 1758–1946*, Brit. Mus. (Nat. Hist.), London, 1951. (*Note*: this includes the mammals of North Africa down to the parallel of 20°N.).

ELLERMAN, J. R., MORRISON-SCOTT, T. C. S. & HAYMAN, R. W. *Southern African Mammals, 1758–1951: a reclassification*, Brit. Mus. (Nat. Hist.), London, 1953.

HARPER, F. *Extinct and Vanishing Mammals of the Old World*, Spec. Publ, Amer. Comp. Int. Wild Life Prot., No. 12, 1945.

MABERLY, C. T. A. *Animals of East Africa*, Timmins, 1962. Cape Town. *The Game Animals of South Africa*, Nelson, Johannesburg. 1963.

MEESTER, J. & SETZER, H. W. *The Mammals of Africa. An Identification Manual*, Smithsonian Institution Press, Washington, 1974.

RICHARD-VINDARD, G. & BATTISTINI, R. *Biogeography and ecology of Madagascar*, Dr. W. Junk Publ., Hague, 1972.

ROBERTS, A. *The Mammals of South Africa*, Trustees of 'The Mammals of South Africa' Book Fund, Johannesburg, 1951.

ROOSEVELT, TH. & HELLER, E. *Life-histories of African Game Animals*, 2 vols., Murray, London, 1915.

ROSEVEAR, D. R. *Checklist and Atlas of Nigerian Mammals*, with a foreword on vegetation. Govt. Printer, Lagos, 1953. *The Rodents of West Africa*, Brit. Mus. (Nat. Hist.), London, 1969. *The Carnivores of West Africa*, Brit. Mus. (Nat. Hist.), London, 1974.

SCHOUTEDEN, H. *Faune du Congo belge et du Ruanda-Urundi: 1. Mammiferes*, Tervuren, Ann. Mus. Belg. Congo, 1948.

SCLATER, P. L. and THOMAS, O. *The Book of Antelopes*, 4 vols., R. H. Porter, London 1894–1900.

SHORTRIDGE, G. C. *The Mammals of South-West Africa*, 2 vols., Heinemann, London, 1934.

SMITHERS, R. H. N. *The Mammals of Rhodesia, Zambia and Malawi*, Collins, London, 1966.

STEVENSON-HAMILTON, J. *Wild Life in South Africa*, Cassell, London, 1947.

SWYNNERTON, G. H. & HAYMAN, R. W. *A Checklist of the Land Mammals of the Tanganyika Territory and the Zanzibar Protectorate*, J. E. Af. Nat. Hist. Soc. *20;* 1951: 274–392.

WALKER, E. et al *Mammals of the World*, 3rd edit., 2 vols., Johns Hopkins Univ. Press, Baltimore, 1975.

WILLIAMS, J. G. *A Field Guide to the National Parks of East Africa*, Collins, London, 1967.

Index of Scientific Names

Figures in **bold** refer to the plate on which a coloured illustration appears

Index of English Names

Figures in **bold** type refer to the plate on which a coloured illustration appears